FORUM

WITHDRAWN BY
WHITMAN COLLEGE LIBRARY

FORUM

CANADIAN LIFE AND LETTERS 1920-70

SELECTIONS FROM *The Canadian Forum*

EDITED BY J.L. GRANATSTEIN
AND PETER STEVENS

UNIVERSITY OF TORONTO PRESS

©University of Toronto Press 1972
Toronto and Buffalo
Printed in Canada
ISBN 0-8020-1909-9 (cloth)
ISBN 0-8020-6168-0 (paper)
ISBN Microfiche 0-8020-0247-1
LC 75-166930

The following poems were published by The Ryerson Press and are reprinted by permission of McGraw-Hill Ryerson Limited:
'Poem on Canada' from *The White Centre* by Patrick Anderson; 'Political Meeting' from *The Rocking Chair and Other Poems* by A.M. Klein; 'Boy Remembers in the Field,' 'The Hawk,' and 'The Plowman' from *The Collected Poems of Raymond Knister*; 'And Give Us Our Trespasses' from *The Unquiet Bed* by Dorothy Livesay; 'Manzini: Escape Artist' from *Breakfast for Barbarians* by Gwendolyn MacEwen; 'Fidelia Vulnera Amici' and 'Battle Hymn for the Spanish Rebels' from *The Ill-Tempered Lover and Other Poems* by L.A. MacKay; 'Orpheus in the Underworld' from *Black and Secret Man* by Eli Mandel

Acknowledgment is made of permission to reprint the following:
Northrop Frye: 'Canada and Its Poetry' from *The Bush Garden: Essays on the Canadian Imagination* to The House of Anansi Press; John Glassco: 'The Entailed Farm' from *Selected Poems* to Oxford University Press, Canadian Branch; David Helwig: 'Winter of the Daffodils' from *The Streets of Summer* to Oberon Press; Irving Layton: 'Lady Enfield,' 'Sheep,' 'Whatever Else Poetry is Freedom,' 'Côte des Neiges Cemetery,' and 'There Were No Signs' from *Collected Poems* to The Canadian Publishers, McClelland and Stewart Limited; Alden Nowlan: 'Rivalry' from *Bread, Wine and Salt* to Clarke, Irwin & Company Limited; Michael Ondaatje: 'Peter' from *The Dainty Monsters* to The Coach House Press; E.J. Pratt: 'Silences,' 'The Fair-grounds, Columbus, Ohio,' and 'The Shark' from *Collected Poems* to The Macmillan Company of Canada Limited; Al Purdy: 'The Wine-Maker's Beat-étude' from *Wild Grape Wine* to The Canadian Publishers, McClelland and Stewart Limited; 'Poem for One of the Annettes' from *Poems for All the Annettes* to Contact Press and The House of Anansi Press; James Reaney: 'Klaxon' from *The Red Heart* to the author and his literary agent, Sybil Hutchinson; A.J.M. Smith: 'The Lonely Land' and 'Swift Current' from *Collected Poems* to Oxford University Press, Canadian Branch; Raymond Souster: 'Rags-and-Bones Man' from *So Far So Good* to Oberon Press.

CONTENTS

Preface / xiii

THE 20s

November 1920 / F.H. VARLEY *The Colliery Accident* / 3
March 1921 / HUNTLY K. GORDON Canadian Poetry / 3
April 1921 / J.S. WOODSWORTH Unemployment / 5
June 1921 / M.H. STAPLES The Genesis of the United Farmers / 7
September 1921 / LAWREN HARRIS *Slums and Shadows* / 9
October 1921 / C.B. SISSONS The Farmers' Case / 10
October 1921 / FRANK CARMICHAEL *Man with Scythe* / 12
November 1921 / EDITORIAL Our Next Parliament / 13
December 1921 / A.J. CASSON *Decorative Landscape* / 14
April 1922 / J.S. WOODSWORTH The Labour Movement in the West / 16
December 1922 / HENRY WISE WOOD In Defence of Group Politics / 18
January 1923 / E.J. PRATT 'The Shark' / 20
June 1923 / R.S. KNOX A New Canadian Poet / 21
November 1923 / EDITORIAL / 22
March 1924 / J.S. WOODSWORTH Besco / 22
June 1924 / J. ADDISON REID Secession in Canada: Quebec / 24
June 1924 / THOMPSON-HARDY Secession in Canada: The Prairies / 26
July 1924 / DAVID MILNE *Camp Porch* / 27
November 1924 / J.S. WOODSWORTH Mobilizing Progressive Opinion in Canada / 28
March 1925 / ROLAND-GILLES MOUSSEAU A Letter / 29

August 1925 / J. ANSEL ANDERSON *The Coward* / 30
October 1925 / A.Y. JACKSON *A Winter's Night* / 33
January 1926 / A POLITICAL CORRESPONDENT Politics, Parties, and Leaders / 34
February 1926 / EDITORIAL Peaceful Penetration / 36
May 1926 / GRAHAM SPRY Europe's Conception of Canada / 37
May 1926 / EDWARD SAPIR 'Advice to a Girl' / 38
July 1926 / THOREAU MACDONALD *Northern Summer* / 39
August 1926 / EDITORIAL The Constitutional Issue / 39
December 1926 / DOUGLAS BUSH Making Literature Hum / 40
January 1927 / WATSON KIRKCONNELL A Letter / 42
February 1927 / DOUGLAS BUSH A Reply / 43
January 1927 / EDITORIAL Mr King's Luck / 43
January 1927 / J.E.H. MACDONALD *Paul Bunyan Takes an Evening Stroll in Algoma* / 44
July 1927 / A.J.M. SMITH 'The Lonely Land' / 45
October 1927 / B.R. BROOKER 'Energy Is Eternal Delight' (Blake) / 45
October 1927 / HUNTLY K. GORDON The Nudes at the CNE / 46
October 1927 / RICHARD DE BRISAY A New Immigration Policy / 46
October 1927 / JEAN BURTON *Phyllus* / 49
November 1927 / EDITORIAL Phyllus / 54
December 1927 / MALCOLM H.V. CAMERON A Letter / 54
December 1927 / FRANZ JOHNSTON A Letter / 54
January 1928 / ESCOTT M. REID Canada on the Council / 55
April 1928 / A.J.M. SMITH Wanted: Canadian Criticism / 56
June 1928 / FRANK H. UNDERHILL Canadian and American History – and Historians / 58
August 1928 / A.J.M. SMITH 'Cavalcade' / 60
January 1929 / CARL SCHAEFER *Snowbound* / 59
July 1929 / FRANK H. UNDERHILL O Canada / 60
July 1929 / A.S. WHITELY The Oriental in British Columbia / 61
August 1929 / LEO KENNEDY 'Split Me These Gull Throats' / 64
September 1929 / DOROTHY LIVESAY 'Parrot of Night' / 64
October 1929 / ROBERT FINCH 'The Metro Breakfasts' / 65
November 1929 / C.L.E. 'God's Absolutely Against It' / 65
December 1929 / FRANK H. UNDERHILL O Canada / 66

THE 30s

April 1930 / FRANK H. UNDERHILL O Canada / 71
June 1930 / EDITORIAL The Group of Seven / 71

June 1930 / E.J. PRATT 'The Fair-grounds, Columbus, Ohio' / 72
June 1930 / A.J.M. SMITH 'Swift Current' / 72
July 1930 / DOROTHY LIVESAY 'If It Were Easy' / 72
August 1930 / EDITORIAL Unemployment Must Be Tackled / 74
August 1930 / F.R. SCOTT 'Proud Cellist' 'Sunday' / 74
August 1930 / A.J.M. SMITH 'Testament' / 74
February 1931 / J.F. WHITE Police Dictatorship / 75
March 1931 / EDITORIAL 'The Intellectual Capital of Canada' / 77
June 1931 / E.A. FORSEY Montreal is a Quiet City – 'And It Must Remain Quiet' / 80
October 1931 / FRANK H. UNDERHILL O Canada / 84
December 1931 / L.A. MacKAY 'Fidelia Vulnera Amici' / 86
December 1931 / EDWARD ARTHUR BEDER *Wattman* / 88
January 1932 / F.R. SCOTT Communists, Senators, and All That / 91
January 1932 / DOROTHY LIVESAY 'Morning in Autumn' 'Alienation' / 94
January 1932 / MARY QUAYLE INNIS *Holiday* / 95
April 1932 / FRANK H. UNDERHILL The League for Social Reconstruction / 98
June 1932 / J.F. WHITE Socialism without Doctrine / 99
July 1932 / J.F. WHITE Deportations / 101
August 1932 / A.M. KLEIN 'Soirée of Velvel Kleinburger' / 103
August 1932 / FRANK H. UNDERHILL The Cooperative Commonwealth Federation / 105
September 1932 / RAYMOND KNISTER 'Boy Remembers in the Field' 'The Plowman' 'The Hawk' / 107
May 1933 / FRANK H. UNDERHILL Canada and War / 107
May 1933 / LEO KENNEDY Archibald Lampman / 109
July 1933 / EDITORIAL Liberals and Liberty / 111
September 1933 / F.R. SCOTT The CCF Convention / 112
October 1933 / EDITORIAL Thanksgiving / 114
January 1934 / H.M. CASSIDY Is Unemployment Relief Enough? / 115
February 1934 / EDITORIAL The Pre-War Era / 116
February 1934 / ANGUS MacINNIS More about the British Columbia Election / 116
April 1934 / J.E. KEITH The Fascist Province / 120
September 1934 / FRANK H. UNDERHILL The CCF Convention and After / 122
November 1934 / J.H. GRAY Battle of the Winnipeg Cenotaph / 124
November 1934 / FLORENCE RHEIN *Beauty Parlour* / 129
January 1935 / ALAN CREIGHTON 'Barbarous Epoch' / 131
February 1935 / J.R. McLEAN Bennett of Tarsus / 132
March 1935 / F.R. SCOTT 'Social Notes' / 133
April 1935 / G.V. FERGUSON An Alberta Prophet – 1935 Model / 135
August 1935 / GRAHAM SPRY Politics / 137

November 1935 / MALCOLM MacKENZIE ROSS 'Nationale' / 140
March 1936 / FRANK H. UNDERHILL On Professors and Politics / 140
March 1936 / E.J. PRATT 'Silences' / 142
March 1936 / QUEBECER French-Canadian Nationalism / 143
June 1936 / HUGH GARNER Toronto's Cabbagetown / 145
September 1936 / A.J.M. SMITH 'The Face' / 148
October 1936 / L.A. MacKAY 'Battle Hymn for the Spanish Rebels' / 148
March 1937 / FRANK H. UNDERHILL The Debate on Foreign Policy / 148
March 1937 / EARLE BIRNEY 'Grey Rocks' / 151
June 1937 / FELIX LAZARUS The Oshawa Strike / 151
July 1937 / NORMAN BETHUNE 'Red Moon' / 153
September 1937 / KING GORDON The CCF Convention / 154
November 1937 / RALPH GUSTAFSON 'Rhyme for the Modern Child' / 156
February 1938 / FRANK H. UNDERHILL To Protect Our Neutrality / 156
February 1938 / ANNE MARRIOTT 'Prairie' / 157
May 1938 / EUGENE FORSEY Under the Padlock / 157
May 1938 / RUFUS II Another Month / 161
June 1938 / A.M. KLEIN 'To One Gone to the Wars' 'Toreador' 'Sonnet without Music' / 162
August 1938 / F.R. SCOTT Canada the Ammunition Dump / 162
August 1938 / A.M. KLEIN 'Barricade Smith: His Speeches' / 164
January 1939 / L.A. MacKAY Glacial Stream / 167
February 1939 / JOHN SMALACOMBE A Protest / 168
March 1939 / DAVID ANDRADE 'Dust Patterns after Revolution' / 168
May 1939 / HENRY PAUL I am a Transient / 169
June 1939 / EDITORIAL Canadian Censorship / 172
October 1939 / FRANK H. UNDERHILL Peace Aims / 173
November 1939 / G.M.A. GRUBE Freedom and War / 176
December 1939 / F.R. SCOTT The Real Vote in Quebec / 178

THE 40s

January 1940 / EARLE BIRNEY To Arms with Canadian Poetry / 183
February 1940 / F.A. BREWIN Conscription in Canada / 185
February 1940 / H.E. BERGMAN *Along the New Highway* / 186
June 1940 / LOUISE SMITH HARVEY Anti-Semitism in Quebec / 187
August 1940 / F.R. SCOTT Social Planning and the War / 189
September 1940 / FRANK H. UNDERHILL North American Front / 191
October 1940 / EDITORIAL Winning the War / 193

December 1940 / RAYMOND SOUSTER 'Last Act, Last Scene' / 194
February 1941 / CARLTON McNAUGHT Democracy and Our Universities / 194
October 1941 / FERGUS GLENN The Conscription Build-Up / 196
December 1941 / EDITORIAL Freezing Injustice / 201
January 1942 / EDITORIAL Meighen Redivivus / 203
June 1932 / F.R. SCOTT What Did 'No' Mean? / 206
September 1942 / P.K. PAGE 'Bed-sitting Room' / 208
October 1942 / EDITORIAL Maligning the CCF / 209
January 1943 / EDITORIAL The Pro and Con Party / 211
January 1943 / JAMES WREFORD 'Winter Weather' / 214
January 1943 / IRVING LAYTON 'Lady Remington' / 214
October 1943 / MARGARET AVISON 'Mutable Hearts' / 214
December 1943 / NORTHROP FRYE Canada and Its Poetry / 215
April 1944 / MIRIAM WADDINGTON 'The Sleepers' / 221
June 1944 / PATRICK ANDERSON 'Poem on Canada' / 221
July 1944 / A.J.M. SMITH A Letter / 227
July 1944 / CARLYLE KING The CCF Sweeps Saskatchewan / 227
December 1944 / P.K. PAGE 'Draughtsman' / 229
January 1945 / EDITORIAL National Unity / 229
August 1945 / EDITORIAL The Boys Come Back / 231
May 1946 / F.R. SCOTT Labour Learns the Truth / 234
September 1946 / A.M. KLEIN 'Political Meeting' 'The White Old Lady' / 236
March 1947 / F.R. SCOTT Alignment of Parties / 237
April 1947 / GRACE MacINNIS Immigration? On What Basis? / 239
May 1947 / F.R. SCOTT 'Orderly Decontrol' / 242
May 1947 / JOHN GLASSCO 'The Entailed Farm' / 242
August 1947 / NORTHROP FRYE Toynbee and Spengler / 243
October 1947 / L.J. ROGERS Duplessis and Labour / 246
February 1948 / FRANK H. UNDERHILL Liberalism à la King / 248
April 1948 / JAMES REANEY 'Klaxon' / 250
August 1948 / LOUIS DUDEK 'Upstate Tourism' / 250
May 1949 / W.R. TROST *The Buster* / 251
November 1949 / MILLER STEWART Canada's Pollution Problem / 255

THE 50s

September 1950 / S.W. BRADFORD The CCF Failure in Foreign Policy / 261
October 1950 / FRANK H. UNDERHILL Canadian Socialism and World Politics / 263

November 1950 / S.F. WISE Canadian Football / 266
December 1950 / F.R. SCOTT Mr King and the King Makers / 268
May 1951 / EDITORIAL The United States: Canada's Problem / 271
August 1951 / FRANK H. UNDERHILL Notes on the Massey Report / 271
August 1951 / GAVIN WHITE Canadian Apartheid / 274
March 1952 / MARTHA CHAMPION RANDLE The New Indian Act / 276
April 1952 / FRANK H. UNDERHILL Power Politics in the Ontario CCF / 278
April 1952 / FRED SWAYZE 'Spring Song' / 281
December 1952 / FRANK H. UNDERHILL Turning New Leaves / 281
January 1953 / DOROTHY LIVESAY *Matt* / 283
July 1953 / FRANK H. UNDERHILL How to Vote / 285
August 1953 / J.B. CONACHER A Canadian Social Scandal / 288
October 1954 / LOUIS DUDEK The State of Canadian Poetry: 1954 / 289
March 1955 / A.R.M. LOWER The Question of National Television / 292
July 1955 / CURT LANG 'History Lesson on Point Grey' / 294
August 1955 / JEAN INGLIS 'And the Green Hills Laugh' / 294
August 1955 / LOUIS DUDEK 'Keewaydin Poems' / 298
October 1955 & November 1955 / MILTON WILSON On Dudek and Layton / 299
November 1955 / PAUL FOX The Liberal Party / 302
May 1956 / MILLAR MacLURE Poets in Review / 305
May 1956 / A.J.M. SMITH 'On Reading Certain Poems and Epistles of Irving Layton and Louis Dudek' / 305
July 1956 / A.G. CHRISTOPHER A Letter / 306
July 1956 / EUGENE FORSEY Pipeline and Parliament / 308
August 1956 / PHYLLIS WEBB 'The Idiot Birds' / 310
October 1956 / IRVING LAYTON Layton on Layton / 306
January 1957 / A. VIXEN The New Conservative Leader / 310
February 1958 / IRVING LAYTON 'Sheep' 'Whatever Else Poetry is Freedom' 'Côte des Neiges Cemetry' / 312
June 1958 / JOHN PORTER Political Parties and the Political Cheer / 314
June 1958 / MICHAEL OLIVER Duplessis and Quebec's Intellectuals / 316
July 1958 / DONALD V. SMILEY One-Partyism and Canadian Democracy / 319
September 1958 / E.W. MANDEL Frye's *Anatomy of Criticism* / 320
November 1958 / MILTON ACORN 'The Tolerant Philistine' / 323
December 1958 / PAULINE JEWETT Mr Diefenbaker's Proposed Bill of Rights / 323

The 60s

May 1960 / MILTON ACORN 'Restaurant Scene' / 331
June 1960 / JOYCE WIELAND *Circus* / 331

August 1960 / HERBERT F. QUINN Defeat in Quebec / 331
September 1960 / A.L. LEVINE The US and the Canadian Economy / 333
October 1960 / MILTON ACORN 'I Will Arise and Go Now' / 335
February 1961 / ALDEN A. NOWLAN 'Wasp' / 336
March 1961 / KENNETH McNAUGHT J.S. Woodsworth and the New Party / 336
May 1961 / RAMSAY COOK The Old Man, the Old Manifesto, the Old Party / 339
August 1961 / MALCOLM LOWRY 'Tashtego Believed Red' 'Nocturne in Burrard Inlet' / 342
October 1961 / PAUL STANDING Nipples on the Newsstands / 342
October 1961 / IRVING LAYTON 'There Were No Signs' / 344
January 1962 / LAURIER L. LAPIERRE Le Séparatisme and French Canadians / 344
February 1962 / A.W. PURDY 'Poem for One of the Annettes' / 347
September 1962 / DONALD V. SMILEY Canada's Poujadists: A New Look at Social Credit / 348
November 1962 / DAVID HELWIG *The Winter of the Daffodils* / 351
May 1963 / JOHN MEISEL Election Outcome: A Breather / 354
May 1963 / KENNETH McNAUGHT Uncle Sam Again / 357
June 1963 / MARGARET ATWOOD 'Mad Mother Ballad' / 359
July 1963 / RAMSAY COOK A Time to Break Silence / 359
October 1963 / H. BLAIR NEATBY The Present Discontents: A Proposal / 361
October 1963 / A.W. PURDY *The Undertaker* / 363
November 1963 / GWENDOLYN MacEWEN 'Manzini: Escape Artist' / 368
December 1963 / E.W. MANDEL 'Orpheus in the Underworld' / 368
January 1964 / MARSHALL McLUHAN Murder by Television / 369
July 1964 / MELVILLE H. WATKINS The Canadian Quandary / 371
July 1964 / ABRAHAM ROTSTEIN The Canadian Quandary / 373
July 1964 / DAVID BROMIGE 'The Great Lover' / 377
July 1964 / PADRAIG O BROIN 'Railing at Byzantium' / 377
October 1964 / EDITORIAL In the Bourassa Tradition / 377
January 1965 / A.W. PURDY 'The Wine-Maker's Beat-étude' / 381
June 1965 / LIONEL TIGER Bennett and the Power and the Glory / 382
August 1965 / ABRAHAM ROTSTEIN and MELVILLE H. WATKINS The Outer Man: Technology and Alienation / 384
March 1966 / bp nichol 'to islands rowboats stand on' / 386
March 1966 / GEORGE BOWERING *The House on Tenth* / 386
May 1966 / RAMSAY COOK 'Un Québec fort dans une nouvelle Confédération' / 392
June 1966 / DAVID W. SLATER Gordon's New Book / 395
June 1966 / DOROTHY LIVESAY 'And Give Us Our Trespasses' / 397
July 1966 / MELVILLE H. WATKINS Is Gordon's Game Worth the Candle? / 398
August 1966 / HELEN GOWANS *An Awfully Mature Person* / 400
December 1966 / ALDEN NOWLAN 'Rivalry' / 404

March 1967 / MICHAEL ONDAATJE 'Peter' / 404
April 1967 / RAYMOND SOUSTER 'Rags-and-Bones Man' / 406
January 1968 / EUGENE McNAMARA *To Burn* / 406
April 1968 / ALDEN NOWLAN 'The Unnatural Son' / 408
May 1968 / PAUL FOX The Liberals Choose Trudeau: Pragmatism at Work / 411
May 1968 / GAD HOROWITZ Trudeau vs Trudeauism / 413
June 1968 / JOYCE WIELAND cover illustration / 416
December 1968 / HANS WERNER 'Sonnet for Monica' / 416
February 1969 / DALTON CAMP Canadian-American Interdependence: How Much? / 417
February 1969 / PAUL BIDWELL 'God Bless Americaw' / 419
March 1969 / GLEN SIEBRASSE 'La Plaza de Toros, Madrid' / 420
May 1969 / ABRAHAM ROTSTEIN Running from Paradise / 420
May 1969 / DAVID McFADDEN 'Get Your Feet Off the Coffee Table' / 424
October 1969 / ABRAHAM ROTSTEIN The Search for Independence / 424
January 1970 / COLLEEN THIBAUDEAU 'February 20th' / 428
January 1970 / KENNETH McNAUGHT The Permanent Colony / 429

PREFACE

The Canadian Forum is unique. No other serious monthly in Canada has ever survived fifty years of continuous publication. No other periodical has regularly published prose and poetry of quality alongside articles of political and social commentary. And no other magazine has so consistently pressed for progressive policies and defended civil liberties, political dissent, and artistic freedom. This in itself is a proud record, but what makes it even more striking, if not amazing, is that the *Forum* has survived virtually without advertising, sometimes with regrettably few subscribers, and always with very little money. Month in and month out for a half-century the *Forum* has appeared, the product of voluntary labour by a dedicated editorial board; month in and month out the *Forum* has consistently produced some of the best writing in Canada.

A group of faculty and undergraduates founded the *Forum* in 1920 at the University of Toronto. The magazine was the offspring of a tiny periodical, *The Rebel*, also published at Toronto, and the credo of *The Canadian Forum* in many ways resembled that of its parent: rebellion against convention, not against society. The first editorial board had Barker Fairley as literary editor and C.B. Sissons as political editor, and their goal as announced in the first issue was to make *The Canadian Forum* a national magazine. Too much of our news was coloured and distorted, the editors maintained, before it ever reached the Canadian press; too often our convictions were borrowed from London, Paris, or New York. Real independence was a spiritual thing, not a product of tariffs or treaties. No country had ever reached its full stature that made its goods at home but not its faith or philosophy. *The Canadian Forum* was avowedly nationalist in 1920 — and so it is still in the 1970s.

Equally important to the editors of *Forum* in 1920 was that their magazine should live up to its name. The first editorial statement defined the role of the magazine: 'The Canadian Forum had its origins in a desire to secure a freer and more informed discussion of public questions and, behind the strife of parties, to trace and value those developments of arts and letters which are distinctly Canadian. Consequently it invites the expression of opinion on the part of its readers.' The pages of *The Canadian Forum* were always to be open to anyone who could express himself with 'conciseness, point, and good-nature' and for fifty years this, too, has remained true.

But this did not mean that the *Forum* lacked a point of view. Right from the first issue, the magazine developed a deliberately progressive attitude toward politics and culture. It published short stories that defied the puritanical morality then so solidly embedded in Canadian life, and poetry that was aware of newer and more modern modes. From its beginnings, the *Forum* encouraged unknown authors who later became well-established figures in our literature. Often the pages of the magazine were the places where poets tried out their ideas, and readers looking back can see early versions of well-known poems (Smith's 'The Lonely Land' and Layton's 'Whatever Else Poetry Is Freedom' are just two examples, both reprinted here as they first appeared in the *Forum*) as well as poems and stories by writers who have declined for a variety of reasons to resuscitate them from the pages of *The Canadian Forum* into their collected work. These works have a historical and literary interest, and this volume contains such poems by Smith, Scott, Livesay, Birney, Klein, Atwood, and others. The *Forum* also published graphics that broke sharply with the conventions of the day, including work by the Group of Seven, those notorious painters incapable of representational art.

Most notably, *The Canadian Forum* published articles of opinion that pressed hard against the accepted wisdom of the day. This has always been so, and this surely is the enduring value of the *Forum*. During the 1920s, for example, *The Canadian Forum* published numerous articles by J.S. Woodsworth, that dangerous agitator who had been involved in the Winnipeg General Strike of 1919. The *Forum* also poked fun at the foibles and follies of Canadians, commenting wittily on the preoccupations of their leaders, their newspapers, and their businessmen. Most often, however, the tone was serious. There was so much wrong with society, so many social evils, so much repression. Some very able social critics found in the *Forum* their first and best platform. So it was for Frank Underhill, the *Forum*'s most published author and probably its best, for Frank Scott, for Eugene Forsey, for Mel Watkins, and for Abe Rotstein.

The critical shafts were usually aimed from the left of the political spectrum, but *The Canadian Forum* was never a party organ. For its first seven years, the *Forum* was completely independent, financed by its subscribers and its board members. For the next seven years, J.M. Dent and Sons, the publishers, met the magazine's annual deficits and paid the salary of a full-time editor, J. Francis White. In the depths of the depression, however, Dent was forced to withdraw its support and for a year the magazine was run by a group of liberal Liberals under the editorship of Steven Cartwright. In 1935 this group abandoned control, and the magazine was rescued by Graham Spry, then the secretary of the Ontario Co-operative Commonwealth Federation. The next year direction passed to the League for Social Reconstruction, the intellectual precursors and 'idea men' of the CCF. Upon the League's dissolution, an independent board of directors was established and this method of editorial control has continued ever since. Since the Second World War, *The Canadian Forum* has had as its editors Northrop Frye, James Giffen and Stefan Stykolt, Milton Wilson, and Abraham Rotstein. Many of the people involved in the *Forum* were deeply committed politically, but to their credit they retained the breadth and disparity of view that has so characterized the magazine throughout its life.

Apart from its continuing concern with society, certain themes have recurred with striking regularity in the *Forum* decade after decade. National independence is one. How could Canada become a nation? The question was raised in the 1920s as contributors examined the effects of the British tie; it was raised in the 1930s as *Forum* contributors searched for ways Canada could avoid the war that they could see fast approaching; it was raised in the 1940s as Canada's growing dependence on the United States became evident; and it has been raised ever since as the *Forum* and its writers sought to escape the smothering embrace of the military-industrial complex and the multinational corporation.

Hand in hand with the independence issue went the discussions about Canada's proper place in the world. Should Canadians be satisfied to remain 'ready aye ready' as part of the British Empire? Was there not something more to life than that? Could Canada be neutralist? Frank Underhill and others asked in the 1930s. By the 1940s, of course, the tone had changed to whole-hearted support for collective security, to one of wondering that Canadians could ever have been so foolish as to contemplate neutrality. For a few years, the cold warriors sometimes seemed to dominate the pages of the journal. Still, the *Forum* was often ahead of the public mood, and by the time of the Korean War contributors were beginning to ask if Canada – and Canadian socialists in particular – should search for another course than mere loyalty to the dictates of Washington. By the end of the 1950s this theme would be dominating the discussions in the pages of *The Canadian Forum*.

Mackenzie King was another perennial subject. For the first thirty years of the *Forum* there was scarcely an issue that did not curiously examine the Liberal Prime Minister as a unique wonder of the Western world. How did the dumpy little wizard from Kingsmere do it? He offered no leadership, he had no principles, no charisma. All that he did possess was a native cunning and great good fortune, and the *Forum* published a host of articles that speculated about the secret of his uncanny success. Frank Underhill, in particular, was fascinated by Mr

King, but so were the *Forum's* anonymous 'political correspondents' in the 1920s, Frank Scott, Eugene Forsey, and others. In many ways King dominated the pages of the *Forum* until 1950, much as he dominated the country.

Certainly the *Forum* is an indispensable source for a King-watcher. In fact the *Forum* is an indispensable source for anyone interested in Canadian history, politics, society, and culture in the last fifty years. No one subscribes to the *Forum*, its editors sometimes complain, but every scholar cites it in his work. There is more than a little truth in that statement. Generations of students and scholars have referred to and will continue to refer to the *Forum* as a reliable source of comment and criticism on all aspects of Canadian life. So many people who had something to say said it in the *Forum* that in a very real sense the backfiles of the magazine are a national treasure. Since 1920 *The Canadian Forum* has been Canada, a mirror of its whims and errors, its social conscience, its strength. That is no mean record.

The editors of this anthology have had to be rigorous in selecting pieces for inclusion. The range of choice was enormous, and we were forced to operate on certain principles. Generally, material that has been reprinted widely was omitted, apart from a few selections to indicate where some famous poems and articles first appeared. Generally, articles that discussed foreign phenomena were similarly excluded, and the emphasis throughout is deliberately focused on Canada. And, generally, articles from as wide a range of contributors as possible were selected.

The arrangement of sections is by decade, and a chronological sequence has everywhere been followed. As does no other arrangement, this gives the reader a sense of the richness and the scope of the material published by the *Forum*. Because we believe that the *Forum* had its greatest influence in the 1930s, this decade receives a disproportionate amount of space. We regret this not at all; our only regret is that so much excellent material had to be left out and we can only encourage readers to return to the bound files of *The Canadian Forum*.

Most of the contributors to *Forum* have been very generous in allowing us to publish their early work, some of which they now find immature, derivative, or otherwise far short of their present standards. Where used, pseudonyms have been maintained; occasionally, writers' real names are added in footnotes. The editors made every effort to locate authors and to secure permission to reprint material in *Forum*. Where we have not been successful in locating individual authors or artists, it was not for want of effort. Finally the editors would like to thank the Canada Council for a small research grant, Mrs Linda Forrest Grayson, Virgil Duff, and Fritz Logan for their assistance in selecting this material, and Joan Murray for choosing most of the art work that graces these pages.

THE 20s

Discussion of the 1920s today usually focuses on flappers, bathtub gin, constitutional crises, and boom. What is sometimes forgotten is that most of the post-war decade was a period of high prices and unemployment, of terrible discontent in the mines and factories, and of separatist rumblings on the prairies and in Quebec. No reader of the *Forum* in these years could have been unaware of this other side of life in Canada. To read the articles written during these first ten years of *Forum*'s life is to comprehend the anger of J.S. Woodsworth at the treatment meted out to the strikers at BESCO by an insensitive, illiberal government; it is to share in the rage of Henry Wise Wood and the Progressives at the treatment of farmers by the 'interests' of the East and to understand their search for new forms of governmental organization; and it is to understand that secession is not an issue peculiar to our own time. The public may have been mired in smugness, but the *Forum* was not.

Certainly the literary criticism appearing in *The Canadian Forum* during these years castigated Canadian complacency in the arts. There were pleas for more rigorous critical standards in judging our literature, most notably in A.J.M. Smith's 'Wanted – Canadian Criticism.' There was a sense of mission in the publication of Jean Burton's 'Phyllus,' a story that was presented as yet another critical attack on an outmoded and unrealistic narrow-mindedness. And there was an awareness of the emerging new poets. Poems by Pratt, Livesay, Smith, Kennedy, and Finch appeared during this decade, a good list for any decade in fact.

HUNTLY K. GORDON
Canadian Poetry

Despite flattering reviews of 'excellent and truly Canadian poetry,' English Canada fails to produce a distinctive verse of literary value. New volumes appear continually and are, for the most part, as quickly relegated to their deserved limbo. Nothing depresses the Canadian lover of poetry more than these exhibitions of verse making and he soon learns to despair of finding a poet who will picture for him characteristic scenes and people with that sure touch which calls them up, living and vivid, before his mind's eye. Only by the reality of its impression can poetry succeed, and seldom does Canadian poetry achieve reality.

I do not here speak of the French poetry of Quebec, the *habitant* songs of Drummond and others, nor of the unauthored songs of camp and trail. That they have a true and distinctive spirit and poetic merit I am ready to believe, but am unfitted to judge. It is the verses of known and English speaking authors that are so profoundly disappointing that one is tempted to conclude that they are neither poetry nor Canadian. They leave the poetry lover more unmoved the more he delights in their subjects. There is something fundamentally wrong in such poetry.

Nevertheless we have poets of decided, though not of outstanding ability – Lampman

F.H. VARLEY *The Colliery Accident – Anxiety at the Pit-head* Nov. 1920

at the head, Bliss Carman, Duncan Campbell Scott, Marjorie Pickthall, and many would name others. Lampman and the Canadians as a whole feel deeply the distinctive beauties of prairie and mountain, bushland and farm, and love their people and their ways. But one sometimes wonders whether they do not 'see, not feel, how beautiful they are,' so insincere sounds the sincerity of their praise, and so unreal is their description. Even their most personal subjective verses fail to touch the reader home. It is in this insincere, this unconvincing expression that one must seek the fault that destroys our claim to a distinctive poetry.

Lampman is perhaps the truest singer and the most Canadian of our poets. He knew the wide waters and islands of Temagami when it was scarcely heard of in southern Ontario. The silent rivers and the tangled bush of the North filled him with that sense of beauty which struggles for poetic expression, while many of his poems give us vividly enough pictures of the exceeding heat and cold, drought and storm, and the changing labours of Ontario farm life. They call up the mental vision, but from a prolonged reading of his poetry we turn away disheartened. His expression is continually marred by words and phrases which recall customs and scenes as foreign to us as are the subjects of his 'classical' verses. For instance, the really fine poem 'In November' has these lines on the dead mulleins in a typical bush clearing:

Not plants at all they seemed to me,
But rather some spare company
Of hermit folk ...

The one word 'hermit' destroys the unity of impression of the poem. It is expressive of medieval Europe, but in Canada there 'ain't no such animile.' This criticism may sound petty and cavilling, but the use of such words demonstrates that Canadians have not a sure native touch in their expression. Had there existed a sound tradition when Lampman began to write, or had he been great enough to found and follow scrupulously one of his own, he might have achieved much. As it was he found no well worn road for his guidance and no Burns has arisen to deepen and correct the path left by this straying Ferguson.

If this false Canadianism is true of Lampman, it is much more depressingly so of others. In a short essay there is no room for discussion author by author, but *The Oxford Book of Canadian Verse*, our best anthology, may be taken as a fair representation of Canadian verse. Its introduction announces as the standard of selection truly Canadian verse of high literary quality. Yet, though the majority of its 251 poems deal with Canadian themes, a half-dozen at most give delight over familiar things revivified by the writer's insight. The rest are for the most part heavy, solemn, and sometimes drearily Shelleyesque. One asks for bread here and receives a stone.

Take 'The Whitethroat' for instance. No bird song is sweeter or more characteristic of our southern spring and northern summer than that of this little sparrow. You may hear his sad and lonely call any evening in the Georgian Bay, ringing out from some pine-darkened channel among the islands, and to many he is the very voice of the North. Here is what Theodore Harding Rand does with him:

Shy bird of the silver arrows of song,
That cleave our northern air so clear,
Thy notes prolong, prolong,
    I listen, I hear:
'I – love – dear – Canada,
    Canada, Canada.'

O plumes of the pointed dusky fir,
    Screen of a swelling patriot heart,
The copse is all astir,
    And echoes thy part! ...

And so on. No picture of the silent Northland will arise at this. Take also 'The Canadian Herd Boy.' As a youngster I have fetched the cows from the river bank through bush and rail-fenced fields but find nothing familiar or real in Mrs Moodie's verses except one word, 'Cobos,' a somewhat unhappy member of this Scott-like poem.

To repeat, there is nothing more Canadian than these subjects and nothing less Canadian than their treatment. The same is true of the great mass of our poetry. The truth is there is scarcely material for a pretentious Canadian anthology. If a new one of any worth is printed it must be extremely small and exclusive, including perhaps only fifty poems. Everything, however, is to be gained by waiting till there is a larger body of writers and a higher standard of work.

The cause of unreality in Canadian verse is not far to seek, though its cure may not be so simple. Lampman gives us the key to the weakness of the rest. His finest verses often failed through a false or exotic expression. Those who followed him, far from avoiding his error, have in many cases exaggerated it grossly. It is scarcely necessary to mention the authors of *Scottish Canadian Poets*. Despite the theory that the Canadian is more akin in his sentiments to the Scot than to the Englishman it is obvious to the most casual reader that these verses are neither Scottish nor Canadian in sentiment or expression. They serve, however, to point the faults of authors writing in English. These might with equal justice be called English Canadian poets and likewise their work is neither English nor Canadian. Such expressions as 'bosky dell' and 'grove' are as foreign to us as are 'corrie' and 'shaw' and yet expressions such as these, descriptive of typically English scenery, are the stock in trade of our poets. For the most part they ignore the native for English expressions, and those by no means the purest and most universal.

This outland phraseology is all the more obvious because we seem to set ourselves almost consciously to write on native subjects. One almost expects to find 'Made in Canada' on the last page, so direct and obvious is the treatment. But one looks in vain for that loving familiarity by which British writers take the distinctive characteristics of their countrysides in the stride of their poems. A strange corollary of this is found in our subjective poems. The charm of a vast number of English lyrics of this nature can be traced to the well-nigh unconscious use of familiar, almost local, sights or sounds to interpret the mood. Such a deep knowledge of Canadian life does not seem as yet to run deeply and unconsciously through the being of our poets and their work is the loser by much charm and simplicity, and above all by that reality and concrete value without which no school can prosper for long.

We come to the conclusion of all this unpleasant fault-finding. Before a poetry can achieve universality it must paradoxically attain nationality. All countries producing great poetry have left their indelible stamp upon it and Canada as yet is content to derive her forms and expression from England. I do not infer that there should or can be any drastic break with English literary traditions; our language is basically the same and the example of those who are most akin to us must be our safest guide. Yet, if we are to produce poetry of any value, we must shun derivative expression and sentiment as we would the devil and follow our characteristic bent as eagerly as we are learning to do in other spheres. We have our own expressions and names for the features of the countryside ('bush' is as poetic as 'grove') and above all we have a characteristic spirit. We must learn to use and purify them, and develop a native tradition, or die to literature.

J.S. WOODSWORTH
Unemployment

Away down the street from the civic relief office stretches the queue of men awaiting their turn to obtain meal tickets. A long parade of respectably dressed men march from their suburban homes to join the down town workers in a huge demonstration on Cambie Street grounds. Such are the outward manifestations of unemployment in Vancouver to-day.

In a small city, ten thousand unemployed. What an economic loss! If these men were on strike what volumes of righteous indignation would be poured forth from the disinterested citizens! These citizens now content themselves with grumbling about giving relief to men who, no doubt, wasted their earnings in riotous living.

But what does this unemployment mean in terms of human welfare? The district nurses tell a heartrending story of under-nourished children, of unwelcome babies coming into homes in which there is no clothing in which to wrap them, of weary struggling mothers and discouraged or embittered fathers and of broken homes.

Is this Canada – the Canada of which we have been so proud? In the old world, poverty always had been and was taken almost as a matter of course, but in 'this land of opportunity' have we so soon come to this?

Of course we have had unemployment and bread lines before now. In 1913 in Vancouver the situation was even more acute, if less serious. Then came the war. Thousands of men enlisted at once in a spirit of enthusiasm, but thousands of others were compelled by economic pressure to enlist. Production was artificially stimulated. A good market, high prices, public and private 'graft' and unlimited credit brought a period of so-called 'prosperity.' But now the war is over. The bills are coming due. The old trouble is re-asserting itself with increased intensity.

What is the worker thinking about it? His thoughts are not the thoughts of the business man. He looks at things from an entirely different angle. In fact, he lives in a different world. There lies one of the most dangerous factors in the situation. The ordinary well-to-do citizen fails to recognize that, since the war, we are living in a new world of ideas. He, unfortunately, is still living in the past. While he may talk of re-construction, he thinks of this as construction on a larger scale along old lines. The worker dreams of a new heaven and a new earth.

This new view of life which is held by an ever-increasing section of the working-class leads to a repudiation of the hitherto accepted leadership. The professional politician may wax eloquent over 'our wonderful natural resources' but this stimulated passion leaves the working man cold. He knows that he has been fenced off from these resources. He knows that, as a matter of fact, the richest resources in British Columbia are held by American syndicates. The patriotic 'spell-binder' is to-day powerless. 'War – ah, it's a lovely war!' He has been there. 'If *they* want to fight *they* can do the fighting themselves next time – *Our Country* – the world safe for Democracy – Bah! Two meals and a lousy bed is all *they* give you when you get back. Russia for me.'

Even the business man is no longer listened to. The business man is not yet aware of this. He still dominates the Board of Trade and City Council. He still listens to self-laudatory speeches in the Canadian Club or the Rotary Club. He still commands the subservient press. But the heart of the people is far from him. 'Immigration, the greatest need of Canada.' The immigrant worker laughs scornfully as he thinks of a still longer bread line. 'More British Capital.' He knows that already we cannot pay even the interest on the money we have so recklessly borrowed and squandered. 'Production.' That was the last slogan to which he responded. Now he knows that the yards are stocked with lumber, the warehouses with clothes, the cold storage plants with food – yet his family has not adequate food, clothing or shelter. Now there comes the latest word of wisdom, 'deflation' – 'liquidation.' It simply makes him angry. He turns in disgust from the wisdom of the business man.

The church has ceased to offer him anything that will appease either physical or spiritual appetite. The daily press is absolutely discredited. The university is under suspicion or too remote. Perhaps he remembers that even as modern an economist as Jevons attributed recurrent unemployment to the spots on the sun!

The old leadership rejected, the workers of the West are rapidly accepting the Socialist analysis of society. In the present distress, they believe they are experiencing the birth pangs of a new social order. Undoubtedly there is, with a vast number, a sense of expectation – a feeling akin to that of the religious enthusiast who was convinced that the 'Day of the Lord is at hand.' With many, belief in the inevitableness of the Revolution has led to a sort of fatalism. They can do little to hasten the event. Or again, ameliorative measures are not to be encouraged as they may somewhat retard the approaching climax.

Eagerly they scan the papers for news from Soviet Russia, for signs of a break-up in Middle Europe, for a more aggressive movement in Great Britain. In their halls, all day long they debate the merits of "direct action,' 'the dictatorship of the Proletariat,' or speculate as to whether there is any possibility that in this country the change might be brought about without violence.

In the meantime, the situation grows steadily worse and little of a constructive character is being attempted. The Vancouver member of the Federal House – who is said to be slated for a cabinet position – expressed the opinion that if only a vigorous campaign were carried on in the Rotary and Kiwanis Clubs, it would be discovered that many members had odd jobs in their back yards. These, if made available through a well-conducted Bureau, would go a long way toward solving our unemployment problem! This valuable suggestion ought surely to be passed on to similar clubs in Toronto and Montreal. A thousand pities that it has not been cabled to New York and London and Vienna!

What can be done? Let us at least lay down some fundamental principles.

1 The large proportion of *unemployment is involuntary*. Granted that a percentage of the men are lazy or shiftless, the fact is that six months ago most of the unemployed were at work and would be at work to-morrow if work were available. With modern large scale production the individual is helpless. A lumber worker cannot himself open up a camp; a miner, a coal mine; or a dismissed railroad worker start up a second CPR system.

2 Under these conditions, when private enterprise fails, the *State is under obligation to*

provide work. If the State with all its resources finds itself unable to do so, the case for the private individual is indeed hopeless.

3 Until suitable work is found, the *State should provide adequate maintenance.* This is not as a matter of charity but as a matter of simple justice. A more fully developed industrial state would provide a system of unemployed insurance. The Minister of Labour tells us that it would require several years to build up such a scheme. In the meantime the underlying principle, as in the case of workmen's compensation, should be recognized, namely that Industry should carry its own charges.

4 *Any work provided should be productive in character and should be carried on under prevailing conditions* as to hours, remuneration and control. We have surely gotten beyond the mere work-test. We should realize the futility, economic and moral, of mere relief works. We must not permit employers under the guise of charity to lower the standard of living built up at so great a cost during the past hundred years.

5 *The financing of such enterprises should be a first charge on the natural resources and credit of the country.* In law, private ownership has never been absolute. In a society, where social production becomes prevalent and the monopolistic element enters, private ownership of the very means of life reduces us in time to the servile state. We have admittedly abundant natural resources, we have the credit of the country – the capitalized labour power of the people – that on which alone our whole modern financial system is based. Why not bring natural resources, credit and workers, together?

6 If in the midst of abundant resources *any administration fails even to feed its people it ceases to command their loyalty.* It has ceased to function as an organ of democratic government. When once this becomes apparent it needs no prophet to foretell that all the legislation and all the repressive measures will not long hold down a free and intelligent people.

In Canada, as elsewhere, we face strenuous times. It may not be given to the business and professional men to decide whether or not we are to enter upon a new social order. It does seem to be in their power to decide whether the transition period be comparatively easy or a long drawn out struggle marked by violence and general dislocation. The present attitude of the American business man is not reassuring.

M.H. STAPLES

The Genesis of the United Farmers

'It has been the immemorial custom of the Canadian Farmer to put on what is called a poor mouth, and to represent himself in season and out of season as the long-suffering goat of the body politic. ... At the present moment the farmer is engaged in a political movement designed to free him from the necessity of paying customs taxes. ... Returns show that in 1918, out of a total of $62,687,258.02 collected under the Income War Tax Act, the farmers contributed the imposing sum of $957,980.27. ... Motor cars have been purchased and other usually reliable manifestations have given the lamentations of the farmer a hollow ring. ... It is perhaps unnecessary to say that the success of the farmer in evading his share of taxation increases the burden which other classes must bear.'

The above quotations are selected from the editorial columns of one of our leading Canadian journals. They give expression to views widely held concerning the farmer and his efforts. One wonders if it ever occurs to those who hold such views to ask whether the facts concealed in the statements quoted might not bear an altogether different construction.

The year 1918 was one of the most favourable years that agriculture has ever experienced, yet few farmers earned enough to pay income taxes under the law, in spite of the fact that they toiled on an average twelve hours a day, Although such enlightening figures were not available until last year the tiller of the soil has felt that somehow he and his wife were not receiving just recompense for their labour. He complained, but he worked on and as he worked on he became more restive. Phrases such as 'poor mouth' did not tend to soothe his feelings, and when the great delegation to Ottawa in 1917 was met with closed doors, his resentment was fanned to a white heat.

Immediately, what the farmer leaders had already seen began to engage the attention of the rank and file. For the last ten years the rural population had steadily declined, great areas were being turned to pasture, and the sons and daughters of the land were flocking to the city. In the absence of young folk and with the declining population community spirit and social intercourse sank to a low ebb. Along with this there had developed a strange lack of interest in public matters and a tendency for each farmer to confine his attention to the affairs of his own farm. There was scarcely a farmer sitting around the board in any of the Councils of the land above that of the local municipality. These were the actual conditions. The average farmer had not bothered much about them, but when he did waken up, what he learned came to him with somewhat of a shock.

Immediately he began to connect these discoveries with his grievances, in the relationship of cause and effect. It had been his belief that the fiscal policy of the Dominion operated immediately to his disadvantage. In the urban centres he had seen the market for his products frequently so glutted or manipulated that he could not afford to produce for it, while at the same time foreign products were coming in to satisfy the demand, and he concluded that the men to whom he had left all marketing arrangements had made a miserable failure of their undertaking. Then the educational system was so ordered that none but the well-to-do farm boy could take advantage of the higher instruction with any hope of returning to the farm, since by the time he had completed his course he had exhausted his capital and must turn to some occupation requiring little money at the start. Even the primary school had been very little changed for the last forty years and what change there had taken place seemed to many to be for the worse rather than for the better. Suddenly, almost, the farmer saw these as the result of his failure to take an active interest in public affairs.

Then, for the remedy. How were manufacturers able to maintain the tariff in the face of such stout opposition as was offered in 1911? How were professional men able to lay down a standard fee for services rendered? How could financial institutions operate so nicely under a uniform policy? Obviously it was through organization, purely class organizations at that. Then the farmer must have a class organization too. Only those who know rural conditions and who understand something of the farmer's habit of thought have any idea what a stupendous undertaking it was to form an independent association of farmers, but the farmer believed that it had to be done, and now it is an accomplished fact.

In the fifteen hundred branches scattered all over the Province of Ontario the United Farmers meet fortnightly to conduct business and to discuss public matters. Questions of the day are keenly debated, often with the assistance of material supplied from Head Office. When one considers how large a place legislation plays in the regulation of business, in shaping the fiscal policy, in the method of raising revenue, and in ordering the educational system, he needs no extended explanation as to why the organized farmers became interested in politics. Their discussions were neither learned nor profound, but they bore directly on questions of legislation and administration.

In developing their organization the farmers copied a feature from the association of manufacturers - a feature which had led to much confusion of thought, both within and without their ranks. The manufacturers frankly admit that their organization exists primarily for making the will of manufacturers effective in legislation and administration. From a perusal of the Constitution and By-laws of the United Farmers it seems evident that at first the farmers scarcely thought of politics, and certainly not beyond making their wants known through established channels; but as their association grew in experience they were forced to deviate somewhat from their projected path. They found that mere petitions were not very effective. They recalled that when the Laurier régime was ushered in on a low tariff policy in '96 the promised reform never developed. They remembered that the Liberal naval policy of 1911 was rejected at the polls only to be endorsed in substance shortly afterwards by the victorious party. They saw that the reins of government were given into the hands of urban representatives who naturally legislated in their own immediate interests. They lost faith in the old political parties and they took independent action.

Now electors are accustomed to think in terms of the old political organizations and consequently it is not surprising that from all sides the United Farmers are regarded purely as a political party. Because of this they are likely to suffer somewhat, for no field is more perilous to tread than the field of public service. But in the turmoil of political onslaughts let no one overlook the twenty million dollars worth of business done in the clubs last year, the many new assembly halls erected in newly acquired athletic fields, the hundreds of successful picnics held and many kindred activities. Here is the main business of the UFO.

If one keeps these activities in mind and the philosophy of the state which they presuppose he is not likely to be misled by a pamphlet such as that recently published by the Canadian Reconstruction Association entitled, 'The Non-Partisan League of North Dakota, a Study of Class War and Its Disastrous Consequences.' It is likely to catch the unwary and the man who is prejudiced in favour of its implied contentions, but the thinking man will ask what can be the reason for such a publication emanating from such a source. Scarcely anyone in Ontario is interested in the Non-Partisan League. In the West the Non-Partisan League has been killed effectively, and the United Farmers were foremost at the killing. Therefore, the farmers do not need to be warned against a threatened danger, nor do manufacturers need to be set on their guard against farmers. It is a deliberate and subtle play upon public psychology. The suggestion is: The agrarian class movement has been tried out in North Dakota and has been disastrous. See, you farmers of Canada, where you are heading. Beware! You have neither the experience nor the brains.

To see the utter folly of the comparison and the inference, one has only to contemplate the two-year record of the farmer-labour Government of Ontario. Farmers of Canada are not socialists, nor do they seek to attain their ends primarily through state machinery, nor is politics their first and chief interest.

They have fastened on another method, namely, co-operation, and this is full of menace to many business interests who, to-day, are operating in more or less of a preserve. Happily they have not their eyes fixed for guidance upon an experiment that has ended with 'disastrous consequences.' Co-operation in Great Britain, an old country, and in New Zealand, a new country, has met with astounding success. Co-operation has met with serious reverses in America, but still it survives and with experience grows in strength. Its genius is such that 'it will not down.' It is full of menace to certain fea-

LAWREN HARRIS *Slums and Shadows* Sept. 1921

tures in the present order of society, where the underdog is mercilessly exploited, because it involves an active campaign of education and the bringing to light of information which is now suppressed. It is full of hope for the future because it depends for its success upon enlightened action, each individual bringing to the assistance of his fellows whatever means or talent he may possess. This is vastly different from what we have been accustomed to, namely, a magnified game of cock-on-the-rock, where the strong man thrusts the weak man off, with such a resultant dust of fiscal laws and administrative confusion that he has little difficulty in retaining his vantage ground. Nor is it a socialistic machine which would lodge men in with regulations, making it impossible for them to go astray. Rather for the whip of authority it substitutes the hand of fellowship.

Such is the vision which the farmers have caught; such are the methods by which they would follow it. In its pursuit they stumble over countless obstacles both natural and artificial, and in the turmoil the vision grows dim, but let no man mistake confusion for hesitation. The vision abides and periodically becomes clearer. Privilege calls their progress class war. Well – let us have more of such wars.

C.B. SISSONS

The Farmers' Case

On the morning of the twenty-first of October, 1919, the Canadian public awoke to find that a new force had arisen in Canadian politics. On the previous day the provincial elections had been held in Ontario. Without the support of the daily press, without candidates in many ridings, the United Farmers elected more members than either of the old parties and almost as many as both the old parties combined and were able by an alliance with the labour members to form a government. That was almost two years ago. Yet it is doubtful if any considerable number of urban electors know why the farmers are in politics or what they want. Mr Meighen in his London speech admitted that they were his most formidable opponents because they were in earnest, and he professed to know their aims and purposes, but surrounded as he is by lawbooks and privilege he too fails to appreciate their position.

The greatest weakness of the farmers' movement lies just in this. It lacks the means of expressing itself to the urban electorate. Through its picnics it has revived the useful practice of public discussion. But these picnics are for farmers. Through the *Grain Grower's Guide* and the *Farmer's Sun* it disseminates the opinions which have united the farmers in class endeavour. An occasional town weekly takes up the tale. Quite recently, whether from conviction or scenting the future, certain city dailies have become not unfriendly. On the whole, however, the movement has failed to secure, in press or on platform, an approach to city people.

When Cobden was engaged in a work similar to that which the leaders in the farmers' movement have now undertaken, he was not satisfied with making himself solid with Manchester and the factory towns. In the face of strong opposition, even threats of personal violence, he carried his message into rural England. By force of argument, by sincerity and earnestness, he convinced the agricultural interests bitterly hostile to the repeal of the Corn Laws and the withdrawal of protection from their industry, that the policy which was wiset for the manufacturers was also wisest for the farmers, that the economic interests of England were one and indivisible. The cities of Canada to-day await the zeal and faith and clear thinking of a Cobden.

The present alliance of the farmers with organized labour is one rather of common hostility than of community of interests. Both feel that the business of the country has been predatory and that they are its victims. Some of the labour leaders, it is true, are convinced that a protective tariff naturally encourages the manufacturer and business man to develop predatory instincts. Within the past two years a convention of the Independent Labour Party carried a Free Trade resolution, with one dissenting voice. But in this the leaders have yet to show that they carry the rank and file with them, and superficially at least the farmer has little in common with the type-setter who strikes in these times because he is refused a dollar an hour in wages, or with the railway employee whose annual salary equals the price of a farm and makes transportation charges so high as seriously to impair farm profits. Recurring periods of unemployment and profiteering behind the tariff wall, however, are combining to prepare the mind of the labour man for the seed. Ready also is the mind of the professional man and the clerk.

What, then, is the attitude of the agrarian party to trade and industry, as set forth in the New National Policy? It insists on the 'development of our natural resources.' Farming, mining, fishing, lumbering, the industries concerned directly with nature, which has been so lavish to the people of Canada, these it would stimulate. Take the lumbering industry, for instance. To-day there is stagnation. The mills are shut down. Lumber camps are closed. Yet people are suffering for want of houses. Marriages are deferred. Children are being herded in apartments. Barns and stables lack repairs. Carpenters are idle. The lumbermen control the natural resources, and the immediate means of exploiting these resources. The lumbermen's association controls the prices, and has been slow to make reductions, thus inviting the conclusion that production is being curtailed in order to maintain high prices. The agrarian policy would encourage the use and conservation of our great forest wealth. If gentle means failed, then foreign competition, the cancelling of licenses or severe taxation would be invoked.

While it would stimulate natural industries, the farmers' platform nowhere shows hostility to manufacturing. Its quarrel is simply with the principle of protection which, it claims, 'fosters combines, trusts and gentlemen's agreements, unduly handicaps the basic industries, is a chief corrupting influence in our national life' and is 'the most wasteful and costly method ever designed for raising national revenue.' The farmer remembers the village and town industries of a generation ago. In many ways they served his needs better than the highly organized industries of to-day. He obtained better wagons from the local wheelwright, better ploughs from the local foundry. He believes that the protective tariff is a misfortune to the manufacturer: it has suggested the watering of stock and the production of inferior goods. He knows that two industries for a quarter of a century have had an opportunity of showing what Canadian manufacturers and workmen could do without state aid, and that both these industries have succeeded. He knows through his farm papers that last spring, when unemployment was general in Brantford, the Brantford Cordage Company was running full strength and shipping bindertwine to Ireland, the home of the industry, and to various foreign countries. He has faith in Canadians. He has been compelled to sell his own products in world markets at competitive prices. He thinks that the manufacturer should do the same. He believes that it would be good for the manufacturer's moral and mental health if he were compelled to do the same.

If at times farm leaders have been factious and class-conscious it is because they know that too often it has been the practice of business, big and little, to sell the farmer what he must buy, virtually the raw material used in the production of farm produce – the land, the sun and the air being the gift of God – at the United States price plus duty and freight. In this way farmers have been compelled to pay twenty or thirty or forty or even fifty per cent more for their essential commodities than their competitors in world markets have had to pay. If farmers grow restless and protest that this is not a fair game they need hardly be decorated with the horns and tail of Lenin.

The city man is now in a position where he can appreciate the farmer's point of view. He too has felt in his own person the effect of this practice of selling at the United States price plus the duty and freight. When he wishes to buy a new car he looks longingly across the border. He reflects, however, that he can recover the few hundred dollars added to the price of the car by marking up the price of the real estate or bacon or neckties he has to sell. His market is a sheltered market. Once, indeed, since the war even the dullest of city folk had the effect of the tariff brought home with striking emphasis. Sugar had been hoarded in Canada. The world price fell, and sugar could be imported from the United States, duty and freight and exchange considered, to undersell Canadian sugar. The Federal authorities intervened. Through the Board of Commerce importation was stopped. Then the voice of unsweetened public opinion was heard in the land. The Board of Commerce – that *deus ex machina* – was smashed as an unlovely idol. It was the most telling lesson in economics city people had ever received. Then for the first time many of them became familiar with a law under which farmers, west and east, had long worked and suffered, and which for some years they had thoroughly understood.

No responsible agrarian leader has ever insisted on immediate free trade in all articles. The New National Policy declares for 'an immediate and substantial all-round reduction of the customs tariff.' It advocates also an attempt to secure reciprocal trade in natural products with the United States. Now in reciprocity there are always two parties to the bargain. Under any reciprocal arrangement it would certainly be pro-

October 1921

FRANK CARMICHAEL
Man with Scythe Oct. 1921

vided that the agreement could not be terminated suddenly, but only after notice of two or more years had been given. The dislocation of business caused by the Fordney tariff could thus be prevented by the giving of time in which to secure other markets, unless indeed the exchange of products proved so satisfactory that it became permanent and a part of the general pacific policy of the North American continent. The free entry of farm machinery and certain similar products is also advocated, though it is not stated that this should be made immediate. Free trade with Great Britain within five years is included. This clause suggests that the idea of a gradual approach to free trade was in the minds of the Council of Agriculture, as well as possibly a shrewd attempt to impale the imperialistic manufacturer on the horns of a dilemma.

The fourth plank of the farmers platform deals with the means to be employed for raising revenue. In view of the contention of Mr Meighen and others that the farmers are out-and-out and immediate free traders the first sentence of this section is interesting. It begins: 'As these tariff reductions may very considerably reduce the national revenue from that source, the Canadian Council of Agriculture would recommend...' Then follow the proposals for direct taxation on unimproved land values, incomes, inheritances, and profits of corporations. It thus appears that an agrarian government would still collect revenue from customs duties, eliminating, however, the protective idea from the tariff and giving free trade in certain essential commodities. When confronted with the task of raising revenue the new Finance Minister would not find his task light. Nor does the present minister; hence possibly the General Elections. The matter of finding the value of Ontario farm land, without improvements, is by no means easy. It is perhaps safe to say that more than half the farms of Ontario can be bought for less than the replacement values of their buildings and fences, On the other hand land without buildings has considerable value, as is shown when a farmer wishes to add to the size of his farm by purchasing fields from his neighbour. The assessor would be required to accommodate these two factors in arriving at an estimate of unimproved land values. Again the application of the income tax so as to bear equally on the salaried man who buys everything he requires to keep him warm and fed, and on the farmer, who produces much of his living and inevitably adds to capital much of what might be regarded as profit, is a very delicate task. The present Finance Minister comes nowhere near success in it.

But these are questions of the future. The farmers would appear to be right in concluding that hot-house methods of encouraging industry will never give Canada permanent prosperity. Natural wealth we have in abundance. Natural industry, whether on the farm or in the factories, industry developed by Canadians who trust themselves, without fearing or despising others, is to be the industry of Canada in the new era, if the farmers win their case.

EDITORIAL
Our Next Parliament

The present political situation is unique in the history of Canada. We have had third parties before, but they have originated in religious or racial impulses. To-day we have a third party, possibly stronger than either of the old parties. Its origin is neither religious nor racial. It includes within the ranks Canadians of all creeds and origins. Its leaders with one or two exceptions are native Canadians of the Protestant faith. but they are not men who seek political capital by emphasizing this fact. Their appeal has been made to economic interest and not to racial and religious prejudice. For the first time in many years we are to have an election fought mainly on economic issues.

The government of the day faces the electorate under the title of the National Liberal Conservative Party. The encyclopaedic name, however, has not been accepted by the press or the people. It is called what it is – the Conservative party. It is the avowed champion of protection and the avowed opponent of radical or even liberal tendencies. The government consists, with two or three exceptions, of lawyers and wealthy business men. Mr Meighen makes his appeal to the cautious and conservative elector who hesitates to interfere with existing business and social conditions.

Mr King, on the other hand, calls himself, and is, a Liberal of some sort. He denounces privilege, and in softer tones, protection. But he seldom refers to the platform of the Liberal party as adopted at the Ottawa Convention where he was chosen leader. This platform in its trade policy very nearly paraphrases that of the Agrarian party. In Quebec and in the Maritime Provinces he has been even less bold in his attack on protection than he was in Toronto. His lieutenants both in Ontario and Quebec have been appealing to the city voters by using the old Conservative argument that removal of protection would shatter our industrial fabric. Mr Pardee in Brantford went as far in his defence of the principle of protection as Mr Meighen himself could have desired. Mr Lemeiux has done the same thing in Quebec. It is a significant fact that the latter has been rebuked by his leader for his advocacy of the Shaughnessy railway policy, while no reference was made by Mr King to tariff delinquencies. The campaign speeches of Mr King and his followers indicate a tendency to regard the straight-forward pronouncement of the party platform as something which can readily be forgotten when the battle is to be fought with privilege. Mr King distinctly creates the impression that he is leaving the door open to those who profit by protection, and placing a light in the window.

Mr Crerar as head of the Progressive party stands definitely pledged to the gradual reduction of the tariff and the renunciation of the principle of protection. He has not been very explicit in his statements as to just how his policy would work out. He appears to believe that

A. J. CASSON *Decorative Landscape* Dec. 1921

legitimate Canadian manufacturing would actually be encouraged by a lowering of the tariff. A considerable number of commodities are now so highly protected that the volume of imports of such articles is inconsiderable. Naturally production will be increased and industry will be revived, if the duties on what may be called foundation goods are reduced or entirely removed. Agricultural implements, fertilizers, cement, oil, for example, the raw material of industry, would be lowered in price by being made subject to foreign competition. It is more than doubtful if these industries would be driven out even if protection disappeared. Certainly other industries which are dependent on them would benefit by reduced costs.

In this way manufacturing would be made more efficient as well as cheaper. Too frequently the quality of goods declines as competition is shut off. Even the opening up of a branch factory of some American firm does not necessarily mean that the Canadian consumer has reaped an advantage. Generally speaking he must pay the price of the United States plus the duty, freight and exchange, while the quality of the goods sometimes noticeably declines. The term 'made in Canada' under the new policy would become a term of pride, a mark of workmanship that can face the world, not workmanship that shrinks behind a tariff wall and seeks a market in an appeal to patriotism.

The Progressives would turn industry once more into natural channels. Our farms, 'the top six inches of the soil,' our forests, so often neglected and pillaged, our mines, hardly scratched as yet, our lakes and extensive sea-board, teeming with opportunities, these solid industries will attract capital now devoted to hot-house production. On them will be built a more stable economic structure than is possible when industries are stimulated by artificial means.

One other anticipated effect of the proposals of Mr Crerar is that the volume of our exports will be increased. High protection tends to increase costs of production to a point where competition in world markets is impossible. Only by exports can we pay our very large obligations abroad. Farmers have so developed their business that they can compete in foreign markets with all-comers. Certain manufacturing industries not far removed from the primary industries, such as lumbering, paper-making, and packing are also on a more or less competitive basis. Of those manufacturing industries further removed from the primary industries the only two which have no protection, those of binder twine and cream separators, sell a considerable part of their products abroad, while the manufacturers of agricultural implements (which have enjoyed less protection than most of our manufacturing industries) are also large exporters. Our manufacturers during the war found they could succeed in shell-making. Canadian munitions in time gained an excellent reputation. What was done in war can be done in peace, under the permanent stimulus of competition. At any rate the farmers are unwilling that agriculture should continue as the only considerable exporting industry. They insist that the manufacturer should do his share to pay the interest and principle on our large debts abroad.

The Railway policy and the Tariff policy form the issues which divide the people of Canada into opposing camps. To-day there appear to be three camps; after the election there will probably be only two. Under our present parliamentary system, which requires cabinet solidarity, almost certainly a coalition will be necessary if the business of the country is to be carried on without a second election. It is not at all probable that any one party will have a sufficient number of members to form a cabinet without assistance. A Farmer-Labour alliance such as obtains in Ontario is hardly likely to control a majority in parliament, although this is possible. Neither of the old parties has the remotest chance of so doing, unless something remarkable happens within the next month. A year ago the most natural coalition would have appeared to be that of Mr King and Mr Crerar, but the indecision and even reactionary position of the Liberals on the Tariff have made this impossible. In Quebec and the Maritime Provinces Mr King has burned his bridges. There are, however, some stalwarts among the Liberals, such as Mr McMaster of Brome, who are not likely to bend the knee to Baal, and who may be willing to join the Progressives if a few votes will mean a majority in the House.

On the other hand all indications point to a union of Protectionists, Conservative and Liberal. During the present campaign, indeed, for some little time now, Mr Meighen has said nothing to provoke hostility in Quebec. The high priest of conscription one would expect to be a difficult idol for the people of Quebec, but less unlikely things have happened than that a temporary alliance should be formed between the Conservative party and the friends of Sir Lomer Gouin who believe protection essential to Canadian prosperity. The imperialist followers of Sir Robert Borden and the Nationalist followers of Bourassa, remembering 1911, will testify to this.

Should it prove impossible to form a government under any of the three leaders, and should it appear that progressive ideas prevail in the new house, it is quite possible that Mr Drury may be asked to go to Ottawa. As the first Secretary of the Canadian Council of Agriculture and the first President of the United Farmers of Ontario he stands solid with the Farmers. His resolute position on Hydro radials has given him the confidence of many of the business men of Canada, and created the impression that he has administrative ability to match his unusual powers in public debate. In Quebec too he has some strength owing to his repeated castigation of racial intolerance and national ill-will. His type of mind is essentially antithetic of that of Mr Meighen, and the Parliament of Canada would regain some of its prestige lost during recent years were two such able exponents of opposing schools of thought to shape Canadian policy as first minister and chief critic.

This much is clear. There never was a time when the individual character and views of a candidate should be more carefully scrutinized. In a contest in which three comparatively equal parties are involved the pressure will be very great to induce members to shift their allegiance to the right or to the left. Especially in the case of Liberal candidates, electors would do well to assure themselves of the real complexion of their candidate. If the two wings of the Liberal party should fall apart in the new House, the individual preferences of ten private members may determine the fate of Canada for years to come.

J.S. WOODSWORTH
The Labour Movement in the West

In order to gain an intelligent idea of the Labour Movement of Western Canada it is necessary for the outsider to rid himself of the grotesquely false conceptions gained from the press reports of the Winnipeg strike of 1919.

For years among labour men, as among farmers and business men, the Western outlook and spirit have differed somewhat from that of the East. In labour circles the protest against the dominance of the Eastern ideas became so strong that at the Trades and Labour Congress, in 1918, the Western delegates met by themselves and decided to call a convention of the Western delegates to discuss specifically Western problems.

This conference was held in Calgary early in 1919. Among many resolutions introduced was one urging a new type of organization. There had been a growing feeling that policies were too much under the control of the headquarters of unions situated in Eastern American cities. More serious than this was the fact that the development of industry, while breaking down the old craftsmanship, had built up a strong centralized management. It was realized that, to meet the newer and more effective forms of capitalistic organization, labour must effect a closer organization. Radical enthusiasts proposed to call this the One Big Union. It was decided to submit the proposal to a referendum vote of all members of trade unions in the West and, if possible, in the East; and a provisional committee was appointed to carry on the educational propaganda, to take the vote and to give effect to the decision, which it was considered would be overwhelmingly favourable. After passing other resolutions, including a fraternal greeting to the Workers' Republic in Russia, the conference adjourned. A verbatim report of the proceedings was published in a special edition of the Winnipeg *Tribune.* No special indication in all this of a secret conspiracy to overturn the Government of Canada by force!

In May the Winnipeg General Strike broke out. It arose from a local dispute affecting the Metal Workers and the Building Trades, and was concerned with wage schedules and an interpretation of a principle of collective bargaining. It differed from other strikes, however, in the unanimity with which it was supported by the whole trade union movement. All offered to 'down tools' – even to the policemen.

This exhibition of solidarity thoroughly frightened the citizens generally. The Board of Trade, backed by the associations of employers, opposed itself solidly to the organized workers. Hysterical reports were skillfully used to play upon the nerves of a people still unstrung by the strain of the war. Russia still connoted the nationalization of women, even though the *canard* had already been exposed. The demand for a new social order was translated to mean a bloody political revolution.

In this novel emergency the authorities seemed helpless. Finally the Federal Government took action, and, disregarding even constitutional forms, clubbed the workers into submission. A Citizens' Committee, an extra-legal body, had been formed at the Board of Trade. Volunteers were enlisted, by whose authority is not clear. Legislation was rushed through in the Federal House, depriving citizens born outside Canada and not naturalized, including British-born, of the right of trial by jury. Provincial rights were overridden by the appointment of a Federal Deputy Minister of Justice in Winnipeg. The strike leaders were arrested at midnight and rushed in high-power automobiles to the Federal penitentiary. In an effort to prevent a suggested parade of returned men, the mounted police were ordered out and in the rioting that ensued shot into the unoffending and flying crowds whom curiosity had drawn to the scene. The labour paper was suppressed without adequate grounds, as the subsequent trials showed. Houses were searched, including Canon Scott's room, on general warrants, and lawyers selected papers and books that they thought might later prove of value in the prosecution.

Contrary to the general impression, the strike was not a One Big Union affair. The One Big Union had not yet come into existence. The voting on the principle of One Big Union organization had not yet been completed. The strike was called by the Trades and Labour Council. The Chairman of the Strike Committee was, and is, a strong American Federation of Labour man. The Secretary of the Strike Committee was, and is still, the Secretary of the Trades and Labour Council of the American Federation of Labour. The wonderful solidarity of the workers of Winnipeg was attained under International forms of organization.

At this juncture, however, it seems as if the authorities adopted the policy of "divide and conquer." A bitter campaign was begun against the One Big Union, the organization of which had just begun after a favourable vote was reported. The officials of the American Federation of Labour in their eagerness to maintain their organization against the One Big Union secessionists lent themselves to this policy. In the Crow's Nest, for example, we had the outrage of the check-off. The American Federation of Labour officials joined with the coal operators and Government commissioner in forcing the miners who wished to have the One Big Union form of organization to pay dues to an American organization. The Minister of Labour, an American Federation of Labour partisan, in official documents published the most unjustified attacks on the One Big Union. An intensely bitter factional fight ensued in which the One Big Union as an organization has outside the city of Winnipeg, been almost wiped out. The American Federation of Labour unions, weakened in numbers and morale, are now being successfully attacked in their turn.

The One Big Union failed to attain its objective not merely because of outside attacks but because it was forced into precipitate action. The enthusiastic leaders over-estimated the readiness of the rank and file for class action. In my own union, Vancouver International Longshoremen, the vote went two to one in favour of the One Big Union principle. After the general strike had failed, the men, fearful of losing their jobs, or of having trade diverted to the port of Seattle, revised their vote, going two to one against going over to the One Big Union.

Further, the One Big Union policy oscillated between a thorough-going Industrial Unionism and an organization capable of 'mass-action.' This, with personal quarrels, led to the split between the Loggers' Industrial Union and the One Big Union.

The One Big Union in Winnipeg to-day is simply like the Canadian Brotherhood of Railway Employees, a rival of the American Federation of Labour. The Street Railwaymen, whom you may see wearing a One Big Union button, are the same men and have much the same general ideas of life as they had up to the day when by a majority vote they decided to affiliate with the One Big Union instead of remaining affiliated with the American Federation of Labour.

The divisions in the industrial field have been more or less reflected in the political effort of labour. The eddies and cross-currents within the labour movement are so complicated, and the situation is subject to such kaleidoscopic changes, that any detailed description would be likely to baffle the general reader. Even an outline of development in a single city may be difficult to follow, but may afford a general idea of the forces at work.

Several years ago there was organized in Winnipeg the Manitoba section of the Dominion Labour Party, which latter never existed even on paper. In the municipal elections of 1920 the bitter antagonism between the members of the American Federation of Labour and the One Big Union led to a split in this organization. It was claimed that the Trades and Labour Council officials tried to dominate the political organization. The Independent Labour Party was formed by those who held that under existing conditions the political end of the movement must be entirely free, and the membership open equally to Internationals or One Big Union men.

The Socialist Party of Canada, numerically weak, maintained its teaching of doctrinaire Marxianism and its policy of non-co-operation.

At the last Trades and Labour Congress held in Winnipeg there was formed the Canadian Labour Party. Each province was left to work out its own form of organization. In Winnipeg an attempt was made to secure, through this new body, at least co-operation between the Dominion Labour Party and the Independent Labour Party. The partisan feeling, however, was too strong and the effort failed.

In Centre Winnipeg the Independent Labour Party nominated its candidate, who was unopposed either by the Dominion Labour Party or the Socialist Party of Canada – hence an overwhelming victory. In North Winnipeg, 'Bob' Russell was nominated by the Socialist Party of Canada. His personal popularity, notwithstanding the weakness of his party, would probably have carried him to overwhelming victory, had it not been for the opposition of a small Communist group, who insisted on affiliation with the Third International. Ironical, surely, that Russell, sent to penitentiary on the charge of attempting to set up a Soviet government in Canada, should go down at the hands of a Communist group!

In South Vancouver, Tom Richardson, nominated by the Federated Labour Party, an organization similar to the Independent Labour Party of Winnipeg, was opposed by Jack Kavanaugh, who was nominated by the Socialist Party of Canada but ran as a Communist.

In Calgary, William Irvine was nominated by

the Dominion Labour Party and, receiving the endorsation of the Progressives in the rural part of his constituency, was elected.

Since the election there has arisen the new Workers' Party. The left-wing socialists have been mostly members of the Socialist Party of Canada. Under the rebuke of Lenin and in accordance with the action of the Red Trade Union International, the 'left-wingers' have decided to become less academic and uncompromising and to participate in rank-and-file movements.

This change of front is leading to some curious results. Secessionist movements are admitted to have been a mistake. Converts to the new policy now discount the One Big Union, which recently they championed, and denounce their former colleagues in the Socialist Party of Canada. Whether or not the new organization will carry out the policy of 'a united front' or, in its efforts to dominate, simply add one more to the existing political factions remains to be seen.

Unity was never so sorely needed as at present. But while organizations, industrial and political, are so chaotic and impotent, the movement itself goes steadily forward. Education proceeds apace. The workers in Canada were never so class-conscious as to-day. Wise leadership or a great emergency will readily weld together the scattered groups.

HENRY WISE WOOD

In Defence of Group Politics

A army is composed of a certain number of men, but these men, unorganized, acting as individuals, would not have much military strength. Thoroughly organized, each supporting the others, all acting together, their full strength and efficiency are developed. As an unorganized military group has low efficiency, so also has an unorganized citizenship group.

During the past century certain citizens have been organizing themselves into group units for the purpose of dealing more effectively with economic and political affairs. These groups have been organized on the basis of an interest that was common to all the members of the group. This basis is economic.

The primary efforts of the group have been directed towards the advancement of the group interests. These interests, being economic, are affected very largely by legislation; conquently the groups have been very active and, where well organized, very efficient in influencing legislation. This perverting of legislation in the interest of certain economic classes has done much towards throwing economic relationships out of balance, thereby causing great injustice to the unorganized masses.

This process has had a tendency to create a cleavage between economic elements, with organized classes on one side and the unorganized masses on the other. In the resulting competitive conflict, unorganized individualism has been continually losing ground before the steady, systematic advances or organization. The unorganized forces were much superior in numbers, but their potential strength had not been developed.

Among those who saw the hopelessness of unorganization trying to stand against organization were the farmers. They saw that unless they could develop organized strength to protect the interests of agriculture, agriculture would be reduced to hopeless impoverishment by those who had developed organized strength. With a clear vision of this necessity before them, they began to try to solve the problem of democratic, economic group organization. This was a much greater enterprise than farmers had ever undertaken before. The true principles of such organization were not understood, such organization never having been developed to any degree of efficiency. A lack of this knowledge has done more to retard organization among farmers than any other cause, and full success will never be achieved until these principles are thoroughly understood and adhered to. But while the farmers have met many difficulties and not a few defeats, the unrelenting hand of necessity has been steadily driving them on to renewed efforts, and the hope of success now seems greater than ever before.

Democratic organization among the people means that the people must organize themselves, and organize in such a way that they can initiate, direct, and control all the activities of the group thus organized. This is distinguished from autocratic organization by being self-governing, or governed from the 'bottom up' instead of from the 'top down.' If the farmers succeed in establishing organization on this basis to stability and efficiency, it will be the first successful attempt to develop democratic organization to any considerable extent. Heretofore they have proceeded along the lines of right principles up to a certain stage of organization, and after reaching that stage they have almost invariably departed from the true principles. This departure has frequently occurred in undertaking commercial activities, but the most lamentable instances have occurred when the farmers have undertaken to exercise their citizenship strength and influence, or in other words, when they have undertaken 'political action.'

In the past, in undertaking political activities, invariably they have reverted to the unorganized political party system. And just as invariably their organization has met with disaster. This was the only result that could logically be expected, as in so doing they violated the principles of both organization and democracy. The political group, under the political party system, is not an organization of the people. The people acting in it as individuals are unable to exercise any controlling influence; hence the party is not democratically controlled. On the contrary, it is autocratically controlled by a little group of self-organized politicians at the top. Democratic organization cannot be developed in such a group, neither can democratic citizenship function efficiently therein. The individual still remains the citizenship unit, with no citizenship strength, as useless as hewn stone or bricks before they are placed in the building.

Our social system is founded on the basis of competition. Competition is the law of force, of destruction. As long as competition was carried on by individuals it did not become very destructive. The competitive unit – the individual – had very little destructive efficiency. As the unit was raised from the individual to the mob it became more efficient. As it was raised from the mob to the organized group it became still more efficient. When raised to a co-operation of a number of organized groups operating as one unit, it will pass into the highest stage of efficiency.

The Great War marked the progress that had been made in the development of this process up to that time. Military competition has become so efficient that the nations have been trying to build a co-operative league or unit of themselves, ultimately to contain all, or at least a preponderant majority of the nations, and thus stop military competition. But they are trying to build a temple of peace over the crater of the live volcano of commercial conflict, which is liable at any time to belch forth military strife. Nations cannot stabilize their relationships on a permanent co-operative basis until after economic interests, both financial and industrial, have been permanently adjusted on that basis.

But how are the people to bring harmony, system, and co-operation among the discordant, warring elements of an economic system established on the basis of competitive conflict? These interests or institutions are inanimate things and cannot speak for themselves. Individuals as such cannot speak for them, because individuals as such do not control them. When all the individuals dependent upon a particular interest or institution build themselves into a group unit, and develop group intelligence and a group understanding of their common interest and how it is related to other interests, the group becomes articulate and can speak for its own interest in the adjustment of relationships with other groups.

It is true that in doing this the groups will develop greater capacity for destructive competition. But there is reason to believe that when this competition becomes sufficiently destructive, its very destructiveness will force the groups to develop systematic co-operation with each other as a means of self-preservation. As a result of efficient military competition nations have been driven to begin to seek international co-operation. This, however, will be impossible until economic co-operation is established. May we not reasonably expect that organized, highly developed economic competition will eventually force warring economic elements to make a like attempt with better results. With the warring economic elements reconciled on the basis of systematic scientific co-operation, nations will have nothing to quarrel or fight about, and will irresistibly be drawn together into a world-wide brotherhood league.

The economic classes whose interests are best served by the operation of the law of competition have already made much progress in the development of group intelligence, and in making the group articulate. With these groups organized, carrying on systematic destructive competition, while the other elements remain unorganized, inarticulate, with no resisting power, we can never hope for economic co-operation, but can only look forward to economic oppression and exploitation ending in economic ruin and social collapse.

Man is designed as a social being. His mission

is to build a perfect social structure – a true civilization. Through systematic co-operation men construct; through competition they destroy. The only hope of building strength and solidarity, and establishing peace, prosperity and contentment lies in co-operation. The great menace to constructive progress is competition.

The individual is the smallest social unit. As individuals build themselves into groups the unit is raised, and becomes more efficient, whether engaged in co-operative construction or competitive destruction. Some of the organized economic groups composed of a comparatively small number of individuals, but controlling large amounts of wealth, think they can best serve their selfish interests under competitive operations. The actions of these groups are the primary cause of wars, and their operations in the economic field threaten the overthrow of the social system. Mammon has led them to the mountain-top of organization, shown them the kingdoms of the economic world, promised them conquest of these kingdoms if they will worship at his altar and obey his destructive commands. These organized groups seem determined to obey Mammon's mandates, though they wreck the social system, and they themselves go down in the ruin.

Other economic groups, composed of larger numbers of individuals but smaller amounts of wealth, are organizing. These groups cannot hope to serve their best interests under the operation of Mammonistic competition. In fact, their best interests demand systematic co-operative construction of a true social system throughout, which process involves the overthrow of Mammonism and the abrogation of its laws. As these latter groups develop strength and efficiency, conflict between them and the plutocratic groups is inevitable, unless Mammonism can be induced to capitulate to democracy and join the constructive forces in building a civilization in harmony with Nature's laws, dedicated to the service of humanity and to the glory of Nature's God.

This 'showdown' between the Mammonistic and the humanistic forces will not develop to the final stage until the elements of each force are thoroughly mobilized through systematic organization. The Mammonistic forces have already made much progress in the process of mobilization. They have shown the basis on which that mobilization can be accomplished. The democratic or humanistic elements are adopting the same basis, and they have made some progress in the process of mobilization through organization. While the basis of organization is the same, the method of procedure must be entirely different. Mammonism is autocratic and must proceed in an autocratic way, governed always from the top down. Humanism is democratic and must proceed in a democratic way; by wisely selected leadership, advised, guided, and served from the top down, but controlled always from the bottom up.

These two organized forces will join issue on every part of the social field, more especially on the political and economic; and lost is that force that goes into the final conflict unorganized and unmobilized.

E.J. PRATT

The Shark

He seemed to know the harbour,
So leisurely he swam,
His fin,
Like a piece of sheet-iron
Three-cornered,
And with knife-edge,
Stirred not a bubble
As it moved
With its base-line on the water.

His body was tubular
And tapered
And smoke-blue,
And as he passed the wharf
He turned,
And snapped at a flat-fish
That was dead and floating.
And I saw the flash of a white throat,
And a double row of white teeth,
And eyes of metallic gray,
Hard and narrow and slit.
Then out of the harbour,
With that three-cornered fin
Shearing without a bubble the water,
Lithely,
Leisurely,
He swam, –
That strange fish
Tubular, tapered, smoke-blue,
Part vulture, part wolf,
Part neither – for his blood was cold.

A New Canadian Poet

It is something of a paradox that at the present time, when more poets than ever seem to clamour for a public hearing, so many of them should be content to sit aloof, ensconced in nut-shell worlds of their own. For the fashionable cult is still of the inward vision. The poet, turned towards himself, hearkens and bids us listen to his little soul-cries or delicately records the peculiar images which life has thrown on his moody mind. *Quicquid agunt homines*, when the men are others than the poet himself, is held to be an almost antiquated interest. The obsession with self has, indeed, tended to limit poetry to the art of the exquisite lyric.

To those, however, who still find pleasure in a more objective utterance, for whom there is also poetry in the bright display of scenes and actions, this volume of Mr Pratt's, so long looked for, will be very welcome (*Newfoundland Verse*: E.J. Pratt; The Ryerson Press; pp. 140; $1.50). Not that Mr Pratt has denied himself his lyrical or reflective moments. Some of these, indeed, are beautifully transcribed, like the impression of Dawn where, in keeping, one feels, with the poet's healthy temperament, the interest of the fisher breaks upon and blends with his feeling for the morning's glory:

Dawn!
Gold-minted –
The monarch of the morn,
Awake –
Shadows withdrawn,
A sheet of glass rose-tinted –

The lake!
Splash!
A coral ring
Studded with rubies and agates and gold,
Finely wrought out.
A vision of a silver flash.
Lost! Was it a grayling,
Or a rainbow-trout?

One might also point to 'Snow on the Battlefield' and 'Before a Bulletin Board,' or to this war echo called 'Before an Altar':

Break we the bread once more,
    The cup we pass around –
No, rather let us pour
    This wine upon the ground;

And on the salver lay
    The bread – there to remain.
Perhaps, some other day,
    Shrovetide will come again.

Blurred is the rubric now,
    And shadowy the token,
When blood is on the brow,
    And the frail body broken.

But the great things in the volume are unquestionably the narratives. With these Mr Pratt lifts himself to a place among the best of recent story-tellers in verse. 'Carlo' and 'The Ice Floes' are in their kind masterpieces. The former is the simple story of a dog's heroism; but for clear crisp narration and for the happy humour of the compliment it could not be bettered. Mr Pratt throughout the volume proves himself the master of various measures but the neat handling ... of the octosyllabic couplet is especially fine. ...

'The Ice Floes,' which describes an incident from the strenuous life of the Newfoundland sealers, shows the same clean vigorous workmanship and is even more notable for the vividness with which the scenes have been imagined. Another of the longer pieces that make pleasant reading is the conversation between the old Salt and the Scholar in 'Overheard in a Cove,' rather daringly told in heroic couplets. The sanity and the sense of humour which never let Mr Pratt lose himself in mere sentimentality are nakedly displayed in this admirable satire on the youth who has displaced the homely wisdom of his fathers by the educational veneer and jargon of the schools. One can only hope that there are more of these narratives to come.

There is much else that will be enjoyed and treasured among these Newfoundland verses. As would be expected, such a regional collection is rich in the poetry of the sea. Its lure, its cruel dealing, and its double harvesting of life and death for the fisher folk are variously chronicled in the lesser poems and in the longer narratives. It is, however, in 'Sea Variations,' the semi-lyrical poem which fitly opens the volume, that Mr Pratt has expressed most magnificently its beauty and its terror. The whole poem is built into a cunning rhythmical pattern, and for a foretaste of its quality one cannot do better than offer the opening lines:

Old, old is the sea to-day.
A sudden stealth of age
Has torn away
The texture of its youth and grace,
And filched the rose of daybreak from its waters.

The appeal of the volume, it may be added, has

Editorial

Canadians who have a national point of view cannot fail to be concerned with a certain tendency which is developing rapidly among manufacturers. Within the past month two large Canadian concerns, the Canadian General Electric Company and the Goldie-McCullough Company have been reorganized as admitted annexes of larger American companies. The already long list of companies doing business in Canada and paying dividends in the United States is thus increased. We may well pause and ask ourselves whether, after all, this business expansion is a matter for congratulation. It is the result of a desire to avoid the Canadian tariff wall as well as to secure the advantage of British preference. If it has the effect of building or maintaining factories whose main business is the assembling of parts manufactured in the United States, and whose profits go partly to Canadian workmen but mainly to American investors and such Canadians as they associate with themselves for the purpose of manipulating the tariff, that is to say if the industries are hothouse in character and chiefly concerned in exuding a yearly tribute across the border, we doubt if they are any improvement on the handy foundries and work-shops which a generation ago did service in our villages and towns. At any rate, they are a poor fruit of the National Policy, invented by the Conservatives and fostered by Mr King.

been enhanced by the really beautiful decorations given it by Mr Varley.

J.S. WOODSWORTH
Besco

What is the root of all this trouble in Nova Scotia? Bolshevism among the foreign miners? No, that is not an adequate answer, though an easy way of disposing of any industrial difficulty. The miners in Nova Scotia are chiefly of Scotch-Canadian stock and there was similar trouble long before Lenin came upon the international stage. No case can be summed in a word, yet there is one word that is much nearer than Bolshevism; that is 'Besco' – the common sobriquet of the British Empire Steel Corporation. For years we have been studying the miners and are puzzled because we cannot find a solution to the trouble. Suppose we devote our attention to the other factor. Better still, suppose we study the relations of the two factors.

Another Royal Commission has reported. It has been studying the miners; only incidentally has it studied Besco. Can its recommendation then prove other than futile? The Commission finds that the military were needed to cope with the situation at Sidney. Property rights were endangered and the Government had to step in. The papers feature this. But what of the primary human rights that have been disregarded until the men are rendered half desperate? On this point the report is couched in the most general terms. Certain obvious reforms are recommended, notably the abandonment of the eleven- and thirteen-hour shifts which involve, every fortnight, twenty-four hours continuous work.

But when the Commission reports to the Federal Government, the Federal Government disclaims any power to enact legislation along these lines, claiming that this is a provincial matter. Possibly growing public opinion may force the Nova Scotia Government to take action. A year ago Besco informed a delegation from a local ministerial association that Nova Scotia would not move until Judge Gary made the change!

Other investigators have reported on the situation but without bringing about material improvements. In 1920 the housing and sanitary conditions were described by a Royal Commission as being 'with few exceptions absolutely wretched.' Two years later a Board of Conciliation admitted that the company's houses were 'not in a satisfactory condition.' The minority report made went further describing the sanitary conditions as 'absolutely wretched.' Another two years and still no change in this or other conditions of life and labour.

In a series of articles which appeared a year ago in the *Toronto Daily Star,* Mr F.A. Carman puts his finger on one of the sore spots:

Fourteen companies of various grades of importance go to make up Besco. When the fourteen went into the cauldron they owned in stocks of various kinds a little under $83,000,000. When the merging process had been completed these $83,000,000 had been transmuted into just under $102,000,000. ... To pay dividends on nearly $102,000,000 of stocks should be a sufficient task for the men *who have to manage an industry which must meet the world competition in the steel and coal trade. But before they can begin to do this they have to meet prior charges of over $31,000,000 of mortgages of various sorts. ... In the Besco process common stocks were reduced from 63 to 24 million while preferred stocks rose from 19 to 77 million. ... The result of this transformation process has been the addition of charges of over $4,000,000 to the annual liabilities of the industry. ... The recent watering down of the stock of these companies was not the first operation of the kind. ... This original $15,000,000 of common 'watered' stock is represented in the existing issues of Besco stock by $6,000,000 of common stock and by $13,500,000 of 7% second preference on which the dividends are a cumulative liability. Which shows us in epitome how what was originally merely a speculative 'flyer' may by skilful financing be transmogrified into the next thing to a bond.*

'Skilful financing' - aye, and unscrupulous financing. One transaction has recently been dragged to the light of day. At a time when important negotiations were in progress between the Newfoundland Government and the Company, ex-Premier Squires received $46,000 from funds of the Dominion Steel Co. This action according to the evidence was approved by Roy Wolvin and other high officials (See *Montreal Star*, Jan. 31st, 1924.) Such is Besco!

In vain have the workers appealed to Provincial and Federal Parliaments for legal redress or assistance. Besco was well represented in the Government councils. A year ago, when a deputation asked Mr Mackenzie King for the provision of pension for worn-out miners - a part of the pre-election programme of the Liberal party - all they received from the Prime Minister was a copy of his book *Industry and Humanity*!

In vain have the workers appealed to Provincial authorities to obtain representation in Parliament; constituencies were gerrymandered, an industrial county being united with a county peopled largely by farmers and fishermen with a two-member constituency. Then on the eve of the election 'roorbacks' were issued – 'false tales' concerning the candidate J.B. MacLachlan who went down to defeat.

When two years ago, the miners resorted to the 'strike on the job', the Press entirely misrepresented the situation. Even Mr Meighen recognized the merits of their policy:

What have these men done? They have been requested, we will put it, to accept a wage reduction of 32-1/2 per cent. They have declined to do it. They say, 'No it is not a living wage, we cannot support our families, we cannot send our children to school, we do not want to go on strike or go out.' ... They say 'Here you are giving us two-thirds of a day's pay and we will give you two-thirds of a day's work, and only that; we don't pretend to give you any more.' (Hansard, March 30th, 1922)

At that time, the Government refused the Royal Commission asked for by the Mayors of the mining towns, but a little later sent down troops notwithstanding the protests of the local authorities that there was no need. So the struggle has gone on with growing bitterness. Last summer driven back to work by starvation, the steel-workers in a notable statement declared that every man's hand was against them. Within the last few weeks the coal miners have been forced into the pits, against their will, by the reactionary American officials at the head of their own union. But that is too long and too complicated a story to be even outlined here.

In the meantime the miners' leader is serving a two-year sentence in Dorchester penitentiary convicted of seditious libel. What had he done? In a circular letter he staged that the Provincial Police had brutally ridden down men, women, and children on a Sunday night when most of them were coming from church.

One old woman over 70 years of age was beaten into insensibility and may die. A boy of nine years old was trampled under the horses' feet and had his breast bone crushed in. One woman beaten over the head with a police club gave premature birth to a child. The child is dead and the woman's life is despaired of.

The coal operators gave this letter to the papers. Then MacLachlan was arrested and taken to Halifax charged with unlawfully publishing a false tale and also with seditious libel. The charge of publishing a false tale was withdrawn; the tale was all too true. MacLachlan's letter is substantially corroborated by statutory declaration and by the evidence given before the Royal Commission. But in the case of seditious libel, as the Attorney-General pointed out, the truer the statement the worse the libel. So J.B. MacLachlan is behind the bars because he dared to criticize the brutality of the Provincial Police of Nova Scotia.

That is technically true. But under this obsolete and discredited law of seditions any of us might be convicted. Mr Meighen might be sent to the penitentiary for criticizing the Liberal administrations. Why then was MacLachlan the victim? Because in fighting in the cause of the men he had incurred the enmity of the powerful British Empire Steel Corporation. They were out to 'get' him, and since he was irreproachable in his personal character and well within the law in his official activities, they invoked this old law that dates back to witch-burning days.

Even then MacLachlan did not get the fair play of those early times. He was not allowed a trial in his home county but was taken to Halifax where for years the minds of the people have been poisoned against the miners.

When an appeal was taken for another trial, the trial judge was a member of the Court of Appeal. Of the six judges on the Bench, four, before the time of their elevation to the bench, had been connected with the Steel or Coal companies subsidiary to Besco.

Were anything lacking in the proceeding to inspire in the workers a contempt for law it was more than made up for by the congratulatory telegram from the General Manager of Besco to the Attorney-General.

Is there no public opinion in Canada that dares challenge such high-handed action? These injustices we neglect at our peril.

Secession in Canada

These two articles throw some light on the attitude of at least part of the populations of Quebec and of the Prairies towards Confederation. In the light of these particular opinions the approaching National Holiday takes on greater significance.

J. ADDISON REID

I Quebec

The possibility of a Separatist movement in French Canada is one that must always be reckoned with by any far-sighted political thinker. The latest expression of this phase of Canadian thought is embodied in a volume entitled *Notre Avenir Politique*, published by *L'Action Française* of Montreal. *L'Action Française* is a monthly journal published in the special interest of French Canadian thought and aspirations. The book is a symposium of articles by various contributors produced during the twelve months of 1922.

The first of the contributors, Louis D. Durand, foresees the breaking up of the British Empire as the result of revolutionary forces now operating in the British Isles; that Canada will cease to be a part of the British Empire by reason of circumstances which she has no part in bringing about and over which she has no control. If the Empire falls apart, there is, he believes, no cohesive force in the Canadian Confederation that can hold it together. It remains only for the French Canadians to plan their course accordingly.

In the contribution by Anatole Vanier on 'The French State and the United States,' one begins to get the measure of some of the leaders of this movement. Here we have youth free to let the imagination soar without limit and unrestrained by any practical considerations. The new French state, which he takes for granted, will need to form alliances, and of course the United States will be a desirable international associate. It is useless to waste time considering the preliminary or preparatory stages of national evolution – or revolution. 'Whatever may be the next stage of political transformation, it will only be transitory if it does not permit Quebec to take her place in the international world in the capacity of a sovereign American French state.'

Father Villeneuve, OMI, writes of 'Our Brothers of the Dispersion.' What will happen to the French Canadian settled in the other Provinces, in Ontario, in the West, and in the United States, if Quebec sets up for herself an independent nation? These people were ill advised to have left Quebec for the precarious situations in which they now find themselves, but nevertheless Quebec will not fail in her duty to them. Though they will be under an alien government Quebec will still look after them and protect them. It is possible that some among us would welcome separation as freeing the English-speaking provinces from Quebec interference in their educational affairs. But evidently that would bring no relief. 'That would be to forget recent facts which have revealed to us one and all of what deeds our national fraternity, despite its imperfections, renders us capable,' says Father Villeneuve. 'The Ontario question, Green Valley, Gravelbourg, to mention only some names, are an eloquent demonstration of this. ... It is our opinion that independence which would give us a country more our own, would develop by that very fact a more enterprising and more extended citizenship.' And there follows, later on, the not too subtle suggestion that there is an English-speaking minority in Quebec in whose welfare the Protestant and English speaking majorities of other parts of Canada may have a lively interest, which they will not wish to imperil by too severe treatment of the French within their jurisdiction.

Space will not permit the examination of each contribution in detail, and, for the rest, merely the general ground taken by these advocates of separation will be indicated.

The territory of the new state must include more than Quebec. One might think that if there is to be a separation between Ontario and Quebec, the Ottawa River, being a natural and existing boundary, would remain the boundary. But the new French state must include the French communities on the west bank of the Ottawa and the boundary will be fixed on an ethnic and not on a geographical basis. It must also include the Maritime Provinces. 'An independent eastern Canada with Quebec as the central pillar,' says Durand, 'implies the union with Quebec of a certain territory to the west of our Province and of the three Maritime Provinces.'

As for the forces which are working to break up Confederation, there is first the natural incongruity of the sprawling disjointed skeleton of Provinces stretched clear across the continent. The western provinces are frankly both a financial burden and a political incubus. Our enormous burden of railway debt, increased by annual deficits, has been incurred and is being borne for the benefit of the West. Eastern Canada could support its railways without deficits. The western provinces are also constantly agitating for a fiscal system which would be ruinous to the east. It would be a distinct gain to slough them off in any case.

Then there is the instinctive and inevitable antipathy between Ontario and Quebec. The people of Ontario are not Canadians; they are colonists of England and think and act not as Canadians but as colonists. In their attitude toward their large French populations they are merely persecutors and religious fanatics.

Any rights which other Canadians may think they have to perpetuate Confederation, simply do not enter into the question at all. But most of these writers seem convinced that in spite of their apparent attachment to the Empire, Ontario and the West are progressing steadily and surely, consciously or unconsciously, toward annexation to the United States. French Canada is the only part of Canada that can or will resist this tendency.

A people who have three hundred years of existence [says Durand] who have their customs, their traditions, their language, their religion and who are strongly rooted in the soil as ours, have better to do than to dream of letting themselves be namelessly swallowed up in the Yankee melting pot.

Now, to what extent does this book represent the attitude of the people of Quebec generally? I believe that for the present these writers represent only a small band of crusaders with an inconsiderable following. But they are offering definite and aggressive leadership to the French Canadian people and there is no similar body of men offering definite and aggressive leadership in the other direction. It is not inconceivable that, though indifferent now, the French people might in a time of national crisis when their feelings are highly wrought upon, accept this leadership with something like unanimity. Abbé Groulx says:

The aspiration continues to live, inextinguishable in the depths of our souls. It requires only a breath of wind to rekindle it. Let a tempest arise, let the nationality feel itself in peril and the idea would spring up like a flame.

It has remained for one of the oldest and best tried leaders of Quebec particularism to offer the most forceful opposition to this school of thought, and he a man whom English-speaking Canada has always regarded as the chief of the separatist movement. Henri Bourassa has evidently watched this movement getting out of bounds and decided that it was time to call a halt and bring these extremists back to earth. He took the occasion in an address delivered before the Catholic Commercial Traveller's Association in Montreal on November 23rd last. He endeavours here in the strongest terms to call them back to a sense of reality and to rebuke them for expending their energies in vain dreams to the neglect of the numerous duties of the hour. He says:

Whatever may happen, the whole of the Canadian Confederation is, none the less, at the hour, the country of all Canadians, ours as well as that of the Anglo-Canadians; it imposes on all the same duties, it commands the same love, not perhaps of heart, but of conscience, of honor and of right.

At the end of a particularly strong passage he says:

June 1924

To oppose the policy of England simply because it is English, or because it is displeasing to France, even if it favor our interests, even if it be just in itself, is not nationalism, extreme or moderate, nor nationalism of any sort; it is foolishness, the foolishness of hate, and all forms of hate are barren by nature. This I have written on many occasions; I repeat it this evening with a conviction that strengthens from day to day. If we wish victoriously to resist our enemies, let us learn to conquer our own weaknesses, and cease to behave like badly raised children.

These brief extracts do not pretend to represent the whole of Bourassa's viewpoint, nor should they be taken as indicating that he has adopted English-speaking Canada's attitude to these questions, for nothing could be further from the truth. The viewpoints of both separatists and anti-separatists are outside the orbit of our thinking. With the intransigents there is no hope of coming to an understanding so long as they remain intransigent; but they are comparatively few in number at present. With their opponents it is quite another question and with them it may be easier than we think to find a common ground.

THOMPSON-HARDY

II The Prairies

Old ghosts never die, and the spectre of secession is one that promises to bob up periodically in the prairie provinces. An obvious truism is that the West is a geographical unit bounded on the east by a wilderness of rocks and Tories and on the west by Banff, Lake Louise, and the glories of Canada's California. Equally obvious is the statement that Hard Times, that most uncomfortable of devils, is always prodding the God of Things as They Are into restlessness. Combine Hard Times with Geography, and in the West, secession – to lead ultimately to annexation – pops out of the box.

It is difficult, of course, to put one's finger on an evasive thing like talk of annexation or secession. Memories of the imperialistic fervour of wartime are long-lived. In spite of this, however, a considerable amount of discussion about these elusive topics can be heard. The very fact that at the last convention of the United Farmers of Alberta in January, a motion favouring secession was put forward shows clearly that a wind is blowing somewhere – even although the motion was voted down. The writer himself has heard an Englishman – who three years ago on arriving in the west pooh-poohed the idea of union with the States – declare forcibly this fall that annexation is the only solution of the Westerner's difficulties. Nor is this man unique. Again and again, in the privacy of their homes, many perfectly good citizens of Anglo-Saxon stock have been heard to affirm that the West would find the United States a far better teammate than Eastern Canada. A month ago a prominent Western editor declared that a man who came out with a secession or annexation plank in his platform would have a surprisingly large following. Secession, therefore, may be more than a passing bugbear. It may, on provocation, take on flesh and substance to become an active factor in western politics. Mencken's declaration in the *Smart Set* last year that Canada must ultimately join the States is, possibly, not all mere romancing.

The Easterner, at this point, will, probably, remark that the Westerner is a damned fool who doesn't know when he is well off, and that, if he sees a better 'ole, let him jolly well go to it. Yet there are, perhaps, some justifications for the prairie farmer's point of view. These are firstly economics, secondly economics, and lastly economics. A man's means of livelihood is the tenderest part of him. As things are now, the Westerner is continually having this sensitive organ prodded and disturbed. High transportation charges, to be blamed on the eastern-controlled railroads; high rates of interest, due to eastern banking and investing methods; high cost of production, chargeable to the eastern manufacturer and protectionist, who maintain the (to the Westerner) outrageously high tariff on implements and other necessities—these combine to keep the prairie farmer tottering on the brink of financial collapse. The well-established agriculturist claims that he is producing at a loss, the pioneer is often in actual want and poverty – witness the home in which, when cold weather comes, only one member of the family can be outfitted warmly enough to venture outside, or the countless shacks that lack all but the most primitive of furniture. No wonder that some Westerners feel that they are paying too dearly for a sentimental unity with the East.

To irritate them further, the eastern-controlled Dominion Government has kept the Natural Resources of the West dangling before the three prairie provinces like the carrot before the proverbial jackass. The reader will recall that, when the prairie provinces were organized, the Federal authorities kept the Natural Resources and the revenue therefrom, paying in lieu of them to the provinces a fixed indemnity. This arrangement, at first, worked in favour of the West, but for a considerable period the scale has dipped the other way. Hence for several years the prairie premiers, collectively and individually, have been crawling to the Seats of the Mighty, begging for a return of the alienated resources. It is not our part to unravel the intricacies of the negotiations or to act 'sweet reason' to the warring standpoints; but, in passing, it might be pointed out that the delay and the somewhat stingy proposals heretofore advanced by the Federal Government have given another indictment to the Westerner on which to feed fat his ancient grudge against the East.

In one other Dominion policy the West is vitally interested – the attitude towards immigration. This side of the Lake of the Woods, two questions, of the 'hen *versus* egg' genus, share the theorist's affections. Does the immigrant bring prosperity, or does prosperity bring the immigrant? Kindred to this is the battle between the qualitatives and quantitatives, with the balance, I fear, inclining on economic assumptions towards the latter, although a goodly number still argue sturdily that only certain kinds of immigrants have any practical value for the West. But all factions are inclined to agree on one point, that the Federal Government has mismanaged the whole affair miserably in the past, and promises no immediate sanity for the future. In fact, in all matters the West is not merely distrustful but is cynically bored with the gifts which the East bears.

These are some of the factors which appear to be instrumental in keeping secession and annexation live topics on the prairies. There are many Americans in the West, and they and their Canadian-born neighbours have but to look to the south to see a land, materially speaking, flowing fatly with milk and honey – a land, too, where the costs of administration are said to average five dollars per head as opposed to an estimated eighty in Canada. Economically, he is likely to believe – although he may be wrong – that wealth and ease lie just across the border, and to feel that the struggle to develop and pre-

DAVID MILNE *Camp Porch* July 1924

serve a distinctive economic and political unit by means of two or three strands of steel is not worth while.

Economic, then, are the arguments which support secession and annexation. The contrary position is usually based on more or less intangible things that do little to fill one's stomach when – to quote Plautus – 'one's insides are rattling' for lack of food. It may be urged that the establishment and preservation of a definite Canadian character is valuable, that our connection with Great Britain gives us an historical depth and background we should otherwise lack, and that the Yankee has many undesirable qualities which we do not crave, but which must be swallowed along with prosperity. The latter somewhat Pharasaical argument is, however, subtly undetermined by American-made movies and magazines and it must be admitted that British traditions, while indubitably strong, have not nearly so great a hold on the West as they have on the East, or at any rate on Ontario. It seems that the Westerner's living conditions must be ameliorated before secession and annexation will cease to agitate him. Good harvests, unless accompanied by a lowering of the costs of production and transportation, will not wholly down the spectre. In Alberta, it might be buried by the development incident upon a real discovery of oil or iron, but this, in spite of the promise of the oil-well 'brought in' last fall at Wainwright, is not yet assured.

In the final analysis the immediate solution of the problem seems to depend on the East. Since Sir Lomer Gouin's resignation the West has had some hopes of a Liberal Progressive alliance with its consequent concessions to the prairies. Hope deferred has stiffened their distrust, not only of the old political Parties and shibboleths, but of the whole East as well. This distrust only the East can cure. A sympathetic attitude to the peculiar difficulties of the prairie farmer might go far toward repairing the frayed bonds of Canadian unity. Otherwise the Westerner may claim, with some show of reason, that, while the East blooms with millionaires, he, alone, foots the bill for a 'Dominion from sea to sea.' He may still wonder whether the West, of which the contribution in wheat and livestock has often been assessed, will be allowed to make its greatest contribution to the Dominion – that of a distinctively Western character to temper the somewhat cautious and crabbed disposition of the East.

J.S. WOODSWORTH
Mobilizing Progressive Opinion in Canada

This article by one of the few real Progressives in our House of Commons will commend itself to all readers of progressive opinions. Mr Woodsworth's project is a difficult one and the means will have to be created. We invite correspondence from those interested who have suggestions to offer.

The unsatisfactory condition of public life in Canada must be recognized by all thoughtful men. The old objectives are gone, the old ideals are inadequate, the old parties do not command the enthusiastic and loyal support of even their own adherents. We are awaiting a lead, but no leadership is evident.

Following the war-time efforts and excitement and the post-war revival of hope – whether that hope was for a return to 'normalcy' or for re-construction or for social revolution – there has come over all classes an apathy toward public affairs. With some, there is a sense of bewilderment – of helplessness in the midst of forces that are too great to be comprehended, much less controlled. With others, there has developed from disillusionment a sort of cynicism: 'Tomorrow is uncertain, let me live as well as I may today. A good car for myself and the family; let those who enjoy it worry about world affairs!'

Such an attitude is not confined to Canada. Yet in many other countries, new winds are beginning to fill the sails. In Europe, dire poverty and nationalistic strife have forced attention upon political issues. In the United States, prosperity and growing financial power are developing a new imperialism. In Canada, we are marking time. As, for the past five years, we have drifted down the river of time we have confidently hoped that prosperity was just around the next point. Our leading public men content themselves with the old party watchwords. When and from what direction will the new wind come?

A number of factors contribute to render very difficult the formation and expression of new ideas and policies in Canada. There is a lack of the sense of national responsibility. We have not outgrown either our colonial status or the colonial psychology. In international affairs, the most the nationalist hopes for is the chance of keeping free from European complications or of having the right to endorse, or to refuse to endorse, the action of Great Britain. On the other hand, economically and socially we live under the shadow of our great southern neighbour. Our young life is drained off to the American cities; our intellectual leaders are constantly tempted toward larger fields.

The heterogeneous character of our population prevents cultural unity. The population of the city of Montreal may be three-quarters of a million. Exclude the French and Jewish and other non-British groups and judged by the standards of Toronto, Montreal is about the size of Hamilton. In the West, there are large unassimilated blocks of Europeans who live in Canada in the flesh, but spiritually live still in the old world. Ultimately these various cultures may blend into something new and higher. At present, they are almost mutually exclusive.

The problem is further complicated by our vast distances, geographical barriers, and provincial institutions. Maritime or Montreal or Winnipeg papers are read very little in Ontario, and, what is not so clearly appreciated in Ontario, Toronto papers exercise very little influence in either the East or the West. Canada has attained constitutional unity before she has developed a national ideal.

Progressive opinion in Canada is not much in evidence. In England for the past quarter of a century there has been a very considerable body of men who have set themselves the task of studying with an open mind the pressing social problems which confront the world. The constructive record of the Fabian Society shows what may be accomplished by a small group. In the United States, *The New Republic* and *The Nation* must have found a considerable constituency. Why should it be only in other countries that forward-looking men are drawing together for political action? In Canada, let *The Canadian Forum* confess how general its appeal has been!

One of our political parties has adopted the name 'Progressive.' Surely only a very limited number of individuals within the party may rightly claim to be classed as progressive in outlook or policy. In contrast with British Labour, our Canadian movement has had narrow horizons and its radicals – chiefly non-Canadians – have been too doctrinaire and dogmatic to make a popular appeal. Our business men do not think, but actually pride themselves on their ready-made opinions from which they have not even taken the trouble to remove the trade-marks. Our professional men are mostly business men – at least in their mentality. Among journalists, one finds considerable independent thought, but for well-known reasons this rarely finds expression in their writings.

Within the universities the students affect the 'open mind,' but in practice this means a spongy mind. Few graduates have real convictions on matters of public policy or are fired toward the national welfare. In our State or privately-endowed universities, academic freedom, when shown, is often of a rather imported character, reflected or exotic in type. It is not born of the soil and does not spread rapidly.

There is no progressive group, but, in all classes, there are individuals with independent, self-hammered-out progressive opinions. One meets them in various nooks and corners down in the Maritime Provinces and in British Columbia. In Montreal they sometimes gather in modest private clubs. The 'Reconstruction Groups' were a genuine manifestation of at least a forward impulse. In Ottawa, the civil service contains not a few who keep alive the sacred flame – by their own firesides. The 'New Canada Movement' is a reaching out to others like-minded. In Toronto, university-trained young business men are wishing there were some independent and constructive political movement in which they could find a place. In the Western cities, one may discover little groups – sometimes somewhat academic in character – drawing their inspiration from progressive British and American journals.

How can these scattered opinions be organized? How brought to bear on our urgent practical problems? This, may we venture to suggest, is one of the tasks to which *The Canadian Forum* might apply itself. First these individuals must find one another. Then there must be some arrangement for the exchange of ideas. Probably this could hardly be done from one centre but from a dozen local centres loosely federated. Once raise a new standard – once create a skeleton organization, and the rapidity of the development might astonish even the most sanguine.

Canada is awaiting a lead. Public opinion is awaiting organization and direction.

To the Editor, *The Canadian Forum*

Sir:

Last summer you published an article by Mr Addison Reid, entitled 'Quebec and Secession,' in which the author dealt extensively with the separatists of the so-called nationalist school. In fairness to every one, an opportunity must be taken to summarize the actual situation and see whether or not the 'secessionist movement' is making any headway in this province.

As stated by Mr Reid, there is in Quebec a certain 'intelligentsia' under the influence of an organization called 'L'Action Française' that has adopted as its political platform 'the establishment of a French free state on the shores of the St Lawrence River.' This doctrine implies an independent eastern Canada with Quebec as central nucleus, including a narrow strip of Ontario to the west and the three maritime provinces.

It may be common belief in the English-speaking provinces that these ideas mostly originated from influential quarters, and that no effective attempt is being made to check the attack upon the very spirit of the federative pact. But the movement is not widespread, and it is likely to die a natural death as a result of public apathy.

The rural population, the backbone of the province, is in absolute ignorance of the activities of the separatist organization. In fact, the overwhelming majority of the voters of the province have not been reached by the secessionist move. Nor is any serious partisan of the movement to be found in the circles of government, industry, commerce, or finance. Now for the university world. First of all, the new evangel was proclaimed chiefly by persons whose connections with the University of Montreal are well known; and that was sufficient to rouse the direct and immediate opposition of Laval University in Quebec. Quebec, as a rule, sincerely professes to see white whenever Montreal sees black. Nevertheless, it would be far from true to say that the University of Montreal is unanimous. It is an open secret that the few fervent advocates of the founding of a French free state are only a handful of crusaders, not even forming the responsible element of the university. Dissensions later broke out among the secessionists themselves; and the attitude of Henri Bourassa sounded the death-knell of the movement. He emphatically showed himself the most serious opponent of what was once his own nationalist party. As he said recently, 'Whatever may happen, the whole of the Canadian confederation is the country of all Canadians, ours as well as that of the Anglo-Canadians; it imposes upon all the same duties, it commands the same love, not perhaps of heart, but of conscience, of honour, of right.'

Yours, etc.,

Montreal   Roland-Gilles Mousseau

J. ANSEL ANDERSON

The Coward

'Mike, you lazy, low-down son of a wall-eyed cayuse! Get up in your place and stay up, blast you!'

The ends of the lines flirted out and caught the unsuspecting horse on the rump with a sharp crack. He plunged ahead, and the whole team quickened its pace.

'Of all the aggravating jobs,' muttered the man, 'this business of driving a twelve-horse outfit on a hot day takes the ribbon by a good neck.'

He glanced up at the sun and guessed the time – four o'clock – twice more up and down the milelong furrow before he could think of quitting for the night. The twelve horses plodded steadily along, six abreast in the lead and six on the pole. Twelve heads bobbed up and down in front, and behind the big four-bottom plow ripped through the baked sod. The smell of sweat and dust was everywhere. A wheel squeaked for oil, trace chains jingled, the iron whippletrees rattled and banged, and, underneath, the steady drumming of twelve sets of hoofs added to the sound. Presently Mike, the big bay off-wheeler, dropped back again. With a curse Jack pulled up the team and got down to shorten up the laggard's traces. He had been mad when he came out from dinner, and three hours of sitting up there on the high hitch-cart, in the heat, nagging at his team or staring ahead up the long furrow through the cloud of dust that hung above the horses' heads, had not improved his temper. An irritable driver makes a ragged team, and a ragged team a still more irritable driver.

He climbed back to his seat, started the team with a whistle, and lit his pipe on the move. Half an hour later he was back at the same old thought. Suppose he wouldn't ride a bucking horse! Well, what of it? Lots of men wouldn't. Just because they were good riders they had no right to chaff him, and showing him up at the dinner table in front of the women was the last straw. The thought rankled in his mind. He wasn't a coward; he wasn't afraid of– . Now, was he? Perhaps he was scared. Perhaps he was really a coward. The thought fascinated him. He tried to put it out of his mind, shouted to his horses, and lit his pipe, but it came creeping back, and with it a host of old memories. Perhaps he was scared. How about that business down East? It was almost five years since that had happened; since he had shaken the dust of the Eastern city from his feet, left civilization, education, and position behind him, and fled West. It all came back to him again as he sat there on the high seat with the lines dangling listlessly from his hands. He cursed himself for a fool; cursed the girl who had lost control of the car on the hill; cursed the kindly providence which had saved his life when he jumped and hurtled the girl to her death. But, most of all, he cursed the friends and parents who had branded him 'coward' and made his life in the old hometown unbearable. What did they know of it anyway? What else could he do but jump? It was only luck that had saved his life. Why hadn't he tried to save her? How could he? Couldn't she jump as well as he? To hell with their civilization! He had left it for good and come West to work on the farms.

Coward, coward, coward – now it was cropping up again. Perhaps he was scared, but bucking was cruel sport anyway. Perhaps he was scared; another man might have grabbed the girl and thrown her out – yes, another man would hardly have left his future wife hurtling to her death. Poor Nina – had he really loved her? He would hardly have jumped if he had. Why, he thought more of Iseult than he had ever thought of Nina, and Iseult was only a horse. His attention came back to the team.

'Hike, you pie-biters! Noble, May – slacking there – cut it out. High, you bull-headed bronc, steady up. Easy there, Iseult.'

Stars, but she was some little mare! Just been broken a month and working up there in the lead like a fool, a good head in front of the rest. That was the way to train 'em. That was the kind of a leader that made a fast outfit. He'd have to watch her or she'd strain herself. What wonderful animals horses were. Such willing workers, always on the job, never grumbling; they'd give most men pointers. For some time he watched Iseult, glorying in the rippling muscles of her thighs, the swing of her shoulders and her arched neck. Wonderful little mare, he thought, take the bit all day, no slack lines for her – it was a pleasure to drive horses like that. He remembered breaking her –what a fight she had put up – great little mare, intelligent as a man and twice as friendly.

The outfit reached the end of the narrow land. Jack always took a pride in making these figure-of-eight turns, no easy matter with a large team. He yanked on the rope of the power lift, and the plows came out at the exact moment. He gathered up the lines, pulled slightly to the right, and with a shout to the off-side leaders, brought the whole team round in a narrow circle. The big grey on the off-side broke into a trot, the middle horses edged round, with ears laid back, and Iseult danced impatiently, the pivot of the whole team. Jack let the lines run through his fingers, and the outfit surged ahead. Another jerk and the plow was back in the ground. He pulled up to rest the horses and climbed down.

It had been a hot, close afternoon, but now the wind was picking up. He strolled round to Iseult and sheltering beside her lit his pipe. The little mare rubbed her nose against his shoulder, snuffed at the smoke, and turned back with ears pricked forward to watch a bunch of horses taking a playful gallop in a pasture two miles east.

Jack climbed to his seat and gathered up the lines. Without waiting for the word the team started. They knew as well as he did that another mile would make it quitting time. The wind was rising steadily, blowing the dust away in front close to the ground. Jack rolled down his sleeves, leaned back in his seat, and puffed contentedly at his pipe. This was the time of day he liked best. There was some satisfaction in a big day's work well done. This job of driving a big team got hold of a man; something in the control of immense power which thrilled a fellow. He was startled out of his reverie by a wrench on the lines. The big grey had taken a jump. Nervous, scary kind of a horse, he thought, too high-strung for safety in a big outfit, but a great leader. Funny how panic would spread through a team if one horse got scared – herd instinct – by advantage when things went smoothly, but when things went wrong – the big grey lunged forward again.

'Easy there, High! Steady, old man!' A sudden gust of wind lifted the words away over the horses' heads. Jack looked round and swore. Away in the west the sky was turning grey, little spurts of dust leapt from the tops of the distant hills.

'Going to have a dust storm,' he told himself philosophically. 'Here's hoping it isn't a bad one.'

The horses seemed to sense the storm and quickened their pace almost to a trot. Jack tightened up the lines and held them down. He glanced back; no doubt about the storm, he could see the low-lying cloud of dust just topping the hills on the horizon. Take about ten minutes to come up at the rate the wind was blowing, he judged. Coolly, he surveyed his position and calculated his chances. No good trying to unhook now; the horses were far too excited. Darn that rattle-headed grey, he'd yank the arms out of a man.

'Steady, then, babes! Easy now, easy!'

Nothing like talking to a horse in a pinch, gave 'em confidence. If he could only get across the road and let the plow into the mile of summer fallow leading south to the house, he might be able to hold them. Lucky there were no fences around this halfsection, and the gate into the yard would be open. He looked back again; the black wall of dust towered almost on top of him. He yanked out the plow, and as the outfit ran up on the horses' heels over the hard road, the storm caught them. They broke into a trot, crossed the road, and were on the run before he could get the plow back in. The wind roared in his ears, and the whole landscape was blotted out by driving dust. He scrambled to his feet and leaned back on the lines, but nothing could stop that wild stampede. He could see the plunging horses through the dust; the two greys bounding along in huge leaps; Iseult running like a hare. Boys, but she could travel! The whippletrees banged and clattered above the roars of the storm. The high platform rocked and pitched. Heaven help the horse that went down. Should he jump? What if he fell beneath that bounding plow? Better jump while the jumping's good! Not he – have to be there if they smashed into a fence. A wheel horse went down, dragged a few yards, and made its feet again. Jack screamed out a curse. Through a break in the dust he caught a glimpse of the house a couple of hundred yards ahead. The horses had swung round in a huge half circle and were making straight for the gate. They'd never get through; it was only just enough for six abreast, not a foot to spare. Better jump – no, stay with it. He leaned back on the lines, pulling with all his might, feet braced wide, swinging to the bucking platform.

It was over in a second. A huge post sprang out of the dust, a black horse reared high in an attempt to jump the wire. Came a crackling of splintering cedar posts, the whine of a tight wire breaking, and high above the storm the agonized scream of a terrified horse. Two of the head team were down and dragging. The struggling mass surged on a few yards and subsided, the rear six piling up on the leaders. The poles broke with a crack like a double-barrelled gun. For an instant Jack balanced above twelve struggling horses, then he jumped clear.

A moment he hesitated, and he was in the midst of it. God, what a mess! If he could only get them out of it before some horse was smothered or broke a leg! In amongst the threshing heels of the leaders he worked like a fiend, choked by the dust, wrenching out and unhooking traces. The off leader was up with his halter broken, rearing in the tangled wires, held back by his traces. Scrambling over heads and flanks Jack was at him and had him loose. Back he went, tugging, wrenching, soothing, cursing; now holding a horse down with knee on head, now kicking one to its feet. Gee, how they groaned!

'Steady, then, babe! Whoa then, so then!'

Four of the lead horses were free; two of them fighting in a mass of tangled lines. Let them fight, they'd break free!

'Get off that head, ye devil!'

With both hands on a halter he heaved at a horse's head. Biting son of a gun, couldn't he see he was trying to help him. Lord what a mess, and Iseult under it all. The halter broke, he reeled back, a frightened horse struck him in the back with its fore foot in a frenzied effort to rise. Blast their hides. Easy now, babes – he must keep cool. Better undo the wheeler's traces. His head swam from the kick, but he plunged in amongst their heels once more. Iseult heaving like a bellows –

'Who in hell invented these whippletrees anyway, curse 'em! Here you kicking, cut it out!'

All but four of them up and the worst to come.

'Get up, Mable, get up.'

Kick the brute –kick, kick –with a heave she reached her feet still fastened to the neck-yoke.

'At a babe! Pull back, you old rascal!' She did, and yanked the horse on the other end of the neck yoke out of the mess. Two left and in bad shape. Ted all in and lying on Iseult. Dragging at the halter pulled over his head; hanging onto the tail he braced his foot against the broken pole and heaved over his rump. Just his luck to get Iseult under it all. The big horse would come round, but Iseult lay groaning with head and neck stretched out, and one hind leg bent under her. He pulled it out with a yank.

'Broken, by all the seven devils! – the best little horse in the bunch!'

He dropped to his knees beside the brown colt's head. The big eyes looked up at him imploringly. The reaction set in. Ten minutes of high tension, of working like a fiend, unmindful of kicks and falls, had sapped his strength. He buried his face in his hands. Iseult as good as dead – the best little horse in the bunch.

He got slowly to his feet. The storm had passed. The rolling level prairie looked grey and dreary. He turned and went up towards the house to get a gun. The boss met him in the yard.

'Did you break much?' he asked.

'Not much, some harness, I guess, but Iseult's broken her leg.'

'Too bad,' said the boss, 'but I'd just as soon it were her. Wild, useless little cayuse. Plenty better'n her on the range.'

'Useless', muttered Jack. 'Iseult useless. She's dead.' He turned towards the house.

'Here, the gun's in the shed.'

Jack got the rifle and came back. He raised it to his shoulder and sighted on the colt's white star, hesitated a moment, and dropped the butt to the ground.

'Here you are, boss,' he muttered.

The farmer took the gun without a word and stood watching his hired man. The ragged, hatless figure slouched on towards the barn. One arm showed white where his sleeve had been ripped from collar to cuff. Something in his dogged walk and the set of his curved shoulders spoke of utter dejection to one who knew Jack's usual briskness.

'Well, I'll be damned!' the farmer burst out. 'You can't never tell these honest-to-God horsemen. Might have been his best girl the way he takes on. Gol-ding it, he doesn't even own the horse.'

A.Y. JACKSON *A Winter's Night* Oct. 1925

January 1926

A POLITICAL CORRESPONDENT
Politics, Parties, and Leaders

These are the times that try men's hearts, and far and wide the cry for a political saviour goes up in the land. The King Government lives on in a state of suspended animation and not even its warm supporters pretend that in its present dilapidated state it is capable of giving the country decent administration. Often before in the history of politics in the Anglo-Saxon world the leader of one of two rival parties has incurred great unpopularity with both his followers and the country, but never before, surely, have two leaders enjoyed the whim or experience of being simultaneously the target of a steady flow of vitriolic criticism from their followers. If there were in existence to-day in Canada bodies parallel to the British organizations known as the National Union of Conservative Associations and the National Liberal Federation, both Mr King and Mr Meighen would soon be served with notice, endorsed by overwhelming majorities, to vacate their high estates. But their several offences are of a completely different character.

Apart from a pleasant voice and a mastery of the formal technique of platform oratory, Mr Mackenzie King has few serious qualifications for the Premiership of Canada, and it is an open secret that if he had not been almost the only politician of the Liberal faith who combined an Ontario birthplace with Scotch Presbyterian lineage, and a record of hostility to conscription, his claims to leadership of his party would have received scant consideration in 1919. In opposition, his platform gifts were useful and his deficiencies could be concealed, but the limelight and responsibilities of the Premiership speedily revealed the pitiable inadequacy of his equipment for his exalted position. Quebec elected him leader to win back the lost Liberal legions of the English-speaking provinces, but his success in this task can be gauged from the fact that in neither of the two general elections which he has fought has he been able to poll more than 25 per cent of the voters of English-speaking Canada. To-day, according to credible report, life for him is all dead-sea fruit, and he keeps himself in almost monastic seclusion in Laurier House, his days given over to gloomy melancholy. Meanwhile, across the Ottawa River in Hull, where prevail the more tolerant liquor laws of Quebec, any day in any bar there can be found groups of mutinous Liberals – members, defeated candidates, and party workers – engaged in a dolorous analysis of his deficiencies and plots for his deposition. Ottawa teems with tales of his vanity and pomposity, his love of ceremony and pageantry, his Edward II-like predilection for strange and unworthy favourites, his old-maidish obsession with petty problems of etiquette, and his naïve comprehension of the realities of politics. His followers crave for some bold political Bayard who can ride the storm and face the whirlwind, and instead they find a bewildered and harassed figure, lamenting the ingratitude of the public and shrinking from his imminent doom. Mr King would make an admirable social secretary to some American multi-millionaire who had a humanitarian interest in labour problems, but as Premier of Canada he is an absurd and preposterous person, and, what is more, his colleagues and his followers know it and make no secret of their knowledge.

The case of Mr Meighen is altogether different. He has immense qualifications for success in the field of politics – courage, character, a keen analytical mind, great capacities both for parliamentary debate and administrative work, and in addition a thorough grasp of the practical problems which form the staple of Canadian politics. But he is a misfit as leader of a Conservative Party. His is a restless, critical mind which likes movement and change and is always ready to discern faults in the existing order of things. His early life in St Mary's and Portage La Prairie gave him the democratic social philosophy of Main Street, and his consistent and almost admirable contempt for all social forms and pretences grates upon the nerves of the Conservative elect who dwell in such favoured regions as Rosedale and Sherbrooke Street. They feel, with some justification, that Mr Meighen is singularly lacking in the atmosphere and graces which should be the proper adornment of a Conservative leader. President Coolidge creates the same impression among a large element of Republicans, but he happens to be a natural-born and proven conservative.

How far removed Mr Meighen is from being entitled to this designation has been demonstrated by his recent *démarche* at Hamilton, reiterated and expanded during the Bagot by-election campaign. His new policy that Canada should never be committed to active participation in a war until the will of the people had been ascertained at a general election was a bold move, obviously planned for the appeasement of Quebec, but it constituted a sharp breach with the traditions of the Conservative Party, which has always championed the idea of Imperial solidarity and was wont to denounce as a disloyal traitor even the Sir Wilfrid Laurier who laid down the doctrine that if Britain is at war Canada is at war. It failed to make any serious impression upon Quebec, but, if it had succeeded in its main object, a very far-reaching change in the fundamental basis of our politics would have been achieved by Mr Meighen. Any party which he led would have brought to an acceptance of a protectionist-nationalist creed; it would be in a position to attract a great deal of support in Quebec, but it would also be exposed to a dangerous flank attack at the hands of some enterprising Liberal leader of the calibre of Mr Dunning.

The obvious move for the Liberals would be to sail upon the opposite tack and, if they coupled advocacy of free trade within the Empire with a policy of close co-operation in the political sphere, in a short time a healthy and vitalizing readjustment of our political life could be accomplished. There would be a substantial transference of French-Canadian votes to Mr Meighen, but, as compensation, thousands of other voters would withdraw their allegiance from him. Mr Meighen, always a realist, is the first Conservative politician to realize that economic protectionism and political nationalism go hand in hand, and his effort to bring some coherence into the policy of his party does not deserve the abuse with which it has been greeted by the Toronto *Telegram* and other papers. Conservatives will sooner or later have to make up their minds that if they want a full-blooded protectionist policy, they can only secure it by becoming stern nationalists; and Liberals, on their side, will have to grasp the lesson that every fresh encouragement of political nationalism simply sets up buttresses for the protectionist system.

On the surface, the Conservative position is vastly stronger than the Liberal, and it is difficult to see how they can fail to arrive in office within the next year. The Progressive Party may give Mr King support to beat off the initial Conservative attack, but they will certainly not keep him indefinitely in office pursuing such a policy of passive negation as would not trouble the dovecotes in Quebec. The price which the Progressives will certainly demand for their support – after the first sessional indemnity has been earned by attendance –will be unpalatable to a substantial contingent of Mr King's Quebec supporters, and down will come his Government. But, once in office, the weaknesses of the Conservative position will soon disclose themselves. Lacking a majority in the House of Commons and possessing very inadequate French representation in his Cabinet, Mr Meighen will be compelled to seek an early dissolution. He would go into it committed to a policy in Imperial relations which is acutely repugnant to a large element in his own party, and there will probably be a marked abatement of the sympathetic support which many Liberals and Independents gave him on Oct. 29th last by way of protest against the vindictive personal campaign waged against him in Quebec.

Taking the Bagot election as evidence that his new policy has not won for him forgiveness in Quebec, the prospects are that he could not achieve more than a trivial improvement of his position; he has probably reached the zenith of his strength in Ontario and would be certain to lose seats in Manitoba and the Maritime Provinces, and his Quebec gains would probably not counterbalance these losses. His only chance of salvation would lie in the failure of the Liberals to change their leader, for English-speaking Canada has finally made up its mind about Mr King's pretensions to the rôle of statesman. There are many experienced observers who believe with Senator David that another general election fought under the same leaders will yield appreciably the same result and will not terminate the present deadlock, and Sir Lomer Gouin is credited with the statement that the party which first has the wits to change its leader will prevail and obtain a secure spell of power. Obviously it is difficult for the Conservative Party to discard a leader who has just won sixty-odd seats and towers above any possible successor in political ability and experience. Therefore, by a strange paradox, the setback suffered by the Liberals opens the way for an improvement in their fortunes by the path suggested by Sir Lomer Gouin, and it also happens that they have available in Mr Dunning, Mr Lapointe, or Mr MacMaster a trio of potential leaders, each of whom would be infinitely more effective and appetizing to the public than Mr King can ever be. But the law of inertia may prevail; Mr King may remain titular head of the Liberal Party and the state of deadlock continue for years.

Remains the Progressive Party, whose commanding position makes it the object of an ardent courtship by both the older parties. It is sadly reduced in numbers, but its average quality has gained enormously by the disappearance of a tribe of incompetent and self-satisfied rural Babbitts who had utilized the Progressive insurgency of 1921 to ride into Parliament on false pretences. In their ranks the percentage of casualties was happily very high, but, on the other hand, excepting Mr Good, who did not stand for re-election, the voters sent back every member of the radical group which withdrew in 1923 to a separate tabernacle by way of protest against Mr Forke's complacent subservience to the King Government. The plain conclusion is that many rural constituencies are still willing and anxious to return genuine Progressives who stand fast by their professions, but will not waste their suffrages on flyblown Liberal politicians masquerading as Progressives. If the life of the Canadian Parliament were a fixed term like that of the United States Congress, the radical Progressives would gleefully assist the Conservatives to eject from office Mr King, who was foolish enough during the recent campaign to brand them as 'political outlaws'; but the $4,000 indemnity is a magnificent form of assurance against a Government's defeat on the floor of the House of Commons within fifty days of the opening of a session. If, however, the Progressives act with shrewdness and courage they can, and should at an early date, force issues which will end the present artificial and unhealthy alignment and bring new life to our politics by opening up clearer avenues for the expression of liberal and conservative opinion.

EDITORIAL

Peaceful Penetration

We are unable to acquiesce in the point of view expressed by Sir Vincent Meredith, who, in the course of an optimistic address at the annual meeting of the shareholders of the Bank of Montreal, commented on the large sums coming to Canada from the United States for investment in manufactories and other enterprises. He said, 'I do not share this fear, but rather welcome the flow of money, which must assist in the development of our natural resources, give employment to labour, and increase our exports to other countries.' No objection whatever can be raised to the exchange, on a moderate scale, of investment capital between one country and another; but what may be beneficial in moderation may be distinctly dangerous if carried to excess. Accurate figures are nowhere obtainable, but there is no doubt that a large proportion of Canadian industry is owned or controlled by American capital, and estimates have been made placing this percentage as high as forty or fifty per cent of the total. Imagine the consternation that would prevail in Great Britain if it were found that nearly half of her industrial organization were in the hands of some foreign nation. If we are to regard with equanimity the alienation of half of our natural resources and technical equipment, are we to be equally complacent while the balance of our industry is annexed by our neighbours? It is an amusing paradox that many of our fervid patriots who would fight to the last ditch rather than allow one foot of Canadian soil to be occupied by a foreign force, see no objection to the disposal of our economic wealth in instalments to the highest bidder.

One of the strongest arguments that can be made in favour of government ownership of our natural resources is that this implies Canadian ownership. If the Hydro-Electric System of Ontario were not the property of the Province, it is certain that some at least of the units would have been purchased by American investors. The United States is now the wealthiest country in the world; the total profits of industry in that country can be expressed in billions, and there are not at present a sufficient number of openings for capital investment, at an attractive rate of interest, to absorb all this surplus wealth. In consequence, the Americans are looking to the foreign investment field, and Canada, with a stable form of government, an industrious population, and a great wealth of undeveloped resources, is a fertile field for the predatory dividend hunter. If this flow of capital from the United States to Canada continues at the same rate for another ten years, practically all our manufacturing plants and the greater part of our mines and timber limits will be owned or controlled by American capital. Under such a régime the successful young Canadian will aspire to the position of branch manager of an American corporation, while the less ambitious will become day-workers in a plant controlled by absentee owners. This picture may seem overdrawn and fantastic, but such an end is well on its way to consummation, and once American capital assumes a dominant position in our industrial life it is idle to imagine that we can retain complete control over our political destiny.

GRAHAM SPRY

Europe's Conception of Canada

Europeans long ago gave up the effort to understand Anglo-Saxons, and many of the finest minds that ever applied themselves to constitutional questions utterly failed to comprehend the British constitution. De Tocqueville, for example, did his best – and a very good one – yet he half came to the conclusion that *'ce n'existe point.'* For evidence of what other people understood or misunderstood the British constitution to be, we need only consider the sad travesties of parliamentary government which were set up on the British model in the last hundred years. To-day the British and the British constitution have been more or less given up as impossible.

The British Commonwealth is a term that has only added to the mystification. To explain to Europeans that the Dominions such as Canada are legally and willingly subjects of 'George V by the grace of God, King,' yet not constitutionally bound in any way to carry out his will or that of his English ministers, is utterly impossible. Article IX of the Locarno Pact, embodying that apparently contradictory principle, is left severely alone by many of the sagest commentators on that treaty. Some hazard a guess. There are those who say that the Commonwealth *'n'existe plus.'* There are those who interpret it as simply the artful method by which *'Albion perfide'* limits her responsibilities. But most give up in the utter hopelessness of one who has found an incomprehensible as great as life itself.

It is the delight of Canadians in Geneva to ask Europeans their opinion of Canada. Canada is a concrete case; no one, not even a De Tocqueville, could say Canada does not exist; there in the League Canada sits and says her say, and on the governing body of the Labour office has representation as the fifth industrial power of the world. Time after time I have asked people here what they considered the position of Canada to be. The greatest number confess they do not know and shake their heads in kindly amazement. The rest, who essay an answer, can be divided into two classes – those who are sure we are Americans; those who have no doubt that we are English. When President Harding died, the good Frenchmen of the pension I was staying in at Grenoble shook my hand sympathetically and expressed their condolences. That a Canadian could be anything else but an American, coming from the same continent, seemed impossible. This represents the first view. The other view, the view of those who consider Canada part and parcel, a chattel and no more, of Great Britain, is expressed in the words of a Greek passport official. Examining with some doubt a Canadian passport, and for some moments in vain trying to solve the doubt, he at last remarked, *'Ah, oui, le Canada, c'est en occupation de l'Angleterre, n'est-ce pas?'*

The truth is, indeed, that a greater part of Europe never thought of Canada as an entity in itself until after the war. The part that the Canadian army played was not taken as an expression of Canadian nationality, but as the almost feudal contribution of a subject people. Certainly that was the view of the central powers. When the peace came, and, due to the persistent efforts of Sir Robert Borden and General Smuts, Canada took her place in the peace conferences and later in the League of Nations, even then there was no change of view. The European thought largely as the United States thought. He believed that the presence of the Dominions as full members of the League was simply a means by which Great Britain multiplied her voting power. That the Dominions were capable of independent action or would take independent action seemed unlikely and impossible. The incident in which Canada and Belgium opposed France and Great Britain at Versailles in the name of small powers was overlooked. Even in 1922 there was misunderstanding which caused quite a little battle between Canada and Italy at the Labour Conference in Geneva on the question of Canada being both British and Canadian. The question was whether Canada, as the fifth industrial power of the world, was or was not entitled to a seat on the governing body of the Labour Organization. Italy said Canada was represented by Great Britain. For one day it seemed as if the Italian view would prevail. Then Ernest Lapointe appeared, and in a speech that is still remembered in Geneva he utterly destroyed the Italian thesis and justified Canada's claim. Canada won her seat, and, for once at least, there could be no doubt that the representation accorded was accorded in virtue of Canada being Canada.

But is there no sign of understanding? Slowly it is coming, and it is coming almost entirely through Canada's participation in the League. Here, in Geneva, either through the Assembly, or commissions of the Assembly, or the Labour conference, or the quarterly meetings of the Labour office governing body, or the scores of less imposing, less heard of, international conferences at Geneva, the existence of Canada both as an entity and as a partner in the British Commonwealth is slowly becoming understood. The members of the League are having increasingly numerous contacts with Canada and Canadian representatives. Canada, as never before, is becoming a reality to the statesmen of the world, and is making it more and more possible for these statesmen to understand, or at least to accept the existence of national unity and Imperial unity side by side. They are realizing that on questions of security the Dominions are practically at one with the Motherland, and that the slightest suggestion of weakening any member of the Commonwealth unites all of them. They are equally realizing, these statesmen, that on other questions the Dominions go their own way, and sometimes utterly disagree. In the Opium conference, for example, Canada voted against Great Britain. In the last Assembly of the League, Canada and Ireland went a step farther than Great Britain on the question of compulsory arbitration. Then there is the great case of Article IX of the Locarno Pact. The cases could be multiplied, and with the example of this strange existence before their eyes, a practice, an actuality, foreign nations, whether they understand or not, at least acknowledge that the fact exists – that there is in this world a medley of people who create an institution no one else can account for, an institution which is united one moment and disunited the next, yet never changes its fabric, its appearance, its loyalties. The presence of Senator Dandurand in the chair of the Assembly itself helped enormously. And the fact that he, a French-speaking Canadian, should be sent from Canada, and then be proposed as chairman by an English delegate, revealed the truth of the British claim that the Commonwealth represented no racial dominance. Yes, Europe and the world are slowly beginning to accept, to acknowledge, even vaguely to understand the British Commonwealth, and by understanding the Commonwealth they come to understand the position of Canada.

With knowledge there has come, too, a certain respect. For the names of Canadian delegates to the League, names such as Rowell, Foster, Lapointe, and Dandurand, stand high with other delegates. There is, indeed, no recommendation to compare with a good delegate to the League. And there is another aspect. The relative importance of small nations is far greater to-day than ever before. The war greatly weakened the great powers. The League has strengthened the little. Canada occupies an intermediate position between great and small, and of these intermediate powers of similar population Canada, as the senior of the British Dominions, as a neighbour and an interpreter of the United States, as a nation composed of peoples speaking the two official languages of the League, above all (for without them these other sides would not be seen) through the quality and character of some of her delegates to the League or the Labour conference, Canada occupies a leading place – a position of real influence quite disproportionate to her power or the share she is willing to take in world affairs.

EDWARD SAPIR

Advice to a Girl

Slip steel into your love;
    Give grudgingly;
Let in your very passion
    Hardness be.
Be not of those sweet ones
    Who stand revealed,
But with a swift sword parry
    And a shield.
Fear not the sharp thunder
    Of a jest,
Lightning in the surchargèd
    Air is best.
These for your safety and
    For my reproof;
There is ever a day coming
    With ominous hoof
Charging in grievous storm,
    Then were it best
To have your love with steel
    Alloyed in jest.

EDITORIAL

The Constitutional Issue

Mr King's speech of July 23rd made it plain that the constitutional issue is to dominate all others in the election campaign, but unfortunately he befogged the real issue at stake. Taken by itself this issue is clear enough, and it is to be hoped that it will not be obscured through any considerations of political expediency on either side. Lord Byng's action in refusing Mr King's request for a dissolution has been debated comprehensively throughout the past month, and we do not now propose to discuss it at length in these columns; but two points regarding it deserve consideration. In the first place, all the precedents for such an act on the part of a governor-general are only to be found in colonial days, and therefore no longer hold good. Secondly, the status of Canada since the war is admittedly that of an independent nation, a co-partner with Great Britain and in the British Commonwealth. Consequently, it is obvious that the Governor-General, as the King's representative in Canada has no prerogatives here that the King has not in Britain. Technically, of course, the King still has the right to refuse to accept the advice of his Prime Minister, but he has not excercised it for a hundred years, and, according to the peculiar way in which the British constitution grows and develops, it is therefore considered that such a thing is no longer 'done.' If the King surprised his people by refusing his Prime Minister a dissolution under the succeeding election, the British people would return that Prime Minister's party to power, thus making plain their feelings on the point. The King's position would be as secure as ever, and he would still have the respect and affection of his subjects; but he would not refuse his Prime Minister's advice again, and the precesimilar circumstances to those which arose at Ottawa last month, it is quite certain that, at dent established by a hundred years of practice would be confirmed.

This is the spirit in which we regard the matter, and certainly the feeling of the Canadian people towards Lord Byng is quite as cordial as ever. It must be remembered that while a king is trained from the cradle for his peculiar career, a governor-general – who has the same position and responsibilities as a constitutional monarch – is often as not offered the job after a lifetime devoted to some other and more ordinary pro-

THOREAU MacDONALD *Northern Summer*

fession. With the best will in the world he is apt to make mistakes on occasion, and his position is the more difficult in that the Dominions have been rapidly developing during the past century from the status of crown colonies to that of fullfledged nations at which they have just arrived, whereas the relative positions of the monarch and the state of England have remained unchanged. A good deal of nonsense has been talked about the effects of Lord Byng's action. To say that it will give impetus to separatist forces in the Dominion is just as absurd as to hold that all those who take exception to it are working for separation from the Commonwealth. In some quarters a cry has been raised for a Canadian governor-general in future; but we feel sure that the proposal will meet with little approval. The reason why the King is so popular in Britain is that he is above and outside political life – he is a man apart. What chance would we have in Canada of getting a man who would not only be that, but who would never be suspected in any quarter of being anything else? As things are, we choose our governor-general and get a man who is free from bias in Canadian affairs as no Canadian could be. It may not always be pleasant for the Englishman in question, but we shall continue to demand that one be sacrificed to our needs all the same. The present issue is not one of Canadian nationalists asserting their independence against 'British' interference; it is a matter of the citizens of a democracy asserting the limitations that must govern the constitutional head of their State.

But if Lord Byng was constitutionally wrong in refusing Mr King's request for a dissolution, Mr King was morally wrong in asking for it. And, in seeking that means of escape from the vote of censure that was hanging over his head, he offended not only against the canons of political morality but against those of good taste and sportsmanship as well. This does not in the least affect our opinion that Lord Byng should have followed his advice. On the contrary, by granting the dissolution he would have enabled the electors to pass judgment on Mr King at the polls – and in a democracy it is assuredly the people who should judge their leader in such a case as this. Now, had Mr King's request that he be allowed to appear before the bar of public opinion been granted, it is quite certain that judgment would have gone against him. From a political point of view, his position would have been hopeless; both the Liberal and Progressive rank and file would have resented the poor generalship which deprived them of their seats and involved them in the expense and turmoil of another election within the year; the Tories would have had a clinching case against him on the customs issue from which he had fled; and the large floating vote, which is affected by personalities and issues and is the determining factor in every election, would have swept Mr Meighen into power with a swingeing majority.

Whatever other results Lord Byng's action may have had, it is certain that in refusing to be guided by Mr King's advice he saved the bacon of the Liberal party. As events have turned out, the Liberals' claim that no party could satisfactorily carry on the King's Government has been vindicated; their ill-starred Ministry has had the vote of censure passed on it, and many voters will feel that in suffering that indignity, and also a short sojourn in the wilderness, the Liberal chieftains have been adequately punished – for no one seriously believes that they were 'partners' of a gang of bootleggers, however deplorable the slackness in the customs department may have been. Moreover, by refusing the Liberals their dissolution, the Governor-General unwittingly supplied them with a constitutional issue which will throw the customs scandal into the shade in most parts of the country. If the Liberals had been allowed to present themselves to the electors when they requested, they would have appeared under a heavy cloud of suspicion and cut but a poor figure; as things are now, they will appear in chariots of fire as the bright defenders of the people's rights and liberties. Their heaviest handicap is Mr King, and they would have been well advised had they substituted another and more admirable figure for their present leader; but, even as things are, they should recoup some of the losses suffered at the last election.

DOUGLAS BUSH

Making Literature Hum

As each Canadian Book Week or gathering of the Authors' Association recedes into the past and the echoes of mutual adulation roll comfortably from soul to soul, there rises insistently in one's bosom the impolite query: 'Do Canadian authors ever read anything?' It would seem incredible that intelligent persons who were abreast of the contemporary movement could hold the opinions which most of our *literati* exuberantly express about their own work and their friends'. Every year one hopes to hear the last of our windy tributes to our Shakespeares and Miltons, and every year the Hallelujah Chorus seems to gorw in volume and confidence. In fact the Canadian literary world – with the exception of a few sceptics, to whom one humbly bows in passing – reminds one of nothing so much as the New York of Jefferson Brick and the Watertoast Gazette. Inflated rhetoric used to be left to the politicians, its rightful exponents, for use on the first of July; during the last few years it has become the language of literature, and one learns on all sides that Canada is taking its permanent seat in the literary league of nations.

This happy conviction is not at all disturbed by the fact that most of the few Canadian books which find their way to American or English reviewers are at best dismissed as negligible; a very few receive tempered praise – as good for Canada. This attitude of competent foreign judges (if not mere jealousy) might, one would think, lead to some sort of self-examination, some wonder if we are so good as we say we are. But self-reverence survives self-knowledge, and the only result of occasional deflations is that certain domestic critics become unpopular.

The trouble is that, born to hew wood and draw water, we are trying desperately to be literary, to have a real renaissance. In the literary way Canada is probably the most backward country, for its population, in the civilized world, and the quickest way to get rid of this unpleasant family skeleton is to abolish critical standards and be a booster. We don't know what to write, but by jingo if we do we have the pen, we have the ink, we have the paper too. And so we have bulky histories of Canadian literature appraising the product of every citizen who ever held a pen; bulky anthologies preserving almost everything metrical that has sprung from a Canadian brain; little books celebrating the genius of people who in another country would not get beyond the poetry corner of the local newspaper; reprints of Canadian 'classics' which not even antiquity can render tolerable; respectful consideration of inferior Zane Greys as literature – in short, an earnest and sincere desire to establish a completely parochial scale of values.

This attitude may serve to win repute at home, for a time, but it is not likely to carry conviction abroad. Its vicious results have been sufficiently evident for years; in the dearth of Canadian anthologies one might make a very pretty collection (it would need to be in two or three volumes) of the more fantastic critical comments of the last decade – the most patriotic soul would be surprised at the number of Shakespeares in our midst. Our standards of judgment not only lead us to worship the small but to neglect the big. Witness the slowness of Mr D.C. Scott's conquest of an audience –while Robert Service, after a sensational welcome, settled down in the pleasant role of a Canadian classic. Mr Scott, though not a major poet, possesses qualities which Canadian verse, now as always, lacks and apparently despises, a sense of form, restraint, austerity of thought, feeling, and phrase. Mr Wilson MacDonald, to mention a new reputation, has a very small tincture of those qualities. Resolved to be a minor Whitman, Mr MacDonald abandons himself to vague, undisciplined, and rather naive emotion; his poems have verbal fluency and energetic rhythms, but almost no intellectual content. Mr MacDonald is better than a good many Canadian poets, but his defects illustrate the vices of Canadian verse in general – an inadequate and untutored critical instinct, lack of intellectual grip and intellectual background, a Swinburnian inclination to invertebrate rhapsodizing, to the accumulation of sounds without any particular meaning. One may except such an individual poet as Mr Pratt, whose *Cachalot*, first published in *The Canadian Forum*, confirmed the author's possession of a sinewy and arresting style, and a masculine imagination at home among the elemental energies of the sea and its creatures.

The salvation of Canadian literature would be a nation-wide attack of writer's cramp lasting at least a decade. Some years spent in reading great literature of the past and present might, in the first place, cause a number of Canadian writers to desist altogether from vain wooing of the muses, which in itself would be a gain for letters and for our disappearing forests. It might also – at least nothing else can – strengthen and inform the intellects of the more resolute survivors. Men of the Renaissance did not attempt self-expression until they had nourished themselves on the greatest literature available. In our renaissance, the interpreters of the Canadian soul – to use a popular if question-begging phrase – mostly prefer to skip the stage of education and assimilation. For us, as Professor Lowes once said of sentimental poets in general, it is enough to drop into the slot-machine a sunset or a heart throb and the poem falls warm and soft into your outstretched hand. Our statesmen commonly assume that a reference to the vast physical resources of our fair dominion is a satisfactory substitute for an idea. Our writers think that tourist enthusiasms before mountain or rivulet make cultivation superfluous; indeed they seem to fear that some fundamental brain-work would take the bloom off their spontaneous emotions. Canadian authors simply do not know enough. How would it be to turn the annual week for buying Canadian literary products into a week for reading a great non-Canadian book – even if one 'has a book'?

To the Editor, *The Canadian Forum*

Sir:

In your last issue an otherwise comparatively unexceptional and platitudinous article by Mr Douglas Bush was marred by an introductory sneer at the Canadian Authors' Association which showed so grave an ignorance of the aims and activities of the CAA that a word of protest is imperative.

Mr Bush assumes that the annual conventions of the Association are mawkish with mutual adulation and that a Canadian Book Week is conducted for the purpose of extravagant self-praise. This is the sort of distorted conception which is perhaps natural to an ex-Canadian, writing from an exalted seclusion among the Brahmins of Massachusetts; but it constitutes a most regrettable libel.

The Canadian Authors' Association was founded in 1921 for the specific purpose of opposing an iniquitous Copyright Act by which certain sinister interests had robbed the native author of a clear title to his own work and had disgraced Canada in the eyes of foreign authors. For five years the Association has been breaking lances in this fight for justice, and the end is not yet. Of all this, Mr Bush knows, or says, nothing.

It was assumed also that such a nation-wide organization might achieve subsidiary ends (a) by annual educational campaigns, seeking to give the Canadian public a nodding acquaintance with the literature that we already possess and so build up a sympathetic audience for the writers of the present and the future, (b) by fostering mutual acquaintance and encouragement, and (c) by a joint study of literature and the problems of authorship. In the prosecution of these ends the Association has been frequently compromised by certain nondescript camp-followers – utilitarian scribblers, rhapsodical spinsters, and pushful dowagers, as well as by the left-handed co-operation in Book Week of certain publishers, whose purposes are naturally mercenary and whose weapon is the blurb. I can assure Mr Bush, however, that most of the leaders of the CAA have been men with as few illusions as himself regarding the shortcomings of Canadian literature. Among these, some of Canada's most eminent men of letters, the academicity of whose own writings proves the absence of ulterior motives, have gratuitously given countless hours of laborious and unselfish service to the Association. They have toiled for justice in the present; for an intelligent public sympathy that would find harvest in the future. And in the three last annual conventions, while mutual good-fellowship has prevailed, there has been little evidence of reciprocal back-scratching and head-patting, little disposition to rate Canadian work above a creditable average. Of all this, Mr Bush knows, or says nothing.

As for Canadian Book Week, the general aim, especially in recent years, has been educational, and the greater part of the effort, so far as the CAA is concerned, has been exerted by members with no commercial interest in the field. There has, of course, been frequent zeal without knowledge; there have been fatuous utterances by embarrassing allies; but once again those in the responsible councils of the Association have been singing 'Whispering Hope' rather than the 'Hallelujah Chorus.' To indict a nation for the perversities of its jingo press is far less culpable than to indict a well-meaning Society for the aberrations of some of its members. Of all this, Mr Bush knows, or says, nothing.

Even in his legitimate strictures on Canadian literature in general. Mr Bush's adolescent love of salt has betrayed him into deluging the dish beyond all reason. It is true that we have poets without intellect. It is true that we have critics who will glibly quote Croce in order to sneer down any wistful academic pleas for absolute standards in literature. Let Mr Bush pillory these to his heart's content. But it is surely treasonous for him to say sweepingly that the best that Canadian books can hope for abroad is 'tempered praise, as good for Canada,' when Canadian history, economics, and science are given almost equal credit with the work of the Old Land, when Denison's dramas are accredited in Moscow, and the *Times Literary Supplement* has just hailed Miss de la Roche's latest novel as 'Hardyesque' and 'a striking book,' Moreover, Mr Bush gives no credit to the long line of devoted Canadian scholars, from MacMechan in Halifax out to Clark in Vancouver, whose teachings and work have set forth with equal penetration and far more sanity and balance the cultural ideal for which he pleads.

But this slight remonstrance over looseness and rashness of statement is not my main purpose. I have written rather to protect the Authors' Association from the superciliousness of smart ignorance.

Yours, etc.,
Winnipeg   Watson Kirkconnell

To the Editor, *The Canadian Forum*

Sir:

... Mr Watson Kirkconnell writes in such a state of moral incandescence that he is neither consistent nor relevant. If my youthful remarks (by the way, is it not time to retire that ancient controversial gag about adolescence?), if my remarks were mostly 'unexceptionable and platitudinous,' the gentleman doth protest too much, methinks. Not to mention the private letters of approval which I have received from Canadians who speak with authority. ... But most of Mr Kirkconnell's fervent outpourings have nothing to do with the case. I was writing a brief piece on Canadian literature and the pulmotor method of criticism, I was not writing about the Canadian Authors' Association (much as I should like to). Yet Mr Kirkconnell, building up his charges like ballads, with incremental repetition and a refrain, blames me for not having given a detailed account of the Association and all its activities, including a history of the Canadian copyright laws. Of logic, it would seem Mr Kirkconnell 'knows, or says, nothing.'

As for the justice of Mr Kirkconnell's defence of the critical zeal of the Authors' Association, that may be safely left to readers to estimate. If Canadian literature is not being nourished by puffery, why have there been protests against it from such men as Professor Broadus, Mr Jacob, Mr Murray Gibbon, Mr Eayrs – to name a few whose strictures I have read? I refrain from producing documentary evidence, since it would fill blue-books. The most visible effect of the parochial propaganda which Mr Kirkconnell calls 'mutual acquaintance and encouragement' has been that Canadian literature and criticism are overspread with a mildew of sickly self-consciousness, and the feeblest songster who, yielding to 'request of friends,' declares 'Go to, I will make a poem,' is certain of applause. So long as this condition prevails there seems to be room for platitudes, especially as they can scarcely be heard for the patriotic voices proclaiming with Gilbertian iteration that 'all is right as right can be.'

Yours, etc.,
Cambridge, Mass.   Douglas Bush

EDITORIAL

Mr King's Luck

Mr King's luck is extraordinary. Six months ago he seemed to have come to the end of his tether; his Government was in bad odour with its own followers, he could no longer command a majority in the House of Commons, and he invited catastrophe by asking for a dissolution under circumstances which would have provided a Roman holiday for the Tories. What happened? Lord Byng refused him a dissolution, presented him with a constitutional issue which threw the customs scandals into the shade, and he was returned to power with a stronger allied force under his banner than any Liberal leader had commanded for years. Immediately after the election came the Imperial Conference. Mr King was in an uncomfortable position, for the following which gave him his new majority was composed of two main divisions sharply divided on the very issues which he knew would be foremost at the Conference – inter-imperial relations and Canada's status. Quebec did not want any tinkering with the British connection, yet the large section of Liberalism that comes within the orbit of the *Manitoba Free Press* was pressing for a declaration of Canada's full nationhood and absolute equality with Great Britain. Mr King's luck again held good. Without lifting a hand or committing himself either way, in fact approaching the Conference with a statement that Canada had no particular demands to put forward and had merely sent him there in a spirit of goodwill to all, he returns to us with an imperial recognition of Canada's status which satisfies western Liberals and for which no Quebec faction can reproach him, since it was presented to him as a free gift by imperial statesmen whom the eloquence of Gen. Hertzog had persuaded of its advisability before he got there.

In the field of domestic politics, fortune has been no less kind to our lucky Premier. He has before him the reasonable prospect of five years in office; he begins his new lease of political life at a time when the country is entering on a period of prosperity which may well prove to be unprecedented; the West has recovered from its slump and has just harvested a paying crop,

J.E.H. MacDONALD *Paul Bunyan Takes an Evening Stroll in Algoma* Jan. 1927

industry is flourishing in the East, our exports of manufactured goods at last exceed our imports, our favourable trade balance is steadily increasing, immigration is already stimulated, and government revenues show such a promising increase that tax reductions should be easily practicable. Best of all, perhaps, from the politician's point of view, Mr King's following is now so divided that its reactionary and progressive elements can be brought to meet each other half way on economic issues, instead of the left wing having to go all the way as has been the case with every Liberal Government prior to 1925. Again, circumstances have removed from the opposition the keenest mind and the greatest obstructive force it possessed, and in the first clash between the Premier and the new leader of the opposition, Mr King's superiority in debate was clearly demonstrated. We do not wish to criticize the Premier before he has had a chance to prove himself under these new and favourable circumstances; but we regret that in the first debate of the new Parliament he showed a greater pre-occupation with party feuds than with constructive policies. Under the conditions which governed the last Parliament this would have been understandable, but conditions have changed and the people who put Mr King in power with a safe majority would like to see him recognize the fact by forgetting the petty squabbles of the past and concentrating on the rich possibilities of the future. If Mr King has it in him to conceive and carry out a policy in harmony with his oft-expressed Liberal aspirations, he will never have a better chance. The country is with him and his luck is in.

A.J.M. SMITH

The Lonely Land

Cedar and jagged fir
Uplift accusing barbs
Against the grey
And cloud-piled sky;
And in the bay
Blown spume and windrift
And thin, bitter spray

Snap
At the whirling sky;
And the pine trees
Lean one way.

A wild duck
Calls to her mate,
And the ragged
And passionate tones
Stagger and fall,
And recover,
And stagger and fall,
On these stones,
Are lost
In the lapping of water
On smooth, flat stones.

This is a beauty of dissonance,
This is a desolate splendour,
This resonance
Of stony strand,
This smoke cry curled over a black pine.

B.R. BROOKER
'Energy is Eternal Delight' (Blake)   Oct. 1927

These are the poems of Canada,
Resinous scent of the balsam,
Cold sting
Of blown spray,
Cry of wild duck over Long Lake

When the wind bends the pines
South
And curdles the sky
From the north.

July 1927

HUNTLY K. GORDON

The Nudes at the CNE

The Toronto press and public have made another exhibition of themselves – an exhibition all the more absurd in the face of that city's calm assumption of the leadership of the Dominion in the aesthetic field. The hanging of two or three 'nudes' in the Art Gallery of the CNE gave those local papers which seek publicity at all costs the enviable opportunity of 'creating a sensation' without cost to themselves. Two or three skilfully emphasized and suggestive reviews, and a few hundred of their readers – perhaps one half of one per cent – decided that the Art Gallery was for once worth visiting. The reporters assigned to the 'job' carefully noted the increased attendance – with their well known conservatism. Editorials, articles, and reproductions of the pictures followed. Letters to the Editor began to crowd the correspondence columns, and the public suddenly found itself involved in an acrimonious and puerile discussion. Those who protested against the pictures declared that they were indecent, immoral, and a cause of perversion to our pure Canadian youth. Those who defended them declared they were outstanding and representative works of art of the realistic school. The descriptions of the visiting 'throngs' were as varied as the arguments. One writer said the pictures were surrounded by crowds of 'giggling boys and girls'; another that he had to wait in line half an hour before he could get inside the door and found not a soul in front of the pictures in question, but at a distance numbers of all ages and both sexes casting at them sidelong glances of shamefaced curiosity; and another that unusual interest was displayed by a few middle-aged and elderly people. It would seem obvious to any unbiased observer that the whole humiliating rumpus was caused by the newspapers for reasons best known to themselves. Had the public been left to itself the comparatively few who are really interested in pictures would have visited the gallery and admired or condemned these pictures as they found them, in their judgments, well or badly painted.

The controversy might easily be left as food for Olympian laughter were it not for the possibility of far-reaching and dangerous results, for it has actually been proposed that, since a committee of artists cannot be trusted to select an exhibition of 'decent' and 'moral' pictures, then laymen must be added to their number! The artists, presumably, would contribute the technical knowledge and the laymen the true moral discrimination. Artists are always so indecent and laymen so simon-pure! Such a suggestion surely could have been made only in Toronto or Tennessee.

The whole idea is a contradiction of terms, for art has nothing to do with morality except in the most incidental and philosophic connection. No subject is or can be immoral in itself. It is a question only of good treatment or bad treatment, a good picture or a bad picture, and no artist intent only on producing a good picture can produce an indecent one whether he painted Caesar's Wife or A Scene in a Brothel. Conversely, if indecency is the main impulse in the painting of a picture, the artistic desire to create form will have the less to do with it, and the result will be, indecent if you will, but primarily simply a bad piece of work. It can, of course, be argued that a fine work of art has a spiritual or moral value. Quite so. In their own degrees, a sturdily-made utensil, a perfect machine, or a well-ploughed field have the same effect. The cause is not in the morality of the subject, but in the degree of creative imagination and interpretive skill involved.

RICHARD DE BRISAY

A New Immigration Policy

The amount of immigration into Canada at present is unsatisfactory to most Canadians. During the years of the post-war depression immigration was not wanted since many of our own people had to go to the United States to make a living; but good times have come again and there is a general feeling that they should be exploited to the utmost. A minority exists that is content with the present size and composition of our population, and that minority exercises no small influence over the Government; but most of us recognize the need of a larger population to support our railway and administrative systems, and we are confident that with our natural wealth and an average of 3 souls to the square mile we can absorb tens of millions of new settlers. Our nationalists will not rest content with an immigration policy which promises to keep our nation down to the status of a third rate power, and our imperialists realize that the next few years offer our last chance to secure British stock, for if Great Britain's present surplus is not drawn off, her birth rate will drop so sharply that in the next generation there will be no surplus. Under these circumstances there is bound to be a national demand for a more active immigration policy as soon as it is generally recognized that in the new era we have entered the tide of immigration can not be expected to rise of itself. ...

Immigrants are brought to a new land in two ways: they are either driven or enticed. And in the great days of colonization in North America they were mostly driven. The persecuted Puritans of the seventeenth century had to choose between the devil and the deep sea; the prospect ahead was fearful, but worse lay behind; if they risked being drowned or dying of ship fever by going, they risked being hanged or dying of prison fever if they stayed, and they preferred to dare the Mohawks of New England rather than suffer the tender mercies of the Stuarts and the Bishops at home. In the eighteenth century the UE Loyalists were not threatened with the thumbscrew and the boot, but they were quite sufficiently persecuted to make them face the hazards of a new country where they could be free. In the nineteenth century the great flow of emigrants from the Old World was sustained by the pressure of political persecution in some quarters and of privation and the lively fear of starvation in others. But in the age we live in no pressure forces the western European to emigrate. In Great Britain especially, under the new social legislation wages are high and the unemployed need not fear starvation, while the only persecuted class is a small minority whose members are wanted by nobody but the police. The result is that although generous State assistance is offered to emigrants so few take advantage of it that in the year 1925-6 little more than half a million pounds was spent on emigration compared to 255 millions spent on social insurance.

If King George V were really the bloody tyrant portrayed by Big Bill Thompson of Chicago, it would be a very good thing for Canada. It is even arguable that it would be to our advantage if England were thrown into convulsions by a *coup d'état* to-morrow. If Mr Churchill should come down to the House in a black shirt and with a castor-oil corps of his friends behind him, purge the Commons, proclaim a dictatorship, gaol the Socialists, smash the Unions, suspend the Habeas Corpus Act, repeal all social legislation on the Statute Book, and make it a capital crime for a worker to belong to any organization, attend any meeting, or lift his voice in any criticism of the Government, then indeed we might look for a rush of the right sort of immigrants – men of high spirit and low demands, who would be glad to sweat for their living in a free country and who would be admirably suited to help build up the perfect State in this Dominion. But since we have no reason to hope for any salutary pressure to force the British out, we must consider what can be done by way of enticing them out; and that brings us to a consideration of the immigration restrictions of our own Government which were found by the McLean Report to be a contributory cause of the present stagnation.

Those restrictions are not primarily due to any pressure put upon our Government by the forces opposed to immigration, nor are they only a feature of those post-war years during which immigration on a great scale was not wanted. They are really due to the same general change in social outlook which has been responsible for the schemes of social insurance in Great Britain. We Canadians have adopted the new social philosophy of the Old World, and since we admit the State's responsibility for the sustenance of the individual we are no longer willing to receive immigrants unless there is some guarantee that they shall not become a charge on the community. For a few years after the railways had opened the West we followed the example of the United States and invited all able-bodied men to come into the country, help build it up, and take what advantage they could from their labour, on the tacit understanding that they sank or swam by their own efforts. We did not assume any responsibility: it was up to them. They had their chance in a rich new land and that was considered enough. That was the way the United States had filled up its territory during the whole of the nineteenth century. The philosophy which permitted it was typical of the century of the Darwinians and the Manchester School, and the Yankees boiled it down into one short exhortation: 'Root, hog, or die!' A few thousands died here and there, but the rooters made a great country. Even in our new age that philosophy has survived in the Great Republic; the result is that the USA is the most lawless of civilized nations, the crudest, the hardest. But that is natural to a young country, and the United States has been satisfied to remain young, satisfied to be afflicted with all the faults and pains of youth so long as she has youth's vigour, its extravagant hopes and excitements, its growth. We in Canada take much credit for the superiority of our administration over that of the States, yet it is a question whether we may not lose greatly through having become precociously careful, moral, sedate. But the choice has hardly been ours; we happened to come late and were caught by the spirit of a new age, so that we find ourselves prematurely a nation among nations with all the inhibitions of countries that were grown old before ours was born.

That is our situation to-day. Nothing forces immigrants into our country, and we ourselves must place restrictions on the small number of adventurous souls who wish to come of their own accord. It is true that we can expect some of our restrictions to be lifted in future: at present, for example, we demand agricultural labourers and refuse mechanics as 'assisted' immigrants, and one of the most discussed problems of Empire Settlement is the fact that Great Britain's surplus labour is industrial whereas our need is for agricultural labour. But that problem arranges itself through the progressive mechanization of agriculture: we need not worry about turning mechanics into farm labourers in an age when farm labourers are being forced to become mechanics. Still, the fact remains that every representative Canadian Government in future will maintain stiff restrictions as to the quality of immigrants and their capacity for self-support. It is clear, therefore, that if we want a large influx of settlers we can only get them by making Canada so attractive that we can keep up our new standards and yet secure the numbers we desire. This is not an easy proposition and we can only put it over by adapting our policy to the new conditions of our age. Having accepted the idea of the State's responsibility to the individual, we must go further and make our State the one above all others where the individual producer is most secure and most prosperous, and fortunately we are rich enough to afford it. There can be no such thing in future as 'a vigorous immigration policy' at Ottawa in a water-tight compartment by itself: if we want rapid growth in population, the whole national policy must be readjusted to that end. The tariff on all the necessities of life must be reduced to the point where the margin between the cost of living and the worker's wages in our basic industries will equal the margin in the USA. Public ownership of public utilities and the supply of all essential services at cost must be encouraged, every sound co-operative scheme on the part of the producers must be fostered, generous Government assistance through credits and research must be given to agriculture, mining, lumbering, fishing, and their allied industries, the Labour Conventions of the League must be enforced and old-age pensions established throughout the Dominion. All the surviving, anti-social shibboleths of the nineteenth century must be discarded and a new deal given the producers all round. This national policy would not only attract the right sort of immigrants but would keep them here when they came; it would stop the drift of our own people to the United States and encourage their expansion at home; in this new era it is the only policy of material and spiritual growth, and growth is the first duty of a young country. Any pessimistic reader will be encouraged by reflecting on the advances already made by the provincial Governments of Ontario and the West along this road.

And then, having set our house in order, we must see that its advantages are kept continuously before the peoples of the Old World, and particularly Great Britain. Here, again, the history of the United States' growth is illuminating, for it is undeniable that the USA has consistently thrown Canada into the shade and still keeps its reputation as the most desirable goal of the emigrant. The Thirteen Colonies got away to a good start with their Declaration of Independence in an age when Liberty was the bright lodestar of every thinking European. Having fought for their liberty and won it fairly, the Yankees turned their backs on the bad Old World and went west; but they made a noise in their going that was heard the world over. They took Louisiana and Florida, pushed across the Mississippi, annexed Texas and New Mexico, rolled back the Indians from the western plains, stormed California, and threw open half a continent in the name of Liberty: even when they had to fight the greatest civil war in history to keep recalcitrants within their free Union, it somehow became a war against slavery and the victory of the North was a triumph for Liberty. The oppressed masses of Europe surged over to this land of the free. By the time the Europeans had won liberty at home and had turned to more material objectives, the United States had become El Dorado and the Almighty Dollar proved as sure a lodestar as Liberty had ever been; at the end of the nineteenth century her population was near a hundred millions. In the twentieth century the United States' luck was out, for in a world gone mad over socialism she found herself the supreme capitalistic State, newly built from the ground up on principles which most Europeans had come to loathe. Politically and socially, the USA was no longer desirable; but the twentieth century had produced the movies, the greatest medium for national advertising the world had ever seen; she monopolized the movies, and the shots of her camera men are now heard round the world as clearly as the shots of her embattled farmers in the eighteenth century. Every night and day the people of the Old World are dazzled by pictures reflecting the prosperity, the opportunities, and the excitements of American life, and so strong is the lure that Uncle Sam can pick just the immigrants he wants and turn back the rest from his doors.

We in Canada have never had any declaration of our independence to shout about, nor has our country made a great name in the world as a happy hunting-ground for dollar-chasers; but the fact remains that Canada to-day offers more liberty and more security than the USA, almost as high a standard of living, and a much more congenial social atmosphere. To familiarize the people of the Old World, and especially Great Britain, with the facts and attractions of Canadian life, we must establish a moving-picture industry of our own, by Government assistance to whatever degree is necessary. Technical conditions here are favourable to the production of pictures, and political and economic conditions in Great Britain would guarantee a market. The pictures produced need not be propagandist in character: all that is necessary is that they should be produced here in Canada so that they would reflect our national life in all its aspects. The cumulative effect of Canadian pictureplays seen week after week and year after year by millions of British workers, and, as time went on, by all the peoples of Europe as well, would do more to stimulate immigration than all other agencies put together.

To sum up. In the matter of immigration the United States is our rival, and at present our successful rival. But the social fabric of the USA has the same defect as the architecture of its cities: it is impressive from a distance, but it oppresses the man in the street. If we in Canada extend our national fabric on the broad horizontal lines of co-operation in contrast to the vertical capitalistic fabric of the United States, and if we make our national life as familiar to the world at large as the Americans have made theirs, it can not be doubted that most British and European emigrants in future will choose Canada as their new home in preference to the USA. So will many Americans.

JEAN BURTON

Phyllus

There was nothing particularly pastoral about Phyllus, though her fragility might perhaps have appeared Dresden-like with proper care and proper clothes. This was a new experience for her, and shyness choked her. She was excited and unhappy and fearful, and she could not quiet the hard beating of her heart or still its pain, but all these things were as nothing compared with the cruel shyness that held her in its grip and would not let her go.

And should she call him Jake, or Mr Milton, as usual? What *should* she call him?

She tried to say his name, but it came only as a whisper.

Phyllus felt all earthly woes paled into insignificance beside the appalling fact that she did not know how to address this man.

Phyllus had worked in Jacques' Beauty Parlours – Beauty Salons, really, but Phyllus was uncertain of the pronunciation – on Granville Street for five months before Jake had given any sign of noticing her, but Phyllus was accustomed to being unnoticed, and was not hurt or surprised. She was only very tired.

She was tired of heads full of oil and dandruff, and hot sticky marcels, and the smell of shampoo water. She was tired of the irritable old women, and the rich Jewesses, and the giggling girls. The girls were worst. They expected to be amused. They asked her if she had seen the new show at the Capitol, or the Pantages. God knows she had no money to go to the Capitol, no time to go, no one to go with. But they kept saying oh gee, did you see Colleen Moore at the Capitol, oh gee, did you *see* the new show at the Pan?

Many of them asked for the other girls when they came in to make appointments, for the other girls had seen all the new shows and could also, out of the vastness of their personal experience, offer advice and counsel on the subjects nearest the hearts of their clients.

But in spite of the fact that Phyllus was rarely asked for, she worked very hard at Jacques' Salon, harder, it seemed, than the other girls, for when they were through with a manicure or a shadow wave they picked up their True Romances or their Dreamland Tales and promptly buried themselves in its contents, oblivious, apparently, to the outside world; and so remained until the press of customers became so great that they were forced to emerge, swearing beneath their breath, emerge languidly and disdainfully, patting their elaborate curls, carefully gracious and aloof.

But if Phyllus so much as sat down, with a long sigh of weariness, she knew it would not be many minutes before Estella the red-haired would appear, clacking, 'C'm on, Phyllus, put away that book! Cust'mer.'

Phyllus was very tired. Phyllus had always been tired, but of late, when she had been standing all day, her heart smothered her and she found it difficult to breathe. If it had not been for this, Phyllus would not have commented upon her weariness, but would have taken it for granted, as she had always done.

She said to herself, quoting her mother, 'You're tired. Well, what of it? People've been tired before, and they'll be tired again.'

She quoted also her mother's fragment of the ultimate philosophy, 'We'll all have a long enough rest, some day.'

But of late it did not sound convincing to say 'What of it?'

It was because Phyllus was so tired that she did not observe conditions in Jacques' Salon very closely for some months after she came to work there. She did not have much to say to the other girls, in any case. But one day she was moved to sigh to the languid blonde beside her, gum slowly revolving in time to the andante passage in the fictional adventures of the heroine: 'Gee, I'm tired. Why don't she call you, for a change?'

The languid blonde, showing no resentment, opened violet eyes cased in mascara of astonishing blackness and stiffness.

'Dearie,' said the languid blonde, 'we earn our money, same as you. I mean to say, not the same as you.'

And the blonde put her wise, which showed that she had, at least, a kind heart.

This was the original reason why Phyllus now found herself in a boarding house on Richards street, wondering whether she should address her employer as Jake, or as Mr Milton, and wishing in either case that he would turn out the lights.

It had really not been difficult, up to this point. Phyllus hardly knew yet just how it had happened. It seemed that as soon as she had known about Jake and the girls, Jake knew that she knew, and that was all there was to it.

She had dashed up the steps with the others from the downstairs parlours to see the procession go by. The band thrilled her, and the marching men, and the flags. But not the crowd, for the crowd was indifferent and apathetic, like all Vancouver crowds. Phyllus pressed her way to the front, leaving the other girls behind.

She stood, rigid with patriotism, for a long time, for the procession had been badly arranged, like all Vancouver processions; until the car with the new governor-general and his wife passed, dutifully cheered by a number of young men and boys thoughtfully retained in advance for that purpose, Vancouver crowds being, as those in charge of such events know, untrustworthy and not to be depended upon in the matter of enthusiasm and noise.

The new governor general looked about with polite interest, and his wife, a dark-haired woman with kindly lines about her eyes and mouth, smiled and bowed.

'Ah, gee,' said Phyllus reverently.

She silenced with a glare the small boy beside her who took it upon himself to make facetious comment on the governor-general's moustache, for Phyllus believed in the British Empire.

But it had been very hot, and she felt tireder than usual when she turned down the steps again. At the door Jake was standing, meditatively surveying his gleaming finger nails.

'Well,' said Jake affably, 'fine show.'

Phyllus agreed gaspingly.

Jake added an even higher lustre to the nails of his right hand, by rubbing them against the palm of his left.

'They tell me,' said Jake in the tone of one who relates well-nigh incredible tidings, 'that all them decorations was sent from Seattle up here! Home firms didn't get a look in! How the hell do they expect to see Vancouver grow, when all the time they patronize American industry like that, never even giving the home firms a look in?'

Phyllus found herself in fervent unison with these patriotic sentiments.

Jake, satisfied with the state of his nails at last, transferred his attention to Phyllus' ankles. She did not move away, for Jake had the air of one who has not completed his remarks; and she remained standing, for there was no place to sit. Standing in itself made Phyllus' heart beat hard and fast, and now, coupled with her excitement, the old smothering sensation began to come upon her again. But Phyllus waited, standing, and in due time Jake said:

'We'll have supper somewheres together tonight. How's that?'

As simple as that.

He took her, finally, after driving her around Stanley Park – ah, how often had Phyllus envied the flappers in Jacques' Salon who had talked casually of driving around Stanley Park – to the boarding house on Richards street, and Phyllus, for the first time in the evening, was afraid. Not that Phyllus herself lived in a much more exclusive neighbourhood, her home being on Jackson Avenue, inhabited mostly by negroes, and not so very far from the outer fringes of Chinatown. But it was familiar, and this place was not, and Phyllus had never been clever at concealing her emotions.

Jake said, 'This place is all right. Sure. Under new management now. And it's clean. Good, gosh, did you expect the Vancouver Hotel?'

Phyllus followed him up the stairs, and past the man at the desk, whom Jake greeted as an old friend. She trembled, but that, she thought, was due more to her unreasonable heart than to her fear.

The place was clean, as Jake had observed.

Phyllus was totally innocent of sex, although she had a foul-mouthed father and a mother who, when she was not drunk, was frank enough. When she was drunk, she was sentimental, with the unpleasant and insincere sentimentality of her race.

Phyllus clung at this point to the hope that after all, nothing would happen, maybe. For this hope Jake was responsible. It should be explained that Jake had the soul of an artist. That was why his Salon de Beauté was such a success that even women and girls from Shaughnessy Heights now came to him and trusted him implicitly in the choice of hairdressing styles and shades of rouge. Jake was an ardent admirer of romance and beauty. He read poetry. He had said to Phyllus that maybe they wouldn't try anything the first night. Just lie together and talk and get acquainted. This had seemed to Phyllus an admirable idea.

And to do Jake justice he was quite prepared to follow out this programme, having a flair for the unusual. Partly because he was an artist, and partly because he was very sleepy, the weather being hot. But with his arms about Phyllus his sleepiness departed, and he said, 'Kid, this is simply torture to me. You don't understand.'

Phyllus thought this touching, and she had always been the victim of a nervous desire to please.

Jake regaled her, later, with stories of his previous exploits which Phyllus did not mind, it being tactily understood that from now on Jake was to be true to her alone, although he did happen to have a wife, to say nothing of the other girls in the Beauty Salon.

Jake said, in addition, 'You're as safe as a church, see? I never knew this to fail, see? Anyways, I know a doctor. Just as good as a doctor, anyways.'

Phyllus had never expected very much of life, which was just as well; but during the months which followed, she had her taste of the joy of living. The work, she discovered, was easier. Jake was kind. Once or twice he gave her money above her wages. He took her out to eat.

Once he took her to a show, so that Phyllus for the next two weeks was able to exult to every girl she marcelled, delighting in being able to say the expected, the proper thing, 'Gee, did you see Gloria Swanson at the Capital?' until a *blasé* flapper said, one day, inevitably, 'That's old,' after which Phyllus did not refer to it again.

Jake even took her to English Bay and gave her money to rent a bathing suit, and they lay on the sand, grimy and happy, and ate hot dogs, and Jake feasted his eyes upon her, having the soul of an artist, as he frequently reminded her.

But the highlight of the summer was the Sunday he took Phyllus to Capilano Canyon.

They started early, as they were going to walk and see the scenery. Jake might have taken his car, which Phyllus would have preferred; but Jake explained that it would be much more original, and also much pleasanter, really, to walk and see the scenery as one could never hope to do from a car. So Phyllus met him at the corner of Main and Hastings, outside the library, and they proceeded to the dock, through odorous streets lined with second-hand stores and Chinese lodging-houses and Greek restaurants, tall bleak warehouses and employment agencies, down under the subway, already, at nine o'clock in the morning, filled with jostling crowds of men and women and children on their way to Capilano Canyon for the day, laden with picnic baskets and raincoats and kodaks and babies, and most of them, like Phyllus and Jake, prepared to walk – to see the scenery.

They bought chocolate bars and bananas and gum at the news-stand, and passed through the revolving gate to the wharf.

October 1927

The North Vancouver ferry was half way across the inlet, looking, at that distance, clean and glistening.

She boomed a greeting to the West Vancouver ferry, homeward bound. Phyllus, to whom the sound of drums, of whistles, of thunder, always caused a palpitating flutter of the heart, clutched Jake's arm. Jake was indulgently amused and protective. He gallantly held her elbow while he made a way for her through the scrambling crowd when the ferry docked, and found seats on what would be the shady side of the boat when she turned, as he explained to Phyllus, very nautical and technical. Later arrivals observed their strategic position enviously, as they wandered vainly about in search of any seat at all, or failing that, a place to deposit their parcels. Jake was always efficient in a crowd. He looked well, too, with his dark eyes and black hair, glistening with brilliantine, and the carefully trained foppish sideburns, and the crisp black moustache. He would have looked well even if he had not been, as Phyllus proudly told him, such a swell dresser. Other girls cast interested glances at him, but Jake, though acutely conscious of their attention, was blandly indifferent, as he explained the principles of the boat's mechanics to Phyllus. Phyllus adored him.

Phyllus felt that it was almost too much. The clean blue water, the sparkling sunshine, and she, Phyllus, going to Capilano Canyon for the day with Jake! She wondered what the people who glanced at her so casually would think if they knew that she, Phyllus, were one of those whom romance and adventure had claimed for their own, lifting her out of the rut of ordinary days and ordinary ways, and setting her apart forever, for had not she, Phyllus, known Life?

Phyllus looked at Jake, unhearing, and glowed.

Jake ceased his exposition of naval mechanics, and transferred his attention to the crowd surging restlessly about them.

'Lotta tourists already,' commented Jake. 'Great people, the Americans. The tourists are all right. Sure. Bring business.'

At North Vancouver they took the tram as far as it went, and then started on their walk, Jake waving aside the taxi-drivers who kept up a continuous and cacophonous chorus until they were out of sight.

Phyllus enjoyed the walk, in spite of the fact that she tired so easily and that the sun was hot. Jake discarded his coat, and strode forward, magnificent in a pink silk striped shirt, over the roads damp and spongy from the summer rains, and Phyllus pantingly followed him. The rich dense green of the trees on either side of the road soothed her and promised coolness and quiet, and Phyllus would have liked to stop and explore their depths, and just for this one day to lie on piled heaps of leaves and rest, rest, and listen to the sound of the wind in the branches, and look at the sky, and forget all that had happened to her before she knew Jake. Phyllus' whole being called out for rest. Just for this one day. The trees yearned toward her as she passed, whispering of the coolness and the peace waiting for her, only a few steps from the hot and crowded road. But had they not planned to spend the day at Capilano Canyon, she and Jake, had they not come to North Vancouver for no other purpose, would it not be foolish and ridiculous to change their plans for so idle a fancy as this, to rest for a day beneath the trees at a spot which had no particular name, and was never visited by tourists? Certainly Phyllus knew how absurd it would be. She did not mention it to Jake, but followed him breathlessly, under the hot sun, stumbling over the rough places in the road.

They came, finally, to the long hill that is climbed by two steep flights of steps, with a log railing worn smooth by thousands of clutching hands.

'Race you to the top,' suggested Jake, jocularly.

For a long and horrible moment Phyllus, looking at the steps, thought her heart had stopped beating. She put her hand to her breast, and leaned weakly against the rail.

'It would *kill* me to run up them steps, I do believe,' said Phyllus at length, and Jake, alarmed, looked at her.

'Gosh, kid,' he said, 'you *are* tired. We'll sit down here for a couple of minutes, and take it easy. How's that?'

But even after the rest, Phyllus apologetically explaining how she had always tired easy, and with Jake's hand beneath her elbow as they climbed, Phyllus wondered how she ever got to the top. When she finally accomplished it, they sat again on a fallen log until she had recovered her breath, and Jake bought ice-cream cones from the old woman at the side of the road, and the remainder of the walk to the Canyon was not so hard.

At the Canyon itself, Phyllus won Jake's admiration by walking steadily across the long swinging bridge, glancing all along the way with mild contempt at the stout American matrons who clutched the rail, shrieking that they couldn't take another step, and Jim, take me back! No, Phyllus told Jake with scorn, it wasn't height as made her dizzy. Not while you could walk along on the level, like this. It was climbing as took her breath away and gave her that stitch in her side.

When they had eaten their lunch and given the scenery its due meed of praise, it was time to start for home, if they wanted to catch the second-to-last ferry.

The walk back to the ferry did not appear so long or so tiring, for it was down hill, and the evening was cooler. But it was with a dusty, exhausted company that they silently filed onto the boat and sank upon the nearest benches.

Phyllus would never forget, she knew, the beauty of that night, not as long as she lived, with the loveliness of the clear stars against the dark sky, the gentleness of the water, the cool fragrant air, and the comfort of Jake's arm about her tired body. All about them in the soft shadowy gloom shopgirls and their men unashamedly petted. Some one strummed a ukulele. They sang snatches of jazz:

'I'll be loving you – always – always.'

Jake's hand moved about her breasts, and the pain which lay always in wait beneath them was for the moment quieted and robbed of its power.

Still to do Jake justice, he did know someone who was just as good as a doctor, a specialist, in fact; and if he had not lost so much at poker the week previous he would have seen Phyllus through her trouble, and this, too, without being unpleasant.

But as it was, he had lost the money, and that was all there was to it.

So he said, 'Good God, kid. I told you to be more careful. Listen, do you know what this will cost? One hundred in cold cash! One hundred marcels! Two hundred hair trims. Girl, I wish I could do it for you. I sure do. But the truth is, I simply haven't got – why, I can't pay my own bills. Let alone anything like this. And that new drying lamp to pay for! Now listen, Phyllus, you'll be all right. Lots a girls go through with it, and none the worse and no one the wiser, either. And your job is right here waiting for you, when you come back, any time, Phyllus,' said Jake, thus concluding their relationship as he had begun it, in a burst of generosity.

Phyllus was very uncomplaining and quiet about it. She really did not say anything at all. At least, Jake could remember nothing afterwards, although he tried.

In fact, Jake said later, 'If the kid had only stayed around, I'da helped her out. Sure. I was just thinking how I could manage.' Which was probably true.

But Phyllus was tired. Looking back over her life, she could not remember a time when she had not been tired, the result, most likely, of consistent malnutrition.

Phyllus was not excitable or resentful, and she made her plans very carefully and matter-of-factly, insofar as the plans did not seem, in some mysterious manner, to be already formed, for she did not have to ponder the question at all. There was only one thing to do, and Phyllus knew how to do it.

Her only regret was leaving the twins. Not that she was particularly fond of them, but she did not like the idea of leaving them alone and defenceless. She wondered as she lay awake if it were not her duty to kill the twins first.

She decided that it probably was, but that it would be impracticable. Anyway she was too tired to worry about it. She comforted herself finally with the reflection that at least the twins would have the benefit of her example. They were smart enough kids. She knew they would understand. And there was always the chance, remote though it appeared, that they might find someone to marry them, and get along all right after all. It would be a pity to spoil the chance. She left them her last month's wages, paid in advance by the generous Jake.

Phyllus went for a brief walk by the beach. The water was flat and still and the colour of gun-metal. Phyllus found it soothing.

She felt, on the whole, quite happy, leaving the world with no regrets, which is more than is given to most. But her chief comfort lay in the fact that it seemed inevitable and the only thing to do. There is always a certain joy in doing the right thing at the right time, which is the basis of all convention and civilization; and Phyllus, at this moment, savoured the zest of undeniable correctness.

She drew a long breath and fixed her eyes on the top of the stairs, but as a matter of fact she never reached the top.

She left a note for Jake, feeling that this, too, was the correct thing to do. He received it the next morning, before he had seen the papers, although even so he might have remained unenlightened, for Phyllus did not reach the headlines.

Phyllus merely said, in conclusion, 'I was never strong like you,' and there was by that time no way of telling whether she had written the words in a spirit of irony or apology, although Jake had sufficient intelligence to wonder.

EDITORIAL
Phyllus

Although we do not believe in the principle which is religiously followed by most of the 'popular' magazines of 'giving the public what it wants,' and which in practice means 'writing down' to the lowest intelligence, we are naturally not indifferent to the opinions of our readers. It is with some regret that we receive a letter such as the following from one of our old subscribers:

Kindly discontinue sending The Canadian Forum to my address. I do not wish to subscribe to any magazine which published stories of the character of that in the October number of your journal.

We do not believe that anyone who has followed the fortunes of *The Canadian Forum* for any length of time is likely to accuse us of publishing anything that is needlessly offensive in order to make an appeal to those who delight in salacious literature. Furthermore, we are convinced that Miss Burton had no such idea in mind when she was writing the story *Phyllus*. We accepted the story because in the opinion of those members of our committee who have had some little literary experience it is a work of considerable merit. As a serious sociological study it is a distinct contribution to that field, and as a piece of literary craftsmanship we believe that it ranks with the best Canadian fiction. Phyllus is a genuine fragment of life and it is characteristic of a sufficiently large slice of actual existence to be of social importance. From the psychological standpoint it is interesting that of all the races in the world it is mainly among the British people that this belief in the suppression of all discussion of sex problems is strongly held. It is a taboo that has less force to-day than during the Victorian era, but even at the present time there are numbers of people who feel very strongly on the subject and who are moved to moral indignation whenever this convention is violated. We believe that this is a question of very real importance and we should be pleased to see our correspondence columns used by our readers for a discussion of this matter. Is it really in the interests of morality that this inhibition should be continued? And if we agree that ignorance and innocence are not synonymous, is not fiction a valid medium for the purpose of enlightenment?

To the Editor, *The Canadian Forum*

Sir:
Ever since *The Canadian Forum* made its first appearance I have been its interested reader and warm supporter. I have objected in a mild way to its attitude towards one or two public men whose motives seem to be assumed as questionable whatever their performance may be, but, up to the present, I have never felt sufficiently resentful of anything you have published to develop an impulse to protest. In your last issue you have given space to a short story such as any practitioner of medicine with a gift of expression might have told. It is, however, the kind of story that no physician would have told to an unselected audience. I am informed that such tales have an appeal to a certain class of readers but I had not thought that this class subscribed to *The Canadian Forum*.

Phyllus is so skilfully depicted that her progress from squalour to suicide is much more interesting than it would have been had it been presented by a 'sob sister,' but does this interest make the story of any value, ethical, literary, or otherwise?

Should it be granted that it does possess value, does the bald presentation of details, hitherto avoided by writers who are not elucidating psychopathic problems or filling space in the publications of a certain cult in another country, increase the value or satisfy any demand made by the community to which *The Canadian Forum* appeals?

I sincerely hope that consulting-room confessions are not going to become literature or that the public at large are going to imagine that writers in *The Canadian Forum* are persons in any way qualified by personal knowledge to write such studies as are typified by *Phyllus*.

Yours, etc.,
Toronto   Malcolm H.V. Cameron

To the Editor, *The Canadian Forum*

Sir:
Jean Burton's *Phyllus*, in the October issue of your publication seems to have, amongst a few,

created a tempest in the proverbial teapot. Having heard it discussed by and large, the story was particularly brought to my attention. Deciding to read it again, I realized it was a better story than it had, to me, at first appeared.

The only regrettable thing is that Jake will never read it. He reads the trash that is dished out by carloads with sugar coating. There is something of Ibsen about it – Ibsen hurts too.

With all the manufactured ease and luxury that surrounds most of us to-day, a little bitter truth is hard to swallow. But like most good tonics, its bitterness is stimulating to a realization of some of the conditions that exist commonly, but of which we don't like to know.

Miss Burton's frankness is refreshing. She tells her story looking you square in the eye. The author and *The Canadian Forum* are to be congratulated on having the courage to be unafraid.

Yours, etc.,
Franz Johnston

ESCOTT M. REID

Canada on The Council

To overestimate the importance of the election of Canada to a non-permanent seat on the Council of the League of Nations is an easy task. The importance lies not in the event itself but depends on two factors which are difficult to determine, the reason for the election, and the manner in which the Dominion carries out her responsibilities.

It is gratifying to our sense of national self-satisfaction to say that the election marks an international recognition of the status of the Dominions and Great Britain as coequal nations in a Commonwealth, but it is perhaps untrue. It may be that some of the votes given to Canada were cast not in a desire to grant separate representation to the Dominions but in order to give Great Britain increased representation on the Council. We should not therefore be too sure that our independent status has yet received recognition by the nations of the League. The answer to this question will become clearer in three years' time when Canada's term of office expires and another Dominion seeks to take her place. If the Assembly automatically accepts the candidature of any other Dominion then it probably desires merely to double the British vote; if it limits its choice to those two other Dominions, South Africa and the Irish Free State, which have shown a certain degree of independence of British foreign policy, then it probably has at last comprehended something of the constitution of the Commonwealth.

In another respect the importance of Canada's election can only be determined in the future, for it does not so much depend on the reason for her election as on the manner in which she performs her duties. If she is an efficient and able member of the Council her election may have importance not only as a step in the constitutional development of the Commonwealth but also in the strengthening of the League of Nations. Canada may play a great part in the solution of the problems which threaten the peace of the world or she may be a nonentity at the Council table. The choice between these alternatives lies with herself. It depends on the representative she appoints to the meetings of the Council. He must be a man of the very highest ability; one who has a knowledge of international affairs; one who possesses the confidence and esteem of the Dominion; and one who will by his intellectual attainments and his position at home, receive recognition at Geneva. In short, he must be one of those few leading men in Canadian public life who have a grasp of international affairs. Canada cannot afford to send as her representative a man merely because he is personally popular at Geneva, and can be spared from domestic politics. The Prime Minister as Secretary of State for External Affairs must realize that we cannot accept the honour of membership in the Council and not incur with that honour a great responsibility. The Dominion delegations to the Assembly have on the whole been notoriously weak. We do not wish the Dominion representation on the Council to gain that same notoriety.

The Prime Ministers and Foreign Secretaries of the most important states in the world have in the past attended the meetings of the Assembly and Council of the League. May we not request the Prime Minister of Canada in his capacity of head of the Department of External Affairs to represent Canada in the League. It would be too much to require that he attend the four annual meetings of the Council but he might attend the council meetings before the annual assembly and the Assembly itself. It is demanding a sacrifice from the Prime Minister, but one which he should be willing to give.

As substitutes for the Prime Minister at those three meetings of Council where he would be unable to attend and as second delegate to the Assembly, there are two suitable members of the Liberal Party, Mr Massey and Mr Rowell. Mr Massey, with his experience as Minister to Washington is peculiarly fitted to be what the Canadian delegate must be, an interpreter and a link between the League and the United States. Mr Rowell is recognized as possessing a keen grasp of international affairs and he has served with distinction at the Assembly and at the first International Labour Conference.

If the Prime Minister finds it impossible to be the first delegate of Canada to the Council and the Assembly then he ought to request either Mr Massey or Mr Rowell to accept the position of Secretary of State for External Affairs. The Secretary of State would then be the first delegate of Canada. In any case the Department of External Affairs must be enlarged to cope with the new situation in which international affairs are becoming increasingly important to Canada and Canada increasingly important in international affairs. We must develop a more efficient foreign office, for, call it what we will, such it really is, which will keep the government in touch with international political developments and which will be able to provide it with expert advice on questions which arise at meetings of the League of Nations.

At the present time the old criticism that the Senate of the United States made of the Covenant, that it gave Great Britain six votes, is to a great extent just. And that not because of any obsolete dictation by Great Britain but in a more subtle way through the influences of the frequent joint meetings of the imperial delegations to the Assembly. At these meetings the policy of H.M. Government in Great Britain usually wins the assent of the Dominions even when perhaps they feel it to be mistaken. This is because they have insufficient experience of international affairs and they lack independent expert advice on which to form matured views. It is obvious that a Dominion delegate must find it difficult to oppose the policy of a strong and homogeneous British delegation (particularly homogeneous since Viscount Cecil's resignation) when that policy is backed by the expert assistance of the permanent staff of the British Foreign Office. Yet if Dominion representation on the Council and in the Assembly is to mean anything, the Dominion delegates must be prepared to oppose British policy when it is misguided. To do so they must be in possession of sufficient knowledge to know when it is misguided, and have competent expert advice to assist them in stating their opposition at the imperial joint meetings. We must hope that on grave issues the spokesmen of the Commonwealth at the League of Nations are not divided, but if they are, then we must make sure from the calibre of our foreign office and of our delegates that Canada supports that policy which is in the interest of the peace of the world.

A.J.M. SMITH

Wanted: Canadian Criticism

One looks in vain through Canadian books and journals for that critical enquiry into first principles which directs a new literature as tradition guides an old one. Hasty adulation mingles with unintelligent condemnation to make our book reviewing an amusing art: but of criticism as it might be useful there is nothing. That this should be so at a time when we are becoming increasingly 'Canada-conscious' may seem strange, but the strangeness disappears when we examine the nature of the consciousness in question. This, judging from its most characteristic forms of expression, is a mixture of blind optimism and materialistic patriotism, a kind of my-mother-drunk-or-sober complex that operates most efficiently in the world of affairs and finds its ideal action summarized in the slogan 'Buy Made in Canada Goods.' There is, perhaps, something to be said for this state of mind if cultivated within certain very definite limits, if it be regarded solely as a business proposition and with due regard for economic laws; but when duty and morality are brought in and the above mercantile maxim is held to apply to things of the mind and spirit: that is an altogether different matter.

The confusion is one between commerce and art, an error which a society such as ours has some difficulty in escaping. A small population engaged in subduing its environment and in exploiting the resources of a large new country may very easily develop an exaggerated opinion of the value of material things, and has some quite understandable doubts as to the necessity of artists. Indeed, most of our people are so actively engaged in tilling the soil or scrambling to the top of the tree in the industrial and commercial world that they have neither the time nor the inclination for reading poetry on the back porch – unless it be inspiration stuff or He-man Canadiana. The result is good for business but bad for poetry and, if you happen to think that poetry is the more important, you are tempted to ask what is to be done about it.

To the serious Canadian writer this is a vital question, for to him the confusion between commerce and art presents itself in the light of a temptation to effect a compromise. If he chooses to work out his own salvation along lines which cannot be in keeping with the prevailing spirit of pep and optimism he finds himself without an audience, or at least without an audience that will support him. The one Canadian magazine, it must be noted, for which such an artist would care to write is at present unable to pay contributors, while poor imitations of the *Saturday Evening Post* are ready to pay him handsomely if he will cease to be an artist and become a merchant. This is the temptation with which the devil has assailed the Canadian Authors' Association, and the whole communion has succumbed in a body. There would be little harm in this if everyone knew the nature of the compromise that has been made, if, for instance, the Canadian Authors had the honesty to change the name of their society to the Journalists' Branch of the Canadian Manufacturers' Association and to quit kidding the public every Christmas that it (the public) has a moral obligation to buy poor Canadian, rather than good foreign books.

So far, it is true, literature as an art has fought a losing battle with commerce, but the campaign as a whole has barely begun. Reinforcements are on the way. Young writers like Morely Callaghan and Raymond Knister have contributed realistic stories of Canadian life to foreign radical journals. Mazo de la Roche, having won an important literary prize in the United States, has a firmly established reputation in her native land. E.J. Pratt and Edward Sapir are demonstrating that Canadian themes are improved by modern treatment. All these examples are definite, if modest, successes, but reverses are encountered too. A good poet such as Wilson Macdonald is praised for the wrong things, and seems likely to succumb to the blandishments of an unfortunate popularity, the sort of popularity that appears to be at the command of any poet who hammers a vigorous rhythm out of an abundant assortment of French and Indian place-names. If you write, apparently, of the far north and the wild west and the picturesque east, seasoning well with allusions to the Canada goose, fir trees, maple leaves, snowshoes, northern lights, etc., the public grasp the fact that you are a Canadian poet, whose works are to be bought from the same patriotic motive that prompts the purchaser of Eddy's matches or a Massey-Harris farm implement, and read along with Ralph Connor and Eaton's catalogue.

The picture, on the whole, is one of extreme confusion. There are little skirmishes, heroic single stands: but no concerted action. Without a body of critical opinion to hearten and direct them Canadian writers are like a leaderless army. They find themselves in an atmosphere of materialism that is only too ready to seduce them from their allegiance to art, and with an audience that only wishes to be flattered. It looks as though they will have to give up the attempt to create until they have formulated a critical system and secured its universal acceptance.

What are the tasks that await such a criticism?

First and foremost, as a sort of preliminary spade-work, the Canadian writer must put up a fight for freedom in the choice and treatment of his subject. Nowhere is puritanism more disastrously prohibitive than among us, and it seems, indeed, that desperate methods and dangerous remedies must be resorted to, that our condition will not improve until we have been thoroughly shocked by the appearance in our midst of a work of art that is at once successful and obscene. Of realism we are afraid – apparently because there is an impression that it wishes to discredit the picture of our great Dominion as a country where all the women are chaste and the men too pure to touch them if they weren't. Irony is not understood. Cynicism is felt to be disrespectful, unmanly. The idea that any subject whatever is susceptible of artistic treatment, and that praise or blame is to be conferred after a consideration, not of its moral, but of its aesthetic harmony is a proposition that will take years to knock into the heads of our people. But the work must be done. The critic-militant is required for this; not a very engaging fellow, perhaps, but a hard worker, a crusader, and useful withal.

It is the critic contemplative, however, the philosophical critic, who will have the really interesting work. It will be the object of such an enquirer to examine the fundamental position of the artist in a new community. He will have to answer questions that in older countries have obvious answers, or do not arise. He will follow the lead of French and English critics in seeking to define the relation of criticism and poetry to the psychological and mathematical sciences, and will be expected to have something of value to say as to the influence upon the Canadian writer of his position in space and time. That this influence, which might even become mutual, be positive and definite seems desirable and obvious: that it should not be self-conscious seems to me desirable; but not to many people obvious. Canadian poetry, to take a typical example, is altogether too self-conscious of its environment, of its position in space, and scarcely conscious at all of its position in time. This is an evident defect, but it has been the occasion of almost no critical comment. Yet to be aware of our temporal setting as well as of our environment, and in no obvious and shallow way, is the nearest we can come to being traditional. To be unconscious or overconscious – that is to be merely conventional, and it is in one of these two ways that our literature today fails as an adequate and artistic expression of our national life. The heart is willing, but the head is weak. Modernity and tradition alike demand that the contemporary artist who survives adolescence shall be an intellectual. Sensibility is no longer enough, intelligence is also required. Even in Canada.

FRANK H. UNDERHILL

Canadian and American History — and Historians

We are pretty well accustomed by this time to invidious comparisons between ourselves and our American neighbours. During the recent hard times we have had to listen *ad nauseam* to reflections upon their superiority to us in business methods and organization, upon their outdistancing of us in the exploitation of natural resources, and generally upon their unequalled skill in the technique of getting rich quick. And it was rather poor consolation to point by way of retort to such phenomena as Dayton, or Big Bill Thompson, or Mr Sinclair and his juries. But there is one field of work in which the superiority of the Americans to ourselves is even more marked than in the field of business. It is the field of historical research and historical writing. The contrast between what is being accomplished on the two sides of the boundary line in this very important activity is so striking that it is worth a good deal more consideration than we in Canada have hitherto been willing to give it.

The enormous annual output of historical books and theses in the United States has long been a familiar spectacle; and it used to be our habit to declare that these studies were more notable for their quantity than for their quality. But this criticism is surely no longer valid. A new humanism breathes through the recent work of American historical scholars. No one can read many of their books which have been appearing in the last decade without being impressed by the breadth of their learning, their penetrating insight into human nature and its reactions to its environment, their subtlety of discrimination, their thoroughly realistic temper. The modern school of American professors of history have, in fact, rescued their subject from the two opposite vices to which it is prone in academic hands, either literary dilettantism or dry-as-dust purposeless research, and have made it a living humanistic study.

Why is Canadian history so far behind? Why has it not been touched by this American Renaissance? Why is the output of our historical literature so meagre in quantity and so mediocre in quality? These are questions which should interest more than merely academic circles. For people who do not look backward to their ancestors will never look forward to their posterity; and there must surely be no country in the world where professional historians are doing so little to satisfy the natural craving of their people for enlightenment about their past and for guidance in interpreting the meaning of their national development. We cannot plead our youth. The zeal with which Australians and South Africans study their own country puts us, the senior Dominion, to shame. And why are we not spurred on by the example of our American colleagues? How long shall we have to wait until a Canadian Beard can write of the Rise of Canadian Civilization? At any rate it is high time that we abandoned the intellectual snobbery of no truck or trade with the Yankees and set ourselves to study what American historians are doing in the rewriting of American history. We must be a duller lot than even our current productions would indicate if such study doesn't inspire some of us to a new conception of what the writing of Canadian history might become. ...

The root cause of this lamentable failure of Canadian historians to measure up to their opportunities is that they are most of them suffering from a belated colonialism. One of the curious features of our present-day Universities, upon which our grandchildren will reflect with wonder, is the fact that the history taught in them is predominantly the history of England and Europe, and that the students are encouraged directly or indirectly to despise the history of their own country and of the continent of which it forms a part. Anyone who knows the inside of a Canadian University is familiar with the slightly amused condescension with which the genteel members of its history department greet the suggestion from some outer barbarian that the most important history for Canadians to study is Canadian history, and that the next most important is American history, because the United States forms part of the same continent and the same western world as ourselves. The result of such a state of affairs, which has now lasted for a couple of generations, is that the history which is taught and studied in Canadian universities has ceased to be a living thing, it has become a mere mechanical and pedantic discipline instead of a human study. For the historian, like Antaeus, must constantly renew his vitality by contact with the earth, and the only earth with which we Canadian historians can have contact is North American earth. Both distance and

June 1928

CARL SCHAEFER *Snowbound* Jan. 1929

poverty make it impossible for us to keep in real touch with Europe, and it is only a snobbish colonialism which prevents our historians from recognising the fact and acting accordingly. We must cease to gaze wistfully across the ocean and we must turn our energies to the vast unexplored fields which lie all around us. The greatest need of Canadian historians at present is a Christopher Columbus to discover America for them. ...

A.J.M. SMITH

Cavalcade

If only we had a song
We could get through this shadowy valley
And over the sandy plain.
Then we could pasture our beasts
In the meadows under the mountains,
Forgetting the weeds and the dust,
Forgetting the leagues and the stones –
We could win to the sea in the end:
Had we a song to sing–
Something a horse could prance to,
Something a heart could beat to,
A ballad, canzone, a chorus,
Something the feet could step to.

My father had such a song, He sang it lustily.
It sounds hollow enough nowadays.
It sounds hollow enough to me;
And my mother's voice singing on Sunday
Trails away in the dust.
There was a young cavalier
Who rode with us to the wars:
He knew a good song, he knew a brave song.
But they stopped his mouth with the mud in Flanders
Ah well! The locusts are singing.
The vultures are wheeling overhead
And they too are singing a kind of song,
A kind of grace before meat.
The wind sings too.
We had better get on.

FRANK H. UNDERHILL

O Canada

It is remarkable how much energy we devote in Canada to discussions about our future and how little to discussions about our past. We have always tended to seek inspiration by contemplating what we are destined to accomplish in coming generations rather than by what we have accomplished in those that have gone by. Our Canadian history, as one eminent observer has remarked, is as dull as ditchwater and our politics is full of it. And every Canadian instinctively knows that the observation is true. So we seek compensation for our lack of interesting achievement in the past by indulging in rosy dreams about the next century or by announcing loudly that we are about to arrive. This particular complex is one which modern psychologists have made drearily familiar. It explains both the plague of champion boy orators which infests us every spring and the regularly recurring discovery by the Canadian Authors' Association that we have a national literature. ...

It is time that someone protested against the highfalutin nonsense which is so prevalent nowadays on the subject to Canada's contribution to world peace. That sort of stuff should be left to the boy orators. We should remind ourselves that Mazzini used to talk the same kind of rant in the middle of the last century concerning the function of Italy in the world but that, when the real Italy arrived, its practical policy was based on the 'sacro egoismo' of Sonnino and Mussolini. Our evolution will go along the same lines. Our world policy will depend upon our world business connections; and it will be completely hard-boiled, like that of our American neighbours. When and if the next world war breaks out, we shall go into it to make the world safe for Canadian investments. In the meantime we have no particular interests in Europe and no particular policy to pursue at Geneva. All these European troubles, until we have more investments there, are not worth the bones of a Toronto grenadier. And so our government, which is thoroughly realistic in these matters, signalizes Canada's election to the Council of the League by taking up the question of the Minorities; because there is a general election coming next year and the minorities they are thinking of are located not in Central Europe but in Western Canada. As for the rest of us, we shall reach the international point of view by way of International Pete and International Nickel.

On the subject of Americanism the ordinary

Canadian behaves like a fundamentalist discussing modernism. No one in his senses can deny that the social and economic bonds between the two North American peoples are becoming every day more intimate and more complex. The process is as inevitable as the movements of the tides, and even in Eastern Canada our political Mrs Partingtons with their tariff brooms are coming to be recognized as slightly ridiculous. King St and St James St are more and more dominated by Wall St, and business men pass to and fro between New York and Toronto or Montreal as unconscious of the national boundary lines as they are of the state boundary lines when they pass between New York and Chicago or Philadelphia. There is not a man in Canada under fifty years of age who would not pack up and move to the States tomorrow if he got a good business offer. Most of those patriots who talk so loudly about their determination to remain in Canada have managed to preserve their virtue simply because it has never been exposed to temptation. We are reaching a condition on this continent in which men change their citizenship as easily as they change their wives.

Outside of business hours we read American magazines, listen in on American radio programs, talk American slang, visit American winter resorts, and copy American fashions; while they visit Canadian summer resorts, drink Canadian liquor, and play Canadian hockey. What prevents us from recognizing these facts frankly is the suggestion that they may mean political annexation; and when that dread word is mentioned every good Canadian begins to behave like Anatole France's Penguins. *'Qui dit voisins dit ennemis.'*

The truth is, however, that we are working out on this continent a new kind of relationship between two peoples such as the world has never seen before. We fail to understand it ourselves because our minds are still dominated by political ideas about nationality which were imported from Europe. But the inter-penetration of the lives of the two peoples has already become so far-reaching and so complex that it is absurd to talk to us as if we were like Frenchmen and Germans in Europe. We need a new set of political categories. North America is destined to give the political pluralists of our day a great deal of new ammunition for their guns. Exactly what form the political relationship of the next generation will take no one can predict. The one thing that is certain is that annexation talk on both sides of the border will die away. When the non-political ties have multiplied, as they are bound to do, far beyond what they are already, everyone will come to realize that to abolish Ottawa would be as meaningless a gesture as to abolish the royal veto in England. We on the north side of the boundary line shall have to learn how to reconcile our allegiance to Canada with our acceptance of these other non-political facts. Indeed we are learning already. No one would worry about the matter if our professional patriots would let us alone.

The real problem on this continent is not the political relationship between two supposedly mutually exclusive and independent entities called Canada and the United States, but the economic relationship between the classes who make up the North American community. What is this Americanism about which we hear so much? It is government of the people by big business and for big business. It is the doctrine that a millionaire is the noblest work of God. It is the new economic feudalism which is every day making our political democracy more meaningless. But all these things we have in Canada already. The Canada of our business men is completely Americanized now. But it does so happen that we have developed some other elements in our life which may act as a corrective to this overwhelming capitalism. The Wheat Pools on the prairies, the Canadian National Railways, the Ontario Hydro, are examples of another way of doing things, in which the common man exists for some other purpose than that of being exploited by his betters. The question whether Canada is to become wholly American depends on which elements in her economic life will ultimately prevail. Our big business men are our chief American influences, and the tendency of their activities is not one whit altered by the vigour with which some of them wave the old flag. If they prevail indefinitely Canada will become only a geographical expression.

A.S. WHITELEY

The Oriental in British Columbia

'It is the intention of this Legislature, representing the people of this Province, to do the utmost in its power to prevent further encroachment upon industrial, trading, and agricultural activities within the Province by any race or races whose customs or practices or economic standards of living may threaten eventually to lower the recognized Canadian standard of living.'

July 1929

From a resolution adopted by the Legislature of British Columbia in 1928.

It is not the purpose of this article to discuss the problem of Oriental immigration into Canada. As long as the people of British Columbia maintain their present attitude of antagonism toward these people it would be an injustice to permit their entry. Unjust not so much to the people of British Columbia as to the Orientals who, under such circumstances, would not be given fair treatment. It is rather with the Orientals already residing in the Province that this study is concerned; not with the intention of determining the justice or injustice of the policies which control their activities, but in an attempt to show that the presence of the Oriental simply brings to light conditions that are inherent in the present system of industrial production. In other words Oriental competition emphasizes pernicious conditions that should be attributed not to it but to the haphazard system of control that characterizes extractive industries. The improvement of the situation will be achieved not by the removal of the Oriental, but by the extension of the sphere of social control through legislative action. Social legislation rather than coercive measures against the Oriental will remove the 'serious menace to the welfare of all classes.'

It will generally be found that the competition of low-priced labour is most severe in those occupations which demand unskilled workmen. In British Columbia this type of labour finds its largest field of employment in the extractive industries – lumbering and mining. Reference to the 'Report on Oriental Activities within the Province,' published by order of the Legislative Assembly, will show that the majority of the Orientals are employed in the lumber industries, so that in a survey of these we shall find the 'menace' at its worst. The argument used to support the charge that the Oriental is a menace has a fairly definite form, it is presented in the Report in the following terms: 'the standard of living of the average Oriental is far below that of the white man, thus enabling him to live comfortably on a much lower wage than our white men,' and so he invades 'many fields of industrial and commercial activities to the serious detriment of our white citizens.' To conclude this argument satisfactorily it is necessary to continue in this fashion – if Oriental labour were not available the white workers would not accept the wages that are now offered, and consequently they would be employed at a higher scale of wages. Or to put the argument in another way; the low wages now received by the Orientals are paid not because of the inability of the industry to pay more but because it is the policy of the employers to secure labour at the cheapest price. If this is true, and I believe it is, then the Oriental is only partially responsible for the low wages, and upon the employers must be laid the blame for the unsatisfactory conditions that are now existing. If the employers refuse to adopt a policy that is more consistent with the welfare of the Province, i.e., the granting of higher wages and better working conditions, is it not incumbent upon the Legislature to pass such measures as will force them to make the necessary readjustments? This duty was partially recognized by members of the Provincial House when they enacted the Minimum Wage Act.

While this bill was being discussed the lumber interests made many unsuccessful attempts to turn public opinion against the measure. In vain they pointed out that this was discriminatory legislation, and that the adoption of the Minimum Wage Act would mean the ruination of the industry. In spite of their efforts the bill was passed, and became operative. But the employers did not despair, and after having a series of test cases in the courts they were recently successful in a Supreme Court decision, and the Minimum Wage Act is, for the time being, inoperative. The contention of the lumber interests that the Act placed too great a burden upon the industry can only be estimated by reference to the decisions of the Wage Board. The Minimum Wage decided upon was 40 cents an hour for an 8 hour day – or less than $20 a week. Whatever scale of living one may consider reasonable, all will admit that an income of $80 a month or barely $1,000 a year is not sufficient for a worker to maintain his family in decent circumstances. Yet the employers contend that they are unable to pay even this subsistence wage. How can the Oriental be held responsible for such a position? One is tempted to ask who is really threatening the 'recognized Canadian standard of living,' or do the lumber interests admit that such a standard exists? If the lumber industry is capable of paying only a subsistence wage then those who believe in the superiority of the white race should be the first to admit that it is far better for people accustomed to such standards to be employed than members of the white race. If, on the other hand, one believes in the brotherhood of man then that is sufficient to condemn the employment of any people under such conditions.

Besides the archaic wage policy that still survives in the lumber industry, another, equally out-of-date, is pursued by the employers in the pulp and paper industry. This is the principle of the open shop; supplemented in some cases by ineffective company unions. It is to this industry that the Japanese have turned in some numbers during the past few years, and here, again, they are held responsible for the inimical conditions that exist. The pulp and paper interests are aided in their labour policies by the location of their plants. In most cases the mill towns are situated on the narrow inlets of the coast. This enables the employers to have almost complete control over their workers, outside as well as inside the mills. Shortly after the war it was brought to the attention of the Minister of Labour that certain of the pulp companies were discriminating against union men in their employ. It appears that the companies were resisting the efforts of the men to organize. In other words they were resisting any movement that would tend to increase the bargaining power of the workers. Had the workers been successful, the working conditions in this industry would have been so improved that white labour would seek employment: the very result which the Legislature maintains would be secured by the ousting of the Orientals. If the members of the Legislature were sincere in their desire to curtail the unfair Oriental competition then they should have restrained the pulp companies from stamping out union organization. History records that the Legislature took no action. Consequently the pulp and paper interests were left free to dictate whatever terms they might see fit. The result being, of course, that in certain branches of this industry the wages are so low that Orientals are preferred to white men.

In the same manner I might review Oriental competition in other fields – those of mining, and railroad construction. A few years ago the Canadian Railways issued statements to the effect that they were willing, in fact anxious, to employ white labour on their construction gangs, but they found it impossible to secure the men that they required, and so, of necessity, they employed Orientals. At the time very little comment was made upon these statements, except by the few men who had worked on construction gangs and were able to express their feelings in writing. The public seems to have accepted the statements in good faith, and a few remarked that it was a shame that the pioneering type of labourer had disappeared. The fitting rejoinder to the Railway Companies would have been – Are you willing to pay a wage that will make the Canadian standard of living a reality? To one who knows the rates of wages on construction work, the back-breaking days of labour in the mid-summer heat, and the inadequate living conditions of the men, it is enough to remark that it is surprising that the Railway Companies could secure any labour, let alone that of intelligent white men.

Whatever the menace that one sees in the employment of labour at low wages the cause must be sought not in the presence of the Oriental, but in the toleration by the public of working conditions that should be condemned under any scale of social justice. When the people of the Province of British Columbia realize that the solution of the Oriental problem lies in the forcing of industrial interests to adopt more rational labour policies then the so-called menace will disappear.

The penetration of Orientals into the field of agriculture offers a more complex problem than the one just discussed. In this industry the worker lives and labours in the same narrow area, and so comes into closer contact with his neighbours. The different culture of the Oriental peoples, and the fact that they come from the peasant class of their native land make for considerable friction between them and the white people. It is this which causes white farmers to move out when Japanese or Chinese families settle in their vicinity. The establishment of friendly relations between the two races is not without hope, but it will necessitate a good deal of directive effort. It is a surprising feature of the whole Oriental problem that relatively little effort is made to see just what hope there is in the situation. These settlers from the East seemed to have been condemned without a fair trial. As an antidote to this condition I am going to put forward a plan that may be termed bold to the degree of rashness, and yet because of this very fact may be worthy of consideration. The story of Chinese immigration reveals the fact that the early efforts to reduce the number of these immigrants resulted in the imposition of a head-tax. The amount of this tax was increased from year to year until at last it reached $500. The total revenue derived from this source amounted to $22,523,921. It is my contention that in accepting this payment Canada entered into a tacit agreement with the Chinese, the nature of the agreement being that these people should be given the full rights and privileges of Canadian citizenship. The claim of the Oriental is moral rather than legal – a claim in equity. The responsibility of carrying out this contract has never been accepted by any government, and yet it is implicit in our admit-tance of these immigrants. I suggest that the millions of dollars we have taken from the Chinese should be used to create an Oriental fund. At an interest rate of 4% this fund would secure a revenue of approximately a million dollars annually. This amount should be devoted to the Canadianization of the Orietnal peoples within our borders. A good field of endeavour would be the solving of the problem of the Oriental in agriculture. The mere fact that more producers have entered an industry does not constitute a menace to the Canadian standard. It is the competition of people with the lower standard of life that our farmers fear. The Oriental Fund would provide the means whereby this unfair competition could be removed. Agricultural instructors, preferably of the same race, could be provided. These men would aid the Orientals to enter the various farmers' associations and show them the necessity of accepting the marketing policies that cooperative organizations sponsor. The high intelligence of the Oriental peoples should render this a not to difficult task. Money from our Oriental Fund would be available for the establishment of model homes, so that the Orientals could be encouraged to adopt the same mode of life as their neighbors, and in this way remove a great deal of the friction that now exists.

In the cities the same kind of social work is urgently needed; the efforts of the churches and charitable organizations are far from being adequate. With the aid of an Oriental Fund public health nurses could be provided and the sanitary way of living that is a part of Western Civilization could be demonstrated to these people. Part of the fund could be set aside for educative purposes both for the Orientals and the white people. We know far less about the Oriental than he knows about us, and our ignorance is responsible in large measure for the fear that we now have of these Eastern people.

When the people of Canada realize that they are responsible for the condition of the Orientals and for the progress that they make toward our standard of life then some such programme as I have outlined will be undertaken. The only danger is that it will be left until too late, until our suspicions of these people have become so deeply embedded in our thought that reconciliation will be impossible. Let us keep this thought always to the fore – that in the fields of social legislation and directed efforts at assimilation, a solution of the Oriental problem will be found.

LEO KENNEDY
Split Me These Gull Throats

Split me these gull throats, – let their cry
    be lost
Under the blast of surf, let spume wind-tossed
Dry to salt crystals on the wing of a bird
That vaulting each wave, streams landward,
    and is not heard.

Under these lifting waters there are laid
The sprawling bones of men, who, unafraid
Discerned the beginning and the end of all

Wisdom, found in the measured, ultimate fall
Of water, their lost clarity of soul.
Let it be said that death was beautiful.

Over their quietude the little boats
Scud to the haven of the bar; each floats
Securely at an anchorage in time –
Their sails are glistening with wet and rime
Like the gull wing. Soon the storm goes over.
Morning restores the sea-mew and the plover.

DOROTHY LIVESAY
Parrot of Night

That must be the wind
Pushing at my blind!
That must be the wind
Trying to force his way –
Certainly, the wind!
Who else?

I challenge the taut darkness:
Nothing stirs.
Then – whisper, whisper, whisper –
Someone's trying to speak:
Cackle, mutter, cackle –
Someone nearly laughed.

Phah! It is the blind –
I left my window open:
It is the wind; I understand,
Fumbling at the blind.
All hours I hear it talking, talking,
Like a parrot in a cage,
Mumbling to itself
Words of helpless rage:
Talking, muttering, talking
Fully half the night,
Cackling to a heedless wind
In heedless flight.

A parrot in a cage,
And I too deep,
Too slumber-bound to rise.
Turning, I sleep.

There is someone in the room!
It is you.
I hear your footsepts creaking on the floor,
Your breath about my head.
I hear your fingers fumbling at the door,
Your whisper at my bed.
I hear –
It is you!

Crack crack crackle
Creak!
I hear the parrot speak,
Fumbling and pecking in his cage –
Only a parrot in a cage.
The night and the wind,
The hungry pecking bird,
Hammer their voices through my head:
The night and the wind
Drown out every word

Your phantom might, perhaps might not,
    have said. ...

O certainly, the wind!–
Who else?

ROBERT FINCH
The Metro Breakfasts

Eight o'clock!
The Metro is having its petit déjeuner:
I'm the next mouthful.
Ugh!
Fancy swallowing me down with a breath
    like that!
At the palate I'm sampled and passed with
    a click;
Then a rush, and the stomach appears,
I enter a first-class compartment packed
    full of morsels,
Crusty, peppery, sweet, sour, half-baked,
    hard-boiled,
We mingle mixed in the Metro's enormous
    intestine
Until we're spewed out at the mouth of the
    Opera,
Rejected as indigestible,
Good for nothing
Save mincemeat for buses ...

But why does the Metro take so much
DUBONNET
DUBONNET
DUBONNET
for breakfast?

November 1929

C.L.E.
God's Absolutely Against It

'No,' snarled Mr East,
'God's absolutely against it.'
Mr East is the President of a pig iron works
on Back Street,
and we were riding out to breakfast with him at his Mimico mansion (and incidentally to attempt to induce him to allow his grandfather to hoot out a few French Horn solos over the radio).
'God's absolutely against it.
These awful niggers intermarrying.
I think it's awful, so God's against it.'
Mr East is Scotch and has a lovely kinky curl in his violet coloured hair.
We quickly apologized that Mr Booker Washington was so black,
and that Roland Hayes came out black,
by mistake of course.
We were just passing the abattoir.
'It's awful,' he said,
God's absolutely against it.'
We meekly hastened to remind him that the black man had borne the brunt of the Almighty's wrath for the first few million years and had made possible white man's presence on earth. Oh yes, the Moors with their art and their cunning, with their black blood, had gone into Spain. The Armada had been wrecked and survivors had drifted to Scotland where they had many descendants.
Had Mr East ever heard of the black Scottish beauties,

with their jet-black hair
and their jet-black eyes?
'It's awful,' mumbled Mr East,
'God's absolutely against it.

Say, you know,
I think we should go slow on this here St Lawrence Waterways scheme.'

FRANK H. UNDERHILL
O Canada

An honest attempt to enumerate the points in which our Canadian civilization differs from that of the United States is apt to be almost as brief as the famous essay upon snakes in Ireland. The underlying conditions which have determined the character of the two peoples are so similar. Each is a nation made up of the descendants of Europeans who came and settled in an empty continent that possessed almost unlimited natural resources; the history of each has consisted of the process of exploring and exploiting a half-continent. The factors in their history which have made for differences count for little compared with this fundamental economic similarity. That one of them in the course of its growth had a violent quarrel with the mother-country and severed its political connection while the other grew up to independence without any such political breach is relatively unimportant; and it would be recognized as such by everybody were not our minds dominated by too much study of political history and too little study of social and economic history. It was not the Declaration of Independence which made the Americans a separate people, it was the Atlantic Ocean; and Canada is on the same side of the Atlantic. Most of the superficial differences between the two people on which our good patriots are wont to dwell are due simply to the fact that the Americans have filled up their part of the continent more rapidly than we have ours. They are today more highly industrialized and urbanized than we are. The pace with which they have gone through the revolutionary social changes of the last century has resulted in the restlessness, the volatility, and the riotous exuberance of American life compared with which our Canadian decorum seems either dull or dignified, according to the point of view of the observer. But the pace of our Canadian life is quickening. We shall soon have little to learn from them in the art of getting rich quick.

The most distinctive feature of our Canadian life, one would think, should be our experience in building up a new nationality in the North American environment out of the two races, French and English. Yet, when one gets away from the rhetoric of the *bonne entente* orators, one is puzzled to say what particular quality in our life can be singled out as due to our bi-racial experience. The two races have never coalesced, have never understood one another or tried to understand one another. When they do come into contact each shows its worst side to the other. The French, so we are told, have a native folk literature and art which is a real contribution to the culture of North America; but the only Frenchman most of us ever see is the aggressive Quebec cleric or the jobbing politician at Ottawa. And when they picture to themselves the typical English Canadian he bears a strong resemblance to the Toronto Orangeman. The two races have never solved the most elementary problem of living together, that of education. Contact with each other has only served to accentuate and harden the intolerant qualities of each. They live together in an uneasy balance of power, and we seem as far today as ever from the time when 'Canadian' and *'Canadien'* will mean the same thing. That French-Canadian civilization is different from that of the United States is obvious. But its only effect upon us English Canadians has been to strengthen the qualities which make us like the Americans.

If we are to look for anything distinctively Canadian then, it must be found in the way in which we have handled the social and economic questions which arise in the process of exploiting the resources of our half of the continent. And here one does observe some features in our life which do not appear south of the line. We have not given ourselves up entirely to the unrelieved capitalistic individualism of our American neighbours. In such enterprises as the Ontario Hydro, the Canadian National Railways, and the provincial telephone systems of the West we have experimented in another method of providing public services than that of trusting to the private capitalist in search of profit. Their success has implanted pretty firmly in the minds of a good many Canadians at least a belief in the virtues of the public ownership and operation of public utilities which seems to be entirely lacking in the United States. But the fight for the Hydro in Ontario and for the National Railways in Canada at large is still too recent for anyone to delude himself into an optimistic faith that the cause of public ownership is won in this country. The greatest fights are still in the future. It is still possible to manipulate politics at Ottawa so that the publicly-owned railway is at a disadvantage in competing with the private one for branch lines in new territory. And the enormous development of hydro-electric power which will take place in the next generation makes one strain one's eyes rather anxiously for a second Beck who shows no signs of appearing. Have the Canadian people sufficient alertness as to the future to save themselves from the gigantic Super Power Trust into which the Americans are rushing with such joyous abandon at present? If they have not, it will not make much difference ultimately whether the management of the trust is located in Montreal or in New York. There is no real difference, except in names, between being controlled by a Holt and being controlled by a Morgan. And nothing is more certain than that the Morgan of the next generation will gobble up the Holt of the next generation. The best defence of a distinct Canadian nationality is to make sure that these great strategic public services shall be owned and controlled by the people themselves.

When one moves among Americans one is struck by their fatalistic attitude toward these problems of the relation of the public to its public services. One meets plenty of individuals who would like to imitate our Canadian public ownership enterprises, but the idea that it is possible for the American people in its collective capacity to stir itself out of the slumber into which it has been lulled by persistent private ownership propaganda is accepted by everyone as visionary. That democratic political machinery can be utilized as a fruitful method by which the people can provide for their own future is a faith which has almost died out among intelligent Americans. One of the hopeful things about Canada is that we have not yet come to this complete despair about our politics, and that enterprises like the Ontario Hydro and the National Railways show that we are still capable of using our political machinery for constructive purposes. But when the people of the pivotal province of Ontario go through a general election in which millions of words are wasted on prohibition and hardly a word is said on either side about the St Lawrence Waterway, one begins to wonder whether that particular community is capable of providing for its future.

It is to the Canadian West that one must turn when one looks for a people who have shown that capacity for tackling their common problems in common which is presupposed in all democratic theory. The Hydro in Ontario was too exclusively the work of one man of genius. It has aroused a great pride in the people of Ontario but their experience with it has been too largely passive, and whether they have the positive ability to carry on in the spirit of Beck is still in question. On the prairie the farmers are working out for themselves a genuine co-operative community. They have refused to acquiesce in the exploitation to which agriculture has been subjected over all the rest of the continent. They have organized to sell their own products and will soon be organized to buy co-operatively all that they need to buy. The most hopeful thing about the whole movement is that, with the exception of Mr H.W. Wood of Alberta, it has as yet produced no great outstanding leader. It is still throwing up leaders from all sides as they are needed, a fact which shows how really popular it is and how deeply it has its roots in the life of the people. Whatever one may think about their political theories, there can be no question that the prairie farmers have rescued their provincial politics from the atmosphere of futility which pervades our Eastern provinces; and they are probably right in thinking that no healthy political life is possible in a community which has not emancipated itself from the meaningless bickering of the two old political parties. One is sometimes alarmed at the amount of revivalism which the Western farmers work into their co-operative undertakings. Past experience on this continent has gone to show that messianic prophecy does not mix well with plain business honesty and common sense. But their movement is the most hopeful thing in Canadian life at present.

We have distinguished ourselves also from our American neighbours by our Church Union movement. If Union means that Canadian Protestantism has shown itself able to rise above the dissidence of dissent and the stupid sectarianism which has marked Protestantism through all its history, it is a great and inspiring spec-

December 1929

tacle. The success of the United Church so far in keeping the lid on its fundamentalist fanatics is encouraging. But perhaps Union had really no higher motive than the urge which drives banks and packing companies into mergers. The cloud of emotional rhetoric in which our religious leaders hide their activities is even thicker than that which surrounds our politicians. Someone would do a great service to this country if he would write a realistic study of the United Church.

THE 30s

The depression decade unquestionably marked the high point of *The Canadian Forum*. Times were tough for the magazine, its editors and writers, but adversity evidently stimulated the outpouring of a brilliant array of articles on social and political policy and of poetry by such poets as Klein, Smith, Scott, and MacKay which ranks with the best of Canadian political verse. Short stories also captured the depressing spirit of the times, and the undercurrent of anger was very clear.

Rage at the capitalist system was evident on every page of the *Forum*. The sense of injustice that hung over the land found its major expression here in the writings of Frank Underhill. Scarcely an issue went by without a brilliant editorial, comment, and full-scale article by the Toronto history professor. His style was unmistakable – and so was his good sense. The 1930s also saw the regular appearance of Frank Scott of McGill University in the pages of the *Forum*. Scott was Canada's Renaissance man – a constitutional lawyer, a founder of the League for Social Reconstruction and the CCF and, in addition, a first-rank poet. With Eugene Forsey and J. Francis White, Underhill and Scott shaped and dominated the tenor of the *Forum's* criticism during this dark period. Though still small in circulation, the *Forum* had clearly gained a large influence.

FRANK H. UNDERHILL
O Canada

One of the benefits to be expected from the present hard times on this continent is that we shall see a revival of politics. While the great boom was on, the medicine-men of big business with the constant beating of their prosperity tom-toms succeeded in lulling our political senses into a trance. It was no longer necessary to think about the future. North America would automatically reach the millenium by the simple expedient of letting our business leaders follow their nose for money. Our industrial and financial magnates were the only statesmen we needed. All that the rest of us had to do was to whoop it up for the frenzied course on which they led us of over-production in everything from motor cars to investment trusts. But all that looks a little bit foolish now. We can no longer shut our eyes to the fact of large-scale unemployment. We begin to realize that there were considerable sections of the community who had very little part in the fabulous prosperity of the 1920s. We begin to have doubts as to the social value of unlimited speculation. And slowly it dawns upon us that our business leaders, in spite of their evangelical enthusiasm about the supposed new era in North American economics, had no coherent plans for the future at all. Individually they had an eye for the main chance; collectively they had a programme of crude economic Couéism.

So the Coolidge era is over in the United States. Americans no longer praise their government for doing nothing; and the Hoover administration, which has done more in one year than Coolidge did in his whole two terms, is being blamed not for its activity in interfering with economic processes but for its ineffectiveness. In Canada the King government, which throughout the boom, like the House of Lords throughout the war, did nothing in particular and did it very well, seems likely to find itself at the next election in need of something more constructive than a few microscopic tariff reductions. Evidently on both sides of the border we are going to ask much more of our governments in the 1930s than we did in the 1920s.

The collapse of the stock market has, of course, been the immediate occasion for this critical attitude of the public towards public affairs. But already before last October the discerning observer could point to signs that the period of public indifference to politics was drawing to a close. The candidature of Al Smith in the United States was no doubt a dismal failure; but the excitement that it aroused was due to a general recognition that it portended to a revolt of hitherto inarticulate sections of the community against the established *mores*. The mere shrillness with which the prosperity mongers shouted their gospel that we live in the best of all possible worlds showed that they were conscious of an undercurrent of doubt. In our own country the rise of the various farmer movements with their new conceptions as to the proper economic and political organization of society pointed in the same direction. The war left the whole continent in a state of political shell-shock. Perhaps we really did need to keep our minds off any topics that might worry us. But we have been recovering, and for the last few years one seemed to detect an increasing impatience with soothing phrases.

It has been amusing in Canada to see how quickly the change in popular sensitiveness has taken place since last October. A year ago all the boosters were denouncing poor Mr Forke because the Immigration Department was damming up the stream of immigration which was to bring us boundless prosperity. Cranks like the Western farmers who had to do the actual work of assimilating the new citizens could hardly make themselves heard when they objected that dumping masses of newcomers into a community that couldn't absorb them was not the best way to build up a healthy nation life. Today the same Immigration Department is being blamed for contributing to our unemployment problem by flooding the country with immigrants for whose support no effective provision had been made. A year ago, when a few radicals in the House of Commons raised the question of Dominion-wide compulsory unemployment insurance, they were told decisively by Mr Lapointe that the BNA Act made any action by the Dominion impossible; and the fastidious legal sensibilities of Mr Cahan were so shocked that he deprecated even the mention of unemployment insurance in a parliament that had no powers to deal with it. And now today we have the prime minister telling delegations that this very same question must be tackled in the near future. Evidently laissez-faire is not quite so popular as it used to be, and it is not going to be quite so easy for our national political leaders to shirk national responsibilities.

If this is true, it is interesting to recall that only so recently as in the decade before the War the politics of the United States was dominated by the Progressive movement. Progressivism, whether it took the form of the New Nationalism of Roosevelt or the New Freedom of Wilson, meant essentially a more direct and deliberate activity by the national government in shaping the national destiny. Let anyone today who has lived through the Harding and Coolidge regimes read Herbert Croly's *Promise of American Life*, which was the best exposition of the political philosophy underlying the Progressive movement, and he seems to be reading about another world. Yet the book was written only twenty years ago. It embodied ideas which had been slowly growing up since the 1880s. The emotional storms of the War swept them all away and set back the political clock in the United States for a generation. But the War will be over some day even in the United States.

Progressivism was of course only the American expression of a movement towards socialism which was world-wide in the early 1900s. In the English-speaking world the Australasian communities had taken and were embarked on an ambitious series of experiments in state regulation of industry. In England the feeling that it was the duty of a democratic government to undertake a more active responsibility for the national welfare was what lay behind the movement both of Labour and of social-reform liberalism. Only in Canada, curiously enough, did we remain completely unaffected by these tendencies. It was the time of the Laurier ministry, and Laurier's conception of government was to sit at Ottawa with his famous smile and give away railway charters and natural resources to anyone who asked for them. At his best Laurier was never much more than a Whig. His much-lauded but seldom read speech on political liberalism might have been delivered by Macaulay or Lord John Russell. He remained a mere constitutional liberal to the end and never acquired the interest in social questions and the tendency to expand the functions of the state which marked the English liberalism of his own generation. That such a man should have been able to pass for a liberal in the twentieth century shows how little vitality there was in our Canadian politics.

Yet there were new forces stirring and Laurier was not altogether unresponsive to them. As one looks back now one can see that, but for the War, the 1911 election would have played the same part in our political evolution as did that of 1896 in the United States. It was the first sign in the national sphere of the rise of new classes to political consciousness and the first challenge to the domination of our politics by big business interests. With commendable promptitude our financial and industrial leaders met the challenge, and the result showed how strongly they were entrenched against any revolt by mere farmers and consumers. Our incipient Canadian radical movement was submerged by the War, and we never had the chance of seeing whether it was capable of throwing up a Roosevelt or a Wilson. We can at least take comfort in reflecting that it showed no sign of producing a Bryan. If it was twenty or thirty years behind the American movement in developing, it was also not so thoroughly crushed out by the War. But the effect of the War has been that, so far, it has been confined almost entirely to the Western farmers and has never become a general movement emancipated from class and locality as did Progressivism in the States. However, the War will soon be over in Canada too.

Canadian nationalism since 1914 has expressed itself mainly in the sphere of external affairs. But a movement which is based on the determination to undertake responsibility for our own national destiny can not forever confine itself to external affairs. Sooner or later the same national spirit will produce a strong demand for a more direct and a more responsible activity by our government in internal questions. Then we shall run up against the restrictions of the British North America Act and the objections of all those pundits who maintain that our federal union is a sacred legal contract upon which politicians must not lay impious hands. And then our politics will become real.

EDITORIAL

The Group of Seven

The 'Group of Seven' exhibition which was held during the month of April at The Art Gallery of Toronto and at The Montreal Art Association, this last month, has established without any compromise where the 'Seven' stand on the burning question of Modernism. (Speaking of the 'Seven,' it may be said that they are now eight, with Edwin Holgate of Montreal as the breaker of the magic number.) The Seven are modern and yet have evaded the formulae of modernism. Of all the art groups who, on this side of the Atlantic are called modern, there is probably no other that has escaped so fully the 'academism of modernism' and remained so pure in its inspiration and in the techniques which its various members individually favour. If this should be the only contribution of the 'Group' to Canadian Art, it would be well worth a mention in the art history of this country. On the other hand, from the standpoint of what the 'Group' looked like in that exhibition one must frankly admit that it had all the airs of a posthumous exhibition. The cohesion which one implicitly expects to find in the work of members of an art group did not exist between the paintings in that show. One could not see the parenthood between the various canvases. Only in the work of A.Y. Jackson and in that of Edwin Holgate one did find a kinship of mental attitude, something which was in the nature of a brotherhood of art. The cement which once kept all the stones of this Canadian tower together has dried out and has fallen off, the stones have been disassembled and have been scattered. For the sake of sentimentalism or conservatism, bring them together if you will, but it takes more than the desire to see them, one next to the other, to make of them a unit with a symbol, having a common significance.

Contributions by outsiders which had been selected by the 'Group' were, in the majority decidedly weak, and showed a clannish attitude which is incompatible with the growth of a movement. The paintings by Emily Carr, H. Mabel May, Yvonne McKague, George Pepper, and Sarah M. Robertson were exceptions, and helped to hold up the standard of the exhibition. All in all, however, there were paintings in the collection which, if produced by Americans in the United States, would arouse so much enthusiasm that the public would be given more than a little stale publicity about them, or the impertinent remarks of a few ignorant fools seeking the means of having their names played up in the columns of the dailies. Canadians should awake to the fact that they have great artists interpreting their country and its soul, and they should also be told the truth about those self-styled critics who have only contempt for what is best and finest in the field of art in Canada.

E. J. PRATT
The Fair-Grounds, Columbus, Ohio

Waiting their turn to be identified,
After their fiery contact with the walls,
Three hundred pariahs ranged side by side
Upon the floors along the cattle stalls!

The fires consumed their numbers with their breath.
Charred out their names; though many of the dead
Gave proof of valour, just before their death,
That Caesar's legions might have coveted.

But these, still subject to the law's commands,
Received the last insignia of the cell;
The guards went through them, straightened out their hands,
And with the ink-brush got the thumb-prints well.

A. J. M. SMITH
Swift Current

This is a visible
and crystal wind:
no ragged edge,
no splash of foam,
no whirlpool's scar;
only –
in the narrows –
sharpness cutting sharpness,
arrows of direction,
spears of speed.

DOROTHY LIVESAY
If It Were Easy

Fire creeps into my bones, and drowsily
I lean against the flame and drink
Succour from burning wood.

If it were easy as this
To creep close up to love
And gather strength

There would be none of these
Cold heavy evenings
Storm-bound, outside the door.

August 1930

EDITORIAL
Unemployment Must Be Tackled

With the election over we hope the problem of unemployment will be seen in proper perspective and handled by the Government in a resolute spirit. While the campaign has been on, the evils of the existing situation have been so exaggerated by the opposition and so minimized by the party in power that the public hardly knows what to think. On the whole there has been a disposition to regard our unemployment as more serious than it really is; but once the election results are known there will be no profit to anybody in exaggeration, and probably all the influence at the command of business and finance will be exerted to restore confidence at home and abroad by organized waves of optimism. Whatever government is placed in power will be only too glad to clutch at an excuse for not implementing its wilder promises made in the heat of the fray; but at the same time it will not be able to ignore the necessity for sound remedial action. The fact that Canada has escaped the worst effects of the world depression does not make it any less necessary to relieve the unemployment that undoubtedly exists, and we can count ourselves lucky that it is not greater. The latest figures published by the Dominion Bureau of Statistics show that the number of workers employed in our industries on June 1 was greater than in any other year at that date, with the exception of 1929. This bears out the claim of the financial press that what we are experiencing in Canada is more properly described as a 'recession' than a 'depression.' But in a growing country any recession means a sharper rise in unemployment than would be the case in one more stable in its population. In the past year 163,000 immigrants entered Canada and 29,000 Canadians returned from the United States to settle here. Then, too, it must be remembered that the employment figures of the Bureau of Statistics are necessarily drawn from those organized industries which employ largely skilled labour, and that some classes which have felt the pinch most are not included in the survey.

A civilized country which in the nature of its circumstances is bound to have a certain amount of seasonal unemployment every year should have organized methods of dealing with it. Canada may be a young country but she is not a poor one; we can well afford to indulge in the common humanity of unemployment relief, and the sooner we organize it on a national basis the healthier our national life will be. Industry can do much within itself to stabilize employment, and its leaders are at last beginning to consider means of reducing its present anarchy to order; but while the central Government can assist our industrialists in this task, in the end it must itself accept the responsibility for the unemployed. The pressure of public opinion should be strong enough to make the Federal and Provincial Governments co-operate in some scheme to ensure the immediate relief of the destitute; but that should be followed as soon as possible by national schemes of unemployment insurance and old age pensions. These measures, together with the closer co-operation of Federal, Provincial, and Municipal Governments in constructing public works in slack seasons, would go far to meet the necessities of our case, even in times like the present when unemployment exists, as it were, out of season. The expense of a rational plan of unemployment insurance would be contributed to by the workers, the employers and the Government, but the whole expense of a national old age pensions plan would have to fall on the Federal Government. The fairest way to raise the necessary revenues for these social benefits would be by an increase in the income tax, but we may be sure that when these schemes eventually come to be accepted there will be a determined effort to have them paid for out of increased customs duties – which would mean that those classes fitted to pay least would pay most, and the labourer would, through the years, contribute the entire cost of his old age pension and of his unemployment insurance as well. But however it were done, the country would then be better fitted to meet the strain of hard times than it is at present.

F.R. SCOTT

Two Poems

Proud Cellist

Are there quiverings
of flesh and blood

like taut strings
and hollow wood

stirring to fragile form
that lingers
beneath my agile
bow and fingers?

In no woman
is love lent
so beautiful an
instrument.

None so lovely
in her moving,
none so wholly
lost in loving.

A low note dying and
yet not dead
is a lover's hand
uncomforted.

A low note dying and
sunk to rest
is a lover's hand
still, on a breast.

Sunday

Sunlight
Pouring like white wine from a blue bowl
Quivering on the housetops
Gilding the hard roadways
Making drunk all birds and beasts
And a few wise men
And crowds walking solemnly
Into false-Gothic doorways
Into religious dimness.

A.J.M. SMITH
Testament

It is along the seamed and gnarled
and long-dead riverbeds I take my way,
I, molten, moulded, hardened into stone
rifted with ripples, seamed with sand,
myself more sun-baked, sallow-seamed
with sand and little fine grey dust
in eyes and mouth and matted hair
than any Sphinx or desert god
half sand with so much crumbling age
as broods unwinking out of stony eyes
on cactus and the prickly pear.

Was it an old poet spoke of wells
and green and grass and juicy trees?
Babbled a' green fields on a sable bed
and went dry into the salty soil?

April has the sound of silver bells
or a certain misremembered voice
calling to me out of a child's heaven
to walk with it in waving shade
far from the clotted dust
the bleeding stones.

But I have answered with retreating soles
– diminuendos of good-bye,
and leaning upward from a broken shoe
have come at length, still living, on a land
where hollow bones dream out their tragedy,
stand up in sequence and soliloquize.

...this is no place of indolent surrender,
there is life in this death;
this scepticism has its faith,
this martyrdom its ecstasy.
I am not I, but a generation –
these are the bones of my comrades
that have found with me, in stony sand,
the blood and body of our unknown god.

J.F. WHITE
Police Dictatorship

About two years ago the Police Commission of the City of Toronto announced that it intended to 'stamp out Communism' in this city. As Communism is not yet a crime according to our Canadian statutes the police found some difficulty at first in putting their stamping-out policy into effect, but after a certain amount of trial and error they worked out a very efficient system. The owners of public halls were warned that if they rented their premises to Communist organizations they would probably find some difficulty in obtaining renewals of their licences, and those few hall-owners who attempted to buck the police soon found themselves in difficulties. When the Communists, unable to secure rooms, attempted to hold open-air meetings the police refused to permit them the use of the public parks, and when they met on street-corners they were arrested for 'obstructing the traffic,' 'creating a public disturbance,' 'vagrancy,' and sundry other charges. The police found no difficulty in obtaining convictions in the local courts, in most instances, but the majority of cases when appealed were thrown out by the Appellate Courts. After some months of this kind of thing the Police Commission decided that progress was too slow, and since that time have practically abandoned any pretence at legality in dealing with the Communists. A few members of the force were sent to the United States to observe the work of the 'New York Bomb Squad' and after they returned to their native town they put into effect the strong-arm methods which have been standardized in New York and Chicago, and, in not a few cases, improved upon the technique of their instructors. Only on one occasion have the police suffered a serious reverse, and this was when they broke up meeting during the federal election and were taken to task by the Chief Electoral Officer at Ottawa.

It is probable that, at the outset, the Police Commission believed that it would be possible to outlaw one small section of the community and still maintain, in principle, 'the fundamental right of the British Citizen to free speech and free assembly.' But, having once adopted an indefensible position, they soon found that there is no comfortable way-station at an equal distance between the two extreme points of liberty and rigid dictatorship. They began by pre-judging the Communists, finding them guilty of 'sedition' without recourse to due process of law, and then took it for granted that members of the Communist Party had forfeited all normal rights of citizenship. But the logical course of events carried them far beyond this initial attitude. If the Communist was *ipso facto* a criminal, it was only a matter of time before the 'Communist sympathizer' became a potential criminal, and this greatly enlarged the category of those who might be regarded as outside the law. Certain non-Communist labour organizations and foreign groups who were critical of police policy came under suspicion, and a few of these who actually aided the Communists in evading the official edicts were made to feel the heavy hands of the guardians of the law.

There are in Toronto, as elsewhere, a considerable number of idealists, and a larger group who have some belief in liberal principles, and many of these people came to feel that the existing situation was intolerable. About a year ago two or three hundred individuals, of the most varied religious, political, and social affiliations, came together and founded a Toronto Branch of the Fellowship of Reconciliation. This society is international in scope and pacifist in temper, and its aim is to 'liquidate' all national, religious, racial, and social antagonisms – a rather ambitious programme! Together with other activities the FOR decided to operate an open forum, and in December 1930 plans were made for the first meeting. As the members were strongly in favour of 'free speech' it was decided that this should form the subject for the first debate, and an invitation was sent to General Draper, the Chief of Police, and to Judge Coatsworth, one of the members of the Police Commission, to attend the forum and to present their case to the audience. If they were unwilling or unable to speak it was suggested that they should nominate substitutes who would be capable of taking up the cudgels on behalf of the Police Commission. Rev. Salem Bland, and Rev. John Lowe, of Trinity College, were to speak in opposition and to criticize the actions of Commission. Application was made to the manager of the Foresters' Hall for the evening of January 11th, but a few days before the meeting was scheduled to take place the FOR was notified that this hall would not be available. An attempt was then made to secure the Empire Theatre for the same evening, but on the following day when the President and the Executive Secretary of the FOR called at the Empire they found Detective Nursey – who has charge of 'red activities' in Toronto – in conference with the manager. After some conversation the manager of the theatre announced that 'he could not conscientiously rent the hall, under the circumstances.' In the meantime replies had been received from Judge Coatsworth and Chief Draper. The former wrote: 'It is quite evident that it is a Communistic meeting under a very thin disguise. I must decline, therefore, to be present,' and the Chief replied in a similar strain. Subsequently, when newspaper reporters interviewed Judge Coatsworth, with reference to the letter written by him to the Fellowship he said; 'When I wrote it I had in mind an article written by Rabbi Eisendrath and published in *The Canadian Forum* of June last year. The article was entitled "Russia Versus Religion".' Rabbi Eisendrath is President of the local branch of the Fellowship.

The Police Commission, through over-confidence, made a bad tactical error and probably they would gladly arrange a compromise if it could be accomplished without any loss of 'face.' Their inference that the members of the FOR are 'thinly-veiled Communists' is so manifestly absurd that it will not be accepted by anyone of average intelligence, and even those who would give their moral support to the campaign for 'stamping out the reds,' will be inclined to doubt whether the Commission has sufficient intellectual ability to distinguish between the 'disruptive' and 'respectable' elements in the community. The Fellowship intends to make a strong stand for 'Free Speech' – without qualifications or restrictions – and at the present moment is arranging to send a delegation to the City Council to demand 'the restoration of British rights of free speech and assembly which have been denied by the Police Commission of Toronto,' and they will present a petition asking for a judicial enquiry into the activities of the Police Commission.

The Commission represents an alliance of the militaristic and religious fundamentalist bodies which are strongly entrenched in Ontario. General Draper is President of the very influential local branch of the Canadian Legion, he is a Shriner, and is connected with other lodges and fraternal organizations. Judge Coatsworth is a strong supporter of the Canadian Christian Crusade, an order devoted to the defense of Fundamentalism and the destruction of atheism and communism, which seems to have languished somewhat during recent months. He is also not without influence in the councils of the United Church of Canada. Most of the religious persecutions of history have grown out of similar soil – Cromwell with fire and steel in Ireland, the witch-hunting of New England, the Spanish Inquisition. Communist phobia of today is only a modern version of a very ancient disease. The same type of militant respectability sent Sacco and Vanzetti to the electric chair a few years ago.

While the Commission draws some considerable spiritual sustenance from religious orthodoxy, the Fellowship has the backing of all the liberal elements in the churches, and nearly every congregation in Toronto will be divided in opinion. It is possible to regard this as a renewal, or an acceleration, of the old struggle between Fundamentalism and the New Modernism – the Christian Modernism which has returned to the fundamentals of two thousand years ago.

But there are other and more mundane considerations which must be taken into account. Behind all the moral and legal dialectics there are economic developments which are largely responsible for the clash of ideas. At no time in the past history of Canada has there been such an accumulation of wealth at the top of the social scale, and such an accumulation of distress on the lower levels. This sudden increase of inequality must inevitably produce unrest on the one hand and uneasiness on the other. A small group of men have enormously increased their wealth and their power during the last year or two and this group is the real power behind the throne of the Toronto Police Commission.

EDITORIAL

'The Intellectual Capital of Canada'

For the past few weeks the city of Toronto has been suffering from an acute case of the Communist phobia which in one form or another has attacked all the big cities of this continent since the Russian Revolution. In the last number of *The Canadian Forum* an account was given of the activities of the police commission and of their success in preventing the local branch of the Fellowship of Reconciliation from starting an open forum for the discussion of public questions. On January 15 sixty-eight members of the teaching staff of the University of Toronto wrote a letter to the newspapers protesting against the attitude of the police commission and affirming their belief in the British principle of freedom of speech and assembly. The publication of the letter led to a remarkable outburst of righteous indignation among the 'good' people of the Queen City, including three of the four daily papers, the *Star* alone taking the side of free speech. In rescuing some samples of their outraged virtue from the oblivion which so quickly falls upon daily newsprint *The Canadian Forum* believes that it is performing a service to the social historian of one hundred years hence and hopes also that it is doing a little to relieve the gloom which has settled upon all of us during these hard times.

On January 16 the *Globe* which, ever since George Brown founded it in 1844, has appeared with the famous quotation from Junius at the top of its editorial page – 'The subject who is truly loyal to the Chief Magistrate will neither advise nor submit to arbitrary measures' – burst out:

This matter of 'free speech' which is agitating the fellowship and has brought forth the 'protest' of sixty-eight college professors is but a 'red herring' across the trail. Why is the cause of a group of revolutionary agitators to be preferred to the welfare of a loyal, Christian nation? This is the only point involved in the so-called free-speech issue. When somebody is spreading disease germs, should Fellowships of Reconcilation and college professors protest against those in authority using their best efforts to check the malignant inoculations? This tender-hearted bosh about the Bolsheviki ought to be stamped out once for all by an indignant citizenship. It is not British Canadian, or Christian. Why should red-blooded Canadians soft-pedal before their machinations?

And next day in a leader headed "The Reds or the People' it continued:

Now that the disguise is removed and the attack on the police is admitted to be a battle in behalf of the Communists by so-called liberal minded men, it is timely to give some thought to the overwhelming non-Communist majority of the people. Are they to submit to a policy which will let loose a stench of Soviet propaganda, a campaign against the church and educational systems, the rearing of atheism, a destruction of the economic and political structures of the country? ... We need patriots rather than theorizing pussyfooters, and worse.

On the 22nd the *Globe* issued its call to action:

The University cannot escape its share of the responsibility so long as it fails to disapprove the action. This university is a State institution, the property of the Province. Its Board of Governors cannot ignore a course of action by a portion of its staff who, in the name of 'free speech,' came to the rescue of a section of the population who would pull down our form of government, destroy our economic system, and set up defiance of Christianity and wholesome family life. ...

Interviews poured into papers. Sir John Aird, the President of the Canadian Bank of Commerce, expressed the opinion that professors should stick to their knitting, since the professors of Germany, by not doing so, had brought on the great war – a contribution to the vexed question of war origins which is apt to lead mere historians to wish that our banks would give their presidents some knitting to stick to. Mr Frank Rolph, the retiring, and Mr C.H. Carlisle, the incoming president of the Toronto Board of Trade, both expressed their disapproval of the professors' action. Said the latter:

It is with great regret that I read that some 68 members of the faculty of the University had lent themselves to the opposition of an officer of this city. Every one in Toronto has a right to his own opinions, but when a body gets organised for such a purpose within an institution of the outstanding reputation of the University of Toronto, it is a very regrettable condition. If that goes uncensured, then I would take it that the people of the province would understand that the act is condoned by the governors of the university. I am afraid that situation is more far-reaching than we may realize now. [Star, Jan. 20]

Lesser individuals wrote letters. Thus a Mr J. Swinyard Huxley wrote from Weston to the *Globe* (Jan. 21):

These dons should all be bundled off to Russia, where they would have their eyes opened as to what constitutes free speech. A Congressional Committee at Washington has just presented a report advocating the suppression of radicalism of the Russian kind in the United States, classifying the reds as outlaws, and recommending that aliens of this stripe be deported. A scare of this kind should be thrown into our university staff and from the head down they should be all warned that the teaching and approval of radical doctrines must stop.

What a remarkable variety of talent the Huxley family have exhibited in our day! Incidentally it may be remarked that, as one reads through these letters to the papers, he is struck by the number of stalwart Britishers in Toronto who want to copy the methods proposed by the American Congressional Committee. ...

We have not yet quoted from the unique editorial page of the Toronto *Telegram*. In the earlier stages of the controversy the *Tely* lacked its usual effectiveness, not that it loved the professors more but that it loved the Chief of Police less. But it gradually rounded into form. Witness the following from an editorial on February 3:

If a lot of Toronto professors would take Premier Brownlee's advice [to study Russia] there would be less of this 'free speech' chatter in Toronto. Free speech there [in Russia] is accompanied by war on religion, free love, and free work for the many in order that the few may rule the millions. If a few of Varsity's teachers were sent to Russia, not as tourists personally conducted by Soviet agents, but as toilers in Soviet wheat fields and Soviet factories, they would return to their Canadian jobs with a restrained admiration for the privileges that go with free speech theories put into practice.

The subject reached the pulpits of the city. ... Rev. R.G. Stewart of St John's Presbyterian Church, preaching on the text 'An Old Covenant on a New Cart,' spoke as follows (*Globe* Jan. 26) –

It would seem that 68 professors of the University of Toronto have seen fit to offer a new covenant of communism on the old cart of education. If that is so, then the sooner the Minister of Education in this Province wakes up, the better for the Province of Ontario, and for this Dominion of Canada of ours. If that is so, the sooner the proper authorities line up the men who poison the minds of the young men and women who are to lead this country in the coming years, the better it will be for our country. The sooner the back door is opened to the man, or men, who would bring into this fair land a system of government that has brought bloodshed and misery, that laughs at virtue and religion, that sneers at family life, and has trampled the most treasured traditions of humanity into the dust – I say the sooner such men or such a system is given the back door, the better for our country.

Little wonder that after this refreshing draught of the pure gospel spirit, Mr W. Stewart Thomson was moved to write to the *Globe* (27 Jan.):

In these days of 'pussyfoot parsons' it is inspiring to come across a real old Presbyterian blast, and if the Minister of Education does not see fit to take immediate steps to discipline the 68 professors, it is to be hoped that the Alumni will take action. There is no room in the University of Toronto for tainted teachers.

And on the 31st, Mr R.H. Knowles did his bit. (*Globe*):

Are the 68 professors who advocate free speech believers in Divine teaching, or are they atheist or agnostic in their views respecting religion? The parents and friends of the students of the university will surely be looking for a pronouncement as to whether certain members of the staff are either atheist or agnostic in their views.

Alas, the University Board of Governors failed to take action. Rumour has it that they are divided in opinion. Can it be that there are Reds even among the Governors of the University of Toronto? But the cause of Christianity and Canadianism in the University has still its valiant defenders. On February 4, the venerable Sir William Mulock, the Chancellor of the University, addressing a convention of live-stock breeders (in the stimulating intellectual atmosphere of Toronto all classes and groups just naturally fall into the habit of discussing these questions of high principle), came out boldly where the Governors had failed:

If Canada is content to have her laws made by those who deny the existence of God, who would suppress religion, who would destroy the sacredness of marriage, who would abolish home life, who would rob all citizens by any degree of force, up to that of murder, of their wordly goods, would deprive people of liberty and would make them slaves of the State: if, I say, those are the conditions which Canada is content to have established in Canada, then let her open her doors wide and admit into full citizenship the millions of the people of that class. But if Canada does not wish to become a hell on earth she should rid herself at once of those who would, if they could, make her such. ...

The time has arrived when Canadian public opinion should be made known to the communistic people, our fixed determination to exclude from Canada anyone who would disseminate among us the revolutionary and wicked principles of Russian communism. ...

The people must ever be on guard lest they be deprived of their rights and liberties. ... It is as true today as in the time of Curran that eternal vigilance is the price of liberty – not license, but liberty within the law. ... The issue is one of paramount importance, and now is the time for a united Canada to stamp out the treasonable and insidious virus with which wicked men would inoculate the Canadian body politic.

'Sir William's denunciation,' according to the *Telegram*, 'was all the more enjoyed because, as head of the University, he seemed to be expressing an opinion on the 68. ... Canon Cody, who is chairman of the board of governors, sat at the head table and joined heartily in the applause that punctuated the address.' 'We are glad in Ontario to receive Sir William's message,' said Hon. Leopold Macaulay, the Provincial Secretary (as reported in the *Star*). 'I suppose that some of us may regard that message as a little more agreeable to us than some of those unofficial messages from the university that sometimes hit the front pages of the newspapers.' And Mr C.H. Carlisle added, 'While the universities of the world have often been the breeding places of political troubles, I don't think that the university of this province will go wrong with such men at the head as Canon Cody and Sir William Mulock.' Meanwhile Sir William and the Canon 'laughed and slapped each others' knees at this intimation that the professors were being answered unofficially by the university authorities' (*Star*).

O Canada, Toronto stands on guard for thee!

And the professors' letter? Bless you, we had almost forgotten about that. This is what they wrote on January 15 –

The attitude which the Toronto police commission has assumed towards public discussion of political and social problems makes it clear that the right of free speech and free assembly is in danger of suppression in this city. This right has for generations been considered one of the proudest heritages of the British peoples, and to restrict or nullify it in an arbitrary manner, as has been the tendency in Toronto for the last two years, is short-sighted, inexpedient and intolerable.

It is the plain duty of the citizen to protest publicly against any such curtailment of his rights, and, in doing so, we wish to affirm our belief in the free expression of opinions, however unpopular or erroneous.

E.A. FORSEY

Montreal is a Quiet City

– 'And It Must Remain Quiet' (Inspector Bilodeau of the Montreal Police Department) Torn from its context this looks like an attempt to assassinate Montreal's tourist trade. In reality it is the watchword of a campaign to preserve the city's intellectual virginity from the perils of free speech.

Of course we have 'no objection to free speech in principle' (*Gazette* editorial, Feb. 5); but, to quote Mr John T. Foster, president of the Trades and Labour Council: 'we do resent the attitude of those who construe free speech to mean license to do what they please' (*Gazette*, Feb. 19). 'Free speech in principle' means freedom to express our views, not views which we dislike. Moreover, anyone who advocates free speech for Communists is a Communist. Anyone who tolerates Roman Catholicism is a Roman Catholic. That professors sometimes fail to recognize these facts merely proves the permeation of our universities by Communist influences.

Against these, until lately, Montreal has needed no defence. But the depression has wrought a change. The general election witnessed the horrid spectacle of a French-Canadian Communist standing for Parliament. As if this were not in itself sufficient outrage upon public decency, the candidate actually tried to hold a meeting in a square which Mr Bennett had recently graced with his presence. Fortunately there is a civic by-law forbidding open-air meetings without official permission.

Not until after New Year's, however, did things really begin to warm up. On January 19, the Unemployed Council of Montreal, a subsidiary of the Communist party, called a meeting in the Labour Temple. According to the *Star* (Jan. 20):

... the demands presented to the meeting for consideration and discussion were: immediate grant of cash relief to secure three square meals a day; no eviction of unemployed; free transportation and books for children of the unemployed; free light for the unemployed; abolition of the vagrancy laws. Discussion of these demands was about to begin when a strong force of police entered, placed the speakers under arrest, and asked the crowd to leave, which they did in an orderly manner. There was no attempt at rescue on the part of the crowd outside, and the whole affair was carried out with entire good humour (on both sides).

In the *Gazette*, on the other hand, the lurid light of melodrama plays over the scene. Plain-clothesmen are stationed in the hall to report on the proceedings. The 'demands' quoted by the *Star* disappear entirely, giving place to vague innuendoes and question-begging terms: 'plots against the police,' 'mob,' 'plan of campaign against the police system.' The crowd in the hall is 'commanded' to disperse, several refuse and are 'clubbed,' the police are met outside by a 'volley of snowballs and lumps of ice,' the constables 'wade into' the crowd. These 'polite' methods failing, the police, 'struck on the face with fists and their coats pulled,' made the punishment fit the crime by 'resorting to their clubs.' Poetic justice incarnate in 'forty stalwart constables' overtakes the plotters, caught napping in the very act of 'planning to take the police by surprise.'

This last fact alone is enough to show the kind of men we have to deal with. Happily the then chief of police, Director Langevin, could be trusted to meet the situation firmly. Interviewed after the meeting he said: 'Some time ago I had been asked to give a permit to hold a meeting but I refused. This is about the hundredth time I have refused.' Inspector Bilodeau added: 'If any such demonstration occurs again the police would be obliged to treat the crowd more severely' (*Gazette*, Jan. 20).

After this warning one might have expected that there would be no further trouble. But the Communists cannot take a hint. On January 23 they met again, to celebrate the death of Lenin. ...

According to the *Gazette*:

News of the assembly came to Inspector Bilodeau last week. Twenty detectives and plain-clothes constables were stationed in the hall, and after the meeting had started the officers inside informed the inspector.

The police claim that the speakers denounced the police and encouraged those present to fight them. At this juncture about one hundred constables entered the hall. Several detectives walked on the stage and arrested two men. They then ordered the crowd out. Inspector Bilodeau mounted the stage and told the audience there would be no trouble if they would walk out quietly. Such meetings were against the law and he must see that the law was obeyed. He then ordered his men to arrest anyone refusing to move.

In spite of these commands the crowd refused to vacate. The constables in the hall were reinforced by another hundred men, and started to eject the crowd. Many struck the police in the face with chairs and other weapons. The police in order to protect themselves were forced to use their batons.

Two days later the Roman Catholic Archbishop of Montreal in a pastoral letter admonished his flock against Communism. His Grace warned the faithful that the campaign against religion was merely an 'engine of war' in a general attack on our civilization and particularly on our economic order:

There is no one who has not noticed the reaction of [Communism] on Canadian industries. If the [five year] plan succeeds, we can expect to see other Canadian industries suffer disastrous disorganization. ... Simple good sense would urge all governments to protect themselves against Russian dumping.

A striking forecast! Calling attention to the value of 'religion' as a 'force for social security and balance' the Archbishop says:

Religion cultivates the growth of supernatural sources of hope which are not useless for helping one to accept the miseries and hardships of life. ... Religion develops a personal asceticism which is contented with little and makes men love their labour. ... Do away with God and the first problem rising before the mind is the formidable problem of the inequality of human conditions. ... Christian charity is the remedy for the ills of to-day. In a society which lives under the happy influence of Christian baptism, charity re-establishes the equilibrium between rich and poor.

His Grace repudiates the view that labour is a 'marketable commodity' and endorses the principle of a living wage and social insurance, but warns his hearers that 'the unjustified rise of wages' leads inevitably to the high cost of living (*Gazette*, Jan.26). That the Archbishop's words struck a responsive chord in more than one distinguished breast, ecclesiastical and lay, Catholic and Protestant, is evident from a sort of commination service composed some weeks later by the Montreal Catholic School Commission (*Gazette*, Mar. 4):

Whereas the Commission has noted with disapproval the anti-Christian policy of the USSR and their communistic economic activities ...

Whereas it has noted the position taken against these anti-Christian and communistic teachings and actions by the Archbishop of Montreal, by Sir William Mulock, by the Hon. Mr Carrel, by the Hon. L.A. Tasche-

reau, by the Hon. Athanase David, by Sir Herbert Holt, by Archbishops Casey and Duke of Vancouver, and quite recently by the Government of Canada.

Be it resolved that the Commission unanimously approves of the stand taken by the above-mentioned Canadians and the Canadian Government.

But the Archbishop, charm he never so wisely, cannot charm the Canadian Labour Defence League. (The connection between this body and the Communist party resembles that between certain banks and certain trust companies. There is the same use of interlocking directorates, the same official denial of any connection.) On January 29, the League called a meeting to protest against police interference with the other meetings. The police and the hierarchy proved remarkably successful advertisers. 'Over 1500 persons' were present (Gazette, Jan. 30):

The police were also inside and mingled with the crowd. Plainclothesmen filled the stairway and uniformed police were stationed on the street opposite the hall. The chairman, Miss Gordon, said that the non-workers had suffered enough with the police and a stop should be put to it at once. She asked all those present to fight the police. There was no law against free speech or free assemblies. After having spoken for about ten minutes she introduced Louis J. Engdahl of New York. Mr Engdahl began by say, 'Let us unite together. Let us fight against those who are against free speech and the holding of assemblies.' He then launched an attack on the local police methods. It was outrageous the way the non-workers were treated. He asked the workers to gather and fight 'even with your bodies.' At this stage Inspector Bilodeau ordered three plainclothesmen to arrest the woman and Engdahl. 'Fight, fight, fight,' shouted Engdahl, 'Hurray for the revolutionists.' Inspector Bilodeau told [the crowd] that if they wished to continue their meeting they could do so, and that they would have no police interference provided they did not utter seditious speeches.

The term 'non-worker' in this context is perhaps a trifle indiscreet. To a Communist, 'non-worker' would probably mean not 'unemployed' but 'capitalist.' The events of January 29 produced in the Gazette of February 2 a letter from F.R. Scott, associate professor of constitutional law, McGill University, defending free speech on general principles. Professor Scott pointed out that Communism had nothing to do with the question, that sedition has never been defined by our criminal code with any exactness, that at none of the meetings recently broken up had the crowd been accused of disorder 'until after the police have arrested the speakers and started to disperse the crowd. The British method is to let the radicals blow off steam. At the first meeting broken up there were 250 present, at the last, over 1500. It would be interesting to know how many converts to Communism have been made by this procedure.' Director Langevin promptly replied (Gazette, Feb. 5):

I have given my men strict orders not to break up meetings, but to arrest anyone uttering seditious words. My men have never broken up meetings.

(Note Gazette reports, Jan. 20 and 24) –

But when they are assaulted they have to use force and as a result there is a riot and several arrests. Professor Scott stated that sedition has never been defined by our criminal law with any exactness. All I have to say to this is that when anything is said against law and justice as termed in articles 134 and 88 of the criminal code, it is sedition.* Simply because three or four of those [charged] were sentenced last week is enough to prove that the local police are right and that seditious words are uttered at these meetings.

(No charges of sedition arising out of any of these meetings have yet been tried – April 6) –

According to Professor Scott, the British method is to let the radicals blow off steam, but against this I have my orders. At every meeting over three-quarters of the crowd consists of Communists. I cannot allow this sort of thing to take place in Montreal.

A statement so authoritative ought to have satisfied even the academic mind. But Professor Scott seems to have no sense of reverence. In an interview on the same day he even pits his knowledge of law against that of a chief of police.

---

*Article 88, criminal code: A riot is an unlawful assembly which has begun to disturb the peace tumultuously.

Article 134: Everyone is guilty of an indictable offence and liable to imprisonment for not more than two years who speaks any seditious words or publishes any seditious libel or is a party to any seditious conspiracy.

Director Langevin [says] that Communists are to be denied the same rights as other British subjects. ... If he prevents 'this sort of thing' [as he had done] he is clearly acting illegally, since until our criminal code is altered by Parliament it will remain lawful for Communists to attend any meetings and in any numbers that they choose. If ... they preach sedition or cause a riot they may of course be arrested like any other person. Director Langevin's statement that he intends to forbid one class of British subjects from exercising their undoubted rights itself seems to satisfy one recognized definition of sedition, the utterance of an intention to promote feelings of ill will and hostility between different classes of His Majesty's subjects.'

Professor Scott adds that he would be interested to know who ordered Director Langevin to substitute American for British police methods in Montreal.

This time the chief of police did not reply. Instead the *Gazette* (Feb. 5) administered a dignified reproof:

The statement of the head of the police department should remove any lingering doubts as to the propriety and legality of the police action in dealing with seditionists. ... The public have regarded with approval the efforts of the police of Montreal and Toronto to check Communist agitators. The situation calls for action quite as strong as the police are now taking and there is nothing to be gained by microscopic examination of abstract principles. Police activities in Toronto were recently made the subject of a gratuitous protest by a number of professors at the University of Toronto who talked of the right of free speech, and seemed to forget that abuse of this freedom is in certain instances illegal, and that so-called liberty of the individual places no one above the law.

The *Gazette* makes short work of cant about 'British methods':

The present social and political condition of Britain, a condition which owes its worst features to the spread of Communism amongst trade unionists and others, ought to suggest a rather cautious use of the time-honoured precedent of Hyde Park.

People with a nice regard for the 'abstract principle' of truth, or some faint knowledge of what they are talking about, may tell us that for the last four years at least Communists have been debarred from any important office in British trade unions and from membership in the British Labour party; that Communism has no more implacable foes than the leaders of British Labour; that the British Communist party has never had more than about 10,000 members, is perennially short of funds, and could muster only 25 candidates and 50,000 votes in the last general election. But there is nothing to be gained by microscopic examination of facts like these. On February 25, the Unemployed Council of Montreal made a fresh effort, reported in the *Gazette* as follows:

The international 'red' demonstration in Victoria Square yesterday proved a fiasco when police mixed it [sic] with the crowd. No batons were used, but when men refused to move they were hustled by the free use of fists. None were hurt seriously.

While ordering the crowd to move on, the police noticed a man holding a camera. They claim he wanted to take a picture of the scene for publication in Communistic organs. The police ordered him to move on. Instead he talked back and was arrested. The police broke up a bread-line near Victoria Square. They claimed that in the crowd were several men whom they recognized as Communists. The bread-line formed again and two constables were stationed nearby to see that Communists kept away. Three men were arrested charged with distributing posters announcing the demonstration.

(Civic by-law No. 270, sec. 18, forbids the carrying or distribution of any posters, advertisements, prospectus [sic], circulars, or papers, in, near, or on the streets, alleys, sidewalks, and public places of the city. Restaurants have been held 'public places.' No doubt this is enforced with equal vigour against distribution of pamphlets at Liberal and Conservative election meetings.)

It is reassuring to note in these reports the spy system which furnishes the police with advance information of every 'Communistic' meeting. Experience has shown the value of this method of collecting accurate information and allaying popular excitement. But though the police are guarding us well they are, as Alderman Schubert says, 'not always of the most intellectual type.' As a result some of the fish slip through the net. None of the persons charged with serious offences – sedition, unlawful assembly, etc. – have yet come to trial, but about thirty have come before the courts on minor counts. Of twenty charged with refusing to move on when ordered, six got off; three because of 'inconsistent evidence' by the police. Of eight charged with obstructing the police only two were found guilty. (*Gazette*, Feb. 5, 27, March 9, and other issues)

Clement, 'a Frenchman of old France,' charged with obstructing, attempting to aid in the escape of prisoners, and threatening detective Greenberg (*Star*, Jan. 20) came before Recorder Thouin on January 27. He said he had had no work since March 1929, and no home but the Meurling refuge. The police said that when speakers were arrested Clement 'shouted "Come on, comrades, down with the police." In addition, he began pulling one of the constables by the sleeve, advising him to let go the man he had under arrest.' Unable to raise bail, Clement lay in jail for a week awaiting trial. The Recorder sentenced him to three months' hard labour:

In passing sentence the Recorder deplored unemployment and all who suffered through it, but declared he had 'no sympathy whatever for the lazy good-for-nothing type of individual who was content to take up residence in a refuge and remain there as long as possible at the expense of society.' The fact that most annoyed the Recorder was that Clement knowing he could not find work in Montreal was nevertheless content to remain in the city rather than go elsewhere. (Gazette, Jan. 28)

Pete Mazapa, arrested February 21, charged with 'attempting to incite others to fight the police,' appeared before Judge Lacroix on March 3. (Note the dates.)

When Mazapa asked for bail, Judge Lacroix replied, 'You are in a good country and we do not want your sort. You are dangerous and therefore I refuse to grant you bail.' (*Gazette*, March 4)

God Save the King!

FRANK H. UNDERHILL

O Canada

There is a good deal of talk in the papers and elsewhere about the holding of a National Convention of the Liberal Party for the purpose of giving it a badly needed bath and a fresh suit of clothes. Certainly the party would be the better for what is known in the advertising columns as an internal bath. But some people seem to have the same mystic faith in the efficacy of political conventions as they have in monkey-gland operations. As a matter of fact the connection of party conventions with party rejuvenation has been largely accidental in our Canadian political history. The real function of the great Conservative convention at Winnipeg was to consolidate the control over the party of Montreal big business which had never been quite secure under the erratic leadership of Mr Meighen. It was not the convention but the economic depression which won the election for the Tories. As for the famous conventions of the Liberals, the first came in 1893 at a moment when the Conservative government of the country was decrepit and corrupt after a generation of office; and the second came in 1919 when everybody was sick of the war and the war government, and when not even a cabinet of archangels, much less Mr Meighen's collection of nonentities, could have survived the next election. All that a Liberal convention would accomplish just now would be a fine outburst of sentimental hokum for the benefit of the boobs.

What Liberalism needs in Canada at present is a dispassionate scientific study of the methods by which the modern ideals of the social-service state can be applied to a country like Canada. Such a study, if it is to be organized cooperatively, must be conducted along somewhat the same lines as that which produced the Liberal Yellow Book in England. A political convention is, of course, the last place where such a discussion of ideas can be carried on – or such a programme drafted. A convention will only provide the party with another opportunity for ten years more of Mr King's gush about the necessity of the forward-looking elements in the community getting together. What the party really needs, though there is not the slightest evidence that any of its members are conscious of the fact, is a concrete definition of the goal to which the forward-looking elements are looking forward.

The pathetic belief that there is something mysteriously democratic in political conventions still survives in Canada though we have had the quadrennial experience of our American neighbours to enlighten us on the subject. Any body of several hundred men in a public hall is a mob unless it is guided and its programme cut and dried for it by some managers. And, as everyone ought to know by this time in North America, the men who manage political conventions are not the puppets who do the acting on the platform, but the little unobtrusive group who may be found sitting in their shirt-sleeves in some hotel bedroom. A party convention is also invariably attended by the most stupid and gullible of the party stalwarts and invariably avoided by any members whose IQ is at all respectable. At the Winnipeg Tory convention the intellect of the party was represented by a group of University undergraduates from Toronto whose main contribution to the solution of our national problems consisted in delivering the Varsity yell at intervals. Such a body of men lends itself to manipulation and will certainly be manipulated.

Nothing shows more clearly the intellectual bankruptcy of Canadian Liberalism than the general popularity of the notion that all that the party needs is a fine rousing get-together of its membership. For it must be obvious to any thinking man that what is wrong with Liberalism not merely in Canada but all over the world is not its lack of enthusiasm but the fact that it doesn't know where it is going. The social system of the Western world is under fire everywhere because of its disastrous failure to provide for the ordinary man a reasonable security and a reasonable standard of life. What is to be done about this fundamental problem is the one real question of contemporary political organization. This plain fact is gradually beginning to dawn even upon the capitalistic Bourbons of North America. If the present depression lasts much longer we are faced with the probability of such social collapse, not in North America it is true, but in Europe. And since 1914 we have been painfully aware that what happens in Europe has its immediate repercussions on our happy continent.

What has the Canadian Liberal party to offer as its contribution to the solution of this problem? Even if our present unemployment situation is abnormal the problem will be a continuing one. It is inherent in the demand of democracy for a fair opportunity to everyone to attain to the good things of life. A party which is really forward-looking must be prepared for a far wider communal activity than has ever been dreamt of at Ottawa or the provincial capitals. But such activity will inevitably interfere with the opportunities for speculative profit which now lie scattered about in abundant profusion for financial and other buccaneers. And the financing by the State of extended social services will sooner or later bring the community up against the problem of how much the wealthy classes are to pay. How the Liberal party as at present constituted would react to such situations may readily be inferred from its relations with the Beauharnois gang and with protected manufacturers in general during the last ten years.

There is no escaping the fact that in the twentieth century we are going to have more and more of class politics. Those happy nineteenth-century days of the orthodox two-party system when neither party was conscious of a class bias were possible only because it was the comfortable classes alone who had the vote or who were politically articulate. The invasion of politics by the organized labour movement in all advanced industrial countries except the United States has put an end to all that, and has produced a new era from which there is no going back. In Canadian politics we are just on the eve of the new era. We are finding, as other countries have found, that no parties which depend for their financial support on the secret contributions of wealthy individuals and corporations can possibly be trustworthy agents in looking after the interests of the common man. Sooner or later the democratic masses have to make use of such economic mass organizations as they possess to give them a political counterweight against the entrenched power of wealth. The financial dependence of the Labour Party in England on the Trade Unions may not be an ideal situation but it is the only practicable alternative to allowing politics to be monopolized by parties who depend just as directly upon bankers and manufacturers and brewers and upon wealth in general. A so-called democratic or liberal party which is not based solidly on some such class organization of the masses will certainly prove sooner or later, like the Liberal party in Canada, to be either futile or dishonest, and will probably prove to be both.

In Canada there are two sources from which a movement of protest against the domination of politics by St James St and King St might be expected to be effective – Labour and Agriculture. The farmers' political movement of the last decade didn't get very far except in Alberta because the farmers themselves were still dominated by a Victorian prudery about class politics. Labour as a political movement is still handicapped by the domination of AF of L ideas in Canada. But in spite of all disappointments it still remains true that the only hope for those who want a real democratic alternative to the two old parties with their sham battles is a movement in which the organized farmers will be the senior partner and organized Labour the junior partner. In our modern social conditions no political movement which hasn't behind it the drive of an organized economic class will ever get anywhere. The Conservative party has such an organized class behind it. The necessary alternative to it is a Farmer-Labour movement which would soon attach to itself all the floating body of unattached consumers or intellectuals who now either take no interest in politics at all or limit their political activity to writing futile articles in journals like *The Canadian Forum*.

L.A. MACKAY

Fidelia Vulnera Amici

If to a human head a horse's neck
Your painter sets, proceeding thence to deck
With various plumes a motley lot of limbs
Cribbed from whatever walks, or crawls, or
   swims,
Till in a filthy fish the mixture ends,
Could you refrain a gross guffaw, my friends?
What of a Beaver, then, with budding mane
That still he coaxes and pommades in vain,
While fluffy feathers, the uncivil things,
Insist to clothe his flapping paws in wings;
Who ponders on his own ambiguous tail,
'Is that a tuft, a feather, or a scale?'
And like some baffling beast that dies in
   dreams,
Roars like a lion, like an eagle screams?
Thrice happy beast, if ever he could find
A way to know, or guess at, his own mind!

Well, let us help him. 'Tis a pious task
For Beaver-corpuscles. First then, we'll ask
What's our ambition? Why, we aim to be
The Empire's, nay, the whole world's granary.
A lofty mark, i'faith; to find our place
Just in the belly of the human race.
Nor ever there securely. Ah, the blest
Simplicity of our agrarian West!
What though poor silly Nature failed to grant
Complete monopoly in the precious plant?
We borrow Nelson's telescope, and still
Maintain with dogged syllogistic skill,
'Wealth springs from labour; man's a kind of
   meat;
All flesh is grass: therefore, all wealth is wheat.'
And if it were, what help were that to us,
Who frame our foreign commerce, roughly
   thus:

The right hand asks a price that none will pay;
The left hand pushes proffered trade away?
   What then? Our glory goes no further
      deep
Than roots of grass? Why, not at all; we keep
A second barrel still to shoot at fate.
It is not that happy land supremely great
Which with the wealth of fertile fields
   combines
The inexhaustible riches of her mines
– Which yet, perhaps, may last her buccaneers
With luck, a matter of some thirty years.
There lies the wealth. Root it out all at once.
So we be fat, the devil take our sons!
   Had we so little time, so little faith,
To think the land must die with our own
   death?
Must we leave nothing? Did we reckon then
Ourselves to be the very last of men?
Slow grows the oak; the lank and sappy weed
Shoots limply up with true Canadian speed.
We have no time, we have no time to grow
Well-knit, broad shouldered, vigorous, and
   slow;
We must have Immigrants, that we may sprout
Into a lubberly long anaemic lout;
Nor ask, what did the Dinosaurus gain
Whose body grew so far beyond his brain?
   Say, what remains when mines and
      forests go
The way of beaver, and the buffalo?
Though we renew the woods, restock the lakes,
Where shall we find the magic art that makes
An emptied earth put forth her wealth again?
Our rude forefathers, unenlightened men,
Honoured him who most with armed hand
Ruined and spoiled their hapless neighbours'
   land;

But we, most infinitely wiser grown,
Adore him most who most despoils his own.
And lest too slow ourselves our wealth should waste,
Still bawl and bray, in desperate haggard haste,
Calling the carrion crows of all the earth
To gut the unhappy land that gave us birth.

    We could have kept our hands from this foul stain,
Have cleared the forest, duly tilled the plain,
And worked the mine, to fill our daily need,
In reverence, in worship, not in greed;
Who now, to bring our swollen pride to birth,
Lay impious hands upon our mother Earth,
And blind with selfish lust, from shore to shore,
Ravish her crudely like a hired whore.

    And what's our gain? (a), the familiar curse
Of unemployment; (b) – and rather worse –
Employment, in conditions that reflect
Small enough credit on our self-respect.
Smug squint-eyed slavery, that lays a stain
Less on our heart, perhaps, than on our brain:
Our brain, that shuts its eyes to evidence,
Defies all life, all history, all sense,
And worships as divine eternal truth
An economic system, rude, uncouth,
Wasteful, unjust, unhealthy, that can boast
A few poor hundred years of life at most,
When men, except an odd old-fashioned few
Forgot the simple truth that once they knew,
Honoured the giver less than him that lends,
And set the means of life above the ends.

    What can we do about it? We may shift
At least, our form of servitude, may lift
Our masters' boot-heels from our country's neck
– And place our own there – at the least, may check
This reckless fever of the childish few
That strip our wealth, and know what they do.
Where lies the gain, if Parliaments control
Production, Distribution, – and the Dole?
In this, most likely: that their hands are free
For general action; when they disagree
(As, if the gods be good, they mostly will)
For general inaction, better still.
No greater blessing, but a less offence;
Folly inactive, oft resembles sense.

    'So then,' says one, 'your timorous counsel ends
'In sordid poverty?' Not at all, my friends.
I know the truth the Grecians understood –
'How hardly shall a poor man's life be good.'
I never claimed that famine fostered health,
And still the best manure of Art is Wealth.
I but suggest the interest of the land
Might prosper more, more generally planned,
That we might put our corporate brains to use
Settling how much, and what, we shall produce,
Not bolt, like Lazarus in the holy fable,
The random crumbs from Dives' vulgar table.
I but suggest Ambition shift his goal
Sometimes, from body's growth to growth of soul,
Who now, poor thing, is squashed most sadly flat
Under a jellyfish mound of muscled fat.
We have yet a chance to stand in the world's eyes
For something more than silly wealth or size;
But these we stress so much, men have forgot,
Almost, whether we have a soul or not
Seeing us to some Moloch-god of Matter
Offer our own fat head on a shallow platter.

    But stay, abandoned critic! Dost not know
How fair a spiritual light we throw?
See where three thousand thousand paces shine
Of open, unbesoldiered border-line!
Noble, begad! I never heard the ant
Keep up a guard against the elephant.
The generous Lamb wipes a fraternal tear,
And comforts neighbour Lion not to fear.
Inspiring sight! and inexpensive, too:
But let the credit go where credit's due.
We have our faults; but one we ne'er display
– Too tender justice to the USA.
Poor wildered cousins! whom we fear, and hate,
And envy, and insult, and imitate.

    And yet, towards England, our affection mocks
The wit with more ingenious paradox.
Fondly we cherish her, in filial pride,
So long as all the profit's on our side.
We seek her marts – but Lord, the unholy fuss
If ever she presumes to trade with us! –
And generously make good our loyal vaunts
Offering her everything but what she wants.
Yet one commodity with no thought of price
We lavish – tons and tons of good advice:
And Grandma, tugging slyly at our legs
Demurely learns the art of sucking eggs.
... At that, she might pick up, by paying heed,
Some rather useful dodges: and indeed
I'd rather be, begging the Wheat Pool's pardon,
The world's schoolmaster than its kitchen-garden.

December 1931

EDWARD ARTHUR BEDER

Wattman

I remember how I first met Wattman. I had gone in to a place to ask for a job and he was waiting around in the office. The boss came out and questioned me – where had I been working, what class of work could I do, what did I expect to get – and finally he seemed satisfied and it was fixed up that I was to start in the next day.

Wattman came out with me. 'That's a good firm to work for,' he volunteered. 'You'll be well satisfied there. They do nice work.'

'That so?' I answered. 'I'll soon find out anyway.'

'Yes, that's right too,' he conceded. 'You'll soon find out.'

We walked on a little way in silence. 'I heard you tell him you were a stranger here,' he continued. 'Have you got a room yet?'

'No,' I replied, 'I only got in this morning from Buffalo and I started out to find a job first thing. I can always get a room.'

'Listen ' he said, 'I've got a room you could have. A dandy room, big and lofty, a front room, you ought to see it. It's my own house so I'm careful who comes in. It's easily big enough for a young couple but I'd sooner rent it to a young feller like you – you can understand. Come home with me now – you can take a look at it. And say' – he looked straight at me – 'I can wait till you get a payday.'

That was how I came to room at Wattman's house. The room was all he claimed for it. A big front one with a very high ceiling and two big windows that looked out on a pair of whitewashed cottages across the street. There were no pictures or decorations of any sort on the walls, they were stained a pale green, and no covering on the painted floorboards, but I liked it that way. When you get rooming in different places over a number of years you get tired of the stuffy little holes and the junk that fills them in the regular rooming houses, you get to feeling a dislike of sitting in them, they smother you, you stay out as long as you can to avoid the queer smell that's in them.

Wattman's room took my eye the moment I stepped into it. The big windows were open, the sun poured in in long strong rays that seemed like welcoming arms to me. Its wide emptiness set my nostrils sniffing as though I was out in a park, I could breathe in it, I liked it. For furniture there was a white enamel bed in one corner, an old leather couch facing it across the room, a small table set by the window nearest the couch and a couple of brown kitchen chairs.

Wattman interested me. He was a big man with good shoulders that gave him a fine erect bearing and in his walk – for that matter any time you looked at him – there was a blend of gracefulness and strength that was pleasing to that sense in us that likes to see a man full-sized and active. His face wasn't quite as satisfactory as his frame. The skin was tanned and full of colour, but his nose curved at the end and gave him a rather crafty touch. He never bothered very much about the arrangement of his hair, it usually came straight over and reached with a final sweep toward his eyes, which perhaps might account for the impression I had that his forehead was low. His eyes were small; in conversation his features would crease up readily and then his eyes would dance brightly, they would shine with a merry light in them.

The thing that interested me so much about Wattman was the crafty tip to his nose. It didn't seem to belong. His manner wasn't crafty at all. It was hale and hearty and open. Not too hearty, he wasn't in the least boisterous, rather he was full of fine – picturesque wouldn't be too strong a word – courtesy.

When I got home of an evening, after giving me a little time to rest up and read the paper, Wattman would usually come up to my room. 'How's the boy?' he would greet in his firm, good-humoured voice, with a little toss upward of his chin and smile at me. Then he would sit down on the couch, back erect and head in the air and roll himself a cigarette. He would finish with a quick lick and the cigarette would always flare up a little because of the end not having any tobacco in it. After he took a few puffs he would go on in soft tones that conveyed a feeling of warm, friendly interest, 'How did it go today – lots of work – are you feeling tired?'

He would nod in a dignified way as I answered and now and then, as I went into details of some difficult job, he would say sympathetically, 'I understand – I understand.'

When his third or fourth cigarette would go out on him and remain stuck to one of his lips, like as not he would say, 'Will you have a glass of beer? I've got a barrel of good beer, nice and cold, come on, have a glass of beer!'

Then with a quick motion that emphasized his graceful bulk he would jump up and stride to the head of the stairs. He would call down to his wife in a firm pleasant voice. 'Hannah, my dear, bring a pitcher of beer. Mr Nemo is going to drink with me.' And right away his wife would hurry down to the cellar and draw off a pitcher of beer. She would bring it up all foaming and aswirl from her trip up the stairs and she would put the tray down on the table and set out the glasses in her quick nervous way. Her husband would pat her on the back and I could see she glowed at his touch. 'Thank you, my dear, thank you. You're a good girl, Hannah.'

It was a treat to listen to the way Wattman spoke to his wife and children. That's why I say he was so courteous. In his own house a man sometimes drops the politeness that he shows to outsiders. Not so with Wattman. He was at his best in his own home. There was a charm in the way he treated his wife, he had a way of saying, 'Hannah, my dear,' that captivated me sitting in my room upstairs. His voice was so finely modulated, it shaded off into such a sympathetic tone that was so completely charming, that I can picture how pleased his wife must have felt at his tenderness.

It was all the more extraordinary when you looked at Mrs Wattman. To be frank about it I had a shock the first time I saw her. A small thin woman with a bloodless face and the bones standing out gauntly on her cheeks, her perpetual expression of sheepish obedience was weirdly challenged by a mocking squint in one of her eyes. I never found out which eye it was that rebelled so against the permanent set of her features, I simply couldn't look on that unlovely face long enough.

They had seven children. They came about every fifteen months. It was hard luck on Wattman, they were all girls and the reason he had seven children was that he was trying for a boy. He wanted a son very badly, he had a sort of hunger for a lad of his own. But that didn't make him touchy with the girls. He treated them just as affectionately as he did his wife. He fondled them, he gave them money for ice cream and candies and they worshipped him. At the same time you had to admire the way he ruled them. When one of the children was naughty to such an extent that Mrs Wattman felt obliged to tell on her, Wattman never got angry. He would call out her name in that firm, understanding voice of his and the little girl would come to him, her face white but all steeled to go through with it and Wattman, in his dignified way, would put her over his knee, spank her, and the little girl would run out somewhere in the back to cry.

It was early summer when I took that room at Wattman's. The days were long and bright with a hot sun during the middle part of them, but toward evening it cooled off. The smell of the earth rose up clean and sweet from the watered lawns and there was a fragrance from the growing things that was good to sniff at.

When I got back from work Wattman would usually be sitting on the steps leading to his front door, that was the nearest thing to a porch he could claim, a cigarette between his lips, a hose in his hand, watering the small green space that was spread out before him. He liked doing that, he liked holding the thin rubber tube and playing the quick stream up and down, covering the sidewalk and squirting the water up the side of the house and sometimes flicking a little of it at any of his children who were playing around. They would scream merrily and feel a little proud, too, before the other children, proud that their father played with them so right on the street.

Occasionally I would go and join Wattman on the steps. He would gladly make room for me alongside with a quick inviting shift. Sitting in our shirt sleeves we would smoke and talk; the grass would stand out green and drenched before us and gradually the street would grow darker and quieter. Some of the children would go to bed, others would tire and rest up on their steps or sit patiently on the curb telling stories and speaking softly together, their arms all linked up and their ribboned heads bent low.

There was a magic about this hour of twilight, even the noisiest child felt it and grew quiet in a sort of embarrassed way. At the end of the street the sky would change to purple and plum and blue, the sun would dissolve itself and the heavens would glow with spilt gold. Blue shapes edged with gilt would rise up in all sorts of queer patterns, take on deeper colourings and refashion themselves. Then a blue blackness would spread itself like a cloak and the gold would sink right out of the sky.

Wattman did very little. He explained his method of making a living to me in these conversations we had sitting on his steps. He loafed all summer, he did nothing. Around early September he opened a small fur store in a certain part of the city and took in repair work. He always opened up in the same neighbourhood, trying to get as near as possible to the store he had the previous year. He had built up some sort of connection in this way and he could depend upon getting in a certain amount of work. By the time February came around he usually had about eight or nine hundred dollars saved up, or rather Mrs Wattman did, he turned all the money over to her, he told me. They lived on this money during the summer; Mrs Wattman was very economical, she made the payments on the house and doled him out so much a week for himself. That was the way he preferred it. Generally when the fall came around enough remained to open up the store again. If there had been a lean season or some special expense had cropped up, like sickness or his wife's confinement and he was short in money, why, then he borrowed from his brother-in-law. He only needed a month's rent and a few dollars for small expenses, handbills and things like that. He kept all the fixtures that he needed in the attic of his house.

'I work right in the store,' he said, 'I set up a table on a trestle and work right there. I don't need any fancy fixtures. A lady who wants fancy fixtures doesn't come to me, she goes down town. When a woman come into my place she likes it all the better to see me in my coat and working. She has an idea that my price must be lower – she feels that she is saving money.'

When I asked him why he didn't do something all summer and keep his money instead of eating it up, he shook his head. 'My dear friend,' he said softly, 'what can I do? I don't know any other business – it's hard to go into something you don't understand. How do I know? I might lose all my money in a month. I would have to starve all summer. No, no, this way I know what I have to do. Besides it gets so awful hot in summer, how can you work at anything? It's better as I am.' Then he would go on to speak of some of the things that had happened to him during the years he had kept the store, some of the jobs he had taken in and made money on, and how once in a while a cranky customer made trouble for him.

Wattman took a pride in his back garden. He spent a good deal of time there taking care of it, weeding it out, watering it, sometimes just staring at the plants for long periods and smoking cigarettes. His chief delight was his Indian corn. A pleased look came over his face as he showed the sturdy plants to me. He glowed as the warm sun fell upon them and upon him, his tanned skin glinting ruddily, 'Do you know why I grow corn?' he asked in a proud way. I shook my head. 'When they're ripe it's time for me to open my store!'

He meant it. When the corn stood ripening in his back yard, the waxen heads yellowing in the sun, he opened his store.

I knew about it because one evening when I returned from work the front steps were empty. The small lawn looked parched in the heat and there seemed a silence about Wattman's house. Sitting in my room before an open window I wondered at it. And then there was a knock at my door and Mrs Wattman entered in her hesitating, timid way.

'If you please, Mr Nemo,' she said in a low voice, 'Mr Wattman's taken a store.'

'That's good,' I said.

'If you please, Mr Nemo,' she said nervously, 'he sent an express man to get the couch.'

'The couch,' I said wonderingly.

She indicated it. 'Yes,' she said, 'Mr Wattman always takes the couch with him. Since he's had a store he always take the couch with him.'

'All right,' I said. 'I'll take those things off and then you can have it.'

'Thank you,' she answered gratefully, 'I'll tell the express man to come up for it.'

I cleared off the books and papers that were on it and gave the express man a hand with it down the stairs. It was an old couch and shabby with long use. The springs were half broken and made themselves felt uncomfortably through the misplaced stuffing, and the centre of it sagged badly.

From the attic the express man took down trestles and boards, a couple of figures, a machine and a quantity of iron piping. With the Wattman children standing around and looking very important he got the things on his waggon and drove off with his unwieldy load.

About ten o'clock that night Wattman came into my room. He was in good spirits. His face was red and flushed and smiling, and he called to his wife to bring up some beer. 'Have some beer,' he said heartily, 'have some beer. I took a store today, have some beer.'

We sat and talked and drank the beer. He told me what rent he was paying and how he had arranged with a man to look after the furnace when it should be needed. He was pleased about this as he had a dread of doing this kind of work. He told me of an old customer who had passed by and seeing him had entered the store. She had promised to bring in her coat and also to tell her sister-in-law about him.

He was full of good spirits in his hearty way. His voice retained that courteous tone of his, never reaching a loud note for all his evident exhilaration. His hair fell straight down toward his eyes, his face was flushed, his eyes sparkled. It was hard to reconcile his full soft voice with his rather dishevelled appearance.

'Say,' I said, 'your wife asked me to give that couch that was in here to the express man. What do you need a couch down at the store for?'

He looked at me and smiled. His voice was full of a gracious courtesy. It was quite extraordinary the fine feeling he put into it.

'My dear friend,' he said, 'I like to have it with me. I need it. In the season I'm at the store all the time. Many nights it's eleven and sometimes twelve o'clock before I leave the place. It's hard work. So now and then I like to take a little nap. When I feel like it, after lunch sometimes, I like to take a little nap.'

'Right in the store?'

'What's the matter with you?' he said good-naturedly. 'I get a carpenter to partition me off a little office in the back of the store. Just a little office. I keep the phone there and my bills and I put the couch there too. And when I feel like it I lock the door and take a little nap.

'Suppose a customer wants to come in?' I asked.

'Hah, a customer! There's no customers going around right after lunch. In the evenings I see a few customers. But during the day hardly anyone comes in. Sometimes I don't see a soul, nobody puts their head in the door. Come over when you get a chance. I keep some beer at the store and you'll be company for me. We'll have a talk. Don't forget, now, any time you feel like it, come over.'

I did. I went over to see him one afternoon when I didn't happen to be working. I passed the store on the street car and made my way back to it. It was a poor neighbourhood made up of small stores carrying cheap stocks set out in a drab, ineffective way.

Just before I reached Wattman's place a woman went in. I didn't want to bother him whilst he had a customer so I waited around outside until the woman should come out. It was a fall day with a high blustering wind that swooped savagely down the street, tossing papers and light garbage violently in the air and cutting right through me. After standing about for ten minutes or so the cold affected me. I decided to enter Wattman's store. There was no particular harm in going in even if he was occupied.

The door was locked. I tried a number of times, I rattled the handle and pushed heavily against it but there was no doubt about it, the door was locked. I peered through the glass. I saw a table made up of a board set on trestles, a machine alongside it and several pieces of fur scattered around. At the back of the store a wooden partition rose up. The unpainted boards looked crude and cheap and seemed to accentuate the emptiness of the place.

'Well, that's damn funny,' I muttered to myself. 'I could have sworn I saw a woman go in there.'

I walked away a few yards and thought about it. I crossed the street and took shelter in the lobby of a small picture show. The girl in the ticket booth eyed me suspiciously, but I paid no attention to her.

I thought of Wattman, his fine big figure and the perfect courtesy of his manner. I thought of his wife and her intolerable squint and how she had said simply, 'He always takes the couch with him.' I decided to wait.

At the end of about half an hour the door of Wattman's store opened the the woman came out. Wattman accompanied her to the door. He stood there for a minute, big, suave and attentive. I saw him bow his head with that fine deference that was so much a part of him. The woman smiled and went away.

I smiled too. I identified that courteous trick of his. I couldn't hear what he said, of course, but I knew that motion of his. He always made use of it when he addressed his wife in those perfect tones that had so impressed me. Standing in that small lobby behind the shelter of the gaudy billboards I seemed to hear clearly, 'Thank you, Hannah, my dear – you're a good girl, Hannah, my dear....' I laughed.

F.R. SCOTT

Communists, Senators, and all That

No one can deny that under Mr Bennett Canada has become a leader in the movement of world ideas. Where others have vacillated, we have acted. Hard hit though we were by the depression, and despite the thousands of unemployed starving in our streets, we had the courage and unselfishness to announce that we would not sell our soul – or our machinery – for Soviet gold; that we would not support by interchange of trade a country which maintained a low standard of living and which forced workers to work instead of forcing them to be idle. Recently a Toronto court has held that under Canadian law Communists can be sent to prison for any period up to twenty years, just for being Communists. In banning Russian goods we stood, and still stand, proudly alone. In outlawing the Communist party we are not alone, but the company in which we move is select. Japan, Jugo-Slavia, and Bulgaria have proscribed Communism; Italy permits no right of association to any non-fascist body, whether Communist or Conservative; under the Polish dictatorship no one is allowed to think at all. With Japs, Jugo-Slavs, Italians, Bulgars, and Poles, Canada marches toward a higher social order. Only in decadent and backward countries like Great Britain, the United States, France, Germany, Belgium, Spain, Norway, Sweden, Denmark, Holland, and the other British Dominions can the horrid plots of the Marxian idolators be carried out in the broad light of day.

Canadians must be pleased to discover that they are protected by such a reliable system of laws, and that they have fine, clean-cut stool-pigeons of the type of Sergeant Leopold to see that our British tradition of fair play is not undermined by skulking foreigners. It is true that certain Senators affiliated with Beauharnois are still senators, and that they have not had to undergo any civil or criminal action whatsoever. But these men merely abused positions of high public and social trust to transfer to their own pockets millions belonging by moral right to unsuspecting investors. Whereas the Communists have probably got hold of the wrong ideas about how to make the world a better place to live in. Obviously the two cases are totally different.

A friend of mine – I think he had been an investor in the old Canada Power and Paper Company – suggested that Sergeant Leopold should now be disguised as a cunning fellow and ordered to worm his way into the secret conclaves of the Canadian financiers. But I pointed out promptly that you couldn't do that sort of thing. You mustn't start weakening the faith of Canadians in their financial institutions. If you once give them the idea that the money they keep losing oughtn't to have been lost, they may start asking questions or something. And how can the system possibly work if people start asking questions?

It is shocking to realize that we very nearly had no law at all under which the Communist party could be declared an unlawful association. The totally inadequate criminal law which we inherited from England had nothing in it nearly so efficient as the present section 98 of the Canadian Criminal Code, in virtue of which the Toronto Communists were chiefly sentenced. There was only a vague rule about seditious conspiracies, which had hardly ever been enforced, which no one understood, and for which the maximum penalty was a paltry two years. It wasn't till 1919, after the world – and Winnipeg – had been made safe for democracy, that the new section was added. It was apparently invented by the State of New York, and it suited so well the famous American methods of repressing crime that we thought we had better copy it. But later it very nearly got taken off the statute book. Prosperity seemed to weaken the moral fibre of the public. On no less than five occasions the Canadian House of Commons passed a bill to amend the Criminal Code by repealing section 98. Five separate times – in the sessions of 1926, 1926-7, 1928, 1929, and 1930. If it had not been for our Senate of picked men, who manfully threw out the bill every time it came before them, we should have been in a pretty fix now. In the session of 1929 the bill failed to pass the Senate by only three votes. If two members had been a little sleepier that day, Canadian institutions might be tottering. No wonder we insist that every senator shall own at least four thousand dollars worth of property.

It must not be thought that the Beauharnois senators were amongst those who wanted to maintain section 98. On the contrary, the records show that in 1928 Messrs Haydon and MacDougald voted for the repealing bill. Apparently they were in favour of a fairly lenient Criminal Code.

The idea of deporting Communists and other radicals is another good example of the present government's methods in handling a grave social problem. There is nothing like getting rid of a disease by sending away to foreign countries all persons who have it, so that other people may become infected instead of ourselves. Then we can keep clear of future contagion by asking all immigrants as they enter Canada whether they intend to undermine Mr Bennett and other Canadian institutions. If they say they do, we can turn them away. This is really rooting out the cause of the trouble, isn't it?

Our parlour Bolsheviks had better understand what they are in for if the present law is to be enforced to the full. Canada doesn't need to put up with their nasty new ideas if she doesn't want to. Section 98 creates so many new crimes and establishes so many presumptions of criminality that lots of people who are not actually Communists are liable to prosecution. It is a good red-blooded article, with 115 lines of definitions, offences, and penalties, all so obscurely worded that no one can be sure just how much liberty of speech and association survives – except that it is pretty small. The following examples of its provisions will show what the authorities could do if they really got on the warpath. After defining an unlawful association as one whose purpose is to bring about any governmental, industrial, or economic change within Canada by use of force, or which teaches or defends the use of force to accomplish such change, or for any other purpose, the article goes on to say amongst other things:

(1) *Any person who sells, speaks, writes or publishes anything as the representative or professed representative of such association;*
(2) *Any person who wears or displays anywhere, any badge, banner, motto, button, etc., indicating or intending to suggest that he is a member of or in anywise associated with such association;*
(3) *Anyone who solicits subscriptions or contributions for it or contributes anything to it or to anyone for it as dues or otherwise;*
shall be guilty of an offence punishable by twenty years.

How about that for getting after friends and sympathizers of Communists? The Roman type is used to show the wholehearted way in which Parliament tackled the job in 1919: lots of all-embracing *anywheres, anywises,* and *anythings.* Then comes a still better clause:

(4) *In any prosecution under this section, if it be proved that the person charged has –*
(a) *Attended meetings of an unlawful association; or*
(b) *Spoken publicly in advocacy of an unlawful association; or*
(c) *distributed literature of an unlawful association by circulation through the Post Office mails of Canada, or otherwise;*
it shall be presumed, in the absence of proof to the contrary, that he is a member of such unlawful association.

Just examine that for a moment, all you red college professors. None of your old-fashioned ideas that a man is presumed innocent until he is proved guilty. All the police need do here is to show that you once attended a Communist meeting, perhaps through curiosity, or spoke publicly in advocacy of the party, or distributed literature (presumably any kind of literature) of the party, and at once the Canadian legal machinery gets to work and says you are a criminal liable to twenty years. You won't escape gaol unless you can prove that you are not a member of the party. And think what it will be like trying to make this proof! Obviously no member of the party will dare to testify that you are a non-member, because by coming forward he would at once give notice to the police that he is a criminal. You will simply have to give your own word – and why should a college professor's red word destroy a legal presumption?

This is by no means all. The owner of any building who knowingly permits therein any meeting of an unlawful association *or any subsidiary association or branch or committee thereof*, or any assemblage of persons who teach, or defend the use, without authority of the law, of force, violence, etc. ... shall be liable both to a five thousand dollar fine and to imprisonment for five years. This will stop all nonsense in the way of radical meetings of any sort, Communist or otherwise. For how is the owner of a hall to know whether or not a society is a 'subsidiary' of an unlawful association? He won't take the risk of a five thousand dollar fine and five years in gaol. What about the Friends of the Soviet Union, for instance, a society which actually teaches that we should love and not hate the Russians? Isn't this a subsidiary association, and isn't its teaching tantamount to defense of the use of force without authority of the law? And the Workers' Unity League? And the Canadian Labour Defense League, which collects money to defend Communists in the Law Courts – isn't this a 'branch' of the Communist party, or at any rate does it not solicit money 'as dues or otherwise' for the party so as to make every member of it liable to twenty years? What about all you misguided people who have subscribed to the defense of Tim Buck – aren't you pretty close to twenty years in gaol yourselves?

The section warms up as it proceeds, and new crimes come thick and fast. Here are three more specimens: (1) Every person who prints, circulates, sells, or offers for sale, etc., any book, pamphlet, etc. (there are 13 synonyms), in which is taught, advised, or defended the use of force, or threats of injury to person or property, etc., as a means of accomplishing any governmental, industrial, or economic change; (2) every person who *in any manner* teaches, advises, advocates, or defends such use of force, etc., and (3) every person who imports or attempts to import such literature, shall be liable to twenty years' imprisonment. This really gets down to business, and should rid our radicals forever of the obsolete idea that under the Canadian constitution the personal liberties of the subject give the subject personal liberty. Has any Canadian bookseller ever sold a copy of the Communist Manifesto? Twenty years for him. Has any Canadian professor ever taught a class of students in political science that there are occasions when revolution is morally justifiable? Clap him in gaol with the Communists; defending the use of force in any manner is a crime even if it is done in the privacy of the class-room or home. Has any Canadian citizen ever brought into Canada any book in which the use of force to effect political or industrial change is defended under any conditions whatsoever? Let him shiver in his shoes; Sergeant Leopold, disguised as a friend, may be after him, and a long spell in the penitentiary awaits him.

Just to round out the law it is declared to be the duty of every person in the entire civil service of the Dominion to seize all literature of the prohibited kind, whether found in the mails or in any vehicle or vessel, and to transmit it at once to the Commissioner of the Royal Canadian Mounted Police. It was a happy idea of Parliament to think of this ingenious way of creating a censorship service. Without additional cost to the Canadian taxpayer, at once some 40,000 people were given the job of confiscating dangerous books. And by having a police commissioner as final judge the law is sure to be administered in a manner conducive to the purity of Canadian thought.

Enough of section 98 has been explained to show the citizens of Canada the sort of law which governs them. The best thing for every good Canadian to do, if he wants to keep out of gaol, is to cling to the stock of reliable and well-tried ideas which have made Canada exactly what she is today. If he is built so queerly that he finds he cannot agree with Mr Bennett, try as he will, then let him be radical with Mr King. But that is as far as he can expect to be allowed to go. Canada is a country which has inherited British traditions of law, of justice and of government. It is a land of golden opportunity, where everyone who can do a good day's work will get along fine. We have admitted a lot of foreigners to build our railways and dig up our minerals, but they ought to be grateful to us for letting them live here, and not go about organizing to alter the present system in any way. If they do not like the way we treat them, then let them pack up their belongings and travel back to Europe, via CPR. We won't stand for their talk about the downtrodden masses and the class war. There aren't any classes in Canada; it is a democratic country. And as for Soviet Russia let it be understood once and for all that a state which is run for the workers, where the land and natural resources and means of production are owned by the people and not by financiers, where there are no sharp contrasts of riches and poverty, and where the motive of personal profit has been replaced by that of public service, is a state utterly foreign to Canadian traditions and practice. We won't have it, that's all.

DOROTHY LIVESAY

Two Poems

Morning in Autumn

The day takes hold of me and lifts me up –
O ho! The wind! I feared you in the night.
(The whispering wind, clawing like a cat
At curtains, sneaking through the window's crack
And pulling at the curtains of my room).

Alienation

Feared you ... Feared this? This shivering
   delight,

This laughter blowing back my hair, this voice
That trembles out some secret in my ears?
Never again will autumn startle me,
If with such wind, such a haphazard sun
He plays with me, drives sober thoughts away,
Turns words and conversation into song.

(But Lucifer came down that night, the stars
Precarious ladders for his feet. He met the
   clouds,
Stirred up the running clouds to rain and wind.
Lucifer, the cat, came down to me –
Lucifer, the Wind, the fingers at my blind. ...)

What subtlety of presences other than
This you, asleep beside me! the dark,
The heavy dark I smell, the dream I touch,
The wind a cat-thief mocking at my safety.
No: safety is with you, who lie asleep,
Bound in another world I cannot seize.

(Your breathing is less real than these sharp
   claws
Of rain without, this gnawing of the wind –
These only, see me shivering in their hold,
Naked at last before the naked fear).

Yet see sun patterns on the page, and hear
The chuckling breeze that rustles in the leaves
Unfallen yet, soon to be fallen down.
(So Lucifer once fell – is hiding now?
Hiding till night a darker mantle fall).
Ah no; he's dead! Sun searches out my heart.
Come lover, walk with me
Along the Boulevard.

What was it, after all,
   The night, or the night-scented phlox?
Your mind, or the garden where
   Always the wind stalks?

What was it, what brief cloak
   Of magic fell about
Lending you such a radiance, –
   Leaving me out?

What was it, why was I
   Shivering like a tree,
Blind in a golden garden
   Where only you could see?

MARY QUAYLE INNIS

Holiday

Riding in the car had made her a little faint and unsteady, but now that she was safely inside the big store Mrs Samchuk felt better. My, it was a long time since she had been here – two months anyhow – and such a lot as she had been through. She had earned a holiday. Lydie and Dolly and Jim would be all right with Mrs Jenkins to keep an eye on them till Pete got home. It was silly, Pete tramping from house to house looking for work when there wasn't any. Miles he walked to cut a lawn or carry out ashes for fifteen cents. It just used up his shoes and brought back that pain in his leg where he got hurt in the war. He'd do better to look after the kids and let her get out oftener. But now she was out and she meant to stay a while. She lifted the baby higher in her arms and shuffled along the aisle to the cosmetic counter.

It was one of her favourites. The smells were lovely and the colours made it like a garden. The powder boxes were gold and red and green and black, and there were bottles of bath salts, sparkling pink and lavender, and cakes of soap in the shape of roses and swans. Everything glittered like fire. Even the powder puffs were peach and pink and the little rouge boxes were like rubies. Nettie Samchuk walked round the counter very slowly. She didn't dare touch anything but nobody could stop her looking and smelling the thick, bright scents. It was a wonder some of the homely, old-looking women who bought silver powder boxes and huge pink puffs. You'd think such things would be for young girls but very likely the old ones needed them more.

A salesgirl at the corner of the counter sprayed a lady with perfume out of a tall crystal atomizer and a few of the tiny drops fell sparkling on Nettie's shoulder. She smiled and sniffed them appreciatively. That was nice. Rose, it smelled like, though you couldn't tell. They had such funny names.

Over here were the crepe paper flowers and in the corner the paints and coloured paper for artists. She had liked to paint in school; if she had a paint box now she could dabble in it when the kids were in bed. Suppose the Charities woman found her with a paint box. Nettie almost laughed. Anyhow she was too tired at night to do anything but sleep. For a while she looked at silk stockings and handkerchiefs, gay as flowers, and purses with fancy clasps and your initial cut out of gold and fastened on the corner. Then she took the elevator upstairs. A woman in a big brown fur stared at her and frowned but when she saw the baby she made room. Nettie looked right back at her, not rude but not scared either. A store was for everybody.

Children's clothes – that was another of the places she liked. Of course if she had any money she would go to the basement where the things were that you could really buy, but having none she liked better to stick to places that didn't tempt her. Her favourite game was to dress her children. From the show cases you could choose outfits for all of them and the possibility of having such fine things was too remote to allow any sensation of envy. Mrs Samchuk leaned against the edge of the counter letting the baby's body rest on it while she selected Lydie's costume. That flowered dress with smocking across the front would be swell on Lydie with one of those pale pink angora tams that looked so soft you wanted to put your face against it. And white shoes and stockings. Lydie hadn't ever had white. She'd be lucky now if she had any colour. Dolly would look cute in that red knitted outfit with white ducks on the jersey. She moved slowly round the counter staring with fascinated eyes. That blue romper marked 'Made in France' would be real sweet on Jim. The women in France must have good eyes to do that tiny cross stitch. It made Nettie blink to look at it.

There were stools before the counter and, seeing no clerk near, she sat down gingerly and swung her aching feet free of the floor. These shoes hurt her terribly. They were the right size, too. The lady she worked for last fall had given them to her and she had been delighted because they were her own number. Funny how shoes could hurt when they were the right size. Anyhow they did; the soles of her feet were like a burning fire. She sagged all over resting her tired back and arms, for though the baby was light, still carrying him made her arms cramped and stiff. Quite a pretty shawl the Charities woman had given her for him and the dress wasn't bad, only a little yellow around the neck. The bonnet was too big, though, and made his dark, tiny face look like a withered apple. Funny how such a mite of a baby could make you such a lot of pain. He slept so quietly you would almost be worried if you hadn't had babies before, thinking there was something wrong with him.

'Would you like to look at anything, madam?'

The salesgirl had come up without Nettie's seeing and her voice was icily sarcastic. Horrid little snip. Nettie got off the stool with dignity and walked away, not hurrying, to show that she was as good as anybody. Well, there was a lot ahead of her, she had better be getting on. It would be more pleasure if she weren't quite so tired and shaky but it was something to remember anyway, a real treat for anybody that was kept in so close.

The dresses and hats she had been looking forward to. But no mother of four children could get into a dress like that green one, not if her corset was as rickety as Nettie's. No hips at all to them and the models looked about seven feet tall. That blue velvet one with a cream lace vest – if that wasn't the grandest thing! Nettie's mouth opened in a kind of gape of rapture. The way the skirt swept out in deep blue folds right to the floor. You'd have to have swell slippers with diamond buckles. What would Pete say if he saw her in a dress like that. She sighed and hitched the baby upward again. He kept slipping down so, as if her arms were not strong enough to hold him.

Pete hadn't seen her look nice since the year they were married. This green and orange print she had on was faded to a bilious yellow and her red dress at home wasn't much better. Ma had told her she wouldn't have anything if she married a foreigner like Pete Samchuk. But he had such black eyes and she hadn't paid any attention to Ma. Well, he had done his best. They were on the Charities but still they were a lot better off than some. Mrs Jenkins' husband had left her and Mrs Knebel's was dead of pneumonia only last month and her with eight children and expecting again. You couldn't complain when you had your man even if he didn't earn fifty cents some weeks.

Those little hats that sat on one side of your head like a doughnut were kind of cute. For herself Nettie felt she would prefer the good old pull-down kind. The one she had on had been given to her by a lady she worked for when Dolly was a baby. It was all out of shape now, if it had ever had a shape, and was the colour of the ground, but you always knew you had it on and that it wouldn't slide off unexpectedly. May Jenkins had one of these new one-sided hats with her hair all waved where the hat wasn't. It looked cute on her but the wonder was with Mr Jenkins gone and May out of work these three months where the girl found money to pay for it. Likely there was something queer about it. Mrs Jenkins better keep an eye on her. Nettie took the elevator again.

Here were the hammocks and swings and the sight was too tempting. She slipped in cautiously among them and sat down on a huge sliding couch covered with striped denim. The baby stirred fretfully as she laid him in her lap but he did not cry. My, but it was grand to sit down a minute. Her back was one grinding pain. She lifted one burning foot off the floor and then the other. If you had a couch like this you'd have a swell garden to put it in with grass and flower beds and a shiny silver ball like the one that had been displayed in the store window. Nettie didn't know what they were for but they would look nice with the sun shining on them.

The floor walker was coming. Nettie saw him but she couldn't gather up the baby and get to her feet in time.

'It's against the rules to sit on the couches,' he said sharply.

She moved obediently away. It hadn't been much of a rest but she had as good as seen the green garden with the silver ball in the middle of it.

Groceries. That was another good place. It made you hungry, if you hadn't been hungry before, to see the piles of polished apples, the bright oranges, and pale grapefruit. Then the moist pink cuts of meat and the long marble counter ranged with cheeses and the fascinating wire the man used to cut them. And cakes iced with roses and 'happy birthday' in pink, and the crusty brown rolls. Nettie sighed and leaned against the glass case with a sudden horrible empty feeling. A girl in white was demonstrating a jelly powder, serving out portions of sparkling orange jelly in white fluted paper cups, but she pretended not to see Mrs Samchuk who lingered a little and then hunched the baby up and started on.

That potato salad looked nice now with curls of lettuce all round it and a flower on top made of bits of beet and olive. The Charities' food was all right but a body got tired of oatmeal and beans and turnips and no meat but stewing beef. The kids never liked porridge but they had to get used to it now right enough. Nettie couldn't bear the sight of it herself, but you couldn't complain, at least not to the Charities.

Should she go to the rest room and sit down a while? It would be nice but maybe she'd had enough for today. Pete would be home and the kids fussing. She took the elevator down. Her forehead was all over sweat and really if she had been that kind of a person Nettie would have thought she was going to faint. But once she got into the air she'd be all right. While she was hurrying toward a door, a dreadful thing happened. A tall, horse-faced woman in a mannish suit stood in front of her suddenly, demanding, in a loud, terrifying voice,

'How old is that baby?'

Nettie was so startled that she could only stare and mutter,

'Two weeks.'

'Two weeks! Don't you know you haven't any business to bring a baby as young as that into a place full of germs? Somebody ought to see about it. I never heard of such a thing. I don't see —'

Nettie opened her mouth to tell the woman what she thought of her for interfering with a decent, respectable person, but she felt all at once too tired, too helplessly weak to say a word. Instead she plodded around the tall woman and reached the door.

She was trembling all over. The horrible, prying woman had spoiled all her pleasure. Now she couldn't go home till she saw something nice to take the bad taste out of her mouth. And here it was, in the display window right beside her. Under a white and silver arch stood a bride with a satin train yards long and a veil, cold and cloudy white like a snowstorm. Those looked like real lilies in her hands only of course they couldn't be. Made awfully good, though, to fool a person like that. Nettie's curved arms holding the baby sagged slowly downward while she gazed. Then someone brushed against her and she sighed and hoisted the bundle to the level of her breast.

One hand fumbled for the street car ticket in the pocket of her sweater. No need to carry a purse when that was all she had. The car stop was on the other side of the street. She took her place in the crowd at the corner to wait for the green light. Her knees bent under her with weariness, but she thought that when they saw the baby someone would give her a seat in the car. The kids would be crying and she would have to hurry with their supper. Never mind. She could go on now for a while. She had had her holiday.

April 1932

FRANK H. UNDERHILL

The League for Social Reconstruction

Canada lags behind most other countries in her political thinking. But the experience of the last two years has produced a growing number of men and women, even in Canada, who have become very sceptical about the ability of our capitalistic system to produce an efficient or a happy society. Most of these sceptics are probably still more sceptical about the ability of our particular Canadian leaders in finance, industry, and politics to give us any useful guidance in our crisis. But individual critics are helpless by themselves and there exists no organization in Canada to which such men and women can attach themselves with much enthusiasm.

In the hope of helping to fill this gap a group from Toronto and Montreal held a meeting two months ago and decided to launch the League for Social Reconstruction. The founders of the League conceive of it as a kind of Canadian Fabian Society, although they are quite conscious that it does not include in its present membership any Bernard Shaw or Sidney Webb or Graham Wallas or Beatrice Potter. But they hope that it may form the nucleus around which may gather a good many of those unattached critical spirits who find no haven in either of the two national political parties, and whose circumstances do not make it possible for them to join Labour or Farmer political movements. What is most needed in Canada is a clarification of our political and economic ideas. Even if the members of the new society accomplish nothing much more than to work out by discussion among themselves the practical steps in a socialistic programme as applied to Canadian conditions, they will have served some purpose.

They hope to do more than this. It is intended to publish pamphlets on various aspects of our Canadian problems, and gradually to build up a body of information on such questions as public ownership and the social services, about which there is so much material available in England and the United States but so little in Canada. It is hoped that local branches will be formed in various centres; they are already in operation in Toronto and Montreal.

Membership in the League has been based upon the Fabian model. Active members, who have the right of voting and sharing in the decisions about policy, are required to accept the basis as set forth in the statement printed below. Associate members, who have the right of attending all meetings and receiving all publications of the Society, need only signify their general sympathy with the aims of the organization. For both classes a membership fee of two dollars per year is charged. University students may join as undergraduate associate members for a fee of fifty cents; or they may become full members if they wish, on signing the basis.

Mr J.S. Woodsworth, MP, has accepted the honorary presidency of the League. A provisional executive committee is in charge of its activities for the first year. Its members are Prof. F.R. Scott of the Faculty of Law, McGill University; Prof. King Gordon of the Union Theological College; Prof. E.A. Havelock of Victoria College, Toronto; Mr J.F. Parkinson of the Department of Political Economy, University of Toronto; and Prof. F.H. Underhill of the Department of History, University of Toronto. The secretary is Miss Isabel Thomas, 760 Spadina Ave., Toronto. The following manifesto is being issued by the League. ...

THE LEAGUE FOR SOCIAL RECONSTRUCTION

The League for Social Reconstruction is an association of men and women who are working for the establishment in Canada of a social order in which the basic principle regulating production, distribution and service will be the common good rather than private profit.

The present capitalist system has shown itself unjust and inhuman, economically wasteful, and a standing threat to peace and democratic government. Over the whole world it has led to a struggle for raw materials and markets and to a consequent international competition in armaments which were among the main causes of the last great war and which constantly threaten to bring on new wars. In the advanced industrial countries it has led to the concentration of wealth in the hands of a small irresponsible minority of bankers and industrialists whose economic power constantly threatens to nullify our political democracy. The result in Canada is a society in which the interests of farmers and of wage and salaried workers – the great majority of the population – are habitually sacrificed to those of this small minority. Despite our abundant natural resources the mass of the people have not been freed from poverty and insecurity. Unregulated competitive production condemns them to alternate periods of feverish prosperity, in which the main benefits go to speculators and profiteers, and of catastrophic depression, in which the common man's normal state of insecurity and hardship is accentuated.

We are convinced that these evils are inherent in any system in which private profit is the main stimulus to economic effort. We therefore look to the establishment in Canada of a new social order which will substitute a planned and socialized economy for the existing chaotic individualism and which, by achieving an approximate economic equality among all men in place of the present glaring inequalities, will eliminate the domination of one class by another.

As an essential first step towards the realization of this new order we advocate:

(1) *Public ownership and operation of the public utilities connected with transportation, communications, and electric power, and of such other industries as are already approaching conditions of monopolistic control.*
(2) *Nationalization of Banks and other financial institutions with a view to the regulation of all credit and investment operations.*
(3) *The further development of agricultural cooperative institutions for the production and merchandising of agricultural products.*
(4) *Social legislation to secure to the worker adequate income and leisure, freedom of association, insurance against illness, accident, old age, and unemployment, and an effective voice in the management of his industry.*
(5) *Publicly organized health, hospital, and medical services.*
(6) *A taxation policy emphasizing steeply graduated income and inheritance taxes.*
(7) *The creation of a National Planning Commission.*
(8) *The vesting in Canada of the power to amend and interpret the Canadian constitution so as to give the federal government power to control the national economic development.*
(9) *A foreign policy designed to secure international cooperation in regulating trade, industry and finance, and to promote disarmament and world peace.*

The League will work for the realization of its ideal by organizing groups to study and report on particular problems, and by issuing to the public in the form of pamphlets, articles, lectures, etc., the most accurate information obtainable about the nation's affairs in order to create an informed public opinion. It will support any political party in so far as its programme furthers the above principles; and will foster cooperation among all groups and individuals who desire in Canada the kind of social order at which the League aims.

J.F. WHITE

Socialism Without Doctrine

No really distinctive political philosophy has ever flowered on Canadian soil. That minimal quantity of theory which is required for practical purposes by our active politicians has been imported from abroad, and is the not-quite-legitimate child of British empiricism and American pragmatism. This means that the policies of our statemen have been governed by short-run considerations, and that all of our burnt offerings have been piled upon the altar of the Goddess of Expediency. It is true that some of our eclectic liberals and radicals have, from time to time, made selections from the theoretical store-houses of foreign systems, but none of these transplanted cuttings have rooted themselves very firmly in their new environment. In the period between Confederation and the early years of the present century – while our industrial system was getting well under way – some of our bolder spirits adopted the theories of early nineteenth-century liberalism. Or perhaps it would be more accurate to say that they adapted so much of the theory as seemed to be profitable, and, instead of imbibing the pure milk of free individualism, they achieved a draught of diluted, half-and-half *laissez-faire*. Of this nature was the attempt to combine the ideal of free trade with the practical policy of a tariff for revenue purposes only. The more radical principles espoused by some of our labour leaders and farmer-politicians have also been, in the main, derivative. The guiding beacons of liberty, equality, and fraternity, which had been lighted in Europe, were seized with enthusiasm, but they were sufficiently dimmed so that they would not blind our sturdy pioneer workers, who wished to keep their eyes on the main chance.

Without the guidance of any comprehensive philosophy, it is not surprising that the policies of all our political parties have been almost exclusively opportunist in character. It also explains why the boundaries between the different parties are purely imaginary and artificial boundaries. A Canadian Liberal does not need to experience any ecstatic conversion when he slips over into the Tory fold, and he is not required to pocket any of his principles, because he did not have any principles to begin with. And, of course, this lack of equipment will not in any way embarrass him in his new environment. As with political parties, so with the individual politician. No course has been charted for him and he is therefore able, with perfect consistency, to follow his selfish, immediate, individual and class interests. For the members of the two old parties, which have the common interest of supporting the *status quo*, this is a completely satisfactory state of affairs. They have no wish to make any changes in the system; their one desire is to keep things as they are; but as perfect equilibrium is impossible they see to it that any requisite concessions to the great mass of the people are put into effect as gradually and grudgingly as possible. As the social and economic relationships of society are bound up in a net-work of legal devices, a large proportion of our stand-pat Members of Parliament are necessarily barristers and solicitors.

For our agricultural and labour politicians – whether they carry their banners of protest into the legislative halls, or operate in the more circumscribed regions of lodge-rooms and trades organizations – the path is not so easy. They represent the dissatisfied and unreasonable classes of society who are always demanding an economic return that is not compatible with a perfectly stable system. Pressure from below is constantly forcing these leaders into uncomfortable positions. However, even in these unfortunate situations, the absence of logical formulas is a very present help in time of trouble. They become past masters in the art of confusing the issue, of blunting the edges of criticism, and turning the torrent of revolt into impotent eddies. In return for these services the more efficient and clamorous leaders are rewarded, in due course, by the governing class, which provides them with comfortable positions to which they are permitted to retire. Any historical study of farm and labour movements in Canada will reveal a perfect apostolic succession of leaders who have graduated out of their class into that of the upper levels of the bureaucracy.

As the labels of the political parties are quite meaningless it is not to be expected that there should be any consistency or continuity in their policies. There is nothing really paradoxical in the fact that the Liberal Government of Quebec is the most conservative administration in Canada, except for those deluded people who believe that Canadian Liberalism bears some relation to the English Liberal party of the nineteenth century, nor is it a matter for any astonishment that Conservative governments in Ontario have been more addicted to 'socialist' legislation than the 'progressive' governments of Manitoba and Alberta. It is interesting to observe, however, that the Western Provinces, where there has been, for some time, a strong inclination towards state control of public utilities, have achieved very little along these lines, whereas cautious conservative Ontario has taken the lead in experimenting with Government Ownership.

There is at present no sound theoretical basis for state socialism in Canada. In the case of an important institution such as the Canadian National Railways, this was not socialized because anyone believed in the principle of state ownership and operation of railways, but because it was in the interests of the original owners to have their property taken over by the government, rather than allow it to fall into the hands of a receiver. Most of the smaller experiments in government ownership fall into the same category. They were acquired by the state or by one of the municipalities because they could not be exploited with advantage by private capital. The Ontario Hydro-Electric System is the one important exception to the rule, and perhaps it should be regarded as a historical accident.

Some of our uncritical idealists have written and spoken with great fervour of the tremendous accomplishments in public ownership that have been made in this country. One might gather from these effusions that this Dominion is well on the way to becoming a socialist Utopia. The stranger to our shores may arrive on a government liner, land at a government wharf, and have his baggage carried by a government official to an observation car on a state-owned railway. Arriving at one of our large cities he may take a tour of inspection in a publicly-owned street-car or sight-seeing bus, change his money at a provincial savings bank, and return to lunch at a state hotel, where he may be served with a chop from a lamb which had recently been despatched, in the most efficient and social manner, at a municipal abbattoir.

There are quite a number of our reformers who seem to assume that this process will be extended indefinitely, and that without any struggle or effort the greater part of production and distribution will be socialized, and that we shall pass, pleasantly and painlessly, from a competitive order into a cooperative society.

Unfortunately there are indications that this easy process may be rudely interrupted. There have recently been signs of a turn in the tide, and it seems possible that a process of denationalization is under way. The sudden and unexpected collapse of the Manitoba Savings Bank points to the weakness of the foundations upon which our whole system of government ownership rests. Revelations have been made of the methods by which the Ontario Hydro has been milked by predatory interests, and the new policy of purchasing large blocks of power from privately owned power companies, instead of developing its own power sites, suggests that in the near future private capitalism may get most of the cream and leave the Hydro nothing but a very diluted form of skim milk. Violent attacks have been made on the Canadian National Railways, in the last year or two, both in the House of Commons and in certain sections of the press, and, whatever may be the recommendations of the Commission which is now sitting on this institution, it may safely be assumed that no action will be taken which will enlarge the scope of our state railways.

The late Professor Mavor, in his book *Niagara in Politics*, spoke of government ownership, such as we have it in Canada, as 'socialism without doctrine.' Professor Mavor thought that there was something particularly dangerous and insidious about this practice of socializing industry on the grounds – not of principle – but of political expediency. He seemed to fear that the state might be surreptitiously bolshevized, without any of us realizing what it was all about. There appeared to be a danger that we might wake up some bright morning and find that we had inadvertently planted the red flag over all our government buildings, confiscated all our private capital, and nationalized all our women.

This danger seems to have passed. What needs to be stressed now is the reverse side of this argument, the weakness of government ownership without principle, of socialism without doctrine. In Western Canada the sentiment in favour of cooperation – of collective ownership in place of private – is spreading and is finding some organizational form. In the East, the majority of people who have experienced some form of government ownership regard it favourably, and would like to see it extended. But there is no organized body of public opinion behind it, and unless it finds political expression in the near future the public may find that the only valuable institutions that it really owns are the poor-houses and the penitentiaries.

J.F. WHITE

Deportations

The lot of the foreigner in Canada, in this, the third year of the great depression, is not a happy one. Prior to 1929, for thirty or forty years, the Immigration Department extended a welcoming hand to all the peoples of Europe, and hundreds of thousands of immigrants poured into this country with high hopes of making a new start in life, of finding in this new and freer land greater opportunities for progress, and prospects of a better livelihood. In those expansive days Canada needed the foreign worker. Millions of acres of good farming land were waiting for the plough, labourers were required for the construction of public works, railways, and canals, and the new industrial system needed wage-slaves to groom and feed the hungry machines. There was a tendency, particularly in the larger cities, for the native-born Canadian to turn his back on any kind of manual labour – with the exception of a few highly-skilled and well-paid occupations – and to become a member of the white-collar classes. Rough and unskilled labour was all right for the foreigner, but it was not good enough for any native Nordic who was possessed of average intelligence and ambition. Being an intensively individualistic people, only one generation removed from the pioneer stage, it is scarcely surprising that Canadians feel very little sense of collective responsibility towards the newcomers who have taken on their shoulders much of the heavy work of developing our natural resources. In prosperous times, when there are plenty of jobs to go around, they are tolerated, and are addressed – in a patronizing way – as 'New Canadians.' When times are hard, and the native is forced by economic pressure to compete with the immigrant for any kind of work – including the pick and shovel jobs – then he is treated as foreigners always have been treated, in all times and in all places, with a complete lack of consideration. Then he becomes a 'Dirty Wop,' a 'Hunky,' or a 'Dago,' and is regarded as an interloper who is trying to take the bread out of the honest mouths of our Native Sons. Naturally there are members of the employing class who are not slow to utilize these racial enmities for the purpose of keeping the workers divided among themselves, so that they may be able to play off one group against the other.

In the early colonial days there were very few restrictions on immigration. But as the Dominions secured greater and greater measures of autonomy the rules which regulated the admission of immigrants became more strict, in spite of continued political pressure on the part of the transportation companies, who were naturally anxious to have as free a hand as possible. In recent years only favoured classes were admitted, and intending immigrants were required to undergo medical examinations before being permitted to sail for Canada. Individuals who had known criminal records, who suffered from certain communicable diseases or deformities, professional prostitutes, or those who were likely to become a public charge were denied entrance. These restrictions are all very well, as it is obvious that no country can afford to establish a sanctuary for all the criminal and anti-social elements in the world. But, after examining, questioning, and finally admitting a foreigner, on the assumption that he meets all our requirements, there is certainly an obligation on our part to accept him as a potential citizen, and he should not be subject to discrimination on account of foreign birth. Instead of this, our official policy is to regard the foreign-born as being here only on sufferance. If, at any time, an immigrant is guilty of any infraction of our laws – and naturally the foreigner is less familiar with our criminal code than the native-born citizen – or is suspected of belonging to an illegal organization, or becomes an inmate of a house of prostitution, or is guilty of the supreme crime of poverty, then he, or she, is liable to deportation. This means that the foreigner is subject to a double penalty if found guilty of breaking the law. Some Canadians, who, by the mercy of Providence, have been permitted to be born in this country, also run foul of the law and become thieves, prostitutes, or members of the unemployed, and – if they are caught at it – they pay the prescribed penalty. A certain percentage of immigrants, living in the same environment, follow the same course; but in their case, after the law has exacted the usual punishment, they are turned over to the Department of Immigration and shipped home to their native land. To argue that this is not an additional punishment is absurd. Moreover, there is no dead-line in time beyond which the immigrant is safe. Two or three years ago Mr J.S. Woodsworth tried to get the Federal House to accept an amendment to the Immigration Act, which would provide that after an immigrant had been ten years in this country he would no longer be subject to deportation. Even such a mild and obviously reasonable provision was turned down cold by the House.

According to the *Canada Year Book*, in the twenty-five years between 1903 and 1928, 27,660 immigrants were deported from Canada, and since the beginning of the depression in 1929 these proceedings have been greatly accelerated, more than 7,000 people having been deported in 1931 alone. The reasons for deportation in the 1903-28 period are given as follows: Medical causes 6,977, Public Charges 9,978, Criminality 7,429, Other Civil Causes 2,069, and Accompanying Deported Persons 1,207. According to nationalities, the deportees were: British 14,700, American 7,348, and Other Countries 5,612. Before, and during the War, the numbers were comparatively small, but since 1922 there has not been a year in which less than fifteen hundred people were deported. From the above figures it is clear that more stress is placed upon economic considerations than upon ethnic origins, as the majority of our discards have been of British stock. It is equally plain that the most serious crime that an immigrant can commit is the negative one of failing to 'make good,' as nearly two-fifths of the cases were those of people who had become a 'public charge.' Our immigration officials would probably agree with Mr Bernard Shaw when he says that the supreme crime is that of poverty, although Mr Shaw and the officials would hardly agree as to whether the blame for this condition should rest upon the individual or upon society as a whole. To some degree the foreigner is in a better position than the British-born immigrant, as the foreigner can become a naturalized Canadian, whereas a settler from Great Britain does not need to take out naturalization papers. But even this protection is relative rather than absolute, as provision is made for the cancellation of certificates. The Hon. W.A. Gordon, Minister of Immigration and Colonization, replied to a question at the last session of Parliament, as follows:

I have not before me any detailed information with respect to the question asked by the hon. member, but I can say that the act certainly provides for the cancellation of naturalization certificates in cases where these certificates should be cancelled. I believe that there have been a number of cancellations; if there have not, there should have been.

On May 6th, 1932, in answer to another question in the House (Hansard, p. 281), Mr Gordon gave some information about the boards of inquiry which deal with these deportation cases. He was asked if any specific charge had to be laid against individuals before they are compelled to appear before the board. Mr Gordon replied:

No charge as such is contemplated by the act. A complaint is made to an officer who as defined by the act, may include the municipal clerk of a village, town, or city, an officer of the department, or a peace officer. A complaint is made and then the inquiry is set on foot. After the case is heard pro and con, a report is made to the minister, and if in the minister's judgement the board of inquiry has come to a proper conclusion, and if the person whose case is being investigated, has rendered himself liable, under the provisions of the statute, to being returned to his country of origin, appropriate action is taken.

As the board of inquiry is held, in many cases at the port of embarcation, this means that the investigation may be held hundreds of miles from the place where the immigrant has been living. Under such conditions the cards are plainly stacked against the individual under investigation, from the start. He may be picked up by Mounted Police officers in Winnipeg, or in some small town in Ontario, and rushed to Halifax, without any opportunity to see his friends or relatives, or make any disposition of his personal affairs. But he is not under arrest, he is merely in detention!

During the recent election campaign in the constituency of West York, the Premier of Ontario, Hon. George S. Henry, in answer to a heckler, replied: 'No man will be deported from this country so long as he behaves himself.' (*Mail and Empire*, May 27). Unfortunately for Tory consistency, the *Mail and Empire* published a despatch from Ottawa, which appeared three days later. It ran as follows:

No particular significance is attached to the proposed deportation of 37 foreigners from Kitchener, ordered by an immigration board of inquiry, it was learned at the Department of Immigration here. The same thing was taking place in many municipalities throughout Canada, it was stated, and such cases became more frequent in times of unemployment.

So far as the two old political parties are concerned, there is not much to choose between them, as regards their attitude on the subject of deportations. The present Immigration Act was revised in 1927, when the Liberals were in power, but all its more inhumane provisions were retained. On the other hand the Conservative party, since it has been in office has been much more active in deporting aliens – but this may be merely incidental to the depression. Deportation is one of the weapons of the class struggle, and will be used more and more as this struggle becomes sharper. It is a club held over the heads of the foreign-born worker, in an attempt to keep him docile. It is also used to discourage the unemployed immigrant from applying for relief. It will probably remain until the Canadian workers greatly strengthen their political and industrial organizations.

August 1932

A.M. KLEIN

Soirée of Velvel Kleinburger

In back-room dens of delicatessen stores,
In curtained parlours of garrulous barber-
   shops,
While the rest of the world most comfortably
   snores

August 1932

On mattresses, or on more fleshly props,
My brother Velvel vigils in the night,
Not as he did last night with two French whores,
But with a deck of cards that once were white ...

He sees three wan ghosts, as the thick smoke fades
Dealing him clubs and diamonds, hearts and spades ...

His fingers, pricked with a tailor's needle, draw
The well-thumbed cards; while Hope weighs down his jaw.
    O for the ten spade in its proper place,
      Followed by knave in linen lace,
        The queen with her gaunt face,
          The king and mace,
            The ace! ...
Alas, that Velvel's sign makes eddies in the smoke.
For what's the use?
While the pale faces grin, his brow is hot:
He grasps a deuce ...

A nicotined hand beyond the smoke sweeps off the pot.

O good my brother, should one come to you
And knock upon the door at mid of night
And show you, writ in scripture, black on white,
That this is no way for a man to do? –
What a pale laughter from these ghosts, and 'Who
Are you, my saint, to show us what is right?
Make a fifth hand, and we will be contrite;
Shuffle the cards, be sociable, Reb Jew.'
Then Velvel adds a foot-note to his hoax:
I will not have your wherefores and your buts;
For I am for the Joker and his jokes;
I laugh at your alases and tut-tuts,
My days, they vanish into circular smokes,
My life lies on a tray of cigarette-butts ...

For it is easy to send pulpit wind
From bellies sumptuously lined;
Easy to praise the sleep of the righteous, when
The righteous sleep on cushions ten,
And having risen from a well-fed wife
Easy it is to give advice on life ...
But you who upon sated palates clack a moral,
And pick a sermon from between your teeth,
Tell me with what bay, tell me with what laurel
Shall I entwine the heaven-praising wreath,
I, with whom Deity sets out to quarrel?

But prithee, wherefore these thumbed cards?

O do not make a pack of cards your thesis
And frame no lesson on a house of cards
Where diamonds go lustreless, and hearts go broken
And clubs do batter the skull to little shards,
And where, because the spade is trump
One must perforce kiss Satan's rump ...

For I have heard these things from teachers
With dirty beards and hungry features ...

Now, after days in dusty factories,
Among machines that manufacture madness
I have no stomach for these subtleties
About rewards and everlasting gladness;
And having met your over-rated dawns,
Together with milkmen watering their milk,
And having trickled sweat, according to a scale of wages,
Sewing buttons to warm the navels of your business sages,
I have brought home at dusk,
My several bones, my much-flailed husk ...

    My meals are grand,
    When supper comes
    I feed on canned
    Aquariums.
    The salmon dies.
    The evening waits
    As I catch flies
    From unwashed plates.

    And my true love,
    She combs and combs,
    The lice from off
    My children's domes ...

Such is the idyll of my life.
But I will yet achieve
An easier living and less scrawny wife
And not forever will the foreman have
The aces up his sleeve,
But some day I will place the lucky bet.
(Ho! Ho! the social revolutions on a table of roulette!)

My brother's gesture snaps: I spoke.
His cheeks seek refuge in his mouth.
His nostrils puff superior smoke.
His lips are brown with drouth.

Hum a hymn of sixpence,
A tableful of cards
Fingers slowly shuffling
Ambiguous rewards.
When the deck is opened
The pauper once more gave
His foes the kings and aces
And took himself the knave.

Once more he cuts the cards, and dreams his dream:
A Rolls-Royce hums within his brain;
Before it stands a chauffeur, tipping his hat,
'You say that it will rain, Sir; it will rain!'
Upon his fingers diamonds gleam,
His wife wears gowns of ultra-Paris fashion,
And she boasts jewels as large as wondrous eyes
The eyes of Og, the giant-king of Bashan.

So Velvel dreams; dreaming, he rises, and
Buttons his coat, coughs in his raised lapel,
Gropes his way home; he rings a raucous bell.

FRANK H. UNDERHILL

The Cooperative Commonwealth Federation

Amid the columns of drivel which they wasted over the Imperial Conference our Canadian daily papers were able to spare only a few paragraphs to announce the developments that took place in the farmer and labour movements of Western Canada during July and the early part of August. But one takes no risks in prophesying that what happened in Calgary and Saskatoon will have a much more important bearing upon our national future than all the well-advertised theatrical performances at Ottawa in August.

On June 30 a meeting of the Executives of the United Farmers and Farm Women's organizations of Alberta, along with members of the Provincial Cabinet and private members in the local legislature and in the federal House at Ottawa, issued a manifesto proposing joint action on a Dominion-wide scale of all organizations interested in an advanced social and political programme in Canada. The manifesto with their proposed programme of ten points, which bears a marked resemblance to the programme of the League for Social Reconstruction, was printed in last month's issue of *The Canadian Forum*.

On July 27 the United Farmers of Canada, Saskatchewan Section, and the Independent Labour Party of Saskatchewan met together in Saskatoon, after two days of separate sessions, and agreed to unite in a joint farmer-labour movement in the province, with Mr M.J. Coldwell, teacher and alderman of Regina, as their leader. Each body retains its separate identity, but they will campaign together upon a common platform. In the forefront of their programme they put a planned system of social economy; socialization of banking and finance; social ownership and operation of public utilities and natural resources; social legislation to secure the worker adequate income and leisure, freedom of association, insurance against illness, accident, old age and unemployment, and an effective voice in the management of his industry; and immediate security to the worker in his home and the farmer in his land, with substitution of a use-hold system of tenure for the present insecurity.

On August 1, the Alberta and Saskatchewan bodies met in Calgary with representatives from the Independent Labour party of Manitoba, the Canadian Brotherhood of Railway Employees and the League for Social Reconstruction, and formed the Cooperative Commonwealth Federation. Mr J.S. Woodsworth, MP of Winnipeg was chosen as their leader and Mr Norman Priestly, vice-president of the UFA, as secretary. The new Federation will welcome to its membership all labour, farmer, and other organizations accepting its principles, and it hopes to act as the nucleus for a nation-wide political movement with membership in every province. A provisional Dominion Council has been set up with power to add to its numbers, and there is also to be a council for each province.

The programme of the Federation is contained in eight points:

1. The establishment of a planned system of social economy for the production, distribution and exchange of all goods and services.
2. Socialization of the banking credit and financial system of the country together with the social ownership, development, operation and control of utilities and natural resources.

August 1932

3. *Security and tenure of the worker and farmer in his home.*
4. *Retention and extension of all existing social legislation and facilities with adequate provision for insurance against crop failure, illness, accident, old age and unemployment.*
5. *Equal economic and social opportunity without regard to sex, nationality or religion.*
6. *The encouragement of all cooperative enterprises which are steps toward the achievement of the Cooperative Commonwealth.*
7. *Socialization of health services.*
8. *Federal government should accept responsibility for unemployed and supply suitable work or adequate maintenance.*

This new political movement is much more than a mere revival of the great emotional upheaval which swept the prairies and Ontario in 1921. The sixty-odd 'progressive' members who came to Ottawa in that year spent the next few years quarreling as to whether they represented a separate movement or merely the left-wing of the Liberal party, which as usual ceased to be a movement once it had got into office. They were gradually weeded out by successive elections and by the blandishments of Mr King until there was left only the handful who made up the cooperating independent groups of 1926-30 and of the present parliament. But Mr Woodsworth, Mr Gardiner, and their associates have learnt through this ten years experience the technique of cooperation among autonomous groups in Parliament. The UFA, the only branch of the farmer movement which survived as an effective political force, has worked out a method of combining constituency autonomy with group solidarity, local initiative with central direction, which no doubt is not perfect but does achieve the most complete and real democracy that we have yet seen in Canadian politics. And the men and women who have lived through this experience since 1921 start the new movement in 1932 without any mental reservations in their determination to keep clear of the old political parties. They have also, as the result of ten years of feverish boom and catastrophic depression, worked out a clear-cut programme of socialism as applied to Canadian conditions; and they know what their words mean.

The main difficulty which faces the Federation at the moment is that its membership so far is confined largely to the prairie provinces. Undoubtedly its founders are proceeding along the right lines in emphasizing its character as a federation of autonomous units, each unit based on economic function. No new third party movement will get anywhere in these days if it remains a mere unorganized mass democracy; sooner or later it will be betrayed by its leaders if it doesn't disintegrate of itself when the fine wave of emotion has passed. It is equally true, however, that the weakness of the independent cooperating groups at Ottawa has been that they seemed to be, and could be represented by opponents as being, mere local sectional factions without a truly national appeal. The new movement must attract membership from the East.

And even in Ontario and Quebec things seem to be stirring. The farmer pilgrimage to Ottawa from the two central provinces for the purpose of presenting their demands to Mr Bennett on the occasion of the Imperial Conference is an encouraging sign. The UFO seemed suddenly to come to life, and equally startling was the spectacle of French and English farmers cooperating and fraternising in an economic programme. But we had perhaps better remind ourselves that if the UFO really came to life again and if citizens of Ontario and Quebec (other than Prime Ministers and electric-power barons) really cooperated, two miracles would have been accomplished at once. As for Canadian labour, the energy which its various factions spend in fighting one another would suffice for several social revolutions; in the meantime most of them vote Liberal or Conservative.

The other difficulty which will face the Federation as election time draws near will be the old appeal from Liberal headquarters for the union of all the 'forward-looking' elements against Toryism. Already Liberal interpreters have been drawing the orthodox soothing interpretation from the success of the Bracken coalition in Manitoba. It is sad to see the *Farmers Sun* of Toronto among them. People who were not convinced by the experience of 1921-1930 that the only thing to which a Liberal party under Mr King's mealy-mouthed leadership is looking forward is office, are simply too good for this world. The timidity of Mr King, which allowed Mr Bennett to steal the glory of taking the proper course upon both radio and the St Lawrence Waterway, was a sufficient revelation of his quality as a forward-looking statesman. All Canadian citizens who want a government that will seriously face the momentous social crisis in the midst of which we live should use their energies on behalf of the Cooperative Commonwealth Federation.

RAYMOND KNISTER
Three Poems

Boy Remembers in the Field

What if the sun comes out
And the new furrows do not look smeared?

This is April, and the sumach candles
Have guttered long ago.
The crows in the twisted apple limbs
Are as moveless and dark.

Drops on the wires, cold cheeks,
The mist, the long snorts, silence ...
The horses will steam when the sun comes;
Crows, go, shrieking.

Another bird now; sweet ...
Pitiful life, useless,
Innocently creeping
On a useless planet
Again.

If any voice called, I would hear?
It has been the same before.
Soil glistens, the furrow rolls, sleet shifts,
    brightens.

The Plowman

All day I follow
Watching the swift dark furrow
That curls away before me,
And care not for skies or upturned flowers,
And at the end of the field
Look backward
Ever with discontent.
A stone, a root, a strayed thought
Has warped the line of that furrow –
And urge my horses round again.

Sometimes even before the row is finished
I must look backward;
To find, when I come to the end
That there I swerved.

Unappeased I leave the field,
Expectant, I return.

The horses are very patient.
When I tell myself
This time
The ultimate unflawed turning
Is before my share,
They must give up their rest.

The Hawk

Across the bristled and sallow fields,
The speckled stubble of cut clover,
Wades your shadow.

Or against a grimy and tattered
Sky
You plunge.

Or you shear a swath
From trembling tiny forests
With the steel of your wing –

Or make a row of waves
By the heat of your flight
Along the soundless horizon.

FRANK H. UNDERHILL
Canada and War

It is now taken for granted by nearly everybody that the collective system of maintaining peaceful international relations has broken down and that the world has begun the slow drift into another imperialist war. The only persons who profess to be still fully confident in the League machinery are those who have done the most to defeat and frustrate the aspirations with which the League was started – that is, of course, the governments of Britain and France. Canadians, who were involved in one European war without having the slightest idea of what it was all about, must now ask themselves what they are going to do in the present threat of another collapse of Europe into barbarism.

The post-war British Commonwealth has developed a loose decentralized organization on the hypothesis that ultimate questions of peace and war did not need to be faced. Each nation has been more and more running its own affairs; and, while they have all professed to be devoted to certain common interests, they have carefully avoided defining what those common interests are – from a shrewd suspicion that most of these interests would disappear into thin air as soon as an attempt was made to weigh or measure them. There has been some tendency since the Statute of Westminster to declare that common economic interests are the basis of our union and that the Commonwealth must consolidate its economic bonds now that political and legal bonds have been abolished. But, as Professor Coupland remarked in one of his lectures at Toronto the other day, if it be true that the continuance of the Commonwealth depends upon its economic ties, then the Ottawa Conference begins to look perilously like the Boston Tea Party of the Third British Empire. The fact is that it is impossible to point to any interests which the British nations have in common which are not also interests that they have in common with the rest of the world.

But skilful propaganda is already under way to suggest to us that we must draw closer to the other British nations for the protection of our common civilization. It is not yet quite clear who the common enemy is, but that will emerge in due course. We have already had Lord Lothian as a missionary from England preaching this gospel and we are, no doubt, in for a stream of English missionaries like him. They will all be individuals of the most perfect gentility and they will all present a beautiful idealized picture of British liberal imperialism. They will all stress its fundamentally peaceful aims. They will assure us that Canada cannot remain aloof from Europe and that we will inevitably be affected by what happens there. Anyone who is interested in historical parallels need only look up the speeches of the imperial missionaries of the pre-war decade – Earl Grey, Lord Milner, Mr Lionel Curtis, and their friends. We shall be hearing the same speeches again in the 1930s. In fact, the Round Table movement, which supplied the main impetus to the pre-war drive, has since the war been reincarnated as the Royal Institute of International Affairs and has its Canadian branches consisting of a carefully selected group of the best people in each of our main cities. The Universities are the chosen field for this preliminary propaganda; their historians and lawyers and economists are so useful after a war has broken out in proving that we are fighting for the loftiest ideals. For let there be no mistake about it. What we are being invited to cooperate in by these English missionaries is another war in Europe. And English liberals are always much more effective in this missionary work in the Dominions than are the more swash buckling tories.

It is true that Canada cannot divest herself of interest in Europe. Great Britain and the continent absorb over forty per cent of our exports. We stand to suffer severely if the continent drifts into anarchy. But it does not follow that we have any interest in sacrificing 60,000 more Canadians for the sake of some entanglements in which Great Britain may have been involved by a Simon or a Chamberlain. Of course, the government of which Sir John Simon is so distinguished an ornament is profoundly peaceful in its aspirations. So was the government which had Sir Edward Grey as its Foreign Secretary. But we must let them know in unmistakable terms that the poppies blooming in Flanders Fields have no more attraction for us. If the peoples of Europe cannot settle their own affairs our experience since 1914 has made it abundantly clear that no intervention of Canadians can assist them to any settlement that will be reasonable or permanent.

It is not likely, however, that an attitude of mere aloof nationalism will be sufficient to keep us out of war entanglements once the propaganda of sentimental imperialism gets going at full force. The men who control Canada at present are practically all men who made their pile out of the last war. They were well started on the way to wealth and power in the land and railway boom of the first decade of the century, but it was the war that really brought them into their present position of domination in our financial and industrial institutions. They will be quite willing to preach war to us from the point of view of a proud, self-reliant nationalism and they will find plenty of newspaper editors to assist them. It therefore behoves all Canadians who sincerely believe in peace to set themselves to expose the causes out of which wars really arise. They will not find much help from the University professors. But they may find masses of unexpected allies in the University undergraduates, who have begun to pass resolutions that they will in no circumstances fight for their King and Country. As Professor Coupland remarked in the lecture from which I have already quoted, this resolution of the Oxford Union is only the young men's sincere way of saying what the old men, their rulers, said insincerely in the Kellogg Pact.

LEO KENNEDY
Archibald Lampman

Archibald Lampman shares with Canada's few other talented poets, and most of her untalented ones, the ill-luck to have been written about in terms of excessive nonsense. If his position in what the incautious are pleased to call Canadian literature is falsified, if a four-square evaluation of his work is as yet unforthcoming, the fault may be only partly laid to the poet himself. The chief offenders have been those well-meaning but over-biased friends of Lampman who have permitted themselves hearty splurges into adulatory print, and the leisured, patriotic persons whose self-appointed task it is to create legendary beings and national figures.

For that matter, as long as Canadian writers continue to contract for each other's washing, the critical truth about Canadian literature will be very hard to come by. Whether D.C. Scott and Archibald Lampman scratch each other's backs in '99, or A.M. Klein and Leo Kennedy pick fleas off each other in '33, the principle remains uncomfortably the same, though the phrasing of the interred generation with its coy cupidons and floral fixings, has assumed latter-day roughneck characteristics.

But because the convention has it that talent is discovered, not born, because an artist's intimates are usually most eager and liable, though possibly least qualified, to summarize his ability, this problem of log-rolling presents a quite embarassing dilemma. As literary values are disruptingly relative at best, and as Canadian criticism is too dependent on digestion and similar unliterary influences (Mr Stephen Elyot's excellent essay 'Science and Criticism' has made this painfully clear), the honest sceptic can only hope that the generation-after-next will estimate his contemporary with unfalsified weights. Though these as yet unlicensed critics in their turn may be reactionarily spleened and bigoted in a way that will reflect credit on their predecessors' urbanity. ...

It is all very puzzling.

And it does not help poor Lampman much. Nevertheless, it is a detailed way of saying that the rash panegyrics of 'Canada's Great Poet of Nature,' i.e., Archibald Lampman, may be no more outrageous than today's increasing arguments for his demotion, nor than the restorative monographs which a more obliging posterity will write on him in 1966, when tastes and fashions in poetry undergo another scheduled, cyclic revolution.

Archibald Lampman then – to resume loosened ends – has been too long and too loudly publicized as John Keats' little Canadian brother, with literary kinship to Wordsworth on the tedious side. He has been piously elevated for his idealism, and endlessly whooped for his cinematographic studies of nature. Excessive copy has been made of the fact that he hailed indirectly from the Maritimes – Canada's cradle of literary humanity – and issued from strictly Royalist stock. Like the late Bliss Carman, his name and work have been seized upon by patriotic women's groups, hot for national cultural advancement at any cost. Individuals who appear to have read no literature, but who pronounce the phrase 'Canadian literature' as so much efficacious abracadabra, have made great hay by reading singularly ill-chosen sonnets from *Lyrics of Earth* at writers' clubs, mothers' meetings, and as entree between the soup and roast at business men's boost rallies. In brief, he has been much ill used.

And yet, as implied above, not altogether without blame. For the legendary figure of Lampman, made in the image and likeness of the conventional 'poet' of the last century, a hater of cities, crowds, etc., a worshipper of nature, an advocate of extremely simple living and very high ideals, a solitary dreamer of dreams which are never defined or described ... in short, a seclusive, paranoiac person ... this figure, I say, has been aided and abetted by Lampman himself in poems. The posture has unfortunate connotations, since it is usually accompanied by poetic vapidity. It is invariably found in the opera of the open-road-and-space cult of Canadian versifiers. It is sham-heroic and unadmirable. And it was the dominant note in our poetry up till a couple of decades ago.

What are the qualities of this insularity? It is exemplified by intellectual sterility; a lack of interest in contemporary activity and development; and an unwillingness to make contacts outside of the immediate, provincial little sphere.

These are not in themselves disqualifications to pure poetry, nor are they beyond the personal privilege of a poet. He may write enduring verse with no preoccupations other than those three cardinal staples of the poet's repertoire, love, life, and death. He may live through a revolution of blood and rapine, and write only pastorals, yet be well within his rights. He may, if he cares to, perch on a boulder of Ararat like some inhospitable Noah, oblivious of his contemporaries and their efforts at creative salvation. But he must bring to his work some compensatory qualities.

If a poet is to limit his subject matter to one or two bald and unforgettable truisms, that we live, for example, and that we die, he must be able to contribute his own acceptable variations on these themes. If, as in the case of Lampman, he concentrates mainly on the phenomena of nature, it is not enough to see them with sobriety and poeticalness. He must wring out a meaning that is both personal and universal. Then, for a poet to lack active social virtue may be felicitous and even wise. It does not presume in him less virtue than is discovered in those writers who have a social outlook, and who do not withdraw themselves from current movements and remediable wrongs. But it does presume that he has within himself a sufficiency of strength, vision, and emotional depth. In fine, the narrower the scope he permits himself, the stronger must be his intensity, the more profound his feeling, the greater his ability to communicate his findings.

I am not abusing Lampman because his ideas were commonplace. I am not taking him to task because his verse does not reflect Canadian politics of the '90s. I am not indignant because his sonnets give no intimation that he ever heard of his European contemporaries, of the dazzling, decadent yellow book crew, nor of the Americans, Markham, Lizette Woodworth Reese, and great Walt of Brooklyn, yawping a few miles to the south. But I do say that, since his own personal aesthetic contribution was insufficient for the purposes of art, he should have broadened his canvas, and borrowed from sources that would have benefitted him more.

Lampman's biographers and commentators insist that his vocation was to sing the new country, the new-found land, and on this point if on few others, his work endorses their claims. Yet no one in his senses can say that an apprenticeship to Keats and Wordsworth was the right foundation for such a task.

Norman Gregor Guthrie in his essay *The Poetry of Archibald Lampman* (Musson, Toronto) says that, 'Lampman apparently believed himself in some sense a re-incarnation of the spirit of Keats.' That is a tall statement for any literary ostrich to bolt, though quite in line with the hard things that have been written about Lampman. If this is true, it may explain why the poet developed the Keats strain to the exclusion of others which are found in his poetry, and which are more sympathetic to his own talent. The austerity of Arnold, which appears to have swayed him for a time, is surely more in keeping with the man's reserved character, puritan background, and creative sparseness, than the riotous efflorescence of Keats' imagination; though Arnold, too, is no mentor for a pioneer.

Lampman described natural phenomena with graceful realism. He made trim little etchings of snowscapes, crows in flight, and hepaticas in season, with a skill that points to accurate observation and a sharp sympathy for such things. His knowledge of Canadian flora was acquired in no naturalist's handbook or seed catalogue; he knew and deeply loved the seasons' manifestations. No other Canadian poet has described the country scene with such meticulous detail, but for all his careful observation, little in the form of an emotional climax comes out of it. The late Raymond Knister in a few scattered poems of a few scattered impressions could catch the very spirit of his cornfield or plough land, yet use the minimum of data. For a fair analogy, consider the rural Quebec scenes of Krieghoff beside the landscapes of Morrice.

Lampman wrote in the poetic diction laid down by the second generation poets of the Romantic Revival, a diction with which we today are wholly out of touch and sympathy. It exposes the essential weakness of his verse. Stock abstractions such as beauty, sorrow, despondency, truth, freedom, avarice, and unrest set him off on rhetorical sprees, from which he returned, a little shamefacedly, I hope, to write the simple, honest, thumbnail sketches about snowbirds, timothy, orchards, and song sparrows that he really understood and cared about. His devotion to the rag-tags of the poet's dictionary – the methinks, los, o'ers, bemoans, gats, the second person singular, begones, yesternights and yestereves – is dispiriting and trying.

His preoccupation with a very ridiculous concept of the poet's place in the scheme of things is really laughable. Again and again in the collected poems he suggests that the poet is a vague, witless creature who engages himself in an intolerable amount of dreaming:

Wrapped round with thought, content to watch and dream.

Beyond the tumult of the mills,
  And all the city's sound and strife,
Beyond the waste, beyond the hills,
I look far out and dream of life.

For me the dreamer 'tis enough to know
  The lyric stress ...

One could go on indefinitely. The following quotation, frequently produced as evidence of Lampman's excellence, amply illustrates a number of my charges: it is addressed to *Night*:

Come with thine unveiled worlds, O truth of night,
  Come with thy calm, Adown the shallow day,
  Whose splendours hid the vaster world away,
I wandered on this little plot of light,
  A dreamer among dreams.

This 'dreamer' business has been hailed to high heaven by Comrade Guthrie.

Yet Lampman has, at times, a felicity of phrasing, and a mild flutter of genuine emotion is startled here and there.

And the current generation of Canadian poets, of whom I am a hobbling member, has chucked him out, neck, crop, and rhyming dictionary. Our quarrel is, perhaps, not so much with Lampman as with his time and poetic tradition. The pot-bellied, serene Protestantism of Victorian England which still flourished in Canada during the spruce youth of Edward, and which underlay Lampman's spiritual make-up, causes us to chafe. We are impatient of reading into the face of nature the conservative policies of an Anglican omnipotence. We are principally concerned with the poetry of ideas and emotional conflicts. We have detected, as the Lampmans do not appear to have done, that all is decidedly not right with the world; we suspect that God is not in his Heaven. Uncertain of ourselves, distressed by our inability to clarify our relationship to these and comparative issues, we do not feel superior to circumstances at all.

That is, doubtless, a reason why we reject Lampman and his fellows as exponents of a second-hand poetic inheritance which does not stand the harsh light of our day. Why we are irritated beyond good manners by their acceptance of a too-glib philosophy. Why we are over prone to greet the versified manifestations of both inheritance and outlook with a Bronx cheer.

EDITORIAL

Liberals and Liberty

Mr Mackenzie King has been telling the young innocents of the Twentieth Century Club that the CCF movement tends towards a dictatorship and that socialism in general is antipathetic to that individual liberty which is so dear to all good liberals. His objection is a common one among all the academic arm-chair critics of socialism who are so anxious about the freedom of comfortable middle-class people like themselves and who blandly ignore the fact that present economic conditions make any real liberty impossible for the great mass of the working class. It so happens, however, that there is available a very simple test of the genuineness of this solicitude of Mr King and his party for individual liberty. In almost every urban centre in Canada today unemployed men and women are constantly prevented by the police from exercising the elementary British rights of freedom of speech and assembly because the police and their masters are afraid of inconvenient protests against intolerable social conditions; and working-class organizations who try to help the unemployed in maintaining their rights are similarly treated by the police. What evidence is there of any protest against this outrageous police activity by any of the Liberal leaders? The fight for the right of humble and obscure men to express themselves freely is carried on in Canada almost exclusively by the communists and by the CCF movement. The leadership in the agitation against Section 98 is in the same hands. Of the Liberal newspapers in Canada only the *Toronto Star* shows any interest in steadily campaigning against police repression and brutality; even a paper with the fine traditions of the *Winnipeg Free Press* is apt to adopt an attitude of cynical detachment when reporting police outrages. As for Mr King himself, he remains apparently unmoved by what happens to obscure workmen or helpless immigrants or 'foreigners with unpronounceable names.' He lives apart in a serene paradise above the class-conflict. It will be time enough for Canadian Liberals to worry about the hypothetical dangers to liberty in a socialist state when they have bestirred themselves a little about the real dangers to liberty in the Canada of 1933.

F.R. SCOTT

The CCF Convention

The Regina convention of the Cooperative Commonwealth Federation should be convincing proof that the new party can no longer be considered a temporary alliance between a few visionaries and malcontents. After its inauguration last year as an experiment in cooperation between western farmer and labour parties, with its programme of rather vague socialism, there was some excuse for the feeling that it could never hold together for any length of time. The differences of outlook between organized labour and individualistic farmers had obviously not been completely resolved. When during the year the CCF clubs sprang up, admitting another uncertain element of professional and white-collared workers, the composition of the movement seemed even more heterogeneous. The attempt to fuse the proletariat, the agrariat, and the salariat into a cohesive group on a class-conscious basis was certainly a new departure in Canadian political history. And yet despite these possibilities of disruption, which in theory had the Regina stage all set for sharp conflicts of opinion, the convention was carried through without animosity and with every important decision being taken by large majorities. In addition to hearing the usual addresses of welcome, receiving reports and considering a host of resolutions, the 131 delegates adopted a national constitution and debated and passed a four-thousand word programme, all in the space of three days.

The number and distribution of the delegates showed the national extent of the organization after its one year of existence. There were 16 from British Columbia, 17 from Alberta, 21 from Saskatchewan, 17 from Manitoba, 41 from Ontario and 5 from Quebec. These with 9 Members of Parliament and 5 of the National Executive made a total of 131. A newly affiliated group in New Brunswick sent telegraphic greetings so that it was only the two easternmost provinces that were not heard from. About one hundred visitors attended. Such a gathering in itself was no small achievement in these days of poverty. Most of the delegates came by car or bus; two students hitch-hiked from Toronto, starting five weeks before. The CCF has apparently not yet had time to crush out the individual initiative of its members.

Amongst the delegates, the farmers represented probably the most solid body of opinion. On the whole it was right-wing opinion – right-wing, that is, according to CCF standards. That is to say, while it fully accepted the idea of the necessity of replacing the capitalist system by a cooperative commonwealth, and recognized its own economic difficulties as being attributable to the normal workings of capitalism, it never indulged in and was sometimes baffled by the Marxian phraseology of the socialist labour delegates, and it vigorously supported the principles of constitutionalism and compensation for owners of nationalized industries. It clearly would have voted against nationalization of the land – though not unanimously – had that proposal been made. The Ontario farmers showed themselves to be more conservative than the westerners; they alone objected to the general tone of the new manifesto, and one of them, Mr W.C. Good, cast the sole vote against it.

The labour representatives, particularly those from Toronto and Vancouver, provided most of the extreme left-wing argument. Because of their superior debating powers they exercised an influence out of proportion to their numbers. They never succeeded in carrying the convention, however, though this was in part due to the fact that the general consensus of opinion was far more to the left than they had expected. In particular the radical views of most of the CCF Club delegates – always suspected of being a dangerously bourgeois element – came as a surprise to some of the Marxians. One of the great achievements of the convention was to dissipate to a large degree the very natural distrust of organized labour towards the new recruits who have been brought in by the CCF Clubs. It is likely that in the future the opposition to the formation of similar clubs in the western provinces will disappear.

The principal time of the meeting was taken up with a discussion of programme and manifesto. The CCF was faced with a choice of two policies in this regard. It could either confine its platform to a statement of fundamental principles, leaving detailed plans to be determined later; or else it could attempt to lay down a general and fairly complete plan of action describing the steps to be followed in establishing the Cooperative Commonwealth. The latter policy was adopted. In consequence the Canadian electorate is now offered a four thousand word programme which deals in some way with every important aspect of the social changes which the party proposes to make. Such an appeal to the intelligence of the people has never before been attempted by any political party in this country. It is a venture in audacity that implies at least a profound faith in the attractiveness of the programme itself.

The original eight planks of the old platform have been redrafted, and six new planks added. The last is an emergency programme designed merely to alleviate the intensity of the existing crisis, and inserted with the express recognition that emergency measures are only of temporary value, the permanent cure being the eradication of capitalism. Besides these fourteen points the manifesto contains a preamble, and a short explanation, under each proposal, of the manner in which the changes might be effected. The whole document thus forms a comprehensive statement of ends and means, which should be a potent influence making for unity within the movement. There is no room here to discuss the programme in its details; it is sufficient to remark that it is essentially socialist in character, but adapted to suit the particular factors in the Canadian situation. Its repudiation of violence, its opposition to outright confiscation of industry, its insistence on political and religious liberty and its promise of 'a much greater degree of leisure and a much richer individual life for every citizen,' give the lie to opponents who accuse the CCF of desiring all the evils they imagine belong to Communism.

In the debate on the manifesto there were two points that gave occasion for sharp conflicts of opinion. In each case the attack was led by the left-wing socialists. The first was over the question of violence. The manifesto expressly declared that the CCF did not believe in change by violence, and was seeking to achieve its ends solely by constitutional methods. The Marxian group moved that all reference to constitutional practice be struck out. Their argument was not that force must necessarily and in every case be used to introduce socialism, but that there was no predicting what might happen in the future and that the reference was superfluous. The great body of delegates were of the opposite opinion, however, and the declaration of faith in constitutionalism remained. On the second fight, which arose over the question of the compensation to be paid to owners of expropriated industries, the left-wing attack was more successful. The original draft of the manifesto stated that the CCF did not propose outright confiscation, and that the transfer of industries to public ownership 'should be made at a fair valuation.' On a motion to delete all reference to compensation a lively discussion, such as has occurred at innumerable socialist gatherings took place. It seemed at one time that, had a vote been taken, the clause would have been omitted. The matter was instead referred back to the National Council for reconsideration, and on the following day a new version, revised considerably leftwards was introduced and adopted. Since it had the merit of satisfying both sides, and since it deals with so vital a point in the programme, it may be given here:

In restoring to the community its natural resources and in taking over industrial enterprises from private into public control, we do not propose any policy of outright confiscation. What we desire is the most stable and equitable transition to the Cooperative Commonwealth. It is impossible to decide the policies to be adopted in particular cases in an uncertain future. But we insist upon certain broad principles. The welfare of the community must be placed before the claims of private wealth. In times of war human life has been conscripted. Should economic circumstances call for it, conscription of wealth would be equally justifiable. We recognize the need for compensation in the case of individuals and institutions which must receive adequate maintenance during the transition period before the planned economy becomes fully operative. But a CCF government will not play the role of rescuing bankrupt private concerns for the benefit of promoters and stock and bond holders. It will not pile up a deadweight burden of unremunerative debt which represents claims upon the public treasury of a functionless owner class.

Under such a clause the policy of the party is obviously fairly flexible, but, on the other hand there is a moral obligation to care for individuals whose savings have been devoted to purchasing the only form of security the capitalist system could give them, and for institutions, such as colleges, and hospitals, whose income is derived from similar investments.

The other important task of the convention was the adoption of the national constitution. A national executive, consisting of three representatives from each province, was appointed, and the task of administering the affairs of the party in the provinces was delegated to provincial councils. The CCF came out of the Regina convention, as it went in, a mere federation of parties, not a single organization with individual membership. It has thus not yet attained the cohesion of the two major parties. But throughout the discussions on the constitution it was evident that the sentiment in favour of a unified party was very strong, particularly among the CCF Club delegates and some of the socialist organizations. It showed itself in the general agreement upon the necessity of some form of party discipline. On the other hand, the Alberta and Ontario farmers were insistent upon their autonomy, and fought every attempt to restrict their independence. Clearly the issue is one which will have to be faced at future conventions. It is difficult to conceive of a programme as radical as that of the CCF being put into effect by anything short of a united and thoroughly disciplined political party.

The last work of the convention was to consider the numerous resolutions that were submitted from all parts of the country. Amongst those passed were resolutions against the growth of Fascism, the back-to-the-land policy of various governments, and the employment of single men in labour camps at 20¢ per day; advocating proportional representation, the appointment of a Royal Commission to enquire into Canadian penitentiaries, and the resumption of full trade with the Soviet Union; urging the importance of working out programmes for provincial CCF parties; and opposing all collaboration with Liberal or Conservative governments for the maintenance of the present capitalist order.

On the whole, the Regina convention proved an outstanding success. The spirit of the meetings, the determination amongst all delegates that personal differences of opinion had to be sacrificed to the welfare of the movement, the absence of the doctrinaire approach to problems, made a lasting impression upon everyone who attended. More important still was the recognition that the adopted programme was no final word, and that it would need constant revision and elaboration to suit the needs of Canada in a changing world. The goal remains the same; policies and tactics must be flexible. But the new party is only at the beginning of the road it has mapped out for itself; the real tasks, the acid tests of its ability lie ahead. Regina strengthened its programme and its morale, but left vital questions of organization still unsettled. There is no party press, no party fund, no centralized educational bureau. The national executive is now at work upon these matters. Should the CCF make progress in organization and tactics equivalent to its other successes in the past year it will soon confront the present governing class in Canada with a supreme test of its faith in democracy.

EDITORIAL

Thanksgiving

Let us give thanks that the Prime Minister has discovered that Canada depends upon exports. If we keep him another three years in office he may discover that there is a connection between exports and imports. Let us give thanks that the hot weather and the grasshoppers ruined our wheat crop. If we had had a normal crop we couldn't have sold it anyway. Let us give thanks that nothing much happened this summer except a World Conference in London. We might have had another Ottawa Conference. Let us give thanks that it is only in the United States that wages are being raised. As the Prime Minister has told us, we couldn't sell exports if we paid decent wages here. Let us give thanks that the Radio Commission is specializing on French programmes from Montreal. They might be giving us Orange programmes from Toronto. Let us give thanks that the Canadian Authors Association spent a holiday in England. We have not, within the memory of the oldest inhabitant, enjoyed a summer in which we heard so little about Canadian literature. Let us give thanks that our Finance Minister balanced his budget last April. Otherwise his deficit now might be several millions more than it is. Let us give thanks that our Minister of Trade and Commerce increased our exports of stockings to Great Britain from 3,055 dozen pairs in 1932 to 19,295 dozen in 1933. Otherwise our 1933 total exports would have been even more than $107 million below those of 1932. Let us give thanks for the riots and the upheavals in our penitentiaries. Our whole penal system has been revolutionized and modernized by the issuance of cigarette papers to the convicts. Finally, let us in Ontario give thanks that Mr Henry is still Premier. We might have Mr Price.

H.M. CASSIDY
Is Unemployment Relief Enough?

There are many persons in Canada who point with pride to what we have done for the unemployed during the depression. They presume, I think, that unemployment relief is a necessary evil; but that nothing more can be done now and that presently, as industrial conditions improve, relief will no longer be necessary and all will be well again. I often wonder if they also presume what must follow upon this line of reasoning – that prosperity will again give way to depression, and again the wage-earners and their families will have to beg for public charity.

But is unemployment relief really enough?

It might seem so, from a glance at a few figures. In the two years ending in August, 1932, there was an expenditure of some $150,000,000 of public funds, Dominion, provincial, and municipal, on unemployment relief works. During the same two years the number of people requiring poor relief, or direct relief (as we call it) increased steadily, and expenditures of public funds for this purpose were about $36,000,000. By the spring of 1932 the Dominion and the provinces decided that it was impossible to provide work for the unemployed by digging unnecessary sewers and building roads in the wilderness, and gave up the works policy almost completely. Since then we have carried on with direct relief, our gigantic dole, which supported some 1,500,000 people, or 15 per cent of our population, in the spring of this year, and which has probably cost us something like $60,000,000 for the year ending in August last. Thus our total public expenditures on relief for the last three years amount to some $250,000,000.

During the last few months the number drawing relief has declined materially. Since the Dominion Department of Labour does not publish currently its relief figures (although it does issue monthly reports on the number of hogs slaughtered, the number of freight cars loaded, the number of deportations and many other items of interest), it is impossible to say for certain how large the relief load is at present. Probably it has not dropped below the million mark – and it will certainly rise again, as the normal winter recession in industry occurs. For unemployment is still most serious. The number of unemployed in Canada last spring was probably about 1,000,000, or some 40 per cent of our 2,500,000 wage-earners; and the number out of work must still be more than 750,000.

Thus our public relief effort has been a huge one during the depression – not to mention all that has been done privately. The system has worked, after a fashion, and it has done one essential thing – it has provided a bare livelihood for the destitute, so that none have perished from starvation.

But when one has said this, there is not much more praise to be offered.

On the other side I should like to make only two points. The first is this – that there is a fundamental objection to direct relief (or to a relief work scheme that selects those it will help on the basis of need). For it breeds the very conditions it seeks to relieve – it generates poverty and pauperism. Such a scheme gives assistance only to the destitute – to those who are reduced to a condition where life or health is threatened by an absolute lack of food, clothing or shelter. It penalizes the thrifty workman, for it denies him aid until his savings and property are exhausted; while it gives relief promptly after loss of his job to the man who was careless with his wages while he was at work. It protects and sustains only the very lowest standards of living, not those to which workmen of the better type were accustomed. Thus it denies the worthy and rewards the unworthy – with results that are not hard to imagine. Poor relief has always bred pauper attitudes in those whom it serves. During the last two years I have visited relief offices in six of the provinces of Canada, and I think that from practically every relief officer and social worker I have met I have heard the same story of the progressive growth of dependent attitudes on the part of their clients.

The second point I would make about our system of relief is that it fails completely to solve many of the problems arising from unemployment. Here are some consequences of unemployment in Canada which relief has failed to prevent.

Unemployment has reduced drastically and dangerously the living standards of the majority of our working people. Let us take the deterioration in housing standards, as only one example. In the city of Toronto there has gone on, during the last three years, a tremendous shifting of population, partly in consequence of voluntary moving and partly of evictions, from comfortable houses to poor houses, from poor houses to shacks or flats of rooms, and from 'rooms' to a single room. Recently I have interviewed a large group of partially employed workers in connection with a wage study, and I have been struck with the large number of instances in which married men or women with families have reported living quarters of one room, or of two or three rooms, with makeshift cooking arrangements. The houses in which such people live are likely to be rabbit warrens in one of our oldest districts, the Ward, where five or six families may be crammed into an old nine or ten-roomed house, which has utterly inadequate sanitary facilities for so many inhabitants.

Unemployment undermines health and vitality. While our governmental statistics do not show clearly that the health of our population has been seriously impaired so far, there are enough snippets of evidence to make one suspect very strongly that the depression is taking a real toll. This suspicion is confirmed when one reads authentic reports from the United States, of serious increases in malnutrition and dental defects among school children, and of a distinctly greater incidence of illness among the unemployed and their families than among those who have jobs. We shall probably not see clearly the effects of the depression upon health and vitality for considerable time.

One of the most vicious aspects of unemployment is that it destroys the capacity and the willingness of men and women to work. Imagine the effect of a year or two roaming across the country as a transient upon a young man of 19 or 20, who has not yet settled down to a very disciplined existence. He becomes a 'bum' in the process, becomes unreliable, incapable, indolent, unemployable – whereas he never would have developed in such a way if he had a regular job and a reasonable scale of living. Unemployment, it should be emphasized, creates unemployables. It is true that a certain number of those drawing relief are indolent and incapable. But their critics should not forget that a very large part of their unemployability can probably be explained by the economic insecurity, the privations, and the consequent bad social conditions under which they have been forced to live.

Unemployment also contaminates family life. The strain and worry and nervous tension inevitably associated with it make difficult or impossible pleasant and happy relations between husbands and wives or between parents and children. Broken homes result frequently from the necessity of the husband leaving home to look for a job – or from his desertion to get away from the nagging of his wife. In a great many cases the wife goes out to work when her husband loses his job, and takes upon herself the double task of earning money and running the household – which is impossible – so that she must neglect her home and her children. Children take on odd jobs when they are too young; adolescent boys and girls contribute all of their meagre earnings of eight or ten dollars a week to the family support and lose the opportunities of enjoyment that we consider normal to young people; boys and girls leave school or college, giving up plans for advanced education, to support the family in its crisis; young people cannot afford to marry, but have children anyhow, who are marked forever with the stigma of illegitimacy; and in a hundred and one ways, family life is impaired.

Unemployment kills freedom. No man or woman is free in our society, who lacks the means of livelihood. He is not free to say what he thinks, to do the simple things he would like to do, to function independently as a citizen, if he must bend every step towards obtaining a job or if he must beg for charity. And without freedom, there can be no real democracy. Our democratic institutions are only empty forms when so many of our people are enslaved by economic fears.

In short, unemployemnt in Canada, in spite of the system of relief which has provided the elementary means of life for practically everybody, has been destroying the very human stuff of our population. It has been undermining their health, their morale and self-esteem, their capacity and their willingness to work, their family life, and their capacity for citizenship. Even if it were to cease today, it would leave an appalling legacy of social problems that it would take years to clean up – at the expense of increasing vastly our social services; it would leave us with a working force less capable of efficient productive effort than it was in 1929; and it would leave us also with a people less capable of democratic self-government than it was before.

If unemployment relief is not enough, what then, would be enough? I have space to do no more than suggest four great steps that I think Canada should take.

First, the system of direct relief should be

improved to make it as adequate and as fair as possible. This means a much greater degree of Dominion participation and control than in the past.

Secondly, we should set up as soon as possible a system of unemployment insurance. While insurance could not immediately replace relief, a comprehensive scheme could be inaugurated fairly soon if we wanted it badly enough – and at the very least preparations could be made for such a move, something which has not yet been done by our governments to even a slight extent.

Thirdly, I think that at present extraordinary efforts should be made by our governments, and mainly by the Dominion, to provide work. This would involve huge expenditures on necessary and desirable undertakings – not so much sewers and the Trans-Canada highway as new houses for working people, schools, and public highways that are badly needed. Such a programme could be financed by the Dominion to the great advantage of the whole community, not only the unemployed.

And finally, I think that we should set seriously about the construction of a comprehensive plan to reduce the ravages of unemployment in the future. This means drastic changes in the nature of our economic system, so as to give us a planned economy, rather than the unplanned, chaotic economy that we have at present. Unemployment, I believe, can be lessened very greatly, if the right measures of social control are undertaken.

EDITORIAL

The Pre-War Era

As 1933 passes into 1934 the world passes from the post-war era in which we have been living since 1919 into the pre-war era which precedes the explosion. Appeals to the League spirit are now quite useless unless our League of Nations speakers are to enlighten us on what we should do in Canada about sanctions, whether we should advocate a League air force, whether we should back up the present British government in its sabotage of the League, whether we should revise our settled Canadian policy on Article 10, what is the relation between our economic external policy and world peace, and on other similar difficult concrete problems. But if we were to frankly face the question of the meaning of Canada's commitments under the Covenant it would soon become clear that the Canadian people do not take these commitments seriously, and never have done so. Our radio speakers will therefore probably grow virtuously indignant about armament makers in Europe, about Nazi Germany or militarist Japan. No such respectable group of ladies and gentlemen could afford to face the fact that wars are not caused by some fiendish mischief-makers in some foreign lands but are the inevitable result of our present capitalist system. Unless we are prepared to make over our social and economic institutions and eliminate the reckless economic competition within each national community and between communities, the world will drift into another general war. War is only the final form of unrestricted competition. The expedients which are now being discussed by most League enthusiasts who are reluctant or afraid to face the economic basis of war are measures which may postpone the war but cannot prevent it. Short of a fundamental discussion of the economic imperialism out of which wars arise, all peace discussions are likely to do more harm than good. We can see no evidence on the programme of the League of Nations Society's radio talks that any such fundamental issues are to be approached. The speakers will strike noble attitudes for fifteen minutes and their radio audience will then adjourn for a nice quiet Sunday afternoon nap.

ANGUS MACINNIS

More About The British Columbia Election

The 1933 provincial election in British Columbia was an event of considerable importance. ... the issue, for the first time in a Canadian political campaign was Socialism versus Capitalism. Generally, CCF candidates and speakers emphasized this ussue, and their opponents, unable logically to explain the reason for misery and want in the midst of plenty, resorted to the time-honoured custom of raising irrelevant issues. It is admitted, even by many who do not agree with the CCF that its advocates conducted an educational campaign of which they may indeed be proud.

The CCF in this campaign accomplished at least one thing: They have proved the identity of interest of the two old parties. The CCF insisted that the cause of economic collapse was due, not to the graft or the lack of business ability of the Tolmie government, but to the impossibility of administering civil affairs efficiently in a contracting capitalism. They pointed out that the failure of the system to distribute the fruits of industry on a more equitable basis is due to the purpose for which it is ordered and not to faults in its administration. They further emphasized the point that as long as the people insist on retaining capitalism they will have to accept the consequences of the operation of that system, and that it could not be administered any more beneficially in the interests of the masses by a CCF government than by a Liberal or a Conservative government. If, in future elections, the CCF adhere to this policy, the issue henceforth will be, not a high tariff versus a tariff not so high or any of the other old issues that served the purpose of the two old parties of capitalism, but Socialism versus Capitalism.

There were certain other interesting aspects of the campaign of the Liberal party. ... Their chief speaker, apart from their leader, Mr Pattullo, was Mr G.G. McGeer, KC, better known in British Columbia as 'Gerry' McGeer. 'Gerry' has a loud voice, and a fairly extensive vocabulary. Furthermore, he is a gentleman of considerable astuteness. During the last few years of producers' depression and bankers' prosperity, financiers have come in for a great deal of criticism. Abusing bankers has become a passtime almost as popular as bridge, or as hunting Communists in Toronto. Gerry took up the study of money. He became popular as a speaker at Service Club luncheons. The sharing of sin of the Oxford group also became popular and it is said that Gerry joined the Oxford group.

When the Banking Commission sat in Vancouver he appeared before it on behalf of the Vancouver Trades and Labour Council. He announced that he performed this service without money and without price. Some people thought this rather strange, as, in the past Gerry has valued his services highly, financially speaking. Certain people were mean enough to suggest that the reason for this altruism was because there was an election in the offing and workers have votes if nothing else. The best people, however, claim it was because he joined the Oxford group although they do not overlook the advertising value of three hours before the Banking Commission and a tiff with the Chairman, Lord MacMillan.

As we have noted, Mr McGeer was chief spokesman for the Liberals and his tactics can be understood from the following:

In reporting to the Trades Council his efforts before the Banking Commission he said: 'In addressing a properly constituted, impartial tribunal charged with the great responsibilities that this Commission has undertaken, all will agree that fact and argument should be presented in restrained language, advancing plain reason and simple logic. There is, however, a proper time and place in advocacy for appeal, conciliation, argument and denunciation. Upon this occasion I determined that the course most likely to produce results beneficial to labour called for "an evangelical bombardment of invective" directed at the private money system with which the majority of the members of the Commission are actively associated, and in which they have a profit-seeking and proprietary interest.'

The Liberal tactics in the campaign indicated that Mr McGeer decided and the party agreed that what would best serve the purpose on that occasion also was 'an evangelical bombardment of invective,' directed against what Mr Pritchard, in a moment of youthful smart alecism said fifteen years ago; against opinions expressed by Dr Telford in another connection and against statements which Miss Osterhout did not make in 1933.

These tactics were generally followed by the Liberal party. The Hon. Ian Mackenzie stated at a meeting that three members of the Farmer-Labour group in the House of Commons had been implicated in the Beauharnois scandal. When pressed for names, he mentioned E.J. Garland, MP. Next day, when the CCF threatened a libel suit, he withdrew the statement. Mr Tom Reid, Liberal member for New Westminster, made similar statements, but with more Scotch caution and as little Scotch honesty said he had forgotten the names, but that he had them in his files at Ottawa.

The day before the election the employees of large department stores in Vancouver were circularized to the effect that if a CCF government were elected it would take over the stores and all employees would lose their jobs. The lumber workers were told that the CCF was opposed to foreign trade and that if elected to govern on November 2nd the camps and mills would be closed next day. This canard undoubtedly was responsible for the defeat of Dr Lyle Telford, CCF candidate in a Vancouver Island riding.

While the CCF speakers were carrying on the campaign in 'restrained language, advancing plain reason and simple logic,' the Liberals, and the Conservatives masquerading as Independents, were appealing to every fear, passion, and prejudice that could find a place in the minds of a people not yet freed from traditional superstition and fear.

Mr McGeer had his own policy for the rehabilitation of Canada, a policy which he outlined in a pamphlet entitled *The Conquest of Poverty*. This programme provided for a national banking system and a planned economy under state control. His programme was much closer to that of the CCF than to the vague generalities which served as the programme of the Liberal party, but he thought he could use that party to advance his own ideas. The Liberal party had no use for Mr McGeer or his programme but they felt that the Liberal machine could make use of Mr McGeer's special qualities. However, the inevitable happened: The machine triumphed over the individual. When Mr Pattullo formed his cabinet, Gerry was left out in the cold. He said that he had been promised the position of Attorney-General, but that post was given to a young stripling from the office of the legal firm whose head is said to be the boss of of the Liberal machine. So Gerry now is in 'opposition.' 'He would rather be a doorkeeper in the house of the Lord than to dwell in the tents of the wicked.'

There are many other features of the election which might be noted if space permitted. The most pleasing aspect of the election was the consistent vote given the CCF. This indication of an understanding of the real issues involved was most clearly shown in Vancouver East where the two CCF candidates were elected. Although the total vote of each was nearly 11,000, there was a difference of only 3 votes between them. In the other city ridings the CCF totals, though not so close, were much closer than those of any other party.

All but one of the candidates elected are members of the Socialist Party of Canada which is affiliated with the CCF. The only significance that need be attached to this is that these candidates ran in constituencies where socialist organization and education had been carried on, in some instances, for many years. Had CCF club members been nominated in these ridings they too would have been successful. The results show, however, that organization and education count on election day.

Mr Connell, the Associated CCF club member, elected in Victoria, is a retired Anglican clergyman. He labels himself 'Marxian Socialist', pointing out, however, that this does not mean an uncritical acceptance of everything written by Karl Marx, but it does mean that in order to get a clear understanding of social and economic problems, we shall have to approach them from the Marxian point of view.

Much was said by our opponents of supposed rifts within the CCF. Actually there was no dissension of any importance. Seventeen members, who had been expelled from the Socialist Party of Canada, formed a new organization and continued to use the old name. They ran candidates in four Vancouver ridings, but the total vote of their five candidates was only 389. The other 'rift' was an organization, formed by a few disgruntled individuals, and calling itself 'The Independent CCF,' surely a contradiction in terms. They did not deceive any appreciable number of the electorate, as their seven candidates in five Vancouver constituencies received only 2,016 votes.

The Liberal party received approximately 151,000 votes and elected 34 members. The CCF received 115,000 votes and elected 7 members. All others received 92,000 votes and elected 6 members. In this last category is included one Labour member, who was not opposed by the CCF, and who will most likely sit with the CCF members in the Legislature.

Steps should be taken by CCF organizations in the other provinces to familiarize their members with all the factors of this, the first real political campaign of the CCF in Canada. They should not rest content with the accounts they read in the capitalist press. The CCF is now an actual factor in the politcal life of the Dominion. If we can forget personal ambitions and aspirations we can build a force that will have to be reckoned with. Regardless of the belittling and pooh-poohing of the press, Big Business and the leaders of the old parties recognize in the CCF the only challenge to their supremacy and to their reign of exploitation.

J.E. KEITH

The Fascist Province

The Liberal government in Quebec is liberal in the sense that the National-Socialist government in Germany is socialist – that is to say, in the non-sense. Its programme, as disclosed by action taken while in office (it does not bother to offer a paper programme) may be described as pure laissez-faire illuminated by touches of fascism.

Mr Taschereau stands for private ownership in industry and public utilities, especially electric power, and is himself closely tied up with the power trust. He has refused to bring the province under the Dominion Old Age Pensions scheme, although advised to do so by his own Social Insurance Commission in 1932. The shamefully inadequate labour legislation which is on the Quebec statute books is not even properly enforced, as recent evidence before the Stevens' Committee made startlingly clear, and ... the Montreal *Gazette*, purest spokesman for high finance, can find no stronger denunciation for the Department of Labour at Quebec than that its activites are 'creating uncertainty where formerly there was a sense of perfect security.' A new law is about to be passed making collective wage agreements, when adopted by an employer, compulsory on all similar firms in that district; the international unions see in the measure a threat to the right to strike and the beginning of the corporative state. No attempt is being made to lessen the gross inequalities of wealth by a fairer system of taxation.

The suppression of freedom of speech is ruthless and persistent. The latest move in this direction, the David Bill, which would make it an offence to distribute circulars calling a public meeting unless the chief of police approved, is merely symptomatic of the general attitude. The iron heel is showing itself with a vengeance. So far to the right is Mr Taschereau that there is no room for the provincial Conservatives except on his left and theirs are the only voices calling – but how faintly! – for a more humane and liberal policy. The party roles are completely reversed.

Four and a half years of depression, in fact, have done little else than reveal how harmonious are the relations between the three persons in the provincial trinity – the Liberal Party machine, the Roman Church, and St James Street. Scarcely a rift has appeared to disturb the equilibrium of the theo-pluto-bureaucracy. The editorials of the Montreal *Gazette* would make ideal pastoral letters for the parish priests to read from pulpits; the episcopal denunciations of Socialism and Communism must turn the *Gazette* leader-writers pale with envy; Mr Taschereau could not denounce the CCF as divinely as Archbishop Gauthier has done it. The totalitarian state could hardly be more united.

It must be admitted that all three powers have handled the difficulties of these latter years with considerable skill. Mr Taschereau rides more firmly in the saddle than ever. The Conservative opposition, with a heaven-sent opportunity, is too supine, too bound by political tradition, to lead a vigorous attack. Being Conservative, it cannot be radical, and only a radical party could break the governing machine. The once-threatening *Fédération des Clubs Ouvriers* is petering out, blind and un-led. To complete the Liberal stranglehold it only remains to deprive Montreal of its self-government and put it under a Quebec-appointed Commission, in order to prevent Mr Houde or some other unorthodox fellow from obtaining control of the city. On the excuse of economy and good government, with full backing from banks and manufacturers, this change is apparently about to be accomplished. Nothing short of a revolution can prevent Mr Taschereau's return to power at the provincial elections of 1935. This is the brand of Liberalism Mr King will have to cope with if he becomes Prime Minister.

On the side of religion, a similar strength prevails. The leaders of the Church have interpreted the depression as a sort of punishment from God upon greedy individuals. It follows that the individual who wants to help matters must contribute more of penance and of pence; he must return to God before he can hope to return to work. It is difficult to know how far this doctrine is believed, but it is certainly preached, and radical movements are denounced far more strongly than the capitalist injustices which produce them. The increased burden of municipal taxes is causing some people to cast critical eyes upon the enormous tax-free properties of the Church, but no hands have as yet been laid upon this source of revenue, except in Ste Hyacinthe, where in consequence a balanced municipal budget was produced in 1933. With the great investments of the Church not only in lands but in utilities and industrial stocks and bonds, it is not difficult to see why the ecclesiastical authorites attack organizations like the CCF which, they fear, would imperil their economic privileges.

No anti-clerical movement shows any signs of appearing. The only champion of that dangerous cause, Albert St Martin, has at last been effectively silenced. Hailed into court time and time again for sedition, blasphemy, and numberless other charges usually employed to suppress opinion, he was assaulted and nearly killed last autumn by a band of French hooligans who broke up a meeting of his *Université Ouvrière* and then attacked him with sticks, cracking open his head. It was his 67th birthday; the police were present in large numbers, but no arrests were made. All is now quiet on the religious front. Mr Gobeil's devastating charges at Ottawa that the University of Montreal actually had atheists on its staff caused a slight upset recently, but the statement was so vociferously denied, and it was so uncontrovertibly established that no one was allowed to teach any subject at the University unless he had been previously approved by a board of clerics, that there is obviously no danger of error from that quarter.

And St James Street? Its position has in many ways been consolidated. The Montreal Light, Heat and Power Company has absorbed some twenty municipal distribution systems since the depression started. Beauharnois power, after the 'cleansing' of the 1930 investigation, has passed quietly into the pockets of the Holt interests. Not one of Quebec's major financial scandals has yet been exposed: Canada Power and Paper, McDougall and Cowans, Price Brothers, etc., have come and gone, leaving ruin for the small investor but no punishment for those responsible. An unusually severe winter will more than pay the fines of the convicted Webster coal companies, assuming the Court of Appeal confirms the trial judgment. One lone Galahad – Harpell – assaulted the financial fortress, but he won only silent sympathy to compensate for his gaol sentence. Even the United Church is feeling pressure from its wealthy laymen for its mildly Christian utterances in favour of social justice. If St James Street is ever to be called to give an account of its stewardship, the call will have to come from outside the Province of Quebec. Not a person here who knows the facts dare open his mouth.

The outlook for progress in the province, then, is dark at the moment. There are currents moving, bodies of criticism forming, but they have not reached the surface. One or two that have are clearly under expert guidance from above. *Les Jeunes Canada*, for instance, have espoused a programme of social reconstruction which goes as far as public ownership of power and a certain measure of social insurance; yet significantly enough, some of its members threatened to break up the meeting at which Mr Woodsworth spoke on March 3rd, shortly after Archbishop Gauthier's denunciation of the CCF. They are potential, if not actual fascists.

If discontent grows too prominent among the French masses we may expect a concerted move to deflect it into fascist channels, and to provide the people with scapegoats lest they come to see where the real evil lies. The increasing anti-semitism of the French-Canadian (where are minority rights now?) is evidence of this, and a natural enough tendency to associate trusts with the English race lies ready for exploitation. If there were any French socialist leaders they could use this lever first, and could show how public ownership is the easiest method by which the French-Canadian may regain control of the natural resources which English and American capitalists have stolen from him. But there are no such leaders yet, and the masses are being taught that all will be well if only English capitalists are replaced or controlled by French ones, and all chain and department stores replaced by small, independent retail merchants, and all unemployed persons set to work on the abandoned farms. So completely is the French-Canadian deprived of literature not approved by authorities that very little of the fundamental criticisms of capitalism available for English Canadians have reached him. His mind is so indoctrinated that one would probably have to go to the Ontario Orangemen to find its equal.

There are two possible ways in which an intelligent reform movement might start. One is that a leader may spring from the people. All one can say of this is that he is not in sight. The other possibility is the CCF might take root, and might provide a rallying point for the progressive forces. The Church's attitude by no means makes this impossible – in fact, it probably assists through publicity. It must not be forgotten that there is no absolute ban on the CCF. The Church as a whole has not spoken, but only one bishop, and he has merely issued a strong warning. The Church made a similar attempt to destroy the youthful Laurier, and failed. The last meeting held by Mr Woodsworth in Montreal, at which over 1,300 French-Canadians were present, was enthusiastic. If French leadership can be found, the miracle might be worked. The political field is wide open for radicals: both the other parties are thoroughly discredited at the moment. One thing is certain. If Quebec should ever adopt socialism, even of the CCF brand, Canada will be an exciting place to live in. We Anglo-Saxons are dull fellows beside the French when it comes to politics.

FRANK H. UNDERHILL

The CCF Convention and After

Last summer the commentators on public events were all agog over the sudden outburst of high-brow tendencies within the two old parties. The Port Hope and Newmarket summer schools were solemnly discussed as indicating a profound intellectual awakening among the younger generation of Canadian Grits and Tories; and oracular pronouncements were delivered as to their ultimate significance in Canadian politics. But since then the Ontario and Saskatchewan elections, coming on top of those of British Columbia, have made the result of the next Dominion election a foregone conclusion; and as our two old parties never think beyond the next election, they have both quickly given up the useless pretence of having anything intellectual about them, and there have been no summer schools this year.

Last summer, the new political movement, the CCF, also made the headlines with its first national convention in Regina. Since it then adopted a platform which has given it plenty to talk about, political old-timers have been puzzled as to why it should hold a second convention this year in Winnipeg. But the annual convention is part of the CCF constitution, and the vigorous discussions of policy which have taken place in the first two meetings have certainly shown the value of this innovation in Canadian political customs. In a country of such wide extent as Canada, where sectionalism is so dominant, the only way of making a national movement which shall be coherent in policy and democratic in control is through these frequent national conventions. Both the old parties have long been thoroughly oligarchical in their control, and the ordinary party member never dreams of anything but the purely passive attitude of a spectator, in the making of his party policy. The CCF, which had its origin in the belief that the ordinary member of the old parties was being shamelessly exploited by the party leadership and by the big interests to which that leadership was really responsible, is attempting to preserve a genuine democracy by financing itself from its rank-and-file membership and by giving its members a full share in the threshing out of party policy. It would be absurd to maintain that it has as yet solved the problem of combining democracy with effective leadership, but it has started out on the right track.

One of the myths about the CCF which needs to be exploded is that of its so-called brain-trust. The stories of how Mr Woodsworth and his fellow leaders were submitting themselves to the crafty influence of a group of intellectual malcontents and revolutionaries who were diabolically guiding the movement towards the upsetting of all our cherished institutions should now be abandoned by our journalists to the editorial page of the *Mail and Empire*, where all good Canadian bogies go when they die. So far as I know, the idea of a CCF brain-trust originated in the fertile imagination of G.V.F. [G.V. Ferguson] of the *Winnipeg Free Press*. He is a genial and likeable cynic who happens to be on friendly terms with most of the professors who have been taking part in the new movement, and in reporting the Regina meeting he decided to amuse himself by taking his friends for a little ride. Hence the story of the brain-trust, which spread all the way to the *London Times*. It has caused so much perturbation among so many worthy souls and has wasted so much time at the meetings of university boards of governors, who are not accustomed to the shock of discovering that professors have ideas, that it has ceased to be a joke at all. Professors have been active in the CCF, but they are accepted in its councils exactly like other members. In the Liberal party professors also attempt to be active, but they are listened to only when they are imported from Britain or the States. In the Conservative party they are listened to only when disguised as contributors to the *Financial Post* or the monthly bulletin of the Bank of Nova Scotia.

The real weakness of the CCF is that it hasn't an effective brain-trust. A movement which is not merely aiming at office but intends to carry through a far-reaching reconstruction of our economic and political institutions needs a type of organization with which neither of our old parties is equipped. It is trying to work out for Canadian conditions a practical socialist policy, to determine the successive steps by which the socialist ideal of a classless society in which production is organized for use and not for private profit may be realized in our country. This is a task which requires first of all a great deal of research and investigation, and secondly a new technique of popular education. Probably the CCF has attracted about all the votes that it is likely to attract by the mere emotional exploitation of our present discontents. What it needs now is not bigger and better tub-thumping, but new methods of organizing discussion and of carrying on propaganda. I think it would profit by following the example of the British Labour party in this respect. The executive of the Labour party has already published the manifesto on 'Socialism and Peace' which it hopes to have adopted by the party in its annual October conference, as well as several 'Policy Reports' (including one on education) which will also come up for discussion there. These have been prepared by specialist committees after months of study and discussion; and after they have been adopted, with amendments, by the Conference they will form the subject of further discussion in innumerable local conferences, summer schools, study groups, and public meetings. Only by such organized education can the electorate be converted to an understanding of socialist doctrines and policies. And it may be taken for granted that, until the majority of the electorate have been converted in this way, no socialist government will be given a real opportunity to carry its ideas into practice. Romantics who dream of an energetic minority imposing itself upon the apathetic masses and introducing socialism overnight are in danger of waking up some morning to find that the energetic minority is in power alright, but is establishing fascism.

The Winnipeg CCF Convention devoted most of its time to drafting a manifesto on immediate policy. The leaders of the movement after their experience in the provincial elections were impressed by the fact that the voters wanted more definite information on what the CCF proposes to do now. In brief, the Winnipeg manifesto is a statement such as Mr Stevens would have gone on to add to his famous speech if he had thought out what were the essential steps to be taken at once to deal with this economic structure of ours which is 'upside down.' 'I do see the eternal justice of a man who is willing to work or who does work, whether he is a farmer or an industrial worker, getting at least a chance to live decently. We are bound to give that. ... The real wealth of the nation depends upon these two groups.' Mr Stevens, however, and his colleagues, as he confessed, 'have not followed our study far enough for that yet.'

The immediate steps to which the CCF is committed include first of all the socialization of our banking and financial machinery (to eliminate 'the extravagance of the gamblers in finance and the rapacious avarice and ambition of certain people'); and then the protection of the farmer from foreclosure by his creditors, the writing down of farm debts, the establishment of an effective publicly-owned rural credit system, and the control of the processing and distribution of farm products; a large-scale programme of public works, especially a national housing scheme; national regulation of wages and working conditions in industry, a nation-wide scheme of social insurance, and effective protection to the workers' right of bargaining through their own unions. If Mr Stevens and his colleagues ever carry their study far enough, they will find themselves driven to each one of these steps. But if Mr Stevens finds himself driven to such legislative measures he will also find himself driven outside the Conservative party. As for the Liberals, the unconquerable inertia of Mr King effectively prevents them from approaching any of these projects.

The Winnipeg Convention also committed itself to a strong declaration on peace. 'The CCF is unalterably opposed to war. If the great capitalist powers drift into another world war, Canadian neutrality must be rigorously maintained whoever the belligerents may be. Canada must refuse to give military assistance to the League of Nations as at present constituted. We stand for the thorough reorganization of the League in order to make it an effective instrument for peace.' I wish I could feel that all the delegates understood the full meaning of this declaration, but it must be confessed that the discussion revealed the usual Canadian muddle-headed sentimentalism on this subject. There were those who were against war but would fight in a defensive war, and there was one old farmer who thought that it might be his Christian duty to fight for his brother, presumably in France. The bulk of the delegates seemed commendably free from the desire to bury 50,000 more Canadians in France in the process of backing up the policy of Sir John Simon under the guise of fighting for British freedom and democracy; but I am afraid a good many of them could have been swept away by an idealist League orator with exhortations about collective security – which, of course, in relation to the actual League, are just more booby-traps like the exhortations about democracy and freedom.

All the active workers in the movement with whom one talked at Winnipeg were certain that they would do better in the Dominion election than they had in the provinces. And the provincial elections have shown that they can collect votes – one-third of the electorate in British Columbia and one-quarter in Saskatchewan. But, of course, no one doubts that the 1935 election is going to be marked by a so-called landslide for the Liberals. They will not sweep the electorate, but under our ridiculous single-member constituency system they will gather in a huge majority of the seats. This being taken as certain, some other things can be predicted with equal certainty. The Liberals will again be false to their low-tariff principles, as they were after 1896 and 1921. No sane man expects anything else, not even the editor of the *Winnipeg Free Press*. For Liberal tariffs, like Conservative tariffs, are made by the people who put up the campaign funds. They will also fail to find the markets abroad about which they are now talking so glibly. After three or four years of office there will be another nauseating scandal like the customs scandal or the Beauharnois affair; for, while Mr King is honest himself, he suffers from a complete inability to distinguish honest men from rogues among his advisers, and his advisers will include the corrupt Taschereau gang from Quebec. Generally speaking, the Liberal Government will drift, as it drifted from 1921 to 1930, with no definite policy or action, because Mr King's conception of leadership is to expose himself to all the pressure groups who concentrate upon Ottawa and then to go in the direction in which pressure is greatest at the moment.

All these things will discredit our democratic system of government, and democracy cannot stand much more discredit in Canada or in other countries. If the world economic crisis continues as it seems likely to do, such cumulative discredit as will result from four years more of King government after the last four years of Bennett government will bring Canada appreciably closer to fascism. The only way to escape fascism is to have a clear alternative to it and to begin now to educate the electors in what that alternative means. Vague talk about preserving our ancestral liberties will no doubt win the next election for the Liberals; but when it becomes clear that the only liberties they are thinking about are the liberties of business magnates to make money as they please there will be a reaction. Then it will seem that the only real Liberals in this country are the socialists.

J.H. GRAY

Battle of the Winnipeg Cenotaph

The Winnipeg Cenotaph is unique! In all the Rt Hon. Jimmy Thomas' 'Grite Breetish Commonwealth of Nyetions' it is unique for it alone stands as an everlasting monument to the effectiveness of that grand gang of nefarious Munchausens – the war atrocity lecturers. The word 'stands' is used advisedly for it was erected ostensibly as a memorial to our citizens who lost their lives in the Great War. This fact does not, of course, militate against the accuracy of my premise; there are countless scores of other monuments to human imbecility extant which are likewise disguised by euphemistic terminology.

Elsewhere the erection of monuments was a prosaic business carried out with all due regard for the amenities of the occasion. In Winnipeg it precipitated a conflict that lasted three years longer than the war being commemorated, engendered an inestimable amount of bitterness, and ended with a complete rout of common decency at the hands of the converts of the war horror fabricators.

It is truly unfortunate that the information is unavailable for it would be interesting to know the actual amount of cannon fodder these gentry supplied. The total must be stupendous. For three long years they paraded up and down the land belching forth their hymns of hatred to capacity crowds everywhere. Their appointed task was to keep our abomination of everything German at a fever pitch and they were master stokers. They answered the every prayer of the home-guard war winners, answered them as no other weapon could have done.

Were the victory bond sales slowing down? Were school children tardy in subscribing for war-saving stamps? Were the farmerettes complaining of sore backs or the citizenry gagging on oleomargerine? Were there unpatriotic rumblings against conscription? Were heretical scholars reading Goethe, Nietzsche and Schopenhauer and refusing to substitute Gilbert & Sullivan for the Ninth Symphony?

Then call out the horror lecturers!

Out they would tumble, disguised usually as Belgian refugees or escaped prisoners, and another battle was soon won for democracy and the sanctity of Canadian real estate. No atrocity tale they could invent was too preposterous to be believed and exaggerated at each second telling. In those hysterical days it was not conducive to continued good health to declare that to believe one per cent. of the tales they told was tantamount to the denial of the existence of a dozen unmolested virgins in Christendom.

To say that third generation Canadians bearing such names as Schwab, Schwartz, and Schmidt had a precarious existence is to state the case too mildly. Thrown out of employment, boycotted commercially, and in constant fear of personal violence, their lives were made doubly miserable by a small army of juvenile heresy hunters who were forever peeking at windows, listening at keyholes, and snooping into wood-sheds in search of bombs.

How deeply rooted our hatred of the fiendish Hun became may best be illustrated by the fact it took but the mention of a German name in the same breath as the Winnipeg cenotaph, seven years after the war ended, to cause our well organized babbitry to give vent to a war-whoop that echoed and re-echoed from coast to coast.

The present cenotaph is the second the city has erected. The first was of a temporary nature, built, during the post-war craze for sentimental masonry, on the property of the Bank of Montreal at the corner of Portage Avenue and Mainstreet – Winnipeg's Fifth Avenue and Broadway. It stood for a very short time and was demolished when that institution gave way to a very unbankerish desire to have a monument of its own. When the populace awoke to the awful fact that the town was without a suitable memorial to its several thousand war dead, the inevitable committees were formed and a concerted effort made to pester the city council into erecting one. But the city fathers had spent a lifetime side-tracking committees and the patriots succeeded only in wasting their time.

But, by 1924, the petitioners who had escaped from their numerous encounters with municipal red tape with a whole skin became desperate. As a last resort they enlisted the services of the Hon. R.D. Waugh, then recently resigned Canadian Saar Valley Commissioner, one time mayor and present boss of the government liquor monopoly. Mr Waugh became chairman of a revamped committee and war was formally declared on the cenotaph front on June 14th, 1924. A front page splurge in the newspapers announced the decision to erect a $25,000 memorial, that a canvass for the necessary funds would get underway at once.

But despite a fanfare of optimistic oratory and the employment of all the artful dodges of the service clubs the campaign for funds failed, dismally. When the books were finally closed the loot totalled scarcely twenty per cent of the quota, and this made up largely by five and ten cent donations from the school children. The city council came to their aid in the end and footed the rest of the bill, and the committee crashed the front pages again a year later with an invitation to Canadian artists to submit designs for the memorial. The designer of the chosen model would receive an honorarium of $2,500 and would supervise the erection of the memorial.

The committee showed laudable modesty in admitting that its membership was incapable of designing the memorial and its only other decent act was to appoint a board of nationally known artists and architects to judge the designs submitted. The chief assessor of the five experts was nominated by the Royal Architectural Institute of Canada. In order to guarantee absolute impartiality the board instructed the committee to have all identification marks removed from the models and numbers substituted before they took them over.

The conditions governing the contest were given wide publication and forty-seven models were received from all parts of the country. Despite this imposing array of entries the judges came to a quick and unanimous decision. They declared that not only was the model of Emmanuel Hahn of Toronto outstanding, it was one of the finest examples of that type of art it had ever been their privilege to behold. Said they, in part, in their report to the committe:

'The outline is of great dignity and picturesque effect. The sentiment is simply and directly expressed in a manner about which no doubt can be felt and no questions need be asked. ... In the shaping of the shrouded figures on the sides of this rectangular, tapering design great prominence is given to the tragic aspect of war, too apt to be forgotten in times of peace. ... It has fine architectural and decorative qualities.' And so on through two closely spaced pages of praise which concluded, 'This board feels that the highest respect is due to the power this designer exhibits in setting forth his fine idea and in carrying out his work on a full scale will develop his thought in a still higher degree.'

It is unfortunate, for the sake of our civic dignity, that the award of the judges was not confirmed by the committee at once. But at the time it was announced a Dominion election was waxing bitter and a quorum of committeemen could not be mustered until it was out of the way. The interval provided the citizenry with the opportunity of mulling the name over in its collective mind.

'Hahn? Hahn? Sounds like a German name, don't it? Naw, it can't be. No Heinie would have nerve enough to put in a design for a Canadian cenotaph. Probaly a Belgian or a Hollander, them foreign names all sound alike anyway. Still he might be at that. It wouldn't do no harm to find out, let's call up the *Free Press*, jest fer fun like.'

They found out. Hahn was of German birth, having come to Canada 38 years before as a boy of seven.

Then came the deluge!

The discovery of Hahn's diabolic treachery in his choice of birthplace released the floodgates of the reservoir of hatred that had been damned up since the departure of the last atrocity lecturer. At the sounding of the tocsin the hundred-per-centers arose unanimously to condemn the designer, the judges, and the committee as vile debasers of the memory of the sacred dead. 'Pro-bono-publico,' 'vox-populi,' and 'constant reader' seized pen and paper and dashed off vituperative epistles to the newspapers. Wherever two persons were gathered together the scandal was discussed and resolution after resolution was passed protesting against awarding the prize to Mr Hahn.

The pursuant publication of Hahn biographical data served only to excite the patriots to a greater effort to have his design thrown out. Hahn came by his talents naturally, being one of a large family of distinguished artists and musicians. He had attended the Toronto public schools as a boy and, when he had received all that Canada had to offer in way of artistic training, proceeded to Europe where he spent three years pursuing his studies in the art capitals of the continent. He then returned to his home in Toronto and at the time in question was head of the sculptural department of the Ontario College of Art. One time assistant to W.S. Allward, designer and supervisor of the great Canadian memorial on Vimy Ridge, Hahn had earned a wide reputation as a designer of war memorials, no less than nine Canadian cities having chosen his work.

That he had applied for his citizenship papers on his twenty-first birthday, that he had lived in Canada for 38 years, that he had made a distinctive contribution to Canadian culture made not the slightest impression on our one-drop theorists. The work of the propagandists had been done too well for that. He was a German with a German name. That was enough.

As the controversy raged through the town some strange facts began to appear. The two local newspapers, which could be depended upon to disagree violently on any subject save the divine inspiration of the profit system, joined hands in defending Hahn and in denouncing the hundred-per-centers. To refuse Hahn's design, they declared, would be to administer an undeserved slap in the face of every foreign-born Canadian citizen.

But stranger than this was the fact that it was not the war veteran organizations which led the assault although they did object. Rather it was the Board of Trade, the Independent Order Daughters of the Empire (the Canadian DAR), and the War Widows' Association. The degree of bitterness shown by the gals and by Kiwanian R.B. Parker, president of the Board of Trade and captain-general of the opposition, was a source of astonishment to many of those occupying the sidelines. They, however, did not reflect that Kiwanian Parker, the Board of Trade, the IODE, and the War Widows were all doing business on the old stand when the lecturers were on the loose. Nor, indeed, did they recall that much of the oratorical snipe shooting was directed specifically at the female of the species.

There was nothing ephemeral about the first great battle of the war. Month passed into month and it raged unabated. The climax was reached on May 13th, 1925, when the committee met in a bitter session that lasted almost until dawn. Acts of violence were narrowly averted when one patriot clambered upon a chair and shouted, 'Rather than be moved to lift my hat when I passed this infamous thing I would be strongly tempted to *spit* upon it.' Another seconded the motion by declaring it to be 'a studied German insult to the glorious Canadian dead.'

When Hahn was appraised of the storm his creation had caused he graciously offered to withdraw it. But, in spite of the pressure brought to bear on it, the committee refused to allow him to do so. Instead it adjourned for nine months with a pious hope that public feeling would moderate.

During the intervening months interest in the project was heightened by another controversy – where was the cenotaph going to be erected? The task of choosing a site had earlier been allotted to a sub-committee of aldermen who had designated a corner of the spacious parliament building grounds as the best available spot. When the cenotaph committee was formed it immediately declared the question open and the city hall was in a constant state of siege as hordes of tax-payers descended upon it – eager to make patriotism pay handsome dividends. In the words of one alderman, the city hall corridors had, for seven months, been knee-deep with owners of corner lots, all intent upon unloading their property on to the city at a satisfactory profit.

When the committee met again, in May 1927, it hurdled its ethnological difficulties very neatly by awarding the honorarium to Hahn but rejecting his design. It chose the site for the cenotaph and decided to hold another contest. This time the rules were made – 'open to any Canadian citizen *born* in Canada, elsewhere in the British Empire, or in any of the late allied countries.' It also stipulated that the prize this time was to be $500 with an additional $2,000 to be paid to the designer for superintending construction. If, for any reason, the winning design should not prove acceptable to the committee it could sever its connection with the winning artist by payment of the $500.

In refusing to confirm the decision of its judges the committee was put to a good deal of trouble pacifying those indignant artists so that they would act again. But they talked fast and won them over at last by promising that this time their decision would be final. Honest, scout's word of honour, it would!

The conditions went out, the designs came in and in November the judges again handed down their verdict. Unanimously, they bestowed the palm, and the $500, upon Miss Elizabeth Wood, also of Toronto. To quote them, briefly: 'The winning design, in our opinion, is remarkable for its originality and by its heroic proportions is bound to attract the attention of the passers by. ... It avoids the similarity of so many war memorials already erected. The rugged execution of the dominant figure (a muscular young man standing erect, stripped to the waist) is outstanding, breathing, as it were, the spirit of the West with its strength and confidence, and at the same time a memory of the past, emblematic of those who answered their country's call.'

The model was set up in various shop windows and the patriots came, and saw, and were gratified. A sigh of intense relief escaped from the committee-men at the mention of the good old anglo-saxon name, Elizabeth Wood. But their moment of ecstacy was all too brief and presently the anguished cries of, 'Oh Death where is thy sting? What, oh what, did I ever do to deserve this?' went reverberating up and down the alleys of the town.

Miss Wood, it was discovered, was the wife of one Emmanuel Hahn, of Toronto, also a sculptor!

Have I previously alluded to a deluge? Then I retract. In comparison to the downpour of contumely the discovery of Miss Wood's marital status caused, it was but the gentle falling of the dew! The veterans of the previous campaign all rushed to re-enlist, and the Board of Trade and the IODE again led the assault of intolerance against decency. Without stopping to examine the facts they jumped at once to the conclusion that the design was Hahn's, that he had merely used his wife's maiden name to circumvent the conditions of the contest. But they were astute enough to realize that something more than an unfounded suspicion was necessary to win the battle and they turned their guns on the design itself. When the War Widows got off the grandiloquent, but quite meaningless, criticism that it did not adequately portray what the boys died for, they made it their battle cry.

The committee was ensnared in a dilemma that cried aloud for a Solomon. It could neither accept the design nor refuse it. If it confirmed the judges' award it would be tortured through all eternity by the thought that the design was really Hahn's – a thought too horrible to hold. To refuse would be to do Miss Wood a grievous injury if the work was her own. It had no complaint with her, save perhaps her questionable choice in husbands, and this was not sufficient ground upon which to reject her creation. It was left for the *cognoscenti* to point a way out through a chance remark that, strictly speaking, Miss Wood's design was not a cenotaph.

What, not a cenotaph?

'Eureka!' cried the committee as it forwarded her a cheque for $500 post haste. At least it had rid itself of the Hahn family, even if it was still without a cenotaph.

Miss Wood thanked them for the cash and then undertook to divest them of their last shred of self-respect by answering the criticism of her work. Right readily did she admit that hers was not a cenotaph, but she pointed to the fact that in the four-page booklet of rules and regulations not a single mention was made of the word. Instead the words 'monument' and 'war memorial' were used repeatedly. Moreover the word cenotaph had been used almost exclusively in the rules governing the first contest. If a cenotaph was wanted then the committee should have asked for it. Surely the learned gentlemen were aware that such subjects as mind-reading and crystal-gazing were not usually taught in a well conducted school of art!

On December 5th, 1927, the committee, now badly punch-drunk, assembled again to get rid of the responsibility that had made it the laughing stock of the country. To hold another contest was more than their shell-shocked nerves could stand. Besides, Hahn might have some sisters or cousins who were Canadian born. It had spent $3,000 dollars on designs and was no nearer its objective than it had been three years before. The idea then would be to take the second best design and get the thing started before there was another war. But the committee was never very long on logic and it skipped the second best design and seized upon the third. Thus, at long last, it gained for Winnipeg the dubious honour of being the only city in Canada to erect, literally, a fourth rate cenotaph!

The fact that English-born Gilbert Parfaitt, its designer, was employed by the provincial government while A.M. Eadie, designer of the second best model, was friendless at court may or may not be significant.

With its official dedication on November 11th, 1928, it might logically be supposed that the cenotaph's career in the public prints would be at an end. Such was sadly not the case. The site the committee chose for it was a most unhappy one.

At the time of selection a town planning craze was running amok in our town. A dog-leg highway was constructed between Portage Avenue and Broadway to give south side residents ready access to the business section located on the avenue. This highway runs due south for one block, takes a wide turn to the west around the University buildings and then continues south past the western limits of the parliament building grounds. A narrow continuation of the straight section of the highway, known as Memorial Boulevard, leads directly to the main door of the parliament building. On it the cenotaph was erected.

How the committee ever came to light upon this particular spot is beyond all understanding. Eighty feet to the east were the back yards of a dilapidated terrace of rooming houses. One hundred and twenty feet south-east was the provincial jail, surrounded by a twelve-foot, weatherbeaten, unpainted board fence. To the south-west was an antediluvian university building also with its hideous board fence. And hemming it in on the west and north was the dirtiest twenty thousand square feet of vacant space in the city, mostly quagmire. A chance visitor to the town might have mistaken it very easily for the city dump, for it was littered from end to end with old rags, discarded boots and auto tires, bottles, newspapers, tin cans and old clothes. Between the mounds of mud, left by the excavators of the street, were scattered piles of refuse, salvaged from nearby garbage cans by stray dogs.

This is the site, aptly described by a local dignitary as 'the frog pond underneath the scaffold in the back yard of the jail,' on which the cenotaph was erected. With the exception of building a hay-wire fence around the muck-heap no effort was made to improve the grounds until eighteen months later. The committee had escaped to a welcome oblivion and the efforts to have the grounds cleaned up were made exclusively by those whose business took them past the site.

These efforts, sporadic at best, accomplished nothing. But, in the fall of 1929, ex-chairman Waugh became embroiled in a newspaper argument with the civic finance committee chairman about who was responsible for the sorry state of the plot and this controversy served to revive the interest of the patriots. The city council, motivated, I suspect, largely by a desire to get rid of their noise, agreed at length to foot the bill for cleaning and sodding the grounds. In 1931 the tenements were demolished to make way for the civic auditorium, the erection of which was undertaken as a relief measure. Our growing population of miscreants necessitated commodious quarters and a new jail was erected elsewhere. The unsightly board fence was torn down and the building remodelled to house the Debt Adjustment Board which gives the war winners shelter against the mortgage companies.

The last clipping in the bulging cenotaph file in the *Free Press* 'morgue' shows vividly how bitterness breeds venom, and intolerance, abuse. It is dated September 1930, and tells of a special policeman being detailed to guard the monument against despoilers! Just prior to its dedication the canvas protecting shroud was set afire and the face of the monument badly scarred. After an interval it was discovered splattered badly with black paint. Then someone tore one of the bronze lion head decorations off and threw it into the street. In all about a dozen attacks were made upon it!

But today all is quiet on the cenotaph front. All that remains to remind the passer-by of the conflict is the hay-wire fence. Somehow that fence seems most appropriate; a sort of cenotaph in itself, standing, as it were, in memory of the type of mind that made the other possible.

FLORENCE RHEIN

Beauty Parlour

'Miss Arthur advised me to give him up,' said Miss Brown.

She pressed my hair down between her second and third finger and inserted another water wave comb. Miss Brown was pretty. Miss Arthur looked at me over the bent shoulders of another customer and screwed up her mouth as if to say, 'I told her, yes, I told her to give him up.' Miss Arthur was grey and dry and her eyes peered greyly from behind silver rimmed spectacles.

'We've been keeping company for five years,' said Miss Brown. 'I left Beaver Dam three years ago and I've only been back once for a holiday. The folks at home say he hasn't gone out with another girl in all that time. But it's no use.'

Miss Arthur had turned her customer over to the third woman in the establishment, Miss Carter, who was an adept at marcelling, and came over to my chair.

'He lost his job, you know,' she said. 'As I said to Miss Brown, "What is the use of being engaged to a man who has no prospects?" She's a sensible girl. She realized there was nothing in it for her. We've all seen girls who gave up their lives like that – to be kitchen slaves. Haven't we, Miss Brown?'

Miss Brown nodded and Miss Arthur moved away, gathering up an armful of towels and brushes to be washed. Her hair looked flat, like a dull grey cap under her grey net which always slid down on her brow in a spidery line.

'You know,' said Miss Brown, 'I think this is the most awful time to live in. Why, young people haven't a chance. With the depression and everything, why, we haven't a chance. I had to give him up. And I'm twenty-eight,' she said.

I looked up at her and noticed that she was still young with a rather buxom but firm figure, and wideset eyes. Her unhappiness was low spoken for fear of disturbing the other customers in the room, but she throbbed with suppressed revolt, pouring her youth into brushings and curlings and polishings to make other women more beautiful. I had known that she was not happy by the way she touched my hair. I can tell a good deal about a hairdresser by the way she approaches my hair. Miss Arthur brushed it dutifully, by the clock as it were, to earn the dollar and a half which she 'felt justified' in charging for an extra heavy head of hair. Miss Brown touched it with jealous skill. I could see her in the mirror opposite me, examining grey hairs. She would bend her dark head and exclaim, 'And you say you are only twenty-six, Mrs Sinclair. Why, I'm twenty-eight and I haven't a grey hair in my head.'

Miss Carter, the third attendant, was silent with a complete reserve. She was one of those women who is physically neither dark nor blonde, old nor young, and whose spiritual make-up is equally indeterminate. She was an excellent hairdresser. She almost caressed each strand as she turned it over the iron, and she was always being 'jumped' by Miss Arthur for taking too long over arranging the customers' hair. In spite of her skill I did not like her to work on me. For one thing, her complexion was not particularly good, and for another she was extraordinarily physical. Perhaps it was only that when she leaned over me I was annoyed by hearing her breathing, or perhaps the smell of starch in her uniform was too insistent.

Miss Arthur had been a hairdresser for almost twenty years. Her diploma, framed in an imitation gilt frame, hung over the washstands. There was nothing up to date about the establishment, but Miss Arthur was a good business woman and by living in dark quarters with old-fashioned plumbing she paid so little rent that this compensated for the loss of customers who demanded sunlight and pink and green booths, and 'operators' in fussy uniforms. Miss Arthur was considered by a number of women to be very thorough, and though the place was gloomy and definitely not smart it had the reputation of being hygienic. It *was* clean. Miss Arthur saw to it that Miss Brown and Miss Carter scrubbed the floors twice a week and all the brushes and towels were regularly put in boilers. There were enough customers to keep four women busy, but Miss Arthur preferred to overwork three women and save on commissions. Since she worked quite as hard herself as did the two assistants, neither Miss Brown nor Miss Carter would have dreamed of complaining, or so Miss Brown told me one day when Miss Arthur had taken time out to go to a lecture on cooking which was being held, admission free, in a nearby moving picture house.

The next time I went in to have my hair washed Miss Brown told me she had had a letter from her young man back in Ohio. 'He wrote me a long letter,' she said, 'but I didn't answer it. What's the use? We neither of us have any money and you know what happens to a girl who marries without something put by. You know what marriage is.'

'I tell her,'' said Miss Arthur, 'that if he writes again she had better not open the letter. It only upsets her and interferes with her work. I tell her she should make it a closed book.'

I was the only customer in the room at the time and Miss Arthur and Miss Carter were both unoccupied. Miss Carter stood, silent as usual, looking out of the window, staring intently into the narrow back yard flanked by grey walls and cluttered with ash cans.

A customer came in and Miss Arthur hurried forward. 'Miss Carter can take you,' she said.

'I'd rather not have Miss Carter,' said the woman. 'I'm not satisfied with the massage she has been giving me lately.'

'Very well, I will take you myself.'

Miss Arthur sent Miss Carter a bridling look of censure, and Miss Brown a conspiratorial glance. Miss Carter turned back to her examination of the alley without saying anything.

That was in December. I then went to France for several months. When I returned to town in April, I made an appointment to have my hair shampooed. Miss Brown took down my hair and shook it loose.

'Your hair is dry,' she said, and began rubbing oil into my scalp.

She was looking thinner, I thought, and her nose was more pointed than I remembered it.

'We'll have to charge you fifty cents extra for the oil,' she said.

'I've been away such a long time,' I said. 'What is the news? What do you hear from Beaver Dam?'

'Oh, nothing, except I got a letter from the family; my boy friend married a girl from Cincinnati last month. Miss Arthur says it's all for the best, now that it is definitely over.'

Her face was not expressive, what prettiness she had was a matter of fine eyes and neat features and youth. She was so calm that I felt she might have been talking about some other woman's lover, not her own, and that her own life had ceased to exist outside of the second story hairdresser's shop.

'And where is Miss Carter?' I asked. 'Isn't she here today?'

'Oh, Miss Arthur had to let her go. She had to let her go after twelve years. The customers weren't satisfied with her work. Miss Arthur told her that if her work didn't improve, if she didn't take more time and trouble with her work, she would have to go.'

'Yes, I warned her,' said Miss Arthur.

She came out of the small room at the back of the shop where the hairbrush boiler stood and moved close to me, her nearsighted face pushed forward, turtle-wise.

'Has she got another job,' I asked.

'Not regular,' said Miss Arthur. 'Though she's taken some of our old customers by saying awful things about us.'

'You know that she had a baby in March,' said Miss Brown.

'I can't see how I could have been misled by her so for twelve years,' said Miss Arthur. 'She used the most awful language to me. And now she rushes up to customers and tells them terrible things about us. You may meet her some day in a trolley car.

'I began to suspect something was queer just about the time you went abroad. Her work was getting awfully slow, and she kept sitting down and staring out the window in such a funny way. She put on weight too. She used to take a thirty-six uniform and then she had to buy a forty-two. She got big all of a sudden. But she didn't take me into her confidence, so of course I didn't speak to her about it.

'It soon became obvious what was wrong. But she didn't see fit to say anything to me. One morning she was sick right there on the floor. Disgusting. Since she hadn't told me anything, I took no notice: just let her clean it up herself.'

Miss Arthur smiled virtuously.

'She told Miss Brown though.'

Miss Brown went on brushing my hair in silence, but I could feel that she was listening to an oft repeated, dearly loved tale.

'She told Miss Brown that she had taken twenty dollars' worth of things to get rid of it, but they only made her feel sick, and Miss Brown very properly told me, for I doubt if I would have suspected anything even though she had got so stout. Why, she'd worked with me for twelve years. I taught her all she knew about hairdressing.

'One of the customers did suspect, and Miss Brown coolly talked to the customer about her husband, saying that she had been married secretly for over a year. She was an awful liar, because she told Miss Brown that she was going to be married in March.

'Miss Brown came and told me that too. We used to have a little joke about that. She wasn't our idea of a bride, a sweet bride she would make, her looking like that.'

Miss Brown and Miss Arthur laughed together over this favoured joke.

'I can't imagine any man looking at her,' said Miss Brown.

'Nor I,' said Miss Arthur. 'All I could do was tell her that if she didn't change her ways I would have to let her go. That if she didn't stop sitting around and shirking, I would have to discharge her. She hadn't said anything about her condition so I couldn't mention that. I felt it was up to her to tell me.

'One day, she came in here and pulled her chair by the window and just stared out. I can't see what she would want to look at in that old alley full of garbage cans and rag men, but there she sat all day and stared and wouldn't even get up to answer the phone. Miss Brown and I went into the lavatory and talked it over. We had to do most of our talking in the lavatory so she couldn't hear us, because of course we didn't want her to know what we were saying. We decided that the time had come for me to speak, so I went in to her. I asked her if she was married. And then she jumped up and began to swear. I had no idea that a woman could swear like that. She called me the most awful names. Miss Brown could hear it all from the lavatory, she yelled so loud. It was terrible the way she swore and shouted at me. Then she rushed about like a mad thing; put on her hat and coat, and went away. She never cried, she just went on swearing oaths.'

'I heard it all from the lavatory,' said Miss Brown.

'Her baby died three days after it was born,' said Miss Arthur. 'And now she goes up to our customers on the street, and begins to talk about the baby. She tells them about the baby, and cries, right there in the street. As I said to a customer, "What does she mean by talking and crying like that?" Why, we know she hasn't a spark of maternal feeling. She told Miss Brown that she took twenty dollars' worth of things to make it go away. Any woman who could do that couldn't have any decency. What does she want to rush up to our customers for and tell them that the baby died?'

ALAN CREIGHTON

Barbarous Epoch

In those days
Men let thudding iron
Shape their muscle.
They drove fast on Sunday,
Covering leaves with dust.
They must have loved suffering
For they let fresh lives
Follow old paths;
With enough for all
They feared leisure.

In their dark scurrying
They supposed themselves angels,
Forgetting they were a race of beautiful animals
That needed tending.
They were wasteful and stupid ...
It was a crude age.

J.R. McLEAN

Bennett of Tarsus

Mr Bennett is extremely clever. His series of radio speeches, which caught the people of Canada unawares, shocked the Montreal *Gazette,* startled the Liberals, and temporarily surprised the CCF into an illicit union. He stole a march on Mr King and on Parliament. In his reply to the Speech from the Throne, however, Mr King made up for his long silences. The recital of his long interest and fruitful work in the field of social legislation was his complete vindication.

Mr Bennett's speeches were not profound. They contained little that has not been shouted at him from all quarters for the past five years. He was always too busy to listen. He made effective use however of the radio technique for the first time in Canadian politics. Nothing sounds so appalling on the radio as a typical stump speech. Mr. Bennett delivered lectures. He did not chat like Roosevelt. He finds it extremely difficult to be human and friendly to strangers. One cannot help but think that he looked on the microphone as a public meeting or a mob. What he lacked in human touch he made up in moral fervour. He had been so recently converted himself that he had all the fervour of an early Christian. He had reached the Straight Street by a road which had many sharp turnings, and the last was the sharpest turning of all. What worries a great many people now is that same doubt which Saul of Tarsus met after he had seen the great light. 'Is not this he that destroyed them which called upon this name in Jerusalem?' One version has it that among the Athenians there were even some who asked like the Montreal *Gazette* 'What is this rag-picker trying to make out?'

Mr Bennett will have to prove his conversion by bringing down all the legislation he forecast in the Speech from the Throne. There is an uneasy suspicion that the legislation has not yet been discussed in any detail by the Cabinet or the Conservative caucus.

It is Mr Bennett's misfortune that his conversion came so late. It must appear in spite of his protests as just another election bid. A very few months ago in a somewhat thinly veiled reference Mr Bennett said that there were some Canadians who would not be missed if they crossed the border into the United States. Mr Stevens had attacked big business and was forced to resign from the Cabinet. And now Mr Bennett is breathing out threatenings and slaughter against the very same groups.

The speeech from the Throne marks more definitely than ever the trend in Canada toward the positive State. If Mr Bennett's legislation is ready and within the competence of the Dominion Parliament we shall make more progress in one session than in all the parliaments since Confederation. Various forms of social insurance, minimum wage laws, improved company laws are all designed to rectify abuses which Mr Bennett has recently discovered. Mr King who has worked on them since 1898 has offered his cordial co-operation.

The Prime Minister pointed to his 1934 legislation as evidence of his conviction even at that date that reform was urgently needed. The establishment of the Bank of Canada, the Natural Products Marketing Act, the Farmers' Creditors Arrangement Act were no mean achievements. The Bank of Canada has not yet begun to operate. How useful an instrument it is likely to be no one can say. Nor is it certain how far its usefulness has been imperilled by its curious constitution. Mr King pointed to the Central Bank as another evidence of Mr Bennett's queer behaviour. It was the determination of the Conservative members of the Banking Committee which made the Central Bank a monster. Does Mr Bennett seriously believe in state intervention?

The Natural Products Marketing Act is apparently proving acceptable to the producers if not to some of the newspapers of Western Canada. Eight schemes have been approved by the Marketing Board, four of them in British Columbia covering tree fruit, red shingles, dry salt herring and salmon, and Lower Mainland milk and milk products. In Ontario flue-cured tobacco and dry beans producers and in Ontario and the Maritime provinces potato producers have had their schemes approved. The Board is considering poultry and livestock schemes for the three Prairie provinces. A poll of the poultry producers is now being taken to find whether a representative majority favours the proposal. The Board has also before it schemes for Jam, Jellies and Marmalade in the Dominion, British Columbia vegetables, and Ontario export cattle. The Liberals will apparently have to accept the Marketing Act as a *fait accompli*. They can at least show one good man and true, Mr Motherwell.

The Farmer's Creditors Arrangement Act under its able and politic administrator, Mr M.A. MacPherson, us just beginning to prove itself. Some 16,000 farmers have been interviewed by official receivers, 2,000 or more applications for adjustment have been made. 700 or 800 final settlements have been reached. Unfortunately like Mr Bennett's reform programme it is late. Improving business, even if it has not yet affected agriculture, will make settlements vastly more difficult to achieve. Everything will depend upon the Boards of Review which have just begun their work. Mr Bennett who still harbours a healthy contempt for economists called them in too late.

For the future of good government in Canada Civil Service reform is a vital measure. Mr Bennett is reported to be studying assiduously all the available literature on the subject. As Mr Bennett's Plan was itself the result of a rather hasty perusal by Mr Herridge and Mr Finlayson of the available literature on planning one may expect something to come of Mr Bennett's own study. There is an urgent need of introducing into the service a larger number of better trained and more versatile brains. Much has already been done especially in the Departments of Finance, External Affairs, Commerce, including the Research Council and the Bureau of Statistics, and the Department of Agriculture on the technical and economic sides. But the functions of government are growing so rapidly that the few competent members of the various departments are overwhelmed with work.

One of Mr Bennett's greatest disadvantages is the strong defensive armour he has build around himself, and another his intolerance. He has been the champion of individual initiative and has permitted little freedom to his colleagues. He has spoken with fervour of our inherited liberties and has curbed freedom of speech and assembly. Almost at the moment that he declared over the radio his determination to maintain liberty his own personal intervention prevented Tim Buck from addressing a meeting in the Little Theatre in Ottawa. The Directors of the Drama League were obliged to cancel the contract when Mr Bennett shouted his threats over the telephone. The net result was that the Prime Minister advertised Tim Buck's open air meeting. 'Opposition from any class which imperils the future of this great undertaking we will not tolerate.' Those are Mr Bennett's words, not Tim Buck's.

F.R. SCOTT

Social Notes

Stevens' Enquiry

How shocked were all the business men
When they found out how low were the wages
They had been paying their employees for years.

Protection

Isn't it lucky we have such high tariffs
To protect the Canadian working-man
From having his standard of living lowered
By the competition of foreign sweat-shops?

Efficiency

The efficiency of the capitalist system
Is rightly admired by important people.
Our huge steel mills
Operating at 25 per cent of capacity
Are the last word in organization.
The new grain elevators
Stored with superfluous wheat
Can unload a grain-boat in two hours.
Marvellous card-sorting machines
Make it easy to keep track of the unemployed.
There isn't one unnecessary employee
In these textile plants
That require 75 per cent tariff protection.
And when our closed shoe-factories re-open
They will produce more footwear than we
    can possibly buy.
So don't let us start experimenting with
    socialism
Which everyone knows means inefficiency
    and waste.

March 1935

Motherhood

Her travail now over
And her brood gone far away
This old woman of fifty
Must go charring at $2.00 a day.

Expert Advice

Have you ever noticed
How many members of monastic orders
Who have taken perpetual vows
Of poverty
And chastity
Now spend their time defending private property
And urging the poor to have large families?

Credit

This delegation of unemployed Canadians
Had just been informed
That if the Government spent any more on relief
So that their children might be decently clothed and fed
The credit of the country would suffer.

Coming Home

The Soviet ship from Leningrad to London
Was called the 'Co-operation,'
But to reach democratic Canada
I travelled by the 'Duchess of Richmond.'

Royal Commission

Three cheers for the Royal Commission!
By the end of fifteen months
We shall have all the facts.
A year later
And the Government will have a plan.
But by that time, of course,
The situation will have entirely changed
And it would be clearly unwise to interfere.

Great Discovery

After ten years of research
This great scientist
Made so valuable a discovery
That a big corporation actually paid him $150,000
To keep it off the market.

Observation

In tonight's newspaper
There were two protests:
One by an Archbishop
Against the spread of communism,
And one by an unemployed man
Who said his children were sleeping four in a bed
To keep warm.

Penology

Do you see this great walled fortress?
That is where we reform our criminals.
To make them willing and able to start life afresh
We place them in charge of a governor and guards
Carefully selected for their politics.
Uniformity of treatment for all ages and types
Guarantees the same results in all cases.
Each one has a small barred cell all to himself,
Twenty minutes exercise a day,
And full permission to write one letter a month.
We provide compulsory labour without wages
And don't molest the wives and children at all.
After several years of this special training
The prisoners are given complete freedom
To start looking for a job.

Government Help

After the strike began
Troops were rushed
To defend property.
But before the trouble started
Nobody seems to have bothered
To defend living standards.

General Election

There is nothing like hard times
For teaching the people to think.
By a decisive vote
After discussing all the issues
They have turned out the Conservatives
And put back the Liberals.

G.V. FERGUSON

An Alberta Prophet – 1935 Model

This is the story of William Aberhart, the Prophet of Social Credit in Southern Alberta. I do not know his whole story. I wish I did. But I am in the class of those 'who knew him when' – when he was no prophet. Hence this brief prologue to my tale.

Just over twenty years ago Alberta was in the throes of its first prohibition campaign; and a mass meeting of boys had been called to rally them to the cause of the Drys. They were mainly boys who were regular attendants at Sunday School. We did not call it Sunday School. It was before the day of the Tuxis Square, but we had some other name for our activity. I was (for reasons into which it is now unnecessary to enter) a prominent junior Dry. William Aberhart, then as now the principal of a Calgary high school, was a figure among the senior Drys, and I well remember (indeed I blush to remember) the praise he bestowed upon me for the quality of my work in the cause of Prohibition.

Since then our paths have diverged. Mr Aberhart became a Major Prophet, and I became a newspaperman. When next we met we were exercising our respective functions in the community, in the month of January 1935. We did not meet personally. I sat at the press table of the convention of the United Farmers of Alberta, and listened all one morning while Mr Aberhart thundered forth his prophecies about Social Credit. It was an occasion I will not forget, for Mr Aberhart is to-day a strange and powerful figure in his adopted province. Many people swear by him. As many more fear him. Very few laugh at him.

William Aberhart was born on an Ontario farm. He comes, I think, of German or German-American stock, but he has lived for many years in the West. He is a school teacher, and a good one. As he has developed his idiosyncrasies of recent years, I am informed, there have been sundry efforts to have him indicted as a Calgary Socrates. But these have failed because his record as a teacher is too good. His students do extremely well, and he has never neglected them or their work, which is astonishing in view of the number of outside activities he has developed.

Before the war, so far as I know, these activities were more or less orthodox: Sunday School, Bible Class, Prohibition, and what not. But during the war, or shortly thereafter, he began to develop a peculiar line of Bible prophecy. You know the kind of thing. Pastor Russell made a good thing out of it in his day. But Mr Aberhart is not a Russellite. He has a line of his own. He interprets the Bible after his own fashion, developing from sundry selected texts his own peculiar explanation of past events, his prophecies of things to come. He early took to radio, and spent much of his time explaining the errors and follies of the orthodox pastors. His own interpretations were much more peppy than those of the professionals, and he quickly attracted a following.

This following has grown to such an extent that a large and impressive building now stands on Calgary's main street, the Prophetic Bible Institute, built by contributed funds, and here Mr Aberhart holds forth. All over Southern Alberta his flock gather around their radios to hear his deep and confident voice expounding the Scriptures, the Law, the Prophets, and Social Credit.

It was not until Mr Aberhart was well established as a religious figure that he took to Social Credit, and it is Social Credit which has made him the acknowledged leader of a fanatical host of Alberta farmers. The fanaticism springs in part from the position Mr Aberhart holds as a prophet; but his Social Credit doctrine is also such as to inspire mankind with enthusiasm.

Such enthusiasms are proverbially easy to start in Alberta. One explanation of this phenomenon was given me by a prominent Alberta politician, and I will pass it on, without comment of my own. Said he, 'A new country is always populated by fellows who have active minds – cranks if you like to call them that – who were unhappy in their old, settled environment. That explains the people of the Prairies. Well, the wilder they were, the further west they went, until they were stopped by the mountains – stuck in the Foothills.'

There is another interpretation, kinder to Alberta, which I prefer. Imagine yourself to be a decent, hard-working farmer who has undergone every kind of agricultural ordeal: he has been made the buffeted plaything of the high tariff manipulators; he has built markets in the United States which have been ruthlessly cut off; he has suffered drought and every other agricultural pestilence from root rot to grasshoppers; he has seen prices drop to incredibly low levels, and he has not even been able to sell what he had at those levels; he is discouraged, down-hearted, and broke. He owes everybody more money than he thinks he will every see again, and because he is a decent fellow, it worries him.

Then he tunes in on his radio, and he hears a voice explaining with unbounded confidence that his troubles can all be simply solved by a little juggling of currency and credit. Jehovah speaking from Sinai could not have spoken with more assurance, and the children of Israel were never so discouraged as the Alberta farmers are to-day. The Israelites had manna. The Albertans have no manna – not yet. But Mr Aberhart has promised them something much better. He has promised them money, cash money in amounts they have almost forgotten. Real, honest-to-God cash in hand, $25 a month. This is the real thing, and who will blame them if they don't tumble over themselves to get on the Social Credit bandwagon.

This is what Mr Aberhart has done. He has a marvellous expository gift. He has taken the recondite Douglas scheme, and made it over in terms which everybody can understand. He has, moreover, improved on it. His scheme, in fact, makes manna look like the poorest handout a deserving people ever got. Mr Aberhart proposes a Social Credit Scheme for Alberta in which the farmer will not get the world price for his produce, but the "just price,' a price to be set by a commission of Albertans. This price will be higher than the world price, a great deal higher; and in order to give people a chance to buy at that higher price, Mr Aberhart proposes a monthly payment of $25 a month to one and all. He calls the $25 our cultural heritage, and at $25 a month he has made culture more popular in Alberta than ever before.

This article is not an exposition of the Aberhart scheme. It is impossible to do justice to the Social Credit House from which all these good things will flow, or to the technique of credit control which Mr Aberhart has worked out. It is enough to say that he has made a piker out of Major Douglas and that he looks on the British North America Act as if it were something the cat dragged in. The details of the scheme, moreover, count for little, for what has made Mr Aberhart a power in the land is the simple doctrine, 'Come unto me all that travail and are heavy laden, and I will give you $25 a month.' Without that appeal, the Calgary Prophet would be just another of those currency cranks whose chief distinction is their inordinate capacity to induce mental fatigue.

Mr Aberhart has indeed become more than a Prophet. He has become a Political Threat. How serious a threat he is I do not know, but that astute body of politicians who guide the destinies of the United Farmers of Alberta and the Province as well are badly worried. Their meetings, for the first time in 15 years, are harried by the Social Creditors who in turn have Social Credit Circles of their own. All over Southern Alberta a man cannot stand upon a public platform without being asked if he is for or against Aberhart. The Prophet meanwhile inveighs against them in the approved and intolerant style of all prophets. All who are not for him are against him. From Calgary south the country has gone for Social Credit in a big way, and recent issues of the *Edmonton Bulletin,* a shrewdly-managed newspaper which knows how most straws stand in the wind, show clearly, by the medium of red ink and display scareheads that Social Credit is invading the north country as well. There is an election this summer. It will be interesting to note how many frightened candidates are pledged to Social Credit before the campaign is done.

My own feeling is that, when the heads are counted at the polls, Mr Aberhart and his friends will not have done very well. But the effect of what they have done will linger long. And the ultimate disillusion will be both great and dangerous. This is, indeed, the sad part of the Aberhart manifestation. Hopes raised so high cannot be dashed to the ground without damage, and the moral and spiritual damage to Alberta will not be slight. This is the reason why I deplore Mr Aberhart, in spite of our joint activities in the cause of Prohibition. He is an honest and sincere man, which makes things worse. He has not profited personally by his own alluring preachments, and I admire him for that. I also admire him for the amusement he has given me. I am grateful for that. But nevertheless, I deplore Mr Aberhart. I deplore him wholeheartedly. I wish that he would stop.

GRAHAM SPRY
Politics

The swords are drawn and the enemies are entering the final combat, but it may be reasonably asked upon what issues is this significant war being fought? The Liberals, with the light of victory in their eyes, feel the path to Parliament Hill illumined and warmed by the funeral pyres that destroyed the Conservative parties in the provinces, but at the time of writing (August 1st), Mr Mackenzie King and his general staff have vouchsafed the public no better cause for voting Liberal than the destruction of Mr Bennett and his party. Mr Stevens and Mr Woodsworth have both issued manifestos very similar in language though fundamentally different in policy and the public, so far as they have reached the public, know in general that they stand for a change. The daily press of Canada, with few exceptions, debates no definite issues and satisfies its readers with emphatic denunciations of rival parties.

Mr Bennett's attempt to make the Conservative party a party of reform has completely failed and even the prayers of Deacon Denton Massey have failed to polish the halo he has replanted, not too firmly, on his leader's brow. If there be one predominating political sentiment it is certainly the sentiment that Mr Bennett does not stand for reform and that he and his party deserve a thorough and prolonged rest. It is not necessary, as Mr King was once alleged to have done, to consult astrologers in order to be endowed with enough prophetic powers to foresee not only the defeat but even the extinction of the Conservative party.

An extraordinary and somewhat pathetic detestation for Mr Bennett is the primary political motive in Canada to-day, and that unusual, somewhat unintelligent, fervour, combined with a vague, real but still un-canalized desire for change form the main elements in a national election which, in the fifth year of the depression in a pre-war epoch, has an importance immeasurably beyond that of almost any election since Confederation. Unless Mr King surprises the public and contributes, through his influential position and the great publicity media which his well-financed party may command, a policy that creates a definite issue, it is not impossible that beyond this desire for a change and this desire to destroy Mr Bennett, the election will reflect no decision on any vital issue and settle none.

It is, perhaps, too much to hope that either the CCF or the Reconstruction Party may make the economic issue the centre of the fray. The CCF has surprised even its own executives by the vigour with which the various provincial organizations have thrown themselves into the campaign. There are more than one hundred official CCF candidates now in the field with a dozen to twenty further nominations still to come from the four western provinces. If Ontario which has so far nominated thirty-five candidates, is able to increase that number by another twenty, the CCF may have as many as one hundred and seventy throughout the Dominion, though it is more likely that the number will be between one hundred and twenty-five and one hundred and fifty. In an election so confused by new parties and movements of every shade from Lenin to Aberhart, the power of a socialist party is not easily estimated. But even with one hundred and fifty candidates, it is unlikely, and from the most impartial national point of view, regrettable that CCF lacks the financial resources to use national broadcasting and advertising sufficiently to make the future of the capitalist system a national election issue. If the Liberal party proved unwise enough to accept the gauntlet of socialism thrown down by the CCF and thereby made capitalism versus socialism the election issue, the election would have a supreme educational value and the results would have an enduring significance. But Mr King's facility for erecting the unimportant into the significant and his capacity for mopping up vague demands for change will most probably ensure that the issue raised by the CCF with the modest means at its disposal, will be obscured in a cloud partly of polite commendation and partly of "red" suspicion.

It is doubtful if either the content of Mr Stevens' party or the items of his somewhat economically contradictory policy will form a real and vital national issue. Mr Stevens, if he were running for the presidency of a republic such as the United States, might well be elected president. He has shown, in his speeches, no mean capacity for interesting almost every reformer in almost every section of the Dominion. In a straight race between Mr Stevens and the Liberal and Conservative leaders, Mr Stevens would lead by a length. But we are not, in this country, electing a president and Mr Stevens' Reconstruction Party has neither time nor organization to meet on terms of equality either of the well-paid machines of Mr King or Mr Bennett, and he will not even have the radical zeal and philosophic ardour that animate the socialists. It will be difficult for him, as the campaign proceeds, to maintain in a hostile press the frequent headlines on page one and, as his platform is analyzed, the normal sectional divisions that form the basis of Canadian politics will assert themselves. It will, for example, be no mean task to convince the western wheat grower, subject for the past fifteen years to the free trade educational endeavours of the Winnipeg Free Press, the Progressive parties, and the Wheat Pools, that the small central Canadian manufacturer is the lamb with whom he should lie down. And with the monetary heretics, such as Wm. Aberhart, and H. Hallatt, rushing to crawl under Mr Stevens' mantle, it is probable that before the election a credit war will raise the mantle to reveal that, after all, Mr Stevens' banking trousers are essentially of an old-fashioned and respectable but unacceptable cut.

Whatever may be the results of Mr Stevens' efforts to create a national political party in two months, he raises no specific and significant issues. He, too, joins with Mr King in exploiting the hate Mr Bennett has excited, and does not differ from either Mr King or Mr Bennett in his essential respect for the capitalist system. Mr Stevens' stock-in-trade is the bogey of the big interests. It is a useful political cry; it has been useful for forty years. It is re-enforced by artful appeals to almost every occupational and sectional grievance in Canada, but through the heroic propaganda of the ill-financed CCF there has been created, not only among its own supporters, but among the public in general, a desire for some more specific formula for ending the domination of these interests than either higher taxation or further commissions of regulation and control.

If this analysis be correct, then, the Liberal party will seek power without definite policies or specific promises. The Conservative party may raise issues but those issues will no more occupy the passers-by than the Latin inscriptions that float from the worn brass lips of departed princes in the cold, grey mortuary vaults of Santa Croce. The Reconstruction party offers only a new emphasis upon an old issue; a nation of shop-keepers may defeat a Napoleon, but a party of shop-keepers will hardly fool even themselves. The CCF though it has the most completely thought-out, most coherent, and most significant policy, a policy that is one side of the dominating issue of the age, is, however, too ill-financed, and has too little command of publicity media to make its issue the issue of the election.

The result of the election, therefore, will only be the defeat of the Rt Hon. R.B. Bennett. This is a consummation devoutly to be wished, but it determines no issue. It leaves the issues that are vital without an answer.

There are vital issues, issues more vital than the railways that keep Sir Edward Beatty awake at Canadian club luncheons, more vital than economy, more vital than mass-buying, more vital than the fate of petit bourgeois manufacturers in Ontario Main Streets or grocers and haberdashers on the street corners. There is, though the Liberal party will not admit it before the election, a more vital issue than freeing Canada from the chains locked by Mr Bennett.

The Liberal party, if elected, will, of course, bring some useful approaches to important problems. Mr King's shoes, softened by the gentle paths of Kingsmere Mountain, have heels that are shod with kinder materials than iron; civil liberties will be safer under his care than under Mr Bennett. In our relations with Britain's pro-Nazi government, Mr King is, again, a safer exponent of Canadian opinion than Mr Bennett; we can be sure that Mr King, if not wise, will, at any passing moment, be safe. He is not an aggressive chauffeur, but as a pedestrian, he never crosses a corner against a stop light. Inevitably the constitution of Canada and the division of powers, if only taxing powers, between the Dominion and the provinces will arise. Here, Mr King will be in his element, but, dependent as he will be on a French-Canadian block, it is improbable that such settlement as he, with, no doubt, Norman Rogers, may make will be able adequately to recognize the growing belief in the more slowly crystallizing demand or the undoubted necessity for a stronger federal government.

In questions of trade, Mr King will proffer a reasonableness that Mr Bennett could not accomplish; but if world conditions remain as they have been, it is not likely that Mr King will accomplish as much as he will proffer. Indeed, Mr King, faced with Canada's peculiar financial problem of selling in the British market and buying in the American, may be compelled, as

Mr Bennett was compelled, to protect our balance of external payments by restricting imports. Given a restricted international market for our exports, given a continuation of our financial problem, it is difficult to envisage any radical departure in tariff matters, however carefully Mr King may peruse the editorials of the Winnipeg Free Press.

So far as more fundamental problems are concerned, Mr King and the Liberals have less than no contribution to make. The Liberals do not and cannot accept the thesis of Mr Bennett that the capitalist system has collapsed, nor of the socialists that it must be replaced. The professors of Queen's may and the editors of the Winnipeg Free Press may induce a friendly attempt to reestablish less planning and more commercial freedom, and the great industries opposed to the regulation of their profits, wages, or trade practices may make the wisdom of these idealists temporarily effective, but the irresistible impact of forces not less 'natural' than the law of supply and demand will make a mockery and a menace of such attempts. Their penultimate results will not be more goodwill in big business or less unemployment; it will be more pressure from the masses who will have to endure both the goodwill and the unemployment and more power for big business.

The concentration of wealth will persist. Even a drastic inheritance tax or a great increase of taxation of unearned income will not seriously change the present situation. Such taxation may be sufficient to provide improved social services and to maintain relief, but even this is very doubtful; the largest incomes may be somewhat smaller; nevertheless, the real control of the Canadian economy will continue to lie with the few principal financial institutions and the real planning, however strongly it is labelled 'freedom' by the Liberals, will continue to be done by the hundred or so corporations which own and dominate Canada. 'Freedom' will be a boon to them, and the end of Mr King's next regime, if he has one, will find the Canadian people still more fettered, still more shackled than even under Mr Bennett.

There will remain, whatever Mr King may do, the insistent and inescapable issue of the future of our economic system. That issue may be obscured, happily for both Mr King and capitalists, by some recovery, some evanescent hue of prosperity, to which Mr King will have contributed little, or less. But it will be a temporary prosperity and it will be the prosperity, not of the Canadian people, but of a few Canadian corporations. Either there will be even no such passing prosperity, or if there is, it will be succeeded by a depression even more shadowed and tragic than the present. Unemployment may rise and fall but it will continue to exist, be there a boom or a continued depression. Wealth, sucked like the air through a ventilator, will concentrate more and more in a single class. The lines between the secure and the insecure will be drawn more harshly, more inescapably. And beyond the frontiers of Canada, the same lines will be drawn between those nations with socialist governments building a new society and those with New Deal governments struggling in futility to salvage an old. A Socialist government in Britain, a second and finally disastrous government of Mr Roosevelt, the crash and collapse of Fascist states in war and revolution in Europe, these will stimulate and hasten the crystallization of the issue in Canada. A Liberal government may be able to blink at, but it will fail to dissolve that issue. If Mr King forms the next government, he will resolve no problem. He will be but an interlude in the coming struggle for power.

Will he form a government? All the palpable evidences write the answer, yes. There are only two other possibilities. The CCF and the Reconstruction party may be far stronger than present evidences suggest. It is certainly more than probable that the CCF will form the official opposition. Will the CCF and the Reconstruction party combined have a strength as great as that of the Liberals? The CCF strength will be in urban Ontario and both the urban and rural west. It will make some impact in rural Ontario, but there Mr Stevens has a more fertile field than the CCF, thanks to the action of Agnes Macphail and Elmore Philpott and the inaction of the *Farmer's Sun*. Assuming considerable strength for the CCF in the west, and a solid Quebec and the Maritimes for the Liberals, the fight between the Liberals and the two other parties will be most significant in rural Ontario. If Mr Stevens makes a serious drive in rural Ontario, and if it is not too late, he may be able to reduce by not a few seats the Liberal possibilities there.

But there is no evident political vitality in the UFO or in the Ontario farmer. Mr Stevens may make some conquests; but no sufficient indications suggest that they will, in rural Ontario, seriously diminish the Liberal strength. Perhaps, as the campaign proceeds, the situation may radically change, Mr Stevens may be a phenomenon that has been underestimated. We think not.

The real issues in Canada will not be fought out or settled in this election. There will be some reflection of those issues and the pattern of the divisions on them will be made more apparent. But the main result will be the crushing of the Conservative party by an ungrateful nation. Mr King will probably hold one hundred and fifty or more seats, Mr Woodsworth and the socialists twenty-five to fifty or more, the Reconstruction party, twenty to twenty-five, and Communists, Social Crediters and monetary cranks, independents and what not, a handful.

This is the shape of things to come. As Cyrano might have said, it is not a very useful shape.

MALCOLM MacKENZIE ROSS

Nationale

'Breathes there a man with soul so dead
Who never to himself has said
This is my own my native land'?
Scott

Not guilty, Sir Walter!
These things I'll show you are my country's.
See! The silver fish in the pink-papered cans
Came all the way from British Columbia,
And are strictly guaranteed.
This bread is from the native wheat.
It grows out west in a big pool, you know,
And is said to make a fine burnt offering.
... That picture on the wall?
A Lawren Harris tree.
No, no, I don't think the Indians scalped it –
Essence bitten off in frost, I'd say.
... No?
Well, it's Canadian!
He went after it with a pack on his back and
    wearing his high boots.
... Oh somewhere in the great Ontario desert.
... No one lives there, no.

On my right is Massey Hall.
MacMillan cast off his baton and his first name
    the other day,
Just like Stokowski.
You should go sometime,
And see the latest Paris fashions
from Fifth Avenue,
And hear the music.
... Quebec?
I don't know French, Sir Walter, and I have
    no money on St James Street.

But their beer is very good.
You can get it over here in the beverage
    room.
... Beverage room?
Oh, the name's to scare away the devil,
    I believe.

... No, I'm from New Brunswick.
There's a sea, too, and docks lying idle, and
    men hanging about the lean grain-shafts!
In King Square they will be sleeping on
    newspapers until the snow comes.

King Square ... Queen's Park ...
Central Park ...
Hyde Park!
Until the snow comes
Where is your difference
And where is your singleness
'O Canada'
Until the snow comes?

But look, Sir Walter. Do you see that line
    three thousand miles
Without a soldier on it?
Well, never mind. Let us sit and watch the
    Fords go by.

FRANK H. UNDERHILL

On Professors and Politics

One of the signs of the slowness of Canada in emerging from the frontier stage of civilization is the shocked surprise with which so many worthy people regard the intrusion of university professors and students into current political discussions. Anyone who reads the history of the nineteenth century in Europe knows that there the universities have always been in the thick of politics; this, in fact, is one of the reasons why European writings on jurisprudence, history, and economics have tended to be so much more vital than the parallel productions of North American scholars. But to the business men of this country universities are still very much like Dutch paintings; they are things to which you point with pride as the proof of culture, especially of its expensiveness, but they have no part in the world of practical affairs.

The intrusion of professors into politics is, as a matter of fact, an old-established British institution. And this should be pointed out repeatedly in such communities as Toronto, which are always boasting of their devotion to British precedents. At the first election to the new reformed Parliament after the Reform Bill of 1832 one of the burgesses from Cambridge was George Pryme, professor of political economy in the University of Cambridge. His successor, Henry Fawcett, was elected MP for Brighton and professor of political economy in the same year, 1863, and continued to combine both activities till the end of his life. A long list of other academic men who have played a part in public life could easily be made out – classicists like Jebb of Cambridge, who sat for his university in Parliament without losing his Greek serenity, and Gilbert Murray of Oxford who would have done the same for his university had the Anglican parsons not refused to elect him; jurists such as Dicey and Anson; historians like Sir John Marriott and Sir Charles Oman; and a host of younger men who are active in contemporary politcs. Far from being regarded as something unusual (and therefore improper), this habit of Oxford and Cambridge men through the nineteenth century was only one aspect of that more intimate relationship of the English universities with public life which has tended to make them schools of statesmanship rather than the breeding grounds of PhDs such as our universities sometimes pride themselves on being.

Nor in times past has the spectacle of the academic man taking some part in public affairs been entirely unknown in Canada. We have yet to produce a greater university head than Principal Grant of Queen's, who during his principalship was, as his biographers remark, a sort of 'consulting publicist.' In the 1880s Dean Weldon of the Dalhousie Law School was a prominent Convservative member of Parliament at Ottawa. As to more recent time, Professor Stephen Leacock has just been reminding us that he and some of his McGill colleagues at the time of the Reciprocity election in 1911 were in politics 'up to their necks.' I am unaware of any volume of protest having been aroused by such examples.

Why then the outraged indignation of so many respectable people at the present activity of a few professors in politics? Can it be that the real offence just now consists in the fact that the professors concerned have mostly taken the radical side? There have been several recent incidents affecting the teaching profession in Canada which make one wonder whether this may not be the real motive behind the solicitude for keeping our institutions of learning out of current controversy. We have the curious coincidence that when Professor Norman Rogers of Queen's goes into politcs as a member of one of the respectable parties no question seems to arise as to the propriety of his actions, but when Professor W.H. Alexander of Alberta tries to run as a Labour candidate his intrusion into politics is immediately discovered to be dangerous to his university. And a school principal in Regina, Mr Coldwell, is forbidden by his board to engage in political activity, while another school principal in Calgary, Mr Aberhart, launches a new party without his right to engage in politics ever being questioned. Did the different rulings of the two schoolboards have anything to do with the fact that Mr Coldwell was a genuine radical and Mr Aberhart was only a sham one, who incidentally, was also assisting powerfully in destroying the farmers' government in the province?

The most curious reaction to the spectacle of professors in politics has been the holy scientific horror of some of their colleagues. The idea that the university is the seat of an esoteric culture which can never be shared with the multitude and that politics is only dishonest demagogery is, of course, mostly held by intellectual snobs rather than by genuinely educated men. The university professor who conceives of himself as an aloof impartial objective scientist, living in an Olympian detachment from human passions and prejudices, seldom in these days deceives anyone but himself. It is the duty of the academic man, insofar as he aims at being scientific, to make himself aware of his own biases and predilections, of the system of values within which his thinking goes on, of his 'inarticulate major premise.' Any social scientist, if he is honest with himself, will acknowledge that he never quite succeeds in living up to this duty. And most of those academic Pharisees who of late have so sanctimoniously been thanking God in our learned quarterlies that they are not as other men, soon display by their own remarks that they are subject to the same weaknesses of prejudice and partisanship which they denounce in the politician.

In our modern large-scale democracies, party is the necessary instrument through which the process of persuading and educating the public is carried on. It is the only device that we have yet discovered through which the participation of the people in making decisions on public policy can be assured with a reasonable degree of continuity. No professor who gives advice in any form on controversial issues can avoid taking sides sometimes on matters about which parties are engaged in controversy. The professor who aligns himself with one party certainly runs the risk that his own intellectual integrity will suffer from the habit of partisanship and from the still more dangerous habit of getting involved in transitory ephemeral issues. These are serious risks. But in trying to avoid them it is not necessary to go to the other extreme and become a fussy academic old maid always in terror lest the virginal purity of one's scientific mind be exposed to indecent assault if one ventures out into the rude world.

At any rate, when he is castigated by the Brahmins of the academic world for his sins, the low-caste politican-professor may comfort himself by reflecting that there are certain vices to which the Brahmins themselves are specially prone. One of these, a much more insidious intellectual danger in the long run than partisanship, is the vice of never making up your mind. We are all familiar with the professor who is so solicitous about his scientific purity that he never comes down off the fence on any issue, that he sees all sides of every question and never commits himself, delaying decision till all the facts are in, in the serene knowledge that all the facts never will be in. This kind of intellectual jugglery is not science it is a caricature of science. The scientist reaches conclusions if his mind is not paralyzed by indecision, but he is bound to hold his conclusions as hypotheses and not as dogmas.

The other danger which confronts the intellectual integrity of the academic man is the danger of respectability. It is one to which economists in this country are especially exposed. For all Canadian economists are divided into two classes; there are, firstly, those who have already served on Royal Commissions; and there are, secondly, those who are still hoping to do so. Now to serve on a Royal Commission one must have achieved a reputation for respectability. But for any reader who is familiar with the inside of our Canadian universities there is no need to develop this point further.

E.J. PRATT

Silences

There is no silence upon the earth or under the
    earth like the silence under the sea;
No cries announcing birth,
No sounds declaring death.
There is silence when the milt is laid on the
    spawn in the weeds and fungus of the
    rock-clefts;
And silence in the growth and struggle for life.
The bonitoes pounce upon the mackerel,
And are themselves caught by the barracudas,
The sharks kill the barracudas
And the great molluscs rend the sharks,
And all noiselessly –
Though swift be the action and final the
    conflict,
The drama is silent.

There is no fury upon the earth like the fury
    under the sea.
For growl and cough and snarl are the tokens
    of spendthrifts who know not the ultimate
    economy of rage.
Moreover, the pace of the blood is too fast.
But under the waves the blood is sluggard
    and has the same temperature as that of
    the sea.

There is something pre-reptilian about a
    silent kill.

Two men may end their hostilities just with
    their battle-cries.
'The devil take you,' says one
'I'll see you in hell first,' says the other
And these introductory salutes followed by a
    hail of gutturals and sibilants are often the
    beginning of friendship, for who would not
    prefer to be lustily damned than to be
    half-heartedly blessed.
No one need fear oaths that are properly
    enunciated, for they belong to the
    inheritance of just men made perfect,
    and, for all we know, of such may be
    the Kingdom of Heaven.

But let silent hate be put away for it feeds
upon the heart of the hater.
Today I watched two pair of eyes. One pair
was black and the other grey. And while
the owners thereof, for the space of five
seconds, walked past each other, the grey
snapped at the black and the black
riddled the grey.
One looked to say – 'The cat,'
And the other – 'The cur.'
But no words were spoken;
Not so much as a hiss or a murmur came
through the perfect enamel of the
teeth; not so much as a gesture of enmity.
If the right upper lip curled over the canine,
it went unnoticed.
The lashes veiled the eyes not for an instant
in the passing.
And as between the two in respect to candour
of intention or eternity of wish, there
was no choice, for the stare was mutual
and absolute.
A word would have dulled the exquisite edge
of the feeling,
An oath would have flawed the crystallization of the hate.
For only such culture could grow in a
climate of silence, –
Away back before the emergence of fur or
feather, back to the unvocal sea and
down deep where the darkness spills its
wash on the threshold of light, where the
lids never close upon the eyes, where the
inhabitants slay in silence and are as
silently slain.

QUEBECER
French Canadian Nationalism

There is a movement on foot amongst the French Canadians that Canadians would do well to study. Unnoticed by the English press, unsuspected by the public at large, it is steadily gaining strength in Quebec. It has its own clubs, its youth organizations, its newspapers. What is of vastly more importance, it has the backing of the Catholic Church.

This is the movement for the creation of an independent French and Catholic republic on the banks of the St Lawrence.

It is well known that the Abbé Groulx has been preaching this idea for many years. The world war gave it popularity amongst a people conscripted to fight other peoples' battles on foreign soil, but during the years of 'prosperity' little more was heard of it. With the depression, however, it has again sprung into prominence, and this time it is a force to be reckoned with. For Paul Gouin, the leader of the Action Libérale Nationale party, which now holds 42 seats in the provincial legislature, has himself publicly voiced the hope of French-Canadian independence. Basing himself on the remarks of Cardinal Villeneuve made in 1922, he recently spoke of the 'supernatural vocation' of the French race in America, where, in the midst of this North-American Babylon, it was destined to become the 'modern Israel.' The hope, he admitted, could not be immediately realized, but it was something towards which his fellow countrymen would never cease to strive.

To understand the full character of the movement, one must read some paper like *L'Indépendance*. This is the official organ of the 'Jeunesses Patriotes,' a youth organization most active in promoting the new nationalism. From the most recently published number, dated February 1936, and specially dedicated to the Abbé Groulx, the following ideas are taken. In case anyone should like to read the material for himself, he should send his five cents for a copy to the office, 1153 Dorchester Street East, Montreal.

In the first place, the call for independence from the Dominion is made in ringing tones. 'The French-Canadian people will not exist as a nation until it has freed itself from the foreign yoke. This is a right we claim, we demand, and we shall acquire.' Confederation is an absurd attempt to bind together provinces divided by race culture, geography, and religion. There is a natural right to secession. A new name is suggested for the state-to-be: Laurentia. 'O Laurentie, terre de nos aieux.'

It is to be a Catholic state. Just what that means in the political field is not very clear, but some idea of how theocratic it will be may be gained from the fact that the present control of the Church in Quebec is apparently considered inadequate. It is notorious that one reason why Mr Taschereau is so near defeat at the moment is because the Church has turned against him.

March 1936

He has not conceded the clergy the full freedom they demand. At present the priesthood in Quebec merely controls all education, the press, the French trades unions, and social behaviour generally. In the new republic it will not be so hampered.

It is to be a corporative state. 'The parliamentary regime can lead us only to ruin, because it requires the existence of parties which dissipate our national energies.' The corporative state is said to be the 'juridical affirmation of the real man,' as opposed to marxist materialism. Democracy is to be scrapped, and in its place will come 'the centralization of power, wherever it may be necessary, in the person of the man who will impose himself and who will symbolize the spiritual unity of the factory, the municipality, the district or the nation.' A long speech of the leading Belgian Fascist, M. Hoornaert, is quoted with the advice that the reader should substitute 'French Canada' for 'Belgium' whenever that word appears; the gist of the speech is that 'authority' must be restored and democratic parties destroyed.

It is to be a country of the petty bourgeoisie. Those two great scapegoats of fascist ideology, the trusts and the chain stores, will be liquidated. French Canadians are said to be naturally adapted to small proprietorship; they will apparently revert to some mediaeval form of social structure, based on peasants, craftsmen, and small traders, governed by a hierarchy of professional men with the priesthood at the top. Very like the province of Quebec today if English and American Capital were removed from it. Industrialism, father of liberalism, marxism, and all things evil, will be utterly cast out.

It will be a thoroughly masculine state, as is appropriate to Catholicism. This particular copy of *L'Indépendance* does not devote any space to the suppression of women's rights, but the idea is gaining ground in the province despite the valiant fight of those who are striving for the women's franchise. Mayor Houde of Montreal from time to time urges that all the jobs now occupied by women in the city be vacated to make room for men. Recently M. Pellisson, representing the Junior Liberal Association of St Roch, complained to M. Taschereau that there were no less than 800 women employed in the Parliament Buildings at Quebec. The charwomen were not included in this figure; no good fascist, of course, could expect men to do dirty work of that sort.

Needless to say, it will be an anti-semitic state. While M. Gouin is pointing out the civilizing mission of his 'Israel in Babylon,' his cohorts will be proving the point by organizing local pogroms. A writer in *L'Indépendance*, commenting on the evil state of present day society, concludes, 'C'est un malaise universel qui n'a qu'une source: le libéralisme juif.'

This ideal state cannot, of course, be achieved just yet. Meanwhile the 'Jeunesses Patriotes' intend to get what they can. All centralization of power at Ottawa is to be fought. Provincial rights are to be extended rather than curtailed, because the more power Quebec can obtain, the more easy it will be to make the transition to independence. Good French-Canadians are asked to take a solemn oath never to use the English language in their own province. All attempts to induce Canada to oppose Italy through the League of Nations must be prevented, since this will merely extend the nefarious influence of the British Empire. If France supports the League's efforts to help Abyssinia, it is only because France is governed by free masons. The word loyalty is quite inaccurate to describe the relations between the French Canadians and the British Crown; the true relationship is one of political expediency. Loyalty was shown in 1776, in 1812, and in 1867 only because it was a necessary condition of French survival, and assisted in the realization of the ideal of independence.

Such are the principal ideas that move the French nationalists today. They have passed the stage of being secret aspirations and parlour revolutions. More and more they are permeating the new political party which, under the leadership of M. Gouin, may shortly be expected to achieve power in Quebec. It would be wrong to suppose that they are shared by all French Canadians; it would be wrong to suppose that they will necessarily prevail. Whether they do or they do not prevail, however, will depend to a large degree upon the way they are received by the rest of Canada. If they are simply met with Imperialist ballyhoo, Orange cries, Protestant bigotry, and Anglo-Saxon conceit, they will prevail. If they are met with sympathy, understanding, and reasonable concessions, they may be satisfied with something less than the break-up of the Dominion. Ideas of this sort do not spring from mere cussedness, but from a frustrated desire for self-expression.

HUGH GARNER
Toronto's Cabbagetown

You strike Cabbagetown as soon as you cross Parliament street on the west, or the Don river on the east. Of course, if you cross the river by the Bloor street viaduct you won't find Cabbagetown. The worthy members of Toronto's citizenry who live in the Bloor district would be horrified if you made the mistake of calling their neighborhood by such a prosaic working-class name, even though some of them are just one generation removed from it. For Cabbagetown lies a short mile below the homes which dot the hills of Rosedale. (Why is it that a house in Rosedale is called a 'home,' while a house in Cabbagetown is just a house, except in obituary columns when it is a 'residence'? But hardly anyone in Cabbagetown ever hits the obituary columns.)

People living east of the river, when mentioning the district, usually say 'over the Don' much as a wealthy dowager would say, 'Put out the garbage, Simpson.' The people who live east of the river in the Riverdale district are working people too, but they wear good suits to work, and then change into overalls. The workers in Cabbagetown can't be bothered changing their clothes like that. They are proud to be recognized as workmen.

The district is blocked off by streets running east and west, north and south. There are numerous little 'places' and 'lanes' interspersed among them, lined by blocks of red brick houses crowding the broken sidewalks into the narrow roads. They are five- or six-room houses, and are supposedly easy to heat. That is why the landlords refrain from the expense of providing a furnace to heat them. Most of the heat is derived from large coal ranges that spread over half of the small kitchens. The heat from these, which seeps through the clothes-lines full of work clothes, underwear, and socks, is sometimes reinforced by small 'Quebec' heaters in the hall or upstairs rooms. Some of the small parlours are decorated with mid-Victorian bric-a-brac that has survived from the weddings, or holiday trips to Margate or Blackpool, of the parents of the large families that inhabit them.

Most of the residents are English or Scotch, with a few Irish and Canadian families. The Canadian families are usually first generation Canadians of British stock. Lately, there has been a small influx of central Europeans into the district, but they stay in their own little colonies south of Cabbagetown proper. When the sons or daughters marry, they move north or east into better residential districts, leaving their parents in the small houses that they have bravely paid for, or grown attached to.

In winter Cabbagetown retreats behind the darned-up lace curtains that cover its front windows. The district becomes gray and dreary. The chimneys send up spirals of coal smoke, and this mixes with the gray, hanging atmosphere, to add to the murkiness of the scene. Some of the boys and men shove their two-wheeled wagons down to the gas-works and collect bags of coke from the slag heaps. The women make weekly trips to Queen street or Parliament street to spend their relief vouchers. These inadequate vouchers are the chief source and topic of conversation over the back fences, or as parlour jokes. The children go to Park or Dufferin schools, or, if they are Catholics, to St Paul's school. Most of them wear brown woolen sweaters and gray wool toques. They receive them in 'Star' boxes, that are given to them at Christmas by a Toronto newspaper. The sweaters itch the children's necks, so usually the neck is slit in front with a pair of scissors, and hangs open like a heavy polo shirt.

In the summer most of the young people go swimming in Lake Ontario at the foot of Cherry Street, or for walks in Riverdale Park, north of Cabbagetown. The small boys roam the streets in gangs and play Cowboys and Indians down on the railroad tracks. Sometimes they float flimsy-looking rafts up and down the muddy river by means of poles. When they grow older they steal watermelons from freight cars, and scrap-iron from junk yards. If they are caught, they are taken to juvenile court, and are handed over to the Big Brother Movement for safe keeping. This works sometimes, but most of them go back to the gang, or haunt the pool-parlours on Queen street. The girls roam through Riverdale park in the evenings until they are picked up by some of the boys who lounge around the foot-bridge that crosses the narrow river. A lot of the marriages are of the 'shot-gun' variety, solemnized when the bride is a couple of months pregnant.

The old people sit on the front steps in the summer evenings, chatting and laughing across the small lawns or from step to step. The men wear blue work-shirts and wide suspenders, and smoke rank-smelling tobacco in their patched-up pipes. The women cover their ample figures with cotton house-dresses, and mend socks while they talk and joke with their neighbours. On Friday and Saturday nights the men retreat to the 'Avion' or 'Shamrock' beer-parlours, where they argue about the merits or demerits of the Conservative or CCF political parties. They are nearly all ex-soldiers, and when they get drunk they talk about the war. They don't usually speak of it when they are sober.

Sometimes the women hobble over to Parliament Street in their unaccustomed cuban-heeled shoes and attend the cheap little neighbourhood movie-houses to see John Boles or Shirley Temple, and collect their free china cup or saucer. On Saturday afternoons the youngsters migrate in hordes to the movies to see Ken Maynard and Hoot Gibson in their latest wild-west thrillers. They buy penny candies on the way, and usually manage to stick themselves and everything around with a mixture of chocolate and caramel stickiness.

The churches of the district hold rummage sales that are well attended by groups of women who mull over the junk-laden counters, to dive victoriously on small items of interest to themselves. The churches and civic authorities combine to bring the people the joys and sorrows of charity. The district is a social worker's paradise, where they tramp from house to house turning on smiles or frowns at will, and trying to spread their own ideas of happiness to the people, who want work and not advice.

The people get orders for clothes at the relief office. These are taken down to the central clothing depot and are filled by a man behind a wooden partition, who glances at the order form and retreats behind rows of high shelves. The room smells like an army quarter-master's stores, and the recipients line up in front of the wicket. There are benches around the walls where shoes may be tried on. These are unnecessary as none of the shoes ever fit. The attendant ties up the order in brown wrapping paper and the recipient hurries from the office and down the street, looking straight ahead until he is clear of the neighbourhood.

Some of the girls bid their boy friends good night under the corner street lights. They tell them that their parents won't allow them to bring boys home, but it is because they are ashamed of their shabby little homes, and the front room where their father holds sway in front of the radio in his stocking-feet.

In summer time the streets are criss-crossed with various household smells, usually the inevitable beef stew. Ever since the advent of the voucher system of relief, there has been a great increase in the making of beef stews in Cabbagetown. Hamburger steak is cheap, and when mixed with vegetables makes a fairly palatable meal which is filling, if not an epicurean dainty. The only drawback is that the meat voucher serves for only one or two meals; hence the relief recipients are practising vegetarians most of the week. Before the advent of vouchers the people had to go to the relief office and carry the week's supply of groceries to their homes. The variety of food was figured scientifically by well-fed dieticians and contained a large amount of oatmeal and beans. Some of the people are still eating the oatmeal they received a year or two ago. Some of it was used to light stoves, but it choked the stove-pipes.

Every year Dufferin School old boys hold their annual reunion, and old Cabbagetowners come down from Forest Hill and Rosedale to make speeches and meet each other. They always refer to their younger days in Cabbagetown, and beam around the banquet halls as if to say, 'and look at me now.' They all claim pride at being old Cabbagetowners, but they never stop in the district more than once or twice a year. Then it is usually to attend an eviction from one of the small houses that they own.

The evictions are lots of fun for everybody. That is everybody but the evicted householder and the bailiffs who are doing the evicting. Sometimes gangs of neighbours come around and carry the furniture back into the house as fast as the bailiffs carry it out.

The women of Cabbagetown deserve honourable mention. It is they who keep the men and children respectable. They are the washers of tattered shirts, the scrubbers of bare flooring, and the hangers of flimsy curtains. What more can be said of a working woman than that she kept her home clean, her husband fed, and her children happy? And she has done this under the stress and strain of unemployment, poverty, oppression, squalor, sickness, and death.

Behind the front windows of Cabbagetown lies drama, pathetic or shocking. There are innumerable quarrels and bickerings, drunken fights, sordid tragedies. There are the quarrels of worn-out parents with the idle and blasé sons and daughters, who, unable to find work, must needs lie about the house all day sunk in cynical boredom. There are the sordid fights of father and son over petty trifles that shatter their weary nerves. There are the tragic arguments over the birth of illegitimate children to the unmarried daughter of the household, who has reached too far toward happiness that comes of lovemaking, and been caught in its web. For love is cheap everywhere. It costs nothing, and costing nothing is the one thing within the reach of all the young. And if the young girls and boys spend their evening hours making love, who can blame them, and what else is there to do?

There is love in Cabbagetown. There is the all-sacrificing love of a mother for her children. Children who grow thin and puny in front of her eyes. Children who go to school in rummage-sale clothes, and clothes cut down from her own. Children who never eat oranges, or go for walks with well-dressed parents. Who never have ridden in a boat, or eaten crackly-nut at Sunnyside. There is the love of children for parents who sit around stoves in the winter and on the steps in the summer, fading away, old before their time. People who a few years ago were the ones who sat next to you on the picnic ship to Port Dalhousie, who rented the cottage next to you at Bala, or crowded you over the record counter at Eaton's or Kresges. They no longer pack huge baskets with food, drag the five youngest children to the Sunday school picnic. They no longer save all winter to rent a cottage for two weeks in the summer. They no longer shop downtown; the neighbourhood stores take their vouchers.

There is sickness in Cabbagetown. A lot of sickness. People who live mainly on potatoes and bread are easy prey for sickness. People who are forced to keep the heat on only during the day are targets for influenza and pneumonia. People who live five and six in a room are very susceptible to germs of all kinds. People who lie awake at night scratching bed bug bites are easily infected.

There is honour in Cabbagetown. It is strange, but it shows what kind of people live there. Most of them still honour God. Some honour the King. A few the government. Nearly all honour their parents, their children, and their friends. They themselves deserve honour.

In some of the houses of Cabbagetown there is squalor. Not in all the houses, but in some. It is that kind of squalor shown by bare board floors or worn out linoleum. It is apparent in torn wallpaper and fly-specked ceilings. It is noticeable in pieces of dry bread on tables, and filmy milk bottles half full of souring milk. There are dark faded curtains hanging between the living-room and the front room which is turned into a bedroom. It contains an iron bedstead covered with a clean patchwork quilt. Everyone eats in the kitchen. The teapot has a broken spout. The stove glows red in places where the packing has long ago burnt out. The back yard is filled with a motley collection of old two-wheeled wagons, lard tins, and rusty wire.

Some of the houses have signs hanging in front of them, reading, Cartage and Express, Seamstress – Work Reasonable, Curtains Washed and Stretched, and Odd Jobs Done. I sometimes read letters in the newspapers about the people on relief not wanting to work.

There are school yards and playgrounds in Cabbagetown, but they close up at nine o'clock at night. The parks and playgrounds that are open all the time are used by young couples as natural parking places, to take the place of non-existent parlours and chesterfields. They find all the dark corners and there they spoon, laugh, and giggle.

Most of the houses have no bath tubs. Nearly everyone bathes in a wash tub on the kitchen floor or goes to the community baths on Sackville Street. People who have no wash tubs, or are sick or too old to go to the bath house, go swimming, or go without a bath. You can still be clean no matter how poor you are. Oh yeah.

In the summer some of the men play quoits or bean-bag in the parks, or play bridge, euchre or rummy on park benches. Some of the young men play baseball or soccer in Riverdale Park. A large number of the people escape the summer heat by walking down to the bench at the foot of Cherry Street. Others are weak, they just sit.

Groups of town-planners, architects, clergymen, and public-spirited people have been seen walking carefully down the dusty streets of late. There is an embryo movement on foot to clear Cabbagetown of its slums. The people who live there don't like it. What is to become of them when the slums are cleared? They will only have to move into other slums. And when the new houses are built, how can they move back into them? They have no money. It will indeed be a miracle if they are taken back into the new houses for the amount of money that the government now allows for rent. They have no visions of a clean, beautiful district for them. They are not ruled by grandiose illusions as to their status. They have not been at the mercy of relief officers for four and five years for nothing. They think that this slum clearance scheme is one to make the sight of poor districts easier on the eyes of the beholder. The new houses will cause the slum-dwellers to move and scatter or, if the undreamt-of happens, the new houses will hide the squalor that lies beneath their masonry. In neither case is the Cabbagetowner satisfied.

At any rate it will soon pass. Some of the old inhabitants will remember its old land-marks with feelings of regret. There will be jovial eulogies made at commencement dinners and old-boys' reunions. The dirty-faced little cherubs will play on other streets, in other parts of the city. The old people will move to their children's homes, or to the old people's homes. Men will still pick coke, and children die of malnutrition. Women will still bravely hang out white lace curtains, and make beef stew. Cabbagetown will pass, but it will live on and on, arm in arm with the cause, poverty. Until poverty is ended there will always be a Cabbagetown. It might move up to Rosedale.

A.J.M. SMITH

The Face

The man with the acid face
   Under the hammer of glass
Imperils the pure place.
   The emotion of the mass,
Inverted, seems to ask
   The jack, queen, king and ace
To do the task.

Wait for a sure thing,
   Card into sleeve blown,
Arm out of sling,
   Friends posted at phone;
Then when trumps are declared
   And partner's strength known
Overpower the guard.

But keep the face mum
   Till the right minute come.
Look left and look right:
   Whose hand will you bite
With the safest delight?
   Whose safe will you crack
With a pat on the back?

   Replace the slave state face
With a face of bread:
   Each shall choose his place,
Be Dead, or Red.
The cards are no way stacked
And he may live by grace
Who wills to act.

L.A. MacKAY

Battle Hymn for the Spanish Rebels

The Church's one foundation
   Is now the Moslem sword,
In meek collaboration
   With flame, and axe, and cord;
While overhead are floating,
   Deep-winged with holy love
The battle-planes of Wotan,
   The bombing-planes of Jove.

FRANK H. UNDERHILL

The Debate on Foreign Policy

Mr Woodsworth's tripartite resolution on foreign policy produced the most general discussion of the subject that has taken place in the House of Commons since the signing of the peace treaties in 1919. In itself it was not an illuminating discussion. Mr King and his fellow cabinet ministers threw no light whatever on the policy that the government is following in its day-to-day decisions. (A few days later, on the estimates of the Department of External Affairs, Mr King and Mr Bennett once more combined to resist Mr Woodsworth's request for a committee to keep in touch continuously with external policy). But the situation in the House produced by the debate provides us with considerable light upon the present position and the future prospects of the Canadian people.

The speeches of the cabinet ministers centred around two points. In the first place they refused to go so far as to commit themselves to a policy of neutrality in an effort to keep free from European entanglements. The government adopts the pose of standing between two groups of extremists, isolationists and imperialists. But it will take no step now to stop the steady imperialist drive, save the verbal step of reiterating that parliament will decide when the issue arises; and this policy of drift means that on the day when Britain declares war the Liberal party will be swept off its feet by a storm of emotion in which it will be impossible to distinguish any coherent voice except that of Britain calling for help. This conclusion becomes inevitable when one considers the second main point which stood out in all the government speeches. The prime minister, Mr Lapointe, and Mr Rinfret, all three of them, had recourse to emotional appeals about the mysterious dangers which threaten Canada, dangers which necessitate the spending of over $36,000,000 for defence this year. When a Liberal cabinet, professing adherence to the traditions of Laurier, starts beating the tom-toms in this manner, they are making it certain that only one decision will be possible when parliament is eventually called to vote on whether we shall join in war.

The debate showed that the CCF is the only group in the House which is prepared to consider a policy drastic enough to hold us firm against the torrent of events and propaganda that will threaten to sweep us into the European maelstrom. If the point of view represented by the CCF had as little support in the country as it seemed to have in the House, we might as well give up discussing foreign policy and start now preparing for the first contingent. But the main reason for the overstrained and slightly shrill rhetoric of Mr King and Mr Lapointe was their consciousness that they haven't a united country behind them in their decision to postpone social reform for armaments.

One of the remarkable features of the debate was the abstention of the Conservative opposition members. In a debate which extended over three days and which brought three cabinet ministers to their feet, only one Conservative took part, Mr Denton Massey. He made an impassioned appeal for national unity, but gave only the vaguest hints as to the policy on which unity was to be founded. As a national statesman Mr Massey is proving himself to be a first-rate bible-class teacher. Or does one do him injustice by such a criticism? Should one rather conclude that the policy which he and his party desire as the basis of national unity is a policy of supporting the Baldwin government through thick and thin, and that they are much too astute to put this forward frankly until the tom-toms have been beating a little longer and a little more loudly?

Mr King's speech represents a distinct retrogression from the position which he took up in his two carefully prepared speeches of last June in parliament and last September at Geneva. On those two occasions he carefully guarded himself against any commitment to join in either a League war or a British war, and he was equally clear that Canada stood aloof from the 'war of opinion' that is dividing the European continent into two camps. Now he talks vaguely about unnamed enemies attacking us, declares that the British Commonwealth is the greatest force for peace in the world, praises Britain as the great pacifier in Spain, talks about the need for solidarity among all those who cherish democratic ideals. These may be mere rhetorical phrases; but when a man begins to talk in this way he has not far to go in order to reach the conclusion (and he encourages many of his hearers to leap to the conclusion) that we must support Britain in her next war for peace, and that if we hear anybody on the other side of the Atlantic shouting the sacred word 'democracy' we must rush across to show our solidarity with him. It is true that Mr King repeated all the reservations of his two earlier speeches, but it is also true that one of his Quebec ministers talked about Mr Woodsworth not being British enough for him. (That fine phrase will be quoted at Mr Rinfret's political funeral one of these days in Quebec.)

The funniest thing in the whole debate was the passionate devotion of Mr Lapointe to the League of Nations. The lofty moral abhorrence which he felt towards a policy of neutrality such as would prevent Canada from fulfilling her obligations to the League was wonderful to behold. It was as if a Burke or a Gladstone had suddenly appeared in the Canadian House. It almost made one forget that this was the same Ernest Lapointe who prevented the Canadian delegate from taking the lead in imposing oil sanctions on Mussolini. But when one does recall that little fact, the spectacle of the present Liberal government's solicitude for our Geneva obligations becomes just too funny for serious discussion.

What all the Cabinet ministers were seeking was obviously to line up the party solidly behind the defence estimates. The real debate on

March 1937

Mr Woodsworth's motion took place behind closed doors in the Liberal caucus. All gossip from Ottawa leads to a belief that there is considerable unrest among the Quebec Liberal members about the increased expenditure on armaments. We can only guess at the arguments which were used by Messrs King and Lapointe to overcome this unrest. But the public debate gives us some clues. One of the participants was Mr Brunelle, the French-Canadian member for Champlain. He admitted that on principle he was in favour of Mr Woodsworth's resolution for neutrality, but he had qualifications to make in practice. And he went on: 'When the national defence estimates are brought down I will follow the dictates of my conscience. I will take into account certain menacing factors now prevailing in this country. For instance I will bear in mind the significance of the recent uprising at Guelph, Ontario, which it is claimed is the result of subversive movements in our Dominion. Recent occurrences in Quebec city will also be taken into account. ... I will take into account the extent to which Spain and other countries have suffered from the activities of these agitators, and I will not forget that we have in the province of Quebec similar principles and institutions to defend.'

Are we to conclude that those two notorious advocates of advanced liberalism, W.L. Mackenzie King and Ernest Lapointe, assisted the Quebec Liberals in caucus to follow their conscience on defence questions by suggesting arguments such as these, arguments which every genuine liberal would repudiate as a betrayal of the liberal spirit? Is the author of 'Industry and Humanity' willing to cling to office by sponsoring a campaign to spend thirty-six million dollars to put down communism in this country – not to mention the several millions which he is already spending in the upkeep of those splendid fellows, the Sergeant Leopolds of the Mounted Police? And are we to conclude that that other holder-up of the banner of advanced liberalism in the Cabinet, the Minister of Labour, approves of the expenditure of all this money on tanks and aeroplanes, when the obvious liberal method of removing the danger of communism would be to spend the thirty-six millions on providing decent houses and living conditions for those who are most exposed to subversive propaganda?

The depressing feature of this debate and of all the current discussion about defence and foreign policy is the exactness of the parallel between the situation today and the situation in the last pre-war period, the years before 1914. In those days Laurier took up the same position as is maintained today by Messrs King and Lapointe and Dafoe. He posed as the moderate between the two extremes of the imperialists on one side and the isolationists such as John S. Ewart, Mr Bourassa, and the French-Canadian nationalists on the other. He repudiated the imperialist thesis of the unity of the empire in defence. He insisted that, whatever defence measures Canada undertook, she must keep complete control of them in her own hands. Messrs Skelton and Dafoe, in their books on Laurier, have presented him as the skilful, obstinate, and successful defender of Canadian national autonomy against imperialist entanglements.

But the fact is that Laurier's success was only verbal. Chamberlain & Co. manoeuvred him into taking part in the Boer War and so set the precedent for future military adventures; when he announced on raising the first contingent (and, incidentally, he did it by Order in Council without waiting to call parliament) that this step should not constitute a precedent, Mr Bourassa retorted with the damning reply: 'The precedent, Mr Prime Minister, is the accomplished fact.' Laurier acquiesced in Canadian participation in the Committee of Imperial Defence. He decided in 1910 to build a Canadian navy, 'Canadian in time of peace and British in time of war' as his Finance Minister put it. Mr King's new defence forces of 1937 merit the same description. Laurier went to the Imperial Conference of 1911 and told the British that Canadians did not think themselves bound to take part in all British wars; Mr King will go to the Imperial Conference of 1937 and tell the same thing. But Laurier always admitted that if Brtain were in serious danger Canada would have to go to her help; and the only British wars that matter for our foreign policy are just those in which Britain is obviously in serious danger. Laurier was unable to find a policy or a formula by which he could avoid these British entanglements, and Mr King faces the same dilemma. Laurier's choice, remarked John S. Ewart, was either ultimatum or compromise; and he was not prepared for ultimatum. Mr King also is not prepared for neutrality. His constant assurance that parliament will decide when the day comes is a verbal pose only. There is no middle path, as he assumes, between two extremes. There are only two alternatives; either we join in the next British war or we stay out of it. Mr King will not take the necessary steps that lead to the second alternative, and therefore we will be forced to follow the hard path to the first.

The most sinister aspect of the parallel between the two periods is provided by developments in Quebec. Laurier's decision to embark on naval expenditures in 1910 undermined his position in his own province. In 1911 he was beaten by an unscrupulous alliance between the Quebec nationalists (the more extreme of whom were shouting about shooting holes through the union jack in order to let the breeze of liberty blow through) and the imperialist Conservative party of English-speaking Canada. Today there is also a raging nationalist movement in Quebec led by men of much coarser fibre than the Bourassas and Lavergnes of 1911; the temptation to Mr Duplessis to complete the overthrow of the Quebec Liberal party by exploiting the province's aversion to imperialist defence measures will be almost irresistible.

Will Mr King be swept aside one of these days and retired to his studies on Industry and Humanity, when the imperialist crisis becomes really acute, by another alliance such as that of 1911? We shall see.

In the meantime the throb of the tom-toms is becoming louder and more insistent. Elderly sadists of the last war are emerging from their obscurity to join the war-dance again, their eyes glistening and their mouths watering as they think of the young men whom they will send to slaughter. We are getting closer to the condition of mass hysteria which will make all sane discussion of our national policy impossible. Already one can almost pick out the heroes who will be in charge of the concentration camps in the next struggle to make the world safe for democracy.

E. BIRNEY

Grey Rocks

Webbed hands of balsam soothed the shore
    that night,
Consoling with a laboured tide, which stirred
With its dark timeless pain, and, swelling,
    blurred
Grey rocks and air into the sea, and might
Have pulled the hills into its level flight
Had not the mummy moon leaned down to
    splash
Her immemorial gay quicksilver sash
Across the withered travail of the bight.

Into the saga bobs the nervous, lean
Lament of ukuleles, and the choke
And belching of a motor. Voices wail
Laconic time. Has an-y bod-y SEEN
My gal? ... The cut sash heals. The shores
    invoke
Once more the old tide's mumbled gnawing
    tale.

FELIX LAZARUS

The Oshawa Strike

At first sight, he looked more like an automobile salesman than an automobile workers' organizer. Slight, neatly dressed, carefully groomed, spats, anything but the popular conception of an 'agitator.' Even on the platform he did not harangue, did not shout nor orate, but spoke quietly and evenly, with no flights of eloquence or signs of agitation. At the time of his arrival in Oshawa no one could have foretold the virtual political revolution his presence would precipitate in Ontario in three short months. No one could have foretold, least of all Hugh Thompson, auto union organizer, himself.

Hugh Thompson came to Oshawa about three months ago on the request of some workers of the General Motors plant there. The Detroit headquarters of the union were busy settling the strike in the United States. Contrary to all the claims of the *Globe and Mail* and the *Financial Post*, the Committee for Industrial Organization was not launching a drive in Canada, and had not picked Oshawa as the entering point for their invading wedge. They were much too busy on their own side of the line. It just happened that at that time, with no union yet organized in Oshawa, a spontaneous strike of about three hundred auto workers had broken out in one of the departments. Some of the men phoned the Detroit union headquarters for assistance and Hugh Thompson, being the only one available at that time, was sent up to look over the situation. That is how it all started. And that's how Hugh Thompson first met the Ontario Government, in the person of Louis Fine, chief conciliation officer for the province.

Mr Fine was busy. He was busy telling a meeting of the strikers that they really should be good boys and go back to work and give the company's new scheme of wage-cutting at least a trial. It is also said that he advised them not to listen to the CIO man who was waiting out in the corridor for an opportunity to speak. The man waiting in the corridor was Hugh Thompson. Apparently Mr Fine's advice was not heeded, for the men listened to Mr Thompson, and all three hundred men at the meeting signed up in the union right then.

In a month there were so many members in the union, Local 222 of the United Automobile Workers of America, that the foremen and straw bosses and 'sups' in the General Motors plant began treating the men like human beings. That was something new, and without precedent. They had just elected their officers but couldn't get a hall large enough to hold the membership for an installation meeting. The hockey arena 'didn't want their kind of an organization.' A subsequent hockey-match was a failure through lack of attendance. The Department of National Defence stalled on renting the armories. The board of education turned a deaf ear to the suggestion that they rent the collegiate auditorium. The union announced that it would hold its membership meeting at the 'four corners,' the busiest corner in Oshawa, at noon on Saturday. They got the Collegiate.

The events that followed are well-known to anyone who does not read the *Globe and Mail*. A bargaining committee was chosen by the members representing each department in the plant. The outstanding demand at the time was a forty-hour week and time and one-half for overtime. The company had promised to introduce it by April first, but they would not even meet the committee to discuss it if Thompson were to be included. They would only meet with a committee of their own employees. The men insisted that they had the right to choose Thompson to represent them, even as the company had the right to employ a lawyer on their side. But the company said no. So Thompson withdrew.

In his stead, Charles Millard, General Motors employee and recently elected local president, who was also an organizer for the UAWA, was made union representative on the committee. The company said it would meet Millard as an employee but not as a UAWA organizer. The men insisted. They took a strike vote by closed ballot (attention *Globe and Mail*) and gave the shop stewards the power to set the time. Three times the company changed its mind about recognizing Millard as a union representative, and three times Thompson pleaded with the men to postpone the dead-line set for strike action. It was postponed. If anyone has ever tried to prevent a strike, it was Hugh Thompson at that time. He almost lost his control over the men. But he kept them from striking.

Enter Mitchell F. Hepburn. The CIO will never be recognized. The citizens of Ontario will never tolerate lawlessness and sit-downs. British democracy must be maintained. And so the strike was on.

The strike has now been settled. The tumult and the shouting has died, except in the editorial rooms of the *Globe and Mail*, and amongst the boards of strategy of the Grits and Tories.

Was the CIO recognized? Nobody ever asked for its recognition. That would be tantamount to recognizing, simultaneously, all the other unions affiliated with the CIO. But the United Automobile Workers International Union, local 222, was recognized, for Charlie Millard signed the agreement as president of the union. That is all that was and is ever asked by any union anywhere. The *Globe's* ignorance in this matter is either stupid or misleading. In either case it's inexcusable.

Mr Hepburn insists that he is not against organized labour. In fact, he says, he thinks labour has the right to choose any organization it wishes to belong to, providing it chooses some respectable labour body like the AF of L. He forgets, of course, or does not know, that the AF of L is no more respectable than the CIO, that its unions have fought some of the bloodiest battles in American labour history, and that violence in labour tactics is not a matter of lack of respectability, but a matter of self-defence for labour. Mr Hepburn's attention, as well as that of the *Globe and Mail*, is drawn to the recent disclosures in the United States of the wholesale corruption and even company-backed murder of union organizers and members by sheriffs and deputies in the mining districts of Hanlan County, Kentucky.

The difference between the AF of L and the CIO is not respectability. The difference is that a CIO affiliate is organizing amongst the miners in the North Country. Says Mr Hepburn on April 19 in the *Globe*, 'Let me tell Lewis and his gang that they'll never get their greedy paws on the mines of Northern Ontario so long as I am prime minister.' He meant, of course, that they'll never get their greedy paws on the mines so long as his friends have their greedy paws on them. Then again, 'If the CIO wins in Oshawa it will get into the mines and send stocks tumbling.' Mr Hepburn will never live that statement down. It seems, then, that what is wrong with the CIO unions is not their foreign origin, Mr Hepburn, nor their lawlessness and sit-down tactics, Mr McCullagh, but their effectiveness. Now if only they were not so effective they would be as welcome as the AF of L.

Mr Hepburn's goal, says the *Post*, is to rout the CIO. To this end he intends to use four weapons. First, through the Industrial Standards Act and the new Minimum Wage Act, he hopes to remove the fertile fields on which CIO agents sow their seeds of discontent, hostility, and disruption. Second, he hints at the use of armed force, not only to preserve law and order, but to 'shake the CIO loose from any foothold it may gain.' Third, a strike-breaking policy of no relief for strikers. Fourth, 'employing existing powers and evolving others ... to ensure that a proper degree of responsibility shall be required of labour organizations in Ontario.'

This last, of course, is a rewording of his threat to license trade unions. But Mr Hepburn himself is sceptical about his plan. When asked what he would do with the old, established unions, that are now affiliated with the CIO, he remarked that such aspects made the problem a complicated one, and that he had arrived at no definite conclusion.

Mr Hepburn's greatest complication will come when he finds that he has prodded into existence a labour party on a serious scale. This is only natural, of course. It is true Mr Rowe is trying to build up a fiction of Conservative love for labour, but this is so foreign to the conscience of true Tories like Col. Drew that that party is split wide open. Nobody, least of all a Conservative, can believe that fiction. It sounds too much like Alice in Wonderland.

A labour Party consisting of bodies of affiliated trade unions in industrial communities is the only logical outcome of the present industrial and political situation in Ontario. This was evident two weeks after the union was organized in Oshawa. When the use of the Collegiate Auditorium and the Armories was refused them, the first thing the men started to discuss was the nomination of union members for municipal offices at the next elections. With four thousand members in their ranks, and with the families and relatives of these members, they knew that their political power was supreme. They learned from actual experience in two weeks what years of propaganda might have failed to teach. From municipal labour politics it is only a step to the provincial and federal fields. Already the strained silence of the local old-party politicians in Oshawa during the strike has condemned them to political extinction. And as the present unionization drive continues and grows throughout Ontario and Canada, so the sentiment for a labour party will continue and grow.

Where does the CCF fit into the picture? The CCF should be the bond between the organized labour and organized agriculture. Workers who voted Liberal and Conservative at the last elections cannot be expected to become Socialists overnight, but when organized into unions they do understand, from the opposition of governments to their unions, the necessity for independent labour political action.

The next Ontario elections will see labour candidates in many ridings. In those areas where the CCF has been active in promoting unionism, CCF candidates will receive labour backing. In some places perhaps, unions will apply for affiliation to the CCF. The farmers generally, as a body, in the opinion of this writer, will stand opposed to labour. But labour will, nevertheless, be well represented in the next provincial parliament, thanks to Mr Hepburn.

NORMAN BETHUNE

Red Moon

And this same pallid moon tonight,
   Which rides so quietly, clear and high,
The mirror of our pale and troubled gaze,
   Raised to a cool Canadian sky,

Above the shattered Spanish tops
   Last night, rose low and wild and red,
Reflecting back from her illumined shield,
   The blood bespattered faces of the dead.

To that pale disc, we raise our clenched fists
   And to those nameless dead our vows renew,
'Comrades, who fought for freedom and the future world,
   Who died for us, we will remember you.'

KING GORDON

The CCF Convention

The first stage of any movement is educational and propagandist. It is usually marked by rapid growth, burning zeal, unflagging missionary enterprise. It is frequently accomplished by millenial hopes and numbers of adherents who look for a rapid crossing of a bone-dry Jordan into the promised land. The strength of a movement in its first stage is frequently overestimated by friends and foes alike. There were not a few who thought that the CCF would be the official opposition in the Dominion House just three years after its birth, and were disappointed when it polled a mere four-hundred thousand votes and sent to Ottawa but seven members. There were others who, thrilled at the extraordinary advance of Canadian socialism within the first three years of the CCF movement, looked with confidence to the steady growth of the movement by means of the same methods of education and propaganda which apparently accounted for its rapid rise. Both groups were wrong in thinking that a movement aiming at the taking of power can achieve its objective by methods suited to the first stage of its existence. A movement that remains too long in the first stage will die. It must move on into the second stage.

Such, in substance, was the central theme in the speech of the Secretary to the Fifth Annual Convention of the Co-operative Commonwealth Federation meeting in Winnipeg, August 26-27. The deliberations of the Convention and the decisions taken, showed quite clearly that the CCF was prepared to advance, in fact had already advanced, into its second stage. To delegates and observers alike, the Convention gave the impression of a socialist party that meant business, a party that had emerged from the stage of theoretical discussions in the field of social and political analysis, and entered into the realm of social and political realities. It was significant that a convention which was the most unreservedly socialist in the history of the movement was also the most realistic when it came to coping with immediate problems in the present Canadian scene. It is perhaps too much to hope that Canadian radicals are at last stumbling upon some of the essential truths first brought to light by those mighty pioneers of historical social analysis, Marx and Engels. 'Too much to hope' because there is still a great deal of vague and ill-defined idealism, still too much – in other quarters – narrow political and economic dogmatism. With such qualifications it is only fair to say that the 1937 Convention represented an important and a very necessary step forward. If the step had not been taken the movement might well have deteriorated, in the national field, into a comparatively small sect of left-wing political purists, and in the provincial field, into a loosely connected chain of opportunistic party machines. Now there is little danger of either fate overtaking the movement.

There are three distinct signs of this advance into the second stage. In the first place, in contrast with the great Regina Convention of 1933 where the Manifesto was hammered out in the form that has remained essentially unaltered, the Winnipeg Convention concentrated its efforts on political and economic subjects of immediate concern. The Convention was held against the immediate background of Western Canadian disaster of the first magnitude. The most powerful speech of the convention was Mr M.J. Coldwell's on the drought situation. The most comprehensive and carefully worked out resolution was on the subject of drought relief and agricultural rehabilitation. The largest delegation was from the province the hardest hit in the Dominion, and Saskatchewan delegates made contributions to the debate which were not only the most poignant but also the most realistic in suggestions for meeting this national calamity. In a similar way the question of civil liberties caught the attention of the Convention – not civil liberties in the abstract as covered by the clause in the manifesto, but civil liberties as concretely menaced by the fascist tactics of a Duplessis or a Hepburn, or by the undercover activity of RCMP and the open violence of provincial and local police. So, too, in the field of industrial activity. Within the Convention, in spite of the preponderance of western delegates, there was a genuine awareness of the significance of the remarkable advances in the field of trade unionism. Ontario and Quebec delegates carried first-hand reports of Oshawa and Cornwall, of sympathetic co-operation between CCF members and clubs and the new and militant trade unionism. The resolutions passed were no formal gestures of congratulation to organized labour in its new gains; they represented genuine offers of co-operation, based upon the recognition of a new and indispensible ally in the struggle for a reconstructed society. For the first time in the history of the labour and socialist movements in Canada there is at least a hope of close co-operation, if not actual affiliation, between the more aggressive sections of organized labour and the radical political movement of Canadian farmers and industrial and professional workers. In each of these decisions of the Convention the line taken was completely in accord with fundamental socialist theory, but in each case there was evident an historical awareness that was absent from the first Convention.

The second indication of advance into the second phase was the marked improvement in the organizational set-up. Taking into consideration the lack of adequate resources, adequately paid staff and organizers, adequate technique of organizational extension, the past record of the CCF has been little short of miraculous. But the movement has suffered tremendously from such lacks, suffered because many of its most valuable leaders have been financially unable to give full time to organizational work, suffered because there have been no funds for literature, no funds for the ordinary activities of a national office. It appeared quite evident to members of the convention that the movement was in for a serious recession unless drastic measures were taken to perfect organization and raise adequate finances. Too long has the CCF congratulated itself upon being a party so free from great interests that it has been carried along by the dimes and nickels of its impecunious members. The CCF will never receive substantial support from those interests that it seeks ultimately to destroy, but until now it has made no serious attempt to place financial responsibility fairly upon the shoulders of its membership and supporters. It came as a shock to delegates to learn that the vastly increased budget proposed for the coming year was less than the budget of many an individual congregation in the larger Canadian cities. ... The budget proposed was of course related to a tremendous increase in activity – travelling national organizers to cover every part of the Dominion, French language organizers, organizers for the women's work, organizers of youth. To direct this organizational advance Mr M.J. Coldwell, MP, was made chairman of the National Council, Mr Woodsworth remaining as President of the CCF and leader of the CCF party in the House.

There was a third indication of advance which was most noticeable to those who followed carefully the debates on the floor as well as the discussions in the lobbies and at the luncheon tables. The greatest gains made by the CCF during the past few years appear to have been made in the provincial fields. In three of the four western provinces the CCF has polled a respectable vote and elected members to the legislatures. In the recent BC election, as noted in *The Canadian Forum* of July, the vote remained solid despite the unfortunate developments within the party during the last year. In Saskatchewan it becomes more and more evident that the CCF will make a strong bid for power in the next election. In Manitoba, while ILP-CCF dissension has undoubtedly held back progress, the last provincial contest revealed surprising strength not only in the metropolitan area but also in rural districts. These advances have led some to believe that the national aspect of the CCF will tend more and more to be obscured by the considerations of expediency which are bound to come into the formualation of provincial platforms and the organization of provincial campaigns. Indeed, there have been a few indications that rifts between provincial and national organizations were widening.

The Winnipeg Convention gave a definite no to such threats of disintegration. Leaders of the strongest provincial organizations gave assurance of their concern in the national movement and pledged the fullest support to schemes for the advancement of the national organization. Such assurances were based upon a growing recogntion of the necessity of a strong national movement to the success of provincial movements as well as upon the frequently demonstrated concern of national leaders to lend all possible aid to provincial campaigns. It is perhaps not unfitting that a socialist movement should give leadership in resisting the trends towards regionalism and provincialism which have characterized Canadian political development since the depression. For there is no sanity in the belief that Canadian problems can be solved upon a narrow regional basis, by socialist or by any other governments. A national plan is necessary for the solution of Canadian problems essentially national in character. A Dominion socialist party in power is necessary to carry the plan into effect. But provincial socialist parties in power can do much in putting into effect remedial measures as well as contributing invaluable assistance to the carrying out of a national plan.

The CCF has entered the second stage of political realism, organizational efficiency and national consciousness. The third stage is planning for power.

November 1937

RALPH GUSTAFSON

Rhyme for the Modern Child

Sing a song of gas-masks
The government supply,
Four and twenty airplanes
Screwing through the sky –
When the planes were over
The bombs began to burst
And all the goggled pilots laughed
Who got there first.
The priest was in the pulpit
Preaching to the blest,
The Commons were in session
Hoping for the best,
The poet in the poorhouse
Pulled the window down –
Along came the mustard-gas
And wiped out the town.

FRANK H. UNDERHILL

To Protect Our Neutrality

Mr King's foreign policy is based upon his general practice of acting so as to alienate the smallest possible number of votes from the government in power. This involves a careful side-stepping of all real issues, since if he commits himself to any particular action he may offend some section of opinion in the country. He glorifies this inaction under the high-sounding principle of maintaining the national unity of Canada. Of course he is gambling upon the chance that no such serious crisis in world affairs will arise as to compel the government to follow one of several rival policies. If such a crisis does arise and he is compelled to take on a particular line of action, the disunity of the country will be much more bitter than need be, because public opinion will not have been prepared by the government to face up to the difficult alternatives with which world conditions are now confronting it.

Such action as the King government does take is usually done furtively or under false pretences. Thus it 'protects our neutrality' on the Spanish issue by passing legislation under which enlistment in either army in Spain or the selling of goods to either belligerent in Spain can be prohibited. This propitiates the Catholic hierarchy and doesn't offend any other important section of the community, because Canada does no very great trade with Spain under any circumstances. The neutrality legislation is not applied to the Sino-Japanese case because there are very important industrial and transportation interests in Canada who want to profit by the opportunity of helping Japan against China through the sale of munitions and metals, and there is no danger of offending anyone of importance on the other side since the Catholic hierarchy doesn't care about China. So also the government embarks on a policy of rearmament which it can present in public to nationalists as consisting of purely local defense measures 'to protect our neutrality,' and which can be explained in private to British imperialists as forming the basis for another expeditionary force to help Britain. And the Prime Minister's military advisers at the Imperial Conference of 1937 cooperate with British defence officials in drawing up elaborate plans for the coordination of Imperial defence, while he himself comes home with the bland assurance (à la Sir Edward Grey) that he committed himself to nothing.

The most dangerous of all these insincerities is the pretence of the government as to its concern for our neutrality. The Hon. Ian Mackenzie is already anticipating the next session of parliament by campaigning for more defence expenditures 'to protect our neutrality.' Mr King constantly adopts the pose, when he is pressed about Anglo-Canadian relations, that the Canadian parliament will be free to take any action it chooses when once Britain gets involved in another war. Defence on our Pacific coast may serve to protect our neutrality in the case of a war between the United States and Japan and to discourage either belligerent from seizing points in British Columbia. But such a war is not likely to come save as part of a bigger and more general war. The real problem which faces Canada today concerns her position in a British war. On this topic Mr King habitually uses phraseology which suggests inferences that are simply untrue.

We have not at present the legal or constitutional power to declare our neutrality in a British war. Mr King has been fond of declaring that economic sanctions shall not be imposed without the consent of the Canadian parliament. But the fact is that, once a British war breaks out, every Canadian citizen is compelled by law to cease all trade and communication with the enemy of Britain; commercial relations with the enemy become automatically criminal. This will be the imposition of economic sanctions with a vengeance. We may, it is true, decide for ourselves not to send troops overseas, but there is all the difference in the world between this 'passive belligerency' and real neutrality. We should be bound to open our harbors to British warships and to close them to enemy ships. We should be bound to take so many positive actions on the British side that we could feel no grievance if the enemy power retaliated against us. All these matters will be decided for us automatically by the action of the British government in entering into a state of war against some other power.

If the King government means what it says when it talks so loftily about Canadian control of Canadian foreign policy, it is bound to take action now, while we are at peace, to clear up this matter of neutrality. It should follow the example of South Africa in passing the Status Act and the Royal Executive Functions and Seals Act. It should insist at the next Imperial Conference upon a joint statement by the British nations explaining to the outside world that no declaration of war by any one of them binds any of the rest of them. And it should cancel the agreement with the British government by which Canada is obligated to perform certain services for the British navy in Halifax and Esquimalt, services which, if once performed during war, would make all talk of our neutrality meaningless.

Our government will no doubt ask parliament during this coming session, in spite of vague assurances to the contrary given at the last session, to spend still more millions on defence. In the present state of the world there is not much use opposing defence expenditures. But the CCF opposition should insist that the money is really spent on its professed purposes, that is on putting our Atlantic and Pacific coastlines in a proper state of defence. And since the particular military steps that are taken for defence depend upon the general foreign policy of the government, it should also insist that Mr King take the country into his confidence on what his policy really is in reference to a war entered upon by the Chamberlain government of Great Britain.

ANNE MARRIOTT
Prairie

The restless, never-sated pagan wind
Shakes its grey bones across the hungry soil,
Mile after mile – grey mile, green mile –
The empty stubble left from last year's toil,
Summer fallow and few threads of wheat,
Old paintless shanty, cows, a gaunt-ribbed
    hound ...
The tinny-brilliant circle of the sky
Like a cookie-cutter slices out a round
Of dusty bareness, centred by a man
Who plods, bent-necked, in tattered overalls;
A dirty-coloured cloud crawls round the west.
(In the next town they're having thunder-
    squalls).
The old wild greedy wind whirls out the oats,
(No crop this year, not even winter's feed)
While over, over, up and down and over,
Bounces the tumbleweed.

EUGENE FORSEY
Under the Padlock

March 24 marked the end of the first year of Quebec's famous 'Act Respecting Communist Propaganda.' As we enter the second year, the offensive against democracy and civil liberties is being pushed with increasing vigour and on a broadening front. To April 15, the Civil Liberties Union had records of five padlockings and seventy-four raids and seizures, including two or three in Quebec City. According to the *Montreal Star* there have been other cases outside Montreal. Not one of the persons or organizations affected has yet been charged with any offence, let alone convicted.

Nor is this the whole story. Those who fondly imagine that the Black Terror is being applied only against 'Communists' would do well to ponder certain recent incidents and speeches.

On February 5, a Japanese boycott parade of cars with banners, organized by the Quebec CCF and the League for Peace and Democracy, was stopped by the city police 'Red Squad' and the banners confiscated. The official explanation was the well-worn 'fear of a riot.' Several previous parades had been held without incident.

On February 23, in a debate in the Legislative Assembly, Hon. T.D. Bouchard, Liberal leader, complained that copies of his newspaper, *En Avant,* had been seized in a raid in Montreal under the Padlock Act and that the provincial police had refused to return them. The Premier tossed the whole thing off with jocular remarks.

On March 2, Jose Pedroso, Spanish rebel, addressed an 'anti-Communist' meeting in the Plateau School. It had been announced that Mayor Raynault and Archbishop Gauthier would preside, but after protests by the Civil Liberties Union and other bodies against this discrimination in favour of the rebels, the Mayor sent his regrets and the Archbishop was represented by Canon Harbour.

On March 23, some person or persons unknown broke into and ransacked the apartment of John MacCormac, Montreal correspondent of the *New York Times,* of whose comments on the Quebec situation Mr Duplessis had complained bitterly in the legislature. Nothing was taken, but Mr MacCormac's papers were thoroughly gone through. The city police displayed an ostentatious lack of interest, and the provincial police, protesting perhaps a trifle too much, hastened to deny that they had raided either Mr MacCormac's apartment or any place in the same street!

Early in April, the provincial police invaded CCF provincial headquarters, carefully inspected a display of posters, and retired with a warning that they were keeping 'a close watch.'

For the moment these delicate hints are evidently considered enough to keep the CCF, the provincial Liberal party, the *New York Times,* and similar subversive influences within due bounds. For the trade unions, however, something more is needed: 'something lingering, with boiling oil in it.' The legislature has obliged with three measures. The first two outlaw the closed shop and give the government power to change at its own sweet will collective agreements made binding under the Workmen's Wages Act. These Acts, and an abortive proposal by a government supporter to overthrow the whole Workmen's Compensation system, evoked vigorous, and ominously united, protests from the international and Catholic unions. The government had promised the unions not to bring down any further legislation affecting labour without giving them notice. But necessity knows no promises. At all costs a wedge had to be driven between the international and the Catholic unions. The method followed was the usual 'smash-and-grab.' On April 8-9 without notice, the government rushed through both Houses a bill making unincorporated unions liable to suit. The Catholic unions, being unincorporated, were already liable. 'The quickness of the hand deceives the eye.'

One further menace to 'the institutions dear to the province' remains to be eradicated: Protestantism. To this holy task the 'Authorities,' civil and religious, have now dedicated themselves. Some months ago the chief of police of Quebec City refused, in writing, to allow the Grande Ligne Baptist Mission to distribute the New Testament by colportage. A new chief, lent to the city by the RCMP, has since added insult to injury by announcing that this is 'the general practice.' Furthermore the Mission has been warned not to hold prayer meetings in private houses on pain of having them padlocked. An isolated case of petty tyranny? Then listen to Cardinal Villeneuve, Montreal, January 28: 'The religious and moral indifference of the state ... perverse liberalism ... The false principle ... of the neutrality of the state between different religions, and different metaphysical, moral and social theories ... The Church ... on a common footing with ... all other religious denominations ... False conception of the liberty of individuals and the role of the state ... Liberty of conscience: does it mean that each person may, at will, render or not render worship to God? ... Odious liberalism! ... Freedom of speech and of the press, freedom of worship, freedom of teaching: liberties true, decent and precious when they are used in free matters and within the limits of the moral good, beyond which they are abuses, weaknesses and destructive principles.... It is never permitted to ask, to defend, to grant, freedom of thought, writing or teaching, and the undifferentiated freedom of religions, as so many rights which nature has given to man. ... These ... liberties may for reasonable causes be TOLERATED. ... Where custom has put these modern liberties, freedom of worship, of speech, of the press, of teaching, etc., into force, the citizens are to use them only for good. ... In short, to prefer for the state a constitution tempered by the democratic element is not in itself against order, on condition, however, that the Catholic doctrine of ... the proper exercise of public power is respected. ... There are perhaps ... strangers to our faith ... listening to me. ... I tolerate you. ... I tolerate you so that you will tolerate me. I tolerate you ... so that you may admire at once the splendour of my religion and the delicacy of my charity. ... I tolerate you in order to have your collaboration in the common good, and when such collaboration stops, when you preach corrosive doctrines and spread everywhere poisoned seeds, then I can no longer tolerate you. Such, gentlemen, is Catholic liberalism.'

Hear also what comfortable words Archbishop Gauthier saith, in a letter read in all churches on March 20 and 27: 'Prohibition ... in ... Montreal of meetings of the Communist party, and throughout the province the seizure ... of the evil literature which it spreads. God be praised! We have been very slow to protect ourselves, but at last the public authorities ... have had the courage to take measures of a pressing necessity. ... Note the ... disguises with which Communism covers itself: ... the campaigns against Fascism, the saving of democratic institutions, freedom of speech and meeting. ... How many minds, in a milieu like ours are touched, even without their knowing it, by the remote eddies of the religious revolution which, in the seventeenth century, put at the basis of its relations with God the principle of free inquiry. ... Human liberty ... can legitimately do everything that is not forbidden to it. ... Let us allow to fall once for all into the discredit it deserves the theory that it is of the nature of liberty to be able to choose between good and evil.' (The Archbishop is evidently imperfectly acquainted with the Book of Genesis.) 'As Bossuet says, 'Liberty is given to man not to throw off the yoke, but to bear it with honour by bearing it willingly.' ... We are limited on all sides by our ignorance, and our prejudices.' (Speaking the truth unwittingly!)

Where the Cardinal and the Archbishop lead, who fears to follow?

In Montreal, on February 26, the Community Hall of the Church of All Nations (United Church of Canada) was visited by four detectives who seized publicity material relating to a concert. One of them said that they were going to close up 'Katsunoff's International Brigade,' by which he seems to have meant the 'International Brotherhood,' one of the religious activities of the Church, under the superintendency of the Rev. R.G. Katsunoff, DD.

In Montreal also, on February 10, the Rev. R.B.Y. Scott, professor at the United Church Theological College, was informed that a meeting he was to have addressed that evening on 'The Peril of Fascism in Quebec' had been cancelled, because the proprietors of the Jewish Educational Institute, where it was to have been held, were afraid of having their building padlocked. It had been visited not long before by a person describing himself as an 'investigator,' apparently from the provincial police. A week earlier a similar meeting, which was to have been addressed by Mr J.K. Mergler, counsel for the Civil Liberties Union, had also been cancelled.

About the same time, Dr Scott, on behalf of the executive of the Civil Liberties Union, applied for permission to use the hall of the Montreal High School for a members' meeting of the Union. Miss Mackenzie, principal of the Girls' High School, herself a member of the CLU executive, readily gave her consent. But when she consulted the Assistant Superintendent of Schools, that functionary demurred, feeling that he must consult certain officers of the Protestant Board of School Commissioners. Two days later, he telephoned Dr Scott, refusing permission, on the ground that the High School might be padlocked.

The Jewish Educational Institute and the Protestant Board of School Commissioners are not the only people who are afraid of being padlocked. Two months ago the McGill Social Problems Club arranged a series of meetings at which representatives of all parties were to present their views. Mr Arcand, leader of the Fascists, had spoken, Mr Buck was to be next. The Students' Council, however, refused the use of the McGill Union for fear of being padlocked. The Students' Society has voted unanimously for the repeal or disallowance of the Padlock Act and has requested the university authorities to take steps to restore freedom of discussion on the campus.

On March 24, CKAC rejected the script of a proposed broadcast on 'The Right to Liberty,' by Mr Hubert Desaulniers, chairman of the Civil Liberties Union, because of its 'English Protestant tone.'

Meanwhile the avowedly Fascist 'National Christian Social Party' continues to grow, unhindered, to say the least, by the state, praised with faint damns by the Church. You ask, says the Cardinal, 'whether I am a Fascist, totalitarian or democrat? I shall answer in the very words of Mgr Bilczewski. ... "I do not recognize the wild, lying, atheistic democracy which reigns to-day in almost all the states of the world. The masonic organizations, secret or avowed, the revolutionaries and the politicians in their pay, the scribblers, the Communist orators who have explained and still explain to the people that chance and a blind majority of votes shall decide the organization of power in the State, fill me with horror. The end pursued by this democracy does not really lead to the sovereignty of the people, but to the absolute power of backstairs financiers and their lackeys."'' (Now where have we heard that before?) Likewise, the Archbishop. Photographs of Fascists drilling, in violation of section 99 of the Criminal Code, appeared in the Gazette and other papers on January 31 and February 1. 'And if,' says Archbishop Gauthier, 'some hundreds of young people are doing physical exercise or quasi-military training, would it not be that in their view there are not being taken against the peril which threatens us the measures which should be taken? ... This is going on at the moment when seven or eight hundred Canadians are returning from Spain, where they went to improve themselves in the good methods of the Red Army, so that they will be the shock troops of which our enemies will dispose. Is it not a matter of elementary prudence that we should be ready for any eventuality? ... What is there to be surprised at in our young people wishing to be at hand, if, some day or other, we are stricken by the same misfortune? ... I am not at the moment defending the National Social Christian Party. There are in the programme ... very mixed doctrines at which a Catholic should look closely before subscribing. It is German Nazism, with its errors and its tendencies ... How could we forget the manner in which Hitlerian Germany treats our brothers in the faith?. ... Be that as it may ... it is much more important for us to know whether the reasoning of our young people does not contain a part of truth, and whether our weakness, our evasions, our undecided attitudes do not in short act to the profit of the Communists ... If it did not exist, our behaviour would bring Fascism into existence.' (All quotations from the Cardinal and the Archbishop taken from *Le Devoir* of January 31 and March 21.)

In an atmosphere like this it is hardly surprising that the city of Sorel has elected a Fascist Mayor and two Fascist aldermen. The swastika occupies a prominent place in the city hall. On February 6, Mr Arcand and the members of the Fascist Grand Council of Montreal journeyed to Sorel in uniform to celebrate the victory. About the same time Fascist delegations from St Hyacinthe and St Ours also arrived in Sorel to present the mayor with a swastika flag. Late in February, one non-Fascist alderman 'resigned.' A week later three more aldermen and the city clerk followed suit. On March 7, the 'resignations' of nineteen city employees were 'accepted.' Mr T.D. Bouchard and Mr Bastien, MLA, declare that youths are being enrolled in the Fascist movement by ,'hundreds, weekly' in Montreal, and that on Christmas day the Fascists of St Hyacinthe paraded openly, in the uniform, to mass. Mr Duplessis' reply is to accuse the Liberal leader of 'insulting' the Church, and to blame all the talk of Fascism on an American newspaper campaign and a Communist 'plot.' 'No one with a head on his shoulders will say that Fascism in Quebec is dangerous.' The Premier says he 'knows nothing' of the Fascist movement. Mr Arcand, leader of the Fascist Party, is the editor of his official or semi-official organ in Montreal, *l'Illustration Nouvelle*. As well might Mr Mackenzie King deny all knowledge of Mr J.W. Dafoe.

Early in April the Fascists opened headquarters, perhaps not inappropriately, in St James Street, where their offices occupy an entire floor.

French-Canadian defenders of the Padlock Act have been remarkably few. Mr Duplessis and Mr Mignault, ex-judge of the Supreme Court of Canada, have compared it to the law which provides for padlocking disorderly houses. They omit to add that disorderly houses can be padlocked only after conviction of their owners in open court for a defined offence. After all, why should an Attorney-General and an ex-judge bother about due process of law? Mr Duplessis also has compared the Act to 'the British law' providing for handcuffing prisoners.

But the main task of defending the Act has been assumed by representatives(?) of the English-speaking minority. The 'first families' are silent. What they think, we may presumably surmise from the statements of their hangers-on and journalistic mouth-pieces. Hon. T.J. Coonan, KC, Minister without portfolio, says the Act could not define Communism because it had to be broad enough to cover 'the many who are Communists without knowing it.' He has also recently broadcast a long speech calling the Act a bulwark of democracy (but carefully refraining from discussing it). Hon. Gilbert Layton calls it 'one of the best pieces of legislation ever passed in the province.' Jonathan Robinson, MLA, stops short of mentioning the Act itself, but says that never has the English-speaking population been so happy and contented as under Mr Duplessis. *The Star* speaks of the Premier's 'quaint' 'Latin' ways, and publishes Mr Coonan's broadcast without mentioning that it was part of a debate. *The Gazette* prints three editorial defences and, under special heading, a very long letter of ingenious casuistry from the senior counsel of the Sun Life. The

United Church and Presbyterian presbyteries, a few dauntless spirits like Dr Lighthall and Mr Calder, and a considerable number of English-speaking trade unions, brotherhoods, women's clubs, student, and other organizations, have protested vigorously. But of most of those usually called the 'leaders' of the English-speaking community, one can only say, in the words of Mr G.D.H. Cole:

*We are called leaders, yes we are called leaders,
    although we can never tell why;
For the last thing we do is to lead anybody, and
    mostly we don't even try.*

The record of the French-Canadians is, all things considered, infinitely more creditable. It takes more courage for a French-Canadian to speak one word against the government than for an English-Canadian to make a dozen speeches. Yet French-Canadians have taken the lead in opposition to the government's labour legislation. A French-Canadian is chairman of the Civil Liberties Union. Thousands of French-Canadians have petitioned for the repeal of the Padlock Act and many of their trade unions have supported the petition for disallowance. To whom little is given, from them little is required. But they have given much.

RUFUS II

Another Month

In Canada the smokescreen of Royal Commissions becomes dense (total cost to date $1,123,967; total action to date, zero) while the fires in our armament factories are being banked for English and foreign orders; shell cases for England from the National Steel Car and aeroplanes for Turkey from Canada Car & Foundry who maintain a stooge in Berlin and whose president, Victor M. Drury, rides in Goering's cars when in Berlin.

At Ottawa divorce and election bills are delayed, Dunning calls Social Credit's bluff by offering to obtain bank charter for them; CNR employees are laid off.

In Ontario Hepburn's double-cross of the electorate is consummated as power bill is approved despite the opposition of Roebuck and Macaulay. Test of public opinion is denied, while the contracts with the Quebec power companies are exempted from the Power Commission Act and the Privy Council Appeals Act. Net result, these companies may sue Hydro at will but private individuals have to get permission of the Attorney-General.

In Quebec, centralised control of Provincial Police with 34 stations throughout province is effected. Pastoral letter is read in all Catholic Churches blaming communism for all the evils of the modern world and merely warning the faithful to carefully examine tenets of fascism before accepting it.

In England, public opinion gives lie to the rude blatherings of Chamberlain as the Labour Party candidate is returned in by-election (Conservative majority last election 3,900). Re-armament programme is speeded up, efforts are made by government to get co-operation of labour but no guarantees are offered in exchange. Lord Swinton escapes court martial for his conduct of the Air Ministry while private profit is put before public interest as 500 war planes are exported from England during the past year. US Senator Nye charges England with supplying Franco with munitions as Chamberlain cabinet refuse to admit, despite conclusive proof from every correspondent (*London Times* to *Daily Worker*) that Franco has recently received colossal supplies of munitions from Mussolini.

Austria, large concentration camp is established for those Austrains who have not yet been forced to commit suicide. The guards to be those Nazis who were imprisoned by previous regime, thus making sure sadism has full play. Schuschnigg's aide is on his way to the States to show Cardinal Mundelein confidential dossier of Nazi activities in Austria, while the Pope reprimands Cardinal Innitzer for his crawl before Hitler which shocked not only Catholics but all the world. One brave bishop in Stuttgart refuses to vote in plebiscite and in consequence has mob roused against him by Nazi orator.

Germany continues to receive 42 per cent of her iron ore and best anti-aircraft guns from Sweden, 33 per cent of iron ore from France, Rolls Royce engines from England, Pratt & Whitney aircraft engines from the US, nickel from Canada, and all manner of supplies from Russia, as her iron and steel production leads the world for the first time.

In France, Daladier is given the decree

powers that were refused to Blum. Strikes in armament factories, which are condemned by both socialists and communists, prove difficult to handle while the French right adopt the attitude of preferring Franco and Hitler to their own countrymen of the left.

A.M. KLEIN

Three Poems

To One Gone to the Wars

For S.H.A.

Unworthiest crony of my grammar days,
   Expectorator in learning's cuspidor,
Forsaking the scholar's for the gamin's ways,
   The gates of knowledge for the cubicular
      door,

How you have shamed me, me the noble talker,
   The polisher of phrases, stainer of verbs,
Who daily for a price serve hind and hawker,
   Earning my Sabbath meat, my daily herbs.

'Tis you who do confound the lupine jaw
   And stand protective of my days and works,
As in the street-fight you maintain the law
   And I in an armchair – weigh and measure
      Marx.

Alas, that fettered and bound by virtues long
      since rusty,
   I must, for spouse and son,
Withhold, as is befitting any prison trusty,
My personal succour and my uniformed aid,
And from the barracks watch the barricade –
Offering you, meek sacrifice, unvaliant gift,
My non-liturgic prayer:
For that your aim be sure,
Your bullet swift
Unperilous your air, your trenches dry,
Your courage unattainted by defeat,
Your courage high.

Toreador

Unfurl the scarlet banner, Toreador
Take up your stance;
Let, then, the bull bicornate for the gore,
Snorting, advance,
To meet your clean thrust, bringing to his knees
The taurine beast.
Let banner upon blood proclaim the peace
Of bull, deceased.

Sonnet Without Music

Upon the piazza, haemophilic dons
delicately lift their sherry in the sun.
Having recovered confiscated land,
and his expropriated smile redeemed,
the magnate, too, has doff'd his socialized face.
He beams a jocund aftermath to bombs.

Also, the priest, – alas, for so much
      bloodshed! –
cups plumpish hand to catch uncatechized
      belch.

The iron heel grows rusty in the nape
of peasant feeding with the earthworm – but
beware aristocrat, Don Pelph, beware!
The peon soon will stir, will rise, will stand,
breathe Hunger's foetid breath, lift arm, clench
      fist,
and heil you to the fascist realm of death!

F.R. SCOTT

Canada the Ammunition Dump

The attempt of the British Conservative Party to bind Canada irrevocably to its foreign policy through enormous purchases of war material seems likely to succeed. Already there are rumours of a hundred millions in gold recently placed on deposit with the Bank of Canada for war purposes; large orders for aeroplanes are apparently being negotiated with Canadian manufacturers and new aeroplane factories are mooted; extensive production of machine-guns has begun in Toronto; thousands of British pilots, it is proposed, are to be trained on Canadian soil, so that we may expect Canadian airports to hum with military activity, Canadian drawing-rooms to be filled with charming propagandists for war, and peaceful Canadian skies to be loud with the drone of bombing planes practising for deadly raids on European cities of unpredictable nationality. All this and more is going on while the Canadian people drift aimlessly on world currents, listening with persistent credulity to Mr King's promises that 'Parliament will decide' (a romantic phrase that will go down to history alongside of President Wilson's 'Too Proud to Fight') and fondly imagining that they will be allowed to select whatever foreign policy they want 'when the time comes,' as if foreign policy were like a neck-tie or shirt that can be changed at the whim of a moment.

The time for making decisions about the next European war has, of course, come already. The selection of a policy for Canada has begun. What we shall have to do in the future is being laid down for us during these pre-war days, but not by the Canadian Parliament or the Canadian people. It is being decided by a political party which speaks for the financial and aristocratic classes in England, by the passive acquiescence (if not active co-operation) of a Canadian Cabinet that has not explained the serious issues to the electorate, and by boards of directors of Canadian and American corporations who are only too thankful, especially during a business depression, to make money out of converting Canadian raw materials into European war materials. Canadian citizens may be ill-housed, her employed ill-fed, her roads ill-paved and her schools inadequate, her constitution may need revising and her economic policies drastic changing, yet not for these needs will her industries be extended nor to these problems will the brains of her scientists and technicians be dedicated. Foreign slaughter is more powerful a determinant than domestic reform. Europe is at war already; the battlefield, now in Spain, may shift at any moment to other areas; in the frantic search for external allies Germany and Italy have secured Japan, England must secure her Dominions and the United States; hence the drive upon Canada and the steady commitment of innumerable Canadian organizations and power-centres to a policy of active intervention in Europe. If the Canadian people cannot resist the present tendencies involving them automatically in another crusade à la 1914, then their chances of resisting the far greater pressures that will come the moment the first English plane takes off for Rome or Berlin with a load of real bombs are just about nil.

For what does this vast programme of British-Canadian armament manufacture mean? Let us consider some of the implications. First, it means that a number of Canadian corporations will become firm supporters of British policy. They will make investments, install machinery, and hire workers so as to supply the needs of a British army prepared for immediate war. If Canada should ever decide not to fight in that war, and were to take the steps necessary to preserve her neutrality, away would go those investments and that employment. The hundreds of millions of British money will thereafter tie those corporations to British governmental policy exactly as any other political patronage binds any other contractors to the policy of the party that pays them. Secondly, it means that Canada's export trade will become more and more filled with war material, so that more ships carrying goods from Canadian ports will become lawful objects of foreign attack in the event of war. Canadian ships and ports will be inviting the raids and bombings which lead to war. Thirdly, it means that foreign spies and agents will be sent to Canada to wreck our factories and ferret out war secrets, thus threatening internal disorder and calling for more Canadian defence. Fourthly, British army officials and experts, as well as the thousands of pilots who are to be trained here, will be constantly in and about Ottawa and Canadian regiments and clubs, exerting a direct or indirect influence always on the side of participation in Europe. And lastly, most serious of all since it will operate whether war breaks out or not, it means that the biggest national effort in Canada during the next few years is going to be directed, not toward solving Canadian problems, but toward pulling the English Conservatives out of the hole they have made for themselves by their peculiar preference for balances-of-power over collective security.

In short, Canada is to become England's ammunition dump. This is to be the result of twenty years development of Dominion status. Canadian racial unity and economic betterment are to be offered once more on the altar of European bankruptcy, and the definite commitments which we as a nation refused to the world society struggling to be born at Geneva we give without a murmur to a political party representing at best one half of the English electorate. This is colonialism with a vengeance.

There is, of course, an argument to be made out in favour of supporting Mr Chamberlain's foreign policy with this kind of blank cheque, an argument as good as (but no better than) that used in 1914. Many organisations and individuals in Canada, ranging all the way from the IODE to the League for Peace and Democracy, are convinced that Canada's first duty is to fight for democratic institutions against fascist aggression. The only difference between the foreign policies of the two organisations referred to is that the IODE believes democracy is only threatened when England is in danger, whereas the League for Peace and Democracy sees democratic institutions in every country that stands in the way of fascist expansion, regardless of its past record. If England gets involved

August 1938

in a war with Russia as an ally against Germany, we shall see Tim Buck recruiting for the Grenadier Guards. The purpose of this article is not to review all the arguments for and against intervention by Canada in the next European war, but to point out that the decision is now being made in favour of intervention by the acceptance of a position inconsistent with any other choice. As Mr King's verbal foreign policy is one of 'commitments' and freedom of action, it is evident that the real foreign policy of Canada is now radically different from the one given to the public.

One thing at least this armament drive has done. It has exposed the hollowness of the Liberal Government's contention that the increased expenditure on defence in Canada in recent years was for the purpose of protecting Canadian shores. British military experts have concluded that Canada is the place for their armament factories because of her immunity from attack, not only in the immediate future but for some years to come. Canadian defence experts have told us that we must double our defence estimates because our former forces could not defend us from the attacks which threaten. One would expect the English experts, who are more experienced and nearer to the sources of danger, to be somewhat better informed. Can it be that the new Canadian bombing planes and tank corps have been intended for use in Europe all along? If not, then the grounds for the Liberal re-armament policy need re-examination.

A.M. KLEIN

Barricade Smith: His Speeches

I Of Violence

What does the word mean: *Violence*?
    Are we not content?
Do not our coupons fall, like manna, from the
    bonds?
Are we not all well-fed?
    Save for twelve months of Lent?
Is it not slander to aver the Boss absconds
With all the embezzled dollars in his delicate
    hand?
Is there not heard a sound
Of belching in the land?

Who, then, would speak of violence, uncouth
    and impolite?
Surely not we, the meek, the docile, the none-
    too-bright!
The askers with cap-in-hand, the rebels,
    Emily Post
Who know too well our place, our manners,
    and our host!

Wherefore, though wages slither, and upward
    soar the rates,
Not we will be the churls rudely to doubt that
    boast
Of Labor and Capital, that Siamese twin
    alright,
One of whom eats, the other defecates.

The Board of Directors sits
And cudgels its salaried wits: –
At cost of life and limb
Show profits, and still be
Unviolent as a hymn.

They syncopate your groans
    on gramophones;
Your muscles throb in their Rolls-Royce;
They triturate your sweat in cocktail-shakers.

But they are not violent, for violence is
    wicked;
And worse than that – I shudder to say the
    word,
That fell indictment –
It simply is not cricket!

Go therefore, tell your wives that the
    breadbox must stay breadless,
The rent unpaid, the stove unheated, you
    enslaved;
Because you *must* be above *all* things, well-
    behaved.
And having uttered these heroic words, slink
    hence
Into some unleased corner, and there vanish –
But not with any violence.

II Of Dawn and Its Breaking

Where will you be
When the password is said and the news is
    extra'd abroad,
And the placard is raised, and the billboard
    lifted on high,
And the radio network announces its
    improvised decree:
You are free?

Where where will it find you, that great
    genesis?
Preparing your lips for a kiss?
Waiting the call of next in a barbershop?
Rapt with the ticker's euphony?
Or practising some negroid hop?
Where will you be?
When the news is bruited by the auto horn?
Holding a pair of aces back to back?
Paring a toe-nail, cutting out a corn?
Or reading, with de-trousered back,
Hearst's tabloid, previously torn?

Or will you be – O would that you should be! –
Among those valiant ones returning to their
    homes
      To tell
Their daughters and their sons to tell posterity
How they did on that day,
If not create new heaven, at least abolish hell.

III Of the Clients of Barnum

Clients of Barnum, yours no even break!
The maestros have you, have you on the hip!
They gloat: they hold you ready for the take:
And you, O rube, fall smacko for the gyp!

Sucker, you stand no chance; the cards are
    nicked,
The factory, believe you me, is one clip joint;
The sadness is you know not you are licked
Come from the cleaners, you have missed the
    point.

Buffalo'd, taken for a ride, you gape;
Say dirty work at the cross-roads, but can not
Articulate its manner, form or shape.

For deadheads, here where X proclaims
    the spot,
Enters Politico, and p.d.q. –
To tell you what a lovely land is ours;
With him, Kid Pedagogue, the champ who
    slew
All challenging low wages and long hours;
Also Don Pulpiteer, to promise you,
Not earthly dwellings – no – celestial bowers!
Is it not time

Before they shove you on an unemployment
    shelf,
Or freeze you in a pension-frigidaire,
That you do get
Wise to yourself?

IV Of Psalmody in the Temple

They do lie heavily upon me, these
Sores of the spirit, failings of the flesh!
Wherefore, O triply-purgatoried soul,
Scram;
And chastened O my body,
Take it on the lam –
To the colossal, suprasuper hideout, blow,
To the lotiferous movie-show!

There I do sit me down in thick upholstery;
I do not want.
A tale is prepared before me: heroine enters,
Slim; and a villain, gaunt:
Also a well-groomed esquire saying I love you –
Fade out, fade in;
Shots of a lot of legs, and a couple of stooges,
Close-up, a grin.
The decent, the fair, win prizes; the wicked
Their just desserts.

The prince weds Cinderella, and virtue
    triumphs
Until it hurts.
O these felicitous endings, sweet finales,
They comfort me –
O bodies' beatitude, O soul's salvation,
Where this can be!
Most surely I shall dwell in this great temple
And take my bliss
Forever out of scenes which end forever
In an eight-foot kiss.

V Of Faith, Hope and Charity

Beware, – spiritual humankind, –
Faith, contraceptive of the mind;
And hope, cheap aphrodisiac,
Supplying potency its lack;
And also that smug lechery
Barren and sterile charity.

VI Of Beauty

Seeing that planets move by dynamos,
And even the sun's burnished well-oiled spring,
What glory is there, say, in being a rose
And why should skylarks still desire to sing,
Singing, and no men hear, men standing close
Over some sleek, mechanic and vociferous thing?

For these there is one beauty; put it on a table:
A loaf of bread, some salt, a vegetable.

VII Of Poesy

Bard, paying your rental of the ivory tower,
With the old coin of hoarded metaphor,
Abandon now the turret where you cower;

August 1938

Descend the winding staircase; and let your
Speech be, not of the thrush's note, long sour,
But of the Real, alive upon a floor.

Let Keats forget his father's stables, smelling
The mythical odour of the asphodel;
Let Wordsworth clutch his sensitive bosom,
   leaping
When he beholds a rainbow he can sell:
Let Butler Tennyson pour out old vintage
For the good knights at Arthur's King Hotel.

But you, O streamlined laureate,
What's Hecuba to you?
How long will you yet bind your fate
With stars archaic and with obsolete dew?

Go out upon a roof, and laud the moon!
Your words are sweet and flattering, as if
The moon were a good corpse, a threnodied
   stiff!
O idiot bard, O frenzied loon,
Such words to blow
Upon that smooth hydraulic dynamo!

For soon, O sooner than the laurel grows –
Will come to you, superior of the mass,
The foreman Death,
To push you into one of many rows
And bodily have you manufacture grass, –
Of your sweet immortality, true token,
Wage of the foreman Death
His time-clock, broken.

VIII Of Soporifics

These be repasts lethean of your kind:
the tabloid whispering, the penny sheet
shouting the scoop that even the richest meet
with mesalliance, murder, maddened mind;
the sermon showing corpses wined and dined;
the radio hour and its jovial bleat;
the circus come to town, a breadless feat;
two weeks of grace for fifty weeks of grind.
These are the brews that are allowed to mull
in crucibles of bone one would call sane;
these are concoctions patented to dull
the too-keen edge of the too-querulous brain,
persuading the cockerel dung is beautiful,
and the bespatted, spit is only rain.

IX Of Shirts and Policies of State

A shirt! a shirt! a kingdom for a shirt!
Open your paper; bargains, if you please!
A principality goes for less than dirt,
The palmiest state for any pied chemise.
A red blouse buys the franchise of the czar;
The brown habergeon claims an Arian realm;
Where once were candid togos, blackshirts are;
Shirtless is but mahatma at his helm.

Wherefore, O Machiavel,
Get you a rag, a shoulder-strap or a brassiere,
And be it but of the right proper hue
And kings will come in trembling and in fear
And peoples, hoarsely obedient, will come to
   you!
Make haste; and use dispatch!
The shirts of the spectrum governance the
   world!
Get yourself, therefore, while you can, a
   patch
Of rainbow silk, of motley linen, and
Declare another philosophic shirt unfurled!

X Of the Lily which Toils Not

You, Tillie the Toiler and Winnie the Worker,
   consider
This fabulous lily – and her milk-fed pride, –
She toils not, no, and neither does she spin!
O not like yours her most egregious skin,
Her epidermis gilt-edged, bonded hide!

For she has been a child most delicate,
Bathed in milk, filched from the wild goat's
   haunt;
She has thrived, has grown, has come to man's
   estate, –
She is the season's worthiest debutante!
Her grandfather sold cheap gawds in quantity;
Non-lilies in their hundreds toiled for them.
Now, dough is no consideration, see, –
The girl must have her court and diadem.

Call the reporters, call the photographers!
Here, for The Sportsman, a snap of Lilia
Patting the groomed posterior of a horse;
And for The Social Star,
Lily and jaguar.
And please, good fellow, print this one
   apart, –
(It goes to show our hot-house Lily has
Not only a big bosom, but a heart.)
Photo of limousine, and background-slums,
Already titled for the typesetter:
Deb and debtor.
Isn't that cute?
Also do not forget to comment on the style of
   her spring-suit.
Have a drink; drink hearty;
Here are passes to the party.

And what a party! Outre, a l'outrance!
Strawberries from the Himalayas, and
Fowl hatched somewhere in some uncharted
    land
And other tidbits, costly all, and all
Prepared by (trumpets) Oscar Cinq of France.

The wine, the flowers, the music, and the
    guests!
The liquor gurgled of Napoleon's wars,
The hired jester made financial jests,
The slick musicians juggled their music scores,
While dignified doormen guarded all the doors
Permitting only the distingue who
Could swear he never laced up his own shoe.

Tillie, it was a glorious sight to see!
Tails and white ties, and gowns, and naked
    backs;
Chrysanthemums, pink, brought from beyond
    the sea,
Tinted, by artists, with bright blues and
    blacks, –
And brooding, like a spirit,
Over the champagne flood that never once did
    ebb,
Lily the Deb!

Of course, I did not see it all myself;
Sadly, I lacked, what millionaires call pelf,
And so I must, in honesty, relate,
That Barry Cade-Smythe did not crash the gate.

But Barricade Smith did love her from afar,
Watched her, in due time, go upon a cruise
And come back, headlined in the nation's
    news,
As wife of the tenth cousin of the Czar.

Whom, in due time, she buried. No one needs
To be reminded of that tragic cut
Of her Paris widow's weeds.

That season over, with the coming of the
    spring
And dividends blossoming on many a bank,
She wedded, being now a lady of rank,
A closer relative of a deposed king,
Whom, in due course,
She did divorce,

And sent him packing, with a little tip,
Two million dollars, and a discarded ship.

And still to-day, Tillie, if you have the time,
And Winnie, if you care, you may,
Ahunting go to Africa, or climb
Some hills Helvetian, yodelling, and find
Lily at play;
Or on the Riviera, or shooting birds of clay, –

Perhaps, however, you cannot get away.

L.A.M. [MacKay]

Glacial Stream

John Smalacombe, who is best known to *Forum* readers for his political lampoons, presents here (in *Viper's Bugloss;* Ryerson Chapbooks; 60¢) a small collection consisting largely of personal verses. These range in tone from a quiet violence to an exceptional and indeed immodest virulence. One of his political pieces is included, and there are three descriptive pieces that have considerable picturesqueness of detail. Mr Smalacombe is unquestionably vehement within his limits, but the limits are narrow. Death and dislike are apparently the only things about which he can get really enthusiastic. At any rate, these themes rouse him to an aptness and a concreteness that make his handling of other themes seem comparatively vague and allusive, though the best of the descriptive work retains much of the decisive sharpness that is Mr Smalacombe's chief merit.

The rhythm is strong, varied, and flexible, and the handling of vowel sounds exhibits no little dexterity; Mr Smalacombe's ear, however, sometimes seems inadequately sensitive to sibilants. It is unquestionably a serious limitation that the verse, however melodious, should be predominantly negative in tone, though it must be admitted that the negation is far from being quiet, colorless or resigned; indeed, at times it is positively noisy. Two poems, 'Hylas' and 'Dochmiacs' strike a strangely contrasted idyllic note, and five 'Epitaphs' of classic brevity further temper the savagery with which Mr Smalacombe has modelled himself on Archilochus (whose victims went and hanged themselves)

In short, the talent displayed in these verses is characteristically cold, narrow, rapid, and hostile as a glacial stream, though somewhat more turbid.

A Protest

The Editor, *Canadian Forum*

Sir:
Your arrogant reviewer informs me that I do not know a sibilant from a snake in the grass. I beg leave to cast the following in his haughty teeth:

SILENCE FOR SERPENTS

Where low a lapping river ran
    Under a bank of gravel,
Wandered a melancholy man
Who, leaning on a log, began
    To mark a bubble travel.

It leapt, it lingered; in one bound
    It cleared a bulky boulder,
Or idly twirling, loitered round
    Where in a moving mirror drowned
    Green weed lay down to moulder.

Reclining on a rocky prong
    Old lore of mortal trouble
He pondered, in a world gone wrong
Late taught to pirouette along
    Light-hearted, like a bubble.

As you, Sir, have undoubtedly observed, this petty jeu d'esprit has dispensed not only with S, Z, and SH, but also with X, TH, the sharp sound of F, and CH, unless sounded as K.
    That ought to hold him.

                             Yours faithfully,
                             John Smalacombe

Note: John Smalacombe is a pseudonym of L.A. MacKay.

DAVID ANDRADE

Dust Patterns After Revolution

Safe now with friends tonight, a thousand
    miles away,
We turn off the radio to listen to the wind.
And I see again the barricades thrown up
Against the guns, the splintering bullets, the
    whirling dust.

I hear again the red flag snapping over me,
Nailed to a broom-handle stuck in a barrel,
And I am deafened with the rattle of home-
    made rifles
And the heavy booming of guns at the end of
    the street.

These are the brave ones
The factory hands, the clerks, the pick-and-
    shovel men
Fighting their unequal battle against the
    charging white cavalry
That breaks over them like a wave, out-
    rhymes, out-harmonizes,
Better weaponed, better equipped, backed by
    a uniform tradition.

And in the morning, on the sea-shore, on the
    cold dry sand,
Where the wind treads down the dune grass
    and the brittle reeds
And the sand-hills smoke with flung dust at
    their peaks,
I feel my hand hurt where I lean on it, and I
    look at it
And see the pattern of the sand and grass
    imprinted on the palm.
And I wonder if my face, if my mind bear
    that same pattern
Pressed with the heavy pressure of the earth
    from where I came.

Now all things combine to uncombine, all
    counsel disintegration,
Scattering lonely thoughts, leaving utter
    loneliness,
And life itself is but one lonely thought.

Note: David Andrade is a pseudonym of Patrick Waddington.

HENRY PAUL

I Am a Transient

I am an unemployed transient; that is to say, I have spent most of the last ten years on the drift. From town to town across the Dominion at least a dozen times and through 40 of the 48 States, by box car, blind baggage and highway, I have kept moving. I have alternated periods of unskilled poorly paid work with living for months at a time on various forms of public relief, or with downright beggary. I am rarely well-dressed and sometimes quite ragged and dirty. I am now 28; I was 18 when I first 'hit the road.' In point of fact I was graduated directly from a Canadian university into the box car.

In December 1929, I was a curiosity, almost a freak. A tramp at that time was a man over 35, semi-illiterate, a beaten hulk of a man with a shady, usually criminal past, and no future. I was a fresh-cheeked, somewhat naive lad with a great faith in what the world held in store for me. Indeed sheer force of physical circumstances alone impelled me to take the first steps. But I was not to remain an exception for long. From towns and villages and farms, and especially from the drought-striken prairies, new recruits flooded in by the thousands.

Their circumstances showed a strong uniformity. Some were, like me, directly from the classroom; most had been living at home in idleness for a year or two, then had left in disgust or had been shown the door by brutal parents who 'had been supporting a family at their age.' The inhuman provision of the relief system, which in many places excludes children over a certain age – usually 14 – from the relief check, forced many either to leave home or take food out of the mouths of younger brothers and sisters. A few left homes to seek adventures, but these were in a decided minority. Most were under 22, some as young as 13 or 14. Virtually none had ever held a decent job or had any work experience; en masse they had no training, trade, or profession to fit them for life in a bitterly competitive world.

Let us consider what happened to these boys – my own case will do as an example; many others would vary only in particulars. I left home in December, boarded a freight and rode 300 miles in bitterly cold weather. My first stop was at a Canadian town of some 15,000 people, which had, and I believe still has, a large sign somewhere in its environs advertising it as 'a friendly city.' It was not such to me. Desperately tired and cold after a 15 hour ride in below-zero weather I stumbled down the main street. Naively enough I turned my steps towards the local headquarters of a certain international religious organization which makes quite a display of its social and charitable ideals, and which operates a men's hostel in this town. On my arrival there I asked for a bed. The cutting wind was no colder than the refusal, when the person in charge discovered I lacked the necessary quarter. Then I recalled that one of the 'stiffs' who had ridden on the train with me had spoken of sleeping at the police station. I turned thither.

On my arrival I inquired timidly of the sergeant at the desk for a bed. I had a vague idea that I would be given at least a bunk and blankets. The sergeant first took my name, address, and other particulars, then showed me to my 'lodgings.' Picture to yourself a room about ten feet by ten feet with no ventilation, with rough stone walls and a cement floor, an open water closet in one corner, a girdle of steam pipes all around, a huge globe burning overhead, and absolutely no furniture of any kind. On the floor there already lay sprawled a dozen, ragged, unkempt men. They occupied all the available space. To get in at all, I had to step over recumbent bodies. But not even the choking odour of unwashed bodies or the swarms of bed bugs could keep me awake. Space to lie down in there was none, so I slept sitting up. I think I could have slept standing too.

I have slept in many such places since, some very little better, some actually worse, but the memory of that 'bed' is still fresh with me. In the morning we were awakened at six. I struggled to my feet; apparently half a dozen more men had come in after I fell asleep. As to where or how they slept, I am not willing to hazard a theory. We filed out of the dungeon and back into the bright freshly-painted offices. The burly sergeant booked us out.

'I want you fellows to get out of town,' he snapped. 'If I catch any of you guys hanging around here, I'll run you in for thirty days.'

The few nearest him nodded meekly and we filed out into the street, for this was no idle threat. I have done a total of 46 days in jail at one time or another for the crime of 'being without visible means of support.'

The cutting cold tore at me. I did not feel

hungry. I had already missed too many meals to feel hungry. But it is possible to feel very, very cold, especially if one's stomach is empty. I was tired too, after the 'rest' of the previous night. By a stroke of luck, I turned a corner and ran into one of the 'road stiffs' who had come into town on the same freight as I.

This man became my mentor for the next two weeks. If I had not met him, I do not know to what desperate steps I might have been driven. He supplied my initiation into the ways of beggary and vagabondage. I do not care to go into the details, which even at this late stage I find disgusting. It was a difficult job, for I was a delicate, sensitive lad, with a streak of honesty which at first made this life unspeakably hard for me.

As I have said we were together for a scant two weeks. I later learned that my pal had a leg cut off under a freight train, a year afterwards. Sardonically enough he was then 'accepted' by the relief office of the municipality in which this occurred. Since that time I have inducted a half-dozen young fellows into the ways of the road. I have found them hungry, bewildered, hopeless. I have rustled them a few meals, broken them into the ropes, then left them. They and I lived miserably, it is true, but by following these methods we were at least able to eat most of the time and generally to get a warm place to sleep.

What is really noteworthy is that these young fellows, like myself, have stayed on the road. I have met them repeatedly in past years, in freights, on the highway, or in flophouses. In fact I may say here that I have never met or ever heard of anyone who has lived this life for any considerable period of time and has been able to rehabilitate himself completely.

The following spring, when I had been on the road about three months, I got a job. I had almost given up the pretence of looking for work. All winter I had gone through one town after another where I knew no one and no one knew or wanted to know me. I never had time enough to get acquainted before the police ran me out to the next town. While I was in one place my whole time was taken up with the question of how to get food and tobacco and a warm place to sleep. Bitterly cold night-rides on freights, horrible restless 'flops' and bad food, filled my whole existence. My clothes too had become ragged, marking me as a 'stiff' and making me an easy prey for ambitious rookie policemen.

Finally I did get a job, a pick and shovel job at enough to pay for my board, clothes, tobacco, and no more. It was gruelling work for my young untried muscles; but I stuck it out for the six weeks it lasted. I then found myself again 'on the bum,' again banging back doors, again being looked at askance by snooty employment bureau clerks for having the temerity to ask for a job in a ragged pair of pants. From time to time I got bits of rough, poorly paid work (this was in 1930-31). Always the end was the same. The lay-off, the road again, futility.

There may be persons of sufficient strength of character to live through the combination of filth, misery, and beggary that I have described without becoming to some extent demoralized, but I have not met them. When I first went on the road, there were few men under thirty; today there are many, and they are not newcomers. They are the children of fifteen to twenty who drifted into this life five or ten years back. Those who believe that these youngsters will all come back into life if and when jobs are opened for them do not know the facts. Many are beaten hulks today on whose very faces there is the stamp of enforced beggary and degeneracy.

Do I mean to say that these men are hopelessly lost? Not at all. But they need a definite program of rehabilitation. To reduce the question to whether the men will or will not work is the purest nonsense. As a matter of fact most of them will – for short periods of time – but they have lost all stamina, will, direction. They cannot steer directly towards a long-range ambition. It is this state which I call 'box-car neurosis,' as true a neurosis as any in the Freudian canon. They have been hammered out of the form of men and have become worthless both to themselves and to the society around them.

Some highlights of my experiences may be interesting, inasmuch as they illustrate general conditions. Very early in my life on the road I learned to stay away from various religious bodies, which professionally undertake evangelization of the 'down and outer.' I am not here attacking religion. Most of the friends of the drifter come from the United and Catholic churches. But there are several religious bodies which have established missions, hostels, and the like. The procedure is almost always the same. The group purchases a building on which of course they pay no taxes. Then they proceed in the name of charity to jam the building with beds at a concentration anything up to five times as great as that permitted by law to private rooming house-keepers. After installing a checker board and a handful of last year's magazines as 'recreation,' they are open for business.

The rates are always just a little below what a private rooming-house can profitably charge for the same service. These places are in no sense charitable. Beds are not given away. In each of these places there is a collection of broken down bar-room flies and other seedy types of stiffs, who in return for a bed can be counted on for a testimony to their changed lives when pious contributors are present. To the man on the road, who still retains some self-respect, these 'rice-Christians'* are untouchables. In fact to be called a 'mission stiff' is a grave insult.

One great solacer the man on the road has – alcohol. I do not mean to say that all men on the road drink, but the proportion of those who are never sober by choice is perhaps as high as one in four. It is a vicious circle. A man drinks because he is miserable, because he drinks and so on. The difficulty of getting money for drink has led to the use of cheaper substitutes. The two principal ones are rubbing-alcohol and canned heat (the alcohol is squeezed out of the latter through a handkerchief).

Any person who cares to inspect the environs of a hobo camp is reasonably sure to find a number of containers of these liquids scattered around. I do not care to describe here the mental and physical effects of these concoctions. Many of the addicts are hardened reprobates of twenty or so.

Since these men are treated as outcasts; it is only natural that they should become such; they have a kind of closed society with its own conventions, groupings, dignities, and even a partially developed argot of its own. This tendency towards seclusion has been aided by the rapid growth of sexual perversion, made necessary by lack of female companionship. (In ten years I have seen half a dozen women on the road, and these highly unattractive.) Perversions of various types, while by no means universal, are now so common as no longer to be considered marked peculiarities.

As might be expected the physical condition of the men is almost as low as their mental states. Exposure, cold, and hunger have taken their toll. Any scheme for rehabilitation must consider this. A stiff percentage would be unable to do a day's work in their present condition, and would require a long process of rebuilding.

I know I will seem to have painted a very black picture but the problem is a vicious one. I have tried here to state it, not to show how it might be corrected. But certainly the first step to be taken is to stop the flood of new recruits. The number of drifters in Canada today is approaching 150,000. (Not all of them are on the road at the same time of course.) There are at least three men adrift today for every one in 1929. That is, we have created at least 100,000 tramps or roadstiffs in 10 years. During this decade about 1,000,000 young Canadian boys came to manhood. We have been making a bum out of one young Canadian in every ten.

What is more, this state of affairs has not stopped, neither is it stopping. You are the father or mother of a boy of fourteen. Today there is actually one chance in ten that within a few years he will be picking vermin off himself in a box-car. If you are a wage worker or farmer, your son's chances are even worse, for it is from the homes of the working class that practically all these boys come – hence the complacency of those in high places.

There is of course only one immediate hope – vigorous governmental action – but how is this to be attained? Those who know the King government's attitude to spending money on social reforms know that unemployment relief will only come through vigorous publicity and agitation; neither the federal nor the provincial governments act progressively on their own initiatives.

The reactionary press in the larger centres maintains a campaign to keep the 'bums' on the move; the Canadian imperialists are particularly anxious to get 'penniless vagrants' out of sight during the King's visit. On the plea of returning them to homes they haven't got, they are to be banished from the route of the royal itinerary. The Vagrancy Act will no doubt be invoked, as in the past, to herd them into Canadian jails during May and June. A colonial survival of fourteenth-century English feudal legislation against revolting serfs, this Act makes it a jail offense to be 'without visible means of support.'

The focus of resistance to all this must be the men themselves. A large percentage is at the moment too demoralized to be organizable, but there is a score of transients who have been able

---

*'Rice-Christians' was originally the name given by white people on the China coast to the hordes of 'converts' with which some China missionaries padded their church membership lists. In return for aid given in building a church, or even in return for occasionally attending church, the Chinese 'converts' were given two bowls of rice per day. The rice-Christians were, in large part, broken-down opium addicts. Among many of them it was the practice to save a little rice each day with a view to trading it for another pipeful of opium when sufficient rice had been collected.

to save some tattered remnants of their self-respect. Amongst these I have observed a steadily deepening consciousness of their position and an unwillingness to permit themselves to be hounded about the country any longer.

When transients in Toronto began mass 'tin-canning' this winter they were thrown into jail – but the consequent public interest and sympathy for their plight resulted in their release and in at least some local and temporary relief.

But, as usual, the support of the liberal press has been sentimental, and more confusing than constructive. 'Human interest' articles, such as appeared in the *Toronto Star*, have represented the mass of the transients as a fine virile Canadian young manhood in need only of some temporary assistance in the way of snow-shovelling or a more elegant but still temporary flop-house. Such propaganda may have all the best intentions but it does not face the facts nor strike at the root of the problem.

What the single unemployed need is not jail and the bum's rush on the one hand, nor mere winter hand-outs on the other. They need work and wages. Moreover the hours and the nature of the work must be adjusted to the endurance of their weakened bodies, and the wages must be high enough so that they can build up physical and moral and mental stamina once more. Nor will this be possible unless the work is of a socially necessary kind. Unemployed camps of the type attempted in the past, and hinted at again by the Leadership League, are simply serf-labour camps to keep the unemployed away from the big centres where they can make their miseries known, and to put him under military control. In this way he is deprived of what democratic rights he has left and turned into a piece of war-material awaiting export to the next world slaughter.

Any effective program for the transient, as for the unemployed in general, must aim at his absorption into normal and useful industry. Initial measures must include immediate and adequate cash relief, clinical and hospital attention, and work-training schools. A federal program of constructive public works must then be created which will provide jobs at union rates. The money can be found; it is being found instead for 'military defence.' Why also should it not be possible, in a country where thousands lack proper food and shelter, for the government to take over idle factories and finance and train unemployed to run them co-operatively? Why can there not be a national housing program, and schools to make carpenters out of useless transients?

Such a method of approach, if coupled always with the demand for trade-union rates, is the only way to arouse the indifferent trade-unions to the realization that their interests and those of the unemployed are ultimately the same. The worker of today is the transient of tomorrow. In the meantime the unemployed must of course build his own independent organization on a militant basis; but he must have the support of the trade-unions, he must feel the solidarity of the working-class movement behind him, if his problem is to be solved.

EDITORIAL

Canadian Censorship

If purity of mind, unthinking loyalty, and marital happiness can be secured by censorship, then Canadians should possess these qualities in a high degree. According to a recent question answered by Mr Ilsley in the House, the Department of National Revenue seized in 1938 no less than 3,917 publications of a 'subversive nature,' while the 'obscene' literature confiscated amounted to the immense total of 26,639 magazines, 3,897 newspapers, 16,040 pamphlets, and 581 books. All this material, of course, is inspected and blacklisted by a few lesser civil servants whose qualifications for this priestly task are unknown, and who never on any occasion have to disclose the standards used in sorting the nice from the nasty. Our readers will remember that when Mr Woodsworth asked for a list of banned books hoping in this way to shed a little honest daylight on this furtive process, his request was refused on the ground that to name the books would be to incite people to buy them! Obviously the Government believes that the Canadian people have already reached the state of pitiable instability which is the inevitable product of censorship.

In addition to this steady schoolmastering from Ottawa there have been two recent examples of the same spirit. One was the banning of the magazine *Ken* for a cartoon about George VI and his suggested visit to the World's

Fair. The sight of this, apparently, would have loosened the imperial bonds unduly. It is quite proper for Canadians to see the Japanese Emperor made fun of in the Mikado, but they must not see their own Emperor made fun of by other people. The other example was the refusal of the Quebec Film Censors to allow the showing of *Wuthering Heights*, on the ground that it portrayed 'infidelity.' A suggestion was made to the producers that they should cut out the offending portion, but these stubborn people would not conform. The film censors do not mind falsifying a work of art; they do not consider this a form of immorality. Eventually a compromise was reached by which, as reported in the *Montreal Gazette*, the scene showing the illicit love between Cathy and Heathcliff has been cut 'so skillfully as to omit the actual wording of their declaration of affection,' without 'leaving the audience in any doubt as to the emotions of the characters.' So morality is saved; though seen, it is not heard. Meanwhile the number of books in the public libraries of Quebec remains at .3 per capita of the population.

FRANK H. UNDERHILL

Peace Aims

This war is already repeating the pattern of 1914 in the extremely vague and negative character of the statements of our leaders about their aims. We are in the war to stop Hitler and Hitlerism and to bring to an end the processes of the last few years in which settlements of international questions have been imposed by force or the threat of force. But of course, while our force may eliminate Hitler and his government, it will not of itself eliminate the social and economic conditions which produced Hitler, and of itself it determines nothing as to the organisation of Europe that is to follow the war. In fact we are no longer accurate, having once gone to war, in saying that we are in the war to prevent the imposition of settlements by force; we are really in the war to see that the settlement is determined by our force rather than by German force. And the vital question on which our statesmen should be giving us enlightenment is that of the purposes for which our force (presuming that it is successful) will be used at the end of the war.

The real issue of this war is whether some organisations of Europe can come out of it which will be tolerable to the peoples on both sides and which will enable them to settle down and live side by side in a reasonable degree of neighbourliness. Moral declamations help hardly at all either in the analysis or in the solution of the complex and difficult questions raised by this issue of the proper organisation of Europe. Killing Germans – and it will be at actual Germans that the allied soldiers will be shooting, not at Hitlerism or any other ism – and breaking the will of the German people to resist our force, these acts bring us only to the threshold of the problem. What kind of a peace are we trying to bring about? What kind of a Europe do we want to see after the peace treaty?

Nothing is more depressing in Canada just now than the almost complete lack of interest shown by our newspapers in this question of our peace aims. We went into the last war on the blithe assumption that once the Kaiser and his military forces had been eliminated Europe would automatically settle down to a decent regime of peace. We cannot have such faith any longer. If we make the kind of peace that we made in 1919 and if this is followed by the kind of statesmanship that ruled Europe for the fifteen years after that, then we may as well make up our minds that Europe will settle down to breed another Hitler. But it seems to be enough for most of our editors that we are following the British lead. At the end of the last war the one newspaper in Canada which showed an intelligent understanding of the problems of European organisation, of the general conclusions towards which British and American discussion was tending, and of the principles of the League of Nations which emerged from this Anglo-American discussion, was the *Winnipeg Free Press*. Today the slightly hysterical editorials in which it heils the 'Peace Front,' and its tendency to substitute such emotional slogans for the hard analysis of a difficult problem, make one suspect that it is uneasily aware that there is not much content to its 'Peace Front.' What real evidence can it produce that the statesmen of Britain and France believe in the kind of international organisation in Europe which it has been preaching since before the League was founded? What evidence can it produce that the government of Canada is organising our efforts in order to support that kind of international organisation?

The last settlement of Europe emerged out of a struggle between militarists and liberals in the governments of the victorious allied and associated powers. On the whole the militarists got their way. Old states were broken up, new states were created and new boundaries drawn, so that the defeated powers would never be able to challenge the settlement without being immediately exposed to invasion from all sides. Germany and Hungary were disarmed themselves and surrounded by a ring of hostile states directed by France and assisted by France to maintain strong armies against any revival of the military strength of the old central powers. Germany was deprived permanently or temporarily of areas which were of economic importance for military purposes, such as Upper Silesia and the Saar, areas in which, curiously enough, the war of 1939 started. The new states were given slices of territory from Germany or Hungary to ensure that they would be on the right side in future troubles. With characteristic militarist stupidity the old Austro-Hungarian empire, instead of being transformed into a federation of equal peoples, which might have been a bar to German advance down the Danube in case Germany should revive again, was broken up altogether. (Or perhaps it was the liberals who were stupid in this case.) The militarists declare now that the real fault of the last peace treaty was that it did not crush Germany thoroughly enough; and there will be plenty of them at the next peace conference to demand that the job be done properly this time. But there will still be 80 million Germans in Europe at the end of the next war. As Bernard Shaw pointed out in 1914, the only way to crush Germany as our militarist fanatics want her crushed is to sterilise all German adults so that no more German babies will be born.

The liberals in 1918 believed that the solution of the European problem was to give separate national independence to each national racial group. They swallowed the partial dismemberment of Germany and Hungary forced on them by the militarists, but they managed to get a long list of new nation-states set up; and they came home rejoicing at this culmination of the work of nineteenth-century liberalism in emancipating 'peoples rightly struggling to be free.' Unfortunately, however, the racial groups east of the Rhine are so mixed up among one another that it is impossible to draw any boundaries which do not leave racial minorities embedded in every state. The new national states, based on the emancipation of races which had long been oppressed, proceeded in turn to oppress the minorities whom they had at their mercy. The liberal attempt to protect these minorities through the supervision of the League of Nations was a ghastly failure, because the League's operations were controlled by politicians of the successful states who were thinking mainly in terms of military power. And the net result was to create a Europe in which racial hatreds reached a pitch of intensity never before equalled.

Any future settlement of Europe which emphasizes boundaries either because of their strategical importance or because of their racial importance will only lead to another Europe like that of the 1920s and 1930s.

But even that Europe was beginning to settle down into tolerable conditions by about 1926. Racial animosities began to soften as the continent recovered from economic collapse. Germany entered the League and was restored to the family of nations. Sudeten Germans began to cooperate with the government of Czecho-Slovakia. It looked as if the continent might at last disarm and devote itself to the ways of peace. But the depression of the 1930s destroyed all these tentative advances, and a Europe which could not solve its economic problems drifted fast towards internal revolution in one state after another and towards international anarchy. The root problem at the end of the next war will be the economic organisation of Europe. Unless some form of an economic United States of Europe can be put into operation, everything else that the statesmen of the peace conference may do will be futile. No one of the national states of Europe west of the USSR is of sufficient size to be economically self-sufficient in any sense. Unless they can all be started together in some form of cooperation towards raising in common their standards of living, they will continue to cultivate their historic hatreds and eventually return again in desperation to the age-long European process of mass murder. One would feel much happier about this war if one could discern signs in either camp of the economic statesmanship which will be needed for the reorganisation of post-war Europe.

What is Canada's policy on these European questions? Mr King, to his credit, has been somewhat more specific on the subject of the organisation of Europe than have the British or French prime ministers. 'The peoples of the continent of Europe must find in some way, through federal relationships or economic partnerships or rebirth of democratic institutions and the spirit of liberty, the art of learning to live together.' This is a sentence tucked away in his long speech of September 8. Let us hope that he will in due course give us more light on what he had in mind in these phrases. Let us hope that his next review of the action of his government will report not merely more details about 'cooperation' with the British government in 'defence,' but the initiation of some discussion between the two governments towards the definition of their peace aims.

What is to be the constitution of the next League of Nations? The first League failed because the governments concerned had no real belief in the new order they were supposed to be building but treated the League simply as an instrument for furthering their own separate selfish purposes; and because the peoples, who were vitally concerned in a world order of international peace and cooperation, lacked the understanding to see in time the direction in which the policy of their governments was headed. Both the Canadian government and the Canadian people must bear some share of the responsibility of this failure. But there is no particular need for us to put on sackcloth and ashes. The success or failure of the Geneva experiment depended primarily on the lead given by the great powers. The chief criticism of Canadian policy at Geneva is that we followed throughout the lead given by one of the great powers and never explored what might be accomplished by closer cooperation with such small powers as the Scandinavian states who stood most consistently for a genuine application of League principles.

But the old League also suffered from certain inherent defects in its structure which must be removed in any new effort. It was too exclusively political in the scope of its operations. Its constitution and the policies of the powers who controlled it inhibited it from developing those schemes of international economic planning which were necessary if the world was to recover from the devastation wrought by the war and by the depression of the 1930s. At its worst the League tended to become a sort of permanent Congress of Vienna with all the delegates intriguing and jockeying for position. The best that most of its self-appointed defenders in Canada have been able to conceive for it was that it should become a sort of international war-office organising 'sanctions' against 'aggressors.' Neither at its worst nor at its best was the League able to attract to itself the loyalty of the common people of the world which could only have been won if they saw it the centre of world efforts for solving their daily problems of poverty and insecurity. A new League must be based upon a much greater measure of pooling of economic resources among the nations who are its members than was acceptable to the leaders of 1919. And pooling in the devastated world of 194— will mean something much more far-reaching than the laissez-faire free trade of the nineteenth century.

But the root obstacle to this international collaboration in the production and distribution of wealth lies in the semi-monopolistic position of economic control which small groups in each country have established for themselves in their own national economy. Their interest lies, or seems to them to lie, in organising the economic resources of their nation, under their own leadership and primarily for their own profit, for a struggle against rival national economies similarly organised. They form the interests in each country who exalt national sovereignty, who use the instruments of education and propaganda to inflame the nationalistic passions of the masses, and who regard the foreign office and the armed forces of their country as existing primarily to push for markets and raw materials and spheres of influence abroad. We shall not get much real economic reconstruction as long as these groups control national governments. The old League was based upon the fallacy that this international economic struggle can be allowed to go on untouched and that the League need only step in when the struggle threatens to take the form of armed conflict. It will be a hard lesson for us all to learn that we must give up the exclusive economic nationalism which has become rooted in our thinking and in our institutions. But unless a new League can become the centre of a great complex of international economic institutions, it will fail, like the old one.

The old League suffered also in effectiveness because it attempted a world organisation in one undifferentiated centralised institution at Geneva. Science and politics have not yet abolished geography. We need more regional international organisations. Most of the controversies which filled Geneva were primarily concerned with European rivalries and hatreds in which the non-European countries were not directly interested. (And on many of these questions Canada's attitude inside the League was quite properly as aloof as the attitude of the United States outside the League.) The present war arises, in part at least, out of a problem which is older than Hitler, older than the Kaiser, the problem of the European balance of power. It is intolerable that non-European peoples should be asked to sacrifice men and materials every twenty-five years because the peoples of Europe cannot find a way of living together in decent neighbourliness. Fundamentally the Europeans will have to learn this elementary lesson in living from their own experience. The necessary preliminary to any successful world organisations in the future is some sort of United States of Europe which the peoples of Europe will have to work out for themselves among themselves.

So far as we Canadians are concerned the essential test of a satisfactory Europe is demilitarisation. A Europe which is armed or arming is not necessarily one which is going to invade us, but it is one in which the Europeans are going fight one another and are going to ask us to join in the fight. A disarmed Europe is one which is returning to the processes of peaceful production. But demilitarisation cannot be imposed on Europe, and certainly it cannot be brought about by merely disarming the unsuccessful combatants as was done in 1919. It will come about of itself in a Europe in which the conditions of life are generally tolerable. The statesmanship that will lead to these conditions will have to concern itself far more with economic problems than did the statesmanship of 1919. And Canada's contribution to the post-war settlement can probably be made far more usefully in forms of economic assistance and collaboration than in promises to employ 'sanctions' against future 'aggressors.'

G.M.A. GRUBE

Freedom and War

War, by its very nature, tends towards repression, rouses primitive passions, and thus creates an atmosphere in which reasonableness, free discussion, and a spirit of toleration are difficult to maintain. War is therefore a dangerous weapon for democracy to use, even in its own defence. This does not prove that democracies should not go to war under any circumstances whatever, for men use dangerous instruments and weapons every day. But, if they are to survive in doing so, they must be fully alive to the dangerous potentialities of their instruments, and learn to control the passions of Mars, to examine carefully the claims he inevitably makes for the restriction of liberty, and vigorously withstand such claims where they are not justified.

If it is true that vital democratic rights must be surrendered in a crisis, then let us be honest and admit that democracy, instead of being the best system of government yet devised by the mind of man, is only a luxury which, like all luxuries, must be given up whenever times are hard. This I do believe. The restrictions required by war are essentially the same as are accepted in peace: the state always takes the measures it deems necessary to preserve the secrecy of its military weapons and plans, and to protect its public utilities and industrial plants; in war time the risks of sabotage and espionage are much greater and the precautions must be correspondingly increased. Similarly in time of peace the state does not tolerate direct incitement to violence; when passions run very high violence is more probable, and greater care and restraint may reasonably be required from the subject. A tightening up of such peace-time precautions against both kinds of offence does not imply any surrender of civil liberties, as long as the law is used only against those against whom it is intended.

Misdirection and abuse of such legal precautions is of course only too likely in war-time. This presents a serious danger to the proper functioning of democracy and must be resisted, but abuse of the law can be proved to be such, and one may hope that such abuse, the danger of which also exists in peace-time, may return to normal proportions when heated passions cool down.

What is more disturbing is that, as soon as war is declared and even before, governments have a way of taking unto themselves vague and undefined powers that are nothing short of dictatorial. The War Measures Act, for instance, gives the Governor General in Council, that is the Cabinet, authority to issue orders in Council and regulations on anything it may 'deem necessary or advisable for the security, peace, order and welfare of Canada,' and some of the regulations already in force are almost as wide in scope. One wonders why Parliament should thus depute its supreme powers (the Act, by the way, dates from 1914 and was merely reinvoked in 1939). The British House, be it noted, has done nothing of the kind. It has been in permanent session since the beginning of hostilities, and has voted on the various war measures required. Miss Ellen Wilkinson, MP, made some pertinent remarks in this connection:

Some MPs have been impatient about all this work being done by Parliamentary Bills instead of doing it by regulation. But regulations are not open to criticism. It is important that when bills affecting the intimate life of every citizen are being rushed through Parliament, they should have at least a rapid scrutiny by the elected representatives of those citizens. The House of Commons has done a good job under great difficulties. Left to itself without scrutiny, the official mind might have restricted liberties of the ordinary citizen beyond anything that was really necessary in a situation where everyone is ready to be helpful.

In Canada the official mind seems to have done precisely that. Geographical considerations may make a permanent session difficult in this country, but there is no sound reason why Parliament should have adjourned after a week, and should not be reconvened for four months. Our government was surely not in so much greater a hurry to get on with the war than the British government? Parliament should sit more often during the war, and when it does meet it should use its overriding powers to insist on at least a brief consideration of the orders in council and regulations now in force, and make amendments where deemed necessary.

Many people feel that the extent of these vague powers and regulations is not so important because they believe that Mr King and his colleagues honestly desire to preserve as much liberty and democracy in this country as they can during the war. I believe this too. But let us remember that, although it is the Federal Government that makes these regulations, the administration of them will very largely be in the hands of the local and provincial authorities, and prosecutions under them will be judged in local courts. In fact the Federal Government is putting these vague and very wide powers in the hands of others, in whose wisdom, restraint, and love of liberty we may not feel the same confidence. Further, governments do not last for ever, and their good intentions are not always inherited by their successors, while their powers are.

Nor do these regulations receive the same publicity as the proceedings of Parliament, and publicity remains the shield of democracy. Copies of the Defence of Canada regulations are as a matter of fact hard to get even today, and prosecutions were actually taking place under certain sections before anyone knew the letter, let alone the spirit, of the law. It is an old democratic principle that the law should be available and intelligible to the citizens. These undefined powers are neither. It is also an old democratic principle that men should not be arrested without charge or kept in custody indefinitely without trial. The Minister of Justice now has the power to do both on the ground of suspicion alone.

All this puts weapons in the hands of those who would like to suppress every form of criticism, however legitimate and however necessary. A man may be prosecuted and sentenced to months of imprisonment, quite legally, merely for having in his possession even a letter containing 'any adverse or unfavourable statement, report or opinion likely to prejudice the defence of Canada or the efficient prosecution of the war.' Any criticism of government policy, of the budget for instance, could reasonably be argued to come under that, and it could be maintained that any adverse news-report, of the sinking of the Royal Oak for example, did likewise. By the same token, many a recent editorial about Russia in our most 'loyal' newspapers could, it seems to me, be thought 'likely' to 'prejudice His Majesty's relations with foreign powers'! Were such regulations used to the full, it is obvious that all opposition could be suppressed. No distinction is drawn between public speeches and private conversations. In Ontario, several people have already been prosecuted for clearly silly remarks made in beer parlours, and an Ontario magistrate has seen fit to advise that it is everybody's patriotic duty to report any such 'disloyal' statements, wherever made.

Seen in this light, these regulations open up most disconcerting visions of often foolish but sometimes vicious informers keeping their ears open for any expression of opinion contrary to government policy – visions of things which we have hitherto associated with the dictatorships and for which we democrats have had a well-founded contempt. Let me repeat that I am well aware that the Federal Government does not intend to make use of these regulations in this manner. But others may. Why have them then? They are both unnecessary and dangerous. Freedom of criticism is essential, in war as in peace. Indeed it is sometimes necessary to change governments in war time – Britain found it so in the last war – and this cannot be done in accordance with the people's wishes unless democratic rights are preserved. In any case, there are too many people ready to greet the sanest criticism with accusations of disloyalty. They should not be thus encouraged.

And there is yet another danger in all this. It is not only that liberties once lost are hard to recover. This longer view may seem academic where victory is the overridingly urgent aim. On the short view also, however, I believe that it is a profound psychological error to adopt dictatorial measures, or measures potentially so, at the very time that men are asked to wage war against dictatorship abroad. In these days of totalitarian war the morale, not only of the armies but of the civilian populations is supremely important. Morale is never improved by repression, and minorities are dangerous only when denied expression and driven underground. We all know, and we are told on all sides, that Germany's great weakness is precisely that her citizens are denied all freedom and regimented against their will, that they cannot speak their mind for fear of spies. Men will never fight for a regime as they will fight for an idea. If our idea is democracy, then let us practice it.

Is it not strange that, while we pin our hopes to the collapse of a repressive system, so many of us should be ready to follow, even though at some distance, on this very road to repression? Liberty has never lost a war. In England, now as in the last war, there is far more criticism not only of government departments but of the very war policy itself, than many Canadian authorities would think healthy or allow. They are wrong. Such freedom will help victory, not hinder it; yes and even greater freedom would help even more. If we look back to the only democracy of antiquity we find, in ancient Athens, the most virulent criticism not only of political leaders but of the war itself, even on the public stage. Such things we admire, but dare not imitate. Modern democracy is a new thing, and in times of crisis we show an atavistic tendency to return to the caveman's club. Or at least to make sure that the club is available when we may feel like using it.

We should frankly recognize that Nazism and Fascism are but an extreme and pathological form of diseases, which affect, in a milder form, every body politic. War brings the tendency to brutal repression to the surface, yes and racial hostilities and anti-semitism also. These are insidious and rapid poisons. Let us beware of encouraging them; they are far more prejudicial to democracy, to the community's morale, and even to the 'efficient prosecution of the war' than any amount of criticism and disagreement, however fundamental.

F.R. SCOTT

The Real Vote in Quebec

Now that figures of the total vote cast in the Quebec elections are available, it is possible to form a fairly reliable estimate of what happened in that province on October 25th. The imperialist press in Canada, as was to be expected, immediately interpreted the Liberal victory as proof that the people of Quebec were solidly behind Canada's war effort. The *Winnipeg Free Press*, the *Globe and Mail* of Toronto, and the *Montreal Star* showed the unity of their war attitude by the similarity of their misinterpretations. Mr Grant Dexter of the *Free Press* summarized the situation in this way: 'Quebec was offered two choices, to unite Canada in unlimited voluntary participation in the war or to withdraw from the war and to resist the war effort of Canada; she chose the first.' The *Globe and Mail* almost seemed to think that the vote justified the introduction of conscription. One and all were as eager and ready to read war approval into the election results as any of the newspapers in England.

This kind of wishful thinking is quite erroneous, and highly dangerous to the very national unity it pretends to understand. The press in English Canada should cease misinterpreting Quebec in this way and trying to promote war policies based on a false assumption; or else another rift may be created in the future even greater than any which has existed in the past. There are certain very definite advantages for Canadian unity which may result from the fall of Duplessis; to try to exploit the situation for purely imperialist ends is to show an ignorance of Quebec and a disregard for the future welfare of this country.

The first requisite to an understanding of Quebec's choice is to look at the vote. Canadian

Press returns for 84 out of 86 constituencies show the following figures:

Party	1939	%	1936	%
Liberal	287,673	52.73	226,006	40.37
Union Nationale	217,460	39.86	315,418	56.33
ALN (Gouin)	24,893	4.57		
Others	15,573	2.84	18,457	3.30
Total	545,599		559,881	

In other words, the Liberals defeated all other parties by some 30,000 votes only, Duplessis and Gouin between them obtained 44.43% of the votes – and Gouin was more anti-war than Duplessis. Even assuming, therefore, that all who voted Liberal did so because they wanted active participation in the war (which is fantastic), it still remains true that the great Liberal majority in favour of Mr Grant Dexter's 'unlimited voluntary participation' amounts to about 8%. There is obviously a great deal of anti-war feeling in the province of Quebec today, no matter what interpretation is placed upon the election result. To ignore it is to overlook a factor of continuing importance.

The next step that must be taken to understand the situation is to weigh the motives that led the voters to support Mr Godbout and the Liberals. This is admittedly a difficult task, since the element of conjecture cannot be eliminated. Certain broad issues, however, are clear. Quebec was not offered the choice of 'withdrawing from the war' by anyone. There was no possibility of any such action, and the ordinary man on the farms and in the street had sense enough to know it. Equally was it true that there was no party in Quebec which made active participation in the war a principal part of its program. Quebec did not vote for war. Certain independent Conservatives in English speaking constituencies did run as imperialists, and they lost their deposits. A number of Liberals in the same constituencies were equally pro-war and were elected, but in the French districts the Liberals were anti-conscription rather than pro-war. The Liberal vote as a whole, in so far as it expressed any idea at all in regard to the war, was primarily an anti-conscription vote. This is why Mr Lapointe's intervention was so supremely important. Once he had announced, in his opening speech, that in the event of a Duplessis victory he would resign with all his French colleagues in the Federal Cabinet, it became clear that a vote for Mr Duplessis would be more likely to bring on conscription than retard it. For Mr Lapointe was opposed to conscription, and if he left the Cabinet was it not likely that the crisis would be met by the formation of a national government, as in 1917, for the express purpose of overriding French opposition? *Le Canada*, the official Liberal paper stressed this argument on more than one occasion; on the morning of the election its chief headline read: 'Votre vote renforcira la position que nous avons prise contre la conscription, déclare M. Cardin.' Quebec preferred to accept the fact of our present commitment to the war, which it could not change in any way, with the repeated promises that all enlistment would remain voluntary, rather than run the risk of having at Ottawa a far more pro-war government managed by imperialists.

But the war issue was only one of the issues in the election, and it is doubtful whether it was even the main issue. No matter how much the war might be introduced, the electors knew well enough that they were choosing a provincial administration to look after provincial affairs. Mr Duplessis had much to answer for. His financial dealings, which had more than doubled the provincial debt in three years, left him wide open to attack, and Mr Godbout centred his campaign round the financial question. It was not difficult to convince the electorate that the war issue had been dragged in as a blind to cover up the serious crisis in the treasury department, and further that if Mr Duplessis were elected he would receive no money from Ottawa and hence would be forced to resort to high taxation. A large part of the Liberal vote can be attributed to this argument alone. Then much of the labour legislation of the Union Nationale, particularly such things as rendering unincorporated trades-unions liable in damages and collective agreements liable to alteration by government decree, were distasteful to labour generally. The farmers had been better treated by Mr Duplessis and supported him more loyally, but even here his promises had outreached his achievements. Mr Godbout, also, is a good agriculturalist. Purely provincial motives of this kind must have determined the votes of a great proportion of the electorate. If Mr Duplessis had been genuinely concerned to protect the autonomy of Quebec, he could have used his large majority and his two more years of power at once, instead of calling an election.

In short, the extreme interpretations that followed the announcement of the election results were decidedly misplaced. The people of Quebec, while willing to support the defence of their shores, no more like the idea of Canada taking part in European wars today than they did six months ago. But they are a sensible people, and the fact that a vote for Duplessis would not take Canada out of the war was plain to everyone. As the popular vote showed, they altered their political alignments very little. So long as Quebec retains the present electoral system, without proportional representation or the alternative vote, changes of government will not give a true picture of the movement of public opinion. Particularly erroneous was a remark in the *Winnipeg Free Press* editorial of October 27th to the effect that 'The present situation in Quebec is in happy contrast to that in the last war.' Actually the contrast is all the other way. In 1914 Canada's participation evoked far less protest than has been seen already in this war. This time there has been no statement approving the war issued by the hierarchy in Quebec, as was done in the pastoral letter issued to the dioceses of Quebec, Montreal and Ottawa on October 22nd, 1914. This time a petition signed by many thousand people was presented to Parliament, opposing participation, and rejected because of its form; this did not occur in 1914. And this time one leading French Canadian politician thought he could secure another term of office by capitalising on the anti-war sentiment; had his domestic record been better, he would probably have succeeded. It is more true today than it was in 1914 that participation in overseas war strains our national unity. Any future attempt to introduce conscription would make that fact abundantly clear.

This analysis of what occurred in Quebec last October still leaves it possible to interpret the vote as being favourable to the concept of national unity, so long as that term is not identified with unlimited participation. Unity and war participation have no necessary connection. A man may favour national unity, and yet believe this war not to be in Canada's interests. Mr Duplessis had pushed too far his idea of provincial autonomy. The vote at least showed that this appeal can be overdone. Non-cooperation from Quebec in such things as unemployment insurance and other matters of national importance has simply meant that the working classes do not get as much protection as they otherwise might get. Separatism means a lower standard of living for Quebec, and probably many people on relief or near it perceive the fact. The bogey of assimilation has served its turn for a while, and it looks as though appeals to such false fears are not as powerful as we have thought. All this is to the good. There is a real opportunity for increased cooperation from the new administration in the solution of national domestic problems, particularly in the matters that will be dealt with in the report of the Sirois Commission on Dominion-Provincial relations. Anyone who endangers this by trying to capitalize on the Quebec vote for imperialist reasons is undermining Canadian unity.

> QUEBEC ELECTION
> *Duplessis became a Communist*
> *Communists became pro-Hitler*
> *Westmount became Liberal*
> *Godbout became God.* [F.R.S.]

THE 40s

The coming of the Second World War faced the *Forum* with something of a dilemma. There was no sympathy with fascism and its crimes, but the long resistance to the approach of war was hard to forget. As a result the *Forum*, while hardly lukewarm, was not completely enthusiastic about all aspects of the Allied struggle, and there was a persistent tone of criticism at the excesses of Canadian and Allied policy. Violations of civil liberties and the War Measures Act under the Defence of Canada regulations were regularly subjected to analysis. Profits and profiteers were watched closely, as were the antics of the red-hot conscriptionists who tried to run the war in a 'Toronto' fashion. Above all there was Mackenzie King, and in the 1940s the *Forum* was obsessed with King as in no other period. Clearly he could no longer be dismissed as an accident of history, and there were several attempts to analyse his influence and role. In many ways, however, the main interest of the magazine was in the CCF. The party had boomed during the war and the socialist millenium seemed to be just around the corner. This rise – and the subsequent collapse of the dreams of 1943 – are chronicled here.

The tone of disillusionment seemed to carry over into the *Forum's* literary work, too. The new literary magazines that began to appear in Canada during this decade started publishing many of the best of the younger poets, and the literary pages, while still showing flashes of the quality of the 1930s, somehow seemed to lack direction.

EARLE BIRNEY
To Arms with Canadian Poetry

Now that we have collected the more obvious enemy aliens behind barbed wire, clapped the soapboxers and the anti-war pamphleteers in jail, and threatened the pacifist parsons with the same medicine, is it not high time we turned our attention to the poets? The body of our loyal citizenry, pre-occupied with the new mass production of airplanes and sox, are plainly unaware that sedition is rife on the home verse front. We should not lull ourselves with the argument that no one reads Canadian poetry, for the fact remains that metrical propaganda is being regularly exposed to the public eye. Moreover, whatever the war aims of our government, some of this verse is not in keeping with them. Worst of all, the most serious offenders are precisely those poets who are said to have some reputation among the intelligentsia. Who knows but what their utterances might become known beyond the borders of our country, and prejudice His Majesty's relations with foreign powers?

Certain exceptions may happily be made at the start. Mr Nathaniel Benson has left no doubt of his patriotism in a stirring appeal entitled 'A Canadian to America!' which appears in the current (October) issue of the *Canadian Poetry Magazine*. Mr Benson justly pictures the distressed shades of Lincoln and Washington sneering at the failure of the United States to enter the war on our side. 'Arise, America!' he concludes, 'Arise, America, and strike!'

But what of Sir Charles G.D. Roberts, Wilson McDonald, and other senior bards? We have heard nothing from them since the war began. In such days as these may not silence be treasonable? Nor will we be fobbed off with wedges of geese in the northern sky or the lisping of unbombed Canadian children. The time has come when nature is not enough.

Some of our leading journals likewise remain in a most disturbing rhythmical lethargy. The post-peace issues of the *Dalhousie Review* and *Canadian Homes and Gardens* contain not a measured line which might conceivably be said to bear upon the present struggle. The October *Queens Quarterly* presents but one poem, 'The Old Eagle,' by E.J. Pratt. Although this makes a to-do about an airplane, the craft is obviously of a simple commercial type without bombing equipment. In the last *Canadian Forum*, it is true, Dr Pratt has printed a long compostion which makes suitably unflattering references to Hitler, but the ditty seems to eschew the time-honoured phrases and images of patriotic poetry, and shows a dangerous tendency to treat war as in itself upsetting.

Miss Dorothy Livesay, from whom we had grown to expect some support of the war of the democracies against fascism, has also disappointed us by contributing to the same journal and by publishing in the *Canadian Bookman* an obscure piece entitled '2000 AD.' Here Miss Livesay asks the future if it will 'comprehend our silence who today stifle the honest word?' Surely Miss Livesay is not implying that there are honest words that cannot now be uttered by any loyal citizens.

The Canadian Home Journal has not, I'm sorry to say, done much better, with the exception of 'A Mother's Prayer' by Faye Gould McLean, which contains at least three satisfying lines:

He came, a soldier, through my door.
'I've joined,' he called, 'they've said I can.
Gee, Mum, I really am a man!'

The ending, however, which I forbear quoting, unfortunately emphasizes a certain reluctance in the Mother to recognize the automatic manhood of her nineteen-year-old soldier-son.

One is happy to record that at least one Canadian periodical is giving space to the poets who fully understand their duty. In the Toronto *Saturday Night*, Mr J.E. Middleton publishes a well-merited 'Protest' against those who 'when Hell is loose again ... prate learnedly of Peace!' The first phrase is perhaps a bit unfortunate, since our scald has not clearly confined the boundaries of Hell to enemy territory, but Mr Middleton clarifies his vision in the following week's issue of the same journal, by an elegy in memory of the missing seamen of HMS Courageous. They are pictured marching up the 'golden way' and receiving a blessing from the wounded hand of Christ himself. This satisfactorily establishes the partisanship of Heaven in the present war and helps to reestablish that grand tradition of piety which made Canadian poetry of 1914-18 forever memorable. Mr William Patterson, of Calgary, manages in the same issue to combine a similar reference to Christ with an ingenious appeal for recruiting:

> *My Work of Mystery...*
> *Ye thought it done; 'Tis but begun.*
> *Now, who will follow me?*

I regret to note, however, that *Saturday Night* has on at least one occasion allowed versifiers of a different stripe to intrude upon its space. I refer to an affair rather cheekily called 'For the Duration,' by one Joyce Marshall. It reads, in part,

> *'I'll never pen A martial ditty,*
> *High in bombast, Low in pity...*
> *I'll never urge The lads I know*
> *To go where I Need never go.'*

This sort of thing may perhaps not actually discourage recruiting but I should think it might be likely to prejudice discipline in His Majesty's Forces (always supposing that it would be likely to fall into Their Hands), and so actionable under the Defence of Canada Regulations.

It is with a genuine relief, therefore, that one turns to the beloved and traditional poetry-corners of our daily newspapers. It is true that even here not all editors have yet learned to discriminate. From September on, the Toronto *Daily Star* has continued to print unseasonable trifles about autumn colouring and love and the like. There is as yet nothing in the War Measures Act which deals with such writings; yet if this example were to be followed by all our poets, would not the effect be definitely to cause disaffection to His Majesty and even perchance to interfere with the efficient prosecution of the war?

To the credit of the rest of Canada, let it be said at once that the apathy of the *Toronto Star* is being daily repudiated by Vancouver's loyal *Province* and the monumental Montreal *Gazette*. I wish there were space here to quote at length the inspiring 'Highlander's Hymn of Hate' and the 'Lament for the Passing of the Kilts' which have appeared in the Sunday supplement of the former. I must content myself, however, with but fragmentary reference to the rich outpourings of melodious patriotism which have steadily graced the editorial page of Montreal's bulwark of our press.

The first days were of course the most difficult for the *Gazette* as for all of us. For some reason best known to the fickle muse, there was a gap of almost two weeks between Britain's declaration of war and the appearance of Canadian poesy properly adjusted to the event. (I cannot help but feel that all this is connected with Mr King's lamentable slowness in declaring Canada herself at war.) But where other editors resorted to their files for rhymes plainly written in what might now be called the disloyal days of peace, the *Gazette's* literary helmsman ingeniously reprinted the glorious calls to battle issued by Rudyard Kipling and other alert Englishmen in the parallel days of 1914.

By September 18th, however, a Canadian poet had leaped into the breach, with a dithyramb in celebration of two 'great captains' of the past. Mr Alan MacLachlan, writing during the unfortunate days when our Allied Command seemed to be hesitating before the Westwall, aptly reminded the Empire that Conde and Turenne 'waited for no German to make the first attack.' On September 20th there followed a beautiful lyric by an old patriot, Vox Populi, entitled 'Floreat Anglia Atque Gallia.' With that fine triumph over logic which gives the poet his peculiar power, Populi declaimed:

> *Canada's a peaceful land.*
> *But shall Canada stand aloof when she hears*
> *the loud-mouthed guns?*

The answer was, of course, No.

No event has been too great or too small to be shirked by the *Gazette's* gallant soldiers of the quill. Mr Richard Callan, of St. Lambert, PQ taunted the Reds for their pact with Russia ('Nazi champagne healed the sore'), and Miss Eunice T. Holbrook Ruel, following carefully our Allied positions, saw

> *Over the forts of Saarbrucken*
> *The great Archangels wing and watch*
> *As once in Bethlehem.*

Mr W.J. King who had made a fine individual sally against the Huns by describing them, in a September Ode, as 'creatures from the jungle,' returned to active service in November with 'The Crusade.' The Germans are now revealed to be prehistoric saurians, and the poet ends finely: 'Once more the dragons fear the cry "St George!"' Even Armistice Day, a theme presenting peculiar difficulties for our battling Pindars, was not shirked. Fittingly, it was the Honorary National Vice-President of the Independent Order of the Daughters of the Empire who stepped into the breach. 'Mayhap,' she suggests, 'the poppies e'en lift an accusing head.' But 'avaunt such thoughts,'

> *And though the very fiends of hell should laugh,*
> *With choicest flowers pile we high the Cenotaph*

And pledge anew our swords to this now holy war.

Another poetess – and it is indeed gratifying how the women of our Dominion have sat typewriter to typewriter with the men in this important work of the home defence – apologizes most charmingly for fellow poets who have not yet fired their poetic rounds at the hated Boche:

*It seems to me there's so much happening
That poets haven't got much time to write.
They watch for rays from heaven to give
them light.*

But is there darkness in this war for right? The answer, of course, is again, No.

In such a veritable Maginot line, such a fortified Parnassus, as the *Gazette's* bards have built and held, it is difficult to single out any one poetic pill-box for especial praise. Were I forced, I should, however, name the Clarion Ode to 'Poland' which appeared on November 17th. Although its author, Mr Wheaton Bradish, subscribes himself 'An English visitor to loyal Canada.' I think it well to quote from him here – I wish I could say 'in extenso' – as a shining mark at which our Dominion troubadours may shoot. The poet sees our fair young nation flying to Britannia's aid,

*The bloody tyrant's will to foil
And force the forsworn fiend's recoil.
The scions of Montcalm and of Wolfe
Will chase with zest the foul werewolf;
Two races in keen rivalry
To slay such noisome devilry ...
The flaming fiery-cross band on
Until it gilds Pacific's bourn ...*

*Escorning Nazi savagery,
Ah! hearken to Britannia's cry:
Poland dies not, without I, too,
Death's portals with her journey through!*

In these accomplished couplets there is immediately evident the alliterative heritage of our doughty Anglo-Saxon (as distinguished from Low Saxon) forbears, together with those bold inversions, audacities of metaphor and unusual twists of word which convince us at once that Mr Bradish is of Shakespeare's land. Gaze, finally, at the couplet with which the visiting scop hails our Dominion

*Unflinching in two holy wars,
Unstinting in old Britain's cause.*

In the surprising triumph of that rhyme there surely speak not only the indomitable spirits but also the authentic accents of the trueborn Englishman.

We need more Wheaton Bradishes. The time is rapidly approaching when we shall be forced, in the interests of an enduring peace, to curb the verse-hoarders, discipline the shirking sunset-fellows, instruct our willing but inexperienced Kiplings, and intern the seditious peace-rhymers. A Poetry Control Board is on the order of the day and I hope that our government will have the perspicacity to recall Mr Bradish to act as its Controller. It is on such poetry as his that our empire rests.

F.A. BREWIN

Conscription in Canada

The prime minister of Canada, speaking in the House on September 8, 1939, made the following statement:

I wish now to repeat the undertaking I gave in parliament on behalf of the government on March 30th last. The present government believe that conscription of men for overseas service will not be a necessary or effective step. No such measure will be introduced by the present administration.

On the following day, the Right Honorable Ernest Lapointe, Minister of Justice, gave emphasis to the Prime Minister's pledge:

The whole Province of Quebec, and I speak with all the responsibility and all the solemnity I can give to my words – will never agree to accept compulsory service or conscription outside Canada. I will go further than that. When I say the whole Province of Quebec, I mean that I personally agree with them. I am authorized by my colleagues in the cabinet from the Province of Quebec ... to say that we will never agree to conscription and will never be members or supporters of a government that will try to enforce it. Is that clear enough?

February 1940

186

H.E. BERGMAN
Along the New Highway   Feb. 1940

alone advocated conscription. They urged an omnibus conscription that was to cover 'finance, industry and manpower.' The details were not disclosed. The leaders of the Conservative Party and the CCF also indicated their opposition to conscription.

In the light of these facts, it might appear that discussion of conscription for Canada is entirely academic, but governments do not last forever and the path to conscription in the past, both in Great Britain and in Canada, has been strewn with broken pledges. Powerful voices will urge conscription in one form or another. Those who think that conscription would be disastrous to Canada may feel that it is wise to let sleeping dogs lie. On the other hand, if one is afraid of the dog, it is probably wise to be armed before the dog wakes up. When the matter becomes acute and violent controversy is aroused, those who oppose conscription may well be accused of 'disloyalty.'

In Canada at least one powerful voice has already been raised. At a joint meeting of the Canadian and Empire Clubs of Toronto, the Right Honorable R.B. Bennett, chairman of the National Service Commission during the last war, expressed warm approval of Great Britain's method of calling troops to the colours. This he described as 'a registration scheme.' Conscription, he said, was a nasty sounding word. Men, when called up, had given no excuses and the richest of English peers had gone to the assembly depot with the village barber. Canadians, he added, should not be unmindful of the possibility that some day it might be necessary for them to share in this equality of sacrifice and service.

Mr Bennett was right. Canadians should not be unmindful of the possibility of conscription or, as Mr Bennett prefers to call it, of registration followed by enforced military service. They should count the cost and consider what conscription did for Canada in the last war. Both in Canada and in Great Britain in the last war, and again in Great Britain before the present war, conscription was preceded by voluntary registration schemes (which governments said had nothing to do with conscription) closely followed by compulsory registration schemes.

The march to conscription was marked by newspaper campaigns and by a gradual process of concession by governments which had originally announced their opposition to conscription. It is, therefore, interesting to find that today The *Globe and Mail* of Toronto, taking Mr Bennett's hint about the nasty sound of the word 'conscription,' is advocating a voluntary national registration scheme to 'ensure the availability of the services of every man and woman where they will be most valuable, if and when needed.'

The question of whether the individual conscience or an exemption tribunal is the best judge of where a man's duty lies in time of war will probably always be a matter of dispute. The military arguments pro and con are many and varied. Cromwell is usually quoted for conscription, the Duke of Wellington against. Of modern military experts, Major [sic] Liddell Hart is the best known opponent of conscription.

The ethical arguments involved are also interesting. But for Canadians these considerations may be of less weight than the recollection of Canada's conscription efforts in the last war. Canadians may recall that conscription came close to wrecking Confederation. Riots and wholesale disobedience to law, not in Quebec alone, flowed from efforts to enforce conscription in 1917 and 1918. As Mr Lapointe said in the speech in parliament already quoted, the conscription issue has sown the seeds of discord of which even today we are reaping the bitter fruit.

To what end were the Dominion of Canada and harmony between French-Canadians and their fellow Canadians nearly sacrificed on the altar of conscription? 549,359 men enlisted in Canada during the last war. 228,751 were British born. During the whole duration of the war, some 83,355 were enrolled under the Military Service Act. In the spring of 1918, when the tide had begun to turn in favor of the Allies, 32,000 men only had been obtained by the draft. How many conscripts saw actual service in the trenches is not clear. The reason for the insignificant number of those obtained by conscription is not hard to find. In Ontario, out of 124,965 who registered under the first draft, 92 percent claimed exemption and all but 8.2 percent were finally exempted by the original or appellate tribunals. In Quebec, out of 115,602 who registered, 113,291, or 98 percent, applied for exemption and the local tribunals allowed all but four per cent of the exemptions claimed. Appellate tribunals increased the percentage of those held liable for military service to nine per cent. It was estimated that 40 per cent of those liable to the draft in Quebec refused even to register and evaded the provisions of the act altogether. In Ontario the equivalent figure of those who avoided the draft was 10 per cent.

The government even found it necessary, in the spring of 1918, to disregard the exemptions authorized by parliament and to employ the decree powers conferred by the War Measures Act to cancel exemptions already allowed.

The church, the politicians, the local tribunals, and the populace in Quebec alike opposed enforcement of the conscription law. Had not the tide of war turned in favour of the Allies and the government's efforts slackened in the face of rising hostility across the whole of Canada, it is difficult to say whether Confederation could have survived.

The positive contribution of Canada's conscription to the efficient prosecution of the last war was, therefore, negligible and the cost in terms of Canadian unity grave and incalculable. Do Canadians wish to repeat this experiment? Before doing so, they should read carefully the history of Canada in the last war.

LOUISE SMITH HARVEY

Anti-Semitism in Quebec

According to the pamphlets issued by the Bureau of Tourism for this province, the inhabitants of Quebec, the English, the French, the Jews and other races live together in mutual love and concern for each other's well-being. They rejoice together over the quaintness of French-Canadian villages; they plow the fertile valleys in unison, and never a harsh word comes between them. These pamphlets play up the goodwill existing between races of different culture, background and religion, until the reader is overcome and feels that the 'entente cordiale' idea has been emphasized too strongly, and that all is not as it should be behind the alluring phraseology of the government literature. If he begins to inquire, he finds his uneasiness well founded; and should he come to Quebec not as a tourist but as an observer, all the illusions so carefully constructed by the Bureau of Tourism melt like spring snow.

Quebec faces a complicated question on the race-minority problem, one only to be solved by long and patient experience. Whenever it seems insoluble, or other problems are not so pressing, anti-semitism crackles into the headlines. The French-Canadians feel they are a minority in the country as a whole; the English feel they are a minority in the province, although a powerful one. The Jews actually represent a small part of the population. To the casual spectator, there is never any feeling against the Jewish people, but scratch the surface and see what happens.

Prejudice against the Jewish race, although often dormant, has existed for many years in the province of Quebec. Recently there have been cases of students who headed their class, and looked forward to a brilliant teaching profession, only to find that because they were Jewish, they always came second on the list. One such student has had to be content with substitute teaching – that thankless job – ever since her graduation eight years ago. There also are little known cases of discrimination in many of the large business offices. These things are so taken for granted that no outcry is made against them. There is nothing dramatic in them. They have no appeal to the tabloid-minded public, no matter how terrible may be their significance.

But within the last few years dramatic episodes have startled the public. With the rise of Arcand, the leading provincial fascist, and at one time a close adherent of Hitler, incidents occurred and are occurring which belie the picturesque statements of the Bureau of Tourism. Early last summer feeling began to smolder. In the cities and especially in the mountain district of the Laurentians, a farming area largely settled by French-Canadians, speakers went from Arcand's headquarters to rouse the people against the 'international enemy of civilization,' the Jew. They began to nurture and build anti-semitism by fiery speeches, pamphlets, and placards. Holiday-makers getting off the Sunday trains to spend a quiet day in the hills would return by the next train to the city, for placards greeted them in the local stations bearing the legend: 'We don't want Jews here.'

All summer the tension increased. On July 31, the fever broke. More than two hundred notices appeared in the town of Ste Agathe des Monts. The English one read: 'Jews are not wanted here in Ste Agathe, so scram while the going is good.' The French version ran: 'Jews are not wanted here; Ste Agathe is a French-Canadian village and we will keep it so.' Following the appearance of the posters crowds gathered on the street. A Montreal man, a Jew, was hauled into court the next day for obstructing traffic on the main street. No one really seemed clear on actual events, but mass hysteria turned Ste Agathe into an arena for rioting of the worst kind. The placards appeared, a Jew was arrested, several pedestrians were insulted by anti-semitic taxi-drivers, who drove slowly behind them calling out insults as they drove. The following day, a Monday, investigations began. The local chief of police claimed that he had expected trouble, for he had heard that a band of young French-Canadians were out to 'do a job on the Jews.' The parish priests indicated that they felt that Ste Agathe must be kept French-Canadian, and that they had told their congregations as much. It turned out that several well known fascists had also been talking in that district, and that they had been discussing the matter with priests. There is also a rumour, and more than a rumour, that these fascists have been given space to store ammunition and other material in one of the nearby palatial hotels, perhaps for their avowed march on Ottawa, perhaps for a fatal onslaught on the Jews. The investigations further proved that the majority of the French-Canadian populace found their Jewish neighbours good business and good friends. Two days later attempts to burn a bridge leading to an island holding a Jewish hotel were unsuccessful due to the amateur methods employed by the incendiaries.

Since actions in this locality received such a cold hostility from the Canadian public, for a time anti-semitism was shelved. War broke out, the cry of unity was raised. The fascist leaders were interned, or went into hiding. People's attention turned to world events.

Then, on December 17, 1939, a Montreal broadcast shocked its listeners. A day later anti-Jewish posters reappeared in Ste Agathe. The broadcast, prepared by a newscaster of station CKAC, of the French daily *La Presse*, opened with five minutes of small news bulletins and continued with a ten-minute analysis of the

Russo-German pact. It referred to high Kremlin officials as consisting mostly of Jews. 'Complaints that the broadcast was anti-semitic in that it tried to prove that Russia was being governed by Jews, and that by doing so it implied that all Jews were communists, flooded the station.' (the Montreal *Gazette*, Dec. 18, 1939) According to the *Canadian Jewish Tribune*, this 'acrobatic rhetoric was designed to prove that communism was but an alias for international Jewry ... intended to hold up the Jewish population of this country to contempt and hatred. ... However, this phillipic is not original. Its statistics are those of Fritz Kuhn; its revelations those of Arcand, and its inspiration derives from Hamburg.' The article, published Dec. 22, 1939, goes on to disprove the statements by Laroche, and file a complaint against such conduct.

Those who heard the broadcast considered it in extremely bad taste, without reason, and with no excuse for its existence. It is obvious that open anti-semitism is not yet tolerated; it is too reminiscent of Germany, with whom we are at war. But the more insidious prejudices continue. A prominent Jewish citizen tried to place his son in the army as an officer, as many of his Gentile confrères were doing, and was finally told that his son could not be accepted at the moment due to his race, but that later he might be accepted. A Jewish family which has lived in the city for years has recently been refused tenancy. A French-Canadian landlady looked at them, jerked out: 'Pas de Juifs!' and banged her door. On the door of the most popular pub in St Sauveur, the ski-mecca, someone within the last two weeks has painted a bright red sign: 'Christians Welcome.' One of the leading English law firms of the city received through the mail a copy of *The Key to the Mystery*, a pamphlet published by the fascists, proving that the Jews by their own words are the international scoundrels of the earth, very much like the pamphlet mentioned in the November issue of *Equality* in an article entitled 'Talmud Falsifications.' This pamphlet indicates that the most rabid anti-semites are at work.

So it goes. In every phase of life one runs across these slight indications of race feeling. Slowly a hatred is being cultivated, despite the attempts of many in and out of the government to root it out. At present, such a prejudice, growing with others which struggle to show their unseemly heads, does not develop at an alarming rate. Things have been too confused and too murky for rapid growth, but the seeds are there, and they have sprouted. Let us hope that the commonsense which is reputed to be a heritage of French-Canadians will force these weeds to wither away before they stifle what little provincial unity there is.

F.R. SCOTT

Social Planning and the War

Five years ago the research committee of the League for Social Reconstruction produced their book *Social Planning for Canada*. It set out to show why the capitalist economy of Canada had become unable to provide steady employment and an increasing standard of living for Canadians; how the growth of monopoly had resulted in a concentration of wealth and economic power which constantly threatened our democracy; and that the proper democratic solution of the problem was for the people of Canada, through appropriate public bodies, to begin planning their economic development so as to achieve social justice and economic security. Laissez-faire capitalism being on the decline, the only choice lay between fascism and a planned democracy.

The LSR book was well received by the general public. Though hard to read and expensive to buy, it ran through two editions. A fortunate attack upon it by a well-connected St James Street pamphleteer gave it some sale even in financial circles. But its teaching fell on stony ground, for the depression was lifting and the old controls in Canada were about to re-establish themselves through the victory of the Liberal party. Governmental inaction was voted into office in 1935 – which meant that financial and monopolistic control carried on. Economic planning for democratic purposes was postponed.

Now the situation has drastically changed. The lessons that sweet reason and academic argument could not instil, have been driven home by the grim necessities of war. Two unplanned societies, France and England, found themselves retreating before the sheer efficiency of a Nazi-planned Germany. To meet that challenge

England, late in the day, has discarded her economic individualism, and entered upon a new phase of war socialism. Socialist members of the Labour party have entered the cabinet in key positions. All property in England is now liable to conscription by governmental decree. The excess profits tax has reached 100%, and more than 15,000 firms are now under government control. Much of the old system remains (too much, as the example of the holdup in tank production showed) but the inadequacy of capitalist methods of war production is fully recognized. National planning has taken their place, using the techniques of capitalist manufacture but supplying new centralized controls directed toward a national purpose. A new industrial revolution has begun.

In Canada, where the imitation of England is accentuated by war sentiment, the same process is underway. So far as the law is concerned, the War Measures Act and supplementary statutes already provide a greater accumulation of statutory authority in Ottawa than was ever contemplated by Canadian planners. The radical suggestions of five years ago are commonplace today. The constitutional difficulties have temporarily vanished through the coming into force of the dominion's residuary and emergency powers. Canada, like England, recognizes that if she wants the maximum wealth in war supplies she must use the methods of economic planning and not those of capitalism. Public bodies and government officials are now deciding what commodities are needed and in what quantities; they also decide where they can best be produced; men in factories then go ahead and produce them. The role of the private business man or corporation in these planned areas is to see that production is efficient – nothing more. Deciding where and what kind of new developments should come is a public responsibility.

This description doubtless over-simplifies the actual situation. We are running two systems side by side at the moment, and economic anarchy still exists in fields that badly need planning. The examples of Henry Ford and the British Columbia oil companies, both of whom sabotaged a governmental program, sharply reveal the dangers that lie in private ownership of essential economic activities. And we are still allowing extra profits to be made by private persons out of the war emergency. The Liberal party swamped the CCF proposal in parliament to impose a 100% excess profits tax. Our war planning is shot through with traditional ideas of property rights derived from the laissez-faire period. This is scarcely to be wondered at when the composition of the planning boards is examined; to a great extent they consist of men with a necessary administrative experience, but with a social philosophy quite naturally belonging to another era. Nevertheless it remains true that the greatest lesson the public of Canada has ever had in national planning is now being given. And the simple fact emerges, that if this is the way to get more guns, it is also the way to get more butter. The methods used to save the country in time of war can be used to restore the country in time of peace.

Since this is the way our society is developing, the new problems confronting democracy in a planned society should now be faced. Such problems should, indeed, be investigated and dealt with by a special governmental board, which would report periodically to parliament on ways and means of safeguarding the maximum civil and personal liberties consistent with efficient planning. Liberty must be planned too, in the world we are entering. If the war is to be won in a spiritual as well as in a military sense such work can not begin too soon. History can supply examples of countries which won wars and lost their domestic freedom at the same time. The effect of the present war upon Canada is to awaken a sense of social responsibility, a desire to serve the state and to face realities, out of which greater national unity and a more secure democracy may be born; but the war also stirs up passions and fears that hamper the free exchange of ideas on which democracy depends, and it gives reactionary elements an opportunity, often under the cover of a 'bloodshot patriotism,' to prepare the instruments of repression. The greater the number of social controls, the greater the danger of tyranny if they fall into the wrong hands; but the greater also is the opportunity of secure and ordered living if they are infused with a democratic purpose and made answerable to a democratic will.

Wars may be fought either by the methods of dictatorship or by the methods of democracy. Germany is using the former methods; we are attempting to make ourselves equally strong for self-defence without sacrifice of the democratic spirit. In adapting our existing institutions to the needs of defence we shall find that fewer limitations than we now imagine have to be placed on freedom of thought and discussion and more than we imagine on our existing rights of property and our present ways of producing goods. Yet most people will part with their freedom of thought before they will part with their investments, and therein lies our danger. The refusal of the oil producers in British Columbia to obey the law – was it not more subversive of democracy than anything that a harmless religious sect like the Witnesses of Jehovah have done? Yet we have proscribed the latter only. Our interference with intellectual freedom in Canada so far has been greater than our interference with property. Our transition to a democratic planned society is going to be rendered more difficult because we have allowed wealth to accumulate to a dangerous degree, and from the owners of that wealth are bound to come most of the ideas and influences opposed to the changes we must undergo. Yet if we are to hold our own in the present world we must acquire the efficiency and strength that can come from the co-ordination of economic resources, and the ordered utilization of our productive capacity. We must plan as intelligently as our rivals, but more democratically.

Social Planning for Canada dealt very fully with the problem of how to keep a planned society democratic. But the planning under consideration there was for the peacetime purposes of social reconstruction, and the book presupposed a 'people's party,' fully representative of farmers, labour and consumers, as the motive power behind the planning. Today we are planning for wartime purposes, with primary emphasis on military organization, and without that kind of a people's party in control. The Liberal party has a majority that justifies it in carrying on as Canada's war government, but even its members must admit that a party which has not held a convention in the past 20 years still has something to learn about democracy. The need for organized thinking about democracy and wartime planning is thus particularly urgent. Here is a field of work, of immediate practical use for the attainment of the end for which the war is being fought, in which governments, the universities and other responsible bodies could coöperate. Nothing would strengthen this nation more than some official action that would symbolize an advance toward a more democratic social order, not after, but during the war. In war as in peace, democratic ideals can be attained, and a democratic war effort is still the most efficient, the most powerful and the most desirable.

FRANK H. UNDERHILL

North American Front

The Canadian Government carried Canada into the European war last September presumably to emphasize and strengthen our close ties with Great Britain. In less than a year the progress of the war has led them to make a defence agreement with the United States which, however much polite phrases may seek to hide the fact, constitutes a recognition that our ultimate vital interest is the defence of North America and that this interest must be pursued in co-operation with our North American neighbour. This is an ironical situation, though our nerves are too strained just now for us to be able to enjoy the irony of history; and our colonials are doing their best to put a good face on the business by making it appear that the Roosevelt-King agreement really represents a joint determination by Canadians and Americans to come to the help of Great Britain. But it is obvious that the agreement would have been superfluous had not Canadian statesmen recognized that a profound change in the balance of power across the Atlantic and across the Pacific is in process as the result of a year of war.

Actually, we have been drifting towards a reorientation of our external policy in the direction of closer relations with the United States for a long time. But Canadian opinion has been slow to recognize the fact because our thinking has been preconditioned in the direction of Great Britain.

Sentimentally, the whole raison d'être of Canada has been hostility to the United States. The United Empire Loyalist tradition has coloured all our thinking. Since 1815 we have lived through more than a century of peace with friction, but the friction has generally been more in the forefront of our consciousness than the peace which we were inclined to take for granted. On the other hand, remaining in the British empire, we have managed to achieve without much friction a position of autonomy that satisfied most of us and predisposed us to think kindly of the British connection and to glorify British statesmanship. Most important of all in its effect upon our prevailing sentiment, our long effort to distinguish ourselves, to separate ourselves off from the Americans naturally led us to emphasize the British character of our civilization. Lacking any very distinct national consciousness we fled to the British connection as the readiest escape from Americanism. We found a quiet British dignity in our own life as contrasted with that to the south of the border, when more realistic critics discerned only an anemic lack of vitality. Escape mechanisms of this kind are of course inevitable when a small and comparatively weak people live next door to a powerful and expansive nation.

More fundamental in determining this anti-American emphasis in our thinking was the fact that the Dominion of Canada represented an ambitious attempt to build up an economic empire independent of New York. Our banks, our railroads, our protected manufactures, were all expressions of this determination. Confederation in fact was primarily a movement to pre-empt the northern half of North America, to fence it off from American intrusion, and to develop it as a closed economic system the profits and the power from which should accrue to business interests north of the border. And these interests found it useful in establishing their position to instill anti-American feelings into the Canadian mind. Such feelings were a bond of union in a new nation in which there was for a long time not much real material basis of union; and in addition they were a powerful assistance to Montreal and Toronto in consolidating their control of the new nation. Under their leadership we got the habit of girding up our loins about once every twenty years and saving ourselves once more from the United States. Nothing is more interesting to the sociologist studying Canada than the thumping success of the anti-reciprocity elections of 1891 and 1911; and nothing can be more significant of some change that was coming about in our communal consciousness than the failure of an anti-reciprocity election to take place in the 1930s.

In addition to this influence was another economic factor. When the Dominion of Canada at last began to go ahead in the late 1890s after almost a generation of depression, it was the development of the wheat-growing west which produced the boom; and this was based upon a seemingly illimitable market in Great Britain. The growth of the British market, as contrasted with the failure of the American market to expand in a similar way, put an end to all the annexation sentiments that had plagued Canadian politics. Moreover the rapid expansion of the Canadian economy in the twentieth century depended upon imports of capital, and down to 1914 these came predominantly from London.

But in the period between the two great wars all these conditions which determined the direction of our thinking were beginning to change. The sentiment of colonial loyalty was being challenged by a new spirit of native nationalism, though down to the present the two sentiments have been able to co-exist in the most curious combinations in most Canadians minds. But as nationalism became more self-conscious more and more Canadians began to realize that socially and culturally they resembled Americans rather than Englishmen, and that in their day-to-day life they got on more naturally with Americans than with Englishmen. What most of all united them with the Americans and distinguished them from everybody else was the common North American standard of living. True, the citizens of Ontario did not use quite as many Bell telephones per thousand as did the citizens of California nor consume quite as many gallons of ice cream per head per year as did the citizens of Iowa; but essentially it was a common standard of living. And a good many Canadians began to realise that if they were to remain distinct from the Americans this could only be achieved through a dynamic native Canadianism and not through the vestigial remains of British elements in Canadian life.

Canadian business also became more and more interlocked with American. After 1918 the capital from outside which came in to develop Canadian industry came chiefly from New York. The fluctuations of Wall St prices became the barometer of Canadian business conditions. It has been amusing in recent weeks to watch the fevered efforts of our patriotic (i.e. pro-British and anti-American) newspaper editors as they grew virtuously indignant at Mr Mooney in the SEP and at the same time tried to hide the fact that he is a high official in the General Motors corporation which so completely owns the Oshawa concern that separate financial statements of General Motors of Canada are not published; or as they grew still more virtuously indignant at Mr Ford and skilfully failed to mention that the B shares in Ford of Canada, which are the only voting shares, are largely controlled by the Ford family of Dearborn, Michigan.

Canadian trade also began in the 1930s to take new directions. What brought Canada out of the depths of the depression was the development of the Laurentian shield in the central provinces, and its forest and mineral products went chiefly to the United States. (The war is temporarily taking some of its minerals to Britain now.) The wheat-growing West which depends on the British and European market has never come out of the depression. After the war the part of Canada which will have flourished most will be the now highly industrialised centre with its American standards, which will dominate Dominion policy even more than it does now and which in every respect will regard British industry, seeking to recover lost markets, only as a rival.

But it is chiefly the shock of the war since May 10 which has revealed to us how predominantly North American our interests have come to be. As long as Great Britain remained as the ruler of a great world empire, a great world power whose position could not be successfully challenged, all these other developments inside Canada would have produced their effect only very slowly. British prestige dominated our thinking and it was impolitic for any Canadian to doubt in public whether British policy was automatically successful. But now, whatever the outcome of the battle of Britain – and we are recovering from the exaggerated pessimism produced by the sudden collapse of France – it is clear that a new balance of power is being created in the world in which Britain will never recover her pre-1914 predominance. The British Empire was based upon a defiance of regionalism. Now there are arising the dim forms of new regional aggregations, supernational continental empires of some kind, which seem likely to divide the world among them. And in this new regional balance of power Canada's security will be found in the geographical region to which she belongs.

EDITORIAL
Winning the War

A year ago, when the war was just starting and we all had time on our hands, it was a favourite occupation to draft schemes for the peace settlement which was to come at the end of the war. Most liberal democrats – and we are all liberal democrats now – seemed agreed that federation was to be the blessed word of the post-war world. They disputed whether the federation which would bring permanent peace was to be one of Europe, or of western Europe, or of the 'democracies,' or of the world. Some energetic professors of political science, with a well-trained eye for the market, rushed books on the topic to the press, only to have them appear just after the collapse of France. The crisis which began with the invasion of Belgium and Holland put all this pleasant Utopianism out of their minds. And today as we look out on the forces which are loose in the world and begin to realize that we are in the midst not merely of a military struggle but of a social and intellectual revolution, we wonder at the naivete of those strange beings of 1939, ourselves, who could believe that the invention of some new political machinery was all that was needed to save our civilization.

During the critical summer months no one felt much heart for considering these questions of the future of our society. France had fallen and Britain was fighting for her life. It was sufficient that she fought for survival. But now the magnificent recovery of the British people from the disastrous campaign on the continent makes it fairly certain that Hitler cannot reduce them to submission. By next year, largely through their own efforts, they will have achieved equality in air armaments with Germany, and gradually with the help of North America they will win superiority. And this will bring us back to the question which was dropped in the pressure of more urgent matters this spring, the question of peace principles.

The military problem of winning the war, as distinct from the problem of beating off German attacks, is serious enough in itself. Granted that the Nazi bid for gaining control of the British Isles fails – and the Germans cannot finally win the war without this control – what are the prospects of a British counter-invasion of the continent? We should beware of the tempting exhilaration which comes from the thought of the European masses rising against their Nazi masters to welcome a British invader. They are cut off from all the news that the English-speaking world gets now, and the British government has no effective contacts with them, or at least none that are publicly known. We may be sure that German propaganda throughout this coming winter will have done its best to inflame European opinion against British planes which drop bombs on them and British ships whose blockade keeps food from them. Moreover, all those who are fighting Nazism need to bear in mind that it is not the enslavement of the European peoples which is most dangerous, bitter though that may be to its victims, but the possibility that German organizing ability may make a going concern out of Europe. By rationalizing production and distribution over a continental area they may promise security and stability to the masses if they will stay quiet and an open career for the talents to those of ambition if they will accept the Nazi system. Against this it will not be enough to promise merely a restoration of the old governments who are now in exile in Britain and who, when in office, except in the Scandinavian countries, were not able to solve their people's problems of unemployment and insecurity.

The answer to these doubts which gives one hope is the electrical change which has taken place in the temper of Britain since the new Churchill-Labour government took charge of things. As R.H. Tawney in his now famous letter to the New York *Times* has put it: 'We are not fighting in obedience to the orders of our government; our government is fighting in obedience to our orders. We shall continue to fight until the job is done or we are. ... We are fighting to preserve a way of life which we value above life. ... We prefer dying on our feet to living on our knees.' The *New Statesman* (Aug. 24) has described the new regime in Britain as the first stage of a democratic revolution, and it goes on to declare that this revivified democracy must continue to advance both on the home front and on the European front. At home, it says, 'we must, next winter, have not another interim budget but a financial policy which brings the Public Schools within the national system of education.' In Europe it wants the ground prepared to launch a great propaganda offensive for a democratic revolution which will win the support not of the exiled governments but of the oppressed peoples. It criticises Mr Churchill and Mr Attlee for their insularity and lack of imagination in this field. And it concludes: 'any future peace will demand as intimate links between Britain and Europe as those now being forged between Canada and the USA.' (Toronto papers please copy.)

What are the chances of a dynamic democracy of this kind in Britain giving a lead to the peoples of Europe so effective that not merely the physical control of Nazi soldiers and police but the moral and intellectual dominance of Nazi ideas may be destroyed? We cannot tell as yet. But at least we can assert that democracy will wither and decay in any atmosphere save that of free discussion, and that Britain is setting a magnificent example to the world not alone by the dogged endurance of her citizens but also by the freedom with which they discuss their public affairs.

In North America, or rather in the northern part of it, a paralysis has fallen upon the discussion of the ideas by which we live or profess to live. Our publicists repeat the accepted slogans in ever more strident tones, but one doesn't need to talk with very many of the younger generation before he discovers that there is a widespread scepticism as to the sincerity of these slogans. 'When a term has become so universally sanctified as "democracy" now is,' says Mr T.S. Eliot, 'I begin to wonder whether it means anything, in meaning too many things; it has arrived perhaps at the position of a Merovingian Emperor, and wherever it is invoked one begins to look for the Mayor of the Palace.'* The weakness of our Canadian war effort so far is not the slowness in producing munitions or in training men, but the persistence with which our leaders avoid all genuine discussion of the 'way of life which we value above life' and sidestep most policies which would make the values of that way of life more actual to the masses of the people upon whom the burdens of the war are bound to fall most heavily. Yet when it comes to the critical point where we have to decide whether the struggle against Nazism shall be carried through to the end, one may predict that it will not be the common people who will want to give up. Defeatist tendencies will show themselves first among those who are now shouting loudest, 'among those classes for whom the social revolution of modern war means the destruction of privilege and comfort.' (We are quoting again from the *New Statesman.*)

The fundamental weakness of our society in facing the challenge of Nazism is not military or economic. It is rather intellectual and spiritual. Dorothy Thompson says it is the decay of a middle-class civilization whose values are no longer tenable. Since she writes for the New York *Herald-Tribune* and the Toronto *Globe*

---

*Mr Eliot says further (in his recent book, *The Idea of a Christian Society*): 'You have only to examine the mass of newspaper leading articles, the mass of political exhortation, to appreciate the fact that good prose cannot be written by people without convictions.' One would think he has been living in Canada instead of in England!

and Mail and has spoken with great acceptance over the CBC we feel that it may be proper to quote her (Sept. 20): 'The whole middle-class world is in a state of neurosis. While it gives lip-service to the values of the last sixty years, it is not convinced by the sound of its own voice. ... The spiritual inertia translates itself into actual physical and mental inertia. ... This becomes particularly noticeable in youth, which behaves like a bystander in society instead of its junior partner and heir. ... It is precisely this middle-class world which, in possession of wealth and technical equipment, has not even been able efficiently to manufacture and distribute weapons for its own defence. ... Tell men in this society ... that the economic and political reorganization of the world is sure to take place and that we shall either contribute to do this ourselves or take the leavings from the gangsters ... and they will call you a communist or a fascist.' As the military war against the Nazis proceeds we are going to find that it is this inner spiritual weakness which is the chief obstacle to our success. To it we should be directing much more of our attention.

RAYMOND SOUSTER

Last Act, Last Scene

Some day,
Maybe not today or tomorrow
Or the day after tomorrow's tomorrow,
Sitting in this room, your room in this city,
Your cell above the traffic and the dark
 night on the avenues,
Your haven, where no phone rings to ask for
 the manager (one moment please).
Your peace, your kingdom; some day,
And it could be tonight or tomorrow,
You will lift your head from the newspaper,
Your interest will leave the radio,
Only for a second, but that is time enough,
A second is long enough to see the walls
 closing in,
The ceiling coming down slowly, a deliberate
 elevator,
A second is too long to see the lights falling,
A second is a life of horror when the floor
 opens on nothing,
Nothing but darkness.

CARLTON MCNAUGHT

Democracy and our Universities

The recent attempt by members of the governing body of the University of Toronto to frighten one of its professors into resigning by the threat of impending dismissal again leads one to ask what notion prevails in such quarters about the university's function in a democracy.

The reasons advanced for seeking the departure of Professor Underhill were (1) public opinion as expressed in the newspapers and elsewhere, (2) pressure from outside and from inside the university, and (3) the opinion of the board that his continued presence on the staff was doing harm to the university. He was asked to consult with his friends and take a week to consider what he should do. At the end of the week he wrote to the chairman of the board refusing to resign.

Inevitably the matter became widely known amongst the professor's friends and colleagues. Since 'public opinion' had been alleged as a reason for sacrificing Professor Underhill, it became necessary to show that there existed a strong body of public opinion opposed to such encroachments on civil liberties and academic freedom. The immediate reaction was such as to cause speculation about the real source of 'pressure from outside and inside the university' for the professor's removal. A large deputation of his colleagues, headed by the Dean of Arts, waited on President Cody to protest against the unwarranted action. A voluntary petition from his former students testified to the notable part he had played in their intellectual development, the inspiring nature of his teaching, and his moderation and tolerance where controversial matters were involved. His present students sponsored a similar testimonial. Graduates of the university, recent and of long standing and in many walks of life, joined in the protest.

Intimations that pressure was being put upon the university by the provincial government were made, or allowed to go undenied, by the authorities. But when this was revealed in the press, a prompt denial was forthcoming from the premier, through his acting minister of education. Responsibility for any action that had been or might be taken was placed, therefore, upon the president and the board of governors.

This source of pressure having been eliminated, it is interesting to examine the other alleged sources. 'Public opinion as expressed in the newspapers' apparently resolves itself into the editorial pronouncements of one Toronto and three or four outside newspapers which raised indignant voices against Professor Underhill last fall, when a partial and rather highly coloured report of his remarks on Canadian-American relations at a study conference sponsored by the YMCA appeared in the press, and a few letters to the newspapers from violently partisan individuals. The accuracy of the press report Professor Underhill publicly denied, and the board of governors apparently accepted his version of what he had really said, supported by the evidence of those who had been present at the conference. What is meant by public opinion 'elsewhere' can only be guessed at. The source of pressure 'from outside the university,' if it does not refer to the government, can also only be surmised. It was a combination of these vaguely-defined 'pressures' that allegedly created the feeling that Professor Underhill's presence on the staff was doing harm to the university.

What seems so extraordinary about the whole matter is that the president and governing body of a university, supposedly pledged to uphold the right of independent thought within and without its walls, should have even contemplated yielding to pressure, from whatever quarter, that challenged this right. Unless one is to subscribe to the Nazi idea of a university as a place where only one set of ideas and opinions shall be permitted currency, it is difficult to understand how the president of a university could consider the suppression of a staff member, much less his dismissal, because his ideas were unpopular in certain quarters. When the unpopularity, or alleged unpopularity, is based on a misrepresentation of those ideas, the wonder grows.

The fallacy that because one professor in a university expresses certain views publicly he therefore commits the university to those opinions, is one that should be dispelled. The way to dispel it is not to forbid professors with unpopular opinions from speaking in public, but to encourage more professors to speak in public. It would then become abundantly clear that universities, the University of Toronto included, have on their staffs professors holding widely divergent opinions on important matters. If it were not so, our universities would be in grave danger of conforming to the Nazi ideal, against which Canada is supposed at the present moment to be fighting with all her resources of mind and matter.

It is time we realized that ordinary Canadians are as much entitled to hear the reasoned views of Canadian scholars in the fields of history, economics, and political economy, as they are entitled to hear the views of our bank presidents, business men, and members of parliament. To the extent that they deny us this right, our universities are doing a real disservice to democracy.

FERGUS GLENN

The Conscription Build-up

Prominent on Canada's war front during the past summer was the attempt of our newspapers, in collaboration with the less intelligent wing of the Conservative party, to create the illusion of a popular demand for conscription.

It is unlikely that historians will give much space to this unsavoury episode. They will be too busy examining why Canada's production of war supplies was hampered by leaving it almost entirely in the hands of monopoly industry and its stooges, the dollar-a-year men; why the Canadian government allowed employers to preserve profits and perpetuate conditions provocative of strikes and lost time; why, in short, a really constructive use was not made of our manpower for Canada's primary war job.

But precisely because the conscription clamour has been used to detract attention from these vital questions, it is worth our examination now. The technique employed is likely to be used again to befog public thinking and lessen our usefulness to the common cause.

It is the privilege of newspapers to promote any policy they see fit. We may deplore their indifference to history, their fuzzy emotionalism, their inability to think clearly. We may believe them prejudiced by party or class interest. Still, they have a right to air their views and to urge their readers to adopt them. But when, for this purpose, newspapers utilize news and correspondence columns to present a picture which is directly contrary to the facts, they prostitute their function, emulate the propaganda press of Hitler and Mussolini, and become a menace to democracy.

In recent weeks, Canadian newspapers, with a few honourable exceptions, did precisely that. They employed the great North American technique of the build-up to fabricate a falsehood. This involved articles camouflaged as news; tendentious headlining; magnifying of news favourable to their policy and minimizing of its opposite; packing of their columns with letters to the editor virtually all on the one side.

To make matters worse, this torrent was turned on in the midst of a campaign to obtain 32,000 volunteers for overseas army requirements, and coincided with a recruiting tour of western Canadian cities by the prime minister. Signs of the gun-priming could be detected in special dispatches, like that from Winnipeg in the Toronto *Telegram* on June 26, which stated:

When Prime Minister King passes the Great Lakes he will be greeted on all sides by demands for immediate conscription. This cry is most insistent in the weekly press and small dailies. Any meeting Mr King may address on his western tour will echo the demand, many leaders of different parties admit.

This disclosed the real source of the 'demand.' The writer, it will be noted, was compelled to rely on the alleged 'admissions' of 'many leaders of different parties' (whom he did not name) for his statement that popular clamor would 'echo the demand.' Nevertheless the *Telegram* prominently headlined this mass of equivocal editorializing disguised as news:

DEMAND FOR CONSCRIPTION
WILL GREET MR KING IN WEST

It was Mr King's arrival in Calgary on June 27 that launched the real build-up. The staff writer of the *Globe and Mail* accompanying Mr King told of the handbill signed by the 'Calgary committee for conscription,' which citizens found wrapped around their milk bottles that morning, suggesting the prime minister be asked to 'answer this simple question: How can Canada fight a total war without conscription?' The handbill was a fact. But what would Dr Gallup say of the method of sampling public opinion thus revealed by the reporter?
The handbill said publicly what many citizens were saying. ... Soldiers in the guard of honour drawn up at the station asked members of the press car: 'When are we going to have conscription?' Taxi drivers, cigar store clerks, local newspapermen repeated the query. It seemed to be the dominant question throughout the city. ... A check through the files of Calgary newspapers showed that for weeks the dominant note in the 'letters to the editor' columns has been an appeal for all-out compulsory service. The Calgary Herald *has been conducting an essay contest on how to win the war open to boys or girls under 25* [sic]. *The contest has just closed and a compilation showed that 25 percent of the essayists, and there were scores of them, called for conscription. ... Mr King was given a cordial reception everywhere. ... But almost everywhere the newspapermen following in the entourage ran plunk against the conscription question mark. ... The men in uniform did not hide what they thought about voluntary recruiting. They have lost all patience with it, including particularly some of the men who take part in recruiting missions. This feeling, the writer was assured over and over again, is rampant right through Alberta. ...*

Assured, one might ask, by whom? The very next sentence suggested a possible explanation of the 'rampant' demand:

One reason may be the conscription campaign that the Calgary Herald *has been running.*

The *Globe and Mail* gave the dispatch this two-column head:

DEMANDS FOR CONSCRIPTION
TAUNT MR KING IN CALGARY

In Vancouver, according to the same reporter, the prime minister faced an audience 'believed to be largely in favor of conscription.' Believed by whom? The audience was largely of business men, a joint meeting of the Vancouver board of trade and service clubs. According to the correspondent:

Reports of the crystallizing of sentiment in favour of conscription here, and word of the intention to hold in Vancouver a mass demonstration in favour of compulsory service, led to the sudden decision by Mr King to make today's speech before the Vancouver Board of Trade the most aggressive defence of voluntary enlistment heard in Canada since the war started. ... Mr King received a great ovation

October 1941

when he entered the ballroom and bursts of applause were frequent throughout the speech, but the applause was far from unanimous. There was no doubt the audience was impressed; but how far opinions were changed was another matter. Immediate debate on the points raised started as the hundreds of Vancouver business men milled their way out of the crowded room.

In Victoria the 'evidence' of a conscription demand was so scarce that the *Globe and Mail* reporter was reduced to saying:

While there was no public discussion of conscription, members of the press party were repeatedly told [again, by whom?] that sentiment in Victoria is overwhelmingly in favour of compulsory military service.

In Edmonton the reporter apparently could find none at all, even inferentially; and in Prince Albert he could only refer pointedly to the New Canadians.

...There are thousands of them in this district and they have been falling behind their fellow citizens in enlistment.

Nevertheless, on the way back to Ottawa on July 11, the *Globe and Mail* reporter undertook to say:

Prime Minister Mackenzie King's seventeen-day tour of western Canada has focussed attention on conscription as the national question of the hour. In all the cities visited there was strong support for out-and-out conscription. It was noticeable in British Columbia ... and the evidence was almost as strong in Manitoba. ... In Calgary there was an organized effort to make a conscription demonstration while the prime minister was in the city, but the feeling seemed just as strong in the other centres visited where there was no attempt at a demonstration. A week-end in Prince Albert revealed that in the prime minister's own constituency the same strong sentiments for compulsory service apparently predominated among the urban voters.

But, as if stung by conscience into tempering this divination with a few offsetting facts, the writer continued:

Mr King's tour did not take him into rural areas where the feeling may be different. While Prince Albert city seemed overwhelmingly for conscription, the writer was told that a vote in the whole riding would likely produce a different result. Business men and newspapermen throughout the west reported that the people they met in daily contact felt that the time had come for conscription, but there has been no way of assessing the feeling over the west as a whole.

The truth at last! 'Business men and newspapermen' giving the views of 'the people they met in daily contact'; but 'no way of assessing the feeling over the west as a whole'! ...

Meanwhile the recruiting campaign was in progress. But, if one believed leading Canadian newspapers, it was doomed to failure. Instead of loyally assisting in the drive, the press of Canada either remained lukewarm or actively hindered it by asserting its futility, and kept up a continuous quacking for adoption of compulsory methods. Only a few papers supported it.

On June 3, when the campaign was just getting into its stride, the Calgary *Herald* said:

The campaign is meeting with poor results. Every province is far behind the quota ... save one. ... If there is any fault to be found, it lies with an entire generation of Canadians right from coast to coast.

On June 19 the *Herald* said:

Canada is trying to obtain 32,000 volunteers for overseas service. The campaign is lagging dismally, with slightly over one-third of the necessary men obtained.

On June 24, under the caption 'Epitaph on a Recruiting Campaign,' the *Herald* said:

There is very little likelihood that 32,000 men will have been enrolled by July 11. ... Speaking at Lethbridge on Friday, Brigadier-General F.M.W. Harvey, VC, DSO, declared: 'There are in Alberta today enough young men to fill the entire Canadian quota of 32,000 men. But they are not coming forward. ...' Brigadier Harvey said that the young men should be made to realize they were living in 'a fool's paradise.' They are indeed. But shall they be drawn out of that fool's paradise by a method of recruiting which has now been proven a failure?

The emphasis is ours. In the same issue, a *Herald* columnist declared:

We might as well face up to the facts. ... The recruiting drive has flopped; it has flopped loudly and dismally and openly. Every Canadian knows that. ...

On July 8, the *Telegram* said of the recruiting campaign:

Almost two months have elapsed since the drive commenced, but its success even now is not assured. ... Either now or later the government must determine whether it will stick to the voluntary recruiting system with all its delays, inequality and threat of collapse or turn to the more effective compulsory service method. ... Prime Minister King refers to Canada's war effort as being a 100 percent effort. Military men know that this is not possible with a voluntary recruiting system.

On July 12 the *Globe and Mail* said:

Conscription is an open question which should be brought to the fore and not tabooed because it might create a situation disconcerting to the government. The voluntary system may, in the long run, produce enough men. But does it produce men of the requisite qualifications in sufficient numbers at the right time? ...

No source was too inconsequential or obviously partisan to draw on for 'evidence.' Resolutions of Conservative ward associations, Orange lodges, and Canadian Legion locals were always good for a splash. The Toronto conscriptionist organs did not boggle at using visiting United States Legionnaires to bolster their campaign. The *Globe and Mail* found one of these who would undertake to say: 'Canada's war effort is commendable but, in my opinion, the United States is more enthusiastic in its program of all-out aid to Britain,' and headlined this single statement:

LEGIONNAIRES CLAIM U.S.
IS MORE ENTHUSIASTIC
IN WAR THAN CANADA

The *Telegram* was similarly fortunate in locating a Legionnaire from Carolina, who was reported as saying coyly: 'Of course, over there we don't want to get ahead of you people in Canada. No, suh, we don't want to get ahead of you in this war in which we are neutrals,' but declaring 'one may see more war activity in half a day in his state than in two weeks here.' Then came the moral: '"We have selective service, what you call conscription," Mr Broughton explained, "and it works very well."'

Nothing, it seemed, even though it meant fouling one's own nest or libelling the more courteous visitors from a friendly neighbouring country, was too shameful for these papers.

Conversely, any statement seeking to place conscription in a proper perspective was minimized. The Alberta convention of the Co-operative Commonwealth Federation on July 15 passed a resolution which concluded:

We believe the only efficient manner of obtaining the weapons for our army is through conscription of industry. Therefore we resist conscription of men for overseas service by every legal means at our disposal unless wealth is also conscripted.

This received minor headlines and position in those newspapers which published it at all. And when Premier Aberhart stated at Edmonton on July 20 that

Conscription of Canada's monetary system is more urgent than conscription of her manpower. ... If our young men are convinced that we have a freedom of individual effort that is worth fighting for and that they will come back to conditions more conducive to the common welfare, there will be sufficient enlistments to eliminate the need for conscription of manpower. ...

This received similarly short shrift. ...

Two things, however, conspired to spoil the conscription build-up. Mr King, arriving in Vancouver on June 30, made (to quote the *Globe and Mail*) 'the most aggressive defense of voluntary enlistment heard in Canada since the war started.'

But he followed this with a statement whose wording may have sprung from a masterly sense of political strategy, or may have been merely another example of Mr King's curious affection for phrases that (like great music) can mean different things to different people. At any rate, what he said was this:

How best the voice of the people may again be heard should a situation develop where the people's representatives in parliament believe there should be a reversal of policy, there will be time enough to consider when parliament itself has declared its views.

What did this portend? To some it hinted at an election on the conscription issue. Hon. W.D. Herridge, that forlorn leader of the 'New Democracy' party, at least was clear as to what Mr King should be forced to do. In Ottawa the next day, Mr Herridge thundered:

We must compel the prime minister to submit this issue to the people ... we must have a general election without delay. ... The time for a showdown has come. The issue is Mackenzie King and his policy on conscription against the honour of Canada and the security of the em-

pire. ... We must constitututionally purge the man and the government who have brought discredit and disunity to our country.

The conscriptionist papers, however, were not quite so sure. It is true they had been trying to show that the Canadian people were overwhelmingly for conscription. But a vote was another thing. So, with mounting fervour, cries arose against any such 'disruption' of Canada's war effort. Said the *Globe and Mail* on July 2:

Mr King ... would stand so severely condemned before the bar of history that we find it inconceivable to believe [sic] *that a politician who is naturally anxious about his place in history seriously contemplates such a cardinal error. A more intelligible interpretation of his utterance is that it was made in the hope of intimidating his opponents to abate their campaign for conscription. ...*

On July 5 the Toronto *Telegram* took up the cry with less of a pleading, more of a belligerent note.

Mr King will head an election campaign to split the country on the issue. He professes to believe that conscription would split the country, but would not be averse to splitting the country on his own terms. ... Mr King himself must be aware ... that he erred when he said the demand for conscription came from but a small vocal minority. ... No election is necessary to inform himself on the feeling throughout the country. ...

So, it seemed, the newspapers were content with Mr King's leadership after all – provided he led in the direction they wanted. ...

The other event which tended to take the wind out of the conscriptionists' sails was the marked success of the recruiting campaign. On July 16 the results were announced in Ottawa. In the two months' drive for 32,000 men, the objective had been exceeded by 7 per cent. All told, 48,000 volunteered, but medical examinations reduced the total accepted to 34,625. All but three of the thirteen military districts had exceeded their quotas. Ninety per cent of the recruits walked in off the street; 10 per cent came from the four-months training camps. Military District No. 5, almost wholly French-speaking, with headquarters in Quebec City, had come fourth for all Canada, exceeding its quota by 22 per cent.

The following day The Canadian Press quoted Capt. J.R. Brown, Ottawa district recruiting officer, as saying that efforts to obtain recruits in the capital were being 'bogged down' in some cases by business firms who refused to co-operate. He said that one firm with 1,800 employees had told several that they would have to resign their positions if they enlisted in the active army and lose their insurance benefits. On July 18, Premier Godbout told a meeting at Rivière du Loup that the dominion government and Quebec's provincial government do not believe that Canadians should be conscripted to fight outside the country. 'Let the rest of the country do as Quebec in voluntary recruiting,' said Premier Godbout, 'and we will win this war.'

Doubtless advised in advance of the probable results of the drive, Prime Minister King in Winnipeg on July 10 was able to say:

I believe my efforts have encouraged and assisted others who have been engaged in the recruiting campaign. I believe, or at least I hope, that in connection with the present recruiting campaign, they have served to remove any excuse for raising in Canada the issue of conscription for service overseas. What has already been attempted in the way of reviving that issue at this time makes only too clear the advantage that might have been taken of a lengthy absence on my part from Canada to force the issue into the arena of party strife. ...

The conscriptionist press did its best to growl off the success of the recruiting drive. Among other things, it feigned to 'smell a rat' in the setting of the quotas for the various districts. The campaign had succeeded, but what about the future?

The Ottawa correspondent of the Vancouver *Province* wired his paper on July 17:

Hardly anyone here expects that [the results of the drive] *will stop agitation for general conscription for service anywhere. ... All that the success of the campaign is likely to do is to stave if off for a while. ... In the meantime, the recruiting results would be more satisfactory if there were any assurance of their continuing repetition. Far from that, the difficulty of getting men to fill the ranks without depleting war industry seems certain to be multiplied.*

The correspondent does not seem to have been aware of the implications of that last sentence. But this and other editorial expressions should be enough to put Canadian newspaper readers on their guard. The light that failed is sure to be rekindled – and rekindled with the same synthetic fuel.

The significance of the conscription claque is simply this: While paying lip service to the idea of complete conscription of Canadian resources – material as well as human – the conscriptionist press has made it clear that what it means by conscription is merely the drafting of men into Canada's overseas army. It is opposed to the compulsory use of wealth, or to any disturbance of private industry's control of war production. The obvious mismanagement and lag in production it ascribes to 'government interference.' It seeks to obscure the real cause of labour disputes by imputing to the workers an unseemly appetite for 'taking advantage of the war' to improve their lot, while closing its eyes firmly to the still comfortable profits being made by industrialists. It belittles Canada's already extensive contribution in air, land, and sea forces. By doing this, and by raising the false issue of conscription for overseas service, it hopes to divert criticism from its masters, the industrial privateers. And since the Conservative party is even less disposed than Mr King and his government to disturb the ancient, solitary reign of private 'enterprise,' the press has its collaborators in that quarter.

The truth is that if Canada were devoting her full energies to the efficient, rapid, and extensive production of war supplies – and no nonsense – we should be doing what is most needed at the moment, and what we are best fitted to do. We should not need to worry about raising more overseas troops. We might even be sure of equipping and adequately training those already in uniform.

Note: Fergus Glenn is a pseudonym of Carlton McNaught.

EDITORIAL
Freezing Injustice

Canada entered this war with a most unjust distribution of national income. During the 1930s we had suddenly awakened to the realization that our country had developed many of the worst features of the older capitalist societies. We made a thorough analysis of certain aspects of these evils in the price spreads report of 1935. From this report it was clear that private monopoly was a characteristic of the Canadian economy, that with this concentrated control went concentrated wealth, and that large sections of the working and farming classes were ground down to subsistence levels by the operation of the system. Mr Bennett's 'New Deal' was an attempt to meet some of these problems, but the privy council told us that the BNA act was primarily a protection for separate provincial sovereignties, not an instrument for national construction; and the one important law that was free from legal obstruction – the New Combines Act – was successfully emasculated by Senator Meighen and other senators of his kind. Then we started again to review the whole situation; we spent three years more gathering information; at last came the Sirois Report with a large and progressive plan for constitutional and economic reconstruction. But already the war was on us, diverting our attention to European affairs. The half-hearted and ill-prepared attempt to introduce the Sirois reforms in 1941 was easily blocked by a few provincial politicians. *The social system with which we began to fight was as unjust and undemocratic as the two royal commissions had proven it to be during the previous decade.*

As regards the internal distribution of national income, the war helped immediately to ease the burden of depression which large sections of the economy had been carrying for so long. Employment increased rapidly under the stimulus of planned war production. Trade unions found themselves once more in a position to bargain effectively and to increase membership, for labour was becoming scarcer. Some sections of the agricultural community were benefited by a rise in prices. Heavier income taxes and excess profits taxes tended to prevent a sudden accumulation in the hands of the already privileged classes. But no one could maintain that the first two years of the war have rectified the original maldistribution of wealth in Canada to any appreciable degree. The rising cost of living nullified many of the wage advances in terms of real wages, and the situation of the wheat farmer has remained extremely precarious. When Montreal steel-workers have to resort to strike methods to improve their wages above 30 cents an hour in 1941, conditions obviously exist comparable to those disclosed by the price spreads inquiry of 1935.

It is against this background that the Liberal government's policy of freezing wages and prices must be viewed. Everyone will admit that war controls of various kinds are a necessity.

Everyone except the most diehard reactionary must admit what the advocates of social planning have been saying all along, that planned production for use is infinitely more efficient and effective than the old capitalist method of waiting until the great economic laws start the depressed economy working again. If the methods of capitalism were allowed to determine our war production, the war would have finished long ago, with a German victory. Everyone, too, will desire to prevent inflation from upsetting the entire price structure and ruining the war effort. For these reasons the general policy of Ottawa, aimed to increase production without unduly raising prices, has been accepted by the Canadian people. War entails sacrifice on the part of everyone.

All this is clear. But it is one thing to say that everyone must accept hardship during a war, and quite another thing to say that one of the hardships they must accept is the perpetuation of privilege in the hands of the few and of injustice on the backs of the many. For a large number of Canadians better treatment is long overdue. They have a right to say that the economy is unfair to them. Chapter and verse of the price spreads and Sirois reports can be cited to support their claim for consideration. To fix wages now in accordance with a 1926-1929 wage level, or to clamp down a general control over all wages and prices, is to perpetuate the maldistribution of national income. It freezes injustice. Certain classes of wage earners, farmers, for example, are thereby told to accept their inferior position for the duration, while highly paid executives and professional groups know that the law tacitly approves their social privileges.

For a government that professes to be concerned with national morale, and claims that a 'way of life' is at stake in this war, such a policy is shortsighted to the point of blindness. When the introduction of the policy is discovered to have been decided upon without the prior consultation and approval of labour leaders who represent the class most directly affected, the whole matter begins to assume a more sinister aspect. For the most immediate and positive effect which the general freezing order seems likely to have, is to take away from labour the advantages which war prosperity offered it, and to destroy its opportunity of increasing its share of national income through the use of its traditional and recognized techniques of organization and collective bargaining.

If there were no alternative ways of achieving the purpose which the wage and price controls are said to be aiming at, then perhaps even the perpetuation of social injustices might be tolerated by many more Canadians as a temporary contribution to the war effort; though just how a country that does not passionately care for freedom and equality is going to be much use in building a better world it is not easy to see. But there were, in fact, many other ways in which the control might have been introduced. They might, for example, have been accompanied by plans for increasing all wages below a fixed point and decreasing all salaries above it. They might have been aimed to hold down prices and salaries while permitting wages to adjust themselves through collective bargaining; and if the increasing purchasing power of labour created too much demand for certain commodities the situation could have been met by rationing. It is strange that England has; though not so strange when the political strength of English labour by comparison with Canadian is recognized. Or better still, the government could have told the Canadian people that now was the time to establish one of the basic ideas underlying the Sirois report – the proposal for a national minimum standard of living below which no one would be allowed to fall, and which would be maintained by a planned diversion of national income from the more privileged classes and areas to the more depressed ones. Without going to the length of a drastic dislocation of existing payments of income, at least the principle of redistribution could have been recognized and the first steps taken to implement it. The present controls are among the least democratic and the least imaginative of any that could have been devised.

So far in Canada the tributes to democracy in the wage controls have been idle words while the fixing of low wages has been mandatory. It is still lawful for employers to fight, obstruct, and malign trades unions, while it is unlawful for them to raise wage rates. Just at the moment when the most drastic controls are announced, Kirkland Lake mine operators and Ford of Canada flout the principle enunciated in PC 2685. Is it any wonder that the suspicion is being widely voiced by labour that the only inflation the government is really worried about is the inflation of trade union power? Is it any wonder that the contrast is being increasingly noted between England, New Zealand, and Australia, on the one hand, where labour is either in control of the entire war effort or substantially shares that control, and Canada, on the other hand, where labour is scarcely even represented in parliament and is excluded from every government board where the really important decisions are made? Is it surprising that *The New Statesman* recently described us as a Tory dominion?

One simple lesson appears very clearly from this national experience. It is that labour, farmers, and white collar workers are going to be treated in wartime just as they are treated in peacetime, unless they combine in a political party to protect their interests. They have been slow to appreciate this necessity, and Canada in consequence is a less useful influence in world affairs. The development of a national people's party, democratically organized and controlled, is nothing less than a national duty at this time. And the CCF, already in the field, tested and tried over ten critical years, recognized by the British and other Commonwealth labour parties as their Canadian counterpart, is the only party which can fill this need. It alone can put a really democratic content into our domestic and foreign policies. With the support of an awakened public, it can unfreeze the present injustices. A few more examples such as the voters of British Columbia have recently given, and we are likely to see a new concern at Ottawa for the common people without whose active aid and enthusiasm neither this war nor the ensuing peace can be won.

EDITORIAL
Meighen Redivivus

He comes of Ulster stock; and some people would say that the bitter intolerant spirit which is what the name of Meighen connotes to most Canadians is just the bad Ulster inheritance becoming more dominant in him each year as he grows older. But it is probably truer to say that it is his Toronto environment which is showing its influence more and more. He settled in Toronto in 1927 when he made his first retirement from public life. We hope that the electors of South York will assist him to make a second retirement in 1942. For it is clear that the Belfast of Canada has always been his spiritual home. The *Globe and Mail* in the mornings and the *Telegram* in the evenings exemplify pretty completely his social and moral if not his intellectual standards.

He is an honest man according to his lights. He has never been able to hide what he really believes. And when he goes out to other parts of Canada and tries to persuade them that he stands for wider and more generous views and policies than are included in the Toronto way of life, he only succeeds in convincing them that he is a jesuitical casuist. So let him stay in Toronto. In the long run both he and the rest of the country will be happier thus. He symbolizes and fanatically believes in everything that makes Toronto detested by the rest of Canada.

As a politician Mr Meighen's great weakness has always been that he becomes so concentrated upon the victory of the moment that he forgets the price at which momentary victories may be purchased. His intensity makes him see very clearly, but it also prevents him from focussing his gaze more than one inch in front of his nose. In the last war he was the chief engineer who devised, for the benefit of the Borden government, the closure, the Military Voters Act, the War Times Elections Act, the coercion of Quebec. For the moment the device of enfranchising just enough women and disfranchising just enough 'foreigners,' and of distributing the soldier ballots in the constituencies where they would do most good to the government, produced a glorious victory. But the events of 1917 left a widespread conviction that Arthur Meighen is a politician who will stop at nothing for the sake of victory, and he has been paying for this ever since.

So again he defeated himself in 1926. He had been laboriously building up the Conservative machine after the disaster of 1921, he had been sedulously courting Quebec – the Hamilton speech came in November, 1925 – and the explosion of the customs scandal in the 1926 session gave him his great chance to recover his reputation as a political leader. But he threw it all away because he was too greedy for a victory at the moment. When Mr King, with a vote of censure facing him in the Commons, failed to get the governor-general's consent to a dissolution, the Tories could not, even for a few weeks, suppress their eagerness to enjoy the spoils of office. They rushed in to support the governor-general's stand, only to find that they also had to ask him for a dissolution within a couple of days; and thereby they supplied Mr King with a magnificent personal grievance and a plausible constitutional issue by which he was able to distract public attention from the customs misdeeds of his own government and to fight the election on the favouritism of the English governor and the iniquity of the Meighen shadow cabinet. Never was any leader so completely outmanoeuvred as was Mr Meighen in 1926.

The same incapacity for looking ahead came out in his handling of the customs scandal itself. Here were revelations pointing to a most serious state of corruption in one great branch of the government service, and calling aloud to all friends of good government for further investigation. But Mr Meighen was interested only in an immediate party triumph. He concentrated his attack upon the unfortunate Mr Boivin, the French-Canadian minister of customs who had taken over a mess in his department and had not cleaned it up vigorously enough. Mr Meighen tore him to pieces and won a brilliant debating victory; but anyone sitting in the gallery could see the French members slowly freezing in hatred of their old enemy of 1917. And when the election came Mr King collected his usual sixty seats in Quebec province.

Mr King wins elections because he is always looking ahead. Mr Meighen wins debates and loses elections because he is always concentrated upon the event of the moment. Fate played him a shabby trick when he convinced himself that he was meant to be a statesman. He was meant to be an advocate in court.

A review of some aspects of Mr Meighen's career in the past shows how unfitted he is to be a leader of Canada in our present situation. Consider his stand on questions of social reform. In 1926 when Grits and Tories were both courting the support of the Progressives, Mr Woodsworth asked Messrs King and Meighen for a statement of their policy on old age pensions. The first promised, if sustained in office, to introduce an old age pensions measure. The second failed to give any satisfaction whatever. So Mr Woodsworth supported Mr King, who in due course carried out his promise. The Conservatives were afraid to oppose the measure directly in the Commons, and contented themselves with sniping at it. In the Senate they used their party majority to throw it out. The old gentlemen of the upper chamber, each of whom was enjoying an old age pension of $4,000 a year, filled the pages of Hansard with their solicitude lest old age pensions might undermine the sturdy independence of spirit of the Canadian working-man. Next year, 1927, after a general-election victory for Mr King, the Meighenites let the measure through.

If you examine Mr Meighen's speeches during the depression you will find that their main theme is his fear lest social legislation to help the unemployed should encourage too many poor people to depend upon government assistance. When, however, the depression hit him himself, and his career in finance was not going so well, he showed no reluctance about accepting a little government assistance in maintaining his own standards of living. And he became a Hydro-Electric commissioner at $10,000 a year and a senator at $4,000. When the government of his party under Mr Bennett adopted unemployment insurance and other 'New Deal' measures, he could do nothing but give them verbal support, though he still harped in the Senate on the danger of encouraging dependence on the state. But just last year, 1940, when at last an unemployment insurance measure was put on the statute books about the constitutionality of which there was no doubt, Mr Meighen divided the Senate against it. He professed approval of the principle, but wanted the measure put off till after the war. If we in Canada, long after most other industrial countries, have made a beginning of old age pensions and unemployment insurance, our industrial population owe no thanks to Arthur Meighen. On the other hand they can thank him for the infamous section 98 of the criminal code, now abrogated in spite of his opposition.

The question on which Mr Meighen's stand has been most enlightening has been that of participation in British wars. The years from 1914 to 1918 convinced Quebec that he was a fanatical imperialist – which he is – and that such a man could not be trusted for the future. In 1922, when the Lloyd George government almost got into another war with Turkey and when they cabled asking if they could count on Canadian participation, Mr King refused to commit himself until parliament had been called and had expressed its will. Mr Meighen declared: 'Let there be no dispute as to where I stand. When Britain's message came, then Canada should have said, "Ready, aye ready; we stand by you."' Naturally, this only confirmed the feeling of Quebec about him, and the pledge of automatic involvement in British wars – for this was what his words seemed to mean – lost him support in many other parts of Canada also. He has been explaining the 'ready, aye ready' speech ever since. His latest effort is contained in the senate Hansard for May 29, 1940:

Senator Meighen – *We should at once have shown interest in that treaty (of Sevres), and stood ready to examine with her (Great Britain) our course of action. Never did I say that we should have been ready to fight at once merely because Great Britain thought of fighting.*
Senator Dandurand – *But my honourable friend said he would have replied 'ready, aye ready.'*
Senator Meighen – *Certainly, but I did not say 'ready, aye ready to fight merely if called upon.'*
Senator Euler – *What did the statement mean then?*
Senator Meighen – *It meant that we would have replied that we were ready, aye ready for an examination, in a sympathetic attitude, of our duty.*
Senator Euler – *Nobody else interpreted it that way.*

So the 'ready, aye ready' speech doesn't sound quite so heroic today as it did in 1922 when it was first delivered before the Toronto Conservative Business Men's club. To be ready to examine our duty in a sympathetic spirit sounds, indeed, a good deal like Mr Mackenzie King. The ultimate fact about Canadian politics is that a political leader who expects to collect votes outside of Toronto becomes a good deal like Mr Mackenzie King.

Mr Meighen quickly realized how few votes 'ready, aye ready' was likely to get him in those parts of Canada which had not been nourished on a daily diet of the Toronto *Telegram*. And after the 1925 election, when the two old parties were fairly evenly balanced without either having a clear majority, he decided that if he were to come into office he would have to make clear to Quebec that 'ready, aye ready' didn't mean what everybody took it to mean. If he could win some support from Quebec – in which province he had not ventured to appear during the 1925 election – he could oust Mr King from the prime ministership. So he took advantage of a by-election in Bagot to make an offer to Quebec. In his famous Hamilton speech of Nov. 16, 1925, he declared that if he were head of the government when another war broke out and if he decided to support Britain in the war, he would dissolve parliament and seek the approval of the Canadian people for his policy before any Canadian troops were sent overseas.

The Hamilton speech failed completely of its purpose. It didn't win Quebec from its attitude of suspicion and hostility; and, since it seemed obviously to be backing away from the 'ready, aye ready' policy, it infuriated the loyalist Tories of Ontario. In vain did the unhappy Mr Meighen explain that it meant no change in his own or his party's lifelong attitude of support for Britain, but only a change in the procedure by which that support would be expressed. In vain did he declare his confidence that a government going to the people on such an issue would receive an overwhelming mandate for its policy, and that an election would occasion no delay in the effective war effort of the country. It was enough for the enraged Tories that he has recognized the right of the Canadian people to exercise an option about participation in British wars. As the *Winnipeg Free Press* put it, 'In the face of this momentous, radical, revolutionary, bolshevist, treasonable proposition, it was futile for Mr Meighen to plead that, with a Conservative government in power, there should be no fear as to how the option would be exercised.' It took years for the Tories of Ontario to forgive the Hamilton speech – Mr Meighen, indeed, had to give up the leadership of the party very largely because of it. And someone should ask him at one of the by-election meetings in South York whether he and the *Telegram* have reconciled their differences about his Hamilton war policy.

And now a few Toronto magnates have foisted him on the Tory party again as leader. The cabal which carried out the coup was led and directed by a little group of northern Ontario mining millionaires, with the *Globe and Mail*, the organ of this gang, supplying the publicity build-up. They are the most sinister social group in Canada today. And Mr Meighen is a fitting choice as their spokesman. Like George McCullagh, like Mitch Hepburn, like all these frustrated Toronto megalomaniacs, he is itching to coerce somebody, to impose on the rest of Canada the Toronto way of running a war. But somehow or other the rest of Canada has never thought much of the Toronto way of doing things.

June 1942

F.R. SCOTT
What Did 'No' Mean?

The important thing for Canadians to understand about the plebiscite of April 27th is not what the 'Yes' vote meant, but what the 'No' vote meant.

The 'Yes' vote itself is obscure enough to satisfy even the prime minister. It was not a vote for conscription, since the question was never asked whether or not Canadians wanted conscription for overseas. That simple question would have been altogether too straightforward to suit our political tradition. The question was whether or not the government was to be free to use Canadian manpower as it saw fit for the future. But there can be no doubt that many who voted 'Yes' did so because Mr King made it appear that a negative vote would have indicated a want of confidence in himself; he thus neatly converted the Conservative and CCF parties, which had urged a 'Yes' vote, into Liberal election machines. Though at the last minute this intention was denied, the impression was not eradicated, as any glance at the newspapers will show. So people voted 'Yes' for many different and even contradictory reasons.

Nevertheless this does not confront the country with any great difficulty or danger. The yes-men will for the most part approve of a more resolute war policy. It is the 'No' votes which should be studied and weighed, because a misunderstanding of this vote, and action by the government based on that misunderstanding, could easily result in grave peril to our country. No man in his senses, even if he is willing to sacrifice the whole future of Canada as a nation in order to increase her present war effort, could wish to take a step which would immediately divide our forces and so weaken the national will. It would be about as sensible as if the English Tories were to start a major drive on trades unions in order to speed up war production, or Chiang Kai-Shek were to revive his former attacks upon the Communist armies now fighting in his ranks. Aggravating internal dissensions is a curious sort of loyalty to the United Nations.

Yet that is what certain groups in Canada have already done by their treatment of the conscription issue, and what these same groups are still doing by their mis-reading of the plebiscite vote. And though French-Canada is not without her own groups who play politics with these vital matters, nevertheless the major responsibility for the difficulty lies with English-Canada. It is English-speaking Canadians who have been in charge of the major domestic decisions in this as in past wars in which Canada has engaged. Seldom has an effort been made to get to the roots of what appears to be a peculiar reluctance on the part of Quebec to see things as Anglo-Saxons see them. Seldom has a sympathetic analysis been made of the currents of thought in French Canada. Every English-speaking Canadian knows that though Mr Meighen and Tim Buck both urged a yes vote in the plebiscite, they did so from very different reasons. Yet how many people can distinguish between those French-speaking Canadians who voted no because they like isolation, and those who voted no because they like Canada?

British people everywhere would do well to reflect on one fact that this war has brought strikingly to light, namely, that the non-British peoples who are supposed to 'enjoy' the blessings of the British empire do not seem to appreciate those blessings as much as we have been taught that they did. The Irish underwent British rule for 800 years, and in this crisis prefer not to fight with Britain at all. The Boer leader, Hertzog, advocated neutrality for South Africa in 1939, and though Smuts found enough support to defeat him there is still a dangerous anti-war element in that dominion. The great Indian leader Nehru was in jail a long time because he refused to fight for India on British terms, and recently rejected the Cripps' offer of dominion status as inadequate. The Burmese, after 100 years within the empire, seem actually to have fought for the Japanese invaders. And now Quebec votes 'no' on the plebiscite. No doubt the Colonel Blimps will say that this all goes to prove the superiority of the Anglo-Saxon over the 'native.' But people possessed of any intelligence and any concern for the cause of human freedom will be profoundly disturbed by these danger-signals, and will take time off for a little self-criticism. There obviously have been serious mistakes in policy. It may not be too late to rectify some of these mistakes.

Now there is one common factor that has been present in all these situations, and which may go a long way toward explaining them. It is the factor of British rule *over* these other races. These curious non-British people seem to like freedom so much that they want to be free even from British rule. Where this freedom has been most conceded, there is less difficulty, and where it has been least conceded, there is more difficulty. There would never have been a General Smuts in South Africa if there had not been a grant of dominion status to his country. Perhaps if Premier U Saw of Burma had been granted the new status he was seeking conditions might have been different there. The Irish do not yet feel they are really free, since Ulster is still under British rule; and though Mr de Valera does not grant bases to the allies he nevertheless suppresses the IRA. In other words, it is generally true to say that the unwillingness of certain parts of the British empire to fall in line with a British idea of 'total war' is at bottom due to a love of liberty. They want democracy at home before they begin dying for it abroad. This attitude can be pressed too far, no doubt, when the enemy is at the gate; nevertheless it is a very human attitude and at bottom a very proper attitude.

How does all this relate to Quebec and the plebiscite? It is very closely related. The large 'no' vote was a protest, not against the war, but against the idea of imperialism.

The people of Quebec have long memories. Is not the motto of the province 'Je me souviens'? They look at each new political event from the point of view of their own special experience. No political issue in Canada is so surrounded by imperialist associations as conscription for overseas service. A country called Canada with European connections has existed for over four hundred years. When was the first expeditionary force of Canadians sent by a Canadian government to serve in an overseas war? Not till forty years ago, in the Boer war. Then Canadians went to assist the empire in imposing its rule upon a small nation against its will. That evil act has been dearly paid for in this country. Even those who may still think it was justifiable will recognize that it started an association of ideas that has never yet been eradicated – the idea that Canadian armies go abroad only in the interests of British imperialism. And if any reader thinks this is opening up an old sore, let him remember that the Boer War produced Henri Bourassa, the founder of *Le Devoir*, and that both of these avowed enemies of imperialism are very much alive and active in this war.

The first World War added another complication in Quebec to the idea of imperialist expeditionary forces. It introduced the idea of compulsory overseas service for French-Canadians at the insistence of the British majority in Canada. And mixed up with the conscription campaign of 1917 was a degree of political corruption and financial scheming (a Union government was needed as much to save railway investments as to impose conscription) enough to obscure even the highest motives. During the interval between the two world wars most of English-speaking Canada came to the view that conscription for overseas service was a bad mistake which ought not to be repeated. That was the official view of every political party.

Then came World War II. From the point of view of Quebec, what had changed? At the outset, very little. The conflict started as a European war: England and France against Germany. The Tories were running England. Should Canadians be conscripted for that? Not another country in this hemisphere considered the issue a life and death struggle between democracy and tyranny. Quebec accepted the factual situation, and certainly cannot be blamed if she was not immediately caught up with the idea of a great crusade. And for all the talk there has been about our free entry into the war, the fact remains that from Quebec's point of view we had no right to neutrality – had not Mr Lapointe said so? – and therefore there was no choice in the matter. In the same way the sending of the expeditionary force to England was accepted as inevitable, even though there was no vote in the Canadian parliament on the question. But when Quebec saw the conscription issue being raised once again by a group of Toronto imperialists and a small clique in the Conservative party, and being used once more as a weapon with which to defeat a Liberal premier and the Liberal party, then Quebec closed its ranks. This was something they knew all about; this was what Mayor Houde had predicted when he marched off to the concentration camp. And no new factors in the world situation, such as Pearl Harbor, the United States entry into the war, or the sweeping Japanese victories, even when added to the fall of France, had altered the internal appearance of the conscription issue in Quebec. Along both shores of the St Lawrence it still looked like conscription imposed by imperialists, run by imperialists, and utilized by imperialists. The ill-considered Canadian expedition sent to Hong Kong at British request did not improve matters. Besides, were not Canadian troops really needed now at home, and had not Australia, South Africa, and

Northern Ireland refused conscription? So history repeated itself. Quebec voted on April 27 not on the question as to whether the government's hands should be freed, but on the question as to whether Canadians should be forced to defend England and the British Empire. It emerged surprised and strengthened by its own unanimity.

Surely all English-speaking Canadians, and people outside Canada, can understand such a result even if they regret it? Surely, if one grants the premises from which Quebec's thinking started, there was no other vote that could have been given by any self-respecting people. There did not seem to be any need for Canada to have any more conscription for her own defence. And surely for all Canadians the remedy is fairly clear. As Mr Leslie Roberts has so well expressed it, Canada has to make up her mind whether she is fighting this war as a British colony or as one of the United Nations. It is the continuing element of colonialism in Canada's war effort, real or apparent, that is causing so much trouble. We have not made up our minds to be an independent nation in world affairs, thinking out our own policy and making whatever contribution that policy requires, and consequently everything we do looks as though it were done for somebody else and not for ourselves. We have failed even to provide ourselves with the symbols of nationhood. Our war posters and publicity are filled with suggestions that we are just a little lion alongside a Big Lion. We pretend that the bravery of Londoners is greater than that of the people of Chungking or Leningrad. We have been guilty of forms of racial pride that are naturally obstacles to co-operation with other races. There is a close parallel between certain difficulties in Canada and certain others in India.

The French-Canadians mean what they say when they say they will do everything necessary for the defence of Canada. They have already accepted conscription of manpower for this purpose, and they do not mind whether this means going to Alaska, Greenland, or Panama. It is a good deal farther from Quebec City to Alaska than from Quebec City to London. Why the difference in attitude toward compulsory service in the two places? Solely because service across the Atlantic represents the imperialist tie, and looks like defence of the British Empire rather than defence of Canada or Canadian interests. Who will decide the use of Canadian troops overseas? Who really decides when they are to go and where they are to go? These questions touch the realities of the problem in Quebec. The more Canada insists on having a voice of her own in the joint Allied councils, the more she gets away from the old military tradition that her part is just to 'offer' troops for Britain to use where Britain wants them, the easier it will be to bridge the gulf between Quebec and the other provinces. This is not a new issue in Canada; it dates from 1763. All that Quebec means by the 'no' vote is that she does not wish her children to die for any country other than their own. This is nothing very startling.

A fair assessment of the whole situation, of course, must include the small vocal element in Quebec that is trying to capitalize on the present discontent in order to gain power and prestige, and that has leanings toward a clerical-fascism of a Spanish and Italian type. There are such people, but they are no more Quebec than Mr Meighen is Canada. There are, shall we say, impure democrats in all parts of Canada, but the ones in Quebec are much less powerful than those outside Quebec, and less misleading because they do not beat the patriotic drum so loudly. The same people who voted 'no' so overwhelmingly in Mr St Laurent's constituency, only a short time ago preferred Mr St Laurent to a nationalist candidate who posed as the 'De Valera of Canada.' A war effort planned by Canadians for Canadians, in conjunction with all our Allies, respecting minority points of view and deeply concerned for the common man in office, field, and factory, will receive all the support that is needed from Quebec no matter where the battlefields may be. But it must be a war effort free from the restricting concepts of race and empire, free from control by vested interests at home, and devoted in deeds as well as in words to the great principles of human liberty and human brotherhood which it professes to be serving.

P.K. PAGE
Bed-Sitting Room

The sun has beaten its palms flat against glass
and, getting no answer, strides like a long-
    legged ghost
over the window-sill and camps on the rug;
releases canaries which perch on the chair and
    table,
hang from a bow on the wallpaper
and sing like a needle.

The woman is cramped in the cupboard of ancient moths
and fondles the smudge of air with a face-cloth face,
breathes down the neck of her blouse
telling her threat of beads
with pin-prick fingers.

In the drawer her friends are launching their own Armadas
of paper boats with home truth ammunition;
the photos duel in their frames,
the smiling boy
hurls his smile like a javelin at the mirror.
The friend who will sit in the South of France forever
has shot her eyes at the class of nineteen thirty.

In the medicine closet behind the screen, the doctor
squats on his own prescription, legs round a bottle,
numb with his game and stiff as a flag-pole sitter;
the authors scream to be set free from their prison.

But the woman becomes a drum with sound and tells
the clock to tick to tea or supper or bed;
the window is faceless and the red brick pout
of the opposite building is the woman's 'now.'

For four walls high is world and just as wide
as the studio couch or the crippled frame of the door
and the woman lost in the cupboard of ancient moths
is pinned to a board in the floor.

EDITORIAL

Maligning the CCF

A recent Gallup poll showed that the CCF now has over twice as many supporters amongst the electorate of Canada as it had in January last, and almost three times as many as voted for it in the 1940 federal elections.

But it did not require a Gallup poll to demonstrate that the CCF is making impressive gains. Apart from the fact that party membership has been growing by leaps and bounds (in Ontario alone it more than doubled during the past five months), the alarmed outcries, coupled with misrepresentation, belittlement, and mud-slinging, that have been pouring from the press of the old parties and of big business would have been convincing enough evidence.

The Liberal organs are the most perturbed, and it is curious to read their anxious exhortations to the Conservatives to inject life into the Tory party and thus preserve the country from the calamity of an entirely new political alignment. The Winnipeg *Free Press* is the frankest in its definition of the danger. After pouring tepid water on the CCF's aspirations, it goes on to say:

Nevertheless, the growth of the CCF is such that the two older national parties ... must face the fact that one or other of them is bound to go down if the CCF makes serious national inroads into their strength. There is not room in Canada for more than two major political groupings, and if the CCF is to be one of them, either the Liberal or the Conservative party will disappear. ... The present strong position of the Liberals makes the danger to its future more acute to the Conservative party. ... But the meteoric ascent of the Progressive party should remain a salutary lesson to the present leaders of the Liberal and Conservative parties, for history in this respect can repeat itself with results which, in our judgment, might easily spell the permanent disruption of Canadian Conservatism, which therefore should address itself without delay – and for the purpose of its own preservation even if for no worthier motive – to the process of reconstruction.

Thus, in the same breath, the *Free Press* expresses confidence in the Liberal party's future, and admits its anxiety over the prospect of having to fight the CCF singlehanded. It would much prefer a foeman unworthy of its steel – if he can be propped up sufficiently long to make a few passes. If he should, by some miracle, land a lucky blow and turn the tables on his erstwhile coach – well, after all, there isn't so much difference between the Liberals and the Conservatives. And anything would be safer than the CCF!

The consequent attacks on the CCF have

taken various forms. Most of the shameless misrepresentations of CCF policies stand self-revealed as such to any intelligent person. All of them emerge in their true colors when the CCF platform or the speeches of its spokesman in and out of parliament are examined.

More curious is the upbraiding of the CCF for being allegedly untrue to its own principles. Says the Saskatoon *Star-Phoenix*, for instance, referring to the recent CCF national convention:

One may question very much whether this note of extreme moderation that has been struck at Toronto, this absence of the fire of socialist enthusiasm, will appeal to a people engaged in war and with the example of the complete socialism of Russia continuously held before them. Halfway measures may not be the right attitude in the post-war period, are not, in fact, a sound policy for any ideological party.

But complaints that the CCF is not socialist enough, advanced by papers which have never shown any enthusiasm for socialism, are not likely to receive serious attention from anyone.

Another and indirect form of attack is the belated espousal by other parties of labor legislation which the CCF has been advocating for years. Witness Mitch Hepburn's proposed 'Wagner Act' and the resolutions of the Port Hope Conservatives. But coming as they do at the eleventh hour, these moves look too much like vote-catching dodges to be convincing.

As for the Communists and their 'fellow travellers,' their sniping at the CCF for being 'lukewarm about a second front' will only serve to recall the fact that the Communist party's first allegiance is to Russia, not Canada, and that it is not so long ago that they were doing all they could to sabotage Canada's war effort. The fact is, of course, that the CCF is just as anxious for an invasion of Europe as any Communist could be, but realizes that, unfortunately, matters of high strategy must be decided by those in possession of all the facts of a world-wide situation.

The latest and most virulent assault on the CCF, however, centres in the charge that it has been 'wooing' Quebec over the question of conscription. It is easy to see why, although the Conservatives are the most horrified, the Liberals are the most enraged by such a possibility; for the Liberal party has notoriously depended on the French-Canadian vote to keep it in office all these years.

There is nothing inherently wrong, as most of those who make the charge admit, in seeking the support of French-Canadian voters. The plain fact is that unless this country is to be split by a racial and religious schism which will undo everything that has been accomplished since Confederation, a course must be mapped which will win the support of *all* elements in our population. If the CCF seems likely to attract an increasing number of followers in all parts of Canada, it is not because the CCF is 'playing politics,' but because it has sensed more acutely than the other parties what are the real needs of the Canadian people, and what is required to unite them in a common national endeavour. The CCF is winning support because it recognizes that what is primarily needed is a reconstruction of our economic and governmental machinery so that it will serve the interests of the people as a whole instead of a privileged few.

The real sting of the charge is that the CCF has deliberately changed its policy on the war to win Quebec support. What are the facts? The CCF has been accused of being 'isolationist.' But this is merely a smear word that has lost any precise meaning. The CCF is, and always has been, nationalist, in the sense indicated by the late Lord Tweedsmuir when he said: 'Canada is a sovereign nation and cannot take her attitude to the world docilely from Britain, or from the United States, or from anybody else. A Canadian's first loyalty is not to the British Commonwealth of Nations, but to Canada and to Canada's king. ... A sovereign people must, as part of its sovereign duty, take up its own attitude to world problems.'

When it became clear that this war was not just another duel between European groups, into which Britain had been drawn by the criminal folly of a ruling class fearful for its position of power, but had become a revolutionary upheaval, in which the whole future of the common people of the world, including Canada, was at stake, the CCF gave its unqualified support to Canada's participation.

It did more. It demanded a total mobilization of our resources, on a scale and according to a plan which would make our effort fully effective. It called the bluff of those who were shouting for conscription of men to fight outside Canada, by demanding that this should be accompanied by full mobilization of our material resources, and that our effort should be organized in such a way that one part would not be expanded at the expense of another. It believed, and still believes, that in view of our population and position, our most important job is production of food, weapons, ships, and supplies. But it demanded a *total* war effort, and is still demanding it – in vain.

Had this policy been followed, it might never have been necessary to raise the question of conscription. Conscription is a word associated in the minds of many Canadians, especially those of French-speaking Canada, with the old kind of war. In this war, French-Canadians have volunteered in large numbers for overseas service. Some of them died at Dieppe. French Canada even consented to conscription for home service. But conscription of men to fight abroad without a full conscription of material resources is a travesty of 'total war,' and is as repugnant to thousands of English-speaking Canadians as it is to their French-speaking fellow citizens. Had there been a genuinely total mobilization in Canada, it is probable that French Canada, like the rest of the dominion, would have accepted it without demur. But Mr King, yielding to the pressure of extremist groups, entered upon a course of political manoeuvring which made it clear that, while he might introduce military conscription in total, he had no intention of using a similar degree of compulsion in respect to material resources and those who still control their disposal. Thus he is fast losing the confidence and support of Quebec.

In its war policy, the CCF has been unwavering and consistent. No shifting of its attitude, no 'political jobbery,' have been necessary to win support amongst the people of all parts of Canada for this, as for its economic platform of justice and equality for all classes of citizens in a land whose productiveness has hitherto been curbed to the advantage of a small minority.

The attempt to foment animosity and disunity by turning the guns of bigotry and racial prejudice against Quebec might be expected from such rabid sectionalist organs as the Toronto *Telegram*. What is regrettable and alarming is to see the Western papers of the Sifton chain, which have hitherto been regarded as liberal minded, adopting the same tactics. If this is to be the result of Mr King's mistaken policy of appeasement towards an arrogant bloc of Tory imperialists and self-seeking industrialists, it is time that more Canadians turned to the CCF, with its policy of genuine Canadian unity and total effort in the face of the mounting world crisis.

EDITORIAL

The Pro and Con Party

So the old lady has gone and had her face lifted again!

The Canadian Tory party changes its name as often and as easily as the Canadian Communist party changes its line. Plus ça change. ...

They began it when the much-contriving John A. Macdonald launched the so-called Liberal-Conservative party in 1854. He chose the double-barreled name in order to insinuate into the public mind the idea that his new combination was sloughing off its old high-tory reactionary elements. And those dear, simple-minded souls, the historians of Canada, have enshrined as an established fact in our history books his claim that his party was a coalition of all the 'moderates' to deliver the country from the violent contests of the extremists – although this moderate party contained all the old Family Compact extremists, and, as time was to show, it also contained the clerical ultramontane extremists of Quebec. In reality, Macdonald's Liberal-Conservative party was the party of big business plus the French Catholic church. It gave successful leadership for a generation, and built up a nation extending from sea to sea which was run by big business primarily in the interests of big business. Laurier's Liberal party took over this function in 1896.

The Tories came back to power in 1911 by a cynical and shameless exploitation of the most fervent British imperialist sentiment in English-speaking Canada and the most violent anti-imperialist sentiment in Quebec. (One of Borden's Quebec ministers after 1911 was a gentleman who on the hustings had expressed his desire to shoot holes through the union jack in order that the breeze of liberty might blow through it.) In 1921, having alienated practically every group in the community except the greediest of war profiteers, the party went down to disastrous defeat. It was on this occasion that it first tried to repeat what it imagined had been John A's formula for success. It appealed to the country as the National-Liberal-Conservative party. This was under the late Mr Meighen, and the incident was the only one in which his statesmanship ever showed any similarity to that of John A. Macdonald. By 1930 it was the good old Tory party again. But in 1940 it was the National Government party – for the duration of the election campaign. And now it is the Progressive-Conservative party. Would one be putting it too strongly if one suggested that this repetitious technique shows a certain lack of creative imagination?

Of course the party managers are operating on Barnum's principle that there is one born every minute. They calculate that the ordinary voter is dull-witted enough to be taken in by a showy name, and since in this war for democracy everybody must profess himself forward-looking, they present themselves as progressives. But they are trying to put over a fake. Nothing shows this more clearly than the fact that at the Winnipeg convention every candidate for the party leadership came from west of the great lakes, though the voting power of the party is almost entirely in the east. There wasn't a single eastern candidate who could be produced with any likelihood of impressing himself on even the most gullible as a progressive. The candidate they chose is a farmer leader, while the voting strength in the east is largely urban, lower middle-class – the social group in the community from which have come all the reactionary and counter-revolutionary movements of our time. Most important of all, the people who supply the campaign funds for the party are neither westerners, nor farmers, nor industrial workers, nor progressives. But it is they who will really determine the policy of the party.

Mr Bracken is a fine fellow. He has been the best prime minister that any province has had during the last ten or fifteen years – though, God knows, to say this is not to pay him much of a compliment. The far-seeing nationalist program which he presented to the Rowell Commission and his vigorous efforts to have the report of the Commission adopted as national policy, as well as his long campaign in the interests of western agriculture against that low machine politician, Jimmy Gardiner, stamp him as having the qualities that are needed in our national public life. Anyone who ever watched him in the old days skipping his curling rink in a close match would know that he is the sort of man who is at his best when the going is hardest. But he has never had any connection with his present party. And the men who put him in his present job did so for the sole reason that he was the only leader they could think of who had a chance of defeating Mr King. They picked him out to beat King, not to introduce a progressive government.

There are three great issues facing Canada at present. The manner in which we deal with them in our war effort and in our post-war reconstruction will determine whether we are to be a progressive national community or not. They provide the acid tests of the claims of any party to be progressive. It is not necessary to read party manifestoes or platforms. Just watch how a party reacts to these tests.

The first is the question of the place and function of the plain, ordinary man in our society. We all agree verbally that any tolerable post-war society must provide security for him – steady employment; minimum standards of housing, health, nutrition; equal opportunities for education. Genuine progressives add that he must be given a real share in the making of the communal decisions which affect his daily life, decisions about labour conditions and remuneration, about how the community services, of which he is the consumer, shall be carried on, all those decisions for which his right to vote in general elections seems so inadequate. Our wartime society is maintaining a high level of employment, but it is not giving the ordinary citizen any real share in making policy at all. All practical experience shows, and the conclusion is buttressed by the theoretical analysis of economists, that post-war society, if it is to maintain a high level of employment and production so as to make possible a high level of social services, must be one in which government planning and control of the economy have replaced the old system of private capitalist enterprise. Our Canadian Conservatives and Liberals profess to agree with the end, but they refuse to accept the means; they are all for preserving the noble system of private enterprise. They will fight in the last ditch for 'freedom,' meaning the freedom of business men to get rich in the way they see fit, freedom of business from government regulation and taxation. It ought to be clear enough by this time that free business enterprise cannot produce security, and cannot even produce steady prosperity, but only violent alternations of boom and depression. And the record of our big business men in running industry during this war or in running the dollar-a-year jobs at Ottawa shows what they really think of giving the common man a voice in policy. Neither the Conservatives nor the Liberals can meet this first test of progressivism.

It is true that in Britain the shock of war has shaken many a tory out of his old beliefs in nineteenth-century capitalism. But if one examines the transformation in beliefs which is going on there one will find that most of the leaders of the new-school tories are aristocrats, or intellectuals, or scientists, or churchmen. They are not business men. There are no aristocrats in Canada; and, while our acquaintance may be limited, we have never discerned in Canadian toryism any elements which struck us as being distinctly intellectual or scientific or Christian. Our less intelligent business men want 'no government in business' after the war. Our more intelligent ones are coming to see that what they should really aim at is a paternal government controlled by business.

The second great issue is that of Canada's relations to Great Britain. Everyone agrees verbally that, if this war is not to be fought in vain, it must end in some world settlement which makes future wars impossible and which produces conditions under which democratic institutions can flourish everywhere. What we want is a United Nations world that stands for peace and democracy. Within the United Nations the chief obstacle to the realization of such ideals comes from two sources. First, there are the British Empire isolationists who are fighting for a restored and strengthened Empire and for nothing else. Second, there are the 'American Century' isolationists who are dreaming of a great American imperialism. Each of these groups has considerable hope of using the other for its own purposes. Each of them hates Russia, and distrusts a revivified China. Our Canadian Tories are instinctively British Empire isolationists. They have never been anything else. They disliked the League of Nations before the war, they denounce criticism of British policy in India by 'outsiders' today. They are bitterly opposed to every step which might enable Canada to consider these questions of peace and democracy from a Canadian point of view. Most of them regret what Sir Robert Borden accomplished towards Canadian autonomy in the last war. They are pure colonials, and the colonialism always at a critical moment gets the better of their interest in broader issues.

The third great issue is that of the relationship of the French and English inside Canada. We may as well admit that that relationship had never been and is not likely to be for a long time very cordial. But the two races have to live together in some reasonable kind of collaboration. In the past this collaboration politically has always taken form in the leadership of some one political party. Under Baldwin and Lafontaine the two races worked together in the Reform party. Under Macdonald and Cartier they worked together for a generation in the Conservative party, and then under Laurier in the Liberal party. In our own day they worked together not too badly for twenty years in the Liberal party again under Messrs King and Lapointe. All these parties were in reality rather loose coalitions of racial groups, each group leaving its partner fairly free to do as it pleased in its own local sphere.

It is to be noted that for a long time, since 1896, this racial collaboration has not been possible under tory auspices. And, of course, since the events of 1917, followed by the troubles of the present war, it is more than ever impossible now. Since Mr Lapointe's death the Liberal form of collaboration is disintegrating, though this Liberal phase lasted longer than any other in our history. When Mr King goes it will disintegrate altogether; and, incidentally, we shall then realize what a really big man Mr King was, when we see the pigmies who succeed him in the Liberal party trying to deal with this most delicate and difficult of all Canadian problems.

Can the two races find a new political form of collaboration? There is only one possibility. Like the English-Canadian members of the CCF, the masses of the French-Canadians are coming to realize the extent to which they are exploited by economic monopolies, and they have lost faith in nineteenth-century capitalism. But, whatever polite palaver our English-Canadian tories may adopt, they cannot work with the French. Their Toronto instincts of racial domination will always get the better of them in times of strain just as their colonial instincts always get the better of them in times of strain when they face international questions.

No, the best that can be expected from the old dame, in spite of the skill with which this last face-lifting operation was done is that she will be a pro and con party. On each of these three great test issues for progressives she may manage to be verbally pro, but her actions will certainly show her to be con.

JAMES WREFORD
Winter Weather

Wintering time and weather with
the mercury low and locked in wrestling
    winds
precipitate upon our breath
snows that are not our sin:
so do not blame the frozen face
and eyes whose very tears are ice,
nor the dipping pole has spoked the race
thrown out of gear the wise
and well bred wonder, love,
the mechanical passion and blue-print kisses
and the streamlined marriage that seemed
    unmov-
ably stable and was not really missed.
For shall he not who backs the wind
and on his left hand feels it know
the storms are near that to the blind
such bitter bleakness sow?
Then not this fanged and fearful frost
green-griming and still balmless blight
but, after all, this putting to rest
and at long last winter quiet;
not the thin blood which God knows He
made for the gardens of Babylon and
moon drenched Cyclades above a tideless sea:
not the environmental and germ-true man,
but blame, if you must, this prime
unreasonable claim against the drift
and masking shadow and the time
turning away from Egypt's cleft
embosoming but embattled love;
the little Shulammite that prized
Solomon above the lilies, and above
the green of Eden, an Eden fossilised.
Blame this, if at all – the dry, unsatiated cry
for lips that yet more red than human are
and for those arms would underly
eternity, but not this hour.

IRVING LAYTON
Lady Remington

Lie down beside her, soldier,
And do but use her well,
And she can ease your passion
With cries and powder smell.
Be reckless in your loving;
Her grace makes no one poor,
For only bullets issue
From such an iron whore.

Note: This poem is now titled 'Lady Enfield' in Layton's *Collected Poems*.

MARGARET AVISON
Mutable Hearts

Now with a rush the children of men
tackle the windswirled slope,
    their olive shirts windplastered to their ribs
    their cries flashing under the throstled sky,
to meet the autumn.

Is it so swift out of mind—
the brambled valley of summer
    that shivers yet in its thin ornaments
left desolate, now,
    till from late silken threads of light
    invisibility be spun complete?

The counterpoint is shabby
that cannot suffer its own ridicule.

Motionless, in the seamurmurous
dark room she sits
intent to focus with her stricken wisdom
    the corded truth
about the son from whom so long
she beat away the leaden angels –
indomitable, lifting her knuckled forehead
to the indifferent sea-salt of the dark.
    Out of that locus though, the boy
    is fleet: perhaps gone forth
not on the windy sea, but down a street
to spit on the warm sawdust in the fish store,
    store,
    or on the mealy cone-strewn forest earth
    to skewer, cinnamon-strong;
    and many a crooked way
till amidst vasty snowfields
the purple shadows shoulder him,
and out of the bright-needled winter wilds
    he returns home:
        to find her gazing out
with wilful wisdom, in her cheated pride;
    to dabble with her dream
that sin is in his flickering, and the sun
            and seasons.

What *is* the drag against the current?
Why does the look of god shine still

above the rushy pool?
while cold swords wait beyond the sweeping
   curve
   of the dark river?

On the blown ridge now tilt the children of
   men
borne in the breathy brown frost-foaming air.

NORTHROP FRYE

Canada and Its Poetry

The appearance of Mr A.J.M. Smith's new anthology *The Book of Canadian Poetry*: A.J.M. Smith, Editor; W.J. Gage & Co. (University of Chicago Press); pp. 452; $4.00, is an important event in Canadian literature. For instead of confining his reading to previous compilations, as most anthologists do, he has made a first-hand study of the whole English field with unflagging industry and unfaltering taste. A straightforward research job is simple enough to do if one has the time: but Mr Smith has done something far more difficult than research. He had to read through an enormous mass of poetry ranging from the lousy to the exquisite, the great bulk of which was that kind of placid mediocrity which is always good verse and just near enough to good poetry to need an expert to detect its flat ring. He had to prounounce on all this not only with a consistent judgment but also with historical sense. He had to remember that a modern poet may hold deeply and sincerely to the more enlightened political views and become so gnarled and cryptic an intellectual that he cannot even understand himself, and still be just as conventional a minor poet as the most twittering Victorian songbird. In dealing with many of the older writers, Campbell for instance, or Carman he had to trace the thin gold vein of real imagination through a rocky mass of what can only be called a gift of metrical gab. He had to remember that occasionally a bad poem is of all the greater cultural significance for being bad, and therefore should go in. In judging his younger contemporaries he had to remember both that a flawed talent is better than a flawless lack of it and that still it is performance and 'promise' that makes the poet, of whatever age.

It is no easy job; but Mr Smith has, on the whole done it. Of course there are omissions, of which he is probably more acutely aware than his readers. In any case anthologies ought to have blank pages at the end on which the reader may copy his own neglected favourites. In my judgment, a few people are in who might well have been out, and a few out who might well have been in: some dull poems are included and many good ones are not; and one or two poets have been rather unfairly treated – including, I should say, one A.J.M. Smith. But no kind of book is easier to attack than an anthology; and in any case the importance of this one is not so much in the number or merits of the poems included as in the critical revaluations it makes. Mr Smith's study of the pre-Confederation poets is the only one that has been made from anything like a modern point of view. In Charles Heavysege he has unearthed – the word will not be too strong for most of his readers – a genuine Canadian Beddoes, a poet of impressive power and originality: and he has given Isabella Crawford enough space to show that she is one of the subtlest poets that Canada has produced. The more famous writers of the so-called Maple Leaf school come down to a slightly more modest estimate, and, though Mr Smith is scrupulously fair to them, he cannot and does not avoid saying that they talked too much and sang too little, or sang too much and thought too little. In any case the supremacy of Lampman over the whole group comes out very clearly. In the next period Pratt gets his deserved prominence, and the younger poets are generously represented. Here is, in short, what Canada can do: the reader who does not like this book simply does not like Canadian poetry, and will not be well advised to read further. Of course, Mr Smith says in his Preface, French-Canadian poetry is a separate job – still to be done, I should think, for Fournier's *Anthologie des Poètes Canadiens* is, as its editor Asselin frankly admits, more a collection of poets than of poems. But we cannot leave the French out of our poetry any more than we can leave Morrice or Gagnon out of our painting, and one can only hope for some French-speaking philanthropist to produce a companion volume.

The thing that impresses me is the unity of tone which the book has, and to which nearly all the poets in various ways contribute. Of course any anthologist can produce a false illusion of unity by simply being a critic of limited sympathies, responding only to certain kinds of technique or subject-matter. But Mr Smith is obviously not that: his notes and introduction show a wide tolerance, and his selections, though bold and independent, are certainly not precious. No: the unity of tone must come from the material itself, and the anthology thus unconsciously proves the existence of a definable Canadian genius (I use this word in a general sense) which is neither British nor American but, for all its echoes and imitations and second-hand ideas, peculiarly our own.

Now admittedly a great deal of useless yammering has been concerned with the 'truly Canadian' qualities of our literature, and one's first instinct is to avoid the whole question. Of course what is 'peculiarly our own' is not what is accidentally our own, and a poet may talk forever about forests and prairies and snow and the Land of the North and not be any more Canadian than he will be Australian if he writes a sonnet on a kangaroo. One of F.R. Scott's poems included by Mr Smith notes a tendency on the part of minor poets to 'paint the native maple.' This is like saying that because the quintuplets are Canadian, producing children in litters is a Canadian characteristic. Nevertheless, no one who knows the country will deny that there is something, say an attitude of mind, distinctively Canadian, and while Canadian speech is American, there is a recognizable Canadian accent in the more highly organized speech of its poetry. Certainly if a Canadian poet consciously tries to avoid being Canadian, he will sound like nothing on earth. For whatever may be true of painting or music, poetry is not a citizen of the world: it is conditioned by language, and flourishes best within a national unit. 'Humanity' is an abstract idea, not a poetic image. But whether Canada is really a national unit in any sense that has a meaning for culture I could not decide myself until I saw Mr Smith's book; and even then one has misgivings. The patriotic avarice that claims every European as 'Canadian' who stopped off at a Canadian station for a ham sandwich on his way to the States is, no doubt, ridiculous; but apart from that, does not any talk about Canadian poetry lead to some loss of perspective, some heavy spotlighting of rather pallid faces? Every Canadian has some feeling of sparseness when he compares, for example, Canada's fifth largest city, which I believe is Hamilton, with the fifth largest across the line, which I believe is Los Angeles. And the same is true of poetry. Every issue of the *New Yorker* or *New Republic*, to say nothing of the magazines which really go in for poetry, contains at least one poem which is technically on a level with five-sixths of Mr Smith's book. With so luxuriant a greenhouse next door, why bother to climb mountains to look for the odd bit of edelweiss? The only answer is, I suppose, that in what Canadian poets have tried to do there is an interest for Canadian readers much deeper than what the achievement in itself justifies.

The qualities of our poetry that appear from this book to be distinctively Canadian are not those that one readily thinks of: a fact which was an additional obstacle in Mr Smith's path. For Canada is more than most countries a milieu in which certain preconceived literary stereotypes are likely to interpose between the imagination and the expression it achieves. What a poet's imagination actually can produce and what the poet thinks it ought to produce are often very different things. They never should be, but they sometimes are; and it is hard to judge accurately the work of a man who is a genuine poet but whose poetry only glints here and there out of a mass of verse on conventional themes he has persuaded himself he should be celebrating. If a poet is a patriot, for instance there may be two natures within him, one scribbling ready-made patriotic doggerel and the other trying to communicate the real feelings his country inspires him with. If he is religious, the poet in him may reach God in very subtle ways; but the man in him who is not a poet may be a more commonplace person, shocked by his own poetic boldness. If he is revolutionary, the poet in him may have to argue with a Philistine materialist also in him who does not really see why so much patriotic, religious, and revolutionary verse is bad.

Now this creative schizophrenia is, we have said, common in Canada, and the most obvious reason for it is the fact that Canada is not only a nation but a colony in an empire. I have said that culture seems to flourish best in national units, which implies that the empire is too big and the province too small for major literature. I know of no poet, with the very dubious exception of Virgil, who has made great poetry out of what Shakespeare calls 'the imperial theme': in Kipling, for instance this theme is largely a praise of machinery, and of the Robot tendencies within the human mind. The province or region, on the other hand, is usually a vestigial curiosity to be written up by some nostalgic tourist. The imperial and the regional are both inherently anti-poetic environments, yet they go hand in hand; and together they make up what I call the colonial in Canadian life.

This colonial tendency has been sharpened by the French-English split, the English having tended to specialize in the imperial and the French in the regional aspects of it. The French are on the whole the worse off by this arrangement, which has made Quebec into a cute tourist resort full of ye quainte junke made by real peasants, all of whom go to church and say their prayers like the children they are, and love their land and tell folk tales and sing ballads just as the fashionable novelists in the cities say they do. True, I have never met a French-Canadian who liked to be thought of as an animated antique, nor do I expect to: yet the sentimental haze in which the European author of *Maria Chapdelaine* saw the country is still quite seriously accepted by Canadians, English and French alike, as authentic. A corresponding imperial preoccupation in English poets leads to much clearing of forests and planting of crops and tapping vast natural resources: a grim earnestness of expansion which seems almost more German than British. The more naive expressions of this do not get into Mr Smith's book. Instead, he sets Isabella Crawford's song, 'Bite Deep and Wide, O Axe, the Tree,' in its proper context, a viciously ironic one; and Anne Marriott's 'The Wind Our Enemy' and Birney's 'Anglo-Saxon Streets' are also there to indicate that if we sow the wind of empire with too little forethought we shall reap a dusty whirlwind of arid squalor.

The colonial position of Canada is therefore a frostbite at the roots of the Canadian imagination, and it produces a disease for which I think the best name is prudery. By this I do not mean reticence in sexual matters: I mean the instinct to seek a conventional or commonplace expression of an idea. Prudery that keeps the orthodox poet from making a personal recreation of his orthodoxy: prudery that prevents the heretic from forming an articulate heresy that will shock: prudery that makes a radical stutter and gargle over all realities that are not physical: prudery that chokes off social criticism for fear some other group of Canadians will take advantage of it. One sees this perhaps most clearly in religion, because of the fact that the division of language and race is approximately one of religion also. Mr Smith has included a religious poem called 'Littlewit and Loftus', which, though in some respects a bad poem, is at any rate not a prudish one in the above sense: it ends with the authentic scream of the disembodied evangelical banshee who has cut herself loose from this world and who has the sense of release that goes with that, even if she is not wholly sure what world she is now in. It is a prickly cactus in a desert of bumbling platitude and the pouring of unctuous oil on untroubled waters; or else, as in Bliss Carman, prayers of a stentorian vagueness addressed to some kind of scholar-gipsy God.

I wish I could say that the tighter grip of religion on the French has improved matters there; but it has done nothing of the kind. In French poetry too one feels that the Church is often most vividly conceived not as catholic but as a local palladium to be defended for political reasons: as a part of the parochial intrique which is given the title of 'nationalism.' The type of prudery appropriate to this is a facile and mawkish piety. In short, the imperial tendency may call itself 'Protestant' and the regional one 'Catholic'; but as long as both are colonial, both will be essentially sectarian. Similarly, the imperial tendency may call itself British and the regional one French; but as long as both are colonial, these words will have only a sectional meaning. It is an obvious paradox in Canadian life that the more colonial the English or French-speaking Canadian is, and the more he distrusts the other half of his country, the more artificial his relation to the real Britain or France becomes. The French-Canadian who translates 'British Columbia' as 'Colombie canadienne' and flies the tricolour of the French Revolution on holidays, and the English-Canadian who holds that anything short of instant acquiescence in every decision of the British Foreign Office is treason, are the furthest of all Canadians from the culture of what they allege to be their mother countries.

But even when the Canadian poet has got rid of colonial cant, there are two North American dragons to slay. One is the parrotted cliché that this is a 'new' country and that we must spend centuries cutting forests and building roads before we can enjoy the by-products of settled leisure. But Canada is not 'new' or 'young': it is exactly the same age as any other country under a system of industrial capitalism; and even if it were, a reluctance to write poetry is not a sign of youth but of decadence. Savages have poetry: the Pilgrim Fathers, who really were pioneers, started writing almost as soon as they landed. It is only from the exhausted loins of the half-dead masses of people in modern cities that such weary ideas are born.

The other fallacy concerns the imaginative process itself, and may be called the Ferdinand the Bull theory of poetry. This theory talks about a first-hand contact with life as opposed to a second-hand contact with it through books, and assumes that the true poet will go into the fields and smell the flowers and not spoil the freshness of his vision by ruining his eyesight on books. However, practically all important poetry has been the fruit of endless study and reading, for poets as a class are and must be, as an Elizabethan critic said, 'curious universal scholars.' There are exceptions to this rule, but they prove it; and it is silly to insist on them. In looking over Mr Smith's book one is struck immediately by the predominance of university and professional people, and it is in the classical scholarship of Lampman, the encyclopaedic erudition of Crémazie which is said to have included Sanscrit, and the patient research and documentation of Pratt's 'Brébeuf' and sea narratives, that Canadian poetry has become most articulate. There is nothing especially Canadian about this, but one point may be noted. To an English poet, the tradition of his own country and language proceeds in a direct chronological line down to himself, and that in its turn is part of a gigantic funnel of tradition extending back to Homer and the Old Testament. But to a Canadian, broken off from this linear sequence and having none of his own, the traditions of Europe appear as a kaleidoscopic whirl with no definite shape or meaning, but with a profound irony lurking in its varied and conflicting patterns. The clearest statement of this is in that superb fantasy 'The Witches' Brew,' Pratt's first major effort, a poem of which apparently I have a higher opinion than Mr Smith. It is also to be found, I think, in the elaborate Rabbinical apparatus of Klein.

American even more than Canadian poetry has been deeply affected by the clash between two irreconcilable views of literature: the view that poets should be original and the view that they should be aboriginal. Originality is largely a matter of returning to origins, of studying and imitating the great poets of the past. But many fine American poets have been damaged and in some cases spoiled by a fetish of novelty: they have sought for the primitive and direct and have tried to avoid the consciously literary and speak the language of the common man. As the language of the common man is chiefly commonplace, the result has been for the most part disastrous. And here is one case where failing to achieve a virtue has really warded off a vice. There has on the whole been little Tarzanism in Canadian poetry. One is surprised to find how few really good Canadian poets have thought that getting out of cities into God's great outdoors really brings one closer to the sources of inspiration. One reason for this is that there has been no revolution in Canada and less sense of building up a new land into what the American Constitution calls a more perfect state. A certain dedication of political responsibility is sharply reflected in our poetry, and is by no means always harmful to it. We can see this clearly if we compare Bliss Carman with his American friend Hovey, who sang not only of freedom and the open road but also of America's duty to occupy the Philippines and open up the Pacific. The Canadian likes to be objective about Americans, and likes to feel that he can see a bit of Sam Slick in every Yankee: as a North American, therefore, he has a good seat on the revolutionary sidelines, and his poetic tendencies, reflective, observant, humorous, critical, and quite frankly traditional, show it.

The closest analogy to Canadian poetry in American literature is, as one would expect, in the pre-1776 period: the Anne Bradstreet and Philip Freneau and the Hartford Wits. We have many excellent counterparts to these, and of the tradition that runs through Emerson, but few if any good counterparts to Whitman, Sandburg, Lindsay, Jeffers or MacLeish. Early American poetry is traditional, but its tradition is a great one: and when the Americans gained security in government they lost some in poetry; for there is an assurance and subtlety in Bradstreet and Freneau that Longfellow and Whittier and many of those mentioned above do not possess. This is not to say that the best American poetry appeared before 1776, but as we seem to be stuck with at least some colonial characteristics, we may as well appreciate what virtues they have.

Nature in Canadian poetry, then, has little of the vagueness of great open spaces in it: that is very seldom material that the imagination can use. One finds rather an intent and closely focussed vision, often on something in itself quite unimportant: in Birney's slug, Finch's station platform, the clairvoyance of hatred in MacKay's 'I Wish My Tongue Were a Quiver', Hambleton's sharply etched picture of salmon fishing. The first poet Mr Smith includes, the Canadian Oliver Goldsmith, makes an accurate inventory of a country store, and he sets a tone which the rest of the book bears out. The vocabulary and diction correspond: the snap and crackle of frosty words, some stiff with learning and others bright with concreteness, is heard wherever there is the mental excitement of real creation, though of course most obviously where the subject suggests it: in, for instance, Charles Bruce's 'Immediates':

> *An ageless land and sea conspire*
> *To smooth the imperfect mold of birth;*
> *While freezing spray and drying fire*
> *Translate the inexplicit earth.*

or in P.K. Page's 'Stenographers':

> *In the felt of the morning, the calico minded,*
> *sufficiently starched, insert papers, hit keys,*
> *efficient and sure as their adding machines.*

But, according to Mr Smith's book, the outstanding achievement of Canadian poetry is in the evocation of stark terror. Not a coward's terror, of course; but a controlled vision of the causes of cowardice. The immediate source of this is obviously the frightening loneliness of a huge and thinly settled country. When all the intelligence, morality, reverence, and simian cunning of man confronts a sphinx-like riddle of the indefinite like the Canadian winter the man seems as helpless as a trapped mink and as lonely as a loon. His thrifty little heaps of civilized values look pitiful beside nature's apparently meaningless power to waste and destroy on a superhuman scale, and such a nature suggests an equally ruthless and subconscious God, or else no God. In Wilfred Campbell, for instance, the Canadian winter expands into a kind of frozen hell of utter moral nihilism:

> *Lands that loom like spectres, whited regions of winter,*
> *Wastes of desolate woods, deserts of water and shore;*
> *A world of winter and death, within these regions who enter,*
> *Lost to summer and life, go to return no more.*

And the winter is only one symbol, though a very obvious one, of the central theme of Canadian poetry: the riddle of what a character in Mair's 'Tecumseh' calls 'inexplicable life.' It is really a riddle of inexplicable death: the fact that life struggles and suffers in a nature which is blankly indifferent to it. Human beings set a high value on their own lives which is obviously not accepted in the world beyond their palisades. They may become hurt and whimper that nature is cruel to them; but the honest poet does not see cruelty: he sees only a stolid unconsciousness. The human demands that Patrick Anderson's Joe hurls at nature are answered by 'a feast of no'; a negation with neither sympathy nor malice in it. In Birney's 'David' a terrible tragedy of wasted life and blasted youth is enacted on a glacier, but there is no 'pathetic fallacy' about the cruelty of the glacier or of whatever gods may be in charge of it. It is just a glacier. D.C. Scott's 'Piper of Arll' is located in an elusive fairyland, but the riddle of inexplicable death is still at the heart of the poem. The same theme is of course clearer still in Pratt's sea narrative, especially the 'Titanic'.

Sometimes this theme modulates into a wry and sardonic humor. In the laughter of that rare spirit Standish O'Grady, who in his picture of freezing Canadians huddling around 'their simpering stove' has struck out one of the wittiest phrases in the book, something rather sharper sounds across the laughter:

> *Here the rough Bear subsists his winter year,*
> *And licks his paw and finds no better fare.*

In Drummond's finest poem, 'The Wreck of the Julie Plante' the grim humour of the ballad expresses the same tragedy of life destroyed by unconsciousness that we find in Pratt and Birney:

> *For de win' she blow lak hurricane,*
> *Bimeby she blow some more.*

Tom MacInnes has the same kind of humour, though the context is often fantastic, and his 'Zalinka' is a parody of Poe which somehow manages to convey the same kind of disturbing eeriness. But whether humorous or not, even in our most decorous poets there are likely to be the most startling flashes of menace and fear. A placid poem of Charles G.D. Roberts about mowing is suddenly punctured by the line 'The crying knives glide on; the green swath lies.' Archdeacon Scott writes a little poem on Easter Island statues which ends in a way that will lift your back hair.

But the poetic imagination cannot remain for long content with this faceless mask of unconsciousness. Nature is not all glacier and iceberg and hurricane; and while there is no conscious cruelty in it, there is certainly a suffering that we can interpret as cruelty. Hence the poet begins to animate nature with an evil or at least sinister power: night in Heavysege becomes a cacodemon, and spring in Dorothy Livesay a crouching monster. Mr Smith's book is full of ghosts and unseen watchers and spiritual winds: a certain amount of this is faking, but not all:

Lampman's 'In November', with its ghastly dead mulleins and the wonderful danse macabre in which it closes, is no fake. The 'crying in the dark' in Lampman's 'Midnight,' the dead hunter in Eustace Ross's 'The Death,' the dead 'lovely thing' in Neil Tracy's poem, the married corpses in Leo Kennedy's 'Epithalamium': all these are visions, not only of a riddle of inexplicable death, but of a riddle of inexplicable evil. Sometimes, of course, this evil takes an easily recognized form: the Indians in Joseph Howe's spirited narrative and the drought wind in Anne Marriott have no spectral overtones. But it is obvious that man must be included in this aspect of the riddle, as it is merely fanciful to separate conscious malice from the human mind. Whatever sinister lurks in nature lurks also in us; and Tom MacInnes's 'tiger of desire' and the praying mantis of a remarkable poem by Anne Dalton have been transformed into mental demons.

The unconscious horror of nature and the subconscious horrors of the mind thus coincide: this amalgamation is the basis of symbolism on which nearly all Pratt's poetry is founded. The fumbling and clumsy monsters of his 'Pliocene Armageddon' who are simply incarnate wills to mutual destruction, are the same monsters that beget Nazism and inspire 'The Fable of the Goats'; and in the fine 'Silences,' which Mr Smith includes, civilized life is seen geologically as merely one clock-tick in eons of ferocity. The waste of life in the death of the Cachalot and the waste of courage and sanctity in the killing of the Jesuit missionaries are tragedies of a unique kind in modern poetry: like the tragedy of Job, they seem to move upward to a vision of a monstrous Leviathan, a power of chaotic nihilism which is 'king over all the children of pride.' I admit that 'Tom the Cat from Zanzibar' in 'The Witches' Brew' is good fun, but when Mr Smith suggests that he is nothing more, I disagree.

In the creepy ambiguity of the first line of Malzah's song in Heavysege, 'There was a devil and his name was I', the same association of ideas recurs, and it recurs again in what is perhaps the most completely articulate poem in the book, Lampman's 'City of the End of Things'; which, though of course it has no room for the slow accumulation of despair that 'The City of Dreadful Night' piles up, is an equally terrifying vision of humanity's Iron Age. In the younger writers the satire on war and exploitation is more conventional and anonymous, but as soon as they begin to speak with more authority they will undoubtedly take their places in the same tradition – Patrick Anderson especially.

To sum up. Canadian poetry is at its best a poetry of incubus and *cauchemar*, the source of which is the unusually exposed contact of the poet with nature which Canada provides. Nature is seen by the poet, first as unconsciousness, then as a king of existence which is cruel and meaningless, then as the source of the cruelty and subconscious stampedings within the human mind. As compared with American poets, there has been comparatively little, outside Carman, of the cult of the rugged outdoor life which idealizes nature and tries to accept it. Nature is consistently sinister and menacing in Canadian poetry. And here and there we find glints of a vision beyond nature, a refusal to be bullied by space and time an affirmation of the supremacy of intelligence and humanity over stupid power. One finds this in Kenneth Leslie:

Rather than moulds invisible in the air
into which petals pour selective milk
I seem to sense a partnered agony
of creature and creator in the rose.

One finds it in Dorothy Livesay's apostrophe to the martyred Lorca:

You dance. Explode
Unchallenged through the door
As bullets burst
Long deaths ago, your breast.

One finds it in Margaret Avison's very lovely 'Maria Minor' and her struggle to divine 'the meaning of the smashed moth' in a poem which makes an excellent finale to the book. And one begins thereby to understand the real meaning of the martyrdom of Brébeuf, the theme of what with all its faults is the greatest single Canadian poem. Superficially, the man with the vision beyond nature is tied to the stake and destroyed by savages who are in the state of nature, and who represent its mindless barbarity. But there is a far profounder irony to that scene: the black-coated figure at the stake is also a terrifying devil to the savages, *Echon*, the evil one. However frantically they may try to beat him off, their way of savagery is doomed; it is doomed in their Nazi descendants; it is doomed even if it lasts to the end of time.

This is not, I hope, a pattern of thought I have arbitrarily forced upon Canadian poetry: judging from Mr Smith's book and what other reading I have done this seems to be its underlying meaning, and the better the poem the more clearly it expresses it. Mr Smith has brought out this inner unity quite unconciously because it is really there: just as in his 'Ode on Yeats' he has, again quite unconsciously, evoked a perfect image of the nature of poetic feeling in his own country:

> *An old thorn tree in a stony place*
> *Where the mountain stream has run dry,*
> *Torn in the black wind under the race*
> *Of the icicle-sharp kaleidoscopic white*
>   *sky,*
> *Bursts into sudden flower.*

Over a smooth beach with hardly a ripple
   to show
The sharp rocks of longing
Buried seven fathoms below consciousness.

And in her there will be a cave of light
Concealed under the eyelids, a world
Springing alive in her fingertips;

And in her a riotous garden
Seven fathoms beneath the world will bloom
Where the white curve of his nostril, the
   carved earlobe
Will blossom to permanent shapes, give form
To her huge longing, and she will spread herself
A sighing caress in the seagreen sunlight
Filtered through oceans of sorrow.

June 1944

PATRICK ANDERSON
Poem on Canada

MIRIAM WADDINGTON
The Sleepers

There will be no square of yellow light
Spilling from the open doorway into the street,
There will be no sudden illumination of man
   and woman
Clasped in a last passionate embrace.
There will be no agony in his eyes
Reaching after her departing figure;
There will be no blackout, no close-up.

But cutting through the prosaic years
Reality's searchlight will pause
On the unrelenting mask of his face, explore
The reasonless dam, not knowing the hurricane
   rivers
Of desire shored up against its walls.
And there will be endless afternoons spinning
   their time out
Pouring light over his face and hands,
Age coming quiet and slow as a tide

1 Pre-Conquest

Young was the land with all a schoolroom's
   colours,
green, pale blue, white, deep red:
chalks that children write on black
of basalt by the waterfalling light
in the cold strenuous air of their childhood:
basalt, black granite, slate–impervious
to children's letters in big loops
like mountaineers strung out, with space
   between.
Wind blowing into space and into ferns
dark green, and drifting paleness amongst
   flowers.
Purple, soft yellow, colours good for posters
or clumsy letters straggling around holes
that children, trapped upon their paper snow,
write out and lose in lone and Indian file.

Say, what did you expect
but wind, cold weather, medicinal gums,
the emptiness in which children live –
bodies, pockets, cruelty and religion?
Folktales – and faces painted with bear's
   blood,
brown paper wigwams on crude skies
and simple poetry:
   'My penknife whispers in the cedar
   strands fine as sea-lion's hairs ...'
The Spirits haunting since first child was made
out of – a clamshell!

What did you expect
but this, the paleness and the liveness –
a window staring at the plotting boys
clotted around the death
of some tight-fitting, small, animal thing ...
the western wind ruffling the nasty habit ...
the whisperings, the shivers in the trees,
notes passed by maples
excitedly, across an empty space.
These cruel, saying
'Ai, ai, my small red man!',

June 1944

mutilating the life they do not understand,
with songs by the campfire.
And, when they're driven out, the summer
drones like an empty school
full of hot resins, sticky varnishes
and the smell of timber –
full of the colours and the windows,
full of light,
and here (of North Ontario) a map
noisy with flies
and there a children's picture singed by
    August ...
trees, rocks, hills, lakes – discovered
by those who find
a wonder almost empty like a boredom.

II The Coming of the White Man

Suppose it, for the last time, in that moment
when being undiscovered it lay quiet
as almost no other country like the sea —
when resinous currents streaked its boughgreen
    waves
and soundless arrows
slipped like fish through fathoms of spruce
    and balsam:
the time of the tent, the shape of light in the
    water,
and the rustred encampment on the gravel
    shoal
with the flow of phosphorous from its deep
    drowned fire:
suppose it then, with its strange and primitive
    stillness
breathed awkwardly, with gills – not broken
by men brocaded with Renaissance lungs.
In that moment, the last in which it tested its
    silence

against the innumerable dialects of flowers
and birds, in pinprick crowds –
and deployed its multitudinous winds
gravely, amongst a few simple savages,
and slept the last immortal sleep of its
    childhood.

And then, when that moment hung like a cliff,
and for miles and miles extended
westward its enormous capacity to be hurt
(for what is weaker than something that needs
only the casual eye to rupture its being
and luck to change it forever?) suppose,
suddenly, out of the haze,
come like a swimmer, the Renaissance man
aware of his Grecian whiteness discovered!
At first his sea-head less important than gulls
then later nearer than ships
and standing out of the east, dripping with
    armour,
this conqueror with the marvelous corrupt
    face, drawing
soft Europe out of the water,
sanguine, scientific with flowers ...
would not every movement of that first
    naked foot
utterly shatter
the white sand with the sound of a thunder-
    bolt?
That moment when l'uomo universale
crying with von Hutten 'It is a joy to be alive,'
captain and cousin of the Roman world,
coined in the delight of the Medici banks,
    leapt
upon the white sand of the continent!
Yet shall we be in error if we say
that then – as though by arrow shot – he fell
down on his knees, God's cripple,

and the clean sands were
disordered by prayer and greed, as though by
    the wounded?
Planted a cross, claimed for a King, and stole
natives like curios, and hid his face
in the great purse of his soul?
        O here
in vast intervention island America
green as a tyro imposed her giant innocence,
huge as the gardens of childhood. Was not
as easy Indies to his lover's hand
but always a trifle frigid like a gauche
but beautiful mirror, seeming shiningly empty
and keen, as a child does.
To which he comes, the prince adventurer,
competes his heart from that anarchic sea
where windy Luther and sleek Machiavelli
in a mess of sceptres a confusion of thrones
rise and are chaos to Christendom. Hacks
his private way, aches at his joint-stock
    frontier,
protests himself religious, prays for grace,
disrupts the forest in his monetary enterprise
and performs his prodigies
for the artists' banks, the commercial houses
    of Shakespeare.
And the moment is not yet
fulfillment ... nor northwest discovery
to those who see in plains the easier islands
only, and plot their rule and real estate
with gun, axe, bible, theodolite,
seignorial tenure ... Yet, historically,
one did what one could. The best was
    competition,
the winds particular, men against the sky,
the merchandise ordered. One was good at
    those things.
Sometimes one regretted the idyllic relations

and there were even those who talked for
    poetry
as Wolfe – before he died at Quebec
'I had rather etc. than take it,' he said
but, as the curfew tolled the knell of parting
    day,
he performed his historical function, and he
    was dead.
Others have also thought 'the Pen is mightier
    than the Sword'
or 'colonies are provincial' but always there
    were
the things to be got; to be more particular
one thousand six hundred Beaver skins (for
    Europe's hats),
six thousand Lynx pelts, five hundred
    (superfine) Buffalo robes,
a quantity of castorum. And if one despaired
of the cutthroat pace, the raccoon and fox in
    the traps,
the pemmican on the trail, one could give
    the job up –
go native perhaps or become a Scottish laird.

And so a long paddle, a hard road
sweat blinding one.
                    On the brave heart's
    investment
of energy sun's summer interest
pouring in palm, the finery of sex
and, cyclical, the slump of Fall – the leaves
devalued in their cashier's grilles – the boom
of early thaw. Spring and the luxury trades!
Powders, and pollens brimming in the heart's
expanding market, August's mounting price
and far off thunder over crazy buying
of love, 'eternal moments,' gilt edged stock
as fine and faithless as the goldenrod.

To own all this and then to own all Winter's
waspish gazette, from the first August rumours
to the inflation of maples, the scarlet spending,
    till
the empty safe, the shot of ice. And then
be tragic Hamlet, damned, Tory with death.
And so a hard and individual road
from the Portage de la Roche Capitaine to
    the Décharge of the Trou
with the water oftentimes awkward in
    channels and guts
of the pointed rocks, the oldest in the world:
a competition of hearts, a cruel journey:
the rapids of Matawoen a fierce lace
and Lake Nipissing a tough blue
and the beautiful hills crackling adventurous
    muscles.
And the Portage Pin de Musique and Mauvais
    de Musique,
many lost there, crushed by canoes,
and the Turtle, one thousand, five hundred
    and thirteen paces.
The far-flung heart in many awkward and
    beautiful
places and awkward beautiful waters before
they chose, at Grande Portage, from the
    pork-eaters
those who must go upon the western journey,
the winterers to the river of the rainy lake.
And the North was. With winter the snow
    came.
Whole folios of it. Yet nothing written
except one thing, a bleak expectancy –
the possible with its strenuous shade of
    whiteness,
where an intuition without equipment
could trek into the faint wind of the future,
getting its silence on the single track.

And the land was. And the Aurora came.
O then below the pale and famished lights
whose powder tremors and electric gales
hurled from the terrible fluted rays,
the will hurt in the breast. For these
lights can illumine nothing but the spirit,
not lights but sketches of light,
naked, distant, uncertain,
to watch whose glacial radiance is an effort
never a peace, which to expect
is to be lone, lost in the spirit's hunger,
And the land was. But locked in all its lakes,
the land unseen. Although
by many needled tracks and snowy trails,
across tough ridges and down distances
of a green fatigue – in valleys of the yawn –
on plains spreading diffusion of desire –
discovered by a failure,
by the great captains of human weakness.
And the land was. And the people did not
    take it.

Wide was the land.
        And North.
                My Aunt bought lakes –
Aunt Hildegarde, living on Lincoln Terrace,
one of the genteel poor, unmarried,
playing at patience, stroked those cards
whose red is scarlet as the tongues of lovers
or as the autumn maples, with their dogs'
    tongues
remembered the years in Ottawa, a Brockville
    childhood,
and sometimes opened the close cedar drawer
under the knicknacks between the aspidistras
and showed me the deed. Crumpled it was
    and dusty –

June 1944

June 1944

deed to five thousand acres no one land ever seen
and three lakes, all unnamed.
    Aunt Hildegarde
had bought this stake in natural Canada
for a thousand dollars, timber and all.

I thought, as a child would, of her trees, her birds –
her streams, her little glaciers and her thaws
and of the beavers of Aunt Hildegarde.
When, as sometimes happened, she grew severe
I dreamt how seriously across her boundaries
a moose had stepped, and stood there gentle and grim.
In Spring she smiled as all her birds returned.
In Summer dozed, consulting butterflies –
an old lady, with a muskeg all her own.
 It does not sleep. Maybe the Indians cross it
as shadows slur her features when she nods
by the parlor fire, reading the *Globe and Mail*.
When she sleeps, I thought, beside her medicine bottles,
When I grew older, I thought of those lakes as mirrors
in which Aunt Hildegarde had never seen herself –
brisk pits to show her soul and Canada's.
And, as a matter of fact, she often declared
she'd visit them one day. But she never did.
A cancer engrossed her, she grew thin and died.
Her lawyers, they say, had a hell of a time
trying to sell that marvelous empty
neck of the woods that no one had ever seen.
And the land was. And the people did not take it.

III **The Country Still Unpossessed**

Though Champlain looked in it for the Lilies of France
and Laval looked in it for the Wounds of Christ,
and the holy sisters found its winters chaste
while the merchants, with the Hurons gliding about it,
declared it merry with flies and mad with waste:
and the Jesuit Fathers wrote of it in Relations,
sprinkling the holy water which always froze
and a boy climbed over the Quebec Stockade
and stared at it too long – and it chipped his nose.
Then, chased by his wife, Frontenac bowed to it
with the silver of Montmorency in his hand,
walking in the blue water as on a parquet
swept by a foam of girls, in his native land
with military honours to beat the band:
but the Iroquois looked in it for a priest to fry –
a string of red hot hatchets about his neck –
while the glory of God and brandy and beads to buy
enriched the pioneer seigneurs of Quebec.

And the explorers found it in new trails to begin
and Wolfe stood there, and felt his receding chin.
But, despite the priests, the North could beat their bible
(enormous, vague and louder than all their prayers)
where the bearded bear would prophesy like Isaiah
and the grey wolves howl – moon haloes on their hairs –
in the pulpit rocks. Or, in ikons of their lairs,
burned those red eyes unlit by any priest,
while down the Gothic glades there bellowed a moose
of agony size, with a crown of thorns like Christ.
And, despite the traders, despite the coureurs de bois
and the voyageurs, and those who slung canals
and fastened bridges above them, or sharpened their dreams
to the wizened and hungry winter of the rails
westward, forever – or fenced and festooned the miles,
this Laurentide land, boosted with waterpower
and blown from the North, was greater and grander by far.
There, grimy with toil, the lightning dipped like a miner
to dig in the precious ores with a pointed flash
while high in their secret mountains on the magnet lakes
drew shining up their loyalties of fish.

And despite the fever in land or timber or wheat,
the country remained, and the people looked into it.

And Mackenzie looked in it for electoral rights
and the popular will, but all that he could see

was Governor Head who was quite prepared
    to fight
'the low-bred antagonist democracy' –
'I would publicly promulgate, let they come
    if they dare!'
the Governor said (a man with important
    curls,
with a scheming brain but a fine crisp head of
    hair
and tight thin lips and eyes that glazed like
    pearls).
Mackenzie, five times elected and five denied,
prepared to fight it out, appealed to the South,
and smiling 'wiped his seditious little mouth' –
blood ran in Toronto's snow and the people
    died.
And Papineau looked in it for the popular will
and was beaten back: with trumpets Lord
    Durham came
and saw division and graft, dissension and
    spoil,
and wrote his notes and left, a dying man:
And in looked the Fathers of Confederation,
profits and 'progress' all that they could
    know –
the bourgeois midwives of a new-born nation –
from cold colony to empty dominion, so –
yet laid the ground where greater changes
    grow.
And Riel, not mad. *Pas fou.* At his own trial
forsook what his lawyers said and madness
    forever
and claimed the great dignity of the conscious
    will
for what he had said and done on the Red
    River
for freedom and the Metis. Gave up his right

to pardon. Was ordered hanged as a traitor.
But they say his body made a great wound
    in the air
and God damn the English judge that put
    him there!
And Laurier looked at it, in the time of war,
and thought of a national future, and died
    before.

And the factories built. And the companies
    seizing the forests,
the companies burning wheat in the prairie
    dust,
the fortunes solemn as coal or fancy as water
while the Regina dead are specks in the Golden
    West,
only by hunger published and soon dismissed.
But the unions formed. The gradual moulding
    of labour
in crisis and slump, the logic that hunger
    inspired –
while over their heads the land was wavy with
    leisure
and lakes were shining days that no one
    explored.

IV The River

Wide is the land.
    The landfall.
        Sprawling here
your soft and teeming contacts, history!
A flood of access welters from the gulf
past Anticosti ... Gaspé. Thrones of waves
deftly dupply the lost, the empty kingdoms:
authorities advance: super-marine
occasions tatter round the toes of kids.

Under their salty angels the dead bob.
A river is as woundable as glass
and simmers softly on the morning light
danger as well as hope, its edges raw
with clots and festers on the fancy water ...
drains ... rainbows – something no one can
    keep clean.
And this as well in gleaming lateral
connects with lakes and rails, connects,
    resumes,
becomes redundant and no more than rut
glutting itself. A river is not our country.
West is the land.
    The passage is
        Saint Lawrence ...
The horns of Kamouraska sound tonight
and pasturing the fog the sea-bloomed bells
resound and rock your cliffs, sad Saguenay!
Angels and ghosts, traitors and submarines.
In summer like a lust's dear avenue
the inflamed water has docked a treachery
by a hollow wharf. Such ease is dangerous,
such brightness has the very look of luck.
For greedy here, the soft deceit of keels
skimmed on the sonnets of the weed,
    dissolved
your rhyming water-beds. O Pelerins,
shadowed these stanzas of the pebble shoal
but left unread the hills' slow noble cantos.

Here came the immigrant, wheat in his eyes,
with arms stretched wide to grasp its kissing
    tops
and was betrayed; here the remittance man,
cocky with mountains, came; and here, aghast,
the Jew set up his city attitude,
his groceries and sorrow in spiritual bags.

June 1944

Below, the faithful salmon focused home.
Quebec ... lights stacked, while cannon with
   foul mouths,
gagging on cellophane, gasp in the air
that's dollar crisp – trademarked with history.

Is it the railway then, is it the river
you hear – when locked in bedroom like a cyst
you would prepare sleep's terrible piety,
tossing in Montreal? That sheet you draw
smells of the soot and salt of the continent,
the foghorns swell your pillow and the train's
desperate sister whistle sobs for land.
You lie, and lean upon your river arms
a mouth adrift, fat as a bale with sleep
and on your railway arms the freight of your
   head
you lean. The wall is dry. Yet you hear water.
Sometimes you thrust your naked leg, an oar,
and seem to steer with it. The while you slip
cross Canada (West is the land – you sleep
in shoals and shallows of the southern shore,
up by Tourmente, and cough and turn, and
   you
are loose upon Superior, or make
narrow with bones through the canals to snore
your black head past the prairies, gold upon
   gold,
and all unrealised. Sometimes half wake
and shout and there the Rockies, leap upon
   leap,
rear their percussive clouds – moan then and
   fall
to those Pacific sands wet with their girls.
Such the soft motor of your sleep to drift
the horizontal of the flaccid dream
which you call commerce. Which is private
   death.

West is the land. And North. And no one goes.

V **Cold Colloquy**

What are you ...? they ask, in wonder.
And she replies in the worst silence of all her
   words:
I am Candida with the cane wind.

What are you ...? they ask again, their mouths
   full of gum.
their eyes full of the worst silence of the
   worst winter in a hundred years
and the frames of their faces chipped round
   the skaters' picture –
what are you ...? they ask.
And she replies: I am the wind that wants a
   flag.
I am the mirror of your picture
until you make me the marvel of your life.
Yes, I am one and none, pin and pine, snow
   and slow,
America's attic, an empty room,
a something possible, a chance, a dance
that is not danced. A cold kingdom.

Are you a dominion of them? they ask,
   scurrying
home on streetcars, skiing the hill's shoulder
and hurrying where the snow is heaping
   colder and colder.
Are you a dominion of them? they ask.
Most loyal and empirical, she says, in ice ironic,
and subject of the king's most gratuitous
   modesty, she says.
What do you do then?
Lumbering is what I do and whitening is what
   I wheat,
but I am full of hills and sadness;
snow is where I drift and wave my winds
and as silence my doom, distance is my dream.
Mine are the violet tones of the logs in rivers,
my tallness is the tallness of the pines and the
   grain elevators
tubular by the scarps of coal, at Quebec.
My caves are the caves of ice but also the
   holes of Cartier
where the poor squat, numb with winter,
and my poverty is their rags and the prairies'
   drought.

What is the matter then ...? they ask, and some
   are indifferent,
What is the matter then ...? they ask.

The matter is the sections and the railways,
   she replies,
and the shouting lost by the way and the
   train's whistle
like wild-life in the night.
The matter is the promise that was never
   taken, she replies,
above your heads the cool land giant air
and the future aching round you like an aura –
land of the last town and the distant point,
land of the lumber track losing itself
petering out in the birches, the half-wish
turning back in the wastes of winter or slums
and the skiers lovely and lonely upon the
   hills
rising in domes of silence. The matter is
the skiers, she replies, athletically lonely,
drowsed in their delight, who hunt and haunt
the centres of their silence and excitement:
finding the cirrus on the high sierras
sluice down the dangers of their dear content –

the matter is being lost in a dream of motion
as larks are in their lights, or bees and flies
glued on the humpbacked honey of
    summertime.

What should we do then, what should we do
    ...? they ask,
out of the factories rattling a new war,
on all the Sundays time has rocked to motion.
What should we do then ...? they ask,
    English and
French,
Ukranians, Poles, Finns, at drugstore corners
of streets extended to the ultimate seas
of their defended but ambiguous city.
Suffer no more the vowels of Canada
to speak of miraculous things with a cleft
    palate –
let the Canadian
with glaciers in his hair, straddle the continent,
in full possession of his earth and north,
dip down his foot and touch the New York
    lights
or stir the vegetable matter of the Bahamas
within the Carib gutter. Let
the skiers go with slogans of their eyes
to crowd a country whose near
    neighbourhood's
the iron kindness of the Russian coasts –
through deserts of snow or dreary wastes of
    city,
the empty or the emptily crowded North.

And see, she says, the salmon pointing home
from the vast sea, the petalled plethora
and unplumbed darkness of the sea, she says:
gliding along their silvery intuitions
like current on its cables, volt upon volt,
to flash at last, sparkling the mountain falls
of Restigouche – spawning a silver million.

The Editor:

Every person interested in Canadian Literature owes you a debt of gratitude for printing Mr Patrick Anderson's 'Poem on Canada.' Here is a serious and exuberant writer coming to grips with the fundamental task of the Canadian poet – the examination of our cultural traditions and the definition of our selfhood — and doing so with an intensity and an imaginative insight that is commensurate with the subject. The poem is on a large and generous scale, and full of specific felicities that dazzle and satisfy. The couplet on Riel, to choose but one of many instances, unites lyrical grace with epigrammatic wit in a manner that must serve as a school and an inspiration to the young Canadian writer.

But they say his body made a great wound in the air
    and God damn the English judge that put him there!

Where (if that is what we are looking for) can we find writing whose substance and texture are more certainly Canadian than here?

The *Canadian Forum* is performing an important service to the cause of a genuine and critical nationalism by making imaginative work of this calibre available to the general public.

When I recall that within the last two or three years you have published Birney's 'David,' Klein's 'Autobiography,' Avison's 'Break of Day,' Page's 'The Stenographers,' Gustafson's 'Epithalamium in Time of War,' Anderson's 'Summer's Joe,' and Pratt's 'The Truants,' I realize that the *Forum* is not only Canada's leading journal of political opinion but a true cultural force. Such penetrating reviews as Margaret Avison's on Livesay and the recent essays on Canadian poetry by Dorothy Livesay and Northrop Frye are an indication that our poets are not without the help of genuine criticism. We are all indebted to you.

Michigan State College   A.J.M. Smith
East Lansing, Mich.

CARLYLE KING

The CCF Sweeps Saskatchewan

One year ago I wrote in *The Canadian Forum* about the postponement of an over-due election in Saskatchewan: 'To-day the Patterson Government has not the remotest chance of getting the approval of the Saskatchewan electorate. Rather, it is generally recognized that an election now will result in a victory for the CCF. Hence the postponement of an election.'

The voting on June 15 has not only verified that judgment, but underlined it with tremendous emphasis. The Liberal Party has received its severest drubbing in the history of the province. Even in 1929 when a coalition of Conservatives, Progressives, and Independents formed a government, the Liberals had still the largest single group of members in the legislature. Now their large majority in the last legislature has been completely swept away, and six of eight cabinet ministers have been defeated. It is not even certain that W.J. Patterson, the premier, has been re-elected; at the moment of writing [June 17] he has a precarious margin of 30 votes. When the final and official results are in, it is unlikely that the Liberals will have more than five members in the next legislature, as against 47 CCF members. The legislative situation will be almost the exact opposite of that of ten years ago when the CCF, making its first appeal to the people of Saskatchewan, elected five members to face an overwhelming Liberal Government majority.

The most surprising feature of the election results was the phenomenal success of the CCF in the cities. Heretofore the strength of the CCF in Saskatchewan had been among the farmers; the cities had always been regarded as tough, if not hopeless, from the CCF point of view. This time the CCF captured every urban seat: the two-member constituencies of Regina, Saskatoon, and Moose Jaw, as well as the single-member constituencies of Prince Albert, Swift Current, Yorkton, Weyburn, and North Battleford. The change in Moose Jaw was most remarkable: here, where three years ago the CCF organization was moribund, the CCF candidates won with such thumping majorities that both Liberal and both Conservative candidates lost their election deposits! The urban worker in Saskatchewan, it is clear, has joined the farmer in regarding the CCF as the political party through which he can best express his desire for security, decent working conditions, and an improved standard of living.

At the same time the election has demonstrated that it is no longer possible, as it used to be, to frighten the Saskatchewan farmer with the bogey of socialism. The chief Liberal propagandists constantly harped on the evils of socialism. They defined the main issue as 'democracy vs totalitarian socialism,' and their campaign slogan was 'Keep Socialism out of Saskatchewan.' But the farmer remained unexcited. He looked under no beds. His flesh refused to creep. For example, in the constituency where I did most of my campaigning the CCF candidate, a pioneer farmer speaking to audiences mainly of farmers, never failed to call himself a socialist or to label his views socialistic. Yet he defeated the speaker of the legislature, a man who had represented his constituency for the last twenty-three years.

It would, however, be a mistake to assume that the electorate as a whole voted *for* socialism. The big vote was a protest vote, a vote against the policies of Liberal Governments in Regina and Ottawa. The Liberals have governed Saskatchewan for the past ten years to the increasing dissatisfaction of the people of the province. The demand for a change was everywhere. Many farmers remarked to me during the campaign, and said they were also expressing the views of their neighbours: 'We're fed up to the teeth with the Liberals. The CCF can't do any worse and may do a lot better. We're going to give them a chance to show their stuff.' A similar feeling was abroad in the cities.

The swing to the CCF was also a protest against the Mackenzie King Government. Federal issues were freely interjected into the campaign by candidates and speakers for all parties, and Ottawa came in for a great deal of adverse criticism. The chief complaints were about the conduct of the war, the manpower muddle, and the agricultural policies of the Hon. J.G. Gardiner.

For the third successive election the Conservatives have failed to return a single member to the provincial legislature. This spring they gave their provincial organization a complete house-cleaning, and found themselves a new provincial leader in Rupert Ramsay, an able and likeable member of the Agricultural Extension Department of the University of Saskatchewan. They put 40 candidates in the field, many of them experienced and well-known agriculturalists, and they played up Mr Bracken as the Farmer's Friend. The result? The Conservatives ran third in every constituency they contested; all but one of the 40 lost their election deposit; and their total popular vote was proportionately less than their total vote in 1938 (the year of the last provincial election). This is a pretty fair indication of the 'success' that awaits Mr Bracken in Western Canada. In Saskatchewan the Conservatives might as well close up shop.

This election also marks the disappearance of Social Credit from the Saskatchewan political scene. In the 1938 election the late Premier Aberhart of Alberta invaded the province in support of a score of his candidates. Two were elected and SC achieved a total popular vote of 70,000. This time neither of the two sitting SC members were candidates for re-election, nor did their constituencies have SC candidates. A lone Social Crediter, in Moose Jaw, although supported by Premier Manning of Alberta, obtained only 237 votes. Four other 'funny money' advocates running as Independents polled less than 200 votes each.

Nor were the Communists (alias Labour Progressive) a factor. They had three candidates, all of whom lost their election deposits and together polled less than 2,000 votes. Significantly, this includes a candidate in Meadow Lake, the core of the Federal Riding represented by Mrs Dorise Nielsen, MP.

The occupational distribution of the members of the first CCF legislative majority may be of interest. The farmers make up by far the largest group: 27 in all, including a farmer's wife. There are also seven school teachers, six railway men, two small-town merchants, one lawyer, and one clergyman.

P.K. PAGE
Draughtsman

He wears his eyes a tattered blue on charts,
watches from square to careful square, the slow
and formless fading of his art.
'For thirty years or more,' he says and stares
far-sightedly at what is there before his nose.

'Space held about by lines,' he says, 'by thin
accurate lines my hand draws on the cloth,
held in and chequered by me all these years –
made like a building almost – lines like steel,
girders against the weight and wind, but cramped.
Space held too tight and close,' he says and squints
near-sightedly at what is dim and far.

Fear sits on his draughting board. His hands
shake as he rules those old straight lines; his prints
don't come so clean now from the quick machine.
Approached, he parries with the laugh he hates
and feels the bottle's beautiful liquid shape
cool in the memory of his youthful palms.

While all the time his fading vision shifts
and far is hot and near, and near so far.

EDITORIAL
National Unity

Mr King's sudden abandonment of his stand against conscription saved us from a general election on the most inflammatory of all possible issues. Whatever may be thought of some of his actions during the critical period of the recent session of Parliament, most Canadians should be thankful to him for that achievement. The rug-chewers of the Toronto *Globe and Mail* and the fanatics across the country who were determined to oust him from office by any means have been defeated, and even if his motives were no higher than to keep these people out of office he deserves our gratitude. Of course the question of reinforcements for our forces overseas may not have been finally settled. If the war continues through the spring and summer with heavy Canadian casualties, we shall find that we have committed ourselves to keeping up a larger armed force than is possible without drastic overhauling of our civilian manpower policy. But perhaps Mr King's customary good luck will save him from this crisis.

The crisis brings an era in Canadian politics to an end. Since Laurier came into office in 1896 the French Canadians have formed an almost solid bloc in support of the Liberal party. In the voting in the recent session of Parliament Mr King held his French ministers except one, and kept a large part of the Quebec membership loyal to him. But everyone knows that public opinion in French Quebec is solid against conscription. The situation has been exactly like that which faced Macdonald in the Riel crisis of 1885-6.

Macdonald had at that time to choose between holding on to his English-speaking followers by allowing Riel to hang or appeasing his French-speaking followers by commuting the sentence; and, just as Mr King has done today, he decided in favor of the English. Like Mr King he headed a party of which the largest contingent came from French Canada. There was a tremendous upheaval in Quebec over the Riel issue, but Macdonald in the critical division held on to his French ministers and to most of the French private members. Chapleau's famous speech in defense of the government's policy was very much like that of Mr St Laurent today. And poor half-insane Riel became a symbol to the fanatics on both sides of the determination of each race not to be dominated by the other, just as the conscription issue has become in our own day. In the provincial politics of Quebec the Conservative government was upset by a nationalist movement under Mercier, just as the Liberal government of today has been upset by another nationalist movement under Duplessis. But in the federal sphere, in the general election of 1887, Macdonald recovered some of his French following as the excitement died down, just as Mr King may recover some of his in the election during this coming year. Yet it is plain to see now that 1885 marked the beginning of the end of the long collaboration of the two races within the Liberal-Conservative party.

The two main national groups in Canada have never co-operated with each other wholeheartedly. At best they reach a temporary form of collaboration which carries them along without too much friction for a decade or a generation. At worst they drift into a crisis such as we have been experiencing, in which the wild men on each side talk of breaking up our national union altogether. André Siegfried described our relationship as 'a *modus vivendi* without cordiality,' and this is what it is likely to remain. But geography has made it impossible for us to separate, and so wise Canadians will devote themselves to considering what the terms of the necessary *modus vivendi* are to be.

One peculiar feature in our history is the phenomenon of a bi-racial political party which seems to be necessary to enable the two national groups to work together successfully in the field of government. The first of these parties was the Reform coalition of Baldwin and Lafontaine which won responsible government in the 1840s and showed the impossibility of Lord Durham's conception of governing Canada through one racial group alone and of anglicizing the other group. The second was the Liberal-Conservative party, constructed by Macdonald and Cartier in 1854, which dominated Canadian politics for a generation. The third was Laurier's Liberal party. The opposition to these successive governmental parties has usually been ineffective because it has been unable to make any impression upon the French part of our population. It is worth noting that Laurier captured the support of his fellow French Canadians from the disintegrating Liberal-Conservative party in 1896 in spite of the fact that he had all of his church, lower clergy as well as bishops, against him on the Manitoba school question. Laurier's bi-racial governmental party has continued into our own generation under Mr King.

Apparently it is only through this technique of a bi-racial party embodying in itself the willingness of the two races to work together for a decade or a generation that the deep cleavages in our Canadian community can be overcome. Only when French and English are bound together in the loyalty of a common political party, held to one another by the pull of party machinery and party patronage, can they overcome the opposite attractions of national and religious prejudices and fanaticism.

What will be the political party which achieves this racial *modus vivendi* in the next phase of our national history? And who will be its leader? Or rather, who will be its joint leaders? For these successful national parties have as a rule been held together by two leaders, one an English Canadian and one a French Canadian – Baldwin and Lafontaine, Macdonald and Cartier, King and Lapointe. It was Laurier's chief source of weakness that, after Blake retired from Canadian public life, he never found another English-speaking colleague to whom he could give his complete confidence. Our two races need not only a common party but this additional feature of joint leadership, unique in the annals of British cabinet government. The two leaders must be intellectually and temperamentally akin so that they remain friends through thick and thin, or else their party will not survive the strain which is put upon party unity by the inherent sectionalism of our Canadian life.

Of course everyone who knows anything about Canadian history, everyone who has read anything beyond the Toronto Tory papers, knows that the cleavage between the two races which is such a problem to us just now does not date from Mr King's day and is not due to his leadership since 1921 as Tory demagogues in Ontario would have it.

Confederation itself in 1867 was an effort to break a deadlock between Upper and Lower Canada which had plagued Canadian politics for a dozen years previously. It was thought that by letting each racial group manage its own local affairs under a federal constitution, and control its own cultural institutions, while they co-operated in the building up of a continental nation, the age-old problem of English-French relations would at last be solved. But Confederation was no sooner achieved than Ontario and Quebec plunged into a new imperialist struggle for the domination of the Canadian West. This broke out with the Red River rebellion of 1869-70 and continued through the rebellion of 1885 (which led to the hanging of Riel), it continued also into the Manitoba schools crisis of the 1890s, and it was still going on when Laurier stirred up a storm in 1905 over the separate schools of the new provinces of Saskatchewan and Alberta. Yet it was noteworthy that popular passions gradually abated during this period, and the last storm in 1905 was a comparatively minor one.

Unfortunately by the time that we seemed to be settling down to deal with our domestic differences in a reasonably calm spirit, a new issue from outside was injected into Canadian politics which has led to even bitterer differences between English and French than the old domestic issues. This has been, of course, the question of Canadian participation in overseas British wars. In 1885 Macdonald refused to send a Canadian contingent to the Soudan expedition 'to get Gladstone and Co. out of the hole they have plunged themselves into by their own imbecility.' But in 1899 Laurier felt himself compelled by pressure from his English-Canadian followers to send a contingent to the Boer war, and the cleavage which began then has been deepened by the two world wars of our own time.

French Canadians refuse to believe that the enthusiasm displayed by English Canadians for plunging into these wars is due to any superior understanding by us English Canadians of world conditions. And they put it down – as does every observer outside Canada – to our inherited English colonial loyalty. Today we seem as far as ever from agreeing with one another on the responsibilities and implications of Canadian nationality. In peace-time there are plenty of English Canadians who agree with the French Canadians, but when war breaks out they are swept by the emotions of group solidarity, and the old racial division re-emerges. In this recent conscription crisis a French-Canadian leader like Mr St Laurent could distinguish himself by appealing to his racial group to make concessions to the other group, but no English-Canadian leader appeared to make any similar appeal to his own group. To get over this deep difference about foreign policy we seem to depend on a world which is fundamentally at peace, a factor in determining our destiny which we ourselves cannot control.

It is worth noting that the policy to which both Macdonald and Laurier had recourse when they tried to calm the storms aroused over English-French quarrels was that of taking our minds off racial and religious differences and directing them towards economic development. Macdonald's transcontinental railway-building and his NP were efforts to find projects on which leaders and members of the two racial groups could work together. Laurier's wheat boom almost made them forget their rival forms of civilization for a moment, for in the great expansion of the early 1900s there were opportunities for both English and French Canadians, and there was no time for them to sit and brood over their historic grievances. In our own day, since the last war, we have failed to find a national policy to take the place of the economic expansionism of Macdonald and Laurier. The prosperity of the 1920s was very unevenly distributed, and the depression of the 1930s gave a new outlet to racial bitterness. In the new industrial revolution of our age Quebec finds her natural resources appropriated by English-speaking capitalists, and it is only too easy for nationalist demagogues to convince their people that the trouble lies with the English rather than with capitalism. When this war is over we shall have to set to work again to find a national economic policy suited to the new social needs of the twentieth century in which English and French Canadians, or a large proportion of them, can alike find opportunities. This will not produce national unity but it will restore a reasonable degree of national health by taking our minds off our national disunity.

EDITORIAL

The Boys Come Back

They're coming home – at last. A few thousands at a time, Canada's fighting men are returning. Spewed from former luxury liners at an erstwhile Eastern Canadian Port, they board the waiting trains and are whisked across the country to relatives and friends they have not seen for two, three, or more years.

Some of them travel on stretchers. Some are on crutches, or walk with a limp. Many carry hidden scars, physical or psychological, such as battle, prison camp, or long miserable months of boredom leave upon a man. But they are home!

These are the lucky ones. Thousands are still exiled, awaiting their share of scarce shipping space. And many who once went away smiling will never return. Not as many as last time; for this was a 'mechanized' war. Only 37,964 this time, whereas before, with far fewer in action, there were 62,817. That does little to soften the ache for those who have lost son, brother, husband, or friend. These have only their memories, their pride, and the slow balm of time – and the resolve, shared by thousands more lucky, that these sacrifices shall not be barren of fruit in the Canada for which their loved ones died.

Spotting the returned men on the street by some overseas insignia, one is apt to be struck at first by their similarity to the others in uniform who have not been away. A deeper tan, perhaps; a looser, jauntier walk; a more ruminative look about the eyes; but otherwise just another soldier, airman, or sailor on leave. Strange, because as V-E Day approached, we were bombarded by books, magazine articles, and broadcasts telling us about the veteran's return, and how changed he would be. War, we were told, would have so altered him that the utmost forbearance and delicacy would be needed to ease his reinstatement in civilian life. He was pictured as a bit of a problem child, who must be given time and tactful assistance in achieving readjustment.

There was, of course, a grain of truth in this. Both we and the men who have been away from home so long are older, and time itself changes. Also, in some cases, the impact of war, physical or mental, does create individual problems of social reaccommodation. All that could usefully be said on this subject was admirably stated in a series of broadcasts by the CBC during the winter of 1944-5, and now published in digest form (*The Soldier's Return:* CBC Publications Branch, Toronto; pp. 48; 25c.). All relatives and employers of returned men would do well to read these talks by leading psychologists, social workers, and personnel officers. Perhaps their chief merit lay in the emphasis placed on the fact that the average returned man is a normal individual eager to resume pursuits which war has interrupted, and quite competent to do so without special coddling if we provide the physical means.

What are the impressions of the average returned man as he looks about him, in the Canada to which he has come back, for signs that these means have been provided?

He is reasonably satisfied with his rehabilitation grants, much more 'generous' than his father received after the last war. Fresh from experience with the results of inflation abroad, he is favourably struck by the way wartime controls have kept down the cost of living in Canada. Compared with overseas countries, ravaged by war, consumer goods are amazingly plentiful. We appear, indeed, to be living in the lap of luxury.

He is apt to be a little taken aback by the want of co-operation in civilian life, a familiar fact which he had perhaps forgotten about during the months of team-play and social solidarity in his fighting unit. The spectacle of people elbowing their way into queues, crowding each other aside in the scramble for elevators, streetcars, and buses, ignoring traffic-lights at intersections, and behaving generally in a manner which would bring opprobrium and punishment, perhaps death, on active service, is a trifle disconcerting. He is used, of course, to chiselling by shopkeepers; some of his less restrained comrades have tangibly expressed their feelings about this good old civilian custom in Halifax and Aldershot. But he is a bit puzzled by the constant grousing among the home folks over the eminently reasonable controls, the shortages of gasoline, fuel, and certain foods, and by the disposition of motorists to flout law and prudence by travelling at fifty or sixty miles an hour, quite aware that they are wasting gas and rubber which it is still necessary to conserve, without visible advantage to themselves. These things strike him as rather grotesque, after the deprivation he has seen in England and Europe and the spirit of co-operation the war has taught people there.

But what he is most concerned about, of course, is – first of all – a job. Will there be one for him, and how soon? Not just a makeshift job, trumped up to 'create employment,' but a real place in the productive life of his country, with reasonable assurance of stability. He has heard about the government inviting private industry to get busy and provide jobs, with the promise that if they find it too difficult the government will take a hand. But he has seen no concrete plans, no assurances, He reads about employers being short of help; but he also reads about hundreds of workers being laid off. He wishes they would hurry up with these 'reconversion' plans everyone refers to so vaguely without explaining how they're coming along. He is a little worried, in short, about how many jobs there arc going to be, and how soon.

His almost equally pressing, or even more pressing, concern is about a place to live. His wife may have been living with her parents;

there may be no room for both of them with the in-laws, especially if they have a child or children. Or he may, reasonably enough, contemplate a long-postponed marriage, or may have married overseas and brought his wife back with him. In any case, he wants, and is (he thinks) entitled to a home of his own.

What does he find? That there has been a succession of housing 'crises' in Canada ever since he left. Shifts of population as wartime industries sprang up or expanded have taxed living space in many communities. And little has been done, except over-crowding, to meet these conditions. His own community is probably unable to house decently its present population, much less provide a house for him. He hears the government has organized something called Wartime Housing Limited, which has built 1,200 veterans' homes for rental, and has 'approved' 2,700 more; that the Veterans Land Administration has under construction 3,000 small suburban houses, mostly for owner occupation or somewhat higher rental; that licenses have been granted private builders for 23,000 more – if they can get the materials. This for all Canada! The government's 'target' or 'aim' is said to be 50,000 new dwellings within the first full year after VE Day. But as a cold fact, there are virtually no low-rental houses going up, much less immediately available. So he has read (or could have read a couple of weeks ago in the *Financial Post*).

And while all this is due partly to scarcity of materials and labor, the main 'bottleneck' (says the *Financial Post*) has been money. The government, it seems, does not want to go into publicly owned housing; it believes in Private Enterprise. Mr Ilsley has been telling the insurance company heads (according to the *Post*) that either they put up the money and get the houses under way, or the government will go into the housing business. 'We've got to have those cheap houses, and we've got to have them now,' he is reported to have told them. 'The government doesn't want to build them – we believe in private enterprise and we want it to retain control of this great industry. But if you don't act, and act quickly, we'll have to act instead. We'll use Wartime Housing, and put up those dwellings, even if it socializes the whole business.'

Horrible thought! The insurance lads are being difficult, at this writing; but who can doubt what their answer will be?

The uncomfortable fact is, however, that even if the insurance companies graciously (or ungraciously) accede to the government's 'request,' the plans will not 'crystallize' until April or May of next year. And those representatives and ornaments of our country's foremost Public Enterprise – the army, the navy, and the air force – will meanwhile have to kick their heels under any old kind of roof (if, indeed, that) while Private Enterprise rolls slowly and reluctantly into action. Meantime, the authorities are planning to utilize government buildings – if furniture can be found – to house veterans' families *en masse*. There are many communities, however, where there are no government buildings.

What the veteran may well be asking himself is: Why was so little done about all this before I got back to Canada? Why weren't materials and labour released, and housebuilding got under way, a year or two years ago, so I could have been sure of a roof awaiting me when I arrived home after long weary years of war? After all, Canada has no 'blitz,' no V-bombs, no incendiaries, no shelling from German guns. She has had for three or four years thousands in the home army qualified to make bricks, fell trees, mix concrete, make bathtubs. Materials could have been released without in the least crippling the war effort. And if it was all a question of money, what about all the money my pals and I put into Victory Bonds? Surely a little of this could have been spared without holding up any of the things needed at the front. As a matter of fact, house-building has been going on – for the wealthy home-fronter. Why not for me?

Cynics might point to the length of time it has taken to get the much-needed hospital building at Sunnybrook Park, Toronto, beyond the foundation-stone stage. That was a government undertaking.

But what good is a rehabilitation grant, or a training credit, if you have no job to go to? What good is a job, indeed, if you have no decent place to live? And what good is your home-purchase allowance, if there are no houses on the market?

And what good is democracy, for which one has been fighting, if it can't provide the things its citizen-soldiers need, even when the country concerned is far removed from the devastation of war, and has had four years to plan for things like reconversion and housing, and at least a year to put the plans into effect?

So when you see a man in uniform bearing on his person the insignia of overseas service, and note that thoughtful, rather puzzled look in his eyes, you may be sure that these are some of the things he is pondering, now he is back in a homeland whose general air of prosperity

F.R. SCOTT
Labour Learns the Truth

Early in April the two Labour Congresses presented their annual list of legislative demands to the Liberal Government at Ottawa. This was only ten months after a federal election during which the Liberal Party, stealing a CCF slogan, was asking voters to 'Help Us Build a New Social Order,' and was promising full employment and various forms of social security along the lines now being requested by the spokesmen of labour. Since a large part of the labour vote, responding to the election appeal, had obviously supported Mr King, it would be an occasion on which some show of governmental gratitude, if not of actual concern for the welfare of labour, might have been expected.

What happened was very different. On April 4 the press reported that Mr Ilsley administered a sharp rebuke to the Trades and Labor Congress for its excessive requests – a rebuke all the more unkind as this body had aided the Liberals by refusing to follow the example of the Canadian Congress of Labor in endorsing the CCF. He used toward the delegates the banker's language of the 1930s. Some of the recommendations, he said, would involve 'great governmental expenditures,' and 'we must prove capable of balancing our budgets during the years of peace,' though in some years this might not be possible. The plea for reduced taxation throughout the country had to be met, he pointed out. Hence there was nothing in the argument that we could use the wartime spending scale as a basis for rebuilding the peace. 'Continued deficits would destroy the value of the bonds which you hold and the wages which you earn.' (Just how it is that Canada has had 'continued deficits' since 1930 and still is not bankrupt was not explained.) The general impression left by his lecture was one of 'no money,' 'sound finance,' and retrenchment. Commenting on the episode *The Montreal Star* gleefully rubbed its multi-millionaire hands and exclaimed that this 'constitutes a completely adequate reason why all recommendations for reckless expenditures over and above Canada's already colossal commitments for social security schemes should be set aside as outside the range of practical politics.'

This disposed of the Trades and Labor Congress. The following day, by a coincidence which cannot have been accidental, Mr King himself issued a warning, in his most moralizing manner, to Mr Mosher and the Canadian Congress of Labour. The fault of the latter seemed to be not in asking too much, but in failing to show that deference which is expected of workingmen when addressing their superiors. The CCL had dared to say that the government had 'made no plans to permit of an orderly transition from war to peace,' and had 'let economic conditions drift from bad to worse until another depression had occurred.' Mr Conroy even went so far as to refer to the promised 'new social order.' This realistic language was altogether too strong for Mr King's make-believe world. It seemed to show a lack of faith in Liberal promises. Moreover it had not the tone that is going to be expected of labour in the postwar years. Not demands and criticism, but humble requests, will apparently be in order. 'If that is what you have to say to me, then I have nothing further to say to you,' said Mr King, pointing to Mr Mosher. 'Here is where you and I part company.' The Congress submission, he added, should be called the 'complaints' of the CCL rather than representations. 'If you come to this government again, and I am still the head of it, I hope you will consider what I have to say about the method of representation.'

So Schoolmaster King calls the little boys to order, and Monitor Ilsley says times are hard and there won't be any more pocket money. Psychologically the stage is being set for a return to the scarcity economy which is daily being revealed as the inevitable outcome of the Liberal Party's 'free enterprise' policy. Labour is now being 'softened up' for the grimmer days ahead. On the industrial front take home pay is being reduced by shorter hours, the swollen ranks of the unemployed are threatening trade union strength, and even the ancient strike-breaking weapon of the labour injunction is being used, as during the National Breweries case in Montreal. The government, expressing in parliament the wishes of big business, is now openly talking the language of big business, and revealing its fundamentally anti-labour position. Decent Liberals may dislike it, but there is nothing they can do about it while they stay with the party and its policy.

Behind this astonishingly sudden and bold change of tone on the part of the government toward the spokesmen for half a million Canadian trade-unionists, lies a basic fact that has not existed since 1939. The war is now over. Moreover, North America has been saved for capitalism. Private profit is again undisputed king. High wages, social security, and full employment, which labour seeks, are not necessary for high profits; indeed they would directly interfere with such profits. So the time for flattery of labour has passed. Let the working class get back where it belongs. The conflict between monopoly capitalism and the common man– who speaks of the 'common man' at Ottawa now? – stands revealed in all its nakedness. Mr King himself helps to take down the pasteboard facade.

In one respect, it must be admitted, the CCL criticism of the government was wrong. It cannot be said that Mr King, Mr Howe, Mr Ilsley & Co. have not a very carefully thought-out plan for the transition from war to peace. Their plan was, first and foremost, to prevent the CCF from gaining power and starting Canada along the road to an economy planned for abundance and social security. Their plan was to make sure that the second World War did not destroy the system of 'private enterprise' which so handsomely rewards the friends of the Liberal Party. As Canadians come to analyze more closely than they have yet done the manner in which Canada's economic war effort was conducted, they will realize how skillfully the plan was carried out from the very first day of the war. Almost the first move was to repeal the 5% limit on profits which Parliament had imposed in 1939. It cannot be too often repeated, because the same men control Canada today, that Canadian capitalists refused to accept 5% as a sufficient inducement to fight Nazism in 1939. They went on strike for big money then, as they are on strike for big profits now, and they got it. What they seemed to be losing in Excess Profits Tax they took back in special depreciations. The bigger the corporation, the bigger the gains. Monopoly has been strengthened, not weakened, by the war. Now War Assets Corporation is making sure that what the people of Canada built and bought with their sweat and savings will pass, if it has any value, into the hands of the preferred list of applicants. Some Canadian indebtedness abroad has been liquidated, but all our gifts to Britain did not buy back the CPR. The Liberal Party railroaded through a whitewash report on the Aluminum deal, though an American court has since found the company guilty of violating American law, and the potential 2,000,000 horse-power at Shipshaw, built by Canadians and paid for by public money, lies at the disposal of a few Pittsburgh financiers. Canada's economic war effort was large, but to save a vicious economic system the public has had to pay and is still paying a huge and unnecessary price.

The Liberals have a plan also for housing, so desperately needed by Canadian workers. This plan is designed to make sure that insurance companies still have a profitable outlet for their enormous investments and that private enterprise is not interfered with. The supplying of houses is secondary. Hence low cost housing is just not going to get built at all, though it is the most needed. Hence interest rates on housing loans must be kept high. Hence insurance companies must actually be encouraged to become builders of houses. Not even the most crackpot professor of economics in his wildest moments could have evolved a more fantastic housing plan than that to which we are committed in order to save private enterprise. But it is our national plan.

Yes, the Liberal Government has a plan, and it is now becoming plain even to people who voted Liberal. The CCF tried to warn that it was coming, but it had not the resources, nor the Canadian electorate the experience, to clear away the confusion deliberately spread by Trestrail, Gladstone Murray, and other well-paid salesmen for the big interests. The Liberal party shrewdly played up the war effort (except the profits being made) as though it were the personal achievement of Mr King, and flooded the country with election leaflets which almost seemed to come from the CCF presses. It had the backing of the LPP, always more afraid of democratic socialism than of capitalism. since the latter will fail and the former will not. Now the whole scheme is becoming clear, and the Canadian public is going to pay the cost in having to go without the things it was promised. As usual, Canadian Labour is in the front line, and gets the first rude shock. Mr King hopes labour will accept his plan for Canada quietly, and not raise any fuss or bother when it finds peace does not mean what he told them it would mean.

In one other respect too the demands of the Labour Congresses were perhaps not rightly phrased. They did ask for very expensive social services, and at the same time for a lowering of taxation. Under capitalism there is a definite limit to that procedure. Capitalism does not exist to provide social security. It exists to provide profits, and if profits are taxed too heavily, capitalists will go on strike and not produce, 'My problem is,' said Mr Ilsley quite correctly, 'how to increase expenditures enormously and at the same time to reduce taxation.' He said he did not know how to do this. This means Mr Ilsley cannot solve his own problem. Nor can any free enterprise finance minister. Labour must realize that, and not ask for the impossible. But a socialist finance minister would have other sources of revenue not available to Mr Ilsley. He would have the profits from monopoly enterprises which would be brought under public ownership. He would know how to use the new technique of deficit financing which Mr Ilsley once seemed to believe in. He would also have the higher yield of taxation resulting from the full employment which Mr Ilsley's policy can never attain, and which national planning could. Sweden, for example, gets large profits from its tobacco monopoly which go to old age pensions. Our tobacco profits, also large, go to private shareholders and only a fraction comes back in income tax. The huge private profits made in Canada out of what are essentially public enterprises should be appropriated, through federal and provincial ownership, to the national welfare. Let labour, and other Canadians who would like more social security, ponder these facts. In time they will want to replace Mr Ilsley, who cannot solve his problem, with a finance minister backed by a government who can.

A.M. KLEIN

Political Meeting

On the school platform, draping the folding
    seats,
they wait the chairman's praise and glass of
    water.
Upon the wall the agonized Y initials their faith.

Here all are laic; the skirted brothers have
    gone.
Still, their equivocal absence is felt, like a
    breeze
that gives curtains the sounds of surplices.

The hall is yellow with light, and jocular;
suddenly someone lets loose upon the air
the ritual bird which the crowd in snares of
    singing
catches and plucks, throat, wings, and little
    limbs.
Fall the feathers of sound, like *alouette's*.
The chairman, now, is charming, full of asides
    and wit,

building his orators, and chipping off
the heckling gargoyles popping in the hall.
(Outside, in the dark, the street is body-tall,

flowered with faces, intent on the scarecrow
    thing
that shouts to thousands the echoing
of their own wishes.) The Orator has risen!

Worshipped and loved, their favourite visitor,
a country uncle with sunflower seeds in his
    pockets,
full of wonderful moods, tricks, imitative talk,

he is their idol: like themselves, not handsome,
not snobbish, not of the Grande Allee! *Un
    homme!*
Intimate, informal, he makes bear's compliments
to the ladies, is gallant, and grins;
goes for the balloon, his opposition, with pins;
jokes also on himself, speaks of himself

in the third person, slings slang, and winks
    with folklore,
and knows that he has them, kith and kin.
Calmly, therefore, he begins to speak of war,

praises the virtue of being Canadien,
of being at peace, of faith, of family,
and suddenly his other voice: *Where are your
    sons?*

He is tearful, choking tears; but not he
would blame the clever English; in their place
he'd do the same; maybe.

Where *are* your sons?
                          The whole street wears
    one face,
grave, wordless, grim, and in the darkness rises
the body-odour of race.

A.M. KLEIN
The White Old Lady

The panic jangles repeated themselves every year.
The neighbours, clutching the black cup, whispered *Police!*
The Côte des Neiges place again! Lights come on, lights go off!
She is here!

And every evening the sergeant, wearily:
  Police.
And heard: She is standing at all of the
  windows at once.
She is pulling down white blinds, but we see
  her shadow.
Monstrosities

go on in that house. The sergeant takes
  evidence.
Report: Someone anaemic is going whitely
  mad.
Ditto: That dwelling is a smuggling place for
  lepers,
  A cache for diamonds.

A smoke-filled den. Seek there your missing
  and dead —
muffled by linens, cased in the white plaster
  wall.
Visitors, we know, have come unseen, and
  there's vice
  that can't be said.

But every time the police came, stepped into
  the hall,
there was only a white old lady, frail, like
  powder,
with a pleasant smile, living alone, and no one
  else at all.

F.R. SCOTT
Alignment of Parties

Canada now has five parties operating in the federal field: Liberals, Conservatives, CCF, Social Credit and LPP-Communist. The two largest parties are the same two traditional loosely-knit conglomerations that have shared the government between themselves ever since Confederation. Their antiquity is rapidly reaching the point of obsolescence, and whatever historic validity may have attached to their earlier differences, nobody now can tell the one from the other on point of principle. Some may think that the problems posed in Canada by the war were handled with more finesse by Mr King than they would have been by whoever was Tory leader in 1939 (I forget), but the war is over and we face changed conditions and new opportunities. Today the Liberals and Conservatives represent a single body, and a reactionary body, of social and economic policy.

It would be fatal to Canadian capitalism, however, if the public ever became fully aware of the fact. They have become aware of it in two Canadian provinces, Manitoba, and British Columbia, and there we have coalition governments. The CCF is the official opposition. The coalition in Manitoba, be it noted, includes the Social Credit members also, since in their basic adherence to 'free enterprise' they too belong in the same camp. In eastern Canada, however, where the national policy is decided, the old political attitudes are better preserved, or at least better controlled from the top by the power of money and publicity. So the old sham battle is maintained. The public is led to believe that it really matters greatly whether one or the other of the two old parties governs. Whereas what really matters is whether this country clings to 'free enterprise' until another economic calamity overwhelms it, suffering meanwhile all the frustrations and injustices that capitalism imposes, or whether it faces the facts of modern life and begins the march toward a new social and economic order based on national planning and social ownership. And when it starts on the new road, it matters enormously whether Canada aims at a democratic socialism or a totalitarian socialism. Here are real and practical issues, part of the air we breathe daily, round which parties should and no doubt will be aligned. No other distinctions are worth bothering about.

We are far from any such party honesty at the present time. The Tories have been deliberately spreading a story that the CCF and the Liberals were about to amalgamate. This is the kind of 'tactic' the old parties use as a substitute for an honest presentation of views. It was calculated to embarrass Mr King by pinning the socialist label on him, and to embarrass the CCF by sowing doubt among its members as to the sincerity of its leaders. It was of a piece with the other Tory statement that the Liberals are already socialists. Mr J.M. Macdonnell, who ought to know better, has been reported as saying that the question is not whether Canada is going into socialism, but how we can 'climb out of it.' If it is a duty in a democracy for political parties to clarify issues for the public, then the Tories have lamentably failed in their duty. Canada is nowhere near socialism. For a second time after a great world war, this country has been handed over to the unimpeded exploitation of capitalist corporations. For a second time a magnificent war effort has been betrayed in order that private interests might be reinstated. After World War I the Tories went 'back to normalcy'; after World War II the Liberals went back to 'free enterprise.' In historic perspective, there is not a fraction of difference between them.

Mr King has, as usual, been much more shrewd than the Tories. He let this idea of amalgamation with the CCF drift round a long time before denying it. Maybe he even thought he might swallow the CCF up as he did the Progressives after 1921. It was to his advantage to appear as much unlike the Tories as possible, so as to try to escape the unescapable fact that the Liberals are, after all, just 'one of the two old parties.' He recognizes, which the Tories don't, that the world has moved and is moving to the left, and that he cannot hope to keep power unless he attracts a lot of left-of-centre votes. He knows that Canada shares the dubious position, along with South Africa and Ireland, of being the reactionary and slow-moving part of the British Commonwealth, while Britain herself, Australia, and New Zealand have broken with the old parties and turned to democratic socialism. He understands quite well that the pattern set in these countries is likely to be followed here as the CCF advances, and that two old parties will become one old party. His political function is to postpone that event as long as possible. Fundamentally a Tory in that he believes in free enterprise, he must dabble in social legislation and 'Liberalism' in order that the old two-party game can be played a little longer. In this he is capitalism's best defender, and Canada's most misleading leader in this post-war world.

Fortunately the political fog has been cleared a little by some recent statements. The CCF has time and again made it plain that it will not ally itself with the Liberals or any other non-socialist party, but the CCF does not command enough publicity to correct quickly the planned campaigns of misinformation in our kept press. Mr Coldwell, however, made his position so abundantly clear at the opening of Woodsworth House, Ottawa, on Jan. 25, and it was so obvious that the anti-government attack of the CCF would appear in Parliament, that Mr King was obliged to speak out. At the banquet given by the National Liberal Federation – that amorphous body of self-appointed notables occasionally summoned to give the appearance of democracy to the Liberal party machine – Mr King tried to distinguish his party from both Tories and CCF. Of the Tories he said:

The old Tory party, I say, has always been watching special interests rather than the general interest. Study the history of the Conservative party and you will find that it is a party that has a great concern for privilege, a great concern for possession, a great concern for power and for those various objectives that mean special privileges for the few but not necessarily subordinating those special privileges to the good of the many. There is not much trouble in distinguishing between the two old parties.

Not much trouble? Some, obviously, even for Mr King. And a good deal more for the humble citizen, for when the Liberal leader went on to denounce the CCF he spoke like any old Tory:

As you study Socialism you will find that more and more it aims, as its leaders will tell you, at socializing industry, production, distribution and the like with the view to substituting political masters for business masters in the great industries and in the economy of the country.

So Liberalism will keep us under our business masters. Later he said:

Begin to regiment trade and manufacture and industry and what results? If industry is to hold its own in world competition, the success of Canada in the future will lie largely in what we can do in enabling our industrialists to compete.

This is good, capitalistic economics. It is not Canada that competes, but 'our industrialists.' They must be helped. Shall it be subsidies paid out of taxes, as for Dosco? Shall it be giving them publicly-built war plants for a song, as with War Assets Corporation? Or shall it be the simple method of holding down wages? Clearly we must not interfere with our business masters or we shall be sunk. Now is it clear how the Liberals differ from the Tories? No wonder Mr Hilton, president of Steel Company of Canada, recently admitted he gave campaign funds to both the two old parties. These distinctions are too fine for him.

To do Mr King justice he made another attempt at a distinction. He went on:

The Tories say let us do away with controls; let us have no more control by the state. The CCF *say they want controls maintained and extended. ... The Liberal party says that the general good be served instead of the good of any particular group or interest.*

This seems to be getting at something, a sort of vague feeling of goodwill to all. But since it presupposes a free enterprise system, with the state aiding 'our industrialists' to compete, it means just nothing that we did not have in the 1930s. And just how little control the Liberals believe in can be seen from the record. Decontrol is the order of the day. So much so that Mr King removed the milk subsidy against the expressed will of parliament. Every day old controls are coming off and prices are still rising. The magnificent state-owned war plants have been almost completely liquidated by war assets, and now are safely in the hands of our masters of monopoly. Federal labour control is ending, and no lead is given toward a national labour code, long overdue. The co-operative movement is now subject to new Liberal taxation – no doubt to help our industrialists compete! Old-age pensions remain a blot on our social standards, and health insurance disappears from sight. The housing situation is a crying shame. This country is setting back the hands of progress, and the Liberal party, being in power, is responsible. Canada's new deal has ended – if it ever began – and our Republicans are in office.

The political alignment is clear. The Tories, Liberals, and Social Crediters support private enterprise and defend a status quo which cannot last. There is no fundamental difference between these splinter groups. The LPP, tied by long strings to Moscow, aims at a totalitarian system that no sane man wants. The CCF intends to start Canada, as it has started Saskatchewan, along the road to economic plenty and security, by combining the best in our traditions of personal liberty and democracy with the modern techniques of national planning and social ownership. Only this road can preserve the spiritual values of the western world in this industrial and atomic age.

GRACE MACINNIS

Immigration? On What Basis?

Once again the question of immigration has come to the fore. Canada needs immigrants, we are told. When we ask why, we are given the same answers that have done duty since the beginning of the century: to people the empty spaces of this half-continent, to replace the farm population that has drifted to the cities, to spread the taxes and increase prosperity. Some humanitarians add that we should take our share of the displaced people of Europe.

Before committing ourselves, we should consider the matter carefully. First, we should make a definite separation in our thinking between the question of immigration and the question of refugees. Immigration, at this stage of world development, is considered from the standpoint of our own country and the welfare of its people. If immigrants are likely to be good for Canada we let them in; if they will have a bad effect, we shut the door. But the refugee issue must be considered from the standpoint of our responsibility as world citizens, regardless of what effect the admission of displaced persons will have on the life of Canada.

Of course the number admitted should be related to the absorptive capacity of the receiving country. It has been suggested that a fair yardstick would be the contribution made by each country to the upkeep of the United Nations, as this amount is based on the productive wealth of each member nation. Measured by any yardstick, Canada's record in the matter of refugees is very poor. Several of the other Dominions, hard-pressed Britain, and some South-American countries have put us to shame. Without further delay we should open our doors to a fair share of the world's refugees.

Now how about immigration? If we are frank, we shall admit at once that our past ideas of what would be good for Canada were exceedingly narrow and selfish, and consequently exceedingly short-sighted. We brought in people to do the dirty, hard work of the country, people driven from their own countries by the lash of poverty and consequently defenceless against the most merciless exploitation here. We have only to remember the central and southern Europeans and the Asiatics who sweated away their lives building the railways and roads of Canada, clearing the bush-and-stone farms of the northern prairies, toiling in the camps and canneries of the West Coast.

Such immigrants were the perfect answer to the prayers of the big corporations for cheap, unorganized labour. Further, they would be useful in helping to keep native-born labour cheap and unorganized. Among the corporations, the CPR was remarkably efficient in exploiting the newcomers. In the 1937 brief presented by the former government of Saskatchewan to the Royal Commission on Dominion-Provincial Relations, this sentence gives a concise summary: 'The Canadian Pacific Railway ... became directly interested in the colonization of the prairie for two reasons: first, for the disposal of its land, second, to provide traffic for its lines.'

But all the land of the great CPR was powerless to hold enough immigrants to offset those who left the country. From 1871 to 1901, more people left Canada than came into it. Between 1910 and 1931, immigration was about 5,085,708, emigration about 3,409,184. Net emigration of native Canadians in the same period seems to have been somewhere between 650,000 and 775,000. In those thirty years of rapid expansion, we proved unable to absorb about a quarter of the natural increase of Canadian-born and about half of our immigrants. 'Since Confederation,' wrote Dr Eugene Forsey toward the end of the 1930s, 'we have brought to Canada at great expense four times as many people as we could absorb.'

Why did we fail to keep them? That is the first question that must be answered before we even consider the possibility of future immigration. The answer lies in the workings of the capitalist system. Canadian-born settlers on the land had found it impossible to make a living. Hence the early migrations from the Maritimes to the eastern United States, followed by the later movements into western Canada. Hence the steady drain, within each province, from the farms to the cities. The motivation was always the same – the compelling need for greater security, better living standards, and wider opportunities. Within Canada this trend is continuing. The Second World War, with its tremendous need for manpower, both in the armed forces and in industry, merely accelerated the cityward trend. For example, the Government's Advisory Committee on Reconstruction reported in 1943 that, since the outbreak of war, 95,000 women had left the farms of Canada. The Report commented: 'Under present conditions young women are leaving the farms and the older women are bearing intolerable burdens. Some way must be found to make rural life less arduous and more attractive to women.'

Suppose we decided to step up this process of pouring water through a sieve. Where would we get the immigrants? There is a great deal of talk these days about 'selective' immigration. If you back the users of the term securely into a corner, you usually discover that their mental picture of a 'selective' immigrant is a person of Anglo-Saxon or Scandinavian origin, endowed with stolidity and integrity, and a determination to stick to the land, come what may. The main trouble about this kind of immigrant is that he'd rather stay in Britain or Scandinavia than come to Canada. Back in 1937, Dr W.J. Black, Director of Colonization and Agriculture for the CNR, told the Vancouver Chamber of Commerce: 'Oddly enough, there is little inducement to encourage the citizens of the United Kingdom to establish new homes on Canadian soil. Business conditions over there are good and agriculture especially so. The farm worker has special benefits which we scarcely can offer. His wages are practically as high as ours, he works five and a half days a week, he has time and a half for overtime, he sees a pension in the offing, and all of these help to hold him to his life-work in the homeland.'

Today, even with the grave shortages of food, fuel, and most other things, there is no indication that British workers are eager to come to Canada as farm labourers or even farmers. They are moving into an economy of planning for security and opportunity, and they have faith in the outcome. It is interesting to find that the Polish ex-soldiers of General Anders' army have been complaining about the low wages, long hours, and lack of social status that are their portion on Ontario farms. Evidently it has not taken them long to pick up at least some of the ideas and techniques of democracy! So it would be with any group of immigrants who came to Canada today – if they *did* come. The golden age of exploitation is definitely a thing of the past.

We might as well admit that immigration for the old reasons and by the old methods is out. The immigrants we want won't come, and even if we could coax a few to do so, they wouldn't stay on the land to be exploited. Their drift to the cities would merely intensify the scramble for jobs and housing.

Is there any new basis for bringing more people to Canada? Suppose we had a government that was determined to build a high standard of living for every man, woman, and child in the country. Suppose such a government decided to work on a long-range plan, to develop the country's resources so as to provide for the needs of its citizens, so that every person would have enough good food and clothing, a modern, well-built home, complete health and social insurance, as much education as he was capable of taking and using. Suppose such a government decided also that Canada should play a leading part in the peace as we did in the war, that we would help produce enough food for all the mouths of a hungry world, help make enough farm implements to get the peoples of the world off relief and producing food for themselves, help provide enough of the other necessities of life to assist them to their feet economically and socially. Suppose we had a government with such a policy. Would we need more people in Canada to carry it through?

Undoubtedly we would need the services, not only of all our own available men and women (married as well as unmarried), but of a great many more. In fact, with a policy of full production to meet the needs of our own people and to help meet the needs of others, there would be no cause to fear the consequences of immigration.

Our absorptive capacity would be limited, not by our economic system as it is today, but by the extent of our resources, which, by proper development, could sustain a much greater population than we have at the present time. In other words, an expanding economy can accommodate more people; a contracting or stagnating one cannot handle even those it already has.

But, you say, we haven't got that kind of government. Quite true. We're hoping for a socialist government some day, but we haven't got it yet. As Karl Mannheim says in his *Diagnosis of Our Time*: 'There is no doubt that our society has been taken ill. What is the disease, and what could be its cure? If I had to summarize the situation in a single sentence I would say: "We are living in an age of transition from laissez-faire to a planned society."' There's our dilemma in the matter of immigration as in so many other matters. A laissez-faire society can no longer afford immigration. A planned society can. We're living between them. What can we do? Well, there is one thing we cannot afford to do, and that is to stand still and stagnate.

Obviously we must press for the planned society and for the expansion that goes with it. We should try now to make agreements with other countries for the kind and number of workers we think we can use, increasing the number as we can force increased production. At the same time we should press for the establishment of an authority under the United Nations to handle population movements in a planned, international way. Canada should have representation on such a body which would determine quotas and standards for admission.

The kind and number of immigrants we can get will be influenced by the way we treat them after they arrive in Canada. Never again must we dump them on the prairie or in the bush and leave them to fend for themselves. Never again must we allow them to settle in racial or religious blocks. Never again must we keep them as second-class citizens, deprived of rights which we native-born Canadians regard as inseparable from democracy. In short, we must welcome them as fellow-Canadians in the full sense of the term. We must be prepared to share all our rights and opportunities with them, and ready to receive their full co-operation in the responsibilities of citizenship.

Only as immigrants become an integral part of the fabric of our Canadian life will they cease to be regarded as a threat to the democratic bulwarks that have been so painfully built by the workers through their unions, by the farmers through their co-operatives, by the small business and professional people through their organizations, by all of us together through the legal safeguards for personal liberty. This, of course, is just another way of saying that freedom is one thing we can have only when we are prepared to see that others get it too. Immigration on this basis will mean greater production, higher living standards, a richer national culture, and a substantial contribution to world peace. But only on this basis.

F.R. SCOTT
Orderly Decontrol

Above all, we must have orderly decontrol.
No foolish rush and scramble to renounce
The prime functions of government. We must show
How carefully and consciously we can steer toward disaster,
Letting the forces of anarchy return one by one
    Through orderly decontrol.

First we must give away all the assets of war;
Stores and equipment, goods of every kind,
And all the factories built with public money.
These must be channelled toward monopolies
Who will most surely exploit them. This we shall call
    Restoring free enterprise.

Then we must care for the housing needs of our people,
The family being so sacred. What we need here
Is the freeing of private contractors, and the highest return
For insurance and mortgage companies. Thus we achieve
Incentives to build the luxury homes and apartments
    Fit for heroes to look at.

Since we are building a new social order
We must raise lower incomes, anchor the cost of living.
So we withdraw all subsidies. Milk is now orderly.
Wages we leave to nine provinces. Labour must learn
Not to cut into profits. Thus we shall win
    The war on inflation.

We are most deeply concerned with the federal problem.
This is one country; the state has new obligations.
So we submit our national responsibilities
To the veto of provincial politicians. We shall worship
At the altar of divided jurisdiction, and thus we shall honour
    The compact of Confederation.

Nor must we forget we are a Middle Power.
Our citizenship shall be defined in a brand new Bill
Which calls us British subjects. Rights, of course,
Must be denied our Japanese citizens, and we must postpone
The national flag and anthem. Then we may all feel proud
    Of the status of our country.

But above all we must have orderly decontrol.
This is the lesson we learned from World War I –
Not to hurry back to business as usual,
But calmly, showing special skill in a planned retreat,
And boldly meeting the future by restoring the past
    Through orderly decontrol.

JOHN GLASSCO
The Entailed Farm

A footpath would have been enough;
This muddy mile of the highway has no purpose
Except as it serves for others to link up
One distant point with another of equal distance –
Crossroads marked on the map with a nameless cross –
From these uncultivated fields of paintbrush
And the mute, sealed house.

Where the Spring's tooth, stripping shingles, scaling
Bare beam and clapboard, probes for the rot below
Gray porch and pediment and blind bow-window
And the wooden trunk with the coloured cardboard lining
Sprawls open, brimful of leaves and melted snow,

As it fell when the windward wall of the tenant-dwelling
Fell down some years ago.

Here a heap of stones is haven for snake and squirrel,
And the stable dovecote for phoebe and willow-wren;
Field-gates are all wired back, and trigged by the swell
Of risen earth like the ground at the bole of a maple,
Opening on places where nothing is raised or penned,
On rusty acres of witch-grass and wild sorrel
Where the field-birds cry and contend.

You tourist, salesman, family out for a picnic,
Who saw the bearded man that walked like a bear,
His pair of water-pails slung from a wooden neckyoke,
Circling the woodshed, here you can spare
The trouble of stopping: knock, and no one will answer;
And if you look for him round at the back
You will not find anyone there...

You might as well expect time's gate to open
On the living past, and the garden bloom again,
The house stand upright, hay-barn's swayback coping
Stiffen, or see the scythe-mown barnyard frame
A spare, black-coated, freehold yeoman watching
Men in the meadow, and a small boy whoopin whooping

The red oxen down the orchard lane!

Or awake the slow, strong greed of that coffined Farmer
Who cleared, stumped, fenced, rotating the sinew and sweat
Of his hinds, salting away their humours and heart
Beating the ploughshare into an honest dollar,
Who planned to cheat his individual night
Through the same white-bearded boy – who is hiding somewhere
Until you are out of sight –

And have left him alone: alone with grief or anger
Or whatever it is that flickers but will not die
In a dull brain where the victim, turned avenger,

Herds rust and ruin inside a barrier,
At war with a shadow, in flight from passers-by,
From us, who are free from all but the hint of attainder,
What can meet a stranger's eye
With a good face, can answer a question, give a reason,
To whom the world's fields and fences stand out plain,
Nor dazzle in sunlight or crumble behind the rain,
From us – with our hearts but lightly tinged with poison,
And only one foot in the cradle – who not in vain
Composed our quarrel early, and in good season
Buried the hatchet in our father's brain.

NORTHROP FRYE

Toynbee and Spengler

The synthesis of modern thought is the philosopher's stone of our age, and any such synthesis would have to contain, if it did not actually consist of, a philosophy of history. The two greatest modern achievements in this field are represented by Marx and Spengler, one a Communist and the other more or less a Nazi. What we want, clearly, is an equally impressive structure which will make room for humane values and established religion and not scare the pants off the middle-class reader. So when the first six volumes of Toynbee's *A Study of History* (A Study of History: Arnold J. Toynbee; Abridgement of vols. I-VI by D. Somervell; Oxford; pp. 617; $5.00) came out in a one-volume abridgement it scored a smashing popular success. This success was due mainly to *Time*, which has a deep interest in all books that promise to draw a cultural *cordon sanitaire* around Marxism.

A Study of History presents an enormous mass of historical material strung along a thin line of argument often represented only by a single word, generally Greek. In the original, one can snuggle down to read endlessly about hundreds of fascinating subjects, with a comfortable feeling that all the time all this is proving something, though we may have to look back at the table of contents to see just what it is. The abridgement, by exposing the lines of communication more clearly, indicates that Toynbee is not writing a philosophy of history so much as unrolling a vast historical panorama. His material does not really 'prove' anything: it provides the detail of his vision, and he leads us toward an imaginative total apprehension which can skip over the logical, and sometimes even the factual, stage. I have read many critiques of Toynbee, ranging from eulogy to invective, and have been struck with the fact that if one is in broad sympathy with what he is trying to do, his errors, however numerous, appear as blemishes in a picture rather than as wrong turns in a chain of reasoning. But if one is not in sympathy with him, everything seems equally pointless, and the whole pattern dissolves in chaos.

Toynbee worked out his plan independently of Spengler, and when Spengler's *Decline of the West* appeared after the last war he thought at first that his work had been done for him. Spengler says that the essential shape of history is neither a chaos of accidents nor a steady linear advance, but a series of social developments which he calls 'cultures.' These cultures behave exactly like organisms: they grow, mature, decline, and die; and they all last about the same length of time. Each begins in a 'spring' of an agrarian economy, a feudal and aristocratic society, and a mystical iconic religion, and matures into a 'summer' of city-states and individualized art, thence into an 'autumn' of urbane sophistication in art and economic expansion. At this point the 'culture' changes to a 'civilization,' and plunges into a 'winter' of huge cities, impoverished agriculture, dictatorships, and annihilation wars. The possibilities of its arts are exhausted, and its great achievements are technical feats of engineering and civil and military administration. The culture to which we belong is a 'Western' one, which had its spring in the Middle Ages, its summer in the Renaissance, its autumn in the eighteenth century, and began its winter with the French Revolution. Previously there had been a Classical culture which went through the same stages. The heroes of Homer correspond to those of our own age of chivalry; the era of Greek city-states to our Renaissance, and the last glories of Athens to our age of Bach and Mozart. With Alexander the 'civilization' phase of world-empires begins, for Alexander corresponds to our Napoleon. The 'decline of the West' has thus reached about the stage of the Punic Wars in Classical times, and the Roman empire and the reign of the Caesars indicate what is ahead of us. In addition to these two great cultures, Spengler deals with an Egyptian, a Chinese and an Indian one, an Arabian or Syrian one (he calls it 'Magian') which began around the time of Jesus and aged into Mohammedanism, and a new Russian one which is just beginning. Apart from these culture growths, human life presents a mere continuity of existence without shape or significance. Primitive societies and exhausted ones alike 'have no history.'

When one culture follows another in time, Spengler says, it does not really learn from its predecessor, and thus there is no general progress in history. When two cultures conflict, the more aggressive one may stunt and dwarf the other, producing what Spengler calls a 'pseudomorphosis.' Classical civilization did this to Magian culture, and Western civilization is doing it now to Russia. But no Westerner can ever understand what goes on in a Classical or Indian mind: he can only guess at it by seeing how all the products of the other culture fit into a consistent mental pattern which is not his. This overall pattern can be grasped, not of course through abstract propositions, but through symbols. Classical culture lives in a 'pure present': it has nothing of our sense of time and history: it thinks of architecture as a columnar mass, of tragedy as stylized attitude, of sculpture as bodily form, of mathematics as integral numbers and enclosed spaces, of music as a relation of single notes, of diplomacy as personal contact. Western culture is characterized by a feeling for the infinite: it thinks of architecture as a soaring structural energy, of tragedy as an analysis of character, of sculpture as a struggle with material, of mathematics as variable function, of music as counterpoint, of diplomacy as cabinet decisions used as long-range weapons. Magian culture is full of domes, caverns, sacred books, and esoteric traditions; Russian culture expresses a 'denial of height' both in its squat architecture and in its social communism, and so on.

A good deal even of this is German romanticism at its corniest, and some more sinister features are involved. We should, Spengler thinks, accept the character of our age, and not sigh for a vanished past or a Utopian future which (Toynbee agrees) is the shadow of a tired mind. We can think up new variations of the arts, but new organic developments are no longer possible, and we should leave them to misfits and get on with our big wars and dictatorships. ... Was the Rome of the Caesars, the Rome of Virgil and Horace and Ovid and Catullus, really interested solely in aqueducts and brass hats? Don't interrupt the professor. The author of Spengler's next book, *The Hour of Decision*, is just another Nazi stumblebum. But his thesis has bitten deeply into us: we are all Spenglerians to some extent, and if the enemy has any ammunition that we can capture, we should fire it back at the enemy.

Much of Toynbee's book, especially the first three volumes, reads like an improved version of Spengler backed up by a far greater knowledge of history. He also isolates the 'civilization' or 'society' as the unit of historical study. The first three volumes trace the 'genesis' and 'growth' of these societies, and the next three decline and 'disintegration,' though in Volume Four he avoids the 'decline' (*Untergang*) of Spengler's title and adopts 'breakdown' instead. Spengler's six or eight civilizations are all included in a much fuller survey of twenty-one. The main improvement on Spengler comes in the role assigned the proletariat in the last stage. To Spengler the proletariat is nothing but a rabble: Toynbee sees that an internal proletariat (the exploited members of the society) and an external one (the barbarian nomads outside) combine to form a 'universal Church' which becomes at once the coffin of the old society and the womb of a new one, so that a real spiritual progress from one society to another can occur. For reasons too complicated to examine here, this gives Christianity a far more satisfactory historical explanation than Spengler gives it.

At the beginning of Volume Four there comes a crisis in Toynbee's argument, the question of the cause of decline, which involves a direct examination of Spengler. But he fails to pass this crisis, and all the rest of his book has the air of a dodged issue. He fires off two very damp squibs at Spengler. First he calls him a 'fatalist,' which is irrelevant: to predict the death of every living organism may be tactlessness, but it is not fatalism. Then he complains that Spengler uses a metaphor as though it were a fact. But *A Study of History*, organized throughout on such figures as 'nemesis of creativity,' 'withdrawal and return,' 'schism and palingenesis,' is a rather glassy house from which to throw this stone. As we have seen, an intuitive response based on an imaginative grasp of the symbolic significance of certain data is demanded by Toynbee as well as Spengler. Toynbee's real answer is that a civilization is not an organism. An organism has a life-span predetermined from the start; a civilization is a way of social life initiated by an environmental challenge and dependent for its continuity on maintaining a social will and judgement sufficient to meet further challenges. If it collapses, there is always a definable and at one time avoidable cause.

Spengler's evidence for the organic nature of culture is of a kind which Toynbee shows himself much less skilful in handling. If, says Spengler, we study the growth of painting from Giotto to Rembrandt, we can see, in its development of interest in landscape, realistic portraiture, and the handling of light, a steady advance in self-consciousness and in the exploring of a certain range of possibilities. It is not getting better or worse: it is simply growing older. If we compare modern America with Classical Rome, we shall see parallels of a kind that do not appear when we compare it with the age of Charlemagne, and these parallels can be accounted for only by a conception of cultural age. Spengler does not say, any more than Toynbee does, that 'breakdown' is inevitable: he says growing older is inevitable, and he is quite as insistent as Toynbee on the importance of 'self-determination' to prevent breakdown at a late stage. And his powerful argument proving that Western culture is a relatively old one still stands completely unrefuted. It will not do to suggest, like a lazy book reviewer, that it may after all rest on nothing but a false analogy. It doesn't.

Toynbee's conception of history is so closely related to Spengler's that when he throws out Spengler's thesis most of his own would go with it, if he did not continually accept in practice what he denies in theory. He is stuck with many organic metaphors which he does not know how to avoid using. The death-and-rebirth rhythm of *The Golden Bough* is an essential part of his structure: he is quite right, and Spengler quite wrong in ignoring it; but it happens to be an organic rhythm. Civilizations still 'grow,' even if they suddenly turn into machines and 'break down,' and then into inorganic substances and 'disintegrate.' He quarrels with Gibbon's ghost for regarding the Antonine age as a real summer instead of an Indian one. He has no class of things with which to associate his conception of civilization, and has to define it in circular terms like 'entity.' Of his twenty-one civilizations, every one except ours has gone through what look suspiciously like organic stages of a 'time of troubles,' a universal state and a universal church; and the constant assertions that ours is an exception are not very convincing even to Toynbee himself, as the troubled cadences of his sixth volume, with its many uneasy glances at the parallels to 'disintegration' in our own time, abundantly show. One has the feeling that he is afraid that the logical consequence of his own argument will land him in Spengler's 'pessimism.' But whatever one thinks of Spengler's pessimism, the optimism of a man who can write in 1939 that it is too early to say whether we have come to our time of troubles yet seems rather woebegone.

Unlike Spengler, primarily a philosopher who picked up his history as he went along, Toynbee is primarily a historian, and his philosophical basis consists largely of his own hunches, some of Bergsonian origin. There are many places where he does not even see that a prior philosophical problem is involved. Thus his survey of the causes of breakdown itself breaks down through ignoring the question of what constitutes a historical cause. Pascal says that if Cleopatra's nose had been an inch longer it would have changed the world's history. Spengler says that different characters might have replaced Antony and Cleopatra, different battles might have been fought, and the course of historical events superficially quite different, but the fundamental relationship of a moribund Egyptian culture, an aging Classical one and a nascent Syrian one would still have been there. This distinction between history and chronicle is one of the profoundest of Spengler's insights. The distinction disappears in Toynbee, and in consequence he takes us back to the old 'practical' view of history as a chaotic sequence of lucky and unlucky accidents, a roulette game in which a gambler's luck may hold if he figures out a system to beat the laws of chance.

Both Spengler and Toynbee talk about Marx as though he were a second-rate thinker: the Nazi calls him a Jew and the English liberal a German Jew. But I suspect that Marx is holding the nutcracker that the reader of both Toynbee and Spengler wants. New instruments of production change the whole character of a society; and the technique for producing new instruments of production at will brought in by the Industrial Revolution has changed the whole character of history. There is now a completely new factor in the situation which cannot be wholly absorbed into a dialectic of separate 'civilizations,' important as that is. The question whether Western civilization will survive or collapse is out of date, like the same question about the British Empire, for the world is trying to outgrow the whole conception of 'a' civilization, and has reached a different kind of problem altogether. Because the Industrial Revolution started in the West, its transformation of the world has looked like the expansion of Western society, and in fact has partly been that, but something else is also happening. The factors which are the same all over the world, such as the exploitation of labour, have always been, if not less important, at any rate less powerful in history than conflicts of civilizations. Now they are more important, and growing in power. Toynbee feels that world peace now is essentially a question of getting the five surviving civilizations to live together in spite of their traditional differences in outlook. But this is the old league of sovereign nations again, the balance-of-power fallacies revised to rationalize the new setup of national 'blocs.' The conception of United Civilizations, like the conception of United Nations, is pretty, but it isn't the real thing.

A Study of History is already something of a museum piece. Volumes Four to Six were the product of the thirties, that horrible period of impotent democracy and rampant fascism, and their general tone of hoping against hope that as much as possible of the *status quo* will 'survive' reflects what we all felt then. Now we have the atom bomb and Russo-American imperialism before us, but some years have elapsed in war work since the completion of Volume Six, and perhaps a fresh start will bring a fresh energy. The great synthesis of Marx and Spengler has yet to be written, but so has half of Toynbee's book.

L.J. ROGERS

Duplessis and Labour

One of the most important prejudices in the mind of Quebec's nationalist Maurice Duplessis is his deep-rooted hatred of international labour unions. If the Quebec premier had his way, these 'outside' labour organizations, whether of the AF of L, the CIO, or the railway brotherhoods, would be banned in Quebec, and replaced by locally controlled unions of the Catholic Syndicate type. As long as federal wartime labour regulations were in effect, Premier Duplessis did not feel free to commence his 'antiforeign union' crusade – but judging by recent indications, this crusade will be announced any day now. Ever since March, when Ottawa stepped out of the labour scene, organized labour has been the victim of a war of nerves in Quebec, and the blitzkrieg stage may be reached at any time.

Premier Duplessis does not feel bound by any laws which he himself has not placed on the statute books. The existing Quebec Labour Relations Act of 1944, which was put through as one of the last measures of the Godbout regime, is not treated as provincial law by either Duplessis's Labour department or his Attorney-General's department. This law provides, among other things, that an employer is required to negotiate for an agreement with the representatives of the employees' association of which the majority of his employees are members. For a time, the Duplessis technique was to grant certifications to unions representing a majority of the employees, but to do nothing further to persuade the employer to bargain in good faith with the certified union, even though this is the clear intention of the Act. Of late, the process of sabotaging the Act has been carried a step further – now applications for certification from legitimate unions are frequently held up in the Labour department for months, seemingly to give company unions an opportunity to intimidate or bribe the employees of the plant into leaving the legitimate union. When this process has been successful, the Department calls for a plant election, on short notice.

Another trick has been to grant certifications, then revoke them without warning and with no other justification than the claim of the employer that the union 'no longer represents the majority of his employees.' This device has been employed in several Quebec strikes, generally at the time when union strength had reached its lowest point after weeks or months on the picket line.

The system of 'collective decrees,' peculiar to Quebec labour law, by which wage scales for an industry are set at three-way conferences of employers, government and labour, is currently being used as a weapon against legitimate unions. Decrees granting wage increases to all workers in the boot and shoe industry of Quebec – except those belonging to the AF of L Boot and Shoe Workers union – were recently issued. True, the increases were very small, but the effect of the decrees was to penalize those workers who belong to a legitimate union.

The latest move against 'outside' unions reported as being considered by Premier Duplessis is an amendment to the Labour Act which would require union organizers to be licensed by the department. Like most of his other anti-labour moves, this step is taken ostensibly against the Communists in the labour movement – but past events have indicated that the Quebec Premier believes at heart that every union is Communist which is not a company union or a unit of the Catholic Syndicate group.

So far, Duplessis has shown his hand most strongly against organized labour in plants and industries controlled by Quebec capital. Industries controlled by 'outside' capital, with which the Premier is presumably not on such familiar terms, are shown no particular favours by the Quebec Labour department – and organized labour in such plants is given good service by the department.

To see how Quebec labour law works for a 'native' employer with good political connections, let's take a look at the story of Local 313 of the United Rubber Workers union (CIO-CCL), at the Chambly plants of Bennett's Ltd. Early in 1946, organizer Jack Lerette went into Chambly to organize the 300 workers at the two Bennett plants, and within a matter of weeks he had a solid membership built among the French-speaking workers there. Organization was not difficult, because the Bennett workers were being deplorably underpaid and, into the bargain, tyrannized by a feudalistic absentee management. Wages averaged little better than $20 a week for experienced men doing fifty hours of skilled work, and some men received as low as $14.50 for a week's work – after deductions by the company for water and light charges in the company-owned houses of this little company town. Added to that, the company refused to tell the employees how their wages were calculated, what their hourly rate and hours of work amounted to, or what deductions were made. Not until the union took legal action against the Bennett management was this practice halted, almost a year later.

When a majority had been signed into the union, application for certification was made by Local 313, and after a fairly lengthy delay the certification was granted on May 11, 1946. When the Bennett management refused to bargain in good faith with the local, the Quebec Labour department appointed a conciliation officer, early in July 1946. This officer, unprovided with any particular rights or powers, failed to accomplish much. He was, in fact, unable to get the Bennett management to agree to any of the clauses of a standard union contract. Even then, the Quebec Labour department took no action to direct the company to bargain in good faith, as required by the Act. Instead, at the recommendation of the conciliator, an impartial arbitration board was set up, as provided by the Act in cases of last resort.

When the board was finally established after months of tedious delay, in November, 1946, it was composed of one representative of union, one of company, and one of government. Before it began its sessions, the management was asked if it would agree that the findings of the board should be binding on both parties. True to form, Bennett's management refused to agree to this. Instead of calling off the whole procedure, now made meaningless, the board solemnly held hearings at intervals throughout the winter. Then on March 30, 1947, it issued a unanimous recommendation calling upon the company to sign a collective agreement with Local 313 without further delay and to grant a wage increase of ten cents an hour to its employees.

This recommendation was unanimous – signed and approved by the company's representative on the board – but Bennett's management still refused to bargain in good faith or even to discuss the matter with representatives of Local 313. The only course left for the union was strike action – and the strike was called on April 15, 1947 – something over a year after the date when the Bennett employees first sought the help of the Quebec Labour department in getting the collective bargaining agreement promised them by the Quebec Labour Act.

This strike was a legal one in every respect – the union having wasted more than a year of time and considerable money in complying with the provincial labour regulations. Yet the Labour department took no action then, and has taken no action to this day – after almost five months on strike – to direct the company to comply with the law of the land.

Instead, the company was provided with the services of one hundred provincial police almost from the beginning of the strike to enable it to convey strikebreakers through the picket lines thrown up by the three hundred strikers. Backed by this costly show of strength, the company combined intimidation and bribery in an effort to get the workers to break the strike ranks – but almost entirely without success. The Quebec courts, presumably after consultation with the Attorney-General of the province, granted the company no less than thirty-five injunctions against strikers and union officials forbidding them to picket the plant, or even to watch it from a distance of a block or more.

This treatment was given to a union holding a legal strike – a union whose leadership has always been known as non-Communist both in Canada and in the United States. At the time this is written the company still refuses to meet with the union, in spite of several union offers, and in spite of the fact that plant production is far below normal both in quantity and quality. The morale of the strikers, backed by contributions totalling more than $60,000 from other URWA locals and the international office, is still high. The rubber workers intend to fight this strike out to the finish – to find out once and for all whether legitimate organized labour has any legal rights in the province of Quebec.

FRANK H. UNDERHILL
Liberalism à la King

One of the pleasant things about our country at the present moment is that we have a prime minister who is also an author. This affords the final proof that we have achieved complete equality of status with Britain. The intellectual level of our Canadian politics would be considerably higher if we had a nucleus of leading politicians, such as Britain has always enjoyed, who find time to write books on politics or economics or history. What gives the British Labour party its easy superiority over the Tories is that the Labour cabinet is full of authors, whereas the opposition can only boast of one, even if he is a big one. But it must be said that this particular book (*Industry and Humanity: The Right Honourable W.L. Mackenzie King*; Macmillan, pp. xxix, 270, $4.00) of Mr King's does little to raise the intellectual standards of our public life.

Mr King first published his *Industry and Humanity* in 1918 when he was not an active politician. In its original edition, with a large equipment of footnotes, it showed that he had been a genuine student of labour problems and was conversant with all the current discussion of the subject by experts in Britain and America. Even so the book that emerged from his studies was mostly a collection of uplifting abstract moral platitudes; and it stood in striking contrast with a work such as that on *Industrial Democracy* by the Sidney Webbs which got down to concrete cases and discussed practical problems in a practical way.

The original *Industry and Humanity*, however, did devote a good deal of space to particular illustrations of the general principles which the author thought so important. There was a long account of how he had himself applied his principles to the Colorado Fuel and Iron Company. There were discussions of the Whitley Councils in Great Britain, of schemes of 'scientific management,' 'profit-sharing,' and 'co-partnership' in industry. And there was a very optimistic explanation of the workings of the Industrial Disputes Investigation Act. All these sections have been deleted from the present revision or drastically reduced. Is Mr King no longer proud of what he accomplished in Colorado, which was denounced at the time by labour as an application of the company-union technique? Why doesn't he tell us more of the constitutional difficulties which his Industrial Disputes Investigation Act encountered, and which make it appear much less significant now than it did in 1918?

What is left is a series of sermons on the so-called Law of Peace, Work, and Health which Mr King derived from a somewhat rhetorical passage of Pasteur. (According to press despatches he made a point of visiting Pasteur's grave again on his recent European trip.) That capital, labour, management, and the community are all partners in industry is an admirable starting-point for a series of sermons; but like most sermons, Mr King's never commit the preacher to anything much beyond abstract general principles. It is difficult to understand why a book of this kind can have gone through so many editions, unless it is widely collected by parsons as a source for sermon material on the labour question. Almost any of its chapters could be delivered verbatim most acceptably any Sunday morning from any Protestant pulpit. And like that too, too famous sermon on sin, these sermons also would leave their audience uncertain about most points except that the parson was against sin.

Perhaps remarks of this kind should be put down simply to the unreasonable bad temper of the reviewer. For the book has undoubtedly found a certain considerable market over the past twenty-five or thirty years. But a reviewer of a book by a prime minister is bound to raise another point. Since the first edition of this book was published Mr King has been in office for some twenty years; he was chosen in 1919 as the Liberal leader partly because of his expert knowledge of labour questions. What has he done since then to apply these noble principles in action? His introduction has a curious footnote (p. xxvi): 'The implications which stemmed from the Industrial Disputes Investigation Act gave a tremendous impetus to the development of collective bargaining in industrial relations. The Act, by its very nature, often led to what was tantamount to collective bargaining, but it was *de facto* and not a *de jure* process. Collective bargaining, in the modern acceptance of the term, was given form and substance, and made compulsory, in the Wagner Act of 1935.' But where is the Canadian Wagner Act? Of course, constitutional difficulties under the BNA Act have been in the way. But what effective initiative has Mr King's government ever taken to awaken Canadian public opinion or to get Canadian public men to face up to these constitutional difficulties and to do something about them?

Mr King makes an admirable point in his book that the solution of industrial relations depends upon the same principles as the solution of international relations. The whole thesis of the book is that in both fields we must strive constantly to substitute reason for force. Now every liberal will agree that a healthy society is one in which reason plays an ever-increasing part and force an ever-decreasing part. But realistic liberals know that there will always remain some element of force as long as human beings are the imperfect creatures that they are. Labour leaders have always known by instinct that this beautiful liberal process of round-table discussion is not likely to yield them much fruit until they come to the round-table with as much effective power in their hands as is possessed by the employers; and so they have set to work to make their unions as strong as possible. Collective bargaining has become a standard process not merely because of appeals to sweet reasonableness but because the labour bargainers now have power in their hands as well as the employers. And in all the bargaining and discussion by which social decisions are made, this element of power, of force, of coercion, is never very far in the background. The liberalism which abhors power politics so thoroughly that it spends its time dreaming (or writing books) of a world from which power will have been eliminated is a liberalism fit only for Sunday sermons.

In the international field in our day this element of power and force has been even more evident than in the field of industrial relations. And Mr King has gone through what should have been an enlightening experience in this international field since he wrote his book in 1918. It was all very well then to talk nobly about substituting reason for force in human relations. We were all naively optimistic about the League of Nations in those days, and everybody in North America was going to abolish the Balance of Power by joining the League or by going into isolation. But since then Mr King has led his people into a second World War. And today, as the prospects grow dimmer of getting a second international round-table that will work, Mr King's Minister of External Affairs and his responsible officials have been hinting broadly that Canada is prepared to join a closer mutual-security organization within the United Nations, the members of which would pool their national military forces for common protection. This does not mean abolishing force but using it in a more effective way.

In international relations since September 1939, Mr King's actions as a responsible statesman (for most of which this reviewer has the highest admiration) bear little relation to the naive Utopian liberalism of *Industry and Humanity*. He has been quite prepared to use force when necessary. In industrial relations, since he was chosen leader on the far-reaching platform of 1919, his activities have been mainly negative. He has not extended even the limited participation of the Community in the 'Partnership of Industry,' which was achieved in his early Industrial Disputes Investigation Act, to the bulk of Canadian industry. As for social legislation, after twenty years in office his government still has a considerable part of the platform of 1919 to carry out, and most of the legislation it has passed has resulted from the lead given by Mr Woodsworth or Mr Bennett. When a politician's literary performance diverges so widely from his practical achievement one is compelled to revise one's first thoughts and to doubt whether Canadian politicians should go in for authorship at all.

JAMES REANEY

Klaxon

All day, cars mooed and shrieked,
Hollered and bellowed and wept
Upon the road.
They slid by with bits of fur attached,
Fox-tails and rabbit-legs,
The skulls and horns of deer.
Cars with yellow spectacles
Or motorcycle monocle.
Cars whose gold eyes burnt
With a too-rich battery.
Murtherous cars and manslaughter cars.
Chariots from whose foreheads leapt
Silver women of ardent bosom.
Ownerless, passengerless, driverless,
They came to anyone
And with headlights full of tears
Begged for a master,
For someone to drive them
For the familiar chauffeur.
Limousines covered with pink slime
Of children's blood
Turned into the open fields
And fell over into ditches.
The wheels kicking helplessly.
Taxis begged trees to step inside;
Automobiles begged of posts
The whereabouts of their mother.
But no one wanted to own them any more.
Everyone wished to walk.

LOUIS DUDEK

Upstate Tourism

Upstate in New York
they hang rambling roses on their porches,
blankets and red rugs of them;
farther, streets of red strawberries will greet
 you,
hills of apples, plums, grapes, cherries
in speckled orchards
(though the brown fields lie fallow,
famous for their rocks)
and you will be aware of daisies
blowing across the fields, and the smell of
 clover
and buttercups ... cricket sounds in the air ...
and waves of shadow that the white clouds
 make
running over the round hills.

But if one is struck amid the generosity of
 nature
by the growing insanity apparent in the
 villages,
rust around the canneries, and the shambles
 the Joads left,
old pails, and lean-to outhouses,

or by the factory of some big corporation
exploding its whistle into the country air;
or the town side-streets falling away
with a clatter of ash-cans
like the tail on a 'Just Married' car;
or a crumbling doorstep where
mysteriously sits a new ragged generation –
bits of flesh torn from their fathers – chewing
   their hands.

Oh, there is still an elm somewhere against the
   clouds,
a distant barn, or a steeple
hard as a stone against the sky, to look at!
They will meet the tourist's eye with a
   promise of plenty
if he should be cooled by the cold wind
or the evidence of a struggle there for survival.

W.R. FROST

The Buster

The carbide lamp threw a dull light down to the floor of the mine at Bob's feet. He plodded heavily, well stooped over to clear the roof, along the wooden tracks. With each step his body jerked and his head bobbed, throwing the glow of the flame rhythmically up on the clay close to his back and shoulders and then down flatly to the ties upon which he was walking. Ahead of him beyond the blackness and between the musty upright props, another light moved. But this one was timed to the sound of heavy quick picking. The two lights tried to reach each other along the wetness of the roof and over the high slack pile, throwing the shadows of the props like flickering fingers at each other. Bob clumped on. It was quiet and rather pleasant here when contrasted with the harshness of the winter above ground. The air was fresh enough to let the carbide lamp burn fairly well, and free of smoke still until the afternoon's shooting would begin. Bob was thinking about his shot, hoping it would be a good one. His coal had been tight the last few feet, and hard going. If this buster would only clear the bottom seam out to the next face he could get six or eight cars out of it and then mine the top coal, or perhaps split through it and knock it down with top shots in either corner.

'Well, hell, things never go that smooth. I'll just have to bull my way through and burn up more damn powder.'

The lights had reached across the roof and the sound of picking had stopped. Bob had come to the working face in his room and there, waiting for him, was his helper. Gus was discouraged, slouching on a block of coal. He scrunched his foot in the slack, splashing water. It was inches deep across the floor.

He screwed his black face up at Bob.

'If that tin-horn capitalist doesn't put a little punch in the pumps soon our chins will be scratching water; and we're still going down hill,' Gus said. He started to roll a smoke, swearing carefully. 'When I get my papers, Bob, I'm gonna get the hell out of here. If I gotta be a gopher at least I can pick my hole. And that's gonna be where they've got a union. Jeezes look at it, water you can swim in, the roof just waiting to smash your head in, lousy air, wooden turn-tables. And if you squawk you get stuck in another room, just as dirty and maybe worse.'

Bob agreed with him, but not enthusiastically. He remembered that he had spent some time in a union mine and hadn't enjoyed it. That had been the only time he had worked away from the town he grew up in, and he had been glad to come back. He took a chew of copenhagen into his underlip and spit the scraps out of his mouth. He started to sharpen the auger and calculated with his eye where he would drill the shot hole to get the best effect. Gus had been looking at him, watching his hands and his big body. Bob was an efficient worker and his deftness and muscular vigour combined so gracefully that even the rough movements required by his work were given a fluidity that was pleasant to watch. Gus began to make the dummies they would use to tamp the shot in, glancing over the news before he rolled the paper into the appropriate shape. Then he filled the forms with clay. Bob had finished boring the hole and after he had prepared the powder pellets and the fuse, he pushed these into the far end and tamped the hole solidly full with the dummies of clay Gus had made. He worked very quickly, for he wished to shoot again, if necessary, before the afternoon was over.

This was the busy season. Normally the empty cars were allocated evenly among the miners. Now, however, everyone could load as many cars as he was able. Bob was considered to be the most powerful worker among the men. He was proud of his leadership and would extend himself, if necessary, to maintain it.

After lighting the fuse Gus and Bob crawled into a cross-cut about a hundred feet from the working face. Bob was listening for the sound of the shot, so that he could tell how effective it had been. When it came the blast of air blew their lights out. Bob grunted. 'That won't be any damn good, it wasted itself.' They plodded through the smoke, poking their lights forward through the haze, and peered at the coal face, standing close against it and moving among the props. The shot had splintered the coal but had not moved it free. Bob rang the coal with his pick, it struck hard and solid. Gus was turning around to walk out for it was so smoky that little could be seen.

Bob said, 'Bring in an empty, Gus, and I'll start mining this out. It's a poor shot but we have to get it out.'

Bob had to work very hard to pick out and clean up for the evening shots. His body steamed through his woollen shirt. He drove himself but he did not get tired. His concentration on his work excluded other things. He took the perfect functioning of his body for granted. He judged only what had to be done, not thinking it necessary to consider whether or not it could be done. He was not surprised when, at the end of the day, his room was in as good condition as if the shot had been successful. He placed two top shots and put the tools away. The fuses were lit and after the shots went off he picked up the empty powder kit and, with Gus, walked up the slope and out of the mine.

Before going home the miners gathered in the shack above the pit. They sat down for a smoke and then put on their mackinaws and mitts and walked together towards town. There were eight of them and they joked with each other and talked as they went along. They walked rapidly, for the wind was cold and sharp against their sweaty bodies, and the town was over a mile away.

For several years now, Bob had been carefully following a body-building program, and he was still joshed about it a good deal. These exercises had produced such excellent results in him though, that he could take their joking equably. Gus told a story about a party he and Bob had been to before Bob had married. Later in the evening they were having lunch at one of the girl's homes. Both of them were a little drunk. Gus said that Bob had stripped to show the girls his muscles, 'and by God, he had one of them tiger skins on you see in pictures. Do you wear it down the mine too Bob, in case the boss's daughter comes around?'

Bob said, 'Hell no, fellows, I took that thing off the day I got married.'

Everyone laughed. Bob had married Maidie, a local girl, three months ago. The marriage had been performed abruptly and she was now already thick through the waist. Such affairs were not unusual in the district and were not condemned. People, it was thought, got married sooner or later to some one or other and raised children.

Bob turned off at his cottage and waved good-night to the men. Maidie, a large rather small-busted woman, opened the door for him. She talked to him while he took off his coat and shoes. She asked him if he'd had a good day. He told her about it as he wrote down his tally, the number of cars he had loaded, the amount of powder he had burnt, and the total up to date of each for the week. She said that the Johnsons were coming over to play rummy after supper. Bob washed himself and then set the table. Maidie said that he was certainly a good man around the house, and smiled at him. Bob said, 'I think the potatoes are burning,' and moved them off the fire.

The Johnsons arrived while Maidie and Bob were still at the table. They talked for a while and then piled the dishes and played rummy. They decided to stake five cents on each game to keep it interesting. Maidie won thirty-five cents and was quite pleased. She said that she was going to save up for a permanent. She sure needed one, she said. Johnson asked Bob if it were true that the deep mines would have to close up if the government stripped coal for the farmers. Bob thought that the stripped coal wasn't good enough to keep a building warm and that the farmers would soon find it out. Maidie said that she didn't win at cards very often, she must have been quite lucky.

Before going to bed, Bob went through his exercises. He stripped and stood before a full-length mirror so that he could watch the action of his muscles as he exercised. No contrivances were used, the course was based, the booklet claimed, on a natural dynamic muscular competition. Bob worked, breathing easily, until he perspired, watching himself closely. He thought his legs were too bulky. They were out of proportion and he would try to reduce their size. When he was finished for the evening he took his measurements with a tape and wrote them down in appropriate columns in a book he kept for that purpose.

At one time Bob had tried to convince

Maidie that she should exercise too. He was afraid that pregnancy would make her go flabby and ruin her figure. He was sure that if she followed his directions he could keep her in tip-top shape and even, he promised her, make childbirth painless.

Maidie said that with two such parents it was more likely the baby would come out doing push-ups, which would not be comfortable for any one. The idea amused her. She teased Bob with it when he became serious, but to please him she would join occasionally in the deep-breathing exercises. She liked to feel her breasts, now swelling to fullness, stretch and tighten over her expanding chest. Bob would say, 'Now Maidie, you're just yawning, you have to try harder than that.' She finally gave it up altogether and would lie in bed and watch Bob as he went through his routine in the mornings and evenings. She thought it was a little silly if your appetite was good without it.

The cottage they were living in was not yet completely finished. Bob started it after his marriage and had as yet finished only two rooms. He had winterized these and added a lean-to, planning to build on other rooms in the summer, so that finally they would have a pleasant bungalow. Maidie had helped him with the plans, and had decided where the sink and the cabinets and so on should be placed. She liked to watch him work, and would stand around and talk with him while he hammered. These afternoons were often agreeable, and Bob would tell her that soon, perhaps in one or two years, when their cottage was finished, he would spend a summer driving a coal shaft and then they would have a mine of their own. Or he would talk about their child, and say that they would have to bring him up right. Or about how long it would take to finish the rooms, and if they would be done before the snow came. When Maidie was unresponsive Bob felt irritated. She seemed to like everything, but this meant nothing, he thought, for she was so often indifferent. She was content to let him talk, but didn't seem to listen to him. He thought she was unresponsive because she was pregnant, women are strange at these times, it would be different afterwards.

By the time the winter's mining was over Maidie was very big. She wasn't bothered, not being often sick, and idled about the cottage comfortably. She was astonished at her size, not used to it, and occasionally swept a cup and saucer off the table as she turned around. But the last month was difficult. Bob stopped building so that he wouldn't annoy her with the noise, and took over the household duties. Maidie was a good patient, she would lie on the couch and watch Bob as he moved about.

Following the baby's birth Maidie rested, waiting for her strength to come back. After the initial surprise she had adjusted quickly to her new dimensions. Without its ballast her body felt itself again. The process that was child-bearing she remembered vaguely or not at all. It had been a vague occurrence, an unusual thing, difficult to cup in one's hand and look at. It had not happened to her. It was neither eating nor sleeping nor the other things that filled her days and nights. She forgot it. It passed out of her memory. And with the dream that was childbirth behind her, she slipped loosely into the life that was about her. The successive days as they passed merged into one another. A wide dilute comfort surrounded her. For now and ever it seemed, she had her husband and her house. If there was anything she didn't want to do she needn't do it. Independence made Maidie pleasant and happily she watched Bob build the extra rooms on the cottage, paint, care for the garden.

That summer Bob had an opportunity to open up a mine for himself. He had arranged to use some land about four miles from town, not far from a main road. The Bank had offered to advance him the money for his rolling stock on a percentage basis of his returns for the first five years. He was excited at the prospect and told Maidie about it. He said that this was just what he wanted, he hadn't hoped it would happen so soon. Maidie said she thought it was nice. She hoped they wouldn't have to move.

Bob spent long hours digging at the shaft that summer. His test holes had shown promise. The coal was about fifty feet down, and the seam was from four to five feet thick. As the summer advanced Bob decided that he couldn't finish by himself. He asked Gus to help him. They drove the slope in from the side of a hill, built the tipple and a rough road. The day they first hit the coal seam, while digging the slope, he carried a sackful home on his shoulder and burnt it in the stove. It was in the summer, Maidie thought it was too hot to have a fire on. She walked outside and sat on the shady side of the house. The coal burnt as well as any produced in the district, Bob thought, and had many favourable features. He decided to call his mine the 'Little Ash' mine.

When Bob began to drive entry, and open up rooms for the miners he planned to hire, he found that the roof was not good. It was soft and wet and dropped easily even when closely propped up. If a shot knocked out a few props, the roof was sure to fall. He thought that this condition was perhaps only very local and would clear up when the workings were more advanced. One afternoon, Gus was knocked over by a small cave. His back was badly bruised and he had to stop work for a few days. Before Gus returned a major cave-in occurred at the bottom of the slope. A large hole extended into the roof over the mound of stone and clay on the track to a distance of about ten feet. Bob could not tell how far back the cave-in extended. When he clambered up on the pile to see if he could get over it and look at the rest of the workings, he could hear ominous noises farther along. The major part of his tools and equipment were locked in behind the blockage. He tried to clear up the dirt and carry it out of the cave. He was sorry that he hadn't boomed the roof up solidly as he would have done if he had thought it necessary. He decided to go on inside.

He had to crawl on his hands and knees to get on between the roof and the loose dirt that had fallen from it. The passage was uncomfortable and so dangerous that he would not have done it under ordinary circumstances. He squeezed his way along stopping now and again to see if he could flash his light to the end of the rubble. He climbed through finally. He heard more roof drop farther in the workings. A prop cracked. The props were taking weight, there must be a water slip somewhere above, Bob thought. He ran on, he wished to get his tools out, but he was afraid, he stopped and turned. The complete silence underground, the clammy feel of the air, the pitiful comfort of the feeble glare of his carbide lamp, isolated him. It seemed to him that his lamp was going out. Could it be, he wondered, that the air was bad too. Perhaps the air shaft was plugged. He was a damn fool to be here. He could be trapped in a minute. He poked his light at the roof above his head. He left the mine as it was and returned to town for help. But the roof continued to come down, and the mine proved unworkable. When he told Maidie about it, she said that it was too bad. After a while she said that it was lucky he wasn't in it when it happened.

Bob spent more time at home now. Working only eight hours a day he had time to finish up the bungalow and to do odd jobs that Maidie suggested. The baby was often quiet and when the sun was warm Bob would wheel it in its carriage to where he was working. The baby would watch him as he worked, quietly moving its eyes, accepting the scene and his own vigour. Bob felt eerie, he would try to make the baby move, or yell. Sometimes he would pinch it, to see if it could feel anything at all. Just like Maidie, he thought. He would frown when he saw the rash spreading over the baby's legs and stomach. Sometimes he would talk to Maidie when he washed the baby's scalp clean again. He was intently aware of his own discontent. He would like to pinch Maidie too, he thought, he wondered if she would jump or scream. He didn't know how he could get her to do the things he wanted her to do. With both of them, Maidie and the baby, it was like walking among fat shadows. It was like the feeling he sometimes had down the mine when he was all alone. He would shout, and the darkness would move with the noise and swallow it and close around him again. The shattering isolation, the lost dismayed feeling, the hint that life had dissolved itself, this is what he thought he felt with his child and with Maidie. Should he pour hot boiling water on them a drop at a time, would they move then, would they do anything?

In the evenings when he tried to stem the tide of weeds that surged in his garden, sometimes he would stop and look through the window at Maidie who would be lying down, dreaming perhaps or doing nothing. And he would feel bewildered. He would look around where the weeds were growing, the careless competition of the garden. And there, just there without any effort, sat the house. In the sun a cat stretched, licked its fur, and walked away. At night Bob did his exercises until sweat stood out on his skin, and the blood was warm in his body. Carefully with a tape he took his measurements and noticed that now his calf muscle had lost enough. He went to bed planning out the next day, calculating his chances to start out on his own again. Beside him, soft-fleshed Maidie looked at him happily. She stretched and smiled and put her hand flatly on the small of his back.

One night Bob came home drunk. It was late, but Maidie had the baby up. She was crooning to it as she rocked it. In the sink, the dishes were unwashed. Crumbs were on the table and bread and jam and butter. Bob stood and waited, swaying in the doorway. Quiet breathing stretched out through the room. The air moved, the room moved, Bob moved, with these slow movements of his wife's body. Freshly painted furnishings reflected back flecks of light. Bob's eyes touched on bric-a-brac and order, at things he'd done and things he'd yet to do. She smiled and looked at him as if she'd said hello. The baby blew its breath between its lips and spluttered, then settled back and rubbed its head against his mother's stomach.

Bob turned and swayed and started for the sink. One by one he washed the dishes and stopped to stir the scum that floated on the water. A platter kept its grease. He picked it up and turned it round. Attentively he looked at it and let it fall. He dropped the dishes one by one. They smashed upon the floor. He washed them clean and dried them and dropped them on the floor.

A cup he clenched his fist about he threw upon the littered floor. He grabbed a shelf above the sink and tore it off the wall. Maidie picked the baby up and left the room. He held his breath, then swore, and hit the wall. His knuckles bled. He took an axe and chopped a chair to little bits, and whittled on the wood. Then with his tape he noted down his measurements. He closed the book, then tore it quite in half, and walked out into the night.

MILLER STEWART
Canada's Pollution Problem

How far is it to good fishing in much of Canada – to safe bathing, to pleasant boating, or to decent living on the banks of our rivers and streams?

Can we return to these benefits in five or ten years of prying, pushing, and pestering our health and conservation departments? Or will it take longer to scare the cautious political pants off their masters, our municipal, provincial, and federal governments?

In this scorching summer of 1949, the sweating citizens of our big eastern industrial cities sweltered beside the cool waters of our Great Lakes – waters that were banned by the ominous signs of 'Dangerous for bathing.' The dry early summer left many of our streams – drainage basins for whole countrysides – chains of stagnant pools stinking with dead fish, rank with decaying vegetation, a menace to health and an offence to the nostrils.

Why was our municipal and industrial housekeeping allowed to sink to this disgraceful level? It is a long story, and one that has been repeated over and over again in many parts of Canada and the United States. For the sake of clarity and simplicity, it may be told like this, using the salmon as old-time miners used canaries.

One of the unforeseen results of the opening of the first Welland Canal in the 1830s was that Atlantic salmon quickly found this means of bypassing the hitherto impassable barrier of Niagara Falls, and were reported as far west as Sault Ste Marie – but not for long. For the opening of the canal heralded and hastened the clearing of the forests and the coming of people and industry. We know from old survey records that over Ontario there was an average of one-and-a-third miles of watercourse for each square mile of country. With the felling of the forests and opening of plowlands, this has fallen to one-eighth of that figure or less than 300 yards per square mile. Saw mills, grist mills, towns, and villages soon started to pollute the sparkling waters, and the lordly salmon, most fastidious of fish, retreated until today they are taken only in a few unspoiled streams in the sparsely inhabited portions of Labrador, Gaspé, New Brunswick, and Newfoundland.

It is as futile and irrational to mourn the passing of the king of game fish from our rivers as to yearn for the countless buffalo of the plains and the myriads of passenger pigeons who fed on the acorns and beechnuts of the levelled forests. But it does emphasize the fact that the Saguenay, the St Maurice, the Richelieu, the Ottawa, yes, and the Ganaraska, the Don, the Humber, the Thames, and the Grand were once as clear and wholesome as the Restigouche, the Miramichi, and the St John still remain. Almost every river from the seaboard to the head of the Lakes except those which are pollution-proof by the sheer bulk of their waters or remoteness from population are polluted to the danger point with human and industrial wastes.

Our rivers are natural resources that are either exhaustible or renewable – whichever our people desire. The cycle of neglect and exploitation that strangles a river starts with a full flowing river, a highway for vessels, a source of clear water, wholesome fish, a recreation asset of great value, and, if used in moderation, a vehicle for removing waste products. In the memory of many Canadians now living, many Canadian rivers filled that description. Cultivation extended, trees were cut down, fields were plowed without regard for erosion, source marshes were drained, and we overloaded the streams with the products of our sewers. As the river strangles on silt and pollution, it fails in all its functions. The spring run-off of winter's snows comes with a rush without the restraining influence of tree shade and the absorptive value of roots and leaf mould. Spring floods result. In the summer the same stream becomes a chain of stagnant pools or a sluggish, reeking gutter on which man turns his back, and holds his nose. Its banks become garbage and trash dumps, its waters dangerous for swimming, unpleasant for boating, sterile of all save the coarsest fish life, and its water drinkable only after expensive filtering and disinfection by chlorine. A full stoppage in our supply of chlorine (a most unlikely happening) would probably put a very considerable portion of our people in hospital in two weeks.

Fortunately a river takes a long time to die by neglect and strangulation. Convalescence is rapid when the process is reversed. When farm woodlots are replenished, when poor farming areas on its banks are reforested, when farm practices combat erosion, when the sources are put back into condition and our filthy municipal and industrial housekeeping improved, the river can be resurrected as a natural heritage of beauty, sport and usefulness.

Of course, we can't put back our felled forests, and if navigability has deteriorated sufficiently it cannot be restored. The pristine purity and volume of the wilderness stream is out of the question, but nevertheless restored rivers can be safe, beautiful, and full of fun for swimmer, boating enthusiast, and fisherman whenever a serious effort at rehabilitation is made. Further, a river in good condition can improve the underground watertable to the point where wells miles from its banks benefit quickly when the river flow is active and clear. A high watertable means improved pastures and increased crop yields. To municipalities a high watertable greatly eases the water supply problem, grave in many places. It doesn't matter whether the water is drawn from wells or from streams or reservoirs.

When John Graves Simcoe came upon the confluence of the north and south branches of the Thames River at the present site of London, Ontario, he declared it one of the most beautiful river sites in a country of great beauty, and proposed that that spot should be the capital of Upper Canada. The summer of 1948, a fully qualified technician, James Johnston of Brown University, described the Thames at the same spot as 'dark and dirty, a highway of pollution.' He backed his statement by sound scientific facts, for the river water at that point proved to contain as much as 6,000,000 coliform bacteria per cubic centimeter – a condition that might well be described as poisonous.

Canada, with one of the greatest drainage and river systems in the world as its heartland – the St Lawrence-Great Lakes Basin – has only a handful of clean rivers left from the Saguenay to the Nipigon. Wherever there are cities or towns, wherever there are mines, pulp and paper mills, oil refineries, gas works, chemical industries, canneries, or food-processing plants, our rivers are in danger of being killed. Only on the prairies where rivers are scarce and precious have we exercised any care in their use. With this exception, we are treating our rivers to one of the worst exhibitions of careless housekeeping to be found in the world. Our municipalities and industries are putting up a stout battle against measures to improve the situation.

Let's treat the municipal angle first. There are in Canada 1,376 civic organizations with waterworks. Of these only 584 have a sewage system, and only 152 have further systems for disposing of their sewage other than dumping it untreated into the nearest river or stream.

One hundred and one of these sewage disposal plants are in Ontario, and only seven east of Ottawa. In Saskatchewan 67 per cent of the municipalities that have water supply have sewage disposal, 57 per cent in Ontario, and 50 per cent in Alberta. There are no disposal plants in Nova Scotia, PEI, or Newfoundland, and very few in New Brunswick or Quebec.

As a rough rule of thumb, a river can safely accept only 5 per cent of its flow volume in waste if its flow is good, and a slow-flowing river can accept only 2½ per cent. In both cases the natural flow of the river will cleanse it again in seven miles.

If you recall that we originally had eight times as much watercourse for each square mile of countryside before deforestation, and that our towns and cities were much smaller, you can understand why so many municipalities transgress the danger point of their river's waste-carrying capacity. For these towns the first essential is a sewage-disposal plant which removes a great part of the solids in the sewage and returns to the river an effluent that it can safely handle. A sewage-disposal plant is expensive – but not having one can be many times as costly. Indeed, it is only because our country has been relatively uncrowded that we have not already paid a high price for our carelessness.

As yet there has been no official study of the

matter in Canada except that the International Boundary Waters Commission which has just completed its sessions has once more shown that the towns and industries along the border are still drawing their drinking water from the same streams into which they pour their untreated sewage wastes, and that cities the size of Windsor still have no sewage-disposal plants.

One of the many things that we in Canada share with our US cousins is our sin of wasting bountiful assets. The story of America's rivers parallels ours with this exception – they have made a real start on the redemption of their rivers. The last Congress, in the dying moments of its reign, passed the Taft-Barkley (not to be confused with the Taft-Hartley) Act which makes substantial grants for study and investigation of various phases of pollution, makes available funds for municipalities to plan sewage-disposal works, and will give up to $250,000 for actual construction of such works as are approved. This act also provides that the federal Department of Health can, upon the instigation of state authorities, prosecute offenders against the pollution code. A number of states have already started to work on the problem, and have gone after both municipalities and industries which flouted the general welfare by maltreating rivers and streams. The United States has been divided into fourteen zones and the states within each zone are encouraged to co-operate in fighting this problem. In general, the anti-pollution methods that were used in the Tennessee Valley Authority have been taken as the model for the new attack on dirty rivers.

A recent issue of the *Saturday Evening Post* carried the story of the attack under this law upon the Schuylkill, for generations one of the outstanding examples of a filthy river. The strong methods and forceful approach used in this case would have been of no avail, as were all previous attempts, without strong federal backing of this kind.

In Canada, we have had federal, provincial, and municipal laws against pollution for many years, but there have been too many offenders to prosecute! A town or industry accused could always point to other offenders who were getting away with it. Recently, however, a pulp and paper company in northern Ontario was fined and assessed for damages to fishing resorts caused by the dumping of 'white water' from its new mill. The case was appealed, but the original punishment stood, although, no doubt, that particular company will feel that it has been discriminated against unless some of the other flagrant offenders in the district are also fined.

Over Canada as a whole there has been more nuisance created by our industries than by our cities and towns because we have tolerated a point of view that did not regard the proper disposal of industrial waste as part of the cost of doing business. Laws against offenders will help, but we cannot meet the problem fully until we evoke the unenforceable law of good neighbourliness. If we think about the other fellow who lives downstream, and treat him as we expect our upstream neighbour to treat us, the problem is solved. There is no phase of citizenship that requires a better spirit of co-operation that the team work that can regenerate a river valley. The task starts largely with the individual who decides that his share in the enterprise is to clean up his little piece of river bank, and, by example and exhortation, to encourage his neighbour to do likewise.

Although streams have no regard for man's political boundaries, the next step is at the community level. Town or township should, when enough public support has been engendered, pass bylaws to coerce the recalcitrant or lazy. But, more important, they should show a willingness to co-operate with neighbouring units in evolving a plan that will harmonize over the whole watershed. This kind of planning involves forming public opinion that conditions could be improved, then getting a clear idea of what is to be done, and developing widespread recognition that co-operation in a planned attack is essential. At this point a Conservation Authority should be set up with each municipality in the watershed represented. Here is where the province will help by providing technical advice with soil, woodland, water, and wildlife surveys, and, in most cases, with grants to further approved plans.

The method of attack on the problem differs with every valley, indeed, it may vary in different sections of the same stream. For instance, in Ontario there are in various stages of organization almost a dozen conservation authorities, and each must meet its problems in its own way. The Humber Valley Conservation Authority's project contained no big dams, no extensive stream-straightening schemes, in fact no large-scale construction of any kind. Farm ponds, reforestation of swamp tracts, permanent pastures on slopes, contour plowing and strip-cropping with gully and stream bank planting were all to be tried on a 1,200-acre tract purchased by the Humber Valley Authority as a demonstrative area, and were to be used as a recreation ground and as a field department of the natural-science branch of the University of Toronto. The project was announced with a burst of publicity. The Acting Prime Minister spoke at a meeting to inaugurate the program. Then, the whole thing was lamely called off. Protests were answered with the usual passing of the buck to federal authorities, but this after it had been announced that the work would go ahead with or without Dominion support. So far no satisfactory explanation has been offered, and in spite of strong condemnation of its timidity by the *Globe and Mail*, the Ontario government stands pat. The cost would have been trifling, but the whole affair is a nasty example of picayune, peanut politics at a time and place where a strong stand could have done much good.

The Thames Valley Authority, on the other hand, will start with an extensive stream-deepening and straightening project on a notorious flood plain and will proceed to build a series of dams which will produce a number of lakes for river regulation which can be developed as recreation areas. Widely different as these schemes are, they both had equal prospects of curing the problems under attack in the opinion of experienced authorities.

Our rivers and stream problems will vary in scope from the run-off rills in the back forty to the mighty rivers that transcend not only provincial but national boundaries, and the degree of co-operation will vary from two friendly farmers working together in a creek bed to the point where Washington and Ottawa meet on the same footing of mutual help and co-operation.

So let us make our rivers useful citizens – not spotless, but fit to live with. The co-operative spirit our efforts will arouse will make better citizens of all of us – and our country a better, richer place to live in.

[Ed. note: Since this article was received a bill introduced into the House of Commons by Rodney Adamson (PC York West), to prohibit the pollution of Canada's navigable waters by the discharge of oil and raw sewage, has been turned down by the government.]

THE 50s

If there is a dark decade in the history of *The Canadian Forum* it may well be the 1950s. Canada was complacent and smug, riding the crest of the boom, a staunch ally and a fast friend of the United States, and a hard-lining foe of world communism. Satisfied apathy ruled in the guise of Louis St Laurent, and to some extent the national mood was reflected in the pages of the *Forum*. Contributors could write about the discrimination faced by Indians and Eskimos in Canada, but no one seemed to care. Frank Underhill no longer appeared with regularity, and by this time he was turning away from the CCF and toward the Liberal party. The fire was gone from his belly – and from the *Forum*'s too. Only at the end of the decade with the emergence of John Diefenbaker and a new Canadian conservatism did some of the old bite begin to reappear.

Canadian literature was in a similar stage of static consolidation. One or two new writers appeared in the *Forum*, and there was some fierce literary feuding among the poets and critics who had matured in the 1940s. Ultimately this testing of critical theories and poetic stances may have led to a resurgence in the 1960s.

S.W. BRADFORD

The CCF Failure in Foreign Policy

It is discouraging to observe that nowhere in this country (outside the Labour-Progressive party) has there been in 1950 any serious radical criticism of the St Laurent-Pearson-Wrong obeisance to Washington. The Conservative press has recently been saying 'too little and too late,' but even here has been using Milquetoast epithets compared to the lashing administered to Johnson, Acheson, and Truman in the United States. And far worse, the CCF leaders have been busying themselves only with suppressing the BC socialist-pacifist point of view in the Vancouver Convention and out-shouting the Tories in calling for greater participation in the Korean conflict. Is it enough for them to be watering down the Regina Manifesto for domestic purposes and to be ignoring the socialist position on war, imperialism, and international armaments? These questions are not simply the echo of the discredited pacifist-isolationism of the 1930s; they beg the further question of what Canadian socialists have to offer as a genuine and original contribution to the formation of a democratic foreign policy aimed at the prevention of atomic mutual destruction. Surely that question has not been adequately considered in recent issues of the *Forum* or of the CCF press.

If Canadian socialists have been skirting this fundamental issue, Labour party and Fabian leaders in the United Kingdom, and progressive pacifists in the United States have been deeply preoccupied with it. They have not been content with the bungling and high-handed manner in which the Department of State administered UN before June 25; nor have they tumbled over themselves crying, 'Me too' when the United States illegally acted in the name of UN in the Korean venture.

In the United States, the most interesting discussion of these questions was published by the American Friends' Service Committee late in 1949 (*The United States and the Soviet Union, Some Quaker Proposals for Peace*, New Haven, 1949). This dispassionate survey of American-Russian relations brought the distinguished Quaker authors to some positive recommendations. Since, they say, both systems, capitalist and communist, are likely to endure as far ahead as we can see, they must learn to live and let live. The tension between the two now is tremendously augmented by the unlimited race for arms superiority. Neither system is as inflexible dogmatically as its opponent suspects, and those in the Western world who believe that a Marxist is everywhere and at all times the same under the skin are gravely mistaken. With these points in mind, suggest the Quakers, our attention should be focussed not upon those aspects of the communist system which differentiate it from ours, and which we condemn, but upon the possible points of contact between the two systems. Particularly should trade between east and west Europe be again permitted and encouraged by the United States. Discussion on a German peace treaty should be re-opened. There must be a fresh approach by the United States to the UN as a body for negotiating the settlement of disputes (and one might now add as a body which must always represent the existing governments of the peoples of the world). In that organization the United States and other non-Communist countries should concentrate upon issues where they could vote with and not against the USSR. There should be a positive willingness on the part of the United States to reduce the burden of armaments and to concede that conventional as well as newer weapons be considered together in this over-riding problem. The development of an international civil service and o-operation with Russia in the economic development of backward areas are further suggestions in the same theme. All this, of course, to our new War Hawks in Canada and the United States, is anathema. But to a socialist who is, or should be, disturbed by the hydrogen bomb and the recent history of China, Formosa, Japan, Korea, Indo-China, and Malaya, the Quaker book must hold an appeal. Or do we all abandon ship in a 'preventive war'?

In England, C.E.M. Joad, an ex-pacifist, outlined some possible British conclusions which might reasonably follow a reading of the Quaker book (*New Statesman and Nation,* June 3, 1950). Granting the validity of the basic Quaker points, writes Joad, how best can the United Kingdom further the process of mutual accommodation between the two great imperial nations? He argues the necessity of Britain's cutting away from partnership in American policies and then, as a declared neutral in the world struggle of Russia and America, and in partnership with an increasing number of neutrals (including, he hopes, other Commonwealth countries), using her weight in the United Nations to bring about a decrease in armaments and an increase in co-operative progressive activity. This seems to be a renewal of the third force idea and, as Joad writes, 'It is surprising, considering the importance of the issues involved and the amount of discussion they evoke, how little consideration has been publicly given to the question whether and on what terms we could keep out.' He suggests the maintenance of the present level of armaments which would provide Britain and other neutrals with a high nuisance value for any potential aggressor. This may be an extreme proposition, but when one considers the position of Britain, now a declared ally of the United States, as a permanent aircraft carrier off the coast of an ill-defined Western Europe, the Joad proposal assumes some of the colour of moderation.

In France and the other countries of Western Europe and Scandinavia the idea of neutrality gains strength daily. At Paris, two leading historians, Etienne Gilson and André Siegfried, are leaders in the advocacy of this policy. They voice arguments similar to those expressed in England by Joad and the more independent Labour party members. All seem to agree that democracy must pay at least as much attention to its social-economic defences against communism as to its military. Many have proposed that the Western European countries should emulate the military organization and purposes of the Swiss and the Swedes. France in particular is coming to understand that Western Europe cannot undertake to fulfil the American plans of military expansion without jeopardizing its social and economic recovery and thereby leaving itself vulnerable to a vigilant communism within its own borders.

One may well ask whether Canadian socialists have pondered these questions – and how Korea affects this 'wild talk.' Are we simply to abandon our scruples, accept the American account of its stewardship in South Korea, and send our forces to the East for General MacArthur to use indiscriminately from Formosa to the conquest of North Korea? What real guarantees has a Canadian socialist that the Korean war is not, after all, just another outbreak in an ever most desperate imperial rivalry between Russia and the United States? The capitalist dictatorship of MacArthur in Japan, the fiercely reactionary regimes of Chiang-Kai-shek and Syngman Rhee, the unrivalled corruption of French colonial policy in Indo-China – is it not more important to revise all this before risking an atomic war in defence of the 38th parallel? How many of the CCF leaders who now call for Canadian troops attempted to learn anything of the South Korean dictatorship's repression of all reform and civil liberty; or of the South Korean Labour party members who opposed Rhee's planned invasion of North Korea and demanded the withdrawal of both Russian and American troops and advisers? These men received jail sentences ranging up to ten years (*New York Times*, March 14, 1950; *New York Herald Tribune*, November 1, 1949). Is the CCF as a party finally condemned to an uncritical defence of the *status quo* throughout the world?

In 1885, Sir John A. Macdonald turned down the British request for assistance in the Soudan with his famous comment that 'Gladstone and Co.' would have to rely on their own resources to extricate themselves from the hole into which they were plunged by 'their own imbecility.' In historical perspective the present policy of the CCF puts it far to the right of the notable old loyalist. Indeed, if the CCF wishes to remain a truly Canadian party it will have to do some very hard thinking about the realities of this world, and not get led down the path of American expansionism which it views at present through the clouded spectacles of 'collective security.' It would do well to study such current criticism as has been noted above, and also to consider Canada's own experience in foreign affairs.

The first fifty years of Canada's national existence were spent in almost unceasing effort to develop national cohesion and genuine independence of action – to cast off the last vestiges of colonial dependence. During that time also, successive Canadian statesmen sought every opportunity to conciliate threatened breaches of the peace between Britain and America – to keep Canada from being ground to pieces between two expansive imperialisms (or, if the reader likes, between one imperialism and one manifest destiny). The belief that the experiment in building a nation was worthwhile sustained much of this effort and most Canadians shied away from any future in which the world would be divided into two great power blocks in which the more liberal virtues of smaller sovereign or autonomous units would be foresworn. Today Canada's relationship to the United States appears to be as much one of colonial dependence as was our relationship to Britain during most of the years after 1867. One seeks in vain to discover any sphere in which Canadian policy abroad, or control of economic (and therefore social) development at home is not basically affected by American investment or influence. This may or may not be a desirable condition, but as the picture comes more clearly into focus one is reminded of Edward Blake's great West Durham letter of 1891 in which he warned his countrymen of just this peril. If union with the United States is inevitable, he wrote, let us discuss the terms on which it will take place. If it is not, let us discover whether we wish to bring it about or not. In other words, let us look the facts in the face and make up our minds about the conclusions that may be drawn from them.

Again, Canadians have always prided themselves on their willingness and ability, while growing in independence, to act as 'interpreter' between Britain and the United States, in the interest of Canadian development and safety. Today, when Russia has replaced Britain as the greatest block to American expansion, is there any less need for Canadians to do a little conciliating – a job which cannot be done while we are riveted to the Eagle? This is by no means a suggestion that Canada withdraw from any developing system of collective security, but it is a plea that CCF leaders examine more closely than they seem to have done the current policies of collective security which, like those of Goering, seem always to place guns ahead of butter. These policies leave great areas of the world open to the real force of Communist aggression which is to be found in infiltration and propaganda in economically depressed or backward areas. They expose not only Britain and Western Europe militarily; they leave Canada destined for the role of first and most devastated battleground of World War III.

Canada presumably wishes to remain independent and to make her contribution to world political and economic development as a nation and not as a satellite. Let us then consider again the practical and moral virtues of the third force (which has nearly died at the hands of 'realist' Ernest Bevin), and work with others, inside the Commonwealth (like Nehru's India) and outside the Commonwealth, for a world which socialists could call free.

Note: S.W. Bradford is a pseudonym of Kenneth McNaught.

FRANK H. UNDERHILL

Canadian Socialism and World Politics

Mr Bradford's article in the last number of *The Canadian Forum*, entitled 'The CCF Failure in Foreign Policy,' threw more light on the state of mind of some of our disgruntled CCF fundamentalists than it did on the issues of foreign policy. In fact, if one admits its sincerity, one has to add that it persistently beclouded most of the real issues by the way in which it coloured facts so as to distort them, or insinuated some malign purpose in American policy (usually by way of rhetorical questions) instead of quite making an open charge that could be refuted.

For example: (1) 'The US illegally acted in the name of UN in the Korean venture,' though he must know that there is a perfectly good answer to this Russian charge of illegality, an answer based on Russian actions in the Security Council. (2) 'Or do we abandon ship in a preventive war?,' though he must know that responsible leaders in the USA and Britain have quickly repudiated a preventive war every time it has been proposed by some hothead. (3) 'Are we to send our forces for MacArthur to use indiscriminately from Formosa to North Korea?,' though he must know that long before he wrote both the British and Canadian governments had dissociated themselves from American action in the matter of Formosa; and since he wrote, President Truman has slapped MacArthur down when that doughty warrior announced a personal policy of his own on Formosa. Mr Bradford's whole article is skilfully coloured by suggestive statements like these so as to give an impression of American devils on one side, followed by their docile External Affairs and CCF satellites in Ottawa, and certain (unidentified) pure and uncorrupted Bradfordite 'socialists' on the other.

Mr Bradford, before he carries this kind of argument any further, should stop a moment and consider the kind of company he is getting into. The two main groups in Canada who are taking this isolationist, neutralist line against our involvement in world power-politics, are the extremists among the French-Canadian 'nationalists' – the Laurentians of the 1930s and their friends – and the Labour Progressive party with their fellow-travellers. What kind of a socialism is it that lands one in such company?

And when Mr Bradford and his strange bedfellows begin whooping up their anti-American cries, they are joined by a select group of our ultra-Tories, who have always suffered from a Freudian longing to creep back into their British mother's womb. It has been amusing, also, to observe the tender solicitude for the British connection which our Canadian Communists have been displaying of late. They'll be recruiting an Allan MacNab-John A. Macdonald international brigade one of these days to fight against the American Franco in Washington. And Mr Bradford had better watch out or they'll be wanting him to join it.*

Mr Bradford is alarmed lest we have already become an American satellite. But readers of *The Canadian Forum* who may not have kept in touch with British journalism should be informed that he himself in this article is functioning as a satellite of Mr Kingsley Martin and the *New Statesman*. The whole article is pure Newstatesmanese. In 1945 the *New Statesman* started the post-war era with the cry that the British Labour government should work with the USSR rather than with the USA. When hard facts made it clear to everyone that the USSR refused all co-operation, it then shifted to demanding a 'third-force' in Europe to hold the balance between the two non-European giants. Now that the idea of the third force has also been shown to belong to the dream world, and again because Russian policy has forced a polarization of world politics into two armed camps – (if two countries ever disarmed, it was Britain and the USA after 1945) – the *New Statesman*, driven back from one position to another, is now fighting in the last ditch of anti-Americanism. It comes forth every week with a new list of American faults, real or imaginary. The fact is that it has no 'socialist' foreign policy for the world as it exists in 1950. It has only a collection of clichés inherited from the 1930s, when even clichés looked realistic as against Chamberlainism. Its real policy is simple negative defeatism. Because it couldn't have the kind of world it wanted after 1945, it behaves like a spoilt child and refuses to come out and play.

And this is what Mr Bradford's Canadian 'socialist' foreign policy comes to also. In an article of three and a half columns he has no positive concrete suggestions at all. He merely objects to everything that is being done by the Canadian government or by the CCF leaders, and rides off on vague phrases: – 'The prevention of atomic mutual destruction' – on what terms? 'Concentration in the UN upon issues where they can vote with and not against the USSR' – what issues? 'Co-operation with Russia in the development of backward areas' – co-operation on what terms, and in what areas? China?

The *New Statesman* it should be added, has been steadily repudiated by the bulk of the British Labour party ever since 1945. Admittedly there are some pretty black spots in Mr Bevin's foreign policy – his treatment of Palestine, e.g., and his failure to get the heavy industry of the Ruhr socialized when the British were in full control there. But the opposition within the Labour party to his general line of policy has shrunk until it is an insignificant splinter-group which hardly dares to divide the House. The overwhelming majority of British socialists are supporting exactly the kind of foreign policy which Mr Coldwell and his lieutenants have supported in the House of Commons at Ottawa and in the CCF convention at Vancouver. And even in France, where defeatism is admittedly rampant, it is significant that Mr Bradford quotes M. Maritain and M. Siegfried as exponents of the pacifist neutralist isolationism which he hints at throughout his article as being the 'original socialist and democratic policy' that he wants. These are two worthy gentlemen, but they are not socialists, and he can't quote the French Socialist party on his side. Nor the Belgian, Dutch, or Norwegian socialists.

Ultimately all this talk along the New Statesman-Bradford line comes down to a question of the nature of the Soviet regime in Russia and of its foreign policy. Surely it is about time, in this October of 1950, for persons of Mr Bradfords's persuasion to produce some evidence that it is possible to co-operate with Russia on the atomic bomb, on Korea, on disarmament, or on any other major issue, on any basis which differs from complete capitulation to Russian terms. In domestic politics most persons left of centre have discovered by painful experiences that the only kind of co-operation understood by the Communist party is complete subservience to communist domination. In international politics since 1945 the attempts of western governments to co-operate with the Soviet govern-

---

*They would, I suppose, put him in a special scout company, to be raised mainly from among Canadian historians, with Captain Lower and Lieutenant Creighton in charge.

ment have all broken down because it follows exactly the same drive for domination in its international diplomacy. Co-operation from 1940 to 1945 was only possible because our armies were in Africa and western Europe, and the Russian armies were in eastern Europe, with the German armies between the two allied groups. From the moment that our armies met their armies on the Elbe, we have disagreed with them on every major issue. And surely it is impossible now to reject the conclusion that, while there were of course mistakes and stupidities on both sides, the fundamental reason for this disagreement is that the Communists have shown that there is no limit to their ambition short of world domination and that they think their ambition is realizable because of our weakness.

These seem to me to be plain undeniable historical facts. If Mr Bradford has another interpretation of recent history, let him get away from pious generalities and tell us what kind of an agreed peaceable compromise settlement he thinks to be reasonable on (say) the atomic bomb or Korea. Then we shall be able to judge concretely whether the Bradford settlement differs in any substantial way from acceptance of the Russian terms; and if it does so differ, we shall be able to judge whether there is any likelihood of Russia's accepting it.

This brings us to the real core of the argument – power politics. Mr Bradford has been careful not to state his position too clearly here, but what he is really objecting to is the process by which Canada has become involved in world power politics. If the analysis which I have sketched above is at all valid, then we cannot avoid power politics, because the application of power in the decisive areas is the only thing that will stop Russia. Mr Bradford speaks throughout as if there were a practical alternative between confronting the Soviet government with our military power and giving economic assistance to the backward areas in Asia and Europe. But the hard fact is that we have to pursue both policies simultaneously.

Liberals and liberal socialists don't like seeing their communities become absorbed in military struggles. And it is our duty to keep insisting that no settlement of Europe and Asia will be secure unless military victory is accompanied by social and economic reconstruction, and unless the nationalities of Europe and Asia are left to determine their own social structure according to their own ideas and not according to the ideas of Republican senators in Washington. But the peoples of Europe and Asia have no alternative to being absorbed under Russian totalitarian domination unless we impose our power to stop this constant Soviet aggression. And if we don't stop it somewhere in Europe or Asia, we shall one day be faced by a threat to our own freedom in America. There is no escaping from power politics in the present world. And this means working in alliance with the power of the United States. Incidentally, has Mr Bradford some 'socialist' program of his own for raising the standard of living in the Far East or in Western Europe which doesn't involve the use of American money?

When faced with this necessity of joining in a world struggle for power, Canadian Liberals and CCFers are admittedly in an embarrassing position. And Mr Bradford skilfully makes the most of this embarrassment. For all our favourite traditions are against such an involvement. In the nineteenth century North American colonial isolation was a reasonable proposition, because in the conditions of those days the Atlantic was a very wide ocean, and Canada was shielded from the impact of European power politics by the protection of the British navy (which was there whether we remained a part of the British empire or not, and whether we contributed to it or not – the United States was equally protected) and by the balance of power on the European continent. By 1914 this twin shield was no longer giving such automatic protection, for Germany was breaking up the European balance and building a navy at the same time. Laurier Liberals found themselves in intellectual difficulties about Canadian aloofness during the decade before 1914, and when the war came they had no choice but to join in. The United States thought it had the alternative of staying out, but by 1917 the German threat to the balance of power forced the Americans in also.

After 1918 it seemed that we could return to isolation and turn our backs on power politics again. It seemed so both to Mr King and to Mr Woodsworth, and to their followers, and it continued to seem so for some years after the rise of Hitler. Even if one did not take the Christian pacifist position of Mr Woodsworth, it seemed that the power of the British Navy and the French army was so overwhelming that the Nazi challenge could be handled within Europe without outside intervention from North America. Of course this reading of where power was really located in Europe turned out in the spring of 1940 to be completely without basis in fact, and we ought not to have been so foolish.* In the end we had to go to war again in Europe.

Today no one can deceive himself into thinking that there is any possibility of a balance of power in Europe unless the armed force of North America is thrown into the balance. And the need for a European balance has expanded into the need for a world balance. Technological developments – the long-range bomber and the long-range submarine, the new guided missiles, the atomic bomb – have made the world a very small area in which we all have vulnerable frontiers. We cannot get away from power politics. The nineteenth-century liberal and nationalistic traditions of Canada are no longer relevant.

This means another thing, that we have to work with the United States. Here again Mr Bradford can enjoy himself by appealing to past Canadian traditions. But he is talking simple nonsense when he claims that our present position vis-a-vis the USA is as colonial as was our nineteenth-century relationship to Great Britain. We are not, in the first place, depending on American power for our protection without contributing some considerable power of our own, as the Canadian colony depended on British power in Victorian days. Most important of all, we do not suffer from a psychological colonial complex. We are not emotionally involved in identifying our personality and our destiny

*I make a present to Mr Bradford of the admission that I was one of the foolish isolationists of those days in the 1930s who wasn't impressed by stories of German planes and German armoured divisions.

with the United States as our grandfathers were emotionally involved in a filial tie with the nineteenth-century 'mother-country.' ('A British subject I was born, a British subject I will die.') Right down to the 1940s whenever any Canadian proposed any action which showed independence of British leadership and control, he had to face a chorus of denunciations from all the respectable part of the community on the ground that he was 'disloyal.' Whenever the world 'disloyalty' was used it meant disloyalty not to Canada but to Britain. We do not suffer from any such complex in our attitude to the United States. A Canadian can tell an American to go to hell without being accused by the Toronto newspapers of disloyalty to the United States. And there is no likelihood of this happy state of affairs changing. The American people have shown no genius for being a 'mother-country.'

So there we are. Socialists or anti-socialists, we cannot escape power politics in this generation. If we want a liberal democractic socialist world, we have first to make sure that we are going to have a free world in which free propaganda for democratic socialism can be carried on. Until the threat of Soviet totalitarianism has been removed, freedom is a more fundamental issue in our world than socialism.

S.F. WISE

Canadian Football

One of the most revealing phenomena of the twentieth century has been the rise to prominence of mass spectator sports, on a scale unparalleled by the gladiatorial contests or bearbaitings of older times. Organized athletic environment on the grand scale dates from the turn of the century, but made its most striking advance in the middle twenties, the so-called 'Golden Age of Sport.' This was the era of Dempsey and Tunney, of Tilden and Bobby Jones, of Babe Ruth and Red Grange, of the two million dollar gate, the six-day bicycle race, and the dance marathon. Today a comparable impulse is under way, this generation showing the same incapacity for amusing itself, although having an infinite capacity for amusement.

During the past half-century a great sports myth has been built up. Not even when the walls of Greek cities were torn down in welcome for the Olympic victor has the athlete been held in so high esteem. Barbara Ann Scott and Joe Dimaggio have become the pedestalled objects of a nation's adulation; in 1940 an American presidential candidate was elected when Joe Louis, after a tense period of hesitation, decided to support him. The romantic, unreal world of sport has captured the imaginations of millions. It appeals, on different levels, to every class, and the glowing deeds of its peerless champions are chronicled, with more than skaldic veneration, by legions of sports writers.

Although the athletic half-world is largely

one of American creation, Canada, as usual, has been just a few paces behind. Thus the emergence of football as a mass attraction in Canada follows by two decades a similar development in the United States, although Canadians have been playing the game, after a fashion, for nearly a century. Montrealers of the 1860s were the first North Americans to be exposed to English rugby from which football on both sides of the border evolved. As played by the officers of the soon-to-be-withdrawn British regulars, teams were fifteen a side, and the ball was put into play by being heeled out from a grunting mass of eighteen men (the 'scrum') into the arms of the fleet half-backs.

McGill University introduced this game to the United States in 1874, playing a scoreless draw with Harvard. The traditional rivalry with the University of Toronto started seven years later. In 1906 the game broke entirely with the English style of play, with the adoption of a national code of rules.

The object of the sport is to advance the ball (a prolate spheroid consisting of a rubber bladder covered with leather) across the opponent's goal-line, by carrying, kicking, or passing it. The field is a hundred and ten yards long, sixty yards wide, with a goal area of varying width, depending on the stadium. The offensive team must move the ball ten yards in three plays (downs) or lose possession.

As in warfare, there has been in the history of football an alternation between the predominance of the offence or the defence. Today, rule-makers, in the interests of higher scoring and thus presumably greater box office appeal, have weighted the game in favour of the attacking side. Such innovations as the forward pass, and the legalizing of blocking out defenders ten yards ahead of the spot from which the ball is put into play have put weapons of great power in the hands of the offence and incidentally, have moved the Canadian game much closer to the American.

The analogy with war has validity in some other aspects. Over the years elaborate tactical systems called formations have been built up to facilitate the attack. Different groupings of backfielders and linemen are employed and out of these arrangements as many as fifty distinct offensive moves may be launched. Although the team is viewed as a tactical unit, each member has his own assignment, whether blocking, carrying the ball, passing, or executing a feint attack to draw off defenders. The 'T' formation, so called because of the deployment of three backfielders behind the quarterback, is now used by nearly all Canadian senior teams, whether college or professional. Thrusts from this formation are devastatingly abrupt, but to function well it requires split-second timing, fast crisp-blocking linemen, driving halfbacks, and a quarterback who, as well as being a brilliant field general, must be able to pass and to handle the unwieldy football with a juggler's skill. Although the 'T' formation is not new, Canadian quarterbacks of the required calibre are almost non-existent, and all eight major professional teams have hired American specialists at this post. Perhaps the most flawless performer here is Frank Filchock of the Montreal Alouettes.

For the spectator many of the sophistications of play are lost. This is perfectly understandable, since the focus of play embraces the whole field rather than, as in boxing, baseball, or track, a limited area at any one time. Thus most people simply follow the ball as it soars in a high, spiral arc from the passer to the receiver, or is carried by a dodging, twisting halfback in the open field. Others are attracted by the violent contacts of the game, the crushing tackles and blocks, the collision of helmets, armoured giants moving at top speed. For sheer colour, few sports can match football – the gaudy uniforms and gleaming helmets of the players set on a green expanse of ground; the officials in their striped uniforms; and the vast crowd itself, rearing many-hued from all sides of the field up to the last row of seats on the rim of the man-made canyon characteristic of the game. And, as with other forms of human expression, it is possible to apprehend football on a higher level than this.

The discriminating fan sees the key block that permitted a rubber-legged back to burst free, notes with true intellectual pleasure the deception on the flank that shifted unwary defenders out of position, and recognizes, too, the physical and mental lapses that resulted in an abortive offensive gesture. Very few football laymen ever reach this peak of appreciation, and indeed most sports writing is on the emotional 'epic' plane. Only rarely is there a columnist who can give a good technical analysis of a game. One such is Ted Reeve, of the Toronto *Telegram*, and even he has used his column as a publicity organ for the Balmy Beach club. Generally, there is a rather nauseating collusion between sportswriter and promoter. (In this connection, most clubs set aside upwards of $5,000 for publicity and 'good will.')

For, aside from the intrinsic visual merits of football itself (which it has always possessed), the greatest single factor in the post-war surge of Canadian rugby has been the application to it of the methods and organization of American big business. To win Canada's national championship it has been estimated that at least $90,000 is required. A winning team has become a financial as well as a popular necessity, and the result has been cut-throat competition for players, the importation of high-priced American players and coaches, and the placing of the sport on a professional and contractual basis.

Before the war the most celebrated import was Fritz Hanson, of the Winnipeg Blue Bombers, who received $1,200 a season plus a job as a candy salesman. Canadians were almost never paid. Today Canadian linemen receive at least $100 a game, and good Canadian halfbacks upwards of $3,000 a season. Americans all receive above $3,500, and most of them much more. Frank Filchock is paid something like $12,000 a season. In the west the salary scale is somewhat lower, but prior to the present season the Calgary Stampeders managed to lure a fine halfback, Royal Copeland, from the Toronto Argonauts for a sum certainly in excess of $7,000 and probably much more.

Due to higher transportation costs and smaller stadia, the western teams (Calgary, Edmonton, Regina, and Winnipeg) have always been in a more precarious financial position than their wealthy eastern rivals, and have, at various times, resorted to public subscription to make up their operating deficit. It still remains true that to show a really profitable season a western club must win through to a trip east for the Grey Cup final at Toronto's Varsity Stadium, largest in the dominion.

Toronto and Ottawa, on the other hand, have always been on the profit side, and Montreal has undergone an amazing recovery since the war, perhaps due to the unprecedented interest in football of the French population. Hamilton, always an enthusiastic football centre, has regained strength after a disastrous experiment with two senior teams. The Ontario Rugby Football Union, although much older than either the Big Four or the Western Conference, has sunk to the farm team level and can no longer be considered as a serious factor in big-time Canadian football.

College football has never been a success in the Maritimes (where rugger is played) or in the west, due both to transportation difficulties and the lack of a reservoir of young players similar to that developed in Ontario. McGill, Queen's, Toronto, and Western all have American coaches and often outdraw the professional clubs. For the university student the football game is only a minor link in the chain of social events built around it.

It has always been the convention of Canadian football pundits that the Canadian game is much better than the American version and that therefore there should be no change of rules in that direction. For a long time, however, many people have suspected that we have clung to our rules because in this way we avoid acknowledging how really second-rate our teams and coaching have been. This suspicion is borne out by the almost complete success of the American player in our game, notwithstanding the fact that the imports we have are by no means the most skillful representatives of American football. American coaching methods stress specialization of talent, meticulous attention to fundamentals of the game, and upon this highly involved structures of play are constructed. The result is a mechanical perfectionism that a Canadian club of the old type is unable to match.

Canadian publicists, unable to grasp this trend, still wistfully endeavour to badger Americans for flattering remarks upon our great game and great players. This is becoming an embarrassing process for both sides. We in Canada will have to accept, as we have so often in the past, another triumph of American technique and aggressiveness.

F.R. SCOTT

Mr King and the King Makers

In politics, as judged by certain standards all too prevalent, mere survival in office seems to be proof of leadership. On this basis Salazar in Portugal is a successful leader, and Duplessis in Quebec bids fair to be. Mr King, we are led to believe, was a great man because he managed to hold on to the Premiership longer than anyone else has been known to do. We are now permitting him, like Queen Victoria, to give his name to an era.

That Mr King had command of many political skills, that he rendered faithful service to Canada during the larger part of his life, none would deny. Only during World War 1 did he leave public employment to take up research in the United States. No scandal ever attached to his name; even the gross corruption shown to exist in his party by the Customs exposures of

1925 or the Beauharnois enquiry of 1931 did not reach him personally. His international reputation mounted steadily with the growth of Canadian industrial and military power. Anyone would be a narrow partisan indeed who did not accord to William Lyon Mackenzie King full credit where credit was due.

A halt should be called, however, when adulation begins to reach a point of myth-making. This process is now in full swing. Almost magical qualities of leadership are being attributed to the man; to him alone it seems we owe the expansion of Canadian population and wealth; his are the policies which have brought us a high degree of national unity; one almost comes to believe that he placed the oil under Alberta and the iron in Labrador. From professional Liberals all this is to be expected, but some of it has crept in to the writing of more discriminating critics. Perhaps it is not too soon to begin an assessment that comes closer to the realities.

Let us look more dispassionately at this question of leadership. In what sense did Mr King merit the term? Without demanding that leaders be forever dramatic, one can at least insist in a democracy that they let you know where they are going. It is doubtful if Mr King did more than decide issues from day to day – or postpone them. Political shrewdness is a quality he certainly possessed; political courage was seldom evident. Professor Underhill has well said that he was the leader who divided us least – but is this leadership? Or is it a skillful way of holding on to power? Is the leader the man who confuses issues, or the one who clarifies them even at the risk of making some enemies? What leadership did Canada get from Mr King during the great depression of the 1930s; what leadership did he give us then as to Canada's role in international affairs? Could Mr King ever have uttered anything as simple and forthright as did Mr St Laurent when he told Quebec that if there was another war Canada would be involved even if 12,999,999 of her 13,000,000 people were opposed to it? Professor Underhill has said that 'this is the kind of leadership, evidently, that modern mass-democracy welcomes and appreciates.' But President Roosevelt gave a very different kind of leadership, and received an even greater welcome from a larger mass-democracy. It is difficult to believe that Canadians could not have responded to a more positive appeal. If we have matured in politics during the King era, we have done it quite as much in spite of as because of Mr King.

The Liberal Party was not created by Mr King either in structure or program; he took it over as a well established orthodox party acceptable to the main power groups in Canada. He maintained it in this position, but he did not liberalize it. It is a more conservative party now than it was when he took it over. This is the real reason for the decline of the Conservatives, and for the rise of the CCF. True, the Liberals have now espoused a number of social ideas common to all parties of our day, but the espousal is always as little as can be and as late as can be. This is the King policy, and it has resulted in depriving the Canadian people of benefits which they can afford and are willing to pay for. Was Mr King's liberalism 'expressing what lay in the Canadian sub-conscious mind' when he adopted a policy of opposition to low-cost housing, price control, health insurance, and old-age insurance in the postwar years? Or was he expressing what lay in the mind – not sub-conscious – of the Canadian Manufacturers Association?

We should examine with equal care the idea that Mr King was the architect of Canadian unity. We may note in passing that the Liberal Party in Quebec has been reduced to a mere shadow of its former self. A special brand of Quebec nationalism came to power under the King régime. It is true that the extreme forms of disunity created by the conscription issue of World War I were avoided in World War II, though if the second war had not ended, for reasons not due solely to Mr King, this might not have been the case. But surely it is obvious that the improved relations between the two racial groups in Canada are much more due to changed international factors than to any King policy. Even *Le Devoir* has difficulty today in proving that every Canadian decision on international affairs is dictated in London. The decline of British imperial power is the basic cause of Canadian unity, as all informed opinion predicted it would be. In the matters of a Canadian flag, the national anthem, and the appointment of a Canadian Governor-General, where a gesture of normal Canadianism would have greatly assisted national unity, Mr King did nothing.

But there is a deeper aspect to this problem of unity, and here Mr King failed lamentably. A unified country has to have a constitution capable of handling national problems in a unified manner. There is a place for provincial autonomy in Canada, but there is place also, and an essential place, for federal responsibility. Mr King was so fearful of raising controversy that he did little to bring Canadians to a realization of the deficiencies in the powers of the national parliament. He did worse; he in effect added to those deficiencies. He was the man who referred the whole Bennett 'New Deal' legislation to the courts *en bloc*, thus almost inviting a declaration of *ultra vires*. He was a past master at using Royal Commissions as an excuse for inaction. He believed in a policy of frequent reference of national matters to dominion-provincial conferences, in which it was clear every province had a veto. He thus wrote the compact theory into the conventions of the constitution, where it now seems firmly embedded. Whether we shall ever be able to escape from this strait-jacket the present Constitutional Conference has tried to decide. This is not national unity. This is treating Canada as a kind of United Nations. And there is always a Malik in the land. Mr King's two great efforts to establish a new basis for national unity, the dominion-provincial conferences of 1940 and 1945, were both complete failures. Canada cannot be governed by replacing parliamentary responsibility with inter-governmental councils operating on the principle of the *liberum veto*. Which is another way of saying it cannot be governed on the King policy of converting provincial autonomy into dominion status.

It seems probable that Mr King's general handling of Canada's external relations will survive later criticism better than some other parts of his policy. His refusal to go along with plans for a unified Empire or Commonwealth, and his recognition of our essentially North American position with its corollary of closer ties with the United States, were sound decisions. They were also inescapable decisions; no others would have been tolerated. It will round out the picture to remember that with them went a slavish copying of the Chamberlain policy toward the League of Nations, and a rejection of any role for Canada in the Pan-American Union, that are difficult to excuse. Mr King may have turned a cold shoulder to Mr Lloyd George in the Chanak incident, but he turned an equally cold shoulder to those who demanded that Canada's right to enter war of her own free will and not automatically as a legal appendage of Britain should be clarified. His famous declaration of war in 1939 was due less to a belief in national sovereignty than to the pressure of the Conservatives and others who were afraid he would leave us uncertain whether we were at war or not. His friendship with Roosevelt made possible, or at least assisted, the growth of a fine form of Canadian-American co-operation. But we may well ask whether he did not start a trend toward Washington that, in economic matters particularly, holds out as much of danger as of promise. Where does co-operation end and dependence begin? The increasing hold of great American corporations over Canadian resources was not something that bothered Mr King still less his lieutenant, Mr Howe. The CCF proposal, and the Saskatchewan government's request, that certain resources would better be developed under joint dominion-provincial management so as to preserve Canadian control has never been entertained.

Another aspect of Mr King's behaviour that needs a great deal more investigation is his whole attitude toward labour. As the author of *Industry and Humanity*, we might have expected from him some leadership in this field at least. True, he built up the Department of Labour, and founded the *Labour Gazette*. But he also invented the Industrial Disputes Investigation Act. This much-heralded statute has received some approval even in labour circles, yet the more it is examined in the light of later developments the more it looks like a skilful attempt to blunt the force of unionism by weakening the effectiveness of the right to strike. It was Mr King who wrote: 'Private rights should cease when they become public wrongs ... Either the disputants must be prepared to leave the differences which they are unable amicably to settle to the arbitrament of such authority as the state may determine as most expedient, or make way for others who are prepared to do so.' It is fairly evident from this ominous incantation that labour would find itself to be the party committing the public wrong. When Mr King was in the United States during World War I, he acted as labour adviser for large corporations, not for unions. His labour policy was the least defensible part of his handling of affairs during World War II. In this matter, as in so many others, he showed his full acceptance of the general philosophy of free enterprise. He scarcely kept pace with, still less led, the social trend.

Mr King's character, like the Canadian character, was very mixed. It is a pity his private diaries will not be fully preserved so that we might understand him better. We know enough to say however, that though dullness seems to be required of our public men, we do not need to fall down and worship at the feet of mediocrity. Mr King was above the mediocre, but we only lower our political standards when we exaggerate his positive achievements.

EDITORIAL
The United States: Canada's Problem

There are, we are told week after week by politicians, editors, and speechmakers of various sorts, ties of a very special closeness and friendliness between Canada and the United States. Seldom a day passes but Canadians are reminded in words painfully overworked that many of their blessings flow from this relationship with their 'great neighbour to the South.' Popular literature on the subject has been plagued with platitude and propaganda rather than sincerity and frankness.

In more normal times, which must mean in times before the atomic bomb, Canadians of independent thought and progressive inclinations were able, with untroubled conscience and some delight, to point up the follies and regressions of America and to insist that the special ties, particularly the economic and cultural ones, were a burden to the Canadian community. But the present danger of global atomic war, the growing recognition that a graver threat to progressive society lies elsewhere, and the ever-growing pressure toward unity of thought and action in the Western world has left the Canadian progressive with little zeal for muckraking and denunciation. Now he tends to be silent, though the dangers of cant, the need of independent thought are greater than ever. What should be said today about the United States of America?

First it should be recognized that the United States in reacting to the strains of world leadership is undergoing a dangerous period of domestic disagreement. American conservatism presents a frightening ambivalence between isolationism and a militant imperialism. It is hysterical and displays little respect for rational and enlightened public discussion. American liberalism on the other hand is more realistic, more cautious. Less willing to crusade violently for freedom, it offers a surer hope of maintaining it. Despite continual attack, it is holding its own, as the recent dismissal of General MacArthur shows. But the struggle between the conservatives and liberals is by no means over and, despite obvious shortcomings, liberal elements in America deserve our support.

The best method of such support is by a liberal and independent Canadian policy. The happenings of the past few months have demonstrated effectively the restraining influence which the frank expression of disagreement can have upon American policy. Since Prime Minister Attlee flew in haste to Washington following President Truman's atomic bomb announcement, there has been a gradual moderation of American policy. The louder screams of its domestic critics should not lead us to throw up our hands in despair. Mr. Pearson's statements on the use of the atomic bomb, his timely distinction between appeasement and diplomatic negotiation, his stand against extending the war to China, and his warning against hysterical action have had, we hope, some influence in Washington.

There are those who claim that so perilous is the present situation that the open expression of difference of opinion among the Western nations can lead only to disaster. This of course would be the case if such differences were coupled with stiff-necked uncompromising attitudes. Fortunately however there seems to exist a recognition of the need of a certain amount of adjustment among members of the Western coalition to each others' particular interests. Because the United States is the undisputed leader, the most powerful member of this coalition, but the one also with the least experience in diplomacy, a special burden falls upon her in this respect. The present mood of Europe and the Far East demands less insistence on righteous action, as it is conceived in the United States, and more understanding.

Finally, the United States must be continually reminded of its inconsistencies. To demand European unification but to maintain an outmoded and trade-crippling tariff structure is an example of the sort of thing that denies respect abroad. Canada along with other allies must keep prodding.

FRANK H. UNDERHILL
Notes on the Massey Report

The chief danger is that the Massey Report will become merely another historical document – like the Rowell-Sirois Report of ten years ago. Both are the products primarily of our university intellectuals. The commissioners themselves, the special investigators who worked for them, and the groups who drafted the briefs that were presented to them, have been nearly all men and women trained in Canadian universities. Future generations of historians, sociologists, and political scientists will pay tribute to their thorough work in searching out and assembling the relevant facts, to their imaginative grasp of their subject, and to their masterly presentation of a program of action. Both reports show what new insights into different aspects of our national problems may be reached through well-directed team-work by men and women of trained intelligence. But the Rowell-Sirois Report still remains a program only, and it is now almost forgotten by the politicians who are responsible for action. The Massey Report may suffer the same fate. It is already being brushed aside by the 'practical men' as the work of long-haired high-brows. There is no other country in the world where intellectuals suffer from such low repute as in Canada.

The report lends itself to this treatment because of one unfortunate fact about it. Apart from the Canadian Association of Broadcasters and its member stations, who showed themselves up for the selfish cynical profit-making agencies that they are, the commissioners do not seem to have had before them many of the usual representatives of the business man's point of view. The magazine publishers were there, dressing up their ambition to corner the mass-circulation market as a noble effort to save our souls from cultural annexation to the United States; but on the whole the business man as such seems to have been conspicuous by his absence or his silence. (I stretch a point by classing the book-publishers among the intellectuals.) There were a good many agricultural organizations and some labour bodies who presented briefs, but such Boards of Trade and Chambers of Commerce as did appear do not seem to have said much that stuck in the memory of the commissioners.

When Royal Commissioners or lesser people write about Canada it is always revealing to find out whom they take to represent the people of Canada. Read such a journal as the *Financial Post,* and you soon discover that it assumes as self-evident the proposition that the Canadian Manufacturers Association or the local Chambers of Commerce express the opinions of the people of Canada. Read the editorial page of the Toronto *Globe,* and it gradually dawns on you that Mr. George McCullagh intuitively senses what the people of Canada are thinking and that there is no need to look further than his intuitions. The members of the Massey Commission seem to have assumed that the 'voluntary bodies' who appeared before them spoke collectively for the people of Canada. But the people of Canada never actually appear in any active role except when they vote at general elections, and even then the functioning agent is the sixty or seventy per cent of the adult population who can be induced to mark ballot-papers. The voluntary bodies who appeared at the Massey Commission hearings did not include the most powerful of voluntary bodies in this country, the business corporations; and, in fact, they represented only the minority of persons who are actively interested in the arts, letters, and sciences. The overwhelming majority of the people of Canada, or even of the radio listeners, were not there at all, because they were not interested enough. Unfortunately this minority who were interested in the subject, and who had very valuable things to say, are a minority who have little financial power and who are not organized so as to make their voting power felt.

The Report is very well written. It is a pleasure to read a document written by individuals who evidently recognize a good sentence when they see it in a brief and know enough to quote it, and who also know how to write good sentences themselves. One doesn't know whether to be struck more by their picture of the poverty-stricken condition of all the activities concerned with the arts and letters in Canada, or by the vigour with which these poverty-stricken groups present their case. But one has an uneasy premonition that the real attitude of the government to their grievances is shown by the price of the volume in which the Report is published. A federal government which took this subject seriously would have subsidized the publication sufficiently to make it possible for the ordinary poorer class of reader to buy it. When Pitt was pressed to prosecute William Godwin for his work on Political Justice, he replied that there was no danger of subversion from a work which cost three guineas the set. So our business men may rest easy.

I enjoyed the polite restraint with which the commissioners set out the shortcomings of the various national cultural institutions at Ottawa. Much more explosive language might have been used, and has habitually been used for the past generation in university circles. But as a university professor in the field of the humanities, I was, of course, chiefly impressed by their chapters on the universities and the humanities. There is nothing here which is very new, even in Canada, but it is said with force and eloquence. Extracts from these chapters should have been far more widely reprinted in our daily press than they have been. (As usual the *Winnipeg Free Press* seems to be the only daily which is giving the Report good publicity. The natural sciences have been steadily fostered in the universities at the expense of the humanities, though we are now conscious that it is not from the sciences but from the humanities that must come the wisdom for the solution of the deepest social and philosophical problems of our age. How often have I heard these things said or read them in official utterances at the University of Toronto!

The commissioners have a very pertinent remark on Canadian university libraries. 'If the size of a university library is not an unfair index of the attention devoted to the liberal arts, and particularly to research in this field, the relevant facts are illuminating. If a list of North American universities were to be arranged in accordance with the number of volumes in their academic libraries, the best-equipped Canadian universities would be distressingly far down in the roster.' When I first joined the staff of the University of Toronto in 1927, one of the first things I remember hearing was a plea from the librarian for more room and better equipment in the university library. It is now 1951, and nothing has been done in the intervening years to improve the facilities of the library. Yet I doubt if historical research could turn up a single speech on general university policy by anyone in authority at the university during that period in which the speaker did not refer in glowing terms to the vital importance of the humanities and did not affirm his determination to keep the university from sinking into a mere utilitarian scientific technological centre. And this illustrates the real trouble with the humanities in Canada. It is not that the Canadian public is apathetic – the masses everywhere are apathetic – but that those in authority, who profess to be interested, seldom feel any responsibility for fitting their actions to their words.

The proposals of the commissioners for federal financial contributions to the universities and for national scholarships at both the undergraduate and the graduate level will meet with universal support from within the universities. Yet here again one must point to some facts which are apt to make university professors cynical. The figures in the Report (page 141) show that from 1943-4 to 1948-9, i.e. during the period in which university expenses went up most spectacularly, the percentage of university income coming from provincial governments decreased from 40.5 to 32.8. At the same time the federal government's contribution to the universities went up from 0 to 10.3 per cent of their income. That is, the provincial governments sloughed off their share of university finance as the federal government increased its share. If the same process continues when the new federal grants are made – as they are already beginning to be made – the financial problem of the universities will not be solved. Their problem is due, not to the failure of the federal authority to do something new for them, but to the failure of the provincial governments to live up to their old responsibilities. And whatever may be the case in other provinces, here in Ontario which has been wallowing in surpluses there is no excuse for this whatever.

There is one theme in the Report about which some searching questions should be asked. The Commissioners seek a national Canadian culture which shall be independent of American influences. Several times they speak of these influences as 'alien.' This use of the word 'alien' seems to me to reveal a fallacy that runs through much of Canadian nationalistic discussion. For we cannot escape the fact that we live on the same continent as the Americans, and that the longer we live here the more are we going to be affected by the same continental influences which affect them. It is too late now for a Canadian cultural nationalism to develop in the kind of medieval isolation in which English or French nationalism was nurtured. These so-called 'alien' American influences are not alien at all; they are just the natural forces that operate in the conditions of twentieth-century civilization.

The fact is that if we produced Canadian movies for our own mass consumption, they would be as sentimental and vulgar and escapist as are the Hollywood variety; and they would be sentimental, vulgar and escapist in the American way, not in the English or French or Italian way. Our newspapers which are an independent local product do not differ essentially from the American ones; the kind of news which the Canadian Press circulates on its own origination is exactly like that originated by AP or UP. Like the American ones, they become progressively worse as the size of the city increases, up to a certain point. Somewhere between the size of Chicago and the size of New York another force comes into operation, producing a different kind of newspaper. We haven't any daily as bad as the *Chicago Tribune*, because we haven't any city as big as Chicago; but also we haven't anything as good as the *New York Times* or *Herald Tribune*. If *Maclean's Magazine* achieved its ambition, and American competition were shut out from its constituency, it would continue to be what it is now, only more so, i.e., a second-rate *Saturday Evening Post* or *Colliers*. It is mass-consumption and the North American continental environment which produce these phenomena, not some sinister influences in the United States.

If we could get off by ourselves on a continental island, far away from the wicked Americans, all we should achieve would be to become a people like the Australians. (And even then the American goblin would get us in the end, as he is getting the Australians.) Let us be thankful, then, that we live next door to the Americans. But if we allow ourselves to be obsessed by the danger of American cultural annexation, so that the thought preys on us day and night, we shall only become a slightly bigger Ulster. The idea that by taking thought, and with help of some government subventions, we can become another England – which, one suspects, is Mr Massey's ultimate idea – is purely fantastic. No sane Canadian wants us to become a nation of Australians or Ulsterites. So, if we will only be natural, and stop going about in this eternal defensive fear of being ourselves, we shall discover that we are very like the Americans both in our good qualities and in our bad qualities. Young Canadians who are really alive make this discovery now without going through any great spiritual crisis.

The root cultural problem in our modern mass-democracies is this relationship between the mass culture, which is in danger of being further debased with every new invention in mass communications, and the culture of the few. The United States is facing this problem at a rather more advanced stage than we have yet reached, and the more intimately we can study American experience the more we shall profit. What we need, we, the minority of Canadians who care for the culture of the few, is closer contact with the *finest* expressions of the American mind. The fear that what will result from such contact will be our own absorption is pure defeatism. We need closer touch with the best American universities (*not* Teachers Colleges) and research institutions, closer touch with American experimental music and poetry and theatre and painting, closer personal touch with the men who are leaders in these activities.

The Americans are now mature enough to have come through this adolescent phase of believing that the way to become mature is to cut yourself off from the older people who are more mature than you are. It is about time that we grew out of it also. I think that the Massey commissioners should use their leisure now to study the Americans much more closely than they seem to have done hitherto.

GAVIN WHITE

Canadian Apartheid

During the summer weather it is pleasant for us to read romantic stories of the Eskimo living a carefree life far from the trials of civilization. However, these trials of our complex society are now being shared by the Eskimo, and unless prompt action is taken he will soon be reduced to the same position as the Indian. While once there were an estimated twenty-two thousand Eskimo living as far south as Saguenay, these have now been reduced to about eight thousand five hundred survivors, almost all of whom are dependant on a declining fur trade closely linked to the whims of our own troubled economy.

Our national policy has been governed ultimately by motives of profit, and the Eskimo has survived largely because he has been useful to us. As far back as 1928, Fridjtof Nansen appealed to the Canadian people to protect and advance the Eskimo after the pattern of Greenland. There, Denmark was blazing the way with a highly successful industrial and educational program for the Greenlanders; but all our government could say by 1934 was that the Eskimo's 'mental capacity to assimilate academic teaching is limited.' The Eskimo are still considered as wards of Canada; unlike the Indians, their affairs are administered not by the Department of Immigration and Citizenship, but by the Department of Resources and Development. But this does not even guarantee their treatment as resources to be developed for profit to whites; for military posts, prospecting camps and weather stations still employ white service crews shipped at enormous expense, while other governments have been able to train Eskimo for much of this work. Meanwhile the Eskimo remain undernourished and uneducated ministering to milady's furs.

For the Eskimo, white advancement in the Canadian Arctic has meant the destruction of his original hunting economy by the introduction of the rifle with the consequent depletion of game. He now lives on a trap-line regimen with its dependance of the trading posts of the Hudson's Bay Company. Years ago the Dominion Zoologist recommended that the government run the fur trade itself for reasons of conservation. In 1931 a Territorial Administration official said of the Eskimo that 'the only hope of preventing their eventual extinction is government control of trading.' But so far the only development has been a Hudson's-Bay-over-all policy. The 'Bay' has delegated to it many of the administrative duties of the too few RCMP, so that in most areas the Company distributes the Family Allowances and the eight dollar per month Old Age Allowance. This latter the Company may supplement with a dole paid at its own expense. So far as education is concerned, the government, until 1947, contented itself with making grants to a few mission schools, and only since then has it maintained a half dozen teachers of its own. There are also the grants and the nursing stations of the Indian Health Service. This Service has struggled for years to serve the Eskimo with a program widely recognized as both unsystematic and inadequate.

Another service we Canadians provide the Eskimo is the Eastern Arctic Patrol of the steamer 'C.D. Howe' which is supposed to superintend the administration and check the health of the natives. This highly publicized patrol was described by Vincent Massey as 'a regular yearly voyage of inspection and assistance to the most distant communities of the Arctic,' but it is also a supply operation for trading posts and weather stations, and when cargo has been discharged the ship has been known to proceed to the next settlement leaving the medical inspections incomplete. At one settlement last year the 'C.D. Howe' doctors made a complete chest X-ray survey in September, but, although regular air service was maintained through the winter with that post, the thirteen tuberculous patients found were not flown to hospital until the following April. Even though the Patrol may be able to hear complaints and supervise administration by visiting each white settlement for a day or so each year, at least one member of its staff stated before the United Nations Association a few years ago that it was more interested in 'keeping an eye on the Dominion's share of the fur harvest.' (The administration official who accompanies the Patrol is also responsible for royalties and the bonding of furs.)

In other areas the Canadian Eskimo have had their own problems. A year ago there were press reports from the Churchill area on Eskimo polio survivors requiring rehabilitation for return to the traplines, and on a government official taking them copies of the 'Book of Wisdom for Eskimos.' The following month Eskimo were reported starving near Ennadai Lake and the government was on the job. Having no food for relief purposes, it sent medical supplies instead.

The Royal Commission on Reindeer and Musk-Ox estimated that a half million reindeer could be grazed on the prairies south of the Beaufort Sea, and the explorer Stefansson urged the establishment of musk-ox herds to provide a sounder economy for the Eskimo. Finally a reindeer industry was built up in the Mackenzie Delta, the district most accessible to visitors and one area in Canada where the Eskimo had no serious economic problem. Meanwhile the Eskimo of Northwestern Quebec live a hand-to-mouth existence eked out by relief, and, although for some thirty years their Anglican missionary, 'Reindeer' Walton, asked for a few hundred reindeer with which they might start anew, the government's plans have come to nothing. A priest from the Coppermine area has recently published a book relating the government's refusal to treat natives with tuberculosis and comparing Canada's indifference to Eskimo survival with Nazi genocide. He draws attention to the Canadian Consul in Greenland during World War II who was able to say of his flight from the Canadian to the Danish Arctic, 'Those five hours spanned the ages, from a land of still primitive nomadic Eskimos to something that seemed to be the frontier of modern Europe.'

Of course, Canadians should not blame this on their government alone, for interested government officials have been crippled by a public feeling that the North would be developed for the white man, and the native could fend for himself. Accordingly, government doctors found it necessary to refuse maternity cases at native hospitals in order to keep their expenditures at a minimum. On the administrative side, no other nation with colonial responsibilities would attempt to supervise the care of a subject people by employing a mere three or four civil servants as Canada has done, especially when two of these must also attend to fur and game regulations.

There has, however, been some improvement in the past ten years. A year ago the vote was given to Eskimos, and, while only a handful can exercise it, this is some recognition of their existence as a national asset to Canada. The Territorial Administration is pledged to bring the Eskimo to 'exercise all the functions of citizenship,' and to do this it must give the Eskimo whatever education may prove necessary for them to deal with whites on equal terms. It must prepare new industries in which the Eskimo may use this education to gain the security and equality they do not have under the present order. The establishment of these industries may be difficult, but if the government does not provide them there will be groups of white men who will, and the Eskimo will be pushed back as the Indians were. Already white men are fishing commercially in waters the Eskimo depend on for food. The miners are not far behind. Furthermore, with a secure economy or network of economies, the health of the now disease-ridden Eskimo may be tackled from a preventive and nutritional standpoint. There are technical difficulties, but these could be overcome if the Administration were given some encouragement. The North could still be developed by men trained to live there in equal partnership with other Canadians.

MARTHA CHAMPION RANDLE

The New Indian Act

Everyone is aware that whatever history may tell of 'the noble Red Man,' most modern Canadian Indians remain unassimilated, relatively poor, and marginal to the dominant white culture, stubbornly Indian in many ways in spite of the adoption of much of the material culture of the white man. Complex historical and psychological factors account for the present situation.

The Indians are set apart from other minorities. Because of treaties and because of popular sentiment (based chiefly on guilt feelings at having deprived the Indians of their aboriginal lands and way of life) this minority has been accepted as a public responsibility and the status of 'wardship' has been attributed to it. The people of Canada have delegated this responsibility to a branch of the federal government, but few citizens know much about these 135,000 wards of the Indian Affairs Branch of the Department of Citizenship and Immigration.

Though 'wardship' was conceived with humanitarian intentions, the results have been dependence, retreat, and hostility on the part of most Indians. Because of their status as 'wards' they were subject to authoritarian controls, which discouraged initiative; they were segregated on reserves, which furnished the basis for isolation and passive resistance; and they were the objects of paternalistic direction and in some cases direct relief, which created dependency on the government.

Indian affairs are centralized in Ottawa and administered according to the Indian Act. The First Act (1876) was so much amended that confusions and anachronisms in it influenced the Parliamentary Committee to recommend its complete revision. This committee, appointed to study the problem in 1946, made an exhaustive report on the more than one hundred agencies dispersed through all the provinces. In summation, they state: 'All proposed revisions are designed to make possible the gradual transition of Indians from wardship to citizenship and to help them to advance themselves.'

In 1950 a revision of the Indian Act was presented in parliament, but withdrawn after unfavourable publicity and agitation by Indians and their friends. With certain unimportant changes, the revision was again presented in 1951. After committee hearings and some legalistic amendments, it became law in September, 1951.

Though the Act was publicized as a New Deal for the Indians, examination shows that the means by which democracy and full citizenship are to be attained are in essence authoritarian. The end envisioned is full citizenship for the Indians if they become Canadians, i.e., form typical Canadian municipalities, governed by Canadian customs. It shows no democratic tolerance, which allows cultural differences and ethnic diversity.

The Indian Affairs Branch deals with every phase of the Indian's life, and likewise the legislation covers most important activities with the exception of the care of health, which is under the jurisdiction of the ministry of Health and Welfare. From the numerous (125) sections of the Act, the following subjects have been selected as most illustrative of its general tenor:

1. *The definition and registration of Indians.* The new Act avoids the insult of the old which defined 'person' as an individual other than an Indian. Now 'Indian' means 'a person who pursuant to this Act is registered as an Indian.' The register, compiled in Ottawa from present band lists, excludes Indian women who marry non-Indians and quarter-Indians coming of age 21 years from now, but includes women, whatever their genetic background, who marry Indians. The tribes have no power to determine their own membership. Membership is a legal, not a social, concept. Where the genetic mixture is as great as it is in the eastern provinces, active participation in tribal affairs, not any fixed and complicated rules of heredity, should be the basis for Indian status.

2. *Reserve lands.* The Indian Department keeps a register of lands, and no Indian is in lawful possession of land in a reserve unless it has been allotted by the Council, with the approval of the Minister. That the land should be allotted by the Indian Council is democratic, but to require offical sanction denies the Council any real authority.

3. *Management of Indian moneys.* The trust fund (about 20 million dollars) is held intact, and only the interest is spent on behalf of the Indians. The Governor-in-Council may, however, relax the control of capital. No provision is made for any group to earn this responsibility by any specific means. At the discretion of the government, at no specified time, these powers may be granted to a Council, and may likewise be revoked.

4. *Band Councils and their powers.* The fundamental principle of allowing the various tribes to set up their own forms of self-government with their own procedures and regulations nowhere appears. The same type of Council, with the same procedures, elected in the same fashion, is provided for all the tribes. 'Whenever he deems it advisable for the good government of a band, the Governor-in-Council may declare by order that ... the council of the band ... be selected by elections to be held in accordance with this Act.' The powers of the Council are limited to minor by-laws in regard to reserve affairs, and even these must await the Minister's approval to become law. Democracy is decreed, at least one form of it, when the Minister thinks a tribe has reached that state of advancement to warrant it, but the Council has no actual power.

At the discretion of the Governor-in-Council, the powers of a council may be extended to cover money powers, such as imposing taxes and penalties, but this possibility is unspecified as to its application, and is revokable.

5. *Exemption from land taxes.* This is one of the historic privileges of Indians – that they do not pay taxes on reserve lands and on income earned on a reserve, but they pay taxes on other income, and car, gasoline, tobacco, and all hidden commodity taxes. Yet exemption from taxation has been the pretext to keep Indians from voting; if they will sign a waiver from tax exemption they are allowed to vote. This *quid pro quo* has kept Indians from voting, except veterans, who may vote without signing.

6. *Regulations in regard to intoxicants.* The only adequate solution to the liquor question among the Indians would be to institute local option such as their neighbours have. The Act attempts a compromise intended to please both wets and drys. The sale, manufacture, and possession of intoxicants on reserves is still prohibited, and Indians are not allowed to buy packaged liquor or beer, but they will be allowed to drink in beer parlours or cocktail lounges away from the reserves, *if* the Lieutenant-Governor of the province in which they live requests the Governor-in-Council to allow it. This provision will do nothing to prevent bootlegging, for the Indians prefer to drink at home, and they do.

7. *Enfranchisement.* This word has come to have a special meaning in Indian affairs, only remotely related to the meaning of 'the right to vote.' 'Enfranchisement,' according to the Minister, 'is the act whereby an Indian is released from the band, obtains the funds that are due to him and a small gratuity from the government, and goes out into the world on his own.' Most Indians view enfranchisement with dislike and suspicion. One young Six Nations man quipped, 'When is an Indian not an Indian? When he's enfranchised!'

In the old Act, lands of an enfranchised Indian had to be sold to another band-member. Under the new Act, such lands may be sold to a non-Indian after a ten-year period. This is one of the most distressing provisions of the Act as it creates the possibility of pin-pointing the reserves with white holdings. If the community of a reserve were invaded in this fashion its cohesiveness and identity would soon be lost.

Enfranchisement is taken a step further in the new Act. If, in the opinion of the Minister, an Indian or a band of Indians is worthy of enfranchisement, a committee to inquire into and report upon the desirability of enfranchising may be appointed. Such a committee, consisting of one judge, one officer of the Indian Affairs Branch, and one member of the band, may decide by a simple majority to enfranchise the Indian individual or band. 'Such a report shall be deemed to be an application for enfranchisement by the Indian or by the band and shall be dealt with as such in accordance with this Act.' In other words, enfranchisement by edict is called enfranchisement by application and will be treated as such. Compulsory enfranchisement is the threat of liquidation to the Indian people.

Though the envisioned transition of the Indians 'from wardship to citizenship' is a complicated social change, made infinitely complex by different social, historical and economic conditions of the various Indian groups scattered from Newfoundland to British Columbia, even this cursory study of the Act shows that no truly democratic or effective procedures to accomplish the desired result have been evolved. Parliament has enacted new legislation for the Indian minority which keeps it still firmly under the discretionary powers of the centralized Indian Affairs bureaucracy. According to this Act, the Indians must remain wards or cease to be Indians.

FRANK H. UNDERHILL

Power Politics in the Ontario CCF

On February 27 last the annual meeting of the Ontario Woodsworth Memorial Foundation was the scene of a determined drive by the provincial CCF officialdom to oust the old directors of the Woodsworth Foundation in Toronto and to bring it under the control of the small group who run the CCF party in Ontario. The Ontario Woodsworth Memorial Foundation was established in 1944 by a group of CCF individuals who aimed to set up a centre in Toronto for educational and social activities which would attract all those who shared the ideals of J.S. Woodsworth. The group raised enough money to buy a house and property on Jarvis Street, and have since then managed to finance their enterprise by hard work and by generous assistance from a considerable number of sympathizers, most of whom were naturally CCFers. They rented the second storey of the house as offices for the provincial headquarters of the CCF. This landlord-tenant relationship led to a good deal of regrettable friction. Bad feeling was increased by the freedom of discussion which Woodsworth House encouraged on socialist doctrines in general and on CCF policies in particular.

The result was the drive on February 27 to purge the Foundation and bring it effectively under official control. The drive was carried out under the direction of David Lewis, the national vice-president of the CCF with an unscrupulous thoroughness that the Communists themselves could hardly have bettered. In the weeks immediately preceding the annual meeting a flood of subscriptions from new members, many of them holding some official position in the trade unions, poured into the Foundation. This voting power was used at the meeting to oust most of the old directors who were up for re-election and to substitute a slate headed by Mr Lewis himself. Proceedings, which were long and disorderly, were delayed by wordy disputes about amendments to motions and rules of order, and every effort was made to bring on the voting for the new board of directors before the old directors had been given a chance to make their reports about the past year. In the end, though the voting power of the Lewis forces was marshalled in admirable discipline, the purge was not entirely successful.

In recent years the leaders of the CCF in Ontario have shown little interest in socialist education. The old directors of the Woodsworth Foundation had believed, anyway, that it is healthy in a democratic socialist movement for some of the educational activities to be carried on by people who, while dedicated to the idea of socialism, don't earn their living by professional party work. One of the things that has kept the Labour party alive in Britain has been the large volume of educational work done for it by voluntary groups who are not under its control, the Fabian Society being the most important and best known example. It is groups of this kind who help to keep socialist doctrine liberal rather than authoritarian, and the socialist approach to new problems experimental rather than dogmatic. Naturally they are apt to irritate the officials who administer party affairs. In fact the irritation is mutual. People who sit in offices giving directives to subordinates always lack confidence in the other kind of people who derive stimulation and amusement from letting their minds play with ideas and from asking inconvenient questions. But the successful political party needs both kinds of people. In fact it needs all kinds of people. One of the unsolved problems of modern democracy is that of getting political parties in which all kinds of people will be interested enough to participate actively. The danger of the bureaucrat is that he too easily flatters himself into believing that the only desirable participation by the rank and file of the party membership is the docile acceptance of his superior directives.

Of course the offical group who organized the purge in the Woodsworth Foundation at Toronto will publicly and piously deny that they were engaged in any such work. In private they will probably tell you that the group who were running the Woodsworth Foundation had become purely negative critics and troublemakers whose loyalty to the movement was doubtful and who simply had to be rooted out for the good of the movement as a whole. But even if their public professions are taken at their face value, the methods they used to attain their ends throw an unpleasantly revealing light upon the nature of the ends themselves. The drive for absolute power over the Woodsworth Foundation was only too evident. The kind of means which men adopt always sooner or later affects the quality of the ends for which the means are adopted.

The CCF in Ontario, to judge from the results of the last two general elections, one federal and one provincial, is in danger of sinking into an obscure little sect. It doesn't frighten the politicians of the old parties any more, and their propagandists hardly worry any longer to devise new smear tactics against it. It has never succeeded in winning any block of Ontario seats in the federal parliament and it has now lost most of the seats it once held in the provincial legislature. Why this weakness in Ontario? If socialism cannot win and hold any significant mass following in the chief province of Canada, the province with the most numerous big urban centres and the largest industrial population, the province with the richest and most diversified agriculture, the province which is the headquarters for English-speaking Canada of the protestant churches, and the province with the greatest concentration of educational institutions – if socialism can make little headway in this community, it has no future as a national Canadian movement.

In fact the weakness of the CCF in Ontario looms up as a threatening omen for the future of the CCF in Canada as a whole. Canadian CCFers have always buoyed up their spirits by referring to the progress of Labour in Great Britain. Because the Labour party after being launched in 1900 had by 1924 supplied a government to the country and in the next two decades entrenched itself as the largest British political party, we assure ourselves with a mystic fatalism that the same destiny must by an inevitable process be in store for us here in Canada. But Canadian politics has a way of repeating American patterns rather than British. And we should remind ourselves of the fate of the American Socialist party. It was founded at almost the same time as the British Labour party, but it had already before 1914 under Debs won the largest percentage of the popular vote that it has ever succeeded in winning in an American presidential election. Since then it has steadily declined, as in incessant factional fights it has cast off one set of deviationists after another. In its early days it was stronger in its popular appeal in the Middle West than it was in the eastern states, just as our CCF has been strongest in Saskatchewan, because in the upper Mississippi valley it built on the Populist tradition just as the CCF on the Canadian prairie built on the Progressivism of the 1920s. And its successful western members never acquiesced very willingly in the supposed ideological superiority of the eastern New York sophisticates.* Today it is only a ghost. The progressive, humanitarian, radical individuals and groups who were once socialist (including some prominent CIO trade-union leaders) now support the New Deal through the Liberal party, or the ADA, or the Democratic party; and they vote for the Democratic presidential candidate, because they want to get something done in their own lifetime beyond enjoying the pleasure of contemplating their own idealogical purity. The evolution of the American Socialist party is an omen that should frighten CCFers in Canada.

Why has the CCF failed so far in Ontario?

April 1952

*See an interesting article by David Shannon on 'The Socialist Party before the First World War,' in the *Mississippi Valley Historical Review* for September, 1951.

There are no doubt many reasons, but one of the chief reasons has been bad leadership. The party machinery has fallen into the hands of a small clique who perpetuate themselves in party office regardless of the ups and downs in electoral results in the province. They have become adepts in the art of managing party conventions and in using democratic forms to centralize power in their own control. They have almost abandoned the work of political education amongst the party membership, a work which is essential in any left party – though perhaps there have been a few recent signs of life in this field. They have failed to devise effective means for carrying the socialist gospel to the unconverted majority of the province. This is, in fact, their great failure. The CCF in Ontario has ceased for all practical purposes to be a missionary party concentrating on winning more and more converts, and it is slowly sinking into a sect whose leaders seem mainly interested in maintaining at all costs their own authority within the sect.

Political parties, like all other human organizations, including churches and trade unions, are always in danger of falling under the control of bureaucracies of this kind. When the first moral fervour which has launched a new movement begins to cool, the bureaucrat and the organizer emerge and take over the management of affairs. Bureaucrats are very necessary functionaries in any association of men and women aiming at practical achievements. But they are dangerous if there is not sufficient vitality in the rank-and-file membership to check their inherent drive for self-aggrandizement. They soon come to identify the good of the movement with their own personal power and prestige. And if it is a movement like the CCF with an original fund of high moral idealism, they may easily develop into a kind of political priesthood. As they tirelessly shepherd the political sheep under their care, their early idealism begins to degenerate into a certain sour self-righteousness. They resent criticism from below, they are quick to stamp out independence in their followers (which they regard as heresy), they begin to feel a peculiarly holy pleasure in punishing erring brethren. As their appetite for power grows, they become the more insistent on monopolizing authority within the sect just because they have failed to broaden the sect into a great national church. Worst of all, since power always tends to corrupt, their inner conviction of the righteous character of their ends gradually makes them more and more careless about the nature of the means they adopt. The reformer in religion or in politics always has a certain amount of fanaticism in his make-up; and the end-result of pure fanaticism is likely to consist in redoubling your effort when you have forgotten your aim.

This subtle corruption is one which peculiarly affects the leaders of reform movements. The political priests who run the old parties are a cheerful, cynical lot, who are usually rather pleasant fellows to meet. They know that they are running a racket, and they wink when they meet each other. These worldlings didn't start with ideals, and they have no ideals to lose. It is the unworldly reformers, the children of light, who are specially liable to the kind of corruption I am talking about, the corruption which overtakes idealists who have concentrated too much on power. *Corruptio optimi pessima.*

Another force which affects the leadership of the CCF is the affiliation of the big CCL trade unions. Having failed in their effort to win the masses of Ontario directly to the socialist faith, they now dream of a mass support to be mobilized behind them through the organized trade unions. At present the party is too much under the influence of the United Steelworkers and its close allies in the CCL. That a socialist party should try to attract trade-union support, on the model of the Labour party in Britain, is perfectly proper. And the pundits in our respectable dailies and weeklies who view with alarm the spectacle of trade unions going into politics – as if manufacturers and bankers and railway companies had not been in politics for years – only make themselves look ridiculous. But it must frankly be said that the big new industrial unions in the CCL have come up a little too easily for their own long-run good. After the first knocks and blows in the 1920s, their rapid success in an economy of full employment has gone a bit to their heads, and they show some signs of being intoxicated by power. It has been so easy to line up their followers for the economic purposes of higher wages, that it has been assumed that they could be lined up for political voting with the same mechanical ease. And the vision of what can be accomplished by a combination of economic and political power has been a little too attractive in the headquarters of the Steelworkers. Power tends to corrupt in trade unions as well as elsewhere.

To quote the now famous editorial about the retirement of Pat Conroy, in the February number of the *Canadian Railway Employees Monthly:* 'Big-hearted and high-principled, he [Conroy] quit because an unashamed drive for power, conceived in cunning and carried forward with craft, was aimed at changing the Congress from a vehicle for the many to a juggernaut for one. Conroy hoped his action would arouse the membership to the danger they faced, the danger the Congress faced.'

Well, the purge in the Woodsworth Foundation was not entirely successful. But doubtless the provincial CCF officialdom will not rest till they have rooted out all heresy and established themselves as the unquestioned expositors of the party line. They are nobly determined to become bigger and bigger frogs in the provincial CCF puddle. The only trouble is that under their leadership the puddle is likely to become smaller and smaller. And it may dry up altogether.

FRED SWAYZE
Spring Song

(Touchstone: 'I press in here, sir, amongst the rest of the country copulatives.')

Spring, Spring, profligate Spring,
Is a walloping trollop with breasts aswing,
Splay-footed, squelching the mud through her toes,
Lustily laughing as Northward she goes
Yanking the blankets from shivering grasses,
Slapping the maples and elms as she passes.

Wholeheartedly pagan, amused and exhorting,
She spreads the contagion of vigorous courting.

The sluttish and ruttish replenish the earth;
The profile in fashion is matronly girth.
Her boldly emblazoned heraldic crest
Is a tip-toe cockerel thumping his chest.

FRANK H. UNDERHILL
Turning New Leaves

For the Canadian citizen interested in current politics, this (*The Incredible Canadian*: Bruce Hutchison; Longmans, Green; pp. x, 454; $5.00) is the book of the year. It is a fascinating study of Mackenzie King's career written by a brilliant journalist who had the opportunity of observing him at close hand over a long period and who must also have questioned everybody concerned in the main events of the story. It is written in high spirits, with wit and imagination. And it achieves what a book about politics ought to achieve: it makes you feel what an exciting, inspiring, disgusting, broad-minded, selfish creature a first-class politician really is. It brings out both the high idealist and the low opportunist who co-existed in Mackenzie King's person. It reveals his intuitive understanding of his Canadian fellow citizens and his passion for preserving as much national unity as possible alongside his dabblings in spiritualism, his gross superstitions, the many examples of his pettiness and meanness. It does not make him a lovable character, but it explains why in a country like ours he was so successful.

In fact, what Mr Hutchison is more than hinting at throughout his four hundred and fifty pages is not so much that King was an incredible Canadian as that we Canadians are an incredible people; like our greatest leader in this past generation, we are extraordinarily complex in our mental constitution, and not altogether admirable. This volume is the sequel to Mr Hutchison's earlier volume, *The Unknown Country*. It is a greatly superior sequel, because it is harder and more analytical, free from the sentimental posing and the self-conscious fine writing of that earlier volume.

Mr Hutchison's insight is so true in the main points which he makes about King's career and character that it does not much matter whether he will eventually be found right in all his specific details (some of which he admits to be guesses). He is right in constructing his biography as one long commentary on *Industry and Humanity,* and in finding in that volume of 1918 the root of all the later King policies and the core of his liberal philosophy. He is right in his presentation of King as having, at his best, more in common with J.S. Woodsworth than with any other contemporary political leader. He is right in his picture of King's chief achievement, that of building up a national political party of the Left Centre which defeated the challenge of the Progressives and the CCF on the Left and was able to absorb all of the Centre because the leaders of the Right – Meighen, Bennett, Manion, Bracken, Drew – never showed an understanding of what a really national political party must be in Canada. He is right in his constant emphasis that King was not a parliamentary statesman, but a leader of the new twentieth-century type, trusting to his intuitive understanding of the people outside parliament. And he is right in reminding us that the modern welfare-providing, war-fighting state necessitates the growth of executive power at the expense of parliament whether the instrument of this growth be a Mackenzie King or not.

This achievement of building up the one successful national party of the last generation is so important that Mr Hutchison's words are worth quoting. (Of course I quote these passages with special pleasure because they agree with arguments of my own which I have frequently presented in the pages of *The Canadian Forum*.) 'Thus, for unexampled power the Liberal Party paid the price of confusion, contradiction and sheer expediency. For the most part it operated not on principles, but on pressures, like most successful governments in America ... It was but a congeries of separate groups in coalition. Men like Gardiner as the spokesman of agriculture, Howe as the representative of industry, Mitchell as the delegate of labour, St Laurent as the leader of Quebec, possessed almost autonomous and sovereign power within the party and could apply, when necessary, a veto on government policy by Calhoun's ancient Law of the Concurrent Majority. In another political system each of these men would have led his own party, making and breaking coalitions with others in the French fashion. By the genius of the Canadian system, and under an unequalled manager like King, the conflicts between the rival groups calling themselves Liberal could be reconciled within the Party ... And the proof that this was a formidable task and an extraordinary achievement could be found in all the other parties. None of them had been able to find his equal or imitate his success.' Mr. King, in fact, achieved as much unity as was possible in a country like Canada, because for thirty years he was the man who divided us least. On another page Mr Hutchison quotes Chubby Power (one of his heroes): 'Not necessarily Mackenzie King, but Mackenzie King if necessary.' And he concludes justly that by the end of his career King 'had made Canada almost a one-party nation with three splinters of opposition.'

While one is quoting it might be worth while to quote some of Mr Hutchison's references to J.S. Woodsworth. On 1921: 'In King's first parliament there appeared, almost unnoticed, a new political force which perhaps he alone could reckon. Its spokesman was J.S. Woodsworth, a former Methodist minister, an ex-longshoreman, a scholar, a saint-in-politics, the conscience of the Commons, and the portent of a new age in Canada.' On the outbreak of World War II: 'Woodsworth, the saint, knew that he had reached the hour of his martyrdom in politics. Like King, he had refused to face in his philosophy the dilemma of force. Unlike King, he could not and would not accept force when the alternative was destruction ... Being himself more Christian than the church, and closer to the spirit of Christ than any Canadian in politics, he looked with loathing upon the slaughter of innocents throughout the world. He was driven away from the world and back to the isolation of North America ... The same sort of choice had faced many saints. For Woodsworth it was peculiarly agonizing. Other saints could abandon the world as insignificant and turn toward another. Woodsworth's work had been in this world, his whole life of labour, poverty and daily suffering had been devoted to the salvation of human beings here and defiant, he had broken with his own party, he had thrown away his leadership of the Left in Canada, he had deliberately jettisoned his career in politics, and he was the most revered member of the Parliament which rejected him. His tragedy and triumph were now complete. They had been ordered from the beginning. In the jungle of these times the path of the saint leads inevitably to the stake. With one side of his diverse nature King must have envied Woodsworth his martyrdom.'

Mr Hutchison's two standards for judging the ultimate moral quality of King's statesmanship are provided by J.S. Woodsworth and J.W. Dafoe. Since he is clear on the weaknesses of the CCF movement, he might have also been a little more critical of the Dafoe type of liberalism. But perhaps this would be asking too much of a *Winnipeg Free Press* man. Still he does bring out that King's isolation of the 1930s, which Dafoe found so wrong, was shared by his chief adviser, O.D. Skelton, who was as clear-headed and hard-headed a Liberal as Dafoe and who also reached his conclusions by reasoning rather than by intuition, unlike the Prime Minister. Skelton spent hours in the early days of September 1939, in arguing with his chief for Canadian neutrality. Maybe there was more to be said for this in the 1930s than a member of Dafoe's staff would be inclined to admit.

There are more things also to be said about *Industry and Humanity* than Mr Hutchison says. Surely he is being slightly fantastic when he declares that it is 'a book of crystal clarity in the writing, if not in the content, quite unlike King's speeches.' On the contrary it is exactly like King's speeches, and will long hold an unchallenged position as the most unreadable book ever published in Canada. Nevertheless it needs to be read – and in the first unabridged edition of 1918. For Mr Hutchison is right in declaring that here is all of King's liberalism. He exaggerates, however, in presenting King as a revolutionary in 1918. All that the book does is to translate into his own cloudy semi-religious, semi-natural rights rhetoric the ideas which were a commonplace in Britain among Fabians and Liberals, which were being spread in the United States by religious and intellectual liberals, and taken up by Wilson and Roosevelt, and which were already firmly rooted in the social service branches of Canadian Methodism and Presbyterianism. King's writing has the mistiness and the unction of the university sophomore intent on uplift. Contrast his book for clarity and concreteness with such a volume as the Webbs' *Industrial Democracy* which preceded it by a few years, and you see how far he has yet to go in practical, adult political thinking. Examine his solution of the troubles in the Colorado Fuel and Iron Company, of which he was so proud in the first edition, but which he eliminated in later editions, and which turns out to be just a moralistic form of company-unionism. Still it must be admitted that King already knew clearly in 1918 that he was not a socialist and knew clearly all the liberal reasons why.

But whether or not you agree with all of Mr Hutchison's points, this is a fascinating and exhilarating book which should be read by every Canadian voter.

DOROTHY LIVESAY

Matt

When Elizabeth first started going to kindergarten she would come home for lunch, stand beside her chair, and refuse to sit. Instead she began to scream. Her mother and the mother's help, Doris, fluttered around her, their words swooping and pecking. They could not quiet her.

'But what is the matter child? Tell us what is the matter?' She did not know. Perhaps gradually she quietened, was persuaded to sit down, and then began the process of stuffing forksful of potato into a mouth already swollen with salt of tears.

It was not as if she refused to go to kindergarten in the morning. She was a dutiful child and whatever was pre-arranged by grown-ups she accepted as inevitable, just as God arranged the sunshine to soak through her blind in the morning. So brushed, and mouth wiped, wearing a clean striped pinafore, she made her way out into the autumn, carefully memorizing ahead of time the correct route to take through those flat prairie streets. Along the back fence, past a row of shabby brown shingled houses to 'the block,' a square red brick building where people lived in suites. Now she must look to the left and the right, dash across the street and walk down toward the Red River. Other children joined her; but to their careless 'Hellos' she replied stiffly, a muffled ''Lo.' She did not know them very well. And she had to keep an eye out for the opposite side of the street, to make sure she was early and well ahead of Matt. He usually arrived at kindergarten just as they were standing up to sing the morning hymn. His mother would open the play-room door and with a quick push, send him reeling to his chair.

Fortunately, he was not at Elizabeth's table. And the early morning routine was something she yearned for eagerly, taking out the coloured strips of paper, so glossy: the bright sky-blue ones and the deep red like blood, combining them together to make a pattern. Or else there would be raffia work to do, weaving real little baskets to take home to mother. Her hands were slow and awkward. She was never finished when the others were. But her hands caressed the square of paper, patted it, smoothed it down. 'There,' she said to herself, the way Doris said it when she put a cake in the oven.

Then the moment came. The teacher clapped her hands and the children ran to put everything away quickly, quickly, and push their chairs in, run to the centre of the room and form a circle. Elizabeth looked around for the little girl with the red dots on her dress, and grabbed her hand. Hot and sticky it was, but preferable to any boy's hand, especially Matt's. The piano started up, and they began moving and singing, 'The Farmer's in the Dell.' That was nice, and so was 'Ring a Rosie.' But next, with panic, she heard the piano sounding out the tune, 'Go In and Out the Window.' In that game the children would get all mixed up, she

January 1953

would have to grab anyone's hand, anyone who came along.

Quick now, she thought, and held her right arm up, using the left one to press the front of her dress so teacher would see. She wriggled from one foot to the other. Teacher looked up. 'All right, Elizabeth, you can surely wait till the game is over.' Her hands fell numb to her sides. She hadn't really needed to go at all. Now she did, now she couldn't wait!

But teacher did not look her way any more and she was swept again into the whirlwind of the game. She was pushed around, handed from child to child as the game grew faster. Ahead of her she could see Matt being pushed along too. The boys knocked him aside roughly with their elbows and the little girl with the red dots made a face when she got Matt for a partner. She soon shook him off and found another child to hang onto. So when the game was ended there was Elizabeth, just like yesterday, standing right beside Matt.

The chords of the piano banged out like a battle. As the children began to move around again in a circle, Matt seized her hand. She wanted to scream, to yank herself away, never again to feel that clammy hand gripping hers like a sponge. She did not dare to look at Matt, his leering face cocked on one shoulder, his open mouth drooling. She tried to look the other way, at the little girl ahead, tossing brown curls. But Matt yanked her this way and that, and suddenly unable to stay another moment, she pulled away her hand as if stung, and ran for the door.

'Elizabeth!' But she did not heed. Teacher let her go. She ran into the dark hall and down to the end, to the bathroom.

Her trouble went on for days, weeks maybe. She could tell no one. How could you explain that you liked kindergarten, yes, but you were terrified of holding a little boy's hand! To grown-ups, she supposed, Matt was just a little boy like anyone else, but to her, merely the sight of that leering tilted face made her feel sick. Then she began to notice what Matt was like outside kindergarten, when he played in the street. He would come around the corner from his street and pass the 'block' on the way to Elizabeth's house. If he saw that the big boys weren't home from school yet he would stand in the lane that ran between Elizabeth's house and the block. She could just see him as she waited on her back porch.

'Ya-a-aw' Matt would roar, tilting his heavy head backwards as he squinted up at one of the apartment windows. Sometimes a window would open, and a woman would stick her head out.

'Well, if it isn't Matt here again – waiting to be fed. How are you to-day, kid!' Matt would bellow again, and the lady would break into a loud laugh and talk to someone in the apartment; then she would throw Matt a bun. The game was, he had to catch it in his teeth as it fell. If he caught it, he got another one. If he missed, he would grunt and fumble in the muddy lane for the runaway bun. 'That's all for to-day, Matt,' the lady would shout at him.

Elizabeth watched, fascinated, from the safety of her back porch. Then, with whoop and a roar, a loud ringing of bicycle bells, the older boys would swoop onto the corner opposite the firehall. There they began their strange boy games of marbles, or baseball, or tag.

Elizabeth saw Matt move along from the lane, along the sidewalk past her house, then out to the front corner. He could not seem to keep away from the boys, but as soon as they saw him they would decide to play tag. 'Matt's It!' 'Matt's It!' the boys would shout in high glee. Matt would lunge, only to run and trip as he tried to catch boy after boy. When he was down they would kick him in the pants; then pull him to his feet and start all over again. 'Here I am, here I am, Matt! Catch me!' An imp would dash just out of Matt's reach, and Matt would begin to roar, his face crimson, his twisted, drooping mouth forming bubbles from rage.

'Matt, Matt, the great big sap,' a boy cried. Others took it up. They slapped themselves with joy, or rolled over and over in a heap, hitting and scuffling between their laughter. Eventually they would tire of the game and run off to another corner, leave Matt alone to sit sulking and wrathful on the curbstone, licking his wounds.

Elizabeth could see him, just sitting and sitting there. But she was restless now, she wanted to go out onto the street and skip. Maybe he wouldn't pay any attention if she kept to the sidewalk. She ventured to the side fence and peered over. Matt wasn't looking at her; so out she went, pushing the empty garbage pail aside as she closed the gate. She began to skip up and down, up and down the wooden sidewalk. Matt was still sitting on the other side of the boulevard grass, right by the road. Now he looked at her stupidly. His eyelids were puffy, his eyes red and rolling in his head like marbles. She skipped right on, afraid of him, yet secure in the feeling of her skipping-rope. And when she felt so safe, even for a moment, another feeling welled in her – a feeling that *she* was sitting on the curb, alone and abandoned, a child who no one would play with. But whenever she skipped too near him that tender feeling vanished; she saw only his stumpy red hands, clawing the air. She was mad at his being there, right in her way; mad as the other children were mad. Faster she skipped, whirring past him. The rhythm of her skipping seemed to take on the rhythm of those words she heard before:

'Matt, Matt, the great big sap!'

'Matt, Matt —' she started softly. Then each time as she passed him the words seemed to fall naturally out of her mouth, more loud, more daring.

'Matt, Matt, the great big sap,
'Doesn't know how to turn a tap —'
'Gimme!'

She whirled around. Matt was beside her.

'Go away. Go away!' she shrilled. She shook her skipping-rope at him.

'Gimme.' The red stubby paw reached out, grabbed the rope.

'That's my rope. You can't have it. Go away. This is *my* sidewalk!'

'G-r-aw' Matt was beginning to mutter. He still held the rope, tugging and tugging. Elizabeth pulled the other way, screaming at him to let go. Then the rope snapped. A handle came off in Matt's hand and he reeled backward, to the ground. She stood over him, waving her rope.

'Now see what you've done! Broken my good new skipping-rope ... Matt, Matt, the great big sap – that's what you are, a great big sap!'

With a roar he was up, he caught her arm. She let go the skipping-rope and ran as fast as the great wall of air pushing against her chest, as fast as it would let her go. Her legs seemed weak; waving in mid-air, but never moving; just peddling away in mid-air.

Somehow she reached the side gate, opened it. Matt was panting behind her. He picked up the garbage can lid and lifted it high, right above her. She yelled, and just as she got the gate open he banged the lid down, WHAM, on top of her head.

'Aw-a-ow!' she screamed, breaking away from him and stumbling toward the kitchen steps. The door opened. Doris came out and picked her up.

Matt still stood at the gate, the garbage can lid dangling uncertain, a shield against his side.

'Get out! Get out, you wicked boy!' cried Doris. Then she took Elizabeth inside and reported the story to mother.

After that, Elizabeth didn't mind going to kindergarten. Matt wasn't there any more. He was locked up in his own yard, behind a fence. She never had to hold his hand again.

FRANK H. UNDERHILL

How to Vote

If we Canadians took our national politics seriously most of us from now until August 10th would be living lives of quiet desperation. For how can any responsible citizen make up his mind for whom to vote this summer? The sense of frustration and futility should be getting us all down.

The Liberals have most of the brains at Ottawa, but their long tenure of office has made them careless and insolent, and their disciplined majority has reduced the House of Commons to unprecedented degradation. If we wish to preserve the traditions of parliamentary government, it is certainly time that the Liberals were transferred to the opposition benches. But can we contemplate replacing them by the Conservatives? There is a healthy revival of conservative philosophy going on all over the western world, but the idea that a party led by George Drew has any understanding of the traditions of Burke and Disraeli must make the gods laugh. And, as for the other opposition parties, the CCF has failed in its ambition to become the second party in the state and has for the present no real hope of being anything more than a splinter group. It may look forward with confidence to having its health-insurance plank stolen from it in the near future by some government, just as so many of its other welfare planks have been stolen since 1932. And if it had only done an effective job in publicizing its ideas on housing, it could look forward to its housing plank being next appropriated. The Social Crediters, fortunately, don't seem likely to spread beyond Alberta and British Columbia this time; and the issues raised by this latest Revolt of the Masses will hardly emerge on the national stage till some election in the late 1950s.

But the Canadian people are, of course, not living lives of quiet desperation. They are happy extroverts enjoying an economic boom that has gone on continuously since 1940 and has not let up much even with the prospects of the end of the Korean fighting. And their attitude to political controversy is one of profound apathy. The coming election seems likely to be the dullest in our history since our first Confederation election in August 1867. Most voters will be thanking heaven this July and August that they can get away from the yapping of politicians because either, as farmers, they are busy with the harvest or, as city-dwellers, they are enjoying or dreaming of their summer vacation.

Mr King pretty nearly turned Canada into a one-party state. By the time he retired there was no other national party left to challenge the Liberals effectively or to compete with them. He accomplished this feat by blurring all issues, by enveloping all discussion in a cloud of rhetorical double-talk, so that his party seemed to offer every group in Canada substantially what any other party could offer. Thus he defeated the CCF's effort to introduce a British pattern into Canadian politics. The CCF's primary aim was not to establish 'socialism' but to bring about a division between a party of the left and a party of the right like that between British Labour and Conservatives. It was correct enough in its analysis of existing Canadian party politics in the 1930s, but it never succeeded in persuading the Canadian people to think of the Liberals as being on the right as much as the Conservatives. Mr King somehow or other brought his party through the crisis of the depression and then through the crisis of war as a praiseworthy association of all-people-of-good-will which was miraculously both on the left and on the right, which was of course 'forward-looking' but could also be trusted by all fearful souls not to move forward very noticeably. So, in spite of all its efforts to get a clear definition of issues, Mr King left the CCF with the general reputation of being a body of impractical doctrinaires. By the same masterly tactics of frustrating any intellectual clarification, he prevented the growth on his other flank of any movement like that of the Mid-West big-business anti-New Dealers who are now in office in Washington – though maybe his success here was not so much due to his own skill as to the fact that our business tycoons had no successful general like Ike to act as a figurehead.

Mr St Laurent has not Mr King's genius for blurring issues. If he is given time he will eventually make it clear that the major premises of all his political thinking are those of a Montreal corporation lawyer; and then the CCF might get its chance. But he will probably win this election as he did that of 1949 because the voters of this country are still in a state of trance. They have not yet cast off the spell thrown over them by the hypnotic gestures of the Incredible Canadian. It will be a drowsy population that hears the election returns over the radio on the night of August 10th.

In the meantime, if any reader can rouse himself sufficiently to follow a political discussion, there are a few remarks about the current scene that might be ventured.

In the first place, we seem to be developing a new pattern of federalism which would have been incomprehensible to the Fathers but which apparently satisfies our contemporary needs. In the old days, when provincial elections started to go against the party in office at Ottawa, this was always taken as a sign that its tenure of federal office was coming to an end. But today, as one province after another breaks away from the Liberals, the federal Liberal government goes happily on, and this ancient sword of Damocles seems to have vanished into thin air. The Liberals do hang on to Nova Scotia and Manitoba – they are 'Liberal-Progressives' out around Winnipeg – but all the other provinces of any significance have turned against them. British Columbia and Alberta have Social Credit governments, Saskatchewan has the CCF, Ontario has the Frostite Conservatives, and Quebec has the Union Nationale. The people of the provinces seem to prefer a local government free from any political ties with Ottawa, so that it can negotiate or fight with the federal authorities from a completely independent position. But then, having elected this provincialist anti-Ottawa government, they seem to feel no inconsistency in voting another way federally.

This produces a strange kind of party politics. It makes possible the wildest and most preposterous rhetoric about 'provincial rights' at one moment; but at the next moment the same provincial electorate, which appeared to be so inflamed that any kind of national unity is impossible, coolly votes for a national party against whom its provincial government has just been inflaming it. An outside observer, unaccustomed to our political mores, would conclude that we are suffering from some form of schizophrenia. But we natives can only speculate whether the end result of all this will be that we shall keep the Liberals permanently in office at Ottawa – to save us from the provincial-rights governments whom we elect in our ten provinces to save us from the Liberals. All that will be needed to keep this modern system going indefinitely will be to invent a few new names for some of the provincial-rights parties in some of the provinces. How encouraging it would be if one could believe us capable also of producing the Canadian Swift who would send out his Gulliver to examine and report upon all the fascinating intricacies of this new politics!

The CCF must be going into this election in no very happy frame of mind. After twenty years of agitation it has succeeded in capturing only one province, and there its appeal, as Lipset showed in his book on Agrarian Socialism, has not been radical, in so far as it concerned the Saskatchewan community, but conservative. It came into office to save the Saskatchewan farmer's way of life against the forces under whose onslaught in the 1930s that way of life was disintegrating. Similarly, Social Credit came into office in Alberta to save the Alberta farmer's way of life. Both regimes have taken local root because they have functioned to the satisfaction of their communities in this conservative sense. The CCF was prevented from winning British Columbia by the Machiavellian coalition of Liberals and Conservatives. And when these two birds of a feather quarreled, the ingenious British Columbia method of preferential voting handed over the province not to the CCF but to Social Credit. The preferential voting system was devised by the Liberals to compel the Conservatives to give their second choice to Liberal candidates – in order to save the province from socialism – and so elect a Liberal government. By an ironical stroke of fate it worked out in 1952 so the CCF voters gave their second choices to Social Credit candidates and so elected a Social Credit government. This served the Liberals right, but it may have lost the CCF their best chance. To the little man in British Columbia in 1952 the CCF and Social Credit looked equally like protest movements on behalf of the underdog. Twenty or thirty years of socialist propaganda in the Pacific province left him unable to distinguish between them. The hope of the Social Credit leaders is that they will move across the country from west to east and capitalize on vague mass discontent to sweep all the little men of Canada into Social Credit ranks.

The CCF leaders have failed to solve this problem of mass communications. In Saskatchewan they had a mass movement ready-made for them based on all the past experience of the wheat farmers in their organized movements to protect their interests as wheat producers. In Ontario they seem to have decided to seek a mass base in the trade union movement. But there is yet no sign that the Canadian, any more than the American, trade union leadership can deliver the union vote in a political election, however solid their support may be in wage negotiations. In Canada, as in the United States, the trade union leadership has shown a maladroitness in its public relations with the non-trade union world which frequently rises to genius. In the United States, moreover, trade union leaders who used to be socialist have abandoned left-wing party affiliations. Their union interests are too vast to be sacrificed in quixotic party adventures at the expense of alienating the two big parties who hold state and national office. We may expect our Canadian trade union leaders to move in the same direction as they become more firmly established. Where does this leave the CCF in Ontario?

Social Credit seems to be the next political movement in this country with an interesting future. It has no program that can be intelligibly explained. It has a new technique of propaganda, the bible school over the air. The CCF, as I say, has failed so far in mass communications. Its national leaders have been first-class parliamentarians, but the masses do not read the parliamentary debates. Social Credit has discovered how to exploit the emotions of our Canadian lower middle classes. If it is successful it will bring about a condition in which all these little sects of fundamentalist protestants who have sprung up in such numbers will function as the Social Credit party at prayer. (Out in Victoria, BC, so I was told last summer, the United Church is the Liberal party at prayer.) If this Revolt of the Masses should be financed politically by money from Bay St and St James St, there is no knowing how far it might go.

But maybe the Social Credit movement is so completely without principles outside of Alberta that it will blossom and die quickly. For, after all, we are not so demoralized as a community like Germany in the 1930s; and our lower middle classes can still hope to rise, a good many of them, into the upper middle class. Thus Social Credit might sink back to be merely the Alberta variant of this 'provincial-rights' movement which has come to determine the pattern of our contemporary Canadian politics, just as the CCF seems to be sinking back to be the Saskatchewan variant and the Conservative party to be the Ontario variant. And then we should all live happily ever afterward, with

J.B. CONACHER
A Canadian Social Scandal

For the past decade Canadians have been more prosperous than at any time in our history. Total national income continues to increase faster than total population and in most cases wages and salaries have increased even more than the cost of living. The great depression of the 1930s is now only a grim memory, holding little meaning to a generation which has since grown up without any direct knowledge of it.

Because of this unparalleled prosperity the majority of Canadians have little awareness of the bleak and sordid social problems that are a part of our apparently healthy society. The number of sufferers is fewer than in other less prosperous times or than in other less fortunate countries, but the hardships of those who live 'under the line' are the greater by contrast. Let us look at the situation in some of the older parts of Toronto in this year of grace 1953.

Thousands of Toronto families are today living in conditions not easily imagined by most of their fellow citizens. Lack of housing for working class families with children drives many of them to take 'furnished' rooms often in filthy tenements that are soon turned into human rabbit warrens. Any social worker will describe the familiar picture that presents itself to a visitor seeking out one of the unfortunate families. There is no doorbell that works, but persistent knocking may at last bring a downstairs roomer with pale face and vacant stare to the front door. After some hesitation you are told that the family whom you seek are thought to be at the back of the second floor. You stumble through a dark and dirty hall and up a steep unpainted staircase. There are no windows and no electric light. The unpleasant smell produced by too many human beings living in close quarters pervades the building. On the second floor landing you pass members in various stages of dress and undress passing to and from the one common wash room. At least one infant is inevitably crying in the background. Through half open doors you can see the crowded conditions under which these folk live, although you will notice how much tidier some rooms are than others. But generally bedroom, living room, and kitchen seem to be all in one, and always the smell of cooking, and washing, and dirty clothes pervades the atmosphere. The room you finally reach is like the others. The tale of hardship is a familiar one. With three or four children (sometimes with nine or ten) it was impossible to get any other place. In this establishment fewer questions were asked but the rent was as high as more fortunate householders and apartment dwellers were paying in other parts of the city for accommodation infinitely better. These people often pay $18 to $25 a week for one or two miserable rooms of this sort. Often an unemployed father will be called on to pay the whole of his unemployment insurance in rent for such wretched accommodation.

The responsibility for these conditions must lie primarily with the landlord who buys up tumble-down houses cheaply in deteriorating districts, and then chops them up into these fragmentary apartments with the shoddiest furniture. Often a ten-room house may in this way bring in an income of over $100 a week, well over $5,000 a year, perhaps the original cost of the house. Taxes would only be a few hundred dollars a year, heating expenses the very minimum, upkeep often nil. The profits on such investments are high, thanks to the price paid in human misery.

There are, of course, innumerable variations to this general picture. The owner may live in the building, he may rent it to a tenant who in turn sublets most of the rooms in this manner, or he may possess many such properties each operated by a caretaker. The condition of the buildings varies, but invariably the rents are out of all proportion to the accommodation offered. Better accommodation is generally closed to large families. Some are only putting up with these conditions for a short time until, by their own initiative or good luck, they get themselves out of it. Others were born and will die in these surroundings. It is easy to accuse them of shiftlessness, of marrying before they could afford to or of begetting families without benefit of marriage (families with common law parents are all too common), but the explanation must largely be that they in turn are the result of the environment in which they were raised. And by closing our eyes to these conditions we are in many cases condemning their innocent children to a similar fate. What can be expected of children living and sleeping day in and day out under these crowded conditions, generally with nowhere to play but the streets?

(And what must their feelings be when they go to school and see how much more fortunate are most of their classmates?)

It is easier to describe the situation than to point out the remedy. Human suffering has always been the lot of the children of Adam and we are likely to have it with us always. But this knowledge is no excuse for us, the community as a whole, to ignore our responsibilities in justice and charity. Governmental rules and regulations will never put an end to all injustice, but in past years some reduction in the sum total of human misery has been achieved by state intervention and it is not difficult to think of other things which should be done. Despite relatively recent additions the Canadian record in the field of social legislation is not impressive. The public conscience has never been stirred in this country as it has been in Britain as long as a century ago when Lord Shaftesbury and his fellow factory reformers brought the consequences of the English industrial revolution to the attention of the voters and forced the British Parliament to do something about it.

Two social problems that demand immediate attention in Canada are the housing problem and the problem of unemployment relief in cases not taken care of by unemployment insurance. The division of powers and responsibilities between federal, provincial, and municipal authorities complicates both issues but does not excuse the inaction of so many years. Our record of subsidized housing for the poorer elements of the population compares unfavourably with many other countries, especially Britain. The Regent Park project in Toronto points the way to slum clearance but it is only a beginning and even it has been bitterly attacked by certain selfish interests. Projects of that sort will go a long way to solve the major problem of overcrowding and exploitation already considered, because the rents which it is necessary to charge to carry these projects, while not low, are no higher and often less than what the families have to pay for the privileges of living in a slum tenement. The reduced cost of social services, of fire and police expenditures when areas have been so transformed is an acknowledged fact. Toronto voted to continue the work at its last civic election but the pace should be stepped up, the federal government should increase its assistance, and other municipalities across Canada should follow suit.

In the meantime provincial and municipal authorities should take strong action to deal with the racketeers who are allowed to exploit the lot of the numerous families who have not been fortunate to find accommodation in a housing project. There may be a case against rent control in general, but in those depressed areas where exploitation is the rule surely the state must step in and assume responsibility. Rackets in other forms of business are made illegal and the law enforced. Where is the need for action greater than where the welfare of so many human beings, especially children, is concerned? It is essential that the rest of the community take steps to prevent such conditions.

Relief is another matter requiring urgent reconsideration. Municipalities such as Toronto refuse to accept responsibility for families where the father is capable of work but unable to get it. In large cities unemployment insurance is insufficient to cover the barest needs of life for a family where there are no other resources available. Where the breadwinner is for some reason not eligible for insurance the lot of the family may be desperate. Private charity can only tide them over brief crises. Public money should be made available to existing welfare agencies to take care of urgent cases which existing insurance or relief does not meet. Ultimately the federal government should probably be responsible for providing the funds. These are issues that the public should not forget in an election year.

LOUIS DUDEK

The State of Canadian Poetry: 1954

Poetry today is not a popular art; Canadian poetry is even less known than English poetry in general; but as art, it is poetry, not prose, which will in the end prove to be the successful literary medium of this century. We should by now begin to realize – what our newspaper reviewers don't even suspect – that the vast majority of books, novels mainly, that reach the public nowadays, have no real pretention and can never have any place as literature, as permanent art.

Poetry, though ignored, is at least made to last. For this reason, a close look at the almost secret activity (so far as the public is concerned) of Canadian poets just now might bring the general reader a little closer to what is more real, even more immediate, than the long-winded entertainments of fiction.

The first thing to observe is that in this country we have, in the last decade and a half seen an amazing wave of creative work in poetry breaking into print. The period is analogous to, and superior to, the first outburst of poetry in Canada during the '80s and '90s of the last century. The following is a partial list of our poets who have come out with their first books within the last fifteen years: A.J.M. Smith, F.R. Scott, Robert Finch, Earle Birney, A.M. Klein, Anne Marriott, P.K. Page, Patrick Anderson, Irving Layton, Ronald Hambleton, Kay Smith, Raymond Souster, James Wreford, Douglas LePan, Anne Wilkinson, James Reaney – and an additional half-dozen recognized poets in the younger age group.

To anyone who has even a bare anthology acquaintance with these names and the work they stand for it is hardly necessary to interpret what this means. Canada has just produced a literature of its own in poetry in this century. Taking this with the late-romantic verse of the '80s and '90s – Carman, Roberts, Lampman, D.C. Scott, Wilfred Campbell, Isabella Crawford – and the work of Drummond, Service, and Pratt in between, Canadian poetry can now stand without a blush, though still a junior, beside English and American poetry of the last seventy-five years. What we need is a critic who will take a survey of our present stature.

Even before the present poetry movement had declared itself, two critics appeared ready to do service to Canadian poetry: W.E. Collin (*The White Savannahs*, 1936) and E.K. Brown (*On Canadian Poetry*, 1943). They wrote their intelligent analytic criticism of the modern movement in Canadian poetry before most of the poets listed above had appeared in book form. (Collin, in fact, worked from the manuscript of *New Provinces.*) Today, when twentieth-century poetry native to Canada has been put on record through books, anthologies, readings, radio broadcasts, and even TV, we do not have a single critic with the necessary equipment who has been willing to undertake the task of interpreting this poetry seriously, analytically. The chapters on poetry in Desmond Pacey's *Creative Writing in Canada* are the best work to date in that direction, but Pacey's is a very simplified treatment.

Our newspaper and magazine critics are ignorant of the poetry they try to write about when they do try. High school and university teachers, for the most part, are too far behind the spirit of our poetry, too timid and conservative altogether, to dare make an honest statement about literature or its relation to life today. Students in most colleges never get the chance to find out: the libraries don't even have the necessary books. And do the professors of English in our provincial colleges (both senses) read or understand the poetry of this century? Or are they still 'anti-Eliot,' 'anti-modern'? Is the literature they recognize as the best of our time Rupert Brooke, Edna St Vincent Millay, John Masefield, and now at last – Edwin Muir? Don't blush, gentlemen! ...

Canada needs a few bright young critics who will roll up their sleeves and make criticism in this country their job. Some of those now plugging for academic credits with ambitious essays on John Donne or T.S. Eliot's concept of 'time past' and 'time future' might do well to turn their eyes on 'time present' and read *News of the Phoenix,* or *The Red Heart,* or the two recent books by Layton, *Love the Conqueror Worm* and *In the Middle of My Fever.*

There are critical finds to be made: berries where no one has picked before. One of the things about which our critics – the few tired voices one hears – are wrong, is the notion that the activity in recent poetry started suddenly in 1940 and finished suddenly in 1945. A bit of reflection on the probable historical position of the new poetry should make it apparent that the activity of 1940 was only a beginning. Modern rhythm, forms, diction, ideas, and imagination, the characteristic attack of contemporary poetry on life, was bound to come to Canada; the thirties were preparing for it in the work of Klein, Scott, and Smith; the forties produced the printed books. This and the next few decades will show the expansion of this poetry in all directions; the process is now going on.

To test the issue, I would offer the reader books recently out or just coming off the press: *Trio*, containing the first poems of Gael Turnbull, Phyllis Webb, and E.W. Mandel; Reaney's *The Red Heart*; Anne Wilkinson's *Counterpoint to Sleep*; my own long poem *Europe*; or Layton's *In the Midst of My Fever.* Among other things, the reader will find that Canadian poets at this moment, in the midst of world chaos, do have 'something to say.' And in this respect they are unlike recent British and American poets.

E.J. Pratt, for example, has something to

say, however unprepossessing and stereotyped the message at the core may seem to some: *Towards the Last Spike* comes on the heels of a long list of whacking solid books, reminding us of a reputation that will not easily be questioned. Earle Birney's *Trials of a City* places modern life on trial before a court which includes William Langland, an old-time sailor, and an Indian Chief – pretty good 'tests to go by' as Robert Frost would say. A.M. Klein published *The Second Scroll* in 1951, a novel and poetry about world Jewry and the Jewish faith. Books have recently come off the press from the pens of Ronald Hambleton, Patrick Anderson, Douglas LePan, and the three heads of *Cerberus* – Souster, Layton, and myself – all of these as angry and concerned about life values and the realities as ever, and no longer to be shelved away easily as 'socialistic' or 'imitative' of English trends. Others, moreover, F.R. Scott, P.K. Page, and Anne Wilkinson, have new books ready for publication. The generation of poets who started out fifteen years ago are still producing, and most of them have shown some development in ideas and forms. Also, a dozen new poets have appeared on the scene in the magazines: these deserve a brief examination.

The new poets are little known because they have mainly appeared in obscure places. In the last few years *Northern Review* has provided less and less outlet to enterprising work of the kind I would call modern, i.e., continuing the lines opened up by poets as varied as Cummings, Williams, Pound, Marianne Moore, Eliot, Auden etc. (The editor of that magazine has recently declared in print that he favours such writers as C.S. Lewis, G.K. Chesterton, and Roy Campbell, rather than Joyce, Eliot, or Pound!)

The new Canadian poets have therefore looked elsewhere, and have gone unobserved even by the small audience which exists for poetry in Canada. *Contemporary Verse* has ceased publication. To make up for the losses in magazines, however, *The Fiddlehead* (Fredericton, NB) appeared in print last year; *CIV/n*, edited by Aileen Collins, was started in Montreal; and *Contact* was started by Souster in Toronto, a mimeographed magazine with a printed cover – as *Preview* and *New Statement* were in their day. Souster's *Contact* has brought to a handful of young poets in Canada the work of *Origin* magazine in the United States, and the poetry of Charles Olson, Cid Corman, Robert Creeley, and other poets of an interesting group now working in the States. Our underlying position in *Contact* (as well as in *CIV/n*, the Montreal magazine) is one of sharp social criticism based on political or economic grounds alone; it is a cultural attack, a criticism of contemporary life in the name of the whole range of liberal values; and the poetry that we make on this basis is as varied as the personalities of poets can be.

The poets who have appeared in these little magazines have, some of them, true talent and serious artistic purpose: Phyllis Webb (from Victoria, BC) is a young writer with a nervous, original style all her own; D.G. Jones (now in Kingston) is developing a skill in a formal style which is just the example we need; F. Fyfe (now in Hamilton) is a young poet with abundant energy and freedom, somewhat like James Reaney in this respect; Gael Turnbull (in Iroquois Falls, Ont.) writes whimsically and almost too wisely, but with an underlying moral earnestness and social concern which produces a unique combination; E.W. Mandel (St. John, Que.) handles Greek myths and legends as if they were contemporary facts, and uses them to interpret modern life realistically, almost violently, in their light; Leonard N. Cohen (Montreal), the most recent arrival, has a sensitive and imaginative mind, and a ballad-maker's imagination and voice. All this new poetry may be described as highly individualistic and imaginative, ranging into high fantasy rather than stooping to prosaic fact. It is a kind of poetry that began in Canada with James Reaney's *The Red Heart*. It is extravagant at times: but it is no less objective in its implied antagonisms to existing culture than was the poetry of F.R. Scott or Earle Birney.

Of the older poets in *Contact* and *CIV/n*, Patrick Anderson has contributed some prose; Ralph Gustafson has given examples of his usual skill; Souster has matured in emotional tone, but retained all the vivid intensity of his first books. Irving Layton, most important, has in the last few years shown a grasp of poetic complexity and a sense of human tragedy which puts him in the very first rank of Canadian poets. This must be seen in his recent books.

But in addition to all the recent and current books and the new poetry in magazines, anthologies can be taken as a barometer of activity. A.J.M. Smith's anthology is to be reprinted in a new edition; and a re-editing of the Ryerson anthology of Bliss Carman and Lorne Pierce as *Canadian Poetry in English* (Ryerson) has recently been published. Contact Press has put on record a new reading, or cross-section, of the literature in *Canadian Poems: 1850-1952*; and Earle Birney, through Ryerson, has edited *Twentieth Century Canadian Poetry*, which for all its lack of balance in selection is a vital exhibition of our contemporary poetry. These books are creating a new audience for poetry in the universities and schools: at McGill alone, some 700 entering students every year are introduced to the principal Canadian writers through lectures and textbooks – a work started by Professor Arthur L. Phelps. If colleges across Canada undertook to introduce Canadian novels and poetry in combination with the regular English survey, we might be getting somewhere.

Finally, one hates to leave an article on poetry without a few lines of quotation. I offer each of the following as picked stones for the reader to dwell on for some time; they may begin to glow and reveal to him something of what I have been saying.

First, from Layton's *Love the Conqueror Worm*:

> *Imagination*
> *Makes nothing happen, being*
> *The shadow of a beggar's plate*
> *On snow.*

This from Anne Wilkinson:

> *I am so tired I do not think*
> *Sleep in death can rest me.*
> *So line my two eternal yards*
> *With softest moss,*
> *Then lengths of bone won't*
> *   splinter*
> *As they toss,*
> *Or pierce their wooden box*
> *To winter ...*

From Dorothy Livesay, in *Fiddlehead*, Nov. 1953.

> *What moved me, was the way your*
> *   hand*
> *Lay cool in mine, not withering;*
> *As bird still breathes, and stream*
> *   runs clear –*
> *So your hand; your dead hand, my*
> *   dear.*

And from my poem *Europe*, because it seems to fit here:

> *The past speaks in the remaining monu-*
> *   ments and a few pages*
> *   of the dead poets,*
> *judging the Esso empire*
> *and the new Milanese*
> *   without mercy.*
> *What should we say, we few,*
> *   who know what we know,*
> *   but for these records?*
> *Where would we get words*
> *   for our recriminations?*

So this is the scene in 1954, or one view of it. I don't suppose that the present list of names and these comments are sufficient information about the whole range of our poetry now. Each must see it from his own position. The poetry must be read to be valued properly. The presentation given here may sound too optimistic; but, who knows, if the reader will go through the books and magazines for himself, he may decide I have not boasted enough for the poets. They rise in power in proportion as you have the power to see them – being spiritual genii.

ARTHUR LOWER

The Question of National Television

For Canadians there are two distinct phases of the television problem. The one is the question of television as a social device, a piece of technical equipment which intimately penetrates our homes. The other is the question long since fought through in the case of radio, that is, whether we Canadians are to be left with any significant control of the new device, or whether it is to fall into American hands, and thus cease to reflect the Canadian scene. By now both aspects of the problem are familiar to us all.

Much has been written on the Television Revolution. Our age is growing more or less used to revolutions. We have had within fifty years not only one but several technical revolutions which have changed our way of life even more drastically than do changes in government. As someone has said, the automobile made the average American into the irresistible force, but television is remaking him into the immovable object. The automobile ruthlessly grinds down beneath its wheels not only the bodies of unlucky cats and skunks but also a whole civilization. We can go anywhere at any time, at any speed. The necessary consequence is that we are discovering there is nowhere to go – except there and back. The automobile which facilitates people getting about, and therefore, one would think, puts them in contact with each other, has, in fact, gone a long way to destroying our sense of community, for in its little metal casket, it isolates one or two people from all the rest of the world.

Television on the other hand, keeps people rooted to the spot. Otherwise it is just as dehumanizing as the automobile, for it brooks no interference with itself. It is turned on, and you gaze. It doesn't make much difference what you gaze at: you just gaze, and nobody interrupts what is being said. I must confess that as one of the minor demons in this new hell, I am not in much of a position to inveigh against it. But I have also been on the receiving end and can recall what might have been two days of pleasant talk at a friend's house ruined because we had to sit and look steadily at Senator McCarthy.

The irrelevance of the whole performance to us Canadians! McCarthy, of course, has been a proper subject of our contempt – thank God, we are not as Americans are – but he is not our responsibility, and we can't do anything about him. We can neither vote for him nor against him. Our combined collective Canadian shout is never heard more than twenty or thirty miles south of the border, so we may as well give up shouting.

I am, of course, frankly saying that there must be a limit to American penetration into Canadian life, if we are going to go on existing as a Canadian community. I really have no idea how much concern there is in Canada for this particular object. It is evident that our national heart-beat is barely strong enough to keep us alive and that the danger exists – and has always existed – that we, as a political community, may die. It may, indeed, be debated whether we have ever been alive.

With such a feeble sense of our own identity and a shameless dependence in every direction on our neighbour, our earmarks have been mediocrity and complacence.

There are a few oases in the Canadian desert, it may be cheerfully agreed. Unfortunately the palm trees growing in them have to do for so many purposes that it is difficult for them to keep alive. Hence our constant resort to united effort – that is, political effort – to keep our national fabric intact. We recognize that only by a general yo-heave-ho can we manage to build transcontinental railways, maintain airways, or have our own means of expression in these newer media, radio and television: that surely was what the Massey Report had to say. This business of having to resort to a united communal effort is more widespread than even the Report suggested. Canadian socialism is not maintained by the tariff alone: our banks, for example, are Canadian by the grace of God and the Canadian Parliament. Left to the free play of economic forces, large American finance should have gobbled them up long ago. That conspicuous example of 'private' enterprise, the Canadian Pacific Railway, is much the same, an aspect of the Canadian state.

So far our people have been interested just enough to permit government to do these things, and no more. There is no surplus of nationalism in Canada. And there is no surplus of taste, our taste being still that of the backwoodsman, heavy and undiscriminating. Hence the average Canadian has no objection to outside influences. Having no standards of his own, he is overborne by those of other people. And for the average man, the Americans are the only other people who exist.

I suppose the same dilemma will continue to exist for us into the indefinite future, but one sometimes does wish that Canadians could make up their minds and decide whether they wished to be alive or dead. If they became Americans they would at least cease to be mere spectators of someone else's fun. If they wish to remain Canadians – and surely they must wish something of the sort or they would not go on cheerfully supporting this enormously expensive governmental structure of ours – then let's hope, they will try to be Canadians. Personally, I hate going round forever as a mere ghost.

Since private television is only another name for Americanized television, national television obviously is one more peg in this tent of national existence, and a pretty big one. Possibly if enough pegs are driven into the ground, sooner or later there may even be a tent for them to hold up. There need be no idealization of the quality of our local product. Whether it proves good or bad, let us remember our Shakespeare: 'A poor thing, but mine own, my Lord.' That is the attitude of those who have recently formed the Canadian Radio and Television League (30 Bloor Street West, Toronto), of which all readers of *The Canadian Forum* are invited to become members. Readers who do so will have the additional satisfaction of knowing that they are at the same time helping to put those most arrant of all Tories in their places, the thoroughgoing no-nonsense men of the opinion 'throwaways' and the *free enterprise is sacred (as long as it puts money in* MY *pocket)* pressure groups.

CURT LANG
History Lesson on Point Grey

The eye sees at night, water tugging at the rocks,
A threat of storm above, reports of gales
Activated north along the coast, cloud formed windows
Pass and pass again along the moon.
In the green warrens of the sea where no bird flies,
Only the heavy headed cod
Sleeps toward the burning of the sands.

No horizon rises, only the sea merged to the sky,
And a foghorn on the unseen farther shore
Calls through the night to some
Unfortunate, invisible sea-fog demented ship.

No colours to say the sun's passing –
Only an ebbing of the timeless, finial light.

The foghorn now a saurian;
Black, glistening, lifting an amazing, evil neck
Into the sightless air.
Calling bass-voiced to what no eye would see.
What might have been red port lights
Are the surfaced eyes of some huge-backed,
Floating, dark, sea-kept immensity.
The dull ocean fumbles at the shore.

Imagine now some gentle and most frightened thing
Thrown to the serpent end of time.
Trapped between dark trees full of horrors
And the waters lying in death before.

Imagine now the dark trees endless, slow, demented shower
Of curled leaves that fall like furtive souls,
Passing like the footfall of an hour.
Imagine the soft half silent spinning of the leaves
And the cold half living whisper of the sea,
The dark, unseen, reptilian company.

Then would prayer unbolt some fire, some light,
Some flame in this black rush of time.
Then should the moon appear.
Then should the golden sun return.
Then should the earth spit up vast skeletons.
And all the voices of the sea gape watery mouths and yell.

But time has slipped away again.
On the mountain's dark we see, processional,
Bright torches carried in a long and flaming row.
Imagine now dark Druids or masked Haidas;
Imagine now dawn man in primal night;
The lizards dead, man born, we see first men
Enact the burial of first man dead.

JEAN INGLIS
And the Green Hills Laugh

'Bonjour, ma belle. Comment ça va?' said Mr Jereau at 4.04 as usual. 'O.K. Cigarette?' said Beth as usual, hoping he had forgotten what she knew he had not forgotten.

A low murmur from the class room next door indicated that Grades 6, 7, and 8 were saying the Lord's Prayer in preparation for their subdued stampede down the hall.

'Dear, dear,' sang Mr Jereau in his soft voice, as he propped his broom against the blackboard and reached for the cigarette she held out to him. 'You teach me bad habits, Bet, you know that?'

Fumbling with his bulging trousers pocket, he squeezed from it a huge apple and a handful of kitchen matches. The apple he placed on her desk on top of *Latin for Secondary Schools*. One match he struck across 'B. Flannigan' deeply carved into the front desk of the window row.

Beth hunted in a lower drawer for her ash tray and set it up beside the apple. Conscious that Mr Jereau had stopped sprinkling dustbane and was gazing out the window at the sunlit bush beyond the tracks preparing a remark on the weather, Beth kept her head bent over a little pile of Grade 9 French tests and went at them with a red pencil.

A thud against her door. Automatically she held her cigarette hidden behind her desk, although every kid in town knew that she smoked. Still, she preferred them not to see her at it so soon after 4.00 o'clock. But the thud was only an unlucky member of Miss Hackitt's room who had been pushed to the wall during the rush out. She heard Miss Hackitt call, 'Stevie – go back into the room and sit down.'

Four failures and three passes later, Mr Jereau finished sweeping and lowered himself slowly, because of rheumatism, into the front seat by the window. Beth put down her red pencil and gave him a smile.

'Well, Bet, – you all set for Sunday?'

What could she say but, enthusiastically, 'Sure I am.'

'That's the chicken – you ketch on this time for sure, eh? – I got one all tied up for you – what you like, ten pound? fifteen pound? twenty pound?'

Fifteen minutes later when he had gone Beth started a letter on a piece of loose-leaf paper:

                The School After Four
Dear Dot,   Friday thank god

Just finished my daily session with Mr J. – my experienced advice to new teachers: never make friends with the janitor – we're going fishing again on Sunday out at his camp. I'm so weak-minded I don't know how to refuse, but things get quite grim. It's just damn AWKWARD because I can't bear to hurt his feelings. I think everybody else (maybe even you) think I'm disgusting, etc. I rush around peeling potatoes and opening cans of beans and try to keep the conversation on the war (Boer, that is) and his bygone girl friends (Clara, Edith, Lucille, etc. - they are legion.) Then I bring in the 'missus' (still laid up with her broken hip). When things get personal I tear off to the john and sit there for ten minutes looking at the scenery thru large cracks in the wall. Anyway Mr J. has provided me with subject matter for all my letters. But enuff of my luff life. What about yours –

As she scribbled on, Beth wondered uncomfortably if anything really startling would happen on Sunday. It was true that Mr Jereau had been the subject of numerous letters to Dot, Mary, Ellen, Jim, and others since early in the fall she had introduced him by saying, 'The janitor is pressing me to go partridge hunting with him – he is Fr. Can. and aged and has no teeth and is the only one in town who calls me by my first name, pronounced Bet which reminds me of Bête – has also invited me up for dinner some night to meet "The Missus".'

She had gone to meet the missus, and in a spirit of social recklessness had accepted a bottle of beer which she drank in the dining room while listening to Mr Jereau tell tales of moose hunts which had taken place years before she was born. The dining room sideboard was cluttered with old snaps of family members supporting strings of fish or deer carcasses, and plaster images in all sizes of the Virgin. The parlour, which she was shown briefly, contained one of the largest, crimsonest, most anatomical-looking Bleeding Heart pictures she had ever seen.

Dinner was served in the kitchen. The missus, an energetic stooped-over little woman with a loud voice, continually bossed Mr Jereau and his large black dog. In her quiet way Beth had enjoyed the strangeness of it all immensely, and wondered what it would be like to live always with fourteen chipped Virgin Mary's on the sideboard.

She had gone partridge hunting too, tramping along behind Mr Jereau through the October bush, with a pocketful of ham sandwiches, apples, and cigarettes. When Christmas came she went home to the city 700 miles away, and was full of tales when five of the girls and a bottle of Scotch came together in Ellen's room for a reunion.

'God,' said Mary, who was civilized to a high degree, 'you and your passion for "sweet characters".'

'Well dammit,' said Beth, 'he is sweet, and terribly kind and the least I can do is drink a bottle of beer with him, even if I don't enjoy the stuff. Mind you I'm developing a taste for it.'

'Is that all you do for a social life?'

'No, I play bridge at the bridge club – and I go to shows and dances with Willy (he's sweet too, Mary) – and most of the time I prepare lessons for school.'

'The old boy sounds alright,' said Ellen, who had taught for one year in a small town. 'There were a couple up at the Bay like that – unenlightened, but good types – interesting – you may as well enjoy them while you can – after all you don't intend spending the rest of your life among people like that...'

Through the pleasant glow the Scotch was producing Beth felt a prick of annoyance. That sounded as if Ellen thought that people like that were – were – what? 'He brings me an apple to school every day, and he never mentions

August 1955

Willy at all cause he's jealous –' she chanted drowsily, 'and his name is – Alphonse – Alphonse and Willy – what a fascinating sex life I do lead –'

'Oh, Beth,' said Dot leaning over and pulling her hair, 'I think this year is being good for our shy little Beth – and you're HIGH.'

In January Beth wrote:

Dear Everybody,
  Mr J. is showing himself to be what Barb would classify as 'a dirty old man.' Went up for dinner, the missus being out of town, cooked potatoes and pork chops, had a slight slug of Scotch and two beers, and he wanted to kiss me. Was shy, shocked, etc. and changed the subject.

Later she wrote to Dot only:

I am rather ashamed – do you mind confessions? I let Mr J. kiss me when we drink beer in the school on Sunday afternoons. I can't do other without being mean. I keep my mouth clamped shut and bear with his stubble against my face for a few seconds. But oh Dot he will die so soon and I feel so sorry for him and what right have I to be dignified – I know Mary would be revolted, and Ellen for all her sociological broadmindedness would SHUDDER. Situations like this are meant for jokes not for real. Sometimes we drink Scotch instead of beer – he brings the bottle up concealed in his overcoat and after he winds the clocks in the other rooms he hauls it out and takes a huge gulp and I take a slight slurp. I don't wipe the bottle of course. Was it Emily Post or Hemingway that said something about that? Anyway I felt this is a little bit of LIFE and it's funny and wonderful. Don't laugh at me Doff.

Beth did enjoy the Scotch in certain ways, although she held each teaspoonful in her mouth till it mixed with her saliva into a sweetish tingling syrup before she dared to swallow it. But it warmed her – the school room could be very cold on a blustery wintery Sunday – and gave her a burning sensation in her knees and made her want to go to bed instead of preparing five geography lessons. It was comfortable and strange to sit in a bleak school room while the afternoon sky darkened, to hear Mr Jereau's soft voice say, 'Well – Bet –.' And it pleased some rebel imp in her heart to be a teacher UP North, and drink (however mildly) in the class room.

One day she could hardly wait to dash off a letter:

Dear Everybody,
  I really feel like a scarlet woman now – Mr J. has proposed as follows – if the missus should ever be taken Bet would you marry an old man like me? – May and December, December two years ago. He'll be seventy-two in August.

And so Beth dreaded Sunday. No doubt it would be worse than the past two Sundays. It would be the last one. At the end of two weeks school would be over and Beth would be returning to the city.

The five mile drive out to the lake Beth enjoyed. They bumped along in a 1927 car over a narrow road through the bush in almost complete silence. It was a grey day with occasional flashes of sunlight and the country looked lonely and wild. Beth smoked, and watched out the window, and occasionally picked up the tin St Christopher medal which bounced off a screw above the windshield whenever they hit a particularly villainous hole.

Occasionally Mr Jereau would say, 'Well, Bet, so you like this kind of life, et? – you be a real bush woman –'

Arrived at the lake Beth unloaded fishing tackle, food, gasoline, cushions, oars, dip net, and fishing poles from the car while Mr Jereau went to fetch his boat which he kept moored in a little bay a few hundred yards away.

All the way across the lake they fished without getting a bite. Then it was chicken soup, bacon, and beans cooked by Beth on the wood stove in his cabin. And then they must have a second bottle of beer. Knowing her troubles were going to begin, Beth lighted a cigarette.

Mr Jereau with his back close to the wood stove was sweating hard. He mopped his face with a red polka dot handkerchief and settled back in his chair, nursing a beer bottle – a slim old man with stiff legs, dressed in the thickest of tweed trousers and vest and a red plaid shirt. His white hair, about three inches in length, hung over his ears and his browned face. It looked like thin cotton wool, not like hair.

Keeping her eyes on the end of her cigarette, Beth tried unsuccessfully to think of something to say.

'Well, Bet,' he said slowly, 'what do you say – are you going to be my little chum?'

She smiled but wouldn't look at him.

'Come on now Bet, speak up – you like me don't you?'

'Yes I do very much.'

'I like you – the missus she does too – she's a good woman Bet – I got a good woman – But if she die Bet I be lonely – lonely – and I want Bet to be my little chum –'

She listened to him, twisting her legs in her baggy grey slacks, sipping her beer, avoiding his eyes. All desire to laugh had left her and she hated herself for those letters she had written.

She heard his gentle voice go on: 'The first time you smile at me, Bet, you drove a spike right into my heart – you don't know what I got in my heart for you Bet – nobody love you like I do – you be mine Bet and you live like a little queen –.' Her heart was torn with pity for him.

'Bet, you give me a nice kiss, et? Do you like when I kiss you Bet?'

He came and sat on the arm of her chair. His face was wet with sweat, his eyes glistened behind his spectacles, he smelt sickly sweet with cigar smoke. She saw the reddish yellow of his eyeballs, his pink gums, and turned her face aside to stare at her shoes. He put his hand on her knee and she stared at it. It was a big strong knobby hand with dark hair curling on it and dirt under the broken finger nails. She felt warmth on her knee, and breathing close to her face, and still she watched the hand. Muscles in her stomach contracted. She swallowed and finally turned her face to him. His grey stubble scratched her cheek. She felt a wet mouth on her own.

When three kisses were over she slipped out of the chair and said smiling, 'Let's go catch a big fish.' In her voice there was no trace of the sudden horror she felt.

They did the dishes, she swept the floor and put away the food, and soon they were out again climbing into the boat moored at his log dock.

He started the engine, leaned back, and headed the nose of the boat out to the end of the point. Since they had first come to the camp, the wind had grown stronger and now it blew steadily with sudden gusts of greater violence at intervals catching Beth's hair and flicking it into her eyes and mouth. Awkwardly, since she was wearing a sweater – two sweaters – a blazer and a coat with shoulder pads, Beth dug out from her pocket a crumpled green kerchief with rust flowers on it, and turning let the wind sweep her hair back from her face. Fumbling with the square till she had it folded into a triangle, raising her arms above her head till the wind streamed the scarf out behind her, turning her face up to the sky while she pulled the scarf tight and tied its ends under her chin – and her head was tied in a cosy silk bundle. The noise of the wind and the engine sounded lower than before, but more powerful and more permanent.

When she turned to face Mr Jereau with a satisfied grin, he was bent down stiffly in the shelter of the engine lighting his cigar.

He straightened up, put the cigar in the right corner of his mouth and said loudly, 'She's blowin' eh?'

Beth bobbed her head three times.

He nodded.

'Scared?'

'Bet she aint scared of nothing is she?'

'Well – not this anyway – it's fun.'

The cabin now looked like a toy. Behind it and all around the bay rose a steep wall of hills covered with dark green trees under whose shadow the boat swayed forward, bobbing when it half turned and hit the little waves in the bay sideways. Between the fishing tackle box and the dip net, Beth sat easily on her leather cushion, with her legs sprawled apart and one red mocassin resting against the side of the boat.

As the boat moved under the shadow of the hills, Beth felt as if she belonged to this hidden sport whose innocence hung about her in silver clouds. Every muscle, every nerve cell, every hair on her head and body relaxed as she looked at the swirling water, the moving hills, the revolving sky. Oh – she was so – unwatched.

'Well, Bet – we give her a try now.'

Nodding Beth handed him back his fishing pole and picked up her own by the wrong end. It vibrated and she had to stretch to grab the handle. Then her body loosened again; she dropped her spinner over the side and watched the silver and red twinkle out of sight in the dark water as she gave out her line.

Now they were past the point and out of the bay and the boat was ploughing into waves that were big from the force of the wind across the lake. Now Beth was swaying, rocking, rolling, shuddering with the boat. Now an extra big wave bumped with the force of a moving tree trunk and water drenched the left sleeve of her coat.

'She's a rough one – so it's fun – fun, eh?'

Beth smiled.

'I know you aint scared – not my Bet.'

'Nope.'

August 1955

'We could have good fun Bet, you and me, eh? What do you say?'

'We do.'

'That's my girl.' Mr Jereau settled back in silence, bobbing his pole up and down with one hand and steering the boat with the other. His old face was turned up to the sky and his eyes stared vaguely far away.

Beth dashed a wisp of hair back with her sleeve and felt against her cheek rough soggy tweed with its dirty smell. She put her left hand back on her pole quickly. It was a bit of a strain for her to move her heavy pole gently up and down the way one should to attract a fish. She liked better to sit peacefully with both wrists bent backwards by the weight. The rolling of the waves pulled her line rhythmically – pull, pull, pull, pull, pull. JERK. Beth's line snapped into a straight line. Both her feet plunked themselves tight together in front of her.

'I GOT one,' she yelled.

Startled out of his revery the old man jumped and his cigar dropped from between his gums onto the floor of the boat. Out of the corner of her eye, Beth saw him fumbling about picking up his cigar, hauling in his pole, while she wound in her wet line into a big bulge in the centre of her reel.

'You got a big one?'

'I don't know.'

'You can hold her, eh? – keep pulling her in – that's the chicken – you're doing good.' The old man was excited.

He was leaning over the side of the boat and with his right hand in the water was controlling her line between his fingers. His hand, distorted by water, was an old man's hand now, with dark wet hairs curling on it. She stared at it and remembered – oh, all his kindness to her, his saneness ('they all got their good points, Bet, Catholic, Protestant it don't make no difference'). And she thought, this is the last time I'll be on this boat, on this lake –

With the end of her pole jammed into her stomach for support, the fingers of her right hand trying to shove over the mass of wet line clogging her reel, the left hand turning frantic circles, half choking with excitement and tears, – she remembered – without shame or horror or pity – what she had felt when that hand was on her knee.

LOUIS DUDEK

Keewaydin Poems

3

What we call nature is nothing else than
the triumph of life other than our own –
the passive unaggressive trees
and the grass, so alien
they can have no animal contact with us
and are therefore safe
to walk through – they and the inert
inanimate –
a world huge and useless, from our point of
    view,
therefore a bore
    (i.e., if you've got something else to do
        that you're glad to do),
or a place for free association,
    for God the Father, Mother Nature,
        and 'our sister water' –
the friendly family (we like to think) of
    things alive;
or better still, that beneficent 'other,'
    a great deal of 'not mankind,'
hence at least a counterweight to human
    ego –
but most of all, a place of freedom, to
    ruminate in, to be
        forever blowing bubbles
            of so-called 'relaxation,'
for fantasy that has not already found its
    images
        of successful art, in living.
But do not say that it brings you
closer to the unity of any process
that we may be part of,
or that to pile on enough vegetables
    and rocks
is the epiphany of philosophy.

4

Yet green is a pleasure to live with,
    among the colours
a kind of world
of straw, on sticks, stirring yet stationary –

the comic vegetation hung out in rags, flags,
    piled in barrows of bushes –
        or a Victorian parlour
in which there is still room
for you, if you don't mind stepping over the
    bodies
growing and dying, gasping for air,
if you, indifferent to murder
    in forms of life not our own,
love the world we live in –
haletant with genocide and innocent
    abominations
        and all the green pleasures.
We need to think of nothing but ourselves,
and it is so. Which we do.
The order of things, everywhere,
takes care of that also:
relax, kill and live.

5

So man, the top killer of them all,
who has brought three-quarters of the birds,
    fish and animals
close to extinction
and now does his slaughtering systematically
(all save man-killing war, murder, and sport,
which still take the natural form),
persists in the Western-Christian idea,
the romantic theory of nature:
    that order rules,
    that love governs.

MILTON WILSON

On Dudek and Layton

October-November 1955

So we play deck tennis, shuffleboard,
we lie wrapped in blankets,
we laugh, and make each other laugh
on our jolly excursion;
    but the sea
begins to torture our bowels
as if it would make us understand:
    possibly without design,
its influence makes itself known
by an internal shudder,
its great spasms contract our little
    stomachs
and in the midst of glee
    we become suddenly sick.

Not even the desire to show how man shrinks as the sea expands gives much significance to something as pretentious and undistinguished as this. But when I reached the twentieth poem and Mr Dudek was still at sea, I had to revise even this third theory, at least in part.

Fortunately, the reader reaches land with Number 27, and the poems stiffen, the 'sentiment and vacuity' (to quote Mr Dudek on English art) acquire some vigour and sharpness. This is particularly true when he is concerned with art, music, and poetry. In fact, the artier Mr Dudek's poetry the better it is. It becomes crisper and lively with curiosity. For all his worship of the Great Mother, at sea he seemed bored to tears; but in a cathedral or the Wordsworth country, he has eyes and convictions, and the influence of Ezra Pound, so deadly when Mr Dudek is not operating at high efficiency, is now life-giving. The passionate concern for art as the measure of civilization reaches its peak in the third section, where the cathedrals of northern France serve him as

... I found Louis Dudek's new book *Europe* (Laocoon [Contact] Press, pp. 139; $2.00; a series of 99 short poems which follow the course of a European tour of 1953), both puzzling and impressive. I am saying here and now that I found it impressive, so as to inoculate the reader against the comparative stringency of the comments which I intend to begin with.

The opening group of poems concerns the voyage abroad. At first, as the long line of platitudes started to file past in limp, undistinguished verse, I was frankly incredulous. I had not supposed that Mr Dudek, whose talent I respect, could be so unabashedly dull. Might *Europe* be simply a pot-boiler? But who today would write a pot-boiler in verse? On second thought I decided that he was writing a contemporary *Everyman*, or *The Canadian White Collar Worker Visits the Old World*, a sort of versified cousin of Marilyn Bell's Diary. But 99 poems were surely more than Mr Dudek would think of building on such a base. Then I decided that it might be a poetic exercise which someone had dared him to. The idea would be to write one poem every day during the trip and to include them all unrevised (the worst along with the best) in a single volume. This would explain the survival of lines like the following:

theme for some of his most effective verse, reaching a climax in Number 52. What is impressive is not any wisdom, any discriminating aesthetic or historical sense (these are notably absent, it seems to me, who am not very close to the 'Pound-Ruskin axis'), but rather the skill and strength with which his belief in the importance of artistic integrity shapes itself. One does not have to agree that 'everything goes to hell after the Middle Ages' or that the imitation of classical models was disastrous or that French classicism was 'the worst taste in manners or in art the world has ever seen' to be delighted by the sweep of these sweeping absurdities, and to be convinced by Mr Dudek's conviction. And yet, when I try to quote (either from these poems or from the ones on Spain, Italy, and Greece which follow), I find that apart from a few striking lines, the main effect is cumulative. Pulled out of their casual context, passages fade and lose much of what I (rightly) thought I saw in them, and the shorter poems are generally inferior. Here is a comparatively detachable fragment, the opening of Number 64:

Our eyes are filled with arches, with marble
   colonnades, campaniles and towers;
when I close my eyes I see them
   vibrating in the after-image
their fixity has made, since the flesh tries
   helplessly to preserve such stillness:
a toy model of Pisa
   stirs in the million-watt sun
on the piazza, the Florentines
walk about in purple tunics
   as whimsical as their tall crenelated towers;
I see Siena shake in the sun, a white facade
   blazing with immense beginnings ...

I put down *Europe* wondering whether the naive opening was perhaps justified. It is, after all, an education piece. The innocent abroad has to be innocent to start with, or just vulgar, when innocence is impossible. The poems of the return voyage (which include some of the loveliest in the book), with their sifting of the past and renewed understanding of home and the future, gain some of their fullness from our memory of the voyage out. Perhaps in the end things are less puzzling than they seemed. One little puzzle remains.

The wedge of ignorance entered Europe
   with a blind idolatry
of Greece and Rome; you can see it
   as a straight line from the fifteenth
     century down,
'art for art,' copying the Greek forms,
shape without sense, imitating
   imitations ...

writes Mr Dudek, impressed by the superiority of Chartres. But, if the applicability of these lines is as broad as it seems to be, and he is not just condemning inferior talents who would be bad whether they classicized or not, in them he denies the validity of his own poetry and that of Ezra Pound his mentor. For Pound, in his own way, is to medieval culture as Ben Jonson or Racine is to Latin comedy or Greek tragedy. Neither is a slave to what he re-creates, but without the model he would not be recognizably what he is. *Europe*, in turn, is an imitation of an imitation, but very much worth doing, whatever its author may have to say in disparagement of such things.

Even if *Europe* had been a good deal less successful than it is, it would have been worth doing. Mr Dudek is not afraid to be prolific and enterprising, to keep writing and hope for the best. Right now, this is probably the chief virtue of a poet. Irving Layton, whose *In the Midst of My Fever* belongs to 1954 and *The Cold Green Element* to 1955, has this virtue in abundance, as well as a good many others. He is our most conspicuous illustration of the advantages of keeping one's hand in. Practice, I suppose, hasn't made perfect, but poetry is an approximate thing at best, and practice has helped to make Mr Layton write in these two volumes poems which are equal to the best written by a Canadian. He has lived to have the last laugh on his critics, who may not have been as wrong then as they seem now, for the development from *Here and Now* (1945) to the poems now in front of me is immense. Even *Love the Conqueror Worm* (1953) is no adequate preparation for the best of his recent output.

When I say that Mr Layton's best poems are equal to the best poems written by a Canadian, I am speaking of such poems as 'Seven O'Clock Lecture,' 'Composition in Late Spring,' 'The Birth of Tragedy,' and 'The Longest Journey', from the 1953 book, and a good many of those from the 1954 one, where the high level is remarkably consistent. I find his poems exciting for a good many reasons: his high spirits, which erupt in bursts of fantasy and sometimes reform themselves into the pattern of a contemporary myth; the truculence which involves the reader in his prejudices; the firm, but supple and transparent lines of his lyrics. What most of all will make me come back to these two books is the combination of poise, severity, and purity with a devil-may-care casualness. He says 'Look! no hands!' as he shoots straight at the goal without a wobble. ... Mr Layton's disciplined insouciance is a feat, indeed. And if his past abundance is any criterion, we should have a lot more of it.

On second thought ... I certainly ought to elaborate on and reconsider seriously what I meant by my too cryptic description of *Europe* as an 'education poem.'

Europe begins in a state of innocence, leavened with a rather inarticulate dissatisfaction. The speaker leaves home without too much baggage, a simple sightseer (it seems), as yet unaware that what he is ultimately looking for is the home he has left behind. Afloat on the river and then on the sea 'bulging with wombs,' he gradually becomes more articulate; the universal questions which have to be answered about man's needs – his happiness, civilization, and destiny – start to emerge, even if they remain only embryonic and in solution, or are stated casually, as if the speaker were as yet only half aware of their import. He is a part of the Ship of Fools, but it is taking him on a special voyage, of whose significance the whole book records the increasing awareness.

The universal questions which emerge are met by a number of standards, or fundamentals, none of which is ultimately satisfying by self. ...

The first standard (which starts to appear right at the beginning) is represented by the sea, which is both man's master and his slave, which he both fears and envies, which he can never hope to equal, both because it is above him and because he is above it. Ever present as both standard and raw material, it nevertheless offers no panacea. At worst it is little more than 'a lot of water' or a threat of dissolution; at best it is a reminder of what man must not forget (and is not allowed to forget throughout *Europe*), or the 'uncreated chaos' which he must start from and keep returning to. ...

After the sea (which merges with related symbols of Nature), there are the standards of Art and Society. Art and the monuments of the past dominate the middle of the book, although the other standards certainly compete with it.

What should we say, we few,
Who know what we know,
  but for these records?
Where would we get words
  for our recriminations?

But what of those outside the self-conscious few? And how do even 'we few' get beyond nostalgic recriminations? Art, like Nature, seems increasingly inadequate, although infinitely important. As the book moves into its second half and the scene shifts from England and France to Spain and Greece, our common human need for justice moves to the foreground, people crowd out statues and buildings and poems, and the standard of Society dominates. 'Good art is the record of a good society.'

From the perfect circle of the sea, through 'the one good line in a poem,' toward the perfect Republic – so, with many undulations, *Europe* moves. And so also it moves home, to America. On the return journey, the difficulties of applying or even recognizing the standard of Society are apparent. Utopia recedes, as its urgency becomes more demanding. And the sea returns. The end of the poem is its beginning, although a new beginning. The individuals on whose 'ethics' and hard work the future depends are left to create it.

The sea has washed out
everything I have written, the fiction of
temporaneity:
we are back with the real, the uncreated
chaos of ocean ...
Getting started is never easy.
We have work to do.
  Europe is behind us.
  America before us.

But how does this impressive conception (which I have, of course, oversimplified) fare in practice? The most difficult and unrewarding section for the poet is likely to be the first (which includes both the tentative point of departure and the emerging standard of the sea). And it is in this section that Mr Dudek's weaknesses are most obvious, as my review (too facetiously) indicated. There ought to be some way to produce the effect of innocence and anticipated knowledge without being insipid or platitudinous; the *tabula rasa* ought to be really fresh and embryonic.

New men and women!
  – The sea is so easily bored!
And treacherous ... in love ...
  like any woman.
Beware, O nations, of her coiled and
  serpentine body.

This is No. 11 complete, and there are many passages no more distinguished. There are others where Mr Dudek almost brings it off, as in the fresh and lovely No. 4 and No. 25, although the former has a silly parenthesis, and the end of the latter is ineptly phrased, so that one almost forgets the fine things that have preceded it, like the beautiful image of the girl

> *eating lunch at St Catherine*
> *and looking so sad*
> *You'd think the whole world was dying*
> *and this was his sister.*

There are also impressive moments when a simple wisdom arises out of the impact of the sea, as at the end of No. 23, or (with more complexity) in No. 19. But there is no use pretending that Mr Dudek solves his difficult problems convincingly in these 26 poems, which constitute a quarter of the whole.

In the remainder of the book the execution is much more adequate to the conception. I spoke last month of the liveliness, curiosity, and intensity of many of these poems, and of the crispness of their phrasing; as I read them again, they still seem impressive. To be sure, some of the kinks in the argument may need straightening out.

> *Monuments fool us, delude us into*
> *believing that once there was energy*
> *married to equity, to raise such buildings.*
> *But there was also pride and oppressive*
> *power ...*

says the speaker in No. 40. I'm not sure how we move from 'art outlives inhumanity' to the statement 'Good art is the record of a good society.' Mr Dudek's aesthetic medievalism gets him into a number of difficulties which he either fails to see clearly or disregards. Or are the lines from No. 40 themselves a delusion out of which the speaker is later educated? In fact, how much of the poem is finally washed out by the sea?

I ask this because it is relevant to what seems at first sight the most dissatisfying aspect of *Europe*. Whereas Mr Dudek is suitably tentative and 'brooding' about the cure for the ills of civilization, he is often narrow and myopic about the disease. Where he is exploratory in one direction, he is rigid and narrow in the other. For sheer exclusiveness his process of elimination in the arts surpasses anything since Pound's *How to Read*. And the ills of civilization are too easily reduced to the mechanical and the usurous. The enemy seems to be simply middle class plutocracy, standardization, and vulgarity. I am not, of course, denying that these targets are fair game. In the plays of George Bernard Shaw we had a searching and infinitely flexible postmortem on the still kicking corpse of the bourgeoisie. In Ezra Pound, for all his great virtues, the tools of attack are blunt and the corpse is a shadow of the real thing. Mr Dudek, unfortunately, is closer to the method of Pound than to that of Shaw, and thus is in danger of falling a victim to the very standardization which he deplores. The comparative narrowness and inflexibility of his recriminations give some of his poems a sweep and conviction which are impressive, but I, for one, am convinced in spite of myself.

Perhaps Mr Dudek intended to educate his speaker out of this too, although I am not satisfied that this was his intention. However, in a sense the education does occur. The mood is left behind if not rejected, and the best of the later poems, with their rich humanity, seem to me wise as well as beautiful.

PAUL FOX

The Liberal Party

The secret of the Liberal Party's twenty years in office is that it is a middle class party in a middle class country. Canadians are by nature and development incurably middle class, and the federal Liberal Party has become the symbol to them of themselves. People vote Liberal because the Tories will smack of big business and the CCF of labour while the Liberal candidate looks like the universal Canadian, a very ordinary average business man or anyone's daddy.

The Liberal Party has been pragmatic in the extreme. Under Mackenzie King the party moved far enough left to cut most of the ground out from under the CCF. Yet it could still garner votes on the right and leave the impression that it was very different from those reactionary Tories. This mixed programme has given the appearance of being a middle way. A little 'left' in social welfare and a lot of good safe 'right' in fiscal and monetary policy. But above all a large measure of whatever common sense, public opinion, and experience indicate is wise at the moment.

This empirical approach seems eminently sensible to most Canadians because it is the way they run their own lives. Moderation, caution, being careful, taking it easy, *surtout point de zèle* are precepts in the bourgeois catalogue of virtues as well as rules of thumb for Liberal politicians. It is not a coincidence that John Locke who esteemed Prudence the first political virtue has been the enduring philosophic influence in the liberal democratic state. The political settlement he justified has lasted more than three hundred years because its virtues are those of the middle class on which it was established. Canada is different from Britain only in that the middle class in this country is nearly all-embracing. If one doubts this, let him ask the first Canadian voter he meets to which class he thinks he belongs. And then let him ask whether the voter believes in socialism, capitalism, or a little bit of both, 'the middle way.'

By good luck brilliant intuition, or crystal gazing the Liberal Party has hit upon the way to the voters' X. Avoid isms like the plague and do what comes naturally. This is enough to satisfy most Canadians who would do the same thing themselves if in power and who ask only not to be bothered by politics. We are an unphilosophical people who are apolitical into the bargain as long as things are going reasonably well. Political theories do not interest us – we do not seem to feel the need for them. We have never produced a political philosopher in this country, a Jefferson, Paine, Burke, or Locke, and wouldn't know what to do with him if we did. We even consider politics a bit distasteful, a rather off-colour subject which nice people don't talk about for fear of hurting feelings or being thought to believe in something. These are middle class traits, part of the pattern of working hard, minding one's own business, being practical, and not having silly ideas.

On these strains in our national character Mackenzie King played with adroitness, wrapping external affairs, for instance, in such a holy cloak of mystery that Canadians have been about as interested in the world outside as Fiji Islanders. With a few exceptions – notably Mr Pearson's earnest efforts to overcome his predecessor's short-sightedness – it can be said in all fairness, I think, that the present Liberal government still prefers to keep people in the dark because it is less easy to see what is going on. Information has to be pried out of Mr Howe at times with a crowbar, and both Harris and Pickersgill have pursued a policy of 'mum's the word' in the Immigration Department. Now decent reticence may be a worthy attribute of the middle class but when practised as a governmental habit it stultifies the democratic process. Canadian politics are abominably dull because no one ever says anything provocative or does anything startling. How few of our politicians even bother to write their memoirs! The Liberal government aims at operating noiselessly, like a respectable mammoth business corporation which fears nothing more than making people aware that it is there. The shadows flit silently along the wall, as in Plato's cave, and the citizen is never sufficiently disturbed to turn his head.

This soporific attitude is not unrelated to the Liberal Party's pragmatic approach to politics. One is more apt to let sleeping dogs lie if he believes in getting through each day as best he can than if he believes passionately in great principles which are worth fighting for.

Pragmatism also brings its own rewards. It obviates all the pains and problems inherent in philosophising. The Party does not have to think out a complex ideology, and lacking that it does not have to worry about doctrinal splits or purity of belief. If there is no dogma, there is less to disagree with. The party can mean many different things to many different people – and no doubt the Liberal Party's motto 'Unity, Security, Freedom' does.

This generous catholicity enables the Liberals to attract a wide range of candidates at election time. Men can be picked for their vote-getting possibilities – because they are popular or well known in their local communities or because of their ability. There is no established test of what a Liberal is, and no rigid stereotype. The Party tag is not hard to wear and there is no official orthodoxy to swallow since Liberalism is more a state of mind than a creed.

The advantages of such a happy vagueness are obvious in the results. Two present cabinet ministers have been recruited from the highest echelon of the civil service, two others were appointed to the cabinet within five years of their first securing elective office, and a number of members of Parliament have been hand-picked for their attractiveness as candidates rather than for their long records as devoted Liberals. Athletes make particularly good candidates for this reason. In another case the retiring Liberal MP suggested to a friend that he ought to take his place and when the surprised friend protested that he had never been active in politics, he was assured that it didn't matter since he was so well-known in the area. The individual ran, was elected, and has continued to hold the seat. Mr St Laurent was appointed Minister of Justice before he ran for office at all. Six years later he became leader of the party and prime minister.

Of course no assessment of the success of the Liberal Party would be adequate without acknowledging that the party has been singularly fortunate in its choice of leaders, Laurier, King, and St Laurent. The importance of leadership cannot be underestimated, and if the party can produce another chieftain of this caliber, its stay in power likely will be prolonged. But what if it chooses badly? Obviously the next leader must be by the principle of alternation as Protestant English-speaking Canadian. Suppose he is not as acceptable to Quebec as Mr St Laurent has been to Ontario?

The Liberals cannot afford to lose an appreciable number of seats in either Quebec or Ontario since those provinces are the source of its strength. The two provinces together possess 160 of the 265 seats in the House of Commons. Now no party has ever won an election by securing a majority in Ontario and Quebec alone, but the Liberals have depended on Quebec in particular for their victories. Quebec has been predominantly Liberal in federal elections since 1891, and in the last twenty years it has never returned fewer than 55 or 65 Liberals out of its total of 65 or 75 constituencies. This is a comfortable nest egg for the Liberals, but it is largely attributable to things other than themselves – to Quebec's bitter antipathy to conscription, which has been the bane of the Conservatives, and to the province's morbid fear of socialism, which has been the bar to the CCF. Failing a party like Mr Duplessis' to support in national elections, the Québecois' only choice has been to vote Liberal. But this does not mean that he is a dyed-in-the-wool Liberal who would continue to vote that way if he distrusted the party as much as the Conservatives or the CCF. Unacceptable leadership by an English Canadian might destroy the Liberals' hold on Quebec as effectively as the entry into federal politics of a provincialist party like the Union Nationale or the appearance of a French Canadian trade union party.

Ontario is only slightly less crucial to the Liberals than Quebec. In the years of their worst defeats, 1878, 1911, 1917, 1925, 1930, Ontario has let them down badly. Clearly, any party wishing to govern the country must carry a substantial portion of the province's large block of 85 seats. But Ontario is the mainstay of the Conservatives; it has never failed to send less than 25 Conservative MPs to Ottawa even in the blackest elections for the Tories in the last two decades. And there is always the possibility that the CCF will make way in urban ridings.

The Liberals have always required support outside of Ontario and Quebec for their victories. During the last twenty years the Maritimes have been much more faithful to the Liberals than they have previously. The three older provinces have elected at least 18 Liberals to their 25 seats in each election while Newfoundland is, of course, a Liberal preserve. There seems little likelihood of major change.

The West has been the least secure of Liberal bastions, having become prey to strange doctrines and un-Liberal-like enthusiasms. In Saskatchewan the Gardiner machine has grown rusty in spite of Liberal oiling by Prairie Farm Rehabilitation Administration appointments. Premier Douglas has proved himself a more adept politician than ex-Premier Gardiner and he has the added advantage of being twenty years younger. In Manitoba both the CCF and the Conservatives have been gaining ground federally lately. Alberta and British Columbia are perhaps least hopeful for the Liberals. Oil and Social Credit have swept away their chances in Alberta while the long period of provincial coalition government in BC discredited both Liberals and Conservatives so much that the CCF and Social Credit have profited enormously.

It would require a rash person to conclude from this brief survey that the Liberal government is apt to be turned out of Ottawa tomorrow. 'People are not so easily got out of their old forms,' said John Locke discounting the possibility of revolutions. Or in view of what has been said at first about the identification of liberalism with the middle class it might be more *à propos* to paraphrase Sir William Harcourt's famous remark in 1881 and say 'We are all Liberals now.'

To what extent this is due to the favourable degrees of prosperity we have had since 1935 I am unable to say. The common opinion is that governments are not put out of power when times are good, and a hasty survey of recent Canadian political history would seem to confirm it. From 1925 to 1940, a period of more or less depression, there were three changes in the Dominion government and 15 turnovers provincially. In the more prosperous succeeding fifteen years there has been no change federally and only six provincial upsets. But such meagre statistics hardly prove the rule, as the Democrats in the United States learned sadly in 1952.

One point is clear. The Liberal Party is not as firmly fixed in power as many imagine. Its smashing victories of the last two decades – 170-odd seats out of 265 – are not really landslides when the popular vote is analysed. In only one election out of five in these twenty years have the Liberals polled more than 50 per cent of the national vote. Plurality wins have exaggerated wildly their narrow victories, as occurs for most successful parties under our system. But it would not require a total shift of more than 15 or 20,000 votes in 37 closely contested constituencies, on the basis of the 1953 election returns, to put them out of power. A few hundred voters in relatively few ridings is a surprisingly small band indeed to threaten the great Liberal legions.

MILLAR MacLURE
Poets in Review

... A poem is an historical act, and graduates in time, like other such acts, from chronicle to history, from cheers or boos to philosophical consideration; but a poem is also a formal structure, as the wing of a luna moth, a motet, and a pyramid are so. In this sense all poems are contemporary poems, or, if you like it the other way, all poems are monuments. Now if one could only keep a comely balance between the poem as history and the poem as paradigm – but that is very difficult, because history keeps sliding into sociology, 'state of our culture' and so forth, and considerations of form keep degenerating into lists of recurring images and other such approximations. Difficult, but one must not give up trying, for the voices of time and shape, river and stone, make up the dialectic of our condition.

Besides, it is not necessary to encourage Mr Irving Layton, to spur him on to write more. He has already written more, and will write more yet. See the list of his published volumes at the front of his latest collection, *The Bull Calf and Other Poems* (Contact Press, 1956). A prolific poet – and the biological, the sexual image is just right for him. The poems are indeed his children, disconcertingly and charmingly both like and unlike each other, as children of a family are, and they are the fruits of love. Not the love of mankind, which turns so easily into contempt and advertising copy, but of what the senses see. Mr Layton is as concrete as Marlowe, as sharply curious and loving in observing 'nature's geometry' as any naturalist. And this is only the foundation for the passionate consistency with which he relates all that he observes to his own being, the compassionate sensual thoughtful violent self. Here is a poet for whom the act of love and a chokecherry tree are forms of logic – and quite wonderful in other ways too. (Some of the erotic poems in this book have a pleasing Ovidian flavour. It would be amusing if Mr Layton were to turn out an *Ars Amatoria,* and be banished – to Toronto.)

More seriously, it is a superb, irritating, persistent talent. The influences are pretty well taken in by this time – Pound, for example – and the idiom is distinctive. No other poet writing in this country can manage so well the marriage of the big word and the little one in a poem, the genius of English for the mixed metaphor. ...

A.J.M. SMITH
On Reading Certain Poems and Epistles of Irving Layton and Louis Dudek

Hail Coprophilia, muse of Layton, hail!
Doxy of Dudek, skoal! who drop'st in pail
Thick steaming words and brownish lumps
   of rhyme –
Manure essential in this barren clime,
Where Saxon critics without guts or gall
Praise these thy sons but little, if at all.
Yet these are they who vindicate they cause,
Who preach thy gospel and affirm thy laws.
Blest pair of poets, put on earth by thee
To sweat and strain and groan to set us free
From Anglo-philistine hypocrisy.

What shovelfuls of praise we ought to pay
These swart forerunners of an Augean day
Let us with candour, clangour, and no taste,
Make haste to proffer, O make haste, make
   haste!
Layton shall how to flatter Layton teach,
And modest Dudek Dudek's glories preach;
Layton shall tingle in Canadian air,
And echo answer *Dudek* everywhere.
In ev'ry quarterly and magazine
Their linked names in squibs and puffs
   be seen;

October 1956

Letters to editors be filled with them,
And gratitude replace each critic's phlegm:
Repentant Wilson, Dobbs, MacLure, and Frye
Shall who can praise them loudest longest, try.

A.G. CHRISTOPHER
Irving Layton

The Editor:

It's at once instructive and entertaining to see how our critics are apt to run after one another. No sooner had A.J.M Smith shown the way with his review praising the Montreal poet, Irving Layton, than lesser lights have hastened to follow. The same Mr Layton whose frequent publications until a short time ago were dismissed as dreary, derivative, or disgusting.

Mr Layton is a poet who has evolved a lively personal style in more ways than one and whose stature, while not so great as now claimed for him, is still considerable. It is certainly a triumph of industry.

But I suspect it's not on his poetic merits that he's now acclaimed but on his vigour as a propagandist. For once the critics are completely on the defensive and are positively cowed into applause. Mr Layton moves to the attack with coarseness and vituperation, massacring the opposition with coprological verse, naming names and sparing none. Let the man who ventures the mildest criticism look to his reputation or lawyer.

This letter is in part inspired by Millar MacLure's review in the May issue of the *Forum*. It is masterly in its euphemism. Mr Layton's frequent and rather suspicious boasting of sexual powers, his intimate revelations, are passed over with the phrase: 'some of the erotic poems have a pleasing Ovidian flavour. His dislike or dismissal of other human values is noted, but Mr MacLure commends this as unsentimentality. The poet lacks true passion but possesses an admirable energy, often an admirable technique and occasional humour. The critic speaks of the 'passionate consistency with which the poet relates all that he observes to himself,' but that's something else entirely. ...

It's all good fun, admirable to observe. There's been nothing like it in Canadian letters in years. I urge only that critics occasionally stand up to Mr Layton or there may be no more balm in Gilead.

A.G. Christopher
Ile Bigras, Que.

IRVING LAYTON
Layton on Layton

The Editor:

Your July correspondent, Mr A.G. Christopher of Ile Bigras, appears to think that for literary success two things are wanted: 'coprological verse' and industry. With the first one mows down recalcitrant critics: with the second – Pegasus having grown Percheron-heavy – one toils at producing inevitable masterpieces. Not joy, not talent, not insight surprising the seer; but mud, sweat, and tears. Yet surely if it's all that rosy simple why doesn't Mr Christopher take a smack at it? Let him set to work with a will and for my part I'll supply him from my copious arsenal any fourletter word he might need to 'cow into applause' those white-livered recreants, Frye, Wilson, Smith, and MacLure. Such effort would prove a lot more 'instructive and amusing' than counting in his sleep the fence-jumping of critics he dreams are running after that old bellwether, A.J.M. Smith.

Mr Christopher is not the first to gag at my frequent use of coprological and sexual imagery. Long ago in a poem, *Ice Follies* I announced that 'in Canada you can't say shit too often.' Crude? Perhaps. But so is shock therapy. Was it some civilized Greek or Chinaman who said, 'What men do, an honest man may write of'? In this land of delicate lumbermen, fishermen, and clean-minded Mounties, and also in Great Britain itself, you still can't buy an unexpurgated copy of *Lady Chatterley's Lover* except under the counter. Canadians, victimized by Protestantism and Anglo-Saxon hypocrisy, are for the life of them unable to distinguish between pornography, and necessary candour. More to the point, perhaps, they are so little interested in ideas or art they'll pounce on anything as a face-saving formula for having sports and money-making as their only genuine concerns. When a grown-up Canadian pretends that his nervous system, so delicately attuned, so sensitive, is shattered by seeing an 'obscenity' in print, I confess, I'm more than a little suspicious. 'A bungalow-dweller,' I say to myself morosely and turn to Rabelais for nepenthe.

It must be said that the critics and reviewers in this country have been of no help to poets battling this pervasive and odious prudery. They may have thought that noticing it would confer upon it a critical status it did not deserve; or they may have been taken up with weightier matters like plumbing the subconscious with an amphibrach or a hypercatalectic; perhaps they believed that the fight was over and all the censor-morons and silly old maids had been routed. Whatever the reason – timidity, academic blindness to live issues – they missed a chance to demonstrate that criticism is something other than that which merely waits and is parasitic upon the creative act. Of course the issue goes much deeper than that. My own feeling is that their values are not too different from the bulk of English-speaking Canadians and those values for good or ill are basically and unavoidably Anglo-Saxon. The Anglo-Saxon is not at home in the world of art. Ecstasy, emotional intensity, candour – a poet is a man with a terrifying need to confess, said Chekov – embarrass and disconcert him. Confronted by them, his strategy as Lawrence so well knew is to convert this raw discomfort-producing stuff into 'ideas' as quickly as possible, into the mumbo-jumbo of the latest psychologies, into safe and restful scholarship. The latter have their uses but only an English professor in a Canadian university is capable of the sickening blasphemy of preferring them to the Dionysian element.

By way of illustrating my point I recall the public spanking I got on 'Critically Speaking' for having written and dared to publish a poem, 'Intransitive Verb', which goes beautifully like this: 'I smell, You smell, We all smell.' Now a Russian, or a Bulgar, or a Jew – I've tried the poem on all three – laughs unashamedly to the skies when he's given such an exquisite mélange of vulgarity, cynicism, and witty phrasing for they are familiar with thousands equally as good and better in their own tongues. Tolstoy's tabletalk, so Gorki tells us, was not meant for virgins nor, let me add, the prissy schoolmarms and juiceless librarians across this vast and desolate dominion. Ways of feeling and speaking that are alien to the dominant Anglo-Saxon culture patterns are apt to be looked upon with mistrust and only too often with contempt. This is unfortunate and perhaps inevitable. English Canadians are not overly gifted with either imagination or sensitivity, or with that wonderful accepting emotionalism which can make good the lack of either and which I think the Russians more than any other people I know have got. Certainly in evaluating the work of non-Anglo-Saxons the 'ideologism' of Frye and the inhibiting classicism of Smith operate as a culture-osmosis, rejecting 'the awkward and alive,' the aggressively novel; preferring to them the inoffensive, the elegantly polished, the elegiac. Thus Mr Frye has exuberant praise for Wilfrid Watson's *Friday's Child* but dismisses Louis Dudek's *Europe* almost contemptuously. To a working poet like myself that makes no sense at all. The one has written old and overworked themes in old and overworked rhythms, the other has captured a novel music that is beyond the competency of any other Canadian poet writing today. Even having a bad ear as Mr Frye has can hardly excuse his insensitivity to the rare beauty of phrasing of poem 95 of *Europe*, nor his failure to applaud with humility and gratitude the significance of its achievement.

It may seem that I have gone far afield and that I've forgotten our poor correspondent who wished to have a bit of fun at my expense. But indeed I have not. Mr Christopher of Ile Bigras is what I'm talking about, talking about all the time. True, it might seem somewhat unfair that I crowd him into the same pew with the critics whom he takes to task for seeing merit in my later work, but that can't be helped. Poetry, to change the metaphor, makes strange bedfellows.

When he refers to Mr Dudek as my 'doppleganger' and reproves him for imitating my 'more unfortunate aspects,' a reference without doubt to Mr Dudek's poem, *Dirty Stuff*, I can't help feeling somewhat bitter. Had our critics and reviewers and professors of English been alert and concerned to free themselves from narrowing cultural prejudices, that sort of silly finger-wagging would in the year 1956 AD, have been impossible. For that poem, published in the winter-spring issue of *Origin*, is not only serious and audaciously beautiful, it says something which English Canadians have most need of hearing. No English Canadian poet would or could have written it. Needless to say, it will never appear in any anthology edited by Messrs Klinck and Watters, or by Mr Smith, though in my humble opinion it most richly deserves to.

IRVING LAYTON

EUGENE FORSEY

Pipeline and Parliament

The pipe line bill was a bad bill, and even if it had been a good one, the way it was rammed through Parliament would have been indefensible.

Why was it a bad bill?

First, because it was a fraud. Mr Howe kept calling it 'all-Canadian.' It didn't even start that way, five years ago. The company was then a wholly owned subsidiary of Canadian Delhi Oil, an American-controlled company. But at that time it was at least going to carry gas wholly through Canadian territory to Canadian consumers. By the time the thing came before Parliament this year, it was still American-controlled (83.4 per cent), but it was no longer going to carry gas wholly through Canadian territory to Canadian consumers. It was going to carry 200,000,000 cubic feet per day down to the American border for American consumers (with a good prospect of another 200,000,000), and perhaps (if the line got built east of Winnipeg) 300,000,000 for Canadian consumers. But the scheme submitted to Parliament contained not the slightest guarantee that the line would be built one inch east of Winnipeg.

When it came to paying, the thing did indeed come fairly close to being 'all-Canadian,' because the Canadian taxpayer was to put up nearly all the funds, to start with, anyhow. The Dominion and Ontario Governments were to build the section from the Manitoba-Ontario border to Kapuskasing, and the Dominion was to lend Trans-Canada Pipe Lines Limited 90 per cent of the cost of the Prairie section, Alberta to Winnipeg. The Americans were to retain control, but the Canadian taxpayer was kindly invited to come and bring his cheque book.

Second, the bill was neither public enterprise nor private, but a hodge-podge. There was something to be said for private enterprise, if the private investors had put up the money and taken the risks. There was something to be said for public enterprise: a Crown corporation can build more cheaply because it can borrow money more cheaply and doesn't have to pay sales tax or income tax. There is little or nothing to be said for public enterprise building the unprofitable or least profitable part of the line, and lending private enterprise the money to build most of the profitable part.

Third, the agreement between the Government and Trans-Canada was not part of the bill. The loan for the Prairie section might be made 'pursuant to *an* agreement in that behalf made ... before or *after* the coming into force of this Act.' The terms of the agreement could be varied, without Parliament having a word to say about it.

Fourth, though the whole scheme was admittedly not only important but complicated, the Government steadfastly refused to submit it to examination by the standing committee on railways, canals, and telegraph lines. So there was no opportunity of finding out (a) whether any other private interests would undertake the project with less Government aid or none, with or without provision for export to the United States, with or without provision for Canadian control; (b) the precise difference in costs between public and private enterprise; (c) which, if any, of the three sets of 'official' prices for the gas in Canada and at the American border was the correct one; and (d) whether Trans-Canada could really get the supply of 34-inch pipe of which one of its American controlling companies, Tennessee Gas, held the whole North American supply. Point (c) was important because Parliament needed to know whether Trans-Canada was going to sell cheaper to Americans than to Canadians. Point (d) was important because one of the main reasons for insisting that Trans-Canada alone could build the line, and that the bill must be passed forthwith, was that Trans-Canada alone could get the pipe. But the agreement between Trans-Canada and Tennessee on this point bound Tennessee to turn over the pipe only *if* Tennessee got the necessary 'certification, licenses and permits' from the United States Federal Power Commission to allow it to bring the gas into that country; and the prospects of the FPC granting such certificates, licenses, and permits before the end of this year are not bright.

There was something very fishy about this refusal to let the bill go to the standing committee. If it was really the masterpiece the Government claimed, why not seize the opportunity to rout the Opposition on the field of its own choosing? But no; the Government chose to force the measure through by holding to Parliament's head the gun of closure, with Tennessee's hand on the trigger.

The Government had a variety of replies to these objections.

First, Trans-Canada wouldn't be American-controlled once the public issue of stock was made, because its agreement with the Government stipulated that it must offer enough of the stock in Canada to make up 51 per cent of the total which would then be outstanding.

This means nothing. Issuing the stock in Canada does not mean that it will be held in Canada. There is nothing to prevent every single share being bought by Americans. Besides, everyone knows that a very small block of shares, well concentrated, can give effective control; so that even if Canadians did hold 51 per cent of the stock, they might have no control at all.

Second, the Government accused the Opposition parties, especially the Conservatives, of hostility to American investment in general. This is simply not true. If the line was to be privately owned, and was to be built in Canadian territory, to carry gas solely to Canadian consumers (exporting to the United States only what Canada couldn't use), few would object even if the Americans owned the whole thing, providing they put up their own money. But when they proposed to put up *our* money to carry *our* gas to *their* country, under *their* control, it was hardly the same thing. This is no more 'American' investment than the pipe line is an 'all-Canadian' pipe line.

Moreover, the process by which Trans-Canada will set its price for the gas it sends to the United States will be just like 'collective bargaining' between an employer and a company union. Tennessee, which effectively controls Trans-Canada, will sit on both sides of the table and bargain with itself; and, as with the company union, it is not hard to guess which side will come out on top.

Third, however, was the Government's trump card: there could be no possible danger in the scheme because the whole thing would be under Canadian law. To this, unhappily, the proceedings on the bill itself supplied the answer. Who makes that Canadian law? Parliament. And who, in this case, controlled Parliament? The Government. Who controlled the Government? Mr Howe. Who controlled Mr Howe? The American owners of Trans-Canada Pipe Lines.

Just look at what happened. The bill was brought down late. At the very outset of the resolution stage which precedes the bill itself, Mr Howe gave notice of closure, before anyone else had uttered one syllable, whether of support or criticism. Closure means that debate ends about 36 hours later. The resolution was carried by closure. There can be no debate on first reading. Second reading was carried by closure after four days' debate. In committee, the most important stage, on six of the seven clauses, not one syllable of debate was allowed. On the first three, Mr Howe spoke 205 words. Nobody else was allowed to say one word. On the last three, nobody said anything: they were simply called, put to the vote and carried. On third reading, the Prime Minister gave notice of closure before anyone else had said a word. To cap it all, the Speaker actually moved a motion from the chair, to make Friday Thursday, and the obedient Government majority passed it.

The Government tore up the rules, turned the Speaker into a party hack, and made a mockery of parliamentary government, all at the behest of a few American millionaires. It even risked having no money to pay salaries on June 15, making no effort to ask for interim Supply till after the pipe line bill had been passed. In effect, Tennessee Gas told the Government of Canada: 'The business of the people of Canada can wait; ours can't. This bill must be passed by June 7, cost what it may.' Passed it was. And with its passage parliamentary responsible government, for the time being disappears.

The most frightening thing about the whole performance is that the Government seems to have no idea of what it has done. To Mr St Laurent and his colleagues, and the Speaker, as they made abundantly clear, parliamentary democracy means simply voting and getting a majority: counting heads instead of breaking them; no question of also using them; of discussion, of debate. The very meaning of the word 'parliament,' a talking-place, is lost upon them. They have no notion of the rule of law, still less of the fact that the whole British constitutional system can function only upon a basis of self-restraint, of fair play, of observing not merely the letter but the spirit of the rules. They are horrified by Opposition members' defiance of 'constituted authority' in the person of the Speaker, though it was he who was defying constituted authority by breaking the rules, and they who were upholding it by their resistance. They are virtuously indignant at 'obstruction,' blandly unaware that it is not only a legitimate but an essential part of parliamentary government. Of course it is not to be lightly used. But, just as a Government defeated in the House on a great issue of public policy appeals to the people, so an Opposition, on a great issue of public policy obstructs the Government and, if necessary, forces an appeal to the people. The Liberals did it in 1881 on the CPR charter, and again in 1896 on the Remedial Bill. The Conservatives did it on the Reciprocity Agreement in 1911, and forced an election on it, and won. The Liberals did it again on the Naval Bill in 1913, for nearly four months, and finally blocked it in the Senate. The Conservatives did it last year, on the Defence Production Bill, and forced the Government to give way.

But surely the majority of the House has rights too? Yes, within the rules, written and unwritten. It has no right to break the rules, in the letter or in the spirit. Specifically, it has a right to invoke closure; but only when there has been ample debate. Mr Meighen, the author of the Canadian closure rule, was asked, when he introduced it in 1913, whether some Government might not some day use it precisely as this one has done on this bill. His reply was that a Government which did would be 'at once insane and vicious.' That, it is to be hoped, is the epitaph which the Canadian electorate will shortly write upon this Government's tombstone.

PHYLLIS WEBB
The Idiot Birds

The idiot birds
strut the lawn,
summer gives them all
they've ever wanted.
They cheep, they chime,
they scratch the dawn.
Idiot birds! Summer is all
they've wanted.

But then the fools
in ignorant bliss
ascend in the singing air
as we like noisy idiots strut
in our summer of despair.

A. VIXEN
The New Conservative Leader

John Diefenbaker's first ballot victory of 774 votes out of the 1,284 cast in the three-way contest for the leadership of the Progressive Conservative party was clearly not 'an overwhelming majority' as some newspapers have reported. In fact he got fewer votes than George Drew did in 1948 when he won the leadership with a first ballot vote of 827 out of 1,242, and Mr Drew at that time was by no means popular throughout all of his party.

Likewise Mr Diefenbaker begins without full party support. His nomination was the only one of the three not seconded by a French-speaking Canadian and when he made his acceptance speech the seats previously occupied on the convention floor by the Quebec delegation were either empty or silent. Throughout the convention Quebec was an island of calm amidst the tumultuous seas of Diefenbaker applause, and an ominous note was struck when the French Canadians paid their highest tribute to Mr Drew – and even to Premier Frost – by singing *'Il a gagné ses épaulettes'* but remained mute for the new leader. His praises were sung in English: 'For he's a jolly good fellow' ... but not in Quebec apparently.

Mr Diefenbaker's inability to carry the whole country with him represents graphically the greatest single weakness of the Tory party. In spite of a genuine attempt at the convention to present a national appeal (no expense or effort was spared to have bilingual signs, chairmen, and working papers, and there was a room full of translators) the Conservative party continues to be by nature intuitively Anglo-Saxon. Its reflex actions are automatically British (note the immediate ardent defence of Britain in the recent Middle East-debate in parliament and outside) though like a man struggling to broaden his limited perspective the party's second thoughts are often more considered and eclectic (the policy resolutions on the Middle East presented to the delegates made no mention of Britain and could have come just as easily from the Liberals or the CCF).

The tragedy of the Tory party is that it cannot free itself from its inherent Anglo-Saxon personality, try as it will, and this inhibition is slowly fossilising it in a country which is working out its own national character compounded of not just Anglo-Saxons but one-third French Canadians and a steady stream of new Canadians to whom Macdonald's battle cry 'A British subject I was born, a British subject I will die' means nothing. A casual survey of the delegates' name tags revealed few foreign names. There were no official words spoken or written in any language except English or French and no indication that the party was even aware of the existence of other people in the country. The sight of so many enthusiastic young persons and women (about 40 per cent of the representatives were women) was proof that the party has tried hard to broaden its approach, but it was sad that nearly all the delegates appeared to be from one community – English, Scotch, or Irish descent, Protestant, well-heeled, upper middle class, or farmers. The Conservatives could profit from the remarks of a group of immigrants in Toronto recently – that they would believe the Tories were not intrinsically pro-British when they nominated some parliamentary candidates with foreign names.

Now Mr Diefenbaker, despite the accident of name, fits into the Tory mould. A fourth-generation Canadian on both sides of the family (his mother's name was Bannerman), he was born in Ontario, raised in Saskatchewan, became a barrister, and is a Baptist and a 32nd degree Mason. He gives every indication of possessing the annoying Anglo-Saxon faculty of being oblivious to any other group. Certainly he is not *sympathique* with the French Canadians, a fact which is undoubtedly the subconscious source of their coldness to him. In his acceptance speech, after beginning with a laudatory reference to 'the principles of Macdonald and Cartier' and a pledge to support them, he tossed off a few sentences in badly pronounced French and then, as though having despatched the obligatory, he went on to express the hope that his desk in the Commons would be shared by – a French Canadian? A Cartier to his Macdonald? No, George Drew! Since the French Canadians hardly regard George Drew as their Cartier, they must have concluded that talk is cheap and this was another of Mr Diefenbaker's platitudes.

In the latter category the new leader excels. He can knock out a ringing platitude with such sincerity that one is inclined to think he believes them himself. His speeches are loaded with them and his first press conference as leader ended with a masterpiece. After ten or fifteen minutes of answering questions without saying anything:

'Would you accept Social Credit support?'

'I will accept the support of anybody who supports me.'

'Does this mean you would accept amalgamation with the Social Credit party?'

'Well, that would have to be a parliamentary caucus decision.'

'And when will the caucus meet?'

'I haven't had time to decide yet.'

He then told reporters to always feel free to come to him for a full and frank discussion of public issues.

Mr Diefenbaker talks a good fight even if he does not know at times what he is talking about. (His performance at the Couchiching Conference last summer was an outstanding illustration. Far from showing himself the expert on foreign affairs which he is reputed to be, he demonstrated in the most embarrassing manner his lack of information.) However, it is true that this has not hurt him with the general public which is impressed with platitudes, especially if they are delivered in an earnest and explosive manner.

The myth has, therefore, grown up, fostered by the press for some reason – the Liberal press perhaps, which wished to depreciate Mr Drew by comparison – that Mr Diefenbaker is not only an expert in external affairs but a tireless fighter for civil liberties and a great leader. This conception is so widespread that the French-Canadian motorman on the street car taking me to the convention Coliseum remarked that he 'sure hoped that Diefenbaker would win – because he fought for the little guys and wasn't afraid to speak up to the big men.'

It is harder to substantiate this record from the facts. Apart from the Etier School case and his annual plea in parliament for a Canadian bill of rights – for which Croll, Coldwell, and Roebuck have fought just as hard – there is not much in his accomplishments to justify his inflated reputation as a modern Milton. Possibly his success as a lawyer in the litigious West spawned the rumours.

With the exception of the prosperous Torontonians who backed his campaign, most of his own colleagues would be the first to admit privately that he has not got the qualities of a leader. He has been a lone wolf, skirting the pack often and skittishly independent and undependable. He does not possess the stability, doggedness, and cohesive power of a good leader, nor the ability to inspire the team, as distinguished from the spectators.

His appeal is entirely to the public, which

has swallowed without realizing it the Diefenbaker Myth. It was for this reason that the party hierarchy acquiesced in his selection. As one disgruntled delegate said, 'They would rather have a man they can win votes with in 1957 than some one they can win with in 1961.' The party has sacrificed long-run returns for quick gains and the Tories will be lucky if this shortsighted decision does not prove disastrous. For once Mr Diefenbaker has run through his fund of popularity – and it may be sufficient to carry the Conservatives in the forthcoming election – his weaknesses will become glaringly apparent. They will be accentuated moreover by the continued indifference of Quebec and the scepticism of new Canadians.

It is a stark indictment of the Tory party that in two decades it has failed to produce one first-class leader, some one with the capacities of Meighen or Bennett, the astuteness of King, or the distinction of St Laurent. Mr Drew came as close as any and was rising above his earlier personal limitations as well as the traditional confines of his Anglo-Saxon party when his career was cut short by ill health. The best the Conservatives have been able to do now is to replace him with a standardized spare part. Until the Tory party can branch out beyond its present inhibited character and develop a personality that grows and changes with the times, it is unlikely that it will be able to attract anything better than a second-class leader.

IRVING LAYTON
Three Poems

Sheep

Like a socialist I knew, a simple soul,
These two sheep, male and female, stare at us
   from their fold;
And their faces are fine, fine and sensitive
With the proper intensity of reserve.
Even the credulity, so water clear in them,
   is attractive.

Yet, indifferent to the impression they make,
They crouch on their mat of dung or with
   the poise of a philosopher seek
The rough part of the post which they know
   well
To scrape against it their purloined fleece and
   fell;
Staring, warily staring, wearily staring, with a
   mien silly and gentle – and cynical.

Amazed. No, but look at those fine musician's
   faces again;
More particularly, the ebony line of the mouth
   curving long and thin.
Do you see it? Would you not say that's the
   smile.
You've caught and watched on the face of
   someone who, while he's too meek to
   defend himself,
Sees through and despises your guile?

I'll tell you something else about sheep
You haven't noticed, see them as much as you
   wish in your sleep;
They're neither-this-nor-thats, half-and-halfs if
   you prefer.
I've asked you to take in they scrub their
   fleece, standing wrapt like a philosopher;
Their itchy, bulky, dung-matted, grey-dirty
   fleece
   yet, look down – what feet! the trim feet
   of a dancer.

And there's also this: they're practical,
   prudent.
Or they seem so, yet they also somehow
   contrive to appear gullible and vacant.
Here again is that unsatisfactory, disdain-making quality: that of the half-and-half, the
   in-between.
I should expect my gifted and temperamental
   daughter
If she flew high, then came down to failure
   to look afterwards as silly and circumspect
As this sheep and his dam.

But Christ, the whole world moves in on this
   fold.
All, all, have become mixtures: alloys, neither
   pure tin nor gold.
Integrity's gone. And I myself at my wife's
   deathbed
Shall, I know, weep: weep like Othello, be
   grief-rent and troubled

Yet note the small cost of some extra flowers or bulbs.

Whatever Else Poetry Is Freedom

Whatever else poetry is freedom.
Forget the rhetoric, the trick of lying
All poets pick up sooner or later. From the river,
Rising like the thin voice of gray castratos – the mist;
Poplars and pines grow straight but oaks are gnarled;
Old codgers must speak of death, boys break windows;
Women lie honestly by their men at last.

And I who gave my Kate a blackened eye
Did to its vivid changing colours
Make up an incredible musical scale;
And now I balance on wooden stilts and dance
And thereby sing to the loftiest casements.
See how with polish I bow from the waist.
Space for these stilts! More space or I fail!

And a crown I say for my buffoon's head.
Yet no more fool I am than King Canute,
Lord of our tribe, who scanned and scorned;
Who half-deceived, believed; and, poet, missed
The first white waves come nuzzling at his feet;
Then damned the courtiers and the foolish trial
With a most bewildering and unkingly jest.
It was the mist. It lies inside one like a destiny.

A real Jonah it lies rotting like a lung.
And I know myself undone who am a clown
And wear a wreath of mist for a crown;
Mist with the scent of dead apples,
Mist swirling from black oily waters at evening
Mist from the fraternal graves of cemeteries.

It shall drive me to beg my food and at last
Hurl me broken I know and prostrate on the road;
Like the huge toad I saw, entire but dead,
That Time mordantly had blacked; O pressed
To the moist earth it pled for entry.
I shall be I say that stiff toad for sick with mist
And crazed I smell the odour of mortality.

And Time flames like a paraffin stove
And what it burns are the minutes I live.
At certain middays I have watched the cars
Bring me from afar their windshield suns;
What lay to my hand were blue fenders,
The suns extinguished, the drivers wearing sunglasses –
And it made me think I had touched a hearse.

So whatever else poetry is freedom.

Note: This poem now has one further stanza in the version printed in Layton's *Collected Poems*.

Cote Des Neiges Cemetery

As if it were a faultless poem, the odour
Is both sensuous and intellectual,
And of faded onion peel its colour;
For here the wasting mausoleums brawl

With Time, heedless and mute; their voice
Kept down, polite yet querulous –
Assuredly courtesy must at last prevail.

Away from the markings of the poor,
On slope and summit, the statuary is vain
And senatorial (now the odour's
A high-pitched note, piercing the brain)
Where lying together are judge and barrister
And some whose busts look on a shrunk estate.

Persuade yourself it is a Warner set
Unreal and two-dimensional, a facade,
Though our mortal tongues are furred with death:
A ghost city where live autumn birds flit
And small squirrels dart from spray to spray
And this formal scene is a kind of poetry.

Especially the tomb of Moise Wong, alien
And quaint among French Catholic names
Or the drainage pipes inanimate and looped
You may conceive as monstrous worms.
Undying paradox! Yet, love and look again:
Like an insinuation of leaves in snow

And sad, sad with surrender are the tablets
For the Chinese nuns; or, a blade between, the rows,
Exact as alms, of les Sourdes et Muettes
And of les Aveugles: – and this, this dear girl,
Is the family plot of Père Loisel and his wife
Whose jumbled loins in amorous sweat
Spawned, these five neat graves in a semicircle.

JOHN PORTER

Political Parties and the Political Career

Political parties are the very stuff of democratic political institutions, and particularly of parliamentary government. The downfall of the Liberals and the ascension of the Conservatives during the last year shows how basically weak our party structures are. The pendulum has not swung, but being out of joint, has taken a violent lurch. Mr Pearson is left to head the Liberal 'rump' with only a fraction of the front-bench men who ruled for so long with an air of indispensibility. Who now is going to 'pick up the pieces' and put the Liberal party together again?

Obviously few of the former leaders can stomach political defeat. At the moment of crisis they desert the rank and file, and become safely bunkered in the corporate world and the law office. When the decisive battle is joined they are not to be found at the front. A few words of encouragement come from the rear, or from Florida, but the party workers must view their lost leaders with something of that bitterness with which Siegfried Sassoon's soldiers viewed their generals.

> *Good morning, good morning,' the general said,*
> *As they slogged off to Arras with rifle and pack.*
> *But he did for them all with his plan of attack.*

Perhaps the reason why the leaders have failed is that they are not political men. After ruling Canada for more than twenty years the Liberal Party chose an ex-bureaucrat as leader in place of a person who had some of the qualifications at least of being a political man. Paul Martin was beginning his career on the hustings at about the time that Lester Pearson was finishing his life as a professor, and about to begin one as a civil servant. In successive Liberal ministries the political outsider – the person who does not devote his life to politics – assumed the top roles in the party in place of the politician. An administrative type of person had been brought in to run the State which never seemed to be in danger of falling into other hands.

The political outsider sees politics as a career interlude, and one which, incidentally, might have great advantages for him. The path to the judiciary or the board room of a large corporation must be considerably shortened by the route through the Privy Council chambers. There is a general feeling, too, that a man is making great personal sacrifices in entering political life, and that he should not be asked to set aside his private interests for more than a short time. As a result Liberal ministries have been built on the principle of cooptation. Men were brought in for brief stints. They were not men with a passion for the political life. Even for the recent pillars of the party, Howe and St Laurent, their time in politics, into which they had been coopted, seemed an interstitial period in careers devoted to the good life of business and the law. In opposition administrators have nothing to administer, but the parliamentary politician comes into his own.

What emerged during the Liberal era was the separation of the parliamentary political life from cabinet leadership. This situation could perhaps be traced to the war years and the march of administrators on Ottawa, or to Mackenzie King's philosophy of a paternalistic state run, not by politicians, but by brilliant administrators. What characterized the higher levels of the bureaucracy characterized also the cabinet, which might be one of the reasons why the two groups got along so well together. As a consequence of the episodic type of political career there is scarcely any parliamentary continuity in the Liberal leadership. There are only two front-benchers, Martin and Chevrier, who came into the House in 1935. It is not only because of the ages of the senior men that the Liberals are left without leadership. Many of the younger former ministers came in, did their stint, and went on to 'higher' things. They were not politicians.

Very few of them had made a career of politics. Fifteen years was a long stint, and Howe's twenty-two years was unusual. Fifteen of the fifty-five ministers between 1940 and 1956 entered the cabinet with previous political experience. Of these seven were drafted from business or professional life, six came in from the supposedly non-political Public Service, and two were from the Senate, to which they had previously been posted from outside politics. A further nine were drawn in directly from provincial politics without previously having seats in the House of Commons. Eight more moved from the back to the front benches within a short time of being in the Commons, and all of these before their second parliamentary term. Of the remaining twenty-three a good number achieved cabinet office before their third parliamentary term. Political training in the House of Commons, which is after all the national forum for national politics, was not during the Liberal regime essential to high political office.

King and St Laurent were not parliamentary men before they were in the cabinet. Neither were Howe, Rogers, Gibson, Pearson, Pickersgill, or Gregg. Men such as Ralston, MacKinnon, McLarty, Abbott, Claxton, Campney, Winters, and Prudham, had only a short acquaintance with political life before getting into the cabinet.

Once in, politics does not seem sufficiently attractive as a permanent venture. Of the fifty-five ministers, including those defeated in 1957 and excluding the ten who died in office or soon after leaving it, ten went to the judiciary, ten went back to business or law practice, four into the Public Service, ten into the quasi-political life of the Senate, one into provincial politics, and one seems to have retired. Only nine fought the 1958 election and only five were still in the House after it. The result is that political leadership for both the nation and the party does not depend on the political man – one who has lived for politics rather than off it. When the party can no longer provide the pay-off with a cabinet post or a judicial appointment the political outsider drifts away, and the ambitious young man is not attracted. The rebuilding of an opposition party and the revitalizing of Parliament will require men who are prepared to make politics their career. Politics is an honourable job in more senses than the Privy Councillor's title.

The question now is whether or not the Conservative Party can avoid the same experience as the Liberals. Only Earl Rowe remains as a link with previous Conservative ministries and he was not given even a titular post after the *risorgimento*. Of the 1957 Conservative ministry only Howard Green and the Prime Minister could be considered parliamentary 'veterans' with twenty-two and seventeen years respectively. Five others came in on the 1945 election. The remainder were in the House seven years or less. Even so they probably represent as many parliamentary seat-years before cabinet appointment as any Liberal ministry. If Conservative cabinets acquire the Liberal pattern in recruitment of administrative types to implement the vision we might expect to see the political outsider come into office prepared to live off politics while the going is good. If the present government could cultivate its parliamentary garden for its future stock of ministers, and at the same time improve its relations with its competent bureaucracy, Canadian political life would be well served.

It can be argued of course that Canadian federalism required regional representation in the cabinet, and therefore cooptation is inevitable, or that when a Prime Minister limits himself to the House of Commons, he must pick some pretty shoddy material if that is all that a particular region has sent him.

Must Parliament necessarily continue to have this low status as the training ground for cabinet leadership? Perhaps the time has come for national parties to do more to control candidates across the country so that a young person bent on a political career could, after some sacrificial attempts, look forward to moving over to ridings where his chances were improved. Local riding associations would probably balk at being told who their candidates are to be. But the local ironmonger or insurance agent is surely less important to the party than one of its leading men who is facing continual hazards in a marginal seat. There is too much in the election literature about the local man who has spent all his dull life in his own riding. Greater control over candidates by national party executives might help to remove some of the risks attached to the political life. The place for democracy in parties is through frequent conventions rather than local control of candidates.

It is probable, however, that most people in Canada want to get rich and parliamentary pay and pension falls far short of what many feel they can make in a lifetime. There are few other material rewards. MPs don't vote themselves railway charters any more, and cabinet ministers relinquish their directorships while in office. Our class system has not provided us with the person of independent means who is prepared to enter politics. Neither is the working class person, to whom ten thousand a year is a small fortune, at home in the two major parties, and the one party which does represent him has failed to catch his imagination.

Now that a charismatically endowed prairie lawyer has fired the embers of our political instincts so long neglected by the Liberals, we might think that we have moved from an administrative to a political era, but unless the personality cult gives way to team leadership, we will be scarcely better off. It will take more than one leader to give our parties vigour and

MICHAEL OLIVER

Duplessis and Quebec's Intellectuals

In Chinese history, one of the signs that a dynasty's fortunes were on the wane was the desertion of the intellectuals. The political distance between pre-republican China and *Union Nationale* Quebec would require some tricky measurement, but French Canada's traditional respect for things immaterial may make the intellectual's attitude to the political regime worth study. Donations from corporations owned by English Canadians and Americans provide the solid bone structure of Quebec's dominant party, and to this adheres a bulk of well-fattened members. But the *Union Nationale*, although sluggish and pallid compared to what it was in earlier years, still has spirit. M. Duplessis retains the enthusiasm of some of the intelligentsia of his province.

The 'elite's desertion from the *Union Nationale* is, however, a striking fact of the present period and this movement away from the party and what it represents must, in part, be explained in terms of profound changes in Quebec society. Intellectuals had to find a place to go if they were to leave the world dominated by a party which claimed to embody the main political tradition of French Canada – nationalism and provincial autonomy. Only since the war have institutions outside the traditional framework grown up enough to provide careers for those who did not conform in their social and political thinking. Most of the escape routes of the past involved a violent de-nationalisation operation which only the most hardy could survive in comfort, and which few relished even if they were capable of withstanding it. Fitting into attractive posts in business or in the federal civil service demanded a quasi-anglicization at least, a severing of ties with the society of family, parish, and school. Those that did make the break lost their influence in the sphere from which they had come. They were thus not a new element in French Canadian society, they were outside it.

The post-war period has, however, created institutions which can be filled by French Canadians *as such*, yet which are largely independent of the traditional forces of church and local and provincial government. The CBC is one of these. No gradual anglicization process is the price in this federal crown company. In fact the French network would have little use for one who had grown too far away from French Canada. The trade unions are another such institution. To a quite remarkable extent, careers within or closely connected with trade unions have attracted Quebec intellectuals, and those who occupy such positions have a much greater stake in remaining an integral part of the French Canadian community than in linking themselves with the English-speaking culture.

Within these purely French-Canadian institutions it has been possible to explore far beyond the social and political boundaries of traditional French Canada. The penalties for unorthodox ideas and behaviour are applied at a much further point of deviation than was (and is) the case in older organizations. When, in 1944, Senator T.D. Bouchard, whose public life had centred on politics, launched his famous attack on the nationalist Ordre Jacques Cartier and the French-Canadian nationalist bias in Quebec schools, he was dismissed from his post as head of Hydro Québec, and never regained his former stature. Yet Pierre Trudeau's attack on the nationalist tradition in a recent book has interfered not at all with his career as labour lawyer, as a perennial CBC panelist and commentator and, generally, as an active force in his province.

The fact that sanctions are not as readily applied is, of course, only a small part of the story. Much more important is the very nature of these new institutions. They not only permit intellectuals to follow careers which require neither anglicization nor direct dependence on the traditional forces of the church and the provincial government, they are also obviously the product of an urban, industrialized society and as such demand attention to a different range of practical problems, and set feasible goals of practical accomplishment. These positive aspects deserve emphasis.

There have been attempts to break away from traditional orthodoxy before, but they have usually borne fruit only in two ways. The first is a rebellious criticism which, because it never gets a chance to act, because it is never faced with the challenge of putting ideas into practice, spends its energies in lone assaults on the existing framework. The careers of critical journalists like Olivar Asselin or Jules Fournier were of this type. So, in a way, was the career of Henri Bourassa, as both politician and journalist. The second is the way of aestheticism. The protests of certain groups in French Canada in the thirties, because they could not be channelled into existing institutions, took the form of individual creative activity in art, in poetry, and in literature. Let there be no mistake about it, these roles are of vital and lasting importance. The rebel and the independent artist are in no way inferior to those who act through collective institutions. But their roles are different – different from that of the trade union leader who faces the tasks of organizing, calling strikes, collective bargaining; different from that of the men responsible for developing a new medium of mass communication. The latter functions are performed through institutions which give opportunities to a much larger number to develop an independent, non-traditional point of view, for it is not everyone who has the capacity for rebellion, or individual artistic creativity, in an unreceptive environment. Furthermore, those who centre their activities about both these modern careers are conscious of accomplishment in a French-Canadian context which is directly comparable to similar achievements in the rest of North America. They are not 'surviving' as French Canadians, they are living and creating something which stands up under any criteria of comparison. Relations with English Canada tend, for this reason, to be easy and confident, and the 'protectionism' of the *Union Nationale* much less attractive.

For the majority of Quebec's intellectuals, however, the traditional institutional framework provides still the most readily available careers. In many such positions, opportunities for critical analysis and for promoting social and political change do exist. A career in journalism always gave some scope to independence. But it could only consistently do so if the journalist was attached to an independent and adventurous newspaper. *Le Devoir* has usually played this role in French Canada, except perhaps for a period from the late twenties to the end of the war, when its nationalism became merely a right-wing traditionalism. Certainly today it must be ranked among the major forums of dissent from the Duplessis régime, and from the narrow formulas of an anachronistic ideology. But its opposition is protest within a nationalist autonomist framework, and in this it differs from the newer institutions open to Quebec's intellectuals.

The universities of Quebec are in a somewhat similar position to a newspaper like *Le Devoir*, in that they are institutions of an older society which are only gradually transforming themselves to meet the challenge of a new era. Once again, by their very nature, they have always provided a place for independent thought. But the bounds of this independence have at times been very narrowly drawn indeed, for the universities and colleges have always been reliant on church and state. Among the newer, non-traditional disciplines – the physical and social sciences – the process of developing new ways of dealing with Quebec's problems has advanced most rapidly. It is no coincidence that the first president of the *Rassemblement* (an organization for education in democracy and reform) came from the Science Faculty of the University of Montreal and the second from the Social Sciences Faculty at Laval.

The desertion of the intellectuals is thus under way. But it is by no means complete. And the deserters lack political form. The provincial Liberal party is in poor shape indeed and it will take more than the coming provincial convention to convince many of Quebec's intellectuals that it is capable of creating a new political atmosphere in the province. The Parti Social Démocratique (Quebec's CCF) has not yet overcome longstanding difficulties in attracting French-Catholic support. The current move of Jean Drapeau, Montreal's ex-mayor, beyond the confines of municipal politics bears watching. But Drapeau's chief force thus far seems to come from clerical sources opposed to vice and political immorality, and disgruntled small businessmen.

Intellectuals who remain with Duplessis may be a dwindling force, but they are by no means negligible. Among them are, first, the truly conservative nationalists. They are a group whose ideas have not evolved appreciably since the days of Bishop Bourget; a group which sees a communist behind every bush (and especially those planted by English Canadians) and which will neither forgive England and English Canada for the Conquest, nor France for the Revolution. Men like Robert Rumilly and Léopold Richer desire the closed society in its most rigorous sense.

Another group of at least quasi-intellectual supporters of Duplessis come from the traditional professions – law and medicine. Substantial careers can be made in both these fields without any appreciable contact with the rest of Canada. Their clientele is often exclusively French-Canadian and no changes in Quebec's social and political structures offer them particular advantages. Their conservatism is based on self-satisfaction and inertia, although patronage considerations as well affect some of the lawyers. When they write or speak, they often echo the values of a past age which the Duplessis regime does little to disrupt.

A third category includes certain secondary school teachers – especially those in orders – and some university professors. Academic willingness to accommodate M. Duplessis is partly based on a realization that Quebec's educational system is badly in need of overhauling, and that drastic change can involve acute discomfort for those who direct its schools. The present provincial régime can be counted on to move so slowly that the stresses of reform will be minimal. In addition, educators are painfully conscious of their reliance on the good will of the provincial government for a major part of their funds, and they know that institutions which question the policies of the government expose themselves dangerously. The tensions between those who share these fears and whose who are anxious for immediate and thoroughgoing change were brought to light dramatically at the provincial conference on education which took place early in February. On one hand, this conference by a vote of 70 to 64 supported the principle of free tuition for all levels of education – a radical proposal indeed. On the other hand, it amended a resolution on the question of state aid to education in such a way as to ensure that 'la Conférence n'ait pas l'air de blâmer le gouvernement provincial.'

In a more general sense, those intellectuals who continue to support the *Union Nationale* share two common features: lack of confidence in French Canada's ability to survive close contact with the rest of North America and a strong attachment to those things which are distinctively French-Canadian. Neither factor in itself is enough. Lack of confidence in French Canada does not necessarily lead to enthusiasm for Duplessis' provincial autonomy position. It can just as well result in a desire to merge with English-speaking North America, a desire to give up the struggle for *survivance* altogether. Again, attachment to those things which make French Canada unique is not enough. The best proof of this is the nationalism of *Le Devoir*. Its editors have again and again pointed out that Duplessis regards provincial autonomy as a possession to be defended rather than a positive duty which must be fulfilled. Many nationalists who realize that they must create a modern, progressive provincial administration if they are effectively to compete (or co-operate!) with Ottawa lost patience with the Duplessis régime's incompetent conservatism long ago.

French-Canadian intellectuals who lack confidence in the ability of their society and its institutions to withstand abrupt change in close contact with English-Canadian organizations are not necessarily the victims of misplaced and illusory timidity, nor does their lack of confidence imply a sense of the inferiority of Quebec's institutions. The problem of sheer weight of numbers in any intimate relationship with English Canada cannot be shrugged off. The feeling that institutions of a minority have to be firmly rooted before they can safely ally themselves, or merge, with those of the majority is not irrational, although it may often be exaggerated disproportionately. Those who have had the disheartening experience of seeing their particular viewpoint overlooked or deliberately ignored simply because it *was* a minority viewpoint are likely to be quite sympathetic to a régime which guards zealously the principles of provincial autonomy. A steadily increasing number of intellectuals believe that M. Duplessis' neglect of the province's social, economic, and educational needs is sufficient reason for opposing him. In others, however, his negative virtue of ensuring that Quebec institutions will be allowed to have their own distinctive development still arouses support.

Perhaps those English Canadians who deplore the difficulties M. Duplessis creates for all Canada can act most constructively by making sure that in joint English Canadian-French Canadian undertakings – conferences, national associations, etc. – the French-Canadian position receives its due weight. They can make certain too that devices like simultaneous translation are used and that the elementary politeness of bi-lingual notices and reports is not neglected. Precautions such as these can never wholly overcome the reluctance of some nationalist intellectuals to enter into associations which presuppose an English-Canadian majority. But they may help to ensure that the defence of provincial and cultural autonomy does not always take the form of Quebec's *Union Nationale* régime.

DONALD V. SMILEY

One-Partyism and Canadian Democracy

Observers of Canadian politics are still staggered by the proportions of the Conservative victory of March 31 and there is a queasy feeling that somehow liberal democracy is not well served by a verdict in which the Government has four-fifths of the seats in the House of Commons. Neither are the pundits able to take comfort in the proposition which was widely held in the days of the Liberal ascendancy that, although the forces to the left of the Speaker were few and scattered, the Canadian public by some form of divine perversity maintained a 'real' opposition to Ottawa in the form of the Duplessis Nationalists and Frost Conservatives. In the Provincial Legislatures too, larger majorities have become the rule; the 1959 *Parliamentary Guide* tells us that in only three provinces (Manitoba, Alberta, and Nova Scotia) do the combined forces of the Opposition number half as many legislators as the party in power. There have of course been only three provincial administrations overturned since 1945. Thus if there is a 'normal' pattern of development in contemporary Canadian politics it is for a party to come into power on a wave of public disgust with its predecessors and to be sustained with substantial majorities for three or four elections. After a decade or so the party begins to become complacent and arrogant, the 'brass' and the 'grass' grow apart, perhaps a scandal or two is uncovered, and the party is finally sent into political wilderness again.

Do big and stable majorities menace any values we may legitimately wish to preserve? The answer must be 'yes,' although it is quite unreasonable to indulge in the facile identification of such majorities with totalitarian one-party rule.

The major charge that can be made against what can be called the one-party dominant situation is that it frustrates intelligent and effective public debate both inside the legislature and out. Under such conditions the major party itself comprises most of the major groups within the community and the most divisive issues are resolved, the most powerful interests conciliated, within the secrecy of Cabinet and caucus. Thus on particular issues the most effective opposition to the dominant group in the Government may well be a minority within the ruling party itself. To the extent that divisions within the majority itself are more significant than those between Government and Opposition, debate on the floor of the House of Commons is less important so far as the resolution of public issues is concerned than that carried on in the Cabinet and caucus.

Large and stable majorities may also frustrate effective reporting of governmental affairs and inevitably of lay debate of public problems. Wilfrid Eggleston spoke skilfully of the inhibition such a situation produces in the working reporter in his article in *The Queen's Quarterly* last winter. Thus long-term one-party dominance may well have the effect of dividing the public into those who can't know and those who can't tell.

Under a situation where one party has dominated a legislature for a period of years or even decades the Opposition is frustrated from playing an effective role. Under the two-party system as it exists in the United Kingdom today the Labour party is in every real sense an alternative government. Many of the Labour leaders held major portfolios between 1945 and 1951 and are well aware that they will in all probability be called upon in the foreseeable future to implement the proposals they have made in opposition; in the case of Mr Aneurin Bevan it appears that the prospects of a particular Cabinet post have had a considerable moderating effect. The institution of the shadow cabinet is well developed and so the electorate can with some degree of rationality assess the consequences for both personnel and policy of a Conservative defeat. Under the one-party dominant system all is quite different. Prior to the federal election of June 1957 only one Opposition MP, the Hon. Earle Rowe, had ever been a member of a federal Cabinet, and he for only a few months as a Minister without Portfolio. A decade of Conservative rule would no doubt bring the Liberals to nearly the same state. Apart from Nova Scotia and New Brunswick, where two-party systems exist, there are only four Opposition members who have held provincial portfolios in the eight Legislative Assemblies. Further, under the one-party dominant system the major Opposition party is in no sense an alternative Government because its leaders are quite unable to speak for the complex of interests that would have to be reconciled should the party succeed to power.

To take a fairly obvious but extreme example, the little band of Tories who with seeming accord adopted the 'Ready-aye-ready' resolution condemning the Liberal policy during the Suez crisis is something quite different from a party with some 50-odd MPs elected with the help of the *Union Nationale*.

Although the Opposition groups in Ottawa and most of the provincial capitals cannot in any realistic sense be considered alternative governments, there is no reason why they cannot make a much more effective job of day-to-day criticism of public policies than most of them are now doing. A partial answer lies in the creation of professional secretaries for the Opposition. If such a reform were implemented, it might be done on a somewhat grander scale than most of its proponents seem to have visualized. The Secretariat could become specialized with a competent official and a small research staff responsible for the surveillance of each major Department. To carry it a step further each such division of the 'shadow bureaucracy' could issue at public expense a periodical critique of Departmental policies, perhaps as an appendix to the Department's annual report. There are of course many difficulties in such a plan, particularly in the field of relations between the Secretariat and the Opposition MPs and between Government and Opposition bureaucrats. However, effective day-to-day criticisms of Government policy can come only through the establishment of large and specialized Opposition Secretariats along with a genuine desire to make the legislative committee system work.

If such overwhelming majorities as those to which we are becoming accustomed are undesirable, we must be willing to consider some reform in the electoral system which produces such majorities. The academicians have for so long been saying 'two-party system good, PR and multiparty system bad' that incantation has been substituted for argument. The orthodox teaching has been that we are faced with the inevitable choice between a political system giving stable government and one which provides some measure of accuracy in the representation of public opinion and that the first alternative is always preferable.

It is not particularly difficult to demonstrate that the single-member district system of election has been strategic in creating the top-heavy majorities in Ottawa and most of the provincial capitals. It is quite true that this system has in the main worked against the 'splinter parties,' in the case of the Reconstruction Party of 1935 and the CCF in an intolerably discriminatory fashion, but in most cases the official Opposition has been also a loser. Perhaps we are paying too high a price for stability.

We should not accept uncritically the proposition that the proliferation of parties makes stable government impossible. The Swedes and Swiss and Dutch and Belgians and Finns have had rather remarkable records with multiparty systems. The failure of democracy in Weimar Germany and the Third French Republic was not so much a result of the number of parties as their narrow and doctrinaire nature. If we wish to discourage doctrinaire groups, PR offers more hope than the single-member district system. It is perfectly possible to devise a PR system which works against small groups while giving those parties with substantial support representation roughly in proportion to their electoral strength – the present West German electoral law, for example, has a provision which discriminates against parties with less than 5 percent of the popular national vote in the distribution of the half of the seats in the Bundestag filled by PR election. On the other hand, the single-member district procedure can work to the advantage of the minor party only if it confines its candidates to sections where it is strong – Social Credit was a major beneficiary of this tendency from 1935 to 1953 – and discriminates against minor parties like the CCF which attempt a national appeal. In brief, an examination of our electoral system is overdue.

Many may feel that the cures for the one-party system are worse than the disease. Unfortunately any major reform will of necessity be inaugurated by the initiative of some party with a large majority itself and it is not easy to imagine such disinterestedness coming from a group of winning politicians except as a result of very considerable public pressures.

E.W. MANDEL

Frye's Anatomy of Criticism

In trouble throughout most of its history as one of the arts of Western Civilization, poetry has always needed beside itself the art of its defenders. Dumb itself, it has won its spokesmen, and sly Plato, indifferent Locke, and ironic Peacock have provoked spectacular passions in defence. But it now appears that this delicate relationship between the offended and the defender needs to be clarified, and the articulate, contemptuous art of criticism itself needs spokesmen. It has found in Professor Frye a particularly able and eloquent one (*Anatomy of Criticism:* Northrop Frye; Saunders; pp. 383; $6.90). Among the increasing number of essays on literary theory, Professor Frye's is especially distinguished by its point of view, the angle or height from which he views his subject: a defence or justification of criticism, not as the nursemaid of wicked or dull-witted poetry, or as 'sonorous nonsense,' but as a coherent and systematic study, a systematic structure of knowledge. His *Anatomy of Criticism* proposes nothing less than to give reasons for believing in 'a synoptic view of the scope, theory, principles, and techniques of literary criticism' and 'to provide a tentative version of it.' Professor Frye pursues these purposes with wit and rigour and with the whole of literature as his familiar province.

Recently this tendency to explain themselves, always present among critics, has become the main stream of the art itself, and though there are parallels enough – the eighteenth-century psychological critics come to mind – the concern of a writer with the foundations of his subject seems curiously modern, and criticism of criticism has a contemporary ring to it. The reasons for that concern might be worth investigating, for it is fairly certain that they could provide a substantial clue to the nature of much significant contemporary thought. But lacking any such insight, we can only observe now that abstraction is, of course, a mighty source of power, and the movement from considering the 'pragmatical pig of the impossible world' to a consideration of considering the pig seems to represent an advance in knowledge or at least a new vision of the subject.

At first reading, then one is tempted to say that in his theory of criticism it is simply power for criticism which Professor Frye seeks, and that his *Anatomy of Criticism* is not really what its title suggests, a skeleton, but a matrix (his own definition of a distinct prose form – the anatomy – is not amiss here: 'creative treatment of exhaustive erudition'); in industrial terminology, Professor Frye has set up the capital moulds or machine tools to produce the machines to produce the product, and one might reasonably expect soon to see – in fact, one is already seeing – parcels of practical criticism wrapped and labelled 'The Archetypal School.' In the *Anatomy* one encounters many frightening statements of this sort: 'If criticism could ever be conceived as a coherent and systematic study, the elementary principles of which could be explained to any intelligent nineteen-year-old, then, from the point of view of such a conception, no critic now knows the first thing about criticism.' Well, perhaps. But does the substitution of system for experience really solve anything? And does Professor Frye want to replace with the standards of an intelligent nineteen-year-old the experience of Dryden, Johnson, and Arnold, to name only the most intelligible (though scarcely the most systematic) of our critics?

But while it is sometimes hard to see what else besides the package deal of practical criticism can be the end of scientific criticism, this is not at all fair to Professor Frye's own humanism, to his brilliant theorizing, or to his valid claim that 'theory of literature is as primary a humanistic and liberal pursuit as its practice,' Criticism is, in fact, presented here as disinterested, an end itself, its own justification; and Professor Frye's analogies between criticism and mathematics or physics – though often puzzling – should merely remind us that while technology accumulates in the presence of science, technology is not science, and we ought not to confuse the scholar or critic with the man who would buy and sell his products by the square yard or in bulk lots.

It is Professor Frye's 'polemical introduction' to the four essays of his *Anatomy* which raises these questions of the end of criticism and which argues for the possibility of a science of criticism, a totally intelligible body of knowledge derived from literature by the intuitions and arts of introduction or acquaintance. And it is here too that he takes a vigorous swipe at value judgments. A demonstrable value-judgment, he tells us, is 'the donkey's carrot of literary criticism.'

In the four essays which follow the introduction, the possibility of a criticism in Frye's sense is explored and the tentative version of it is presented. That version takes shape in essays on Historical, Ethical, Archetypal, and Rhetorical Criticism, and it is only fair to warn the reader that these terms, like many of Professor Frye's other terms, do not mean what one expects. In one sense, his essays are redefinitions of Aristotle's six terms for the elements of literature: plot, character, theme, spectacle, melody, and diction, terms which have lost their lustre in being handled carelessly for so long. The essay on Historical Criticism or Theory of Modes, for example, is not concerned with the relation to history but with the 'epochs of Western literature' defined in terms of the powers of action attributed to characters of fiction. Ethical criticism, contexts within which symbols may be placed and hence with literary significance. Throughout the four essays one is constantly being jolted into new awareness by Professor Frye's individual, precise use of words and by the dazzling (I had almost said fearful) symmetry of his argument.

But in the midst of complexity two central themes run, like golden threads, brightly and clearly. Without radical distortion of his argument, we may state these as first, the centrality of the arts in civilization, and second, the conventionality or 'formality' of art. Art is not only the central human activity but, paradoxically, an imitation of itself. His claim for the central position of art is, Professor Frye recognizes, traditional, and defence of it is perhaps the most significant part of his work. Art is flanked by the world of social action and events and by the world of individual thought and ideas; it is, as Aristotle and Sidney observed, midway between history and science or philosophy, between the will and the reason. The poetic symbol is intermediate between event and idea, example and precept, ritual and dream; in Aristotelian terms, notes Professor Frye, it is *ethos* between and made up of *mythos* and *dianoia*. What we have then is 'a conception of literature as a body of hypothetical creations which is not necessarily involved in the worlds of truth and fact, nor necessarily withdrawn from them, but which may enter into any kind of relationship to them, ranging from the most to the least explicit.'

In critical theory too little has been made of this paradoxical, central position. If art is displayed as existing between the poles of realism and convention (Theory of Modes), and if it derives its significance from its relation to its extremes (Theory of Symbols), it follows that its formal principles will be most apparent when it is least involved in experience, when it is explicitly conventional, mythical, abstract (Theory of Myths). Similarly, if poetry is simply an imitation of nature, then the individual poem is isolated (and so, in fact, critics like R.S. Crane argue), for the poem is 'unique, a *techne* or artifact, with its own peculiar structure of imagery, to be examined by itself without immediate reference to other things like it.' But it is clear that poems may be imitations not only of nature but of other poems. Form, the organizing principle, is thus not only the distinguishing structure of a poem but its convention as well.

From the fact of the central position of art Professor Frye attempts in this way to derive a notion of form. However, the patterns of literary works themselves are derived inductively; hence Professor Frye's definition of archetype: 'A symbol, usually an image, which recurs often enough in literature to be recognizable as an element of one's literary experience as a whole'; and hence too his account of what he calls *mythoi*, 'four archetypal narratives, classified as comic, romantic, tragic, and ironic.' Such patterns, in the sense of repeated structural principles, are said to be an element of literary experience, and a good deal of the two essays on symbols and myths respectively is devoted to a remarkable demonstration of this fact. Whatever one may think of his argument (and in more than one place it *is* mysterious) one cannot help being impressed by Professor Frye's illustrations. He pursues analogies relentlessly and he can spot a dragon-killing myth or a rebirth image in the most improbable places or in the most improbable shape. Tom Sawyer's cave, for example, is like the labyrinth of Theseus, the inside of the Trojan horse, the belly of Jonah's whale, the hell which is harrowed by Christ, and the passing reference in Eliot to the 'toothed gullet of an aged shark.' 'In short,' remarks Professor Frye, 'we can get a whole liberal education simply by picking up one conventional poem and following its archetypes as they stretch out into the rest of literature.'

Such analogies suggest that potentially all literature is identical; in fact, it spreads out from some centre where everything is identified with everything else. For some reason this notion of the unity of art (which is the name of Professor Frye's discussion of the anagogic phase of symbolism) is one which many seem to find particularly shocking or mystifying, though it is implied in certain poems, Shelley's for example, which are thought suitable for school-children, and though it is the only possible meaning of metaphor itself. Ultimately what all archetypal criticism suggests is that if there *can* be an intelligible body of critical knowledge, there *must* be an intelligible form of literature, which in turn implies an intelligible form of nature. Form, in this sense, is not created, but discovered, something, of course, which poets have hinted for a long while now.

In a period in which popular notions of criticism and literature are still based on a naive realism and in which there is, as a result, considerable resistance to the teaching of literature (or criticism) as a civilizing or liberal art, though there is a demand for it as an instrument or technique (teach my engineers to write), the *Anatomy of Criticism* is a work of utmost importance. A systematic account of the conventional nature of art is not only a defence of criticism but a defence of art as well, because it is the sort of account which insists on the integrity of art and the only one which can speak for the dumb arts. If critics go on with their own business, suggests Professor Frye, the social and practical result of their labours will be the re-forging of 'the broken links between creation and knowledge, art and science, myth and concept.'

It is difficult to resist raising a last problem which the notion of convention in art suggests. If the formal principles of art are most clearly displayed in mythical literature, does it follow that they ought so to be displayed in all literature? Or that convention ought to be made explicit? This implies a value-judgment which, if it is not made by Professor Frye himself, is found to emerge from the emphasis of his work: the clearer the archetype, the better the work. One can only answer by pointing out that there is a difference between criticism which is poetic and poetry which is versified critical theory. The sad ghost of Mark Akenside still beckons from the shadows.

Perhaps what is curious about the *Anatomy* is that one finds oneself blaming Professor Frye for implications which he skilfully denies or avoids: that criticism is technology, that all literature ought to be explicitly conventional, that criticism is not concerned with values. But this is only to say that here we have one of those seminal works which is bound to be of enormous influence; it cannot be ignored. One recognizes this as one recognizes in dreams those images which are the critical ones. They are oddly familiar and obviously they are of immense significance, though precisely what their significance is, one cannot always easily say. Reading the *Anatomy of Criticism* one is forcefully reminded of such dream images, like the one, for example, which opens Franz Kafka's *In the Penal Colony:* '"It's a remarkable piece of apparatus,"' said the officer to the explorer and surveyed the apparatus which was after all quite familiar to him.'

MILTON ACORN
The Tolerant Philistine

If behind that toothpaste grin,
one eyeball one way, one the other,
there's an adding-machine going tick-bang,
    click-clang;
if he'd amputate his mother's wedding-ring
    finger
for the price of a girly show:

tolerate it, brother,
tolerate it.
Realize he's human.

And this man makes his wife
a dunghill to crow on;
his 'damn's', 'you did',' and 'you didn't's,'
a fist-full of small flies
eternally at her eyelids:

tolerate it, brother,
tolerate it.
Realize he's human.

If it's all strictly for vultures,
a few smart operators, more cheerful idiots,
and the rest living in a flaccid paroxysm;
its morals and LIFE editorials
a recitation for laughing hyenas:

tolerate it, brother,
tolerate it.
Realize they're human.

But if a student calls Premier Duplicity
a truthful name; if some pickets
hopped up on coffee and empty stomachs
squash a scab; if the man on the wrack
spits back:

never tolerate that!
Why such tolerance could upset
your whole system of tolerance.

PAULINE JEWETT
Mr Diefenbaker's Proposed Bill of Rights

In introducing his bill for the Recognition and Protection of Human Rights and Fundamental Freedoms in the House of Commons on September 5th, Mr Diefenbaker made a good deal of what such a bill would accomplish. It would, he said, 'assure the maintenance of fundamental freedoms in the federal jurisdiction.' It would 'make doubly sure that there shall never be a challenge in the future.' It would 'preserve and maintain rights against the invasion of ... the federal government and Parliament.' It would 'preserve and maintain fundamental freedoms ... binding on the Parliament of Canada.' It would (and here Mr Diefenbaker is quoting one of his earlier speeches which, he says, 'still constitutes my point of view') 'it would establish the right of the individual to go into the courts of this country, thereby assuring the preservation of his freedoms.'[1]

In fact, the bill does none of these things. True, it is misleading in places. For example, the statement in clause 2 that certain human rights and fundamental freedoms 'shall continue to exist' in Canada is persiflage, pure and simple. All the bill does in fact, is (1) express the intention of the government not to abrogate, abridge, or infringe or to authorize the abrogation, abridgement, or infringement of any of the human rights and freedoms outlined in the Act (except in time of war) and (2) provide that all acts of Parliament and all rules and regulations authorized by such acts shall be so construed and applied (presumably by the courts) as not to abrogate, abridge, or infringe or to authorize the abrogation, abridgement, or infringement of any of the human rights and fundamental freedoms set forth.[2]

First of all, then, the bill expresses the intention of the government not to abrogate, abridge or infringe ... any of the human rights or fundamental freedoms outlined in the Act (except in time of war). It is a statement of governmental intentions, the kind of statement more appropriately found in a resolution of both Houses. It in no way binds either the present government or any future government to respect the rights and freedoms proclaimed. The government could, in its very next act of Parliament or in an executive regulation authorized by such act, implicitly or explicitly repeal every article of the Bill of Rights. It could, for example, authorize the Governor-in-Council to take citizenship away from a Canadian if upon the report of a minister the Governor-in-Council was satisfied that such a Canadian had at the time of taking the oath of allegiance not intended to comply with that oath. Indeed, as Mr Pearson pointed out,[3] this is exactly what the government was authorizing 'in a bill which we will be discussing immediately after this one.'

except by due process of law; the right of the individual to protection of the law without discrimination by reason of race, national origin, color, religion or sex; freedom of religion; freedom of speech; freedom of assembly and association; freedom of the press; the right of the person not to be subjected to torture, or cruel, inhuman or degrading treatment or punishment; the right of the arrested person to know the reason for his arrest, to retain counsel without delay and to remedy by way of habeus corpus; the right of a person to a fair hearing in accordance with the principles of fundamental justice for the determination of his rights and obligations.

[3] *Ibid.*, p. 4644.

Similarly, the government could – either the present government or any future government – impose or authorize the imposition of torture, or cruel, inhuman or degrading treatment or punishment or it could limit freedom of speech or of the press. It could do any or all of those things 'recognized and protected' in the Bill of Rights, just as it can do any or all of them now.

An aggrieved individual could, of course, as at present, bring an action in the courts. This brings us to the second point about the bill. It provides that all acts of Parliament and all rules and regulations authorized by such acts shall be so construed and applied as not to abrogate, abridge, or infringe or to authorize the abrogation, abridgement, or infringement of any of the human rights and fundamental freedoms set forth in the Act. It is an instruction to the courts to construe and apply all acts and regulations in a certain liberal way. But already the courts lean over backwards, in most cases, to construe and apply a restrictive act or regulation as narrowly, as favourably to the individual, as possible. The Bill of Rights takes them very little further. If a later act of Parliament, or regulation passed under it, were to rob the individual of any or all of his rights and freedoms, the courts could still inquire only into the meaning of the later act. They could not declare it invalid even if it implicitly or explicitly repealed every section of the Bill of Rights. The aggrieved individual would still have to suffer the consequences of the will of an ordinary majority of Parliament. Further recourse would remain where is has always been – in the political arena, the press, and other public places.

It is nonsense, then, for Mr Diefenbaker to suggest that his proposed bill will *'assure* the

---

[1] *Canadian House of Commons Debates* (unrevised), September 5, 1958, pp. 4638-44.

[2] The human rights and fundamental freedoms set forth include the right of the individual to life, liberty, security of the persons and enjoyment of property, and the right not to be deprived thereof

maintenance of fundamental freedoms in the federal jurisdiction,' that it will *'make doubly sure* that there shall never be a challenge in the future,' that it will *'preserve and maintain* rights against the invasion of ... the federal government and Parliament,' that it will 'preserve and maintain fundamental freedoms ... *binding* on the Parliament of Canada,' that it will *establish* the right of the individual to go into the courts of this country, thereby *assuring* the preservation of his freedoms.'[4] Either Mr Diefenbaker is confusing the issue, or the issue is confusing him.

If Mr Diefenbaker really wants what he says his proposed bill is providing, there are ways he might go about getting it. For example, he might still have the bill enacted as a statute of Parliament but with a proviso that any act of Parliament abrogating, abridging, or infringing or authorizing the abrogation, abridgement, or infringement of any of the provisions of the Act (the human rights and fundamental freedoms set forth), or amending or repealing the Act itself, be passed in accordance with a specified procedure. The procedure specified might be simply that the offending act expressly declare it was being passed contrary to the provisions of the Bill of Rights. Or the procedure might be tougher. It might require that the offending act be agreed to, at third reading, by not less than two-thirds (or perhaps three-quarters) of the total members of the House of Commons. (Should the extraordinary majority procedure be adopted it would be desirable, from a practical rather than a legal standpoint, that the Bill of Rights itself be passed in the same way and a clause inserted in the preamble to this effect.)

Whatever the procedure specified, the result of such a proviso would be a limited entrenchment of human rights and fundamental freedoms against federal encroachment for as long as the Act remained on the statute books. There would be an entrenchment because the courts could inquire, in cases properly brought before them, whether an offending act were in fact an abrogation ... of the Bill of Rights and, if so, whether it had been passed in the manner and form provided. If it had not been so passed, the courts could declare it invalid. It would be a limited entrenchment because so long as Parliament acted in accordance with the proviso its will would prevail.

Now it will be immediately protested that Parliament cannot bind itself or its successors in this way or, indeed, in any way, and that even if it tried to do so the courts would not recognize its action, nor would they look into future statutes to see if the manner and form prescribed was being adhered to. On the first point, however, that Parliament cannot bind itself or its successors, there is a growing body of literature suggesting that for Parliament to prescribe the manner and form in which legislation shall be passed in certain matters is not to limit its own sovereignty; that for Parliament to spell out how it shall exercise its powers in these matters is to define rather than to fetter its capacities.[5] 'Parliament may make any law in the manner and form provided by the law,' and if Parliament in a particular Act provides for a different manner and form for certain matters 'there is no law to appeal to except that Act.'[6] The courts might, of course, refuse to recognize the Act's proviso, or they might refuse to ask if later statutes had been passed in the manner and form prescribed. In the celebrated South African case of *Harris v. Dönges*,[7] however, the courts not only asked if the legislature had been correctly constituted for the passage of certain legislation but also ruled that the entrenched sections of the South Africa Act prescribing alternate methods of legislation for different classes of subject matter were in no sense 'fetters' or 'limitations' on Parliament. It is possible that the courts in Canada, too, might make a break with the traditional concept of parliamentary sovereignty, particularly in a matter of such fundamental importance as civil liberties, provided Parliament itself were to give them a lead.

If, however, Mr Diefenbaker is reluctant to grapple with the 'meaning' of Parliament, or to see the courts do so, there is still another way in which he might entrench his Bill of Rights against federal encroachment. The British North America Act itself could be amended. A section could be added at the end of the Act providing that 'notwithstanding anything in this Act, it shall not be lawful for the Parliament of Canada to abrogate, abridge, or infringe or to authorize the abrogation, abridge-

---

[4] Italics added.

[5] See, for example, D.C. Cowen, *Parliamentary Sovereignty and the entrenched sections of the South Africa Act* (Cape Town and Johannesburg, 1951) and Geoffrey Marshall, "What is Parliament?: The Changing Concept of Parliamentary Sovereignty", *Political Studies* (1954), 193.

[6] Sir Ivor Jennings, *The Law and the Constitution* (4th ed.), 149.

[7] (1952) 2 SA 428 (Appellate Division).

ment, or infringement of any of the human rights and fundamental freedoms herein enumerated' and then listing the rights and freedoms so protected.

Legally, the Parliament of Canada itself could pass such an amendment. By virtue of the 1949 (No. 2) amendment, the Parliament of Canada can amend the Constitution except as regards provincial matters and subjects, constitutional guarantees regarding education and the use of the English or French language, and the parliamentary annual session and five-year maximum term. The Parliament of Canada could, therefore, write a Bill of Rights into the BNA Act against federal encroachment. Such a Bill would not be an invasion of provincial matters and subjects (since it would be a limitation upon the federal Parliament only) nor would it, of course, be an infringement of constitutional guarantees regarding education and the use of the English or French language or of the parliamentary annual session and five-year maximum term. The difficulty about such an amendment, assuming that it contained no two-thirds clause or other proviso, is that it would be just an ordinary statute of Parliament, subject to implicit or explicit repeal by Parliament's very next act. It would be no more binding on Parliament than Mr Diefenbaker's proposed bill, nor would the courts have any further powers under it than they already have.

In order, then, to get rights and freedoms entrenched in the BNA Act against the implicit or explicit repeal by the federal Government, it would seem to be necessary for the Parliament of Canada to ask Westminster to enact the amendment, and also to ask Westminster to enact a further amendment, of the 1949 (No. 2) amendment, excepting the Bill of Rights from the amending jurisdiction of the Parliament of Canada. Legally, this could be done. The Parliament of the UK can still make law extending to a Dominion provided it acts at the request of that Dominion. Politically, however, there might be difficulty. There might be an outcry against returning any formal powers to Westminster. But a Bill of Rights entrenched against provincial as well as federal encroachment would also return formal powers to Westminster. It would enable the Parliament of the UK to state what our legislatures could not do. It would also involve an amendment of the 1949 (No.2) amendment. Yet in all the discussion of such a Bill over the past dozen years, this has not been considered a serious political problem. The only serious political problem has been the invasion of provincial jurisdiction that such a Bill would involve. Indeed, it is because of this invasion, and the anticipated difficulty of getting unanimous provincial agreement, that the matter of a comprehensive Bill of Rights is today no further forward than it was a dozen years ago. If, then, the returning of formal powers to the Parliament of the UK is not a serious political obstacle to writing into the BNA Act a comprehensive Bill of Rights, neither should it be a serious political obstacle to writing into the BNA Act a more limited Bill placing restrictions on the federal Parliament only.

Once the Bill were enacted at Westminster and accompanied by the necessary amendment to the 1949 (No. 2) amendment, it would be binding on the Parliament of Canada unless and until Parliament requested its removal. In the meantime, neither implicitly nor explicitly could the Parliament of Canada abrogate, abridge, or infringe or authorize the abrogation, abridgement, or infringement of any of the provisions of the amendment. If it should do so or, rather, if the courts should decide in cases properly brought before them that it had done so, the offending acts could be stricken from the statute books. The Bill of Rights would be supreme law.

Whether Mr Diefenbaker in fact wants a Bill of Rights with teeth in it is difficult to say. Judging by his proposed bill he does not. However, judging by the claims he has made for the bill, both in the House of Commons and elsewhere,[8] and judging by everything he has said over the past dozen years, one can only conclude that he is in favour of entrenchment, preferably against both federal and provincial encroachment but if this cannot be secured, against federal encroachment anyway. It is to be expected, then, that at the next session of Parliament Mr Diefenbaker will revise his proposed bill in such a way as to make it as effective as possible, either by securing the necessary amendments at Westminster, or by putting in a special proviso such as a two-thirds or three-quarters clause or, if the latter alone seems too speculative, by a combination of the two.

If, however, Mr Diefenbaker decides that all he wants is to indicate to Canadians the kind of rights and freedoms they enjoy and the intention of the government not to infringe these rights and freedoms, and to remind the courts

---

[8] As in his speech at the Bowater Awards dinner when he said that his bill would *ensure* the freedom of the press. Reported in the *Ottawa Journal*, October 18, 1958.

of the role they can play in dealing with infringements, he should withdraw his bill entirely and replace it with a more appropriate instrument, such as a resolution of both Houses. It would be far better to have no bill at all, or to have simply a resolution of the two Houses, than to have a bill which serves only to raise false hopes and false fears.

THE 60s

In its fifth decade *The Canadian Forum* found itself again. Once again there was a readily identifiable 'villain' in the economic and military power the United States wielded over Canada, and once again the old outrage, the old nationalism, the old concern with Canada's role in the world, began to permeate the pages of the *Forum*. Mel Watkins and Abe Rotstein began to appear regularly, calling for nationalism, socialism, and independence, while Ramsay Cook brought a concern for French Canada and an understanding of its problems and strengths to the discussions about separatism and a new constitution. Once again the *Forum* spoke in a clear, strong voice for reform. There was no uniformity of ideology or ideas, but there was a concern for the future of the country that in many ways presaged the emergence of nationalism as a major issue of the 1970s.

The literary work in the *Forum* was similarly rejuvenated. Older poets found new strengths, and the *Forum* was open to all kinds of new writing. It is difficult to discover any significant omissions of work by the writers and, in particular, the poets who flourished through this decade. As its first half-century drew to a close, *The Canadian Forum* had begun to reacquire the influence it wielded in the 1930s.

MILTON ACORN
Restaurant Scene

Take Red the waitress,
scrawny and guts and things
sticking every which way,
but along with her bones she hitches
a corona, a halo of herself.

Take her customer, bitch lady-type,
brains compressed to lips' thinness,
yet in Red's aura her talcumed face
relaxes into humanity; her voice
moves not far from a chuckle.
Now Red's gone and that mouth's
clamped by cruel ropes of muscle.

HERBERT F. QUINN
Defeat in Quebec

The defeat of the Union Nationale party in the Quebec provincial election of June 22nd last, and the return of the Liberal party to power after sixteen years in the political wilderness was undoubtedly one of the most surprising upsets in recent Canadian politics. It is true that the Liberals have only a slim majority in the legislature, as they won only fifty-one seats to the Union Nationale's forty-three. However, if an election is called within the next year or so – a strong possibility – there appears to be little doubt that Mr Lesage's party will increase considerably its representation.

In seeking an answer to the question of why the strongly entrenched Union Nationale party went down to defeat there are two aspects to be considered: first, what was the nature of the policies which were instrumental in providing Mr Duplessis' party with its successive electoral victories over the years; secondly, what were the reasons for the development of the opposition to the régime which was to bring about its downfall.

The ability of the Union Nationale to win every election between 1944 and 1956 was due to several different factors. First of all, in its opposition to the war and to conscription the party expressed the viewpoint of the vast majority of French-Canadians. Secondly, Mr Du-

August 1960

JOYCE WIELAND *Circus* June 1960

plessis' staunch defence of the rights of the province against encroachment by the federal authority during the war and post-war years was bound to be popular among a people who had always looked upon federal centralization as a threat to the survival of their cultural values and way of life. A third and extremely important factor in the Union Nationale's string of electoral victories was that the party's control over the legislature and the administration enabled it to build up a powerful political machine which used the expenditure of government money for purely partisan purposes.

In spite of the success of the Union Nationale in maintaining control over the Quebec administration from 1944 onward it must not be assumed that the opposition to the party over the years was of a negligible nature. Even in the nineteen-forties when the strength of the party was at its peak it still had to contend with opposition from a number of different sources. There was the Liberal party, admittedly in a weakened condition, but still a political force in Quebec politics. In addition, there were two minor parties, the Bloc Populaire and the Union of Electors. The Bloc Populaire was a radical nationalistic party which was in agreement with the Union Nationale's opposition to Ottawa's policies on the war and federal centralization, but was strongly opposed to Mr Duplessis' ultra-conservative economic and social policies. The Union of Electors combined social credit theories with an intransigent nationalism. Neither of these parties ever polled much of a vote in the province as a whole, but they has a certain amount of strength in some of the frontier regions of the province such as Abitibi, Lake St John and the Eastern Townships. Although both parties disintegrated in the late forties, their supporters continued to represent sizable pockets of discontent in different parts of the province.

In the nineteen-fifties opposition to the Union Nationale developed from several other directions. The trade union movement some sections of which had been on fairly friendly terms with the Union Nationale, began to turn against the party because of its anti-labour legislation. A large number of the Roman Catholic clergy were becoming concerned over the administrative and electoral corruption of the Duplessis administration, and were critical of some of its economic and labour policies. Finally, the Montreal Civic Action League, which had originally been formed as a purely municipal political movement, became a bitter foe of the Union Nationale when the latter intervened in the Montreal elections of 1957.

From this brief outline of the various parties and groups opposed to the Union Nationale it is quite clear that by the nineteen-fifties the ability of the party to capture such a large proportion of the seats in every election was due not only to the popularity of certain aspects of its policies, but also to the lack of unity among its opponents. Its strongly entrenched position could not be effectively challenged unless a united front was formed of all the opposing groups. The Liberal party was the only political force which had any chance of organizing such a coalition.

When Mr Georges E. Lapalme became leader of the Quebec Liberal party in May 1950, he inherited an organization which was seriously weakened and demoralized. In the election of 1948 the Liberals had won only eight out of the ninety-two seats in the legislature, and the party's popular vote had fallen to 36 per cent. Under Mr Lapalme's leadership the party was strengthened. A new program was adopted embodying many of the economic, social and administrative reforms demanded by the discontented elements in the Quebec electorate. Mr Lapalme's strategy was to unite behind the Liberal party 'all the forces of the opposition,' that is, the various groups and movements mentioned above which were opposed to the policies of the Union Nationale. In this strategy the Liberal leader was to a considerable extent successful. The Liberals began to receive a certain measure of support from the trade union movement, and some of the former leaders of the Bloc Populaire and Union of Electors joined forces with the party. The Liberals were also backed by the influential Montreal daily, *Le Devoir*, and had a considerable following among the clergy.

In the election of 1956 the Liberals won twenty seats in the Legislative Assembly. Although this was only a small proportion of the total number of seats in the legislature, the party's popular vote had risen to 45 per cent. The discrepancy between the small number of seats and the large popular vote was due to the fact that in a good number of electoral districts, rural as well as urban, the votes polled by the Liberal candidate had just fallen short of a majority.

The completion of the task which Mr Lapalme had set himself of forming a grand coalition of all those individuals and groups opposed to the Union Nationale was to be left to Mr Jean Lesage who succeeded to the leadership of the

Liberal party in 1958. When Mr Lesage embarked upon the election campaign of 1960 he had two distinct advantages over his predecessor. One was that the sudden death of Mr Duplessis in 1959, followed closely by that of Mr Jean Sauvé, had to some extent weakened the party organizationally. At the same time the issue of provincial autonomy, which had been so closely associated with Mr Duplessis, faded into the background. The other major factor in the Liberal's favour was that between 1956 and 1960 the people of Quebec had become increasingly aroused over the political corruption of the Union Nationale administration. This change in public sentiment can to a very large extent be attributed to the tireless campaign waged by the two priests from Laval University, Fathers Dion and O'Neill, against the 'political immorality' which had always characterized Quebec elections.

As a result of these new elements in the political situation, a good number of voters who had reluctantly supported the Union Nationale in 1956, or who had simply not voted at all, swung over to the Liberal party in the 1960 election. It was significant that almost two-thirds of the seats captured from the Union Nationale were in such regions as Abitibi, Lake St John, the Eastern Townships, and the lower St Lawrence, all areas where the Bloc Populaire and the Union of Electors had received substantial support in the nineteen-forties. The Liberals also increased their strength in the northeastern section of Montreal, the stronghold of the Civic Action League. It was obvious that the efforts of the Liberals to unite 'all the forces of the opposition' had at last been crowned with success.

The election of 1960 may be looked upon as a turning point in Quebec politics in two different respects. First, the province has taken an important step forward in the direction of the welfare state. The program on which Mr Lesage was elected to office, and which he has since pledged himself to carry through, calls for increased social security benefits for invalids, the blind, and for widows; a system of hospitalization insurance will be introduced and the government will expand its financial assistance to education at all levels, including the universities. The second aspect of the Quebec situation which deserves comment is that the more extreme forms of administrative and electoral corruption appear to be on their way out. This conclusion is based, not so much on the belief that the old parties are changing their ways, although there is some indication that this is happening, but on the growing evidence that the Quebec voter is no longer willing to tolerate these abuses.

A.L. LEVINE

The US and the Canadian Economy

Canada's national identity is still a pitifully tender shoot. In spite of careful cultivation, it remains pathologically sensitive to a variety of tremors. Is this because we are in the unfortunate position of trying to foster nationalism without the benefit of a national mystique? It does seem that if we could only clutch some myth or ethos, we might even be able to absorb those shocks to our system that our powerful neighbour to the south is wont to administer. Indeed, if we had a sturdy national personality or myth, not every literary current which trickles in from south of the border would be seen as a threat to our sovereignty. But we remain hypersensitive, and the American board members of US-owned Canadian subsidiaries are accused of being incapable of understanding the 'Canadian viewpoint' – whatever that may be.

There are doubtless many legitimate causes for anxiety over American penetration into our cultural, political, and economic life. But how do we separate these from the paranoiac nightmares? What in fact has been the character and degree of the American encroachment? So uncritically have we heeded the shrill warnings which pour forth from the frenzied nationalists that it has become practically impossible for most Canadians to give reasoned replies to this query. Fortunately, there are some exceptions, among whom, one is happy to report, is that group of writers – all but one of them Canadian – who recently set out to examine the nature of the American impact upon our economy. (*The American Economic Impact on Canada:* Hugh G.J. Aitken, John J. Deutsch, W.A. Mackintosh, and others; Burns & MacEachern; pp. 176; $5.75) They have acquitted themselves creditably. They have done much to dispel the half-truths that are still permitted to cloud our thinking. Their joint effort is a judicious appraisal, a nice balance which is neither pap for the super-nationalists nor solace for those who simply ignore the problem. Where the more weird sounds of the anti-American wolf pack need to be silenced, they do so, but where a real menace lurks, they are far from being indifferent. (Some of the authors are in fact much more concerned with the latter than the former.) Noteworthy among the individual contributions are Hugh G.J. Aitken's study of the part the United States has played in shaping the structure of our economy, Clarence Barber's examination of how Canadian agriculture has fared under the impact of US farm policy, Irving Brecher's discussion in depth of the influence of the flow of US investment funds into Canada, and Eugene Forsey's brilliant excision of a number of fallacies which have cloyed popular attitudes to labour organization in this country. To which should be added Maurice Lamontagne's foray into what, to most English-speaking Canadians, is a neglected domain: America's economic impact upon Quebec. It is a pity that this could not have been a lengthier contribution.

The American presence in Canada's economy has certainly not waned over the years. Between 1926 and 1954, American ownership of our industry and commerce grew from 19 to 25 per cent. In manufacturing and mining, the recent percentages are much higher. In 1955, 47 per cent of total investment in the Canadian manufacturing industries was American: in mining, smelting, and petroleum production the proportion was 64 per cent. (Incidentally, while the American share has increased, *total* foreign participation in Canadian industry and commerce has diminished somewhat over the years.) Professor Aitken shows how this great volume of American investment in Canada has encouraged the development of our economy 'along lines complementary to the economy of the United States.' We may not be hewers of wood and drawers of water, *par excellence,* but the cases of pulp and paper, nickel, petroleum, and natural gas indicate that a continuing heavy American investment in our extractive industries will scarcely bring that hoped-for obliteration of our staple-producing status. Secondary manufacturing in this country will doubtless continue to grow, but without seriously diminishing the importance of the primary producer in our scheme of things. So we shall remain dependent, to a greater or lesser extent, upon American markets for our raw materials and partially processed items.

Other worries which have arisen in Canada as a result of the inflow of American investment dollars are examined by Professor Brecher. It is certainly a great catalogue of woe. From it we learn that American exploitation of our natural resources threatens our sovereignty and goodness knows what else, that our sensitivity to the American business cycle is chronically debilitating, that the presence of American corporate giants on our soil hastens the trend to monopoly, that those in control of American companies in Canada are usually heedless of Canada's best interests, and, to make the charge sheet complete, that the American intruders are most niggardly in their contributions to Canadian charities. All this is old stuff to the man in the street. Issues which are rather more complex, and which therefore have not been dinned into our ears to the same extent, include the supposed propensity of Canadian subsidiaries to buy their equipment and supplies in the United State, the alleged restraint placed upon the export sales of Canadian subsidiaries in various of the world's markets, and the attacks by US antitrust men against Canadian operations of certain large American firms.

To a good deal – but not all – of this indictment, Professor Brecher returns a verdict of not proven. The present state of economic analysis and the amount of information available are 'not such as to yield positive results over the whole range of issues pervading the field.' For example, the monopoly issue has become oversimplified: no definite pronouncement is as yet possible. This does not mean that every one of the points at issue is shrouded in uncertainty. In some instances – important ones – a verdict of not guilty is entirely acceptable. Canadian resource development has been accelerated, not retarded, by the activities of US companies. And 'contrary to popular impression,' Canadians are now 'strongly' represented on the boards and executive staffs of Canadian subsidiaries of US companies.

Even in a discussion of purely economic questions, it seems that those irritating metaphysical issues of 'national survival' and 'sovereignty' must intrude. Fortunately, Professor Brecher is on the alert for this kind of nonsense: 'The honest answer to this "sovereignty" question is that there can be no clear-cut answer either way.' It is to be regretted, however, that

Professor Brecher did not bring this same scepticism to bear upon the question of the 'virtual absence of the "Canadian viewpoint" in company decisions,' and, also, upon the perverted solicitousness for our national sovereignty displayed by those who would shield Canadian subsidiaries from the extra-territorial effects of Uncle Sam's antitrust activities. Surely the majority of Canadians were not cut to the quick when certain American corporations were charged in US courts with using their Canadian subsidiaries for setting up cosy little patent pools which were not in contravention of Canadian law. Someone should tell the injured minority to stop flaunting their injured innocence and wounded national pride, and concentrate upon plugging the gaps of their own combines legislation – something which this minority is doubtless disinclined to do.

Professor Barber provides an excellent analysis of the effects upon our embattled agriculturalists of such irritants as the US surplus disposal program, the subsidization of America's domestic producers, and the intermittent imposition of US import quotas on Canadian farm products. 'Serious but not catastrophic' would appear to be the most balanced view of the effects of US agricultural policy, although even 'serious' seems to strike too alarming a note, once the facts of the matter are examined. True, the American surplus disposal program has cut into some of our markets, 'but its overall effects have been less serious than Canadians have been disposed to believe.' As to the subsidization of US producers, this could, for example, result in downward pressure on world wheat prices – possibly a degree of such pressure has already been felt – but this has obviously been offset, to a considerable extent, by American willingness to 'co-operate' with Canada in 'underpinning' world wheat prices. As far as the effects of US import quotas are concerned, these have scarcely been such as to warrant a sense of outrage.

Mr Forsey's performance is nothing short of magnificent. Here is some debunking on the grand scale. The AFL-CIO does not dictate policies to the CLC. Look, for example, at the way in which the two federations differ in the matter of political action. Nor are the Canadian sections and locals of American-based international unions simply run by the latter. It is true, of course, that a Canadian local usually cannot go on strike without the international's approval. But is this such a bad thing? Some of those who foster the myth of the domination of Canadian organized labour by American unions might concede all or most of these points, but this does not prevent them from raising the old chestnut: do not Canadian unions adhere slavishly to the wages policies of their American masters – wages policies which may not be entirely suited to Canadian industrial and commercial conditions? But surely this is an inaccurately drawn indictment. Canadian workers strive to attain American wage levels, not because they belong to the Canadian sections of American internationals, but because they happen to live alongside a healthy, well-paid giant who they do not think differs very much from themselves except in the matter of pay. Covetousness knows no boundary lines. Suppose that every Canadian member of an international were allowed to sever his ties with the American headquarters, what would be the result? Would it not be the same old cry, 'if they get it, we should get it, too'? It is a matter of proximity, not parental prodding.

This is not a book about politics and culture. Still, it should provide food for thought for those who have been wondering about other aspects of the American influence – especially the political. Is it too much to be hoped that the same kind of clearheaded reasoning which informs the present volume, and which reduces to size the great hue and cry about the American economic penetration of Canadian economic life, will now be directed to the way in which we continue to follow America's foreign policy makers to all sorts of questionable destinations? We have certainly not been impoverished by American involvement in our economic life: we will no doubt continue to survive American meanderings in the matter of wheat and natural gas. But will we always remain above ground – this is meant quite literally – if we continue to fall in with every Cold War ploy that comes from Washington?

MILTON ACORN

'I Will Arise And Go Now'

Let's borrow a tent and live on The North
   Shore
Where the wind blows bluff from Labrador
And summer flutters by at half mast,

March 1961

Cut the umbilical cord of the past
While our out-of-work benefits last.

The hungry? Let's not appease them.
If they had the power
They'd only make you paint to please them
And me punctuate my poetry
Let's not mean, but be.

Let's sign a ban-the-bomb petition
To show we're intelligent,
Then let politics go to perdition,
While you tell me and I'll tell you
How sweet we are.

I will read you Henry Miller
And you'll wear your diaphragm.
Selling out the future
And owning no geiger counter,
Let's take it on the lam.

ALDEN A. NOWLAN

Wasp

A wasp on the wrong side
of my parked car's windshield — a thorned
     phallus
stuttering like a machine gun, black and
     golden —
striped on the passive pane. In sudden pity
for him, myself and every other being
beating at unseen walls, and fearing his
sting like a sizzling awl, since I've been stung,
I try to rescue and expel him, not
certain which aim is paramount. A book
threatening to break his back by accident,
I swish a leafy, resilent alder branch
after, over and under him, conceiving
he fears it as a man instinctively
fears giant winged things. Though that things
     fly
shouldn't astonish wasps as it does me.
But he jumps sideways and drops out of reach
inside the defroster, yammering!
His beautiful, masculine body gone
crazy with pitiless confusion.
Motor and fan switched on, he's
blown back still stubbornly probing
the windshield, his fish-scale wings roaring,
his head held down like a drill.
I scoop with the alder,
once, twice, a hundred times. Still he eludes
     me —
as the glass eludes him. What can I do with
     him?
Ignore or kill him? Accept defeat?
Suddenly now it's ridiculously important
that this bug escape his predicament
and not escape me. Holding my breath
I grab him with my bare fingers and hurl
     him out —
out through the open door! Like a hot coal
grasped in the naked hand!
             Foolishly happy,
exhausted, licking my sore paw like a dog,
I sit here, thinking of glass
and the jokes it plays in the world.

KENNETH McNAUGHT

J.S. Woodsworth and the New Party

Woodsworth was one of those rare men whose interior thought was identical with his outward statements. He was also among the very few whose essential principles and goals throughout his career remained consistent. His life is one of the best refutations of the glib shibboleth that consistency is a sign both of weakness and a small mind.

From the earliest entries in the diary which he kept on the prairie mission field in the 1890s to his last statements in the Canadian parliament (although the terminology changed) he was moved by the same primary concern. In his diary in the autumn of 1897 he wrote to himself:

Oh, how prone to wander away. Is this very proneness not yet a remnant of the sinful life? I do not mean an inclination or desire for positive sin, but rather an apathy which does not allow the soul to pray without ceasing ...

Indifference was the one sin – in himself or in others – that he could never forgive. And this is very good theology, both for religious people and for secular socialists. In Christian theology indifference is the ultimate sin – against the Holy Ghost; in socialist thought it is also the ultimate 'sin' – against the brotherhood of man.

To Woodsworth as he passed physically from the prairie mission circuit to city slums and the docks of Vancouver the results of indifference were all too evident. As he moved mentally from the problem of personal, everlasting salvation to that of saving society in this world, indifference remained his prime target of attack. In the Impecunious Society, the society of scarcity in which he lived, he was never at a loss for illustrations of the essential brutality produced by its underlying creed. One of his best achievements was the steady stream of magnificently publicized and usually dramatic evidence, ranging from stark contrasts between the lives of mine-owners and the lives of miners to the relationship of crime to unemployment (a relationship whose ugly face we still must recognize).

Nor did he miss the subtlety of the capitalist system – he had read his Hobson too well. He was quick to see the methods by which a kept press and the power elite (he called them bosses) buttressed their positions in the minds of the people. A bishop blessing a cannon in Vancouver, a prime minister willing to overspend on a peace tower in Ottawa or a minister of finance with his supporting editors sobbing over the burdens placed upon the enterprising middle class – all were seen with the flummery stripped away. Today Woodsworth would undoubtedly be castigating those who think the symbol of a new city hall is more important (or as important) than the reality of low-rental housing. He was very good at discerning and unmasking rationalization, ulterior motive, or conflict of interest. His skill is no less needed in a 'boom' economy.

Of course he had one overwhelming advantage denied to many who live in the soft and cynical years of the second half of this century. He actually believed in two basic principles. He believed that war was an absolute sin; and he believed that social-economic exploitation of man by man was only slightly less wrong than war itself. It was to these two principles that he related all his reading, all his thinking, and all his action. Perhaps, further, one can say that his two principles were really one, namely, that competition amongst men for private gain was the root of the indifference to the social evil he saw all around him.

In our sophisticated age one is almost reluctant to declare that Woodsworth believed in love and co-operation rather than original sin and regulated private enterprise. To do so might make him seem simple-minded and anachronistic. I do not believe he was (or is) either. For all the sophistication of neo-orthodoxy in religion, all the rephrasing of the new sociology (power elite, white collar, alienation) and all the arguments of the counter-cyclical financiers do not mask the underlying cynicism about man which characterizes our age. And to be cynical in this respect is to be willing to permit drift rather than mastery in human affairs.

This brings us to the New Party and Woodsworth's relationship to it.

In the wide range of New Party conferences and discussion groups that have been held, up to the end of 1960, one thing seems to stand out pretty clearly. I wish to illustrate this by reference to three speeches that have been delivered at such gatherings; one by an old socialist, one by an ex-Liberal, liberally-minded independent, and one by a liberal maverick.

The Hon. T.C. Douglas, speaking at the Montreal conference, used the word socialism but his argument was straight out of J.K. Galbraith. We must not, he said, try in the sixties to solve the problems of the thirties with the methods advocated in the thirties. If private enterprise can do the job in significant sectors of the economy, let it do it. The rightward trend, begun in the CCF several years ago, was carried, one felt, to its ultimate conclusion of American progressivism and British Gaitskellism (which are one and the same thing).

Mr Walter Young, speaking at the Toronto conference, declared that if Woodsworth were alive today he would be all for compromise, the acceptance of new political alliances, and the creation of a non-socialist image acceptable to an affluent society.

Professor Frank Underhill, speaking at Toronto, pronounced his benediction upon the middle class. This class, he said, is the only creative class in society and it is therefore to this class that the New Party must direct its attention. He also presented an analysis of contemporary politics which seems to be accepted widely in New Party circles. We are at the end, he announced, of the long conservative trance through which we have been blundering in the fifties. To make this point he indicated the Kennedy victory in the United States – which seems odd on two counts. First, it is odd to select the narrowest electoral win in American history as indicating anything. But more important, to see the Kennedy victory as ending conservatism suggests a peculiar willingness to reinterpret political categories which seems to be epidemic in the New Party. If ever a tory democrat drew breath, surely it is John F. Kennedy.

The point is that socialism has been largely snowed under in the New Party, and has been replaced by the neo-Keynesian doctrines of affluence. To a large extent this has been possible because of the rapid post-war recovery of capitalism, the advance of welfare measures, the debate in British and European social-democratic parties about the virtues of public ownership, and the fears of the cold war. These events have made it politically tempting in Canada to soft-pedal the socialist interpretation, and even the word 'socialism' itself. With so many of us esconced in split-levels and borne in loan-company cars it is comfortable to believe that the boom-bust cycle of capitalism has been eliminated by deft budgeteering, that a government manned by the right people could tame the great corporations and still leave them in the hands of efficient private managers who will happily permit the necessary investment 'in the public sector' while ensuring that a suitable set of 'countervailing forces' prevents the growth of vested interest bureaucracy. With Professor Galbraith's handy intellectual barbiturates available to all, we can forget the old stuff about interlocking directorates (which all economists agree have increased the concentration of economic control rather than lessened it since the war); we can forget the creeping capitalism that is taking over the air-waves inevitably, since it still controls the sources of corporate wealth; we can forget the mass-conformity and abasement of the will secured by billion-dollar advertising budgets which cripple our culture and rival the thought-control of communism. All that is necessary is to follow Galbraith and politely intimate to private business that all this is not a very good thing.

It seems more than probable that those who defend the 'mixed economy' and the belief that the motive of regulated private profit is a better inhibitor of bureaucracy than public and co-operative ownership accept a view of human nature which is even less aware of man's sinful nature than was Woodsworth's view. While it is true that Woodsworth could and did compromise in political situations, there is one area in which he never did and would not today compromise: the area of his belief in co-operation as opposed to competition. And in that area he had no illusions about the basic motives of a capitalist middle class. He would have been no more impressed by the Canadian version of the Galbraith-Kennedy line than he was by the Bennett New Deal. He would have welcomed what it might offer in the way of compensatory amelioration but he would never have accepted a party line which was based on the myth of taming capitalism – upon the implied social philosophy of the joint Stevenson-Kennedy phrase: 'If the free society cannot help the many who are poor, it can never save the few who are rich.' He would still be pointing to the failure of a North American society, called affluent by its beneficiaries, in which (apart even from the present crisis of unemployment) more than a quarter of the population does not share in the 'good life' of the majority. And he would still believe that as long as a significant sector of collective wealth is left in private ownership that sector will ultimately control the press, the pulpit, and the government.

He would not lack illustrations for his argument. He would instance the millions of pounds worth of advertising contributed by the denationalized steel trust to the defeat of the British Labour Party. He would raise questions about a culture which depends upon the advertising imagination of a trust-controlled brewery to provide it with a performing centre for the arts. He would be deeply interested in puncturing the popular belief that the west is no longer 'imperialist'; in analyzing the passage from gunboat imperialism to investment and cold war imperialism; and especially in portraying the militarization of democracy through its economic dependence on the war contracts of private industry. He would relish the opportunity of describing how publicly-owned services have become a part of business-socialism and the non-profit doctrine has been used to create a huge system of subsidization of private industry. And he would certainly underline the impossibility of serving the public sector adequately through tax revenue and 'inducements' to private industry alone.

Apart from social-economic policy his chief concern would be with any evidence he might discern of a tendency to organize for the capture of power *per se*. He never believed that the only, or even the primary, purpose of a political party was to gain office. It is the New Party's compulsion to establish an inoffensive image that would upset him most. Certainly Woodsworth would welcome the new, declared alliance with the trade unions as he would the special appeal to independents. But just as certainly he would accept the new political framework only if it did no damage to his basic principle. An alliance and a program which would express faith in private profit as the motive and regulator of any area of collective wealth he would not accept. In terms of British politics, from which he drew many of his ideas, he would unquestionably side with that wing of contemporary Fabianism which says: 'So far from trying to show that its leaders can manage capitalism as competently as the Tories and reshaping itself in the image of the American Democratic party, the Labour party, if it is ever to return to power with a mandate from the people, must remain a socialist challenge to the established order.'

In foreign policy there can be no doubt about the position which Woodsworth would be taking today. The advent of nuclear weapons with its concomitant possibility of ending all civilization would have swept away any lingering doubts he might have had about his condemnation of war as the necessary continuance of diplomacy. Military alliances outside the United Nations he would be denouncing as the ultimate idiocy which they are. Incidentally, it is interesting to note the usual coincidence of socialist and non-alignment views in New Party meetings. One wonders how far the purpose of image-painting affects foreign policy, as it undoubtedly affects domestic policy discussions.

That which gave Woodsworth his great strength was the ability to define and hold to a basic principle. Talk about countervailing pressures, and a nod in the direction of equality of opportunity would not have satisfied him. An unequivocal declaration of belief in equality accompanied by a clear renunciation of the principle of competition would still have been the *sine qua non*.

He might well have been unpopular were he here today, but for the health of the New Party it is a shame that he is not.

RAMSAY COOK
The Old Man, the Old Manifesto, the Old Party

At last we know who the real conservatives are in Canada. It has long been evident that Mr Diefenbaker is a Populist not a Tory, while Lester Pearson's recent decision to swap his bow tie for a full-length, polka dot cravat has proven his willingness to accept change. No, it's not the 'old' parties that harbour the traditions of Canadian conservatism. Rather it is the New Party, or at least one wing of it – the wing represented by Kenneth McNaught's article, 'J.S. Woodsworth and the New Party.'(*Canadian Forum*, March 1961) It was said of Lord Liverpool, the early nineteenth-century Tory Prime Minister, that if he had been present at the creation he would have cried, 'Conserve the chaos.' Professor McNaught, standing on the threshold of the creation of a new party, has made a firm bid for the mantle of Lord Liverpool.

The general thesis of the article is unexceptional; the New Party must be a left-wing party based on principle – socialist principle – and prepared, if necessary, to place principle before power. Clearly there is no room left in Canada for a third party as amorphous as the present major parties. If a Canadian version of the American Democrats is wanted, then the Liberals offer the potential. For that matter, even the Conservatives, despite the Prime Minister's new pose as the defender of free enterprise against Liberal and New Party socialism, seem to have accepted the limited welfare state with few qualms. Therefore to serve any useful purpose in Canadian political life, the New Party must offer a genuine alternative. Moreover, it must be prepared to serve the function that the CCF and all third parties have served – that of educating the public in the need for change.

It is when Professor McNaught settles down to examining, or rather declaring, socialist principles, that one becomes aware of his inherent conservatism. The implication of his statement is that the Regina Manifesto is a sacrosanct document and J.S. Woodsworth its infallible exegete. Naturally the New Party, as the successor to the party of J.S. Woodsworth, would be false to its past if it failed to pay due homage to its heritage. Undoubtedly the party would benefit greatly if a new Woodsworth appeared in its midst. But to make a fetish of the past, and indulge in excessive ancestor worship can only hamper the growth of a new radicalism. Moreover, it should never be forgotten that among Woodsworth's many excellent qualities, the one that stood out, next to his moral courage, was his insistence that solutions to social and economic problems arose out of careful study of existing conditions. As Professor McNaught has himself demonstrated, Woodsworth was not a doctrinaire, *a priori* political thinker. Rather he was an empirical socialist in keeping with his English-speaking temperament and training. His education and experience, as well as the climate of opinion in the English-speaking world before 1945, led him to a belief in moral progress. To him sin was 'apathy' and 'indifference.' That sin could be overcome if man's environment was altered. In his view an environment conducive to moral progress could be built by the root-and-branch extirpation of competition, and the permament aboliton of war. The first was to be obtained by co-operative and public ownership; the second, by a pacificism in which he was more consistent, but no less naive than W.L.M. King. This may seem harsh, but surely the New Party will be built on weak foundations if it lacks a critical understanding of its past.

What Woodsworth would have said had he been born twenty-five years later, and thus still been here to offer his advice to the New Party, is at least debatable. It is, perhaps, also irrelevant. If the New Party is really to be new, it must be prepared to re-think its position in a world rather different from the one that produced J.S. Woodsworth. Professor McNaught castigates 'neo-orthodoxy' for suggesting doubts about man's moral perfectibility. But the same Fabian, R.H.S. Crossman, whom he quotes with approval in another context, has also written in a perceptive reappraisal of socialism, 'The evolutionary and revolutionary philosophies of progress have both proved false. Judging by the facts, there is far more to be said for the Christian doctrine of original sin than for Rousseau's fantasy of the noble savage, or Marx's vision of the classless society' (*New Fabian Essays*). This admission can hardly be written off as 'cynicism.'

Professor McNaught has no sympathy for those people who want to see the New Party's platform informed by the realism of experience. But surely Premier Douglas has not committed any sin in suggesting that if efforts are wasted in solving the problems of the thirties, there will be very little energy left to solve the ones that beset us in the sixties. One has the uncomfortable feeling that Douglas's real sin is that he won office, tried *some* of the answers of the thirties, found that *some* of them did not produce the promised result, and has had the courage to admit it. Moreover, Professor McNaught's criticism of those who have been influenced by J.K. Galbraith seems unsound. Surely a socialist can make use of the arguments of a non-socialist without fear of contamination. After all, J.S. Woodsworth was apparently able to learn from J.A. Hobson who, like Galbraith, was perhaps more of an economic heretic than a socialist. The New Party should be fully willing to absorb the 'handy intellectual barbiturates' of Galbraith, for let us not forget that the 'Affluent Society' bears many similarities to what that good socialist R.H. Tawney once called the 'Acquisitive Society.'

The British socialist movement, less fearful of American ideas than Canadian socialists, has been willing to assimilate much of Galbraith. This is true of both Crossman and Crosland. Moreover, most sections of the British Labour Party (with the exception of some left-wing elements who are counterparts of the Colonel Blimps on the right wing of the Tory party) accept the idea of a 'mixed economy' which Professor McNaught so disdains. The argument in Britain has been largely over the degree of public ownership. An intelligent left-wing statement on this subject is found in the March 24 issue of the *New Statesman*. There, Harold Wilson, the man whom some left wingers see as an alternative to Gaitskell, argues that within a planned economy a Socialist government would use guaranteed orders, taxation, and public ownership as means of directing the economy. The argument over nationalization, he holds, can be solved if a carefully devised program of economic and social development is worked out and nationalization used where it seems best suited to meet the needs of a good society. Here once more public ownership has been placed in the realm of means where it belongs, rather than being elevated to the status of an end. Certainly the New Party must be a party whose objective is a planned economy – one in which the public sector will not starve while the private sector grows obese, one in which a ten per cent unemployment level will be inconceivable, one in which the problems created by foreign ownership and alienation of natural resources will be approached with hard intellectual labour, rather than loud rhetorical bellows. If public ownership proves to be the best method of gaining these ends then certainly the New Party should be willing to use it. But to declare that the New Party's first article of faith must be to reject Galbraithian economics and the idea of a 'mixed economy,' is simply to ask its members to close their minds to socialist experience both here and abroad since 1945.

The interminable debate on defence in the Labour Party causes one to despair of saying anything about this problem. But the most vigorous, if not the most important, debate at the New Party founding convention will probably be on foreign policy, and Professor McNaught's views will be strongly represented. One of the strong features of socialist thought has always been its realistic recognition of the sources of power in a capitalist society. Unfortunately this perception has too often been accompanied by a blindness to the realities of power in the international world. Nowhere were J.S. Woodsworth's limitations more evident than in his views on international affairs. Yet, Professor McNaught, without adopting Woodsworth's pacifism, suggests that the New Party should denounce all military alliances outside the United Nations as the 'ultimate idiocy which they are' (elsewhere he has referred to the Cold War as a 'spurious military power struggle'). The world balance of terror is not a comfortable accommodation, and one wonders how long it can continue without a smash. But surely the socialist answer to the dangerous chaos of unplanned competition is not unilateral renunciation and withdrawal, but rather acceptance of the challenge to try and bring order and planning into the world. As John Strachey has written in *The Pursuit of Peace*, a pamphlet that should be required reading for all delegates to the Ottawa Convention, unilateralism is 'a turning away, in fear and despair, from the real world with all its difficulties and dangers.' The first step that is necessary for those who write the foreign policy statement of the New Party is to recognize both sides of the paradox of the twentieth-century arms race (as Chester Bowles has recently remarked): an uncontrolled arms race before 1914 ended in war while unilateral disarmament and weakness in the thirties made it impossible to prevent the Second World War. Thus only multilateral disarmament and rational approaches to negotiated settlements of outstanding East-West disputes can carry the world away from the brink of nuclear war. But since the Cold War is about fundamental issues, there is no magic panacea which will end it, and the New Party must be prepared to recognize this fact. (This is what caused Philip Noel-Baker, author of the *Arms Race* and Nobel laureate, to vote against the unilateralist, anti-NATO resolution at last year's Labour Party Conference.) It is easy to give in to the strange combination of pessimism and moral indignation of the unilateralists; it is more difficult to devise a program for multilateral disarmament. But if the New Party is to represent a genuine alternative in Canadian politics it must choose the way that requires intellectual application rather than mere moral exhortation.

It now seems inevitable that the New Party will be embroiled in a debate on the question of unilateralism and non-alignment. This is perhaps a good thing, and may clear the air which has been filled with CLC and CCF sniping. But one cannot help voicing the fear that the effectiveness of the New Party may be paralysed by the same debate which has split the Labour Party. When there is such an obvious need for a clear-headed attack on Canada's domestic problems this seems a tragedy, for in the long run the party's decision on foreign policy can have only a limited impact on the world. Rather than paralysing itself from birth in this struggle it would surely be more responsible for the New Party to adopt a statement on foreign affairs which was infused with the same ideals that caused President Kennedy to remark in his inaugural address, part of which was quoted by Professor McNaught: 'To those people in the huts and villages of half the globe struggling to break the bonds of mass misery, we pledge our best efforts to help them help themselves, for whatever period is required – not because the Communists are doing it, not because we seek their votes, but because it is right. If the free society cannot help the many who are poor, it can never save the few who are rich.'

Throughout Professor McNaught's stimulating article, there is one unifying theme – a fear of the corrupting influence of power. His main attack is quite justifiably directed at those who are overly concerned about the New Party's image. Perhaps it is for this reason that he appeals to the past, hoping to conserve those aspects of the CCF which the Canadian public found least attractive. Being denied power the CCF could at least claim purity – except in Saskatchewan, where Premier Douglas's doctrine may not be pure, but his record is impressive. It may be that past generations of Canadian electors found J.S. Woodsworth's CCF 'right but repulsive' and King's Liberals 'wrong but romantic.' But surely this is to draw a distinction between principle and power which is unnecessary; the New Party must be a party of protest, but if it really believes in its program, it will also have a duty to seek power. Perhaps the most fundamental question that delegates to the New Party founding convention this summer will have to answer is: Will a New Party whose existence only serves to keep the present government in office, as the CCF helped to keep W.L.M. King in power, provide a genuine alternative in Canadian political life in the sixties?

MALCOLM LOWRY

Two Poems

Tashtego Believed Red

A hand comforts held out to one who's
 sinking;
And what founders deeper than a world
 which sinks?
Like a lost ship it never once says thanks,
Since no single hand shall save its timber
 drinking
The poisoned salt its sides awash are flanking,
Thirsty for web of weeds or sift of sandbanks,
Its last music gunshot, its gesture poise
 of tanks
Over the wood where swathes of death are
 ranking...
But witness, the hand is no hand but an arm
Curving itself with the strong swimmer's flex
— A thousand arms which thresh against the
 blast
Of a regressive ocean, even whose calm
Is derelict with that impartiality which wrecks.
— Yet regard, regard, the red banner nailed to
 the mast!

Nocturne in Burrard Inlet

Church bells are chiming on the rail
And wheels the frightful killer whale
The gulls are baaing in the creek
And night is whetting up its beak...

PAUL STANDING

Nipples on the Newsstands

The skin-book revolution is a phenomenon, an encouraging, and, it is to be hoped, an enduring one of the last half dozen years or so. Bosoms, covered or half covered, had formed the staple visual fare of Canadian newsstands for a generation or more, ever since Mae West and others had made them erotogenetic in the early thirties, but for years it had seemed, to our despair, as if there were a maximum permissible exposure limit which did not include any pictorial presentation of their pigmented promontories. For the break-through to open bosoms openly arrived at we had to await the advent of *Playboy, Swank, Gent, Escapade, Caper, Rogue,* and the rest of the skin-books.

Three factors made this development possible, and forced acceptance of the most striking features of these publishing ventures. The first was editorial courage. The second two were slick paper and full colour. There is an aura of solid worth and respectability about coated paper which the skin-book editors have taken shrewd advantage of. Full colour, besides having the same virtue of expense, contributes a deceptively artistic atmosphere to the finished bosom, just sufficient to divert the moralist yet not enough to discourage the scopophile. The point becomes clearer if we compare the skin-books with their newsstand neighbours, the 'men's action' magazines. The editors of the latter still cling to black and white on pulp, and they still demurely cover their nipples and coyly invite their readers to send three dollars to receive, in a plain sealed envelope, what they could get in *Playboy* for fifty cents.

But without yet a fourth factor, a vacancy in the market, no editorial devices, however intelligent and however courageous, could have brought the skin-books to their present position. The process whereby this vacancy occurred is not easy to reconstruct, but seems to have happened in the following fashion. First, the editors of *Harper's* and the *Atlantic* began their titanic struggle, at time of writing still unresolved, to see which could produce the dullest paper. This left open the slot with the reader image of a middle-aged, literate yet not very demanding male, and *Esquire* gradually, almost imperceptibly, moved in. Or it may be that a magazine grows old along with its readers. In any case, when, years later, *Esquire* published a long feature outlining for its public in great detail all the exotic delights that lay in store in, of all things, the *Times Literary Supplement*, we began to suspect the worst, and when a recent issue reviewed the 'Lady Chatterly' trial without even using THE WORD, the truth could no longer be disguised. For *Esquire* the periodical which had given us Petty's drawings, the 'Petty Girls' which had done so much to raise the morale of our boys in the dark days of the war, the periodical which had pioneered the two-page detachable full colour pin-up, for *Esquire* the protracted magazine menopause had run its painful course.

There was nostalgia but not real regret, for over half a decade now the former *Esquire* reader image, the racy, sporty, uninhibited undergraduate, has been well taken care of in terms both of visual and literary content by the skin-books. More important, the successor to the actual reader of *Esquire*, as opposed to the reader image, has been for the first time not overlooked. The actual readers of *Esquire* were, as is well known, boys in grade eight who were trying to find out what women looked like with no clothes on. Contemporary grade-eight boys will never know to what straits their predecessors, as recently as ten years ago, were driven in conducting this facet of the search for truth. Canadian girls, the most ungenerous in the world, were of no help whatever. On the magazine racks the 'Petty Girls' though delightfully complaisant, were always in some measure clothed. *Sunbathing and Health* had its pictures of nudes but the significant data were always obscured. *Popular Photography* also featured nudes, but only the unpromising ones were ever portrayed with even so unsatisfactory a technique as black and white; for the really promising ones the publishers had developed a unique process: black and black. These two frustrating periodicals, both still in business, left the earnest seeker after enlightenment precisely where he started.

There are, it is true, those who felt, quite sincerely, that the dissemination of reliable even if only partial information about what women look like bare naked will have a deleterious effect on society. They point out that there are already three legitimate ways of acquiring this information: one can go to medical school, one can go to art school, or one can get married. The skin-books, they contend, strike at the very roots of these three socially valuable institutions. There is indeed some justification for the fear that with skin-books available for all, fewer boys will feel the call to go to medical school, the doctor shortage will become acute and the cost of health continue to climb. But fears of the effects on art and marriage are, if not absolutely groundless, at least not of the first importance. With a few honourable exceptions, Canadian artists never, after graduation, paint the naked models they went to art school to look at; they confine their mature attentions to the jack pine. Any decline in the institution of marriage, too, can be watched with unconcern by the growing number of people who feel, with the preamble to our Bill of Rights, that the family is the foundation of society, but view with less and less enthusiasm the society of which the family is the foundation.

More realistic is the fear, expressed even by some skin-book readers, that newsstand exposure of the bosom will result in a downgrading of that appendage. They point to the fact that a decade ago bosoms, though still concealed, had a predominant place in the imagination of every red-blooded Canadian, and that the bosom of that time was of proportions noble enough to merit this pride of position. 'Where,' they ask, 'are the bosoms of yesteryear?', noting sadly that the contemporary ideal bosom is appreciably smaller than that of 1950, and that other feminine features have revived and are competing for attention, whereas the bosoms of 1950 had the field to themselves. This feeling must be resolutely combatted wherever it raises its head. It must be kept in mind that the bosoms of 1950 were so monumental as to be absolutely out of hand as well as, naturally, out of reach. Surely too, at a time when the future of civilization itself is in doubt, bosom fanciers can extend the right hand of friendship to those whose backgrounds lead them to a greater appreciation of other female protuberances. Surely, in these times of peril, we can sink our petty differences and strive together for the common good.

Yet another quibble, that a flood of cheap American bosoms is swamping the market and forcing the Canadian competition out of circulation, can be peremptorily dismissed. Parochialism of the narrowest sort, this view does not even take into consideration the question of whether Canadian women have bosoms. The latter have never, to the writer's knowledge, admitted to, let alone given palpable demonstration of, their possession of these items, and until this point is cleared up beyond a shadow of a doubt we would be unjustified even in pressing for skin-books with a 50 per cent Canadian content.

And what of the future? Will *Playboy* turn chicken and go the way of *Esquire*? Will the skin-book publishers rest content with the bosom, if necessary compensating for the ageing of their readers by gradually ageing their models? Or will they advance triumphantly to fresh woods and pastures new? If the latter, what a glorious vision of the future unfolds! For with the problem of what women look like finally and absolutely disposed of, grade-eight boys will, for the first time in recorded history, be able to give their complete attention to other matters, and the prospect opens up of senior matric at fourteen, a good doctorate at sixteen, a decent academic post, with tenure, at seventeen, and the foundation laid for a scholarly, literary, and artistic renascence which could make the twenty-first century indeed the century of Canada. For this prospect we have to thank the publishers of the skin-books; for this hope the publishers of the skin-books, like the breasts which it is their pleasure and pride to present, ought to be supported.

Note: Paul Standing is a pseudonym of T.B. Miller.

IRVING LAYTON

There Were No Signs

By walking I found out
Where I was going.

By intensely hating, how to love.
By loving, whom and what to love.

By grieving, how to laugh from the belly.

Out of infirmity, I have built strength.

Out of untruth, truth.
From hypocrisy, I weaved directness.

Almost now I know who I am.
Almost I have the boldness to be that man.

Another step
And I shall be where I started from.

LAURIER L. LAPIERRE

Le Séparatisme and French Canadians

Our prime minister keeps repeating that the issue of the next general election will be socialism versus free enterprise. This issue has little significance in the Province of Quebec. French Canadians are realizing more and more that they must depend on the state for the direction of most of their collective activities, including their economy. Therefore, although Mr Daniel Johnson, the new leader of the Union Nationale, and Mr Pierre Sévigny, the Associate Minister of Defence, are doing their best to maintain the bogy of greater state control as the road to socialism, I doubt that this question will become a major issue in Quebec.

What does concern French Canadians and what may easily turn out to be the real issue of the next general election in Quebec is what has been called by Premier Lesage 'the re-orientation of Confederation.' Such a reappraisal has been made almost imperative by the increasing emphasis in the past year on 'le séparatisme' or 'l'indépendance du Québec.'

The separatist movement is a part of the upheaval which has been rocking the Province of Quebec ever since the death of Maurice Duplessis and the Liberal victory in June 1960. Quebec is re-assessing its values, its way of life and even its raison d'être. The separatist movement is part of this upheaval, as is the soul-searching of the current Royal Commission on Education, the Salvas Commission, the Mouvement Laïque de Langue Française, the Institut des Affaires Publiques, and René Lévesque. While they are appraising their educational system, their government's use of kickbacks and patronage, the paternalism of their clergy, and the domination of their economy by Anglo-Canadian and American interests, it is only natural that French Canadians should spend some time re-examining the constitutional arrangements which bind them to the entity called Canada. The discussion of separatism has given them this opportunity.

The separatist movement at the moment is made up of three separate organizations, which disagree violently with each other as to the correct solutions of Quebec's problems. The oldest of the three is l'Alliance Laurentienne, headed by Raymond Barbeau. This is an extreme rightist group which advocates a state religion

(Catholic of course), and paternalistic state control of all aspects of life. The middle-of-the-road group, and the most influential of the three, is the Rassemblement pour l'Indépendance du Québec, founded about a year ago by André D'Allemagne, and now headed by the much publicized Marcel Chaput. Dr Chaput has repeatedly refused to outline the method of government to be set up in the separate state he hopes to create. The third group, and the only one with a definite platform, is the socialist group, Action Socialiste pour l'Indépendance du Québec, headed by Raoul Roy. Aside from the issue of independence, much of its program has been adopted by the New Democratic Party. The issue over the words 'federal' and 'national' at the New Party founding convention may point towards the development of a second socialist group in Quebec within the next five years. The total membership of these three groups is now set at 4,000-6,000 but it is obvious that separatism has a much greater influence in the province today than these figures would indicate. At the same time one must recognize the very basic differences between these organizations when one speaks of a separatist 'movement.'

Interest in separatism has been increased in the last three months by the appearance of two books: Raymond Barbeau's *J'ai Choisi l'Indépendance* (Montréal: Les Editions de l'Homme, 1961, pp. 127, $1.00), and Marcel Chaput's *Pourquoi je suis Séparatiste* (Montréal: Les Editions du Jour, 1961, pp. 156, $1.00). Professor Barbeau and Dr Chaput both argue that economically French Canadians are in an inferior and subordinate position. They have lost the ownership of their natural resources and they have been systematically deprived of a decisive influence in the management of the affairs which affect their every-day existence and standard of living. Anglo-American financiers, Barbeau insists, come to Quebec 'chercher du "cheap labour," une main-d'oeuvre à bon marché, des ressources abondantes et des gouvernements qui plient l'échine et dont, en retour, ils remplissent les caisses électorales.' Unable to be 'les maîtres, les propriétaires de leur propre province ou de leurs propre villes,' both men envisage a new order in which an independent Quebec will have the power to decide, to plan, and to effect 'la reconquête de notre économie.'

From this economic consideration comes the social cause of their dissatisfaction. French Canadians have become, Chaput states, second class citizens since everywhere 'nous occupons le bas de l'échelle.' Barbeau argues that for too long have his compatriots been satisfied to be 'les dupes perpétuels de l'impérialism pan-saxon du Canada' and to exist in a 'ghetto confédératif' where the only concession to their existence is 'des bouts de papiers bilingues.' This social inferiority can be seen in that French Canadians are expected to be bilingual while their English-speaking counterparts need not be. In the federal civil service, in the armed forces, in factories, in stores, and even perhaps in the Cabinet, the first criterion for French-Canadian eligibility is the ability to read and write English. Competence becomes a secondary consideration. In the face of what amounts to racial and linguistic discrimination, sanctified by ninety-odd years of practice, is it any wonder that Barbeau concludes that 'avec l'aide de Dieu, en brisant les idoles pancanadiennes et en crevant les mythes pancanadiens, nous nous referons d'abord une patrie digne de nous et un caractère ardent, ordonné, passionné.' Only through independence can French Canadians regain their lost dignity and rejuvenate their social order.

Barbeau and Chaput both believe that Canada's present political structure cannot successfully restore French Canadians' economic and social rights. They feel it is impossible for French Canadians to be politically effective in Ottawa when their representatives make up only thirty per cent of the total membership of the House of Commons. Furthermore, national party politics make inevitable the division of the French Canadian members in the House with the result, as Barbeau suggests, that 'les députés canadiens français divisés entre les partis, ne forment pas une bien solide et puissante opposition au bloc anglo-canadien.' How many times, he asks, have French Canadians been forced to accept policies they opposed and which they considered detrimental to their position within Confederation? The only political action which they can perform successfully in Ottawa, according to Chaput, is to 'retarder l'acceptation des propositions de la majorité.' The separatists therefore advocate complete independence in which the collective needs and aspirations of their people could be dealt with by a government wholly theirs.

Since World War 2, less developed and poorer nations than Quebec have achieved independence. Barbeau and Chaput look at these countries with envy and ask: 'Why them and not us?' Both argue that French Canadians form 'une nation' with all the attributes of a nation. They have six million individuals with a common history, a common language, a geographical territory which has been theirs for the past four hundred years, political and social institutions, and above all 'un vouloir-vivre collectif que même les deux derniers siècles de notre histoire n'ont pas démenti.' This 'nation' must have 'une patrie' where, according to Barbeau, the French Canadian 'pourrait être en parfaite possession de toutes les richesses de la nature et de tous les biens humains et religieux que la Providence lui a départies.' Quebec, then, must become the 'état canadien-francais,' because 'il n'y a que le Québec qui puisse être dit la patrie du Canadien francais parce que c'est le seul endroit au monde où il se sente chez lui ...'

The separatists recognize that a small nation cannot exist in a cultural vacuum, but must be linked to other nations which share a common heritage. A united Canada cannot serve in this capacity, since it represents intellectual, psychological, and cultural colonialism. French-Canadian universities, Barbeau and many others argue, 'sont gangrenées par l'anglicisation.' The majority of text-books, especially in scientific and technical fields, are translations of English texts. Moreover, the French Canadian must earn his living by using 'English' methods, approaches, and know-how. He must absorb, in other words, 'la mentalité anglaise.' The separatist feels that under this barrage the French Canadian is slowly being psychologically assimilated with disastrous consequences for the survival of 'le fait canadien francais' in North America. The only hope, therefore, rests in linking French Canada, not with English-speaking America, but with the twenty-five nations and the 150 million people of the world who use French as their mother tongue. Surely, as Barbeau and Chaput point out, this can only be achieved through the creation of an independent Quebec.

These two books demonstrate the deep dissatisfaction of two individuals with Canadian Confederation. The tragedy is that the disenchantment is not limited to two, but that it permeates almost all the French-Canadian population. For this reason, French Canadians look upon separatism, not as the expression of a lunatic fringe, nor as an exercise in emotionalism, and certainly not as the so-called 'cancer' of Montreal (whatever that is), but as a possible, and, at times, an attractive – if extreme – solution to the problem of 'la survivance du fait canadien francais' in North America. There are probably very few French Canadians who would not accept separatism if it were the only possible means of achieving this end.

Yet many see great weaknesses in the separatist solution. It would create an isolated French-Canadian pocket in the midst of an English-speaking continent, a development which would inevitably endanger French Canada's hopes for self-realization and economic advancement. Nor would it really offer a solution to the task now facing French Canadians: the protection of their minorities outside Quebec, in spite of the separatists' talk of their immigration to the new state. Most serious, I feel, is that separatism is really a denial of French-Canadian history. The most dynamic part of the old French Empire in America never lay on the banks of the St Lawrence. It lay in the vision of opening to civilization a whole continent with its immense forests, its shield, its prairies and rivers, stretching from the Arctic to the Gulf of Mexico, and from the Atlantic to the Pacific. It is a sad commentary on Confederation that the inheritors of this glorious ideal should be prepared to accept such a limited legacy.

One must agree that in the past French Canadians have been reluctant to participate fully in the task of developing Canada, but today this is no longer true. Their educational system has finally begun to produce the economists, engineers, senior executives, and other professionals trained to accept responsibility and capable of operating large industrial enterprises. Their reluctance to participate in their economic development through private investment is gradually being broken down, especially through the creation of the General Finance Corporation, which is designed to encourage French Canadians to invest the two or three billion dollars they now have deposited in banks in the development of their province. There is no doubt that with the help of this agency, they can come to own the larger part of their natural resources and to control the means of their development. In this struggle for what René Lévesque has called 'la reconquête de notre économie,' the co-operation of Quebec's present economic overlords will be necessary; but should it not be forthcoming, Mr René Paré, the chairman of the newly created Quebec Council of Economic Orientation, has warned that French Canadians more and more 'will demand that their governments nationalize the larger business firms that are now in the hands of our Anglo-Saxon compatriots.'

This revival is not limited to the economic field. French Canadians are trying to re-evaluate their role in a pluralist democratic order and they look more and more to the state for the creation of the conditions necessary to their complete 'épanouissement.' A group of professors of l'Université de Montréal has asked the Royal Commission on Education to suggest to the government that the traditional role of the *collèges classiques* be re-assessed and that the French-Canadian educational system be reorganized to follow more closely the system now prevailing in the rest of the French-speaking world. The traditional limited vision of French Canadians is being enlarged as they abandon the idea that the best way to protect their French heritage is to isolate themselves in the confines of Quebec. Premier Lesage has given the province a vision of 'l'état du Québec' while at the same time reinvoking the traditional mission of French Canadians as the guardians of civilization and the protectors of minorities. The Church, occupied with the re-assessment of her role in a pluralist society, has not participated in the separatist debate for once, leaving to the politicians the task of directing the political order.

A re-assessment of the French-Canadian constitutional position has become imperative. Barbeau and Chaput feel that provincial autonomy cannot offer adequate protection. Chaput argues that Ottawa's rights of disallowance and its residuary power, the Supreme Court with its English-speaking majority whose 'mentalité' is 'différente de la nôtre,' and the numerical weakness of French Canadians in all levels of government activity make a mockery of provincial autonomy and render the Quebec provincial government impotent in many decisive areas. Barbeau rejects Henri Bourassa's notion that 'quoi qu'il advienne, l'ensemble de la Confédération canadienne n'est pas moins, pour l'heure, la patrie de tous les Canadiens, la nôtre comme celle des Anglo-Canadiens...'

In spite of Barbeau, Chaput, and others who share their views, the majority of French Canadians are not yet prepared to destroy Confederation; nor are they willing to accept it as it is now understood. Furthermore, they are tired of offers of bilingual cheques, sermons on national unity, and guarantees of entrenched rights. They want fundamental reforms which they hope will secure once and for all 'la survivance du fait canadien français' in North America. The reforms they envisage are the acceptance of bilingualism from coast to coast, the granting of better conditions for the French-Canadian minority outside Quebec, and more effective provincial autonomy through decentralization. These can only be achieved through a complete rewriting of the British North America Act. The federal and provincial governments might be wise to spend less time discussing the 'repatriation' of the British North America Act and devote their energies to a realistic reappraisal of the terms of Confederation.

A.W. PURDY

Poem for One of the Annettes

Which one of you? — oh now
I recognize that tear-stained pro-
Semitic nose shaped wonderfully for
your man Murray's kisses but
he left didn't he?
    Oh Annette
        cry like hell
For Columbus Ohio and Taos New Mexico
where he is and you're not
        As if
the world had ended and
    it has —

Or the Anita with undressed hips that
could break a man in half in bed and
big unpainted Rubens breasts affixed to
    a living woman
swinging high over Montreal
        As if
the whole damn town was a whorehouse full
of literarily inclined millionaires with a yen
for your kind of dirty-story-book love and
    it is —

Or Janine from Poland who's
a citizen of Canada knocked up
in Montreal by a Yank from
Columbus Ohio and
        abandoned and
the abortion took place in The Town of
Mount Royal and the foetus had
        no name —

Cry for your own bad judgment in

loving him with good tears that
    will not
        fall
            but stay
in the blue beginning of every evening when
factory watchmen are coming on duty and
silent lovers are visible as moths hovering on
streetcorners
              in eccentric silver orbit
as permanent as any in
            Maisonneuve's cynical
              metropolis —

Cry the common sickness with ordinary tears
            As if
they would flood the whole quasi-romantic
    town of
Montreal with the light of your darkness and
follow the gutters and sewers glowing down
thru sewage disposal plants by the river and
into the industrial waste of your dreams to
    the sea
        the shapeless mothering one-celled sea —

Oh Anita, they do.

DONALD V. SMILEY

Canada's Poujadists: A New Look at Social Credit

In answer to the charge that his actions in respect to the expropriation of the British Columbia Electric Company made him a dictator, Premier W.A.C. Bennett is reported to have replied, 'No one seems to like us but the people.' This suggestive quip conveys much more about the essential nature of Social Credit than it is likely the Premier intended.

The usual categories of political thought give few clues to an understanding of Social Credit. Despite the fundamentalism of its religious and some of its economic notions, the movement is devoid of the conservative's regard for parliamentary institutions and the rule of law. Its individualism might lead one to interpret Social Credit as a belated variant of liberalism but the movement lacks the respect for rationality and the tolerance characteristic of the liberal temper. Neither is it fair or accurate to regard Social Credit as an incipient totalitarianism because its aims are relatively restricted ones. Manifestly, the usual political categories will not do.

It is my argument that Social Credit is essentially anti-institutional and as such has both radical and nihilistic elements. Otherwise shrewd observers of the movement have assumed that it is basically moderate because of the limited scope of its explicit economic objectives. However, the arbitrary manner by which the Aberhart administration in the 1930s dealt with the creditors of the Alberta community and the methods by which most of the assets of the British Columbia Power Corporation were recently expropriated seem to belie this view. Further, as Professor Mallory has so well described the situation, the Aberhart Government subjected the Canadian federal structure to one of its severest tests and, until a few months ago at least, it appeared that Premier Bennett's headlong pursuit of his resource-development policies was offering Ottawa a similar challenge. Thus in its treatment of the claims of private property and its policies toward the Confederation settlement, Social Credit has been on occasion genuinely radical. However, this radicalism has been basically nihilistic, for unlike communism, democratic socialism, or even some of the variants of fascism, the movement has had no vision, no plan, no real urge to remake society. In spite of its constant appeals to morality, Social Credit is at heart the pursuit of power divorced from purpose – summed up most suggestively in its slogan of the 1960 election campaign in British Columbia, 'Vote for the Government that Gets Things Done.'

To get some understanding of Social Credit, it is useful to analyze briefly how it came to power in Alberta with particular reference to the southern part of the province where the movement had its origins.

Between the days of settlement and the coming of Social Credit, Alberta had developed a complex network of vital and effective rural institutions and had thrown up an extraordinary, able rural elite. Farming communities were highly organized with their United Farmers and United Farm Women's groups, their Wheat Pool locals and other co-operative institutions, their Women's Institutes and their rural municipalities, churches and school districts. Most of these groups had close links with effective provincial associations. Seymour Lipset in his study of the CCF leadership in Saskatchewan in the 1940s has described the characteristic of the same kind of rural elite that, it appears, dominated rural Alberta prior to 1935 – an interlocking directorate composed predominantly of people of Anglo-Saxon and Scandinavian stock, more successful than the average in their own farming operations, overwhelmingly United Church and Lutheran in religious affiliation and who held positions in more than one rural organization. This elite had won control of the provincial Legislature in 1921 and between that year and 1935 had sent extraordinarily able and articulate representatives to the House of Commons in the persons of Robert Gardiner, George Coote, Alfred Speakman, Henry Spencer, and others.

The federal and provincial elections of 1935, and the events surrounding them, saw an almost complete displacement of the Alberta rural elite at the national, provincial, and community levels. The leadership of the United Farmers of Alberta at their annual conventions of 1934 and 1935 had presented a united front in rejecting Aberhart's version of Social Credit despite the ground-swell of support for that gospel in the UFA locals. Aberhart's somewhat delayed response to the latter rejection was to insist that Social Credit candidates for the forthcoming provincial election be persons who had not previously been involved in politics which, in the context of rural Alberta at that time, meant that they would be for the most part people who had not had leadership roles in the dominant institutions of their respective farming communities. Although Aberhart's appeals were successful in alienating the UFA elite from the bulk of the rural population, Social Credit showed no disposition to provide an alternative leadership and the influence of this organization was almost totally destroyed. The intense bitterness which Social Credit brought to rural Alberta was in a very real sense a by-product of the challenge to the position of the rural elite and its sudden displacement from a position of dominance. While the Progressives and later the CCF were built around the existing rural leadership and directed most of their radical urges against institutions controlled in Western Canada, the rise of Social Credit provoked internecine struggles within the Alberta rural communities themselves.

The rural churches in Alberta had been challenged by Aberhartism for nearly a decade before the coming of Social Credit. Characteristically, the fundamentalist sects are more loosely organized than the traditional denominations and rely on frequent appeals to emotion rather than on those of bureaucratic methods. To an even greater extent than other fundamentalist groups active in Alberta at that time, the Aberhart religious movement made little attempt to establish stable rural congregations and its efforts were centred almost entirely in the broadcasting activities of the Calgary Prophetic Bible Institute. The victims of the Institute from the time Aberhart began broadcasting in 1926 onwards were the Protestant denominations, particularly the United Church, with a highly trained pastorate, active lay participation in church affairs, and a liberal and humanitarian ethic which made for close integration with other organizations of the farming communities.

As well as the United Farmers movement and the churches, two other rural institutions, the rural municipality and the local school district, were directly challenged by Social Credit, although their destruction came only after the Aberhart Government came to power. The policies of Aberhart and his colleagues in creating new and larger units of educational and later municipal administration can justifiably be regarded as progressive. However, in the context of this analysis, these measures can be viewed as the destruction of rural institutions which, particularly in the case of the school districts, had played a central if not always beneficent role in the life of agricultural communities. In passing, the vigorous local government policies of Social Credit in Alberta can be contrasted with the more cautious approach of the Saskatchewan CCF to educational reorganization and the hesitant way in which the present Saskatchewan Government is pursuing the reform of its rural municipalities; these differences can, I think, be explained largely in terms of the lack of integration of Social Credit with indigenous rural institutions and the close personal and organizational ties of the socialist leadership with these institutions.

The assault of Aberhartism on rural Alberta was anti-ideological as well as anti-institutional. Under the broad tent of the various farm movements had flourished a large number of social and economic theories. The group government doctrine of Henry Wise Wood, perhaps the nearest thing to an original political philosophy ever developed in Canada, was at one time influential. Some farmers had sought a solution in one variant or other of monetary reform before Aberhart took up Social Credit. Others had accepted low-tariff anti-monopoly economic liberalism as preached by the Manitoba Progressives. They were believers in single tax, direct democracy, socialism, and the gospel of producer co-operation. Such reasoned analyses of the situation in which the rural community found itself, albeit flavoured with a heady utopianism, had no place in Social Credit; one was required to accept the doctrine on faith or not at all. The critical event of the Alberta retreat from reason came in the series of radio debates between Aberhart and Norman F. Priestley, of the United Farmers in early 1935. Priestley was the man of charm, idealism, and intelligence and Aberhart the skilled purveyor of innuendo and irrelevancy, but in the inflamed mood of many Albertans from the deprivations of the depression as aggravated by Social Credit propaganda it was widely believed that the radio-evangelist had won.

Social Credit as it has come to BC in 1952 is different in many essential respects from the earlier Alberta movement. Most strikingly, perhaps, Mr Bennett's party has little of the genuine idealism so effectively manipulated and exploited by Aberhart. However, the two parties are alike in the challenge they have provided to the elites of their respective provinces.

The strategy of Premier Bennett and his followers is the provocation of other centres of power and influence than the British Columbia electorate. Social Credit labour legislation, its supporters claim, is designed to protect the workers against the 'union bosses.' The provincial administration is niggardly in dealing with the financial needs of the municipalities but gives each resident homeowner an annual cash grant of $50; the Premier announced the week before the June 18 election that he would recommend to the Legislature at its next session that this amount be doubled. The highway and hydro-electric policies of the Government are openly designed to the disadvantage of the urban areas of the Lower Mainland and Vancouver Island and the benefit of the over-represented voters in the interior of the province with whose anti-metropolitan interests and attitudes the Premier closely identifies himself. The procedures by which the assets of the British Columbia Power Corporation were expropriated have worried and angered many members of the corporate business community, although they may continue to play along with Social Credit to keep the socialists out. Representatives of such associations as the provincial civil servants, the teachers, the school trustees, the municipalities, the hospitals, and the University of British Columbia find the Premier inaccessible and some of their representatives have been subjected to discourtesies at his hands. The Government revels in the opposition of the metropolitan newspapers. Truly no one seems to like Social Credit but 'the people.'

Social Credit in British Columbia, like Aberhart in Alberta, has challenged not only the existing leadership of the province but also the standards of decorum and responsibility which usually govern the conduct of public affairs in civilized western communities. The Legislature has simply not been allowed to function effectively and the Leader of the Opposition and other Opposition MLAs have been treated with a lack of courtesy by the Premier and his party supporters. The arbitrary nature of the expropriation procedure in connection with hydroelectric development is well known. The Minister of Highways has reaped a rich harvest of personal publicity from his entanglements with the police and the courts of law, an interesting example of the anti-institutional attitudes of a community not far removed from the frontier period. Important governmental decisions are announced by the Premier without consultation with those most directly affected by them inside or outside provincial employment and Mr Bennett has been secretive about many important matters relating to the new public Hydro Authority. After living in British Columbia one might well be surprised that Dicey could consider parliamentary sovereignty and the rule of law to be complementary principles; Dicey of course took it for granted that parliamentarians would be liberal gentlemen – in raw and remote communities on the west coasts of Africa or North America one cannot reasonably proceed on such a sanguine assumption.

An essential difference between Social Credit and other political parties in Canada is that its strategy is based on what I shall call 'electoral policies,' as opposed to 'group politics.' The traditional parties have for the most part drawn their leaders from corporate business, law, and other high-status groups. The democratic left has looked to other elites in the labour unions, farm organizations, the intellectual world, and the liberal Protestant clergy. So long as the political struggle takes place among these groups it is in a sense 'within the Establishment' and at least carried on by participants who, whatever their degree of commitment to social change, are not usually motivated primarily by *personal* resentment against the existing order. Further, the aspiring politician is more likely than not to enter public life with some experiences in the procedures of rational deliberation, accommodation, and the rule of law which influence our private associations as well as government, and some degree of commitment to these procedures. Characteristically then, the political universe of the traditional politicians is one of groups, a universe to be approached through the circumspect treatment of representatives of particular organized interests. The 'electoral politics' of Social Credit is a less complicated business. The movement has drawn its leaders for the most part from persons of lower educational attainment and status than the other parties – chiropractors and evangelists have, for example, been prominent – and it is difficult to name a prominent Social Creditor who has attained a position of eminence in any other field than politics. These men what got where they are through the electorate alone and they thus pursue the voters' support in a most direct and uninhibited way without the deference to centres of influence and the complex balancing of group interests which is characteristic of other politicians. Because Social Credit leaders have shared relatively little in the rewards of status or organizational position outside of politics, they are able to identify themselves closely with the voters' attitudes, particularly as these attitudes embody resentments against the existing order – resentments of the educated by the uneducated, of metropolitan interests and attitudes by rural and semi-frontier areas, of the denominations by the sects, of the private and public bureaucracies by the small entrepreneur, of the fabric of legality by those who regard law as not wholly beneficent.

It is inevitable that rapid social and economic change will give rise to hostilities, frustrations, and anxieties. The Canadian party system has been moderately successful in containing these feelings, to the extent that they have found expression through political activity, within the framework of a liberal and constitutional tradition. Liberals and Conservatives have, in Shaw's words, gathered money from the rich and votes from the poor with promises to protect each against the other, and in delivering on these promises have performed a necessary ameliorating function. The democratic left has also played a conserving and conservative role. By convincing large numbers of dissatisfied citizens that a social order more to their liking could be reached through mild reforms and that these could be implemented through constitutional procedures, high-status socialist leaders have prevented these frustrations, and genuine idealism of course, from being directed into less constructive channels. (In a curious way reactionary groups like the Chamber of Commerce and the Canadian Medical Association have aided the social democrats in the performance of this function by their inflammatory opposition to even the most moderate measures of reform proposed by the democratic left, and so the extremes of right and left have combined to sustain the illusion that such liberals and constitutionalists as Coldwell and Douglas wish to alter in a fundamental way the social and economic relationships of the existing system.) Social Credit, as I have argued, provides an alternative outlet by which anxieties and resentments can find political expression, an outlet which, like Poujadism in France and the various strands of the American radical right, offers a direct challenge to the liberal tradition.

The strength of Social Credit in three of the Canadian provinces raises for Canadians the fundamental question as to whether in the long run our liberal and parliamentary traditions will prove compatible with democracy. In the immediate future the answer may depend on whether conservatives in the business community and public life choose to regard Social Credit as a variant of conservatism. One may reasonably hope that business leaders in British Columbia will be led to modify their conclusion that Social Credit is the only available alternative to socialism in the light of Mr Bennett's record in the past year, including the rapid expansion of provincially-owned commercial operations. And perhaps we can go on to hope that the federal Conservatives will be responsible and discerning enough not to attempt any deals with the party who in the recent campaign in Quebec ran on the radical and nihilistic slogan 'You have nothing to lose.'

DAVID HELWIG

The Winter of the Daffodils

She had lived a life of continued disappointment, and now she was about to die. Her forceful questioning had driven the doctor quickly from his evasions to the truth which he had thought too harsh for her. He was a very poor judge of character, although he spoke with the weighty calm of one who had the gift of prophecy. What he possessed was enough technical ability to make an accurate prognostication. For her he predicted death.

No doubt he pitied her because she was unmarried, and probably, he saw her life as a desert of frustrated virginity. The doctor, who was not over thirty-five, saw her merely as a name, spinster, aged sixty, and had forgotten that she was exactly the age of the century. After the first war, she and enough of her contemporaries to create a myth had championed a new and romantic freedom. She remembered very clearly that on New Year's Eve of 1924, not really New Year's Eve, almost New Year's Day, she had lain on a leather couch in an empty house while a young man tried awkwardly to undress her. As he fumbled with her clothes, she attempted to count the men who had made love to her in the preceding three years, and when she could not, she laughed and told the young man so. For a moment, he looked puzzled, but he shrugged it off and returned to his task. After what seemed an interminable time, he succeeded in undressing her, made love to her (very poorly as she remembered it, but that might be her own dramatic addition), and got her with child.

She had discovered that a candle which burned at both ends could last an unconscionable length of time. Thoughts of her youth were all too often memories of pleasant diversion when she looked for passionate excess. Yet she had tried to be excessive at one time, tried very hard. In a moment of anger one of the friends of her youth told her that she had turned the sex life of Messalina into a simple problem of logistics; the remark still rankled. Her mind was strong and efficient and it steadfastly refused to be overthrown. Prufrock was not Prince Hamlet and she was not Ophelia; nor was meant to be. She had given herself to men known for the passion or perversity of their desires, and yet, somehow, her life had not seemed excessive. These men had given her pleasure: if not, her situation would have been dramatic and moving for her to remember, but her memories were only occasionally distorted by her taste for drama and on this point she was quite clear: the men had given her pleasure.

She tried to couple in her mind the lust of her young body with the death of her old, tired body. The juxtaposition pleased her and she began to recall as many of the literary statements of it as she could remember. Most of them were from her favourite seventeenth-century writers who had clung tenaciously to both terms of the paradox.

In her youth she had even borne a child, the child conceived on the leather couch on New Year's Eve. It has been remarkably easy. The young man paid, she had no trouble, and a healthy child was given for adoption. At the time she had imagined herself, as an old woman, suspiciously peering at young faces, looking for a chance resemblance. But she had never done it. The child would be about the age of the young doctor. She smiled at the delicious irony that the doctor who pitied her her spinsterhood might be her bastard son.

For some reason, she always recalled her casual lusts before the love affairs and friendships. She wondered if she had ever loved. Not her parents: her father she could not remember and she had never been close to her mother. Not Glenn: although she had lived with him for three years, done his typing, kept the accounts for his little magazine and entertained his friends. If she had ever loved anyone surely it was Tonio who was so embarrassed by his broken English that he had scarcely said a word to her during the single week she had known him, when, each day, he brought her daffodils and spoke only with his eyes and his body. After he had made love to her, he would try to tell her that it was beautiful, but the language would not bend to him and he would grow embarrassed and then silent and bad tempered. Finally he walked out and did not come back. When she remembered Tonio she felt a pang of regret.

When she reached the office she went into the coffee shop next door for a bite of lunch. There ought to have been an exhilaration or a great pain as she ate with the knowledge that she had a severely limited number of meals ahead of her before she died. But she felt only the usual sense of slight distaste at the greasy cutlery set before her.

Outside the window of the coffee shop dead leaves and newspapers blew along the street. The pathetic fallacy, she remarked to herself, that she and nature were dying together. Even that was spoiled. The doctor had said she would probably live until early spring.

She was tempted to take the afternoon off as a sort of morbid celebration of 'period of adjustment,' but she had already adjusted herself to the situation. Until her work was completed on the new novel, she would stay on at her job. Then she would announce her retirement, settle down in the country, and wait to die.

Why in the country? There was some obscure idea in her mind of making her peace with life. The usual dramatic nonsense with which her imagination afflicted her. Much the sanest thing to do would be to stay in Toronto and go on doing a little work at home for as long as she could.

When she walked into her office, she stared distastefully at the corrected proofs on her desk. Their author had talent but he was obnoxious. Each proof was covered with blue specks where he had replaced all the excess commas she had taken out of his manuscript. For some reason he seemed to think that commas could be added in the text of the proof instead of in the margin with the other corrections.

Glenn had been possessed by the same mania for punctuations. She phoned the author and tried to come to a sensible compromise about the commas. When he was obdurate, she grew angry and told him that such punctuation was pretentiously literary. He hung up.

From the page in front of her, she removed only the most infuriating commas and went on to the next one. She supposed her attitude was just another example of the tyranny of common sense over her life. One of her greatest disappointments was the discovery that common sense could have its way and order life satisfactorily according to its small measure. As she continued with the proofs, she wondered whether such a discovery was necessarily a disappointment. Glenn had run his life capably on a small and controlled scale and he seemed content; not just seemed, he was content.

She felt a sudden urge to phone Glenn and talk it over with him, but she decided that she did not yet want to announce it to anyone. Glenn would be shocked. For a giddy moment, she thought of taking a taxi over to his office, walking in and announcing that she was dying. Glenn had a weak heart. If only she liked him either more or less and he was not just the sort of friend he was, she would have told him. It was too bad that there was no-one with whom she wanted to discuss her new knowledge.

There was still in her mind the nagging conflict over staying in the city to work and moving into the country to make her peace. If she had never really been at war, was there any need to make peace?

She left work a few minutes early after she decided that she could no longer stomach the unpleasant personality that spattered the proofs. Her argument with herself was still going on. Moving to the country would be absurd; it was as if she thought some sort of mystical tie with the land could bring her peace. It would be another disappointment, besides the fact that it would be awkward.

When she reached her apartment, she looked around her and wondered if she could spend the winter, the rest of her life, in it. The books along the walls included everything she had wanted to read in the last forty years and quite likely everything she could want to read in the next few months. The pictures on the walls she could not have replaced with anything preferable; the furniture could not have been better; but the apartment did not satisfy her.

While she ate supper, she looked around the room with the same expectation she had felt in the coffee shop of seeing everything with new eyes, eyes that had looked into the face of death. The apartment had not changed for her. It was oppressive.

When she had finished her supper and done the dishes, she sat down with a drink, and as she sat, realized that it would be folly to leave Toronto. She went to her desk and began to work.

Two weeks later she had rented a house in a small town on the lakeshore. It was a simple white frame house that had belonged to a fisherman. At the foot of the garden was a wooden frame with a few scraps of net still on it. Before leaving, the fisherman's widow, who was going to live with a son, had enumerated the flowers and fruits that could be expected in the garden, beginning with the snowdrops which grew against the front porch and proceeding through daffodils, summer flowers and fruit to the last chrysanthemums of the autumn, the deepest gold blooms which grew near the back fence.

When she had explained to the fisherman's energetic widow that she had come to the house to die and would need someone to care for her as she grew weaker, there had been a moment's embarrassed silence and then the woman told her of a former nurse a few houses away who could be hired.

Now Mrs Burney, the nurse, dropped in every day and did some cleaning and occasionally a bit of baking.

'My, Miss Taylor,' she said each day, 'this is a grand house you've got here.' And she would show her pleasure in the house by polishing a piece of furniture. Miss Taylor understood Mrs Burney's appreciation of the house. It was clean, neat and orderly, tasteful in a small-town way, and obviously meant to be lived in and enjoyed. She took a vicarious pleasure in the humanity of the house. Nothing in it was her own except a few clothes and a few books. With one of these books, she would spend most of her day, reading lazily and with little concentration in front of one of the windows and looking out the window to the lake or across the backyard. A flow of life seemed to come into her from the house and the carefully worked garden, now sere and rustling but holding in its fertile soil the bulbs that would grow into crocus and daffodils.

The thought of the garden filled with daffodils reminded her of Tonio who had brought her flowers and his impotent rage at the language that had betrayed him. To remember Tonio pained her and she was pleased. The integrity of this small regret was little but something to go with her into the grave. More and more eagerly she awaited the daffodils until she believed she could feel their life in the ground beneath her. She picked up one of her books and leafed through it until she came to Herrick's poem.

Fair daffadils, we weep to see
You haste away so soone;

As yet the early-rising Sun
Has not attained his Noone.
Stay, stay

Somehow she found the plight of the daffodils more moving than her own. They existed only as a given beauty, and when they died, they gave no more. But she existed, still, as the author, auditor and subject of a lifelong soliloquy which could perhaps be brought to a suitable close. The winter of the daffodils was intensely more moving. As she grew weaker, and her mind began to wander, she forgot the source of her feeling about the daffodils and remembered only that she wanted to see them bloom.

JOHN MEISEL

Election Outcome: A Breather

The main and most immediate function of democratic elections is to decide who is to govern. The recent contest served an additional purpose: its outcome was also likely to determine whether Canada was in the process of revising its traditional 'two plus' party system. Now that all the ballots are counted, it is apparent that on April 8th Canadians refrained from giving a clear and ringing answer to either of the problems posed by the election: they accorded no party a majority of seats in the Commons and they did not settle the future role of, and inter-relationships among, the four parties.

Nevertheless, by placing the Liberals within a ballot's width of a technical majority, they enabled Mr Pearson to form a government and to do so without having to engage in a dramatic shadow play with one or more of the other parties. There is now little doubt that Canada will have a government which, unless it becomes thoroughly reckless, will not have to live in constant fear of a non-confidence vote in the House. It is difficult to say whether any policy or course of action received the voters' mandate, since the Liberals obtained only 42 per cent of the votes, and these were distributed quite unevenly across the country. The only unmistakable verdict concerned the Conservative government: over two-thirds of the voters opposed it, although it received more support than any other party in no less than five provinces.

If there was widespread doubt about the capacity of the decimated Diefenbaker cabinet to provide capable government, no such fears are likely to attach to the new Pearson team. It is made up of persons of outstanding talent, and whatever other characteristics they display in the next few years, there is every expectation that they will provide an efficient and incisive administration. But the members of the new cabinet are not only gifted and strong personalities; they have in the past displayed a wide diversity of views. If they are to function smoothly as a team for any length of time, they will have to work out a coherent social and economic philosophy or, if this term is thought unduly to inflate the language, at least a reasonably homogeneous social and political outlook. The failure of the Liberals to win a clear majority will inevitably influence the way in which their leaders seek to shape party policies. Those who belong to what is usually thought of as the right wing will point to the fact that many 1963 Liberal gains were made because normally Conservative voters switched to Mr Pearson. To hold them, so it will be argued, the government will have to pursue a conservative policy. Others are certain to emphasize that it was the continued support for Mr Diefenbaker of what might be termed the non-Tory elements in the Conservative party and the continued urban strength of the NDP which stood in the way of a Liberal majority. Only if the party can capture some of these 'progressive' bastions, so the left wing will argue, can it hope to recreate a genuinely national base of Liberal support. The ambiguity of the election results, therefore, will be exploited by both wings of the party. In these conditions, the leader will be in a particularly advantageous position for pressing his own brand of Liberalism on his colleagues and followers.

But Mr Pearson's skills as a creative politician will have their greatest scope in dealing with the problems now confronting our party system. For the last four elections have shown that it is no longer safe to assume that Canadian Parliaments must, through a 'made-in-Canada' law of political stability, be graced by the presence of a party commanding a majority of seats. Four parties have occupied our national political stage in the last thirty years, and it was either good luck or the skill of the party leaders which gave us majority governments during most of this period. Since 1957, it has become increasingly apparent that either our luck or the skill of the leaders was running out. The 1963 results indicate that we are not out of the woods yet. The centrifugal forces which have prevented the election of majority governments may have been halted but they have certainly not been reversed. Under these circumstances, the politicians will have to acknowledge that there are more ways than one of skinning a beaver: either the 'majority system' must be reinstated or the parties must learn to live in a House of minorities. So far, the politicians of the major parties, as well as large numbers of voters, have refused to contemplate a world in which minority governments are considered normal. There is, therefore, little point in speculating about what adjustments would be necessary, or are likely to be made wittingly or unwittingly, during the present Parliament, for the sake of operating a genuine multi-party system in Canada.

General reluctance to accept anything but a system in which the government relies on a clear parliamentary majority cannot exorcize these cold realities of the recent election: no party won a majority of seats; 26 per cent of the vote (according to provisional results) was cast against the old parties; Social Credit strength in Quebec increased by four percentage points; support for the NDP has not diminished; the rural-urban split in Canada is greater than ever; and the Prairies are as solidly Conservative as in 1962. Given these facts, what are the chances that the traditional party system will be re-established? Powerful forces are at work which, if encouraged, may make majority governments again the Canadian norm. But what appear to be equally strong tendencies may operate in the opposite direction, thus leaving the future still highly uncertain.

Before examining these two possible trends, it should be noted that in the opinion of most observers, the Conservative party will remain on the Canadian scene, but that some time may elapse before it can fully absorb, adjust to, and capitalize on, the changes wrought by Mr Diefenbaker. In view of this, it is further assumed by those who argue that the old party system has been, or is about to be, re-instituted, that only the Liberals can at present, and in the immediate future, become an old-fashioned 'majority' party. To do so they will, of course, have to increase their parliamentary standing when they next go to the people. Several contingencies nourish the hopes of those who expect that the Liberals will obtain a majority of seats at the next election:

(1) The ability of the Liberals and Conservatives to obtain a majority of parliamentary seats has always depended on two factors: the combined strength of the 'third' parties and the gap separating the two old parties. The most significant difference between the 1962 and the 1963 elections, in this respect, is the fact that although the minor parties' representation in the Commons has dropped only by eight, the gap between the Liberals and Conservatives has grown from sixteen to forty-six. Liberals expect that Conservative fortunes will decline further with Mr Diefenbaker's retirement, an event likely to take place before the next election. The reasonable expectation that the Conservative revival will be a slow one consequently leads to Liberal hopes that the gap between their party and their traditional rival will increase before the strength of the minor parties is reduced.

(2) A redistribution of parliamentary seats must be undertaken before the next election and is certain to increase urban representation at the expense of rural voters. This development will probably strengthen the Liberals and weaken the Conservatives.

(3) The Liberals' control of the present government will permit them to introduce policies (and to deploy patronage) which will make their party the choice of a much larger number of voters than was the case in the recent election.

(4) The public's dislike of minority governments, evidenced noticeably during the last stages of the recent campaign, will manifest it-

self again in the future and will further weaken the appeal of the minor parties. This is reckoned to favour the Liberals more than the still disarrayed Conservatives.

(5) Social Credit's instability, particularly in Quebec, will reduce that party's appeal and give the Liberals added strength in French Canada.

(6) On the other hand, the probability that the smaller parties will survive in some form is likely to aid the Liberal party, provided they do not become too strong. By dividing the anti-Liberal votes, as they did so frequently in the period preceding 1957, they will assist the election of Liberal MPs.

Among the circumstances which might prevent Canada from returning to its old 'two plus' party system, the following are particularly relevant in the light of the 1963 results:

(1) Centrifugal economic and cultural forces make it exceedingly difficult for a party to pursue policies which will give it substantial *national* support. The problems confronting the country which must be contained by the party system have become so stubborn that it may no longer be possible for a single party to come to grips with them without alienating important groups of voters. Regional and cultural differences may be too great to be reconciled within even the immense and accommodating bosom of either of the old parties.

(2) Quebec presents a special instance of the general point just made. Regardless of what happens to Mr Caouette and his followers, the parties will find it exceedingly difficult to devise policies which will respond adequately to the nationalist and social awakening of Quebec without offending other parts of the country. And the Liberals, who appear to have re-established themselves in their former stronghold, have in fact obtained no greater a proportion of votes there than in 1958, when they were generally considered to have been rejected by the Quebec voters. That the Dominion and Quebec governments are of the same party complexion will also create an inescapable hazard for Mr Pearson's government.

(3) Despite colossal effort, Liberal strength in the Prairies has increased very little. The Pearson party has a decidedly eastern appearance and will have a hard time competing with the Diefenbaker-Hamilton impact on the Prairies, at least in the next few years.

(4) While the revival of the Conservative party may be a slow one, there is considerable evidence that many traditionally Conservative voters who backed Liberal candidates in the last election did so because of hostility towards Mr Diefenbaker. If, in the next election, the party fights under a different leader, it may regain some of this traditional Conservative support, particularly in the urban centres. This would increase the chances not only of Conservative candidates but also of those running for newer parties, particularly the NDP.

(5) Overall NDP support has not diminished in the recent election. It would be rash to assume that the party is facing anything like the crisis certain to afflict Social Credit. To the extent that NDP voters are concentrated in the cities, the party may cut into Liberal strength in the next election, benefitting from redistribution, inevitable dissatisfaction with the party in power, and a possible revival of Conservative support.

(6) The very success of the Pearson government may, to a degree, weaken its appeal. For if, as is to be expected, the government performs effectively, this will weaken one of the most telling arguments used against the third parties: that a minority government is certain to be inefficient.

It is impossible to weigh exactly the merit of the points briefly noted here, but they must be taken into account when considering whether majority rule will be re-established in Canada. Enough has been said to make it abundantly clear that it would be premature to sit back in the comforting belief that the traditional party system is about to be revived and that we are certain to embark on an era of political stability. All that has happened in the recent election is that Canada has been granted a breather. How it is to be utilized will depend on the effectiveness of the politicians. Mr Pearson's greatest test may not be in how he and his team run the country, but in how he leads the Liberal party. For if he neglects this latter aspect of his office, he may find that his administration will not have time enough to complete the tasks upon which it is now embarking. He is well supplied with able executives, administrators, and intellectuals. Time alone will tell whether he and his colleagues are also blessed with the skills of the professional politician that in the past have maintained a reasonably stable party system.

KENNETH McNAUGHT
Uncle Sam Again

At the peak of the February crisis of confidence in the House of Commons Mr Robert Thompson reminded us that 'the Americans are our friends, whether we like it or not.' While slips of the tongue are not entirely unprecedented amongst Social Credit spokesmen, this one was singular in its revelation of the Canadian frame of mind. Mr Thompson's remark should be enshrined beside another aphorism: 'Americans are benevolently uninformed about Canada; Canadians are malevolently informed about the United States.'

The grain of truth in such comments explains why it is possible for Mr Rusk, and what is left of the American State Department, to make quite substantial errors of judgment about Canadian politics; it also explains the unhappy tendency of Canadians to anticipate all sorts of slights and pressures. Even so, and following the barrage of earnest warnings from our business leaders to avoid anti-Americanism, it is well to recall some aspects of our North American past that are bound to influence contemporary Canadians, either consciously or unconsciously.

For some 145 of the 188 years since the outbreak of the American Revolutionary War Canada lived in recurrent fear of conquest by the southern giant. The actual invasions of 1775 and 1812 were followed by successive waves of manifest destiny sentiment in the United States, complicated by Irish-American anti-British irritability. The border in the 1830s, 1840s and 1860s was crossed many times. In the last quarter of the nineteenth century influential Americans regarded Canada as an inevitable area of their manifest destiny. In 1903 Teddy Roosevelt was willing to swing the Big Stick over the Alaska Boundary Commission and thereby spark one of the biggest explosions of 'anti-Americanism,' the aftermath of which was the defeat of the Laurier government in 1911.

Beyond question, the survival of Canada in the nineteenth century was the result of British sea power, a fact noted sadly by the American naval expansionist, Captain A.T. Mahan. Until 1920, what organization there was of Canadian military defence was based upon the assumption that any conceivable threat would come from the United States.

Through the 1920s and 1930s all this was changed. By the time the American neutrality laws were emasculated following the outbreak of war in 1939 we were ready to enter a military agreement with the United States, in the form of the 1940 Permanent Joint Board on Defence. Thus began what Professor Underhill has bluntly termed 'the American century of our history.' After the war, with the blessing of our continentalists, the military alliance moved rapidly through the broad 1946 military agreements to NATO in 1949 and NORAD in 1957. By these we became committed to the United States far more completely than we had ever permitted ourselves to be bound in peacetime to the British Empire. Thus in military history the American impact has always been decisive: first as a threat, second as the control centre of continental defence strategy.

The political impact has been very similar. French Canada has always fought for survival against the metropolitan controls of the Hudson Valley as well as against the southern social-economic magnetism. And English Canada was founded, in large part, by refugees from the Republican Revolution. Notwithstanding the mutual suspicions entertained by French and English inside Canada, both have consistently rejected political union with the United States, despite the strong, temporary attractions of such a solution in times of depression.

The American Civil War illustrates best the reasons for Canadian political resistance. Ever since the 1763 settlement and the 1774 Quebec Act both British and English-Canadian leaders had eschewed compulsions as a solvent for racial-cultural differences. Thus, when in 1861 Abraham Lincoln called up the first 75,000 men to disprove by force the Southern doctrines of nullification and secession much Canadian opinion was sympathetic to the Southern Confederacy. Canadian softness on slavery did not mean approval of the 'peculiar institution' itself. It resulted from the logical French recognition of where such a policy of force, if approved, would lead in Canada; and from similar English-Canadian recognition that the Lincoln policy expressed pointedly the doctrine that in North America a simple numerical majority must rule. This recognition was sharpened as Lincoln's Secretary of State Seward reiterated his deep faith that Canada should be acquired by the Northern majority as a by-product of the war.

Debating their own future in 1865 Canadians made it clear that they favoured the compromise politics of Henry Clay and John C. Calhoun rather than the Lincoln-Seward principle. Strengthened by a continued Canadian attachment to the pattern of British constitutional evolution, the BNA Act reflected the decision for compromise and entente. Despite a growing tendency to use American terminology in our political conventions we have continued to reject the curious absolutism of American majorities. The American political influence upon Canada, then, has been as important as the military but has been much more negative in nature. Periodically, French Canada threatens to get out of bed, thus reminding us of the un-American nature of our political marriage.

Political and military influences have been conditioned by the love-hate relationship flowing from the social-economic impact of the United States. As the New Frontier writer, Walt Rostow, has brilliantly recorded, American economic growth has always been a couple of stages ahead of Canadian. While we have become increasingly industrialized, in the twentieth century the process has depended more and more upon American investment in Canada. Although the investment has been welcomed, it has resulted in ownership by Americans of a majority of our manufacturing plants and of the great preponderance of our raw materials extracting and processing industry. Concurrently, the higher prosperity and broader economic opportunities south of the border drained off many of our best-trained people each year.

Nor need one labour the obvious impact of mass communications in television, films, and magazines.

Much of what Canadians see and receive from the United States they like; but they hate the implications. Clearly they are no longer real proprietors in their own land, and they are fearful of many of the trends of American life which they suspect foretell their own future in manners and morals.

For purposes of interpreting and projecting the Canadian reaction, it is worth returning briefly to the historical pattern. When we were dependent on Britain for defence, investment and, to a large degree, for markets, we fought British political control with mounting vigour until we got the Statute of Westminster. But it was just as we secured political independence from Britain that we began slipping under the American sway. One may thus expect a steady fight against the application of American *political* influence.

Two differences observable in the new pattern are striking. The American political influence is *following* the economic and military, while in our British relationship the reverse was true. Also, the extent of our economic, social, and military integration with the United States is greater than was ever the case with our British relationship in the twentieth century. Thus the American impact is growing rather than diminishing and the new factors of continental defence will keep adding to the temptation toward a political hegemony.

Present tensions result from growing Canadian awareness of these implications rather than from any underhanded anti-American campaign, as darkly hinted by Underhill continentalists. While liking Babylon, Canadians also fear it, and their resistance will be increasingly on political and historical grounds. For example, although we may not admire Fidel Castro any more than we approved of slavery, we show a real sympathy for the Cuban position. Canadians listened with increasingly quizzical comprehension as the American executive explained after the Bay of Pigs that the only thing wrong with the operation was that it failed. President Kennedy's doctrine that the United States has a right to intervene anywhere in the hemisphere that a government 'incompatible' with the American system comes to power seemed to generalize dangerously from Cuban events.

Compatibility with the American system takes on heightened meaning as we hurtle further into the nuclear age. Because of the nature of the nuclear alliance system the United States is bound to take an ever more intimate interest in our politics just at the time when her indirect influence through mass-media and investment reaches almost the saturation point. Conversely, to retain any real control over either our domestic or foreign policies, Canadians will *have* to be anti-American.

The trouble arises principally from two sources. First, while it is possible to be anti-American in the sense of wishing to regain control of Canada, the proponents of such a policy can be easily smeared as appealing to emotional chauvinism, and some of them are tempted to exploit nationalist emotions stemming from our historical experience. How strong these emotions are was revealed in February when all party leaders found it advisable to label the State Department's clarification of its position on nuclear weapons as interference in Canadian politics. But while such reaction was ill-founded as long as we agree to stay inside a tightly-organized nuclear network it was mild compared to what will happen as the Americans begin to apply more direct pressure.

The second source of trouble is to be found in the growing reluctance of our financial and industrial leaders to accept the kind of economic reorganization that will be required if we decide to recover control of our own country. Recognition of what is implied by genuine independence has already led Toronto's Tory papers to switch their political allegiance to the party that recommends acceptance of continentalism, of obeying State and Pentagon and of joining the Organization of American States so that we may help Uncle Sam keep the banana republics and South America in line also. The revolution in Canadian politics thus reflects directly the American control of our financial system and industrial resources. The kinds of economic planning and collective initiative that alone can recover our independence are not overwhelmingly attractive to Bay Street.

Unhappily the 1963 election campaign, with its party revolution, has obscured the necessary basis of party division. Nevertheless, that basis is likely to become increasingly recognized in the next three or four years, especially as Canadians realize that their defence and foreign policies have been dictated by the real owners of their country.

MARGARET ATWOOD
Mad Mother Ballad

The day after you were born
I found you on a green lawn
Dressed in a sailorsuit;
You were already fullgrown.

I knew you were my son
Because of your scowl, and the hair
Low on your forehead, and the holes
Worn in your shoesoles.

You curled like a child of six
And rested your man's head on my knee
But you had inherited my malice
And my bitter habits:

You closed your mouth on the vein
In my neck, and swelled up like a leech;
You grasped your fist round my heart
And squeezed the pulp from its drained rind.

Now I walk my former paths
Having taken back my heart and blood:
A red strawberry beats in my side
Rain pulses at my wrists.

You are shrunken again from hunger.
I am looking for a green lawn,
Carrying your day old infant corpse
Crumpled in my clenched hand.

RAMSAY COOK
A Time to Break Silence

The motherland for us, is all of Canada, that is to say a federation of distinct races and autonomous provinces. The nation which we wish to see develop, is the Canadian nation, composed of French Canadians and English Canadians, that is two elements separated by language and religion, and by the legal dispositions necessary for the conservation of their respective traditions, but united in an attachment of brotherhood, in a common attachment to a common motherland.

Henri Bourassa
Le Nationaliste, April 3, 1904

It should be appreciated that we have been waiting since 1867. We have been patient. It is difficult to ask a people to keep on waiting when that people has known, since the month of September 1959, a climate of freedom.

Maurice Sauvé MP
House of Commons, May 22, 1963

Time is of the essence ... I know Quebec ... there are a lot of others there thinking – 'What's the use?' – inside four or five years there will be a new Canada or Quebec will be out.

René Lévesque
Toronto, June 1, 1963

More and more the leaders of Quebec speak with a strident impatience about the pressing need for a new look at the essential structure of all aspects of Canadian life. Their impatience is, perhaps, difficult for the average English Canadian to understand. It is at least partly explained by the sharp realization by Quebec's public men that many of the forces that have been let loose in the past four years are now almost out of control. Mr Maurice Sauvé concluded a recent speech by noting that 'if we want to be our own masters at home, it does not mean that we want to separate ourselves from the others, though – and here I am weighing my words carefully – we find more and more in the province of Quebec, people who do not expect anything either from Ottawa or from the rest of Canada.' René Lévesque was even more blunt when he remarked, 'I am a 40 year old moderate – believe it or not – there are young people behind me who make me feel nervous.'

Yet it is not merely the growing strength of separatism and quasi-separatism (the latter existing even in official places as Pierre Laporte's statement in the Quebec Legislature recently indicated) which has caused Quebec leaders to grow impatient. Their impatience is also a reaction to what André Laurendeau has called 'The Silence of English Canada.' Hearing a babel of tongues expressing not always very specifically, Quebec's dissatisfactions, English Canadians have tended to react in two ways. First, some (though fewer than might have some years ago) have concluded that Quebec is just passing through one of its periodic orgies of nationalist breast-beating and should be ignored until it returns to its senses. A second type of reaction has come from those who say: let Quebec list its precise grievances and demands and then we will see what can be done. Sometimes this reply comes from people with a genuine lack of knowledge and confusion, sometimes it stems from a belief that Quebec has no genuine grievances and will have to admit it if specifics are demanded.

While both of these reactions, especially the latter, are understandable, neither is good enough; indeed both are dangerous. It must first be understood that Quebec today is not just passing through a phase of nationalism that will eventually disappear and the *status quo ante* readily be restored. French-Canadian nationalism is much more powerful, much more deeply rooted in the masses, and much more creative and positive than it has ever been before. As a creative force it should be welcomed, not derided or feared by English Canadians. But it could also become destructive, as the fringe groups stretching from M. Chaput's separatist party to the FLQ indicate. It could destroy or at least permanently damage the association between French and English in Canada. That is why it is foolhardy to ignore it.

It is just as dangerous to sit back and await a complete formulation of demands by Quebec itself. The French-Canadian community is in such a tumultuous mood that not even the most influential politicians (except the outright separatists) dare to formulate any final statement for fear of being swept away by the waves of a new, more radical movement within nationalist thought. Obviously this is an extremely dangerous situation, for the mood of discontent is becoming more important than the specific discontents themselves. This is the kind of atmosphere in which emotion could completely replace reason, ultimatums become substitutes for negotiations and even, in the extreme, revolution replace constitutional and legal practices.

The task before English Canadians who desire to prevent their country from lapsing into chaos is to break silence. First we must try to understand what is taking place in Quebec, and why it is taking place. Second, we must try to respond positively by attempting to formulate for ourselves what we believe to be the reasons for the present 'passive resistance' of French Canadians towards Confederation. Having done this, we must then – and this is more important – begin to think about what we are willing and able to do to redress the legitimate grievances of French Canada. There are a number of questions which we must seriously ask ourselves. Are we in the English-speaking provinces willing to re-consider our past, deplorable attitude to public support for the kind of schools that would satisfy the cultural aspirations of French Canadians outside Quebec? Are we ready to reconsider our attitude to the status of the French language in the legislatures, law courts, and publicly-owned corporations in English Canada? Are we willing to explore even the possibility that our federal system may require some radical modification to meet the changed circumstances of the 1960s?

If we could answer yes to all or even some of these questions, we could then formulate a program of specific, prospective reforms which French-Canadian leaders might be able to use – though not necessarily fully accept – to help to reduce the emotional temper of Quebec and to commence a more rational discussion.

Canada is, after all, a country which belongs

to both French and English Canadians. French Canadians are not now satisfied with the manner in which our common community life is organized. Therefore, by definition, English Canadians must bear a share of the responsibility for rectifying the situation, for the problem is not exclusively English Canadian or French Canadian – it is just Canadian.

Prime Minister Pearson's splendid speech on December 17, 1962, advocating a Royal Commission on biculturalism indicated that he had a clear grasp of the roots of our present problem. In his recent contribution to the debate on the address in reply to the speech from the throne, he defined the assumptions from which the next steps should be taken when he remarked, 'Quebec, which is a province different from the other provinces because it is a motherland to people who live in other provinces as well as being a province of Canada, needs the means to remain Quebec ... By the same token ... Canada needs the means to be Canada ... There is no conflict here ... There is merely the need for partnership. The aspirations of Quebec, the cultural identity Quebec wishes to sustain and develop, mastery in our own home, these things which the people of Quebec are asserting would not be possible within a weak country.'

It is easier, as Mr Pearson, Mr Lesage, and every other serious Canadian must know, to state the general position than to provide for its practical implementation. Conflicts do not disappear simply by ignoring them or by declaring their non-existence. Much hard thinking, hard bargaining, creative political leadership, and good will are necessary to resolve our present conflicts. Right now the first necessary step is for English Canada to break silence and admit that the problem does not rest only with the federal government, but with all Canadians. To refuse to make this admission is to deny, implicitly, the existence of Canada as a community. And then the fact may not be slow in catching up with the implied theory.

H. BLAIR NEATBY

The Present Discontents: A Proposal

What do the French Canadians want? English Canadians have followed the activities of Lévesque, Caouette, and the FLQ with fascination; we now have a surprising number of pundits who keep explaining to us why French Canada is dissatisfied. But there is still no consensus on what will satisfy Quebec. As the *Globe and Mail* points out, even the French Canadians themselves are not sure. Until they make up their minds, English Canadians are apparently content to wait.

Instead of waiting to be told what the French Canadians want, we, as English Canadians, should be asking ourselves what we want. The nature of our federal union is at stake. How can we calmly wait for our compatriots to decide the kind of union they want without becoming involved in the discussion? If the Canadian union has any importance for us, the decision should be arrived at by a dialogue between English and French speaking Canadians. If we wait, French Canada has no alternative but to reach a consensus independently and present us with an ultimatum. What happens if we find the ultimatum unacceptable? Can we expect our compatriots to apologize for their presumption and start over again? An ultimatum leaves no room for negotiation or compromise. If we want to preserve the union we must get involved in the debate now.

Our first assumption must be that we cannot expect a union which conforms completely to our desires any more than French Canadians can expect one which conforms completely to theirs. Neither *le fait français* nor *le fait anglais* can be ignored and the union must make possible the survival of both. Union was only possible in 1867 because the Fathers of Confederation understood this; it is only possible today if we understand it.

English Canadians should admit that in the past they have only grudgingly accepted the existence of French Canada. On many occasions we have tried to impose policies which ignored or even threatened its existence. We insisted on participation in the South African war and insisted on conscription in two world wars; we tried to suppress separate schools in Manitoba and instruction in French in Ontario separate schools. It is true that conscription, as an example, would have been put into effect sooner and implemented more effectively if French Canada had not existed but it would be difficult to defend this as an honest compromise.

Our reluctance to accept the French Canadians as equal citizens explains why we are not participating in the present debate on the nature of the union. What we really want is to preserve the *status quo*. We are not ready to discuss possible changes in the union because we would rather keep it the way it is. We admit that French Canadians have survived and, presumably, concede that they will always be with us. We can even take some pride in *our* tolerance and *our* patience which has made this survival possible. But we are not proud to be part of a bicultural country.

Today the French Canadians resent being tolerated. They want to be admitted to a partnership. They want to change the nature of the federal union. They want, in other words, to upset the *status quo*. And if we English Canadians have any political sense, we will realize that their determination is now a political fact. More than a hundred years ago, Earl Grey recognized that: 'It cannot be too distinctly acknowledged that it is neither possible nor desirable to carry on the government of any of the British provinces in North America in opposition to the opinion of its inhabitants.' We have applauded these sentiments ever since; they are enshrined in every oratorical memorial to responsible government. It is time we applied the same principle to the present situation.

If we can accept this principle, we can then discuss with our compatriots what kind of a union is possible. Agreement will not be easy. English Canadians, it is clear, do not want a weak confederacy in which the provinces delegate only the most limited authority to the central government. But this is what many French Canadians are proposing. Is there any acceptable compromise?

One approach, in my opinion, is to have the federal government promote biculturalism. Bicultural crumbs such as bilingual cheques or bilingual civil servants at Ottawa are not a sustaining diet; French Canadians outside Quebec have been starved too long. Let us admit that a resident of British Columbia can be a Canadian citizen even if he speaks French. Instead of a mess of potage let us offer him his birthright. To put it briefly, I think the federal government should take over full responsibility for the primary and secondary education of the French or English minority in each province. In the English-speaking provinces it would provide French-language schools for the minorities there and in Quebec it would administer the English-language schools.

This proposal sounds frighteningly unorthodox. It would extend the federal authority instead of restricting it. Even more outrageous, it would mean a federal encroachment on the sacrosanct provincial autonomy in the field of education. But, radical as it sounds, the proposal at least has the merit of accepting biculturalism as a national policy. French Canadians outside Quebec would no longer be second-class citizens threatened by assimilation. The position of the minority in Quebec would not be significantly altered but the concern of English Canadians for their compatriots in Quebec would be a guarantee of just treatment of the French Canadians in federal schools outside the province.

The assumption is that until biculturalism becomes a federal responsibility it will be nobody's responsibility. Provincial government cannot be expected to give sufficient weight to this problem because, from the provincial point of view, the French-Canadian minority is often less important than other minority groups. It is absurd to think, for example, that Premier Manning or Premier Bennett will ever dedicate themselves to fostering the partnership of English and French Canadians. Quebec, on the other hand, is justly proud of its treatment of the English minority, but no French Canadian will claim that Quebec has been able to do enough for French Canadian minorities beyond its provincial boundaries. The partnership of the two cultural groups must be a national partnership; it requires a national policy.

Partnership must mean more than mere survival. French Canadian minorities should not have to expend all their energies in a struggle for existence. Instead of being tolerated they should be encouraged to be themselves – which means that they must have French language institutions in the areas in which they live. Some of these institutions already exist. Some provinces have separate schools in which the language of instruction is French. There are French television stations outside Quebec and there are French radio stations as far west as the Rockies – in this sphere the federal government has already accepted some responsibility for biculturalism. Federal French language schools would only be an extension of this principle.

Such schools would also make it possible for English-Canadian children to attend French-language schools if their parents wanted them to learn French. For the first time for many of these children there would be an opportunity to become bilingual.

What of the province of Quebec? The first reaction to this proposal would probably be horror at the encroachment on its provincial authority. But Quebec must eventually face the contradiction between minority rights and provincial rights. The extension of provincial powers may mean greater autonomy for the five million French Canadians in Quebec but it means less security for the million in other provinces. Separatism, which is the extreme form of provincial rights, is the antithesis of biculturalism. And even if the province of Quebec is conceded special powers because it is not 'une province comme les autres,' the position of the French-Canadian minorities would not be improved.

The province of Quebec has always shown great concern for the fate of these minorities. Its will to help has often been frustrated by the assertion of provincial rights by the other provinces. If the position of the minorities can be improved in some other way, Quebec should welcome the opportunity. By making the federal government the protector of these minorities, the obstacle of anglophobe provincial governments would be overcome.

The Lesage government might well find the proposal attractive after the first horrified shock. It would, like the other provinces – and to a greater extent than many of them – be relieved of a major expense. Mr Lesage and Mr Lévesque might prefer to use the money they now spend on English-language schools for their ambitious plans of economic development. Obviously, this is a decision which only they can make. But even if they rejected the scheme the federal government could still establish French-language schools in the other provinces. Presumably Quebec would at least approve of this recognition of biculturalism in the rest of Canada.

The Canadian question is too complicated to be solved by any one proposal. Biculturalism is only part of the equation. Minority rights have no necessary connection with provincial rights, and some agreement will still have to be reached on the proper balance between the financial resources and financial responsibilities of the federal and provincial governments. But a national policy to promote biculturalism would at least eliminate one contentious issue from the debate, and would foster the sense of partnership which is the prerequisite for all negotiations. And the co-existence of French and English Canadians in all parts of Canada could mean that when we celebrate our second centennial we will all have learned to be proud of our double heritage.

A.W. PURDY

The Undertaker

They were in love. Joe waited every weekday morning at the footbridge for Beth Holliday to meet him, and they walked the rest of the way to school together. In the warm summer evenings after homework was finished they strolled arm in arm beside the river, where an oily slick from the creosote works rainbowed the water. They had achieved the 'going together' status, which conferred near-adult dignity among other teen-agers.

Beth was a very pale girl of Scandinavian origins. Her manner was serious, none of her schoolmates had ever seen her smile. Blue lakes for eyes, with blue shadows under them; blonde hair worn long – something of the remote princess, the Lady of Shalott. No mirror through which she saw the reflected world, but a heart condition served much the same purpose. Joe never did find out the medical language that characterized this mysterious frailness, and he did not ask. But it awed him, made him regard her with the solicitude of a naturalist for a rare and delicate species not far from extinction. He carried her schoolbooks, elbowed a path through crowds at Saturday night movies, continually interposed his chunky body and florid face between the tall pale girl and the muscular hurrying world.

Probably it was good for him. Joe was an unimaginative youth, but he felt something of a different fibre from himself in the girl; different also from the shrieking, giggling menage of swaying teen-age females at school football games. She talked of books, the poetry of John Keats and Shelley. The romance of Lancelot and Guinivere, Paris and Helen, Abelard and Heloise – people the bewildered Joe had never heard of. She accepted the red-faced homage he bestowed on her, not with any superiority but a solemn eagerness all her own.

There was no doubt that in the pre-Joe years she had been lonely. Medical restrictions prevented the usual games of childhood. Her own temperament as well as illness forced her into the introspection of books and music. And Joe was a red-faced wind devil who inexplicably stopped whirling in order to be near her. Once she asked him 'Why do you like me?' Of course he hadn't been able to answer. 'Because I don't laugh and run like the other girls?'

'I guess that's it,' Joe said, searching his mind earnestly. 'Why don't you laugh sometimes? That wouldn't hurt you, would it?'

'No, but I can enjoy things without laughing. My mother told me the things that make people laugh always come from doing something I can't do. They'd make my heart go too fast. So I got out of the habit of laughing.' She looked at him anxiously. 'Am I too serious?'

The great blue shadows of her eyes turned on him like deep lakes whose meaning was too transparent for Joe to fathom. She put her hand on his, the warm mysterious touch of her illness enthralling him. 'If I kissed you,' he blurted, 'would it – would it –?'

'I don't think so. Do you want to?' Calmly she bent her white face down and touched his lips. Joe was astonished, for the sweet coolness of her face was like rain. It was not like being kissed by a girl at all, with hot freckles and snub nose mashed against his own sun burned face. He was so astonished he did not want to kiss her again, but went home more bewildered than ever by the mysterious attractions of Beth Holliday. His furious nature was stilled in her quietness. He bathed himself in her romantic fancies, cool dreams in which were infinite distance overhung by mists that never allowed him to see the ending of any story.

Gradually he came to feel he had arrived at the finish of a love affair, but the end was the same as the middle and the beginning. As if they had been married a long time and grown old together, all their children gone away, leaving them the timeless calm of aftermath in which was no urgency, but a slow waiting for death. She was 17.

One day in school Joe noticed a pair of legs. They were brown, rather short legs, with a girl attached. She grinned at him and he grinned back. On the weekend they went swimming, Joe chasing her round and round the raft anchored a hundred yards from the beach. He chased her afterwards, down the narrow sandstrip in the sun, pursued her into moonlight, brown legs flashing ahead and waiting to be caught.

He left school that year, having developed sufficient speed of foot to overtake a succession of brown girls, freckled girls, red-lipped girls – pursuing them into streets and restaurants and sometimes grounding them at last in sunless, old fashioned front parlours with 'Thou shalt nots' prominent on faded wallpaper. But he did. For they were always caught. There was some cool quality about Joe's red face that attracted females. He didn't try to figure it out; all the nascent forces of adolescence bursting inside him at once allowed no time for such introspection.

The town's only undertaker at that time was old John Clegg, whose assistant had recently departed elsewhere to set up his own establishment. Old Clegg was touching 70 when Joe applied for a job, and not in the best of health either. Joe's junior matriculation certificate was the open sesame. He took up his new duties with zest and the peculiar coolness he had acquired before leaving high school. After two years of learning the rudiments and niceties of the embalming business at a school in Toronto (graduating second in his class), Joe took over more and more of the duties old Clegg had delegated to his previous assistant. He knew the exact mixture of glycerine and formaldehyde to pour into the round glass water cooler and its pumping apparatus. He sterilized the knives and chrome instruments in the manner of one born to the job.

At first the cadavers had nauseated him. He had to retire to the bathroom when first witnessing the old man's deft slicing of a carotid artery, but recovered in time to assist at his own gruesome initiation. Old Clegg informed him that the carotid was the best place for insertion of a rubber tube that pumped embalming fluid into the corpse.

'Some says it ain't,' the old man muttered, with liver spotted hands steady on the dead man's neck. 'But the carotid's a main artery, easy to find. Now watch!' Clegg slit the dead man's throat like a chicken, cut into the red, fruit-like arterial tissue, deftly inserting the rubber tube. 'Now here's the jugular,' he informed his apprentice with a grin. 'It's right beside the carotid. Shove that other tube in there to take the blood as it gets pumped out by the embalming fluid coming in.'

Joe's mouth and throat were dry, but he did

as he was told. Clegg nodded approval. 'Corpses don't mind much if you can't find that artery first time around, but it makes a messy job. Especially if it's a woman. Ya gotta make damn sure the incision is covered.' He started the pumping apparatus, and Joe watched the level of pale, green embalming fluid descend in its round glass bowl. Later he poured the bucket of blood sloshing down the sink, rinsing afterwards.

Once in those early days of his apprenticeship there was a minor catastrophe. Joe forgot to place the tube carrying outgoing blood into a bucket provided for that purpose. Blood was filmed a quarter inch thick on the floor when old Clegg noticed it, cursing Joe for his mistake with lucid amiability. After mopping and scrubbing for nearly an hour on that occasion, Joe was never so forgetful again.

Ten years after entering the undertaking business Joe was given his own nervous and shaking apprentice, and Clegg went into retirement. 'You do all the work and I'll take the money,' the old man cackled. 'Sides, it's getting so my hands won't hold still long enough to do a job.' He held the shaking liver-spotted hands up for Joe to inspect. 'You'll be doin the same job on me one of these days.' He looked at the younger man shrewdly. 'You got any money? Enough to buy the business, I mean?'

Joe hadn't, but the bank was obliging enough to lend it to him at low interest rates. Two years later old Clegg died, and as the old man had predicted, Joe 'did a job' on him. Standing in the imitation mahogany panelled chapel he considered business matters with some satisfaction. Appreciation of the young man's professional services was rising steadily. He attended the United Church on Sundays (when not otherwise engaged), and sang a good strong tenor, which made the minister shake his hand approvingly after the sermon. Besides, Joe was able to throw a fair amount of business in the reverend's direction.

The church was an excellent place to make business and social contacts, Joe had found. In the coloured sunlight, shaped into curves and rectangles by the tinted glass windows, he sometimes allowed his eyes to rest on a charming face or trim legs, being careful to keep his chin poised at the same upward angle while doing so. Nothing like an undertaker for respectability, he reflected, his good tenor joining the gravel throated congregation in 'Throw out the Lifeline' – then settling down on the oak bench to mentally exclude the sermon, vacant eyes staring into space while the hard pinpoint of his mind centred on a girl's soft neck. She squirmed knowingly, and threw a glance over her shoulder in the midst of a rolling vowel, but Joe did not move a muscle.

Thinking of the girl in front of him, he suddenly remembered bringing in a fresh cadaver with old Clegg, stretching it out on the white enameled embalming table. He had touched the naked body, then jumped back startled. It was hot, almost like fire. The old man grinned. 'Fresh beef, ain't had time to cool yet. Soon as anyone dies their temperature shoots up like a sky-rocket. Dunno why, but that's the way it is. Like they wanted to live some more an that was the oney way they could show it.' – Joe's eyes touched the short hairs on the nape of the girl ahead of him. She twitched in nervous awareness. Her neck looked flushed and hot.

After the service he spoke to the girl and her mother, shook their white gloved hands. Later he saw the mother whisper something to her daughter. He guessed what it was and grinned inside.

At the age of 30 Joe had become a well-rounded figure in his gray trousers and dark jacket. His face was still a healthy red, with blunt features, a manner at once cordial and slightly withdrawn as became his profession. Perhaps the old schoolboy romance with Beth Holliday had something to do with him remaining single. Sometimes he saw her go by the chapel on her way to work at the library. She was in charge of children's books, presiding over fairy tales and science for young people with blond serenity. She always went by the chapel going to and from work, passing on the opposite side of the street and carrying an umbrella whether it was raining or not. He wondered about it once, that umbrella. Perhaps for protection against male advances. He smiled to himself. All that hogwash about Lancelot and Guinivere. The stainless knight of the round table she had expected him to be. The mystery of an illness without outward symptoms, but left her invalid within. That was probably hogwash too. She was no use to any man.

Every afternoon she walked by the chapel at ten minutes after five, passing under the big chestnut tree with pale serious face, a little thinner now, hands clutching an umbrella. He thought of his latest girl friend, comparing the two of them feature by feature. But there was really no comparison at all. Sylvia was dark, all fire and thumping passion, with big white pillows of breasts for a man to lie between. Sometimes she'd bite while they were making love, and bite hard. Later he'd ask her to keep her teeth away from his carotid artery, explaining its significance in his profession. They'd both laugh. It had been a stock joke with Joe for years now.

Lately he'd taken to using the little room off the chapel for his assignments. The room was actually meant for mourners who found themselves a little overcome while paying their last respects to a dear one, but the couch was very useful for erotic passages as well. And he'd discovered the atmosphere of the chapel to have a stimulating effect which caused his partners to give of their best. Naturally such extracurricular guests had to enter by a rear door, left unlocked by pre-arrangement.

Joe sighed a little. Perhaps he was tired of Sylvia's full blown charms. There'd been a new girl in town for the last few days, a waitress at Joe's Café. Came from Montreal, she said, though he didn't believe it. She sounded too much American, a teasing trace of the deep south in her voice, like a cream-fed cat. Her name was Julie. He thought she might be in the country illegally at first, but scoffed at himself for the idea. What American girl would enter Canada illegally? Still, working in a joint like Joe's Café! For Joe Barona was a real tough nut. He'd tried to get him to change the name of the restaurant a while back. It might remind people of the Eternal Rest Chapel and its new proprietor. But Joe Barona wouldn't change a thing. He thought of the black jowelled Italian with distaste.

Julie, working at Barona's dingy little greasy spoon – slender Julie with bold eyes and broad hips, dishing up chow for small town customers. People looked at Julie and sometimes forgot all about their food. A dish. The kind you don't meet in church. He frowned. She'd said 'no' to him twice. But that was to be expected. No girl wants to look easy, and Joe never minced words after a certain stage in his ritual courtship. He put it right on the line. Not baldly stated in so many words, but nevertheless unmistakable. A combination of oblique words and bold admiring glances – Julie would succumb eventually, he was sure.

Outside the sky was black, thunder smacking its lips high among the clouds. Rain began to fall in great drops. A long bar of sunlight touched the green chestnut leaves across the street. It reminded Joe, standing just inside the chapel door, of the stained green glass light in church. But here there was no girl, no sensitive white neck for the sunlight to touch and make aware of his glance. The thought was still unfinished when he saw Beth Holliday coming from the end of the block. Before she reached the chestnut tree black skies unbolted and rain came down in solid sheets. The girl came to a sudden halt under the tree, rain pouring outside the chestnut's periphery, weird green light piercing the leaves and resting on her blond head. She was pretty wet, Joe noted with a twinge of pity. She'd forgotten her umbrella too. He half-turned to go back in the shop and find her an umbrella, then stopped. It might mean the beginning of something for which he had no taste any longer. He stood hidden behind the curtain watching her, while the rain poured.

Beth looked towards the chapel once, pale and serious, the blue shadows under her eyes enlarged enormously. He could see her clearly from the chapel, as it they had been walking across the footbridge together in an earlier rainfall, pearl beads of water spangling her hair, Joe carrying her books as before. Lancelot and Guinivere. Again he turned to get her an umbrella, and came back just in time to see the girl running away down the street. It was the first time he had ever seen her running, the very first time.

Next day was Tuesday, fair and bright, the sky washed clear of rain. Joe and his assistant received a call from the small local hospital in the morning. He was to pick up the body of Beth Holliday. An interne explained what had happened as they wheeled the stretcher into position. 'Rheumatic heart,' he said tersely. 'She got caught in the rainstorm yesterday, and ran to get home. Her heart wouldn't take that sort of thing.' The interne slapped his hands together expressively and said, 'Whoof!'

Once, before they reached the embalming room, he touched her hand. It was fiery hot. He recoiled as if from a leper, noticing his assistant eye him curiously. 'Body heat goes up immediately after death,' Joe explained, and found himself echoing old Clegg almost word for word. 'Don't know why – it's like she wanted to live some more, and that was the only way to show it.' He blinked, not tears, for he didn't feel grief exactly. Just blinked rapidly, and thought of yesterday, her standing in the rain, himself inside. If he'd got that umbrella for her right away, without waiting to think about it, she might be alive – He shrugged himself out of the mood quickly. Just the same it was hard to believe she was dead, even with the draped evidence of her body in front of him.

Later he gave his helper the rest of the day

off, seeing the young man's eyes turn knowledgeable and wise. But that couldn't be helped. He prepared the embalming fluid slowly, shaking his head with dogged wonder at himself. Things he hadn't thought of for years – the girl holding onto his arm, exclaiming at some trifling colour of leaf she'd seen, wanting him to notice it also. The trust she'd had in him, something he hadn't realized at the time, but remembered now. Not really a human girl, for she'd asked nothing from life, and that was exactly what she'd got. But how could he know that without looking into her mind, a thing he'd never done?

Naked on the white table Beth Holliday lost no dignity, as if long expected death had not changed her in any essential way. Awkwardness suggested by clothing was erased, her limbs were liquid white, and belonged to her body like the joined arms of the same moonlit sea. Joe muttered something, listened in on himself to find out what he was thinking. 'She can't be dead,' he heard – but she was. Closed eyes with nightblue shadows, serious sweet mouth, pale gold nipples pointing up at the glaring eye-like two hundred watt bulb, pale pale pubic hair mounded impregnably forever now. He could have wept for himself, but a moment later he had lost the capacity again.

Joe was a furious man, and anger seized him. He took his steel instruments and slit the white throat, finding the carotid with practised certainty, listened to the low chugging of the electric pump push her blood into a galvanized bucket. It made a quiet slurping sound, like a large amount of tomato soup in the mouth of a fat man.

He went out afterwards and drank a bottle of rye whiskey. Then went round to his namesake's cafe to see Julie. The slender perhaps American girl made half-promises, but no firm commitment. Joe was surly. 'Okay,' he told her. 'I been drinkin'. Sometimes I do drink a little too much. But it makes no difference. You know I want you' – And she did know. But Joe didn't look so respectable at this moment. His face was a bright crimson shade from the whiskey, though strangely this seemed to make his blunt features almost handsome with the virility of blood and fascination of that neutrality pact undertakers have with death. He explained to her about the unlocked door of the chapel building. She smiled, her objections seeming to give way suddenly. 'All right, I'll come.'

'You won't be scared?' he asked. The girl said no, she was not afraid. And he knew from her eyes that she was not. 'After midnight then. I'll be waiting.' With no more words he left.

All next day the few friends and acquaintances of Beth Holliday filed into the funeral chapel, signed their names in the book and went solemnly away. Some of them gave Joe a remembering look, but he ignored the glances, stiffly erect in grey trousers and neat dark jacket, so drunk he could scarcely stand. At 11 o'clock that night he locked the front door and went to get another bottle of whiskey before Julie arrived. He managed to obtain only a small 12 ounce bottle from the town bootlegger, drank half of it in an alley and shoved the bottle in his pocket. His mind kept going back to the pale dead girl in her wood box, surrounded by flowers. 'Guinivere,' he snarled aloud. 'Guinivere, and her damned umbrella.' He drank the rest of the mickey in one gulp,

October 1963

heaving the bottle down the middle of the dark empty street. No heads popped out of windows to investigate the clattering sound. The town was asleep, only a vague light here and there behind misty curtains.

Joe went down the alley behind the undertaking parlours, entering the rear door. He flung off his coat, then stumbled over a chair on his way to the mourners' room. 'Too early,' he said drunkenly to himself. 'She won't be here yet.' But she was. A naked girl rose to meet him in the darkness, the streetlight outside projecting tiger stripes through the steel blinds, marking the girl's flesh as if she were a beast. As perhaps she was. For he felt her claws and teeth. The gyrating hips that plunged at him, grating on pelvic bones, made this touching of bodies as much combat as love passage. 'Julie,' he muttered, 'you're a bitch.' He seized her arms and bore her down on the couch.

Drowned in sticky sweat and the musky smell of coupling, he could not think of the dead girl any longer. Julie held him tightly, the swift unison of their plunging movement pushing them together and apart like the courtship of sweating ghosts. There was a brief resistance at first, but over quickly – The pleasure of having his mind blanked out, physical sensation replacing thought, an epileptic freedom that battered at walls of darkness. The girl's body anticipated every movement of his own, a slight hesitation before the downstroke, herself surging up to meet him and hovering momentarily, as if it were a mating of birds in mid-air. Orgasm – all his teeth magically transferred to the loins, and a medieval dentist was pulling them out rapidly, violently, one by one – the bones of his body dissolved in a last convulsive spasm, leaving his flesh collapsed like a limp umbrella spread over the girl.

He felt a fainting sickness suddenly come over him, and broke away from her. 'I'll be right back, honey,' he gasped, running to the bathroom in the rear to pour cold water over his head. When he returned a few seconds later she was gone. Without questioning the girl's disappearance he dropped exhausted onto the couch and slept.

Next morning the sun came up. Joe struggled groggily from the couch, feeling beaten all through his body, but strangely light-headed. He lifted the steel blinds to examine the couch carefully, but the red velour showed nothing. When the young assistant came to work Joe told him to look after things and went back to sleep. At nine o'clock the phone rang, someone for Joe. He got into his clothes hurriedly, dashing into the office under the staring eyes of his helper.

It was Julie. 'Joe,' she said, 'Joe?'
'Ya, whadda ya want?'
'I'm sorry, Joe.'
'You're sorry?'
'I said I'm sorry. I just couldn't make it last night.'
'What!'
'I couldn't make it. Listen I'll come tonight Joe. I'll be there for sure tonight. You're not mad, Joe? Joe –'

He left the phone lying on the desk gargling to itself, and went back to the chapel where the pale girl was lying in her wooden box, surrounded by a kingdom of flowers. He saw that she was smiling.

GWENDOLYN MacEWEN

Manzini: Escape Artist

now there are no bonds except the flesh.
    listen —
there was that boy, Manzini, stubborn with
gut stood with black tights and a turquoise
    penis
leaf across his sex

and smirking while the big
brute tied his neck, arms, legs; Manzini
naked waist-up and white with sweat

struggled. Silent, deliquent, he
was suddenly all teeth and knee, straining
    slack
and excellent with sweat, inwardly

calculating if Houdini would have taken
as long as he, fighting time and the drenched
muscular ropes, as though his tendons were
    worn
on the outside —

as though his own guts were the ropes
encircling him; it was beautiful; it was
Thursday, listen —
there was that boy, Manzini

finally free, slid as snake from
his own sweet agonized skin, to throw
    his entrails
white upon the floor
with a cry of victory —

now there are no bonds except the flesh;
but listen, it was Thursday, there was that boy,
Manzini —

E.W. MANDEL

Orpheus in the Underworld

I

knowing how many had lied
knowing my own lies
knowing those who had gone before

difficult music
to walk through tangled words
soundless to move toward the sounding caves

remembering the omen and the gift
how to count each foot's new pace
ignore the pleading faces in the stone
be silent by the raucous trees
when the crows clamour for my voice

above all to look steadily
to look directly

to look
    where the snake waits
where the unflinching serpent
hunches in his unimpassioned
imperial gaze toward my song

II

northward now
the remembered path
    contemptuous of meaning
      left behind
        with the orators
          beside their monuments and cannon

only the road now
the serpent path
    whatever the others say
      since there was no choice
        never a real alternative

the town far in the past
    despicable, squat
      a huddle of shacks
        like mourning women
like a dark king murmuring about harps
and the road billowing as if its swallowed dead
still lived in it
    like dust
      behind distended cars
which jump and croak like giant frogs,
their drivers black and goggled men

III

as for the end

the reeling plains look southward
and the heat gathers like a beast

the women sweat silently
reading my poems

I watch their faces for the gleam
which tells me that the end begins
that ecstacy in which they burn my lies
and tear from me the poems which I cannot
    write

MARSHALL McLUHAN

Murder by Television

Jack Ruby shot Lee Oswald while tightly surrounded by guards who were paralysed by television cameras. The fascinating and involving power of television scarcely needed this additional proof of its peculiar operation upon human perceptions. The Kennedy assassination gave people an immediate sense of the television power to create depth involvement, on the one hand, and a numbing effect as deep as grief itself, on the other hand. Most people were amazed at the depth of meaning which the event communicated to them. Many more were surprised by the coolness and calm of the mass reaction. The same event, handled by press or radio (in the absence of television), would have provided a totally different experience. The national 'lid' would have 'blown off.' Excitement would have been enormously greater and depth participation in a common awareness very much less.

    Kennedy was an excellent TV image. He had used the medium with the same effectiveness as Roosevelt had learned to achieve by radio. With TV, Kennedy found it natural to involve the nation in the office of the Presidency, both as an operation and as an image. TV reaches out for the corporate attributes of office. Potentially, it can transform the Presidency into a monarchic dynasty. A merely elective Presidency scarcely affords the depth of dedication and commitment demanded by the TV form. Even teachers on TV seem to be endowed by the student audiences with a charismatic or mystic character that much exceeds the feelings developed in the class room or lecture hall. In the course of many studies of audience reactions to TV teaching, there recurs this puzzling fact. The viewers feel that the teacher has a dimension almost of sacredness. This feeling does not have its basis in concepts or ideas, but seems to creep in uninvited and unexplained. It baffles both the students and the analysts of their reactions. Surely, there could be no more telling touch to tip us off to the character of TV. This is not so much a visual as a tactile-auditory medium that involves all of our senses in depth interplay. For people long accustomed to the merely visual experience of the typographic and photographic varieties, it would seem to be the synesthesia, or tractual depth of TV experience, that dislocates them from their usual attitudes of passivity and detachment.

The banal and ritual remark of the conventionally literate that TV presents an experience for passive viewers, is wide of the mark. TV is above all a medium that demands a creatively participant response. The guards who failed to protect Lee Oswald were not passive. They were so involved by the mere sight of the TV cameras that they lost their sense of their merely practical and specialist task.

Perhaps it was the Kennedy funeral that most strongly impressed the audience with the power of TV to invest an occasion with the character of corporate participation. No national event, except in sports, has ever had such coverage or such an audience. It revealed the unrivalled power of TV to achieve the involvement of the audience in a complex *process*. The funeral as a corporate process caused even the image of sport to pale and dwindle into puny proportions. The Kennedy funeral, in short, manifested the power of TV to involve an entire population in a ritual process. By comparison, press, movie, and even radio are mere packaging devices for consumers.

Most of all, the Kennedy event provides an opportunity for noting a paradoxical feature of the 'cool' TV medium. It involves us in moving depth, but it does not excite, agitate, or arouse. Presumably, this is a feature of all depth experience.

The above comments on the Kennedy event may serve as an introduction to an even larger issue involved in our use of the TV medium. It concerns the effects of the TV image on the daily perceptual and learning habits of our children. Starkly phrased, it amounts to this: the TV child cannot see ahead. Why? Because he is too deeply involved in his perceptual modes. Since TV, gone is the speedy, superficial habit of youth in a visually organized world. Today the young are earnest, serious, obsessional. Since TV, they are 'with' things. They 'dig' situations. Measurements recently carried out by Dr Arthur Hurst in Ontario schools revealed an extraordinary shift in reading distance in the primary grades. The average distance from the page in grades 1-3 is now six and one half inches. Before TV the distance had been double, according to the Harmon report. Since TV, that is to say, our children have tried to get *inside the page*. They demand a new relation to the typographic form that they have carried over from their depth involvement in the TV image. The results are most unfortunate, visually, psychically, and pedagogically. Print and TV clash *as forms*. Print does not demand the involvement that the TV image demands. The confusion of these forms is not merely indicated in the pathetic nearness to the page but much more in the clash of attitudes towards the curriculum and the learning process. There is a great drop in motivation. The TV child cannot *see ahead*. It is meaningless to a deeply involved person to explain that he should look ahead as a means of orienting his behaviour. Involvement whether of the artist, the saint, or the *roué*, forbids concern with the price of groceries, or the looking ahead to envision the consequences of present action.

The answer to the problem of why the TV child of today cannot see ahead is to be found in an understanding of the mosaic forms created by electric technology, and encountered at many levels of experience in the electric age. Many readers of *The Gutenberg Galaxy* have expressed uncertainty about the nature of the 'mosaic form' in which the book is presented. It will be well to clarify this matter so far as possible since it concerns not only the habitual modes of visual awareness in literate society, but even more does it concern the new modes of awareness and organization of experience in the electric age. Phonetic literacy is an extension of the body in the way that the wheel or clothing are extensions of the body. Electricity is not an extension of any portion of the body but rather of the central nervous system itself. That is, the instant character of electricity introduces the principle of inter-relation that is antithetic to all earlier technologies which in effect merely fragmented and extended the body by way of specialism and amplification.

The ordinary inability to discriminate between the photographic and the TV image is not merely a crippling factor in the learning process today; it is symptomatic of an age-old failure in Western culture. The literate man, accustomed to an environment in which the visual sense is extended everywhere as a principle of organization, sometimes supposes that the mosaic world of primitive art, or even the iconic world of Byzantine art, represents a mere difference in degree, a sort of failure to bring their visual portrayals up to the level of full visual effectiveness. Nothing could be further from the truth. This, in fact, is a misconception that has impaired understanding between East and West for centuries. Today it impairs relations between coloured and white societies. There is a very large stake in proper understanding of the differences in our sense orientations effected by technological extensions of our bodies and our nervous systems.

Unawareness of the specific modalities of the senses is a great disadvantage, especially when one encounters artistic extensions and amplifications of the various senses. The traditional arts of dance and song and sculpture, iconography and *celatura* extend, heighten, and orchestrate the human senses, as indeed does human speech itself. The arts of any culture in expressing the preferential bias of the culture also channel the perceptions of the culture, providing a basis for the observation that 'nature imitates art.'

The sort of depth participation and involvement indicated by the public response to the Kennedy event on TV has important analogues for the educator. The unique 'mosaic' form of the TV image creates a response in the young viewer that has nothing whatever to do with TV programs. In the same way, the response created by the typographic image (applied to the phonetic alphabet) is quite independent of any 'content.' The content of any medium is always another medium, and the content serves merely to focus the action of the medium itself upon our sensory lives. The effect of TV, therefore, psychically and socially, has been as little heeded or understood as the effects of phonetic literacy and typography. Today it is absolutely necessary to understand these effects since their consequences upon our traditional ways and perceptions do not occur gradually and mechanically, but develop at electric speeds. We have a huge stake in habits of civilized detachment and analytic objectivity. In short, our civilized values are by no means the same as the new habits of total involvement of all men in all men. Such total involvement may well seem utopian to conventional, literate people. In point of fact, it has already happened to us. We are living far ahead of our thinking. As wakeful, rational beings, responsible for a vast heritage, it behooves us to note the dissolving pressures exerted on this heritage by electric technology. Having noted this, we can make a free choice about whether or not to persist in the present patterns of technology. To ignore these patterns and pressures, by merely reacting to them, puts us in the role of automata carrying out automated mandates.

MELVILLE H. WATKINS

The Canadian Quandary

The performance of the Canadian economy over much of the past seven years has been distinctly unsatisfactory. The pained outcry of Canadian economists in these troubled times has been considerable, possibly even surprising when allowances are made for the numbers who have toiled for Royal Commissions and for an academic tradition that seems historically to have sometimes confused silence outside the sanctum with inner wisdom. But no economist resident in Canada has matched Professor Harry G. Johnson, a Canadian teaching at the University of Chicago, in the combined quality and quantity of commentary. Indeed, more than one Canadian economist whose voice has been heard must have drawn strength from Professor Johnson's example and from his significant contributions to the delineation of targets and to the supply of ammunition. Eleven relevant pieces, some previously unpublished, plus a foreword on the disastrous 1963 budget of Mr Gordon, are now collected in *The Canadian Quandary: Economic Problems and Politics* (McGraw Hill; $7.25). The result is a brilliant and sustained attack on Canadian economic policy that should inform and entertain the open-minded while infuriating the rest. Its chief targets are the tariff, Canadianization of foreign investment, and unemployment policy. (Other articles, unrelated to these themes, will not be discussed here.)

'Canadian nationalism as it has developed in recent years has been diverting Canada into a narrow and garbage-cluttered cul-de-sac' (p. 12). This sentence – and there are many others of similar substance and style – aptly states the unifying theme of Professor Johnson's broadside attack on Canadian economic policy. The major target is the tariff, that most obvious symptom of misguided economic nationalism. By permitting inefficient high-cost production behind its wall, the tariff raises prices to the Canadian consumer and lowers his real standard of living. On this proposition there would be close to unanimous agreement among economists. The order of magnitude of the social cost is very probably well in excess of one billion dollars a year. Valid theoretical arguments for tariff protection are hard to come by, and when their assumptions are laid bare their relevance to the technologically advanced Canadian economy seems slight.

The response of the sophisticated Canadian nationalist has always been to concede all this and insist that the burden of the tariff is the necessary price of Canadian nationalism. Professor Johnson properly insists that the proponents of this view must specify the mechanisms by which a larger but more inefficient secondary manufacturing sector maintains national independence. They should also provide criteria by which it can be determined how much a country should pay for any such contribution, with consideration being given to whether any given sum could not be spent to provide more worthy monuments to national independence. Those who have put nationalism behind them can see freer trade as a meaningful manifestation of more responsible international behaviour.

These points are devastating. By giving at least marginal encouragement to US direct investment in Canada does the tariff not feed political apprehension about US control of Canadian industry? Is the average Canadian really happier because he pays more to buy a US automobile manufactured in Canada rather than the US, instead of spending that extra sum on the educational system or on adequate medical care for the poor? Might not freer trade, through compelling Canadian industry to rationalize, lead to more emphasis on native technology and design, thereby increasing the self-respect and feelings of national independence of Canadians?

Professor Johnson's excellent discussion of the Canadian tariff might be criticized for three reasons. Firstly, it is based on an economic analysis which does not explicitly allow for the international movement of labour and capital. Professor John Dales has recently shown that the tariff is just as certain to lower income per head if these movements *are* allowed for. Secondly, because Professor Johnson rests his case almost completely on deduction, he cannot satisfactorily allay the widespread suspicions that movement to freer trade could result in quite considerable dislocation, nor can he tell us how the Canadian manufacturing sector would look under free trade. Thirdly, Professor Johnson sometimes seems to leave the impression that US control of Canadian industry is largely due to the Canadian tariff. But there are undoubtedly other reasons for US direct investment in Canada, and it may well be that the impact of the tariff is more on the structure of industry – e.g., size of firm and output lines – than on the extent of control. I do not think that the abolition of the tariff would in itself substantially lessen US control in any short period.

Professor Johnson directs equally heavy fire at our attempts, largely abortive to date, to 'Canadianize' foreign investment. We appear to fear foreign investment, Johnson suggests, because we assume that the foreign owner (in effect, the management of the parent company) does not maximize profits. Generally, he does not have the Canadian interest at heart. Specifically, he does not hire enough Canadians in top positions and does not export. If the foreign owner does maximize profits, then these complaints fall to the ground, though a failure to export might persist as symptomatic of a high cost industrial structure associated with the tariff. Professor Johnson has thus travelled a long way on the single untested assumption of profit maximization via the allocation of capital without respect to national boundaries. Even if we concede profit maximization, we are still entitled to ask: within what time and space horizons? It is not clear that foreign owners have traditionally operated without regard to national boundaries. It is more likely that it is only with the relatively recent rise of the multinational corporation staffed by men of global perspective that the economist's assumption is becoming generally valid.

In any event, the single assumption of profit maximization does not seem to adequately clear up the basic issue connected with direct investment: why does the investor insist on control? Because by doing so he can export technological and business skills, as well as money, and because he can obtain more of the full economic payoff from these exports. But there are still advantages to the Canadian economy which cannot be fully appropriated by the foreigner, in particular, rising real wages in Canada consequent on the greater productivity of labour resulting from working with more capital and superior techniques.

Given the foreign owner's desire for 100 per cent ownership, devices to encourage 25 per cent Canadian ownership will tend to reduce the income accruing to the foreign owner, to discourage foreign investment in Canada, and to decrease the incidental advantages that accrue to Canadians. To the extent the foreign owners choose to 'Canadianize' anyway, scarce Canadian capital will have been used up buying the shares of companies with certainty that control remains in foreign hands. This should reduce the availability of capital to genuinely Canadian-controlled enterprise. No matter what happens, then, the present approach by Mr Gordon would seem to be economically disadvantageous to Canadians. Also, Mr Gordon's desire, still at the jawbone stage, to shift foreign capital from equity to debt can be made effective only if very considerable incentives and disincentives are provided because it runs counter to the motivation of the direct investor. As to the alleged failure of US controlled firms to export, this is presumably explained by high costs associated with an inefficient industrial structure that has grown up and been able to persist because of the Canadian tariff. The appropriate policy is to abolish the Canadian tariff rather than harass foreign owners. As a minimum, judgment on the net effects of foreign control of Canadian industry should be suspended until that has been done.

Professor Johnson's third target is the whole package of recent Canadian economic policy. In the face of slow growth and high unemployment, the official tendency has been to deny the conventional explanation of the business cycle and to pin the blame on structural deficiencies. The orthodox tools of monetary and fiscal policy can then be dismissed as irrelevant; the authorities can maintain that little can be done in the short-run about inherently long-run problems, or dream up solutions, often very odd, to problems that are probably non-existent.

Such behaviour Professor Johnson properly deplores. To the allegation that unemployment has been associated with special difficulties of a structural nature, the appropriate reply is to first eliminate cyclical unemployment and then see whether any residual exists requiring special remedial action. There has been much talk about special problems in the balance of payments, but the economist is more likely to be struck by the efficiency with which the balance of payments mechanism has operated historically in Canada. The exchange crisis of 1962 was caused not by structural deficiencies but by government blundering.

Professor Johnson has little to say about our recent fiscal policy, though his foreword characterizes Mr Gordon's 1963 move to budget balance as 'economic idiocy.' His fire is concentrated instead upon our monetary policies. Like most Canadian economists, he directs devastating criticism at Mr Coyne's tight money policy in the late 1950s. Mr Coyne must also be indicted because he used the prestige of his high office for the dissemination of economic nonsense and for the promotion of anti-Americanism.

Though my sympathies clearly lie with Professor Johnson, I must register two mild disclaimers to the general nature of the argument of this book. The first is the matter of strategy. One suspects that Professor Johnson is a better evangelist than missionary. He relies almost entirely on deductive reasoning. Though presented with the thrust and cut of a skilled debater, his logic may have limited appeal to many potential readers, and particularly to businessmen – whose influence on economic policy is so important – of pragmatic bent and limited forensic skills. The second is an issue of substance. Professor Johnson takes Canadian nationalism too seriously. It is, after all, only economic. Though deplorable, it is a relatively harmless variety compared to much of what we see in the world today. The moral of these two points seems to me to be that more empirical work is necessary on the nature and causes of Canadian economic nationalism in the hope that we can exorcise this devil from our midst without, hopefully, increasing our susceptibility to worse varieties.

ABRAHAM ROTSTEIN

The Canadian Quandary

The economist has much to learn from the English butler. I have in mind the fine art of running the household without running the lives of the family. The efficiency of the economic process is important, but we might well pause before demands that we reshape our national existence around it.

In his collection of speeches and papers over a six-year period, Professor Harry Johnson relentlessly pursues the arch-villain of Canadian nationalism which 'has been diverting Canada into a narrow and garbage-cluttered cul-de-sac.' His complaint is that nationalism seeks to impose restrictions on American investment in Canada and to maintain the high tariff wall, thus interfering with the operation of the free market for capital and for goods between the two countries. Interferences with the free market in the name of political objectives such as safeguarding national independence, are regarded as spurious since they inhibit economic efficiency. Efficiency is the key to everything and the proceeds will buy all our heart's desire, from slum clearance to bilingualism and independence:

Independence, to my mind, and according to both the empirical evidence and the best tradition of the English novel, comes from the enjoyment of a high income; it is hard to see how a nation can be made more independent by lowering its citizens' standard of living and forcing them to earn their livings in occupations at which they are inefficient. If the public is to be taxed for the privilege of having a national identity – which is what the protectionists are really arguing for – there are far more worthy monuments to national independence than a second-rate manufacturing sector that could be constructed with the money – a decent social security system, a comprehensive public health programme, beautiful cities free of slums, a truly free and high quality educational system, a truly bilingual culture...

The old-new alchemy for our second-rate manufacturing sector is the abolition of the tariff and unlimited foreign ownership. If Professor Johnson is right, it does raise the question of what other national dross can similarly be turned to gold. For example, what of our second-rate defence establishment and our second-rate foreign service? The Americans might run our defence establishment at half of what it costs us at present – they might even do it free – and the English have a proven record of running our foreign service efficiently. Also the banks and the mass media could be made similarly efficient, while Canadians would pocket the proceeds and build monuments to their independence. No doubt we would need them. 'More integration,' Professor Johnson tells us, 'means a richer and more prosperous Canada; and nobody is as independent as a man who can afford to pick up his own cheques.'

In any case, we will become richer as a consequence of more foreign ownership. But Professor Johnson gives us no clear idea as to what we should expect from his proposal of a 'low or zero tariff.' He assures us that we will become more 'efficient,' but should we then expect an expanded manufacturing sector, a truncated one, or no manufacturing sector at all? He offers no evidence to support his mollifying assertion that 'there is little reason to think that such a trade policy would necessarily alter very greatly the amount of manufacturing activity in Canada.' The fragmentary evidence that Professor Johnson does offer is scattered about the book and indicates that a different set of consequences are possible. First he refers to an unpublished paper by Professor J.H. Dales that indicates 'the tariff makes it impossible to tell which of your industries are efficient and which are not.' We are also told of another study by the same author on the question of why Canadian economic growth has lagged behind that of the United States. It appears that

the increasing relative underdevelopment of Canada [is due] to the effects of the tariff, which has steered Canadian productive effort into secondary manufacturing, where not only is production comparatively inefficient, but its productivity has been rising no faster than American manufacturing productivity, and far less rapidly than has productivity in Canadian agriculture. The tariff, in short, has fostered the less dynamic sector of the economy at the expense of the more dynamic.

Presumably then, while we haven't any clear idea which industries will survive a tariff cut and which will not, we suspect that our second-rate manufacturing sector will decline and our dynamic agricultural sector increase. And how is the world likely to receive more Canadian agricultural output? Professor Johnson does give us an answer:

opportunities for development on an agricultural basis are restricted by the policies of advanced countries that would rather protect their agriculture and save themselves a political problem than allow the law of comparative advantage to work itself out.

We are told further about 'the uncertainty of agricultural protectionism and the resulting surpluses in the advanced countries,' the upshot of which is 'a complicated situation in which all countries' policies toward agriculture involve distortions from an internationally efficient allocation of resources.'

This, then, is the basis for Professor Johnson's proposal to turn Canadian commercial policy on its head and thereby provide us with both increased incomes and increased independence.

Turning to the political side of the issue, Professor Johnson would have us believe that the economic benefits of integration carry with them no political liabilities. The arguments do not merit serious attention. For example, his explanation of our failure to recognize Communist China hardly needs further comment – 'the plain truth is that [such recognition is] ... simply unpopular in Canada.'

Then there is a variant of the old theme that laissez-faire brings freedom and intervention restricts it:

But supposing that the development of closer economic ties with the United States might lead Canadians eventually to desire a political union with the United States, is this a valid reason for trying to prevent by government intervention now the formulation of these closer economic ties? ... the present generation, whatever it decides for itself has no right to try to limit the freedom of future generations by depriving them of the opportunity to choose.

Apart from the novelty of the suggestion that a state should pursue a policy geared to its own dissolution, it is difficult to see how a future generation in possession of its own economy would be less free than a generation whose economy is integrated. If the freedom to stay Canadian forms part of the choice, a generation in possession of its economy might be more free. It is a policy of intervention, it seems to me, which increases freedom and laissez-faire which limits it.

Professor Johnson turns to the sovereignty of Parliament as his last bastion for laissez-faire, thereby clouding over the political aspect of the problem with the legal aspect:

neither imports of American goods nor imports of American capital acquire voting rights in Canada, so Canadian independence as embodied in the sovereignty of Parliament can hardly be threatened that way.

American goods and American capital do, however, have voting rights in the United States. Independence, one thinks, is not frozen in institutional sovereignty but has something to do with the political relationship of national sovereignties to each other. Has the US State Department been slow to defend the interests of US periodicals in this country, for example?

The political innocence of the economic liberal is a source of wonder. Since 1950 in Canada, our total foreign obligations have been rising at a rate of some $1.3 billion a year. Americans now control two-thirds of our extractive industries and three-fifths of our manufacturing. Nevertheless, Professor Johnson feels that the economic benefits have no political consequences. If there is an issue at all, it is framed in purely economic terms, namely, does American capital commit economic misdemeanors in this country? If it turns out to be as 'efficient' as Canadian capital, only more so, then that settles the question. The political consequences vanish because somehow the nationality of foreign capital has vanished. For those less innocent, the riddle is intriguing.

In the last analysis, it is the market mentality of the economic liberal which is at the core of his political outlook: The market is impersonal and its participants are anonymous buyers and sellers of the factors of production. These factors, even if they are foreign, have no nationality since the market recognizes only quantity and price and the only criterion for judgment is efficiency. Are American capitalists different from Canadian capitalists? Of course not. Are American workers different from Canadian workers? Is anyone in Canada different from anyone in the United States? Not as long as he is regarded merely as a factor of production on the market. But there is no reason to mistake an economic abstraction, useful in analyzing market behaviour, for a political reality.

Needless to say, independence refers not to income, but to the power to make decisions. No national state concerned with its independence willingly shifts basic decision-making power in vital areas into foreign hands, however friendly and well-behaved these may be. In an interdependent world, such questions are matters of degree. Still, the loss of independence is readily apparent when decision-making power in foreign affairs and defence is shifted outside the country. Why is the loss of independence less apparent in foreign ownership of the economy? Partly because economic power is decentralized, but mainly because foreign ownership takes on a political facade in a market setting. Foreign capitalists are not 'foreign,' they are 'efficient.' From the political point of view, it is as irrelevant whether US capitalists are as 'efficient' as Canadian capitalists, as it is whether the Pentagon would be as 'efficient' in defending Canada as our own armed forces, or whether the English foreign service would be as 'efficient' as the Canadian External Affairs Department. A decrease in independence results from the loss of decision-making power in all three cases. The fact that we have legal sovereignty to alter or revoke the decisions of foreign-owned firms is not unlike our power to abrogate defence treaties or alter our foreign commitments. It does not nullify the political fact. Nor is the loss of decision-making power for the country less real if the shift occurs from Canadian citizens to US citizens – as in foreign ownership – than the shift of power on an intergovernmental basis.

For those not mesmerized by the market, debate on public policy might centre on weighing real economic benefits against equally real political costs. No one can be indifferent to the problems of unemployment and lagging economic growth in this country. Certainly a likely outcome of such a debate is the conclusion that while there are political costs, some of these are worth paying in the light of the expected benefits. But first, both benefits and costs would need to be scrutinized more closely. Yet we have done as little concrete study of the dynamics of Canadian-American political relations as the free traders have of the concrete consequences of the abolition of the tariff.

Once we begin to deal in realities and not fictions, either economic or political, we might be better able to translate a little of Professor Johnson's vaunted sovereignty into effective policy. It is fair neither to the Americans nor to ourselves to allow this capital in under laissez-faire conditions and then start fumbling with ineffective legislation when we begin to realize that incomes and independence are not the same thing.

The problems are complex, and it is naive to rely on simple formulas, least of all laissez-faire. It is true that the economic history of this country has made the problems complex and that some of our problem with foreign ownership, for example, has been brought on by the high tariff.

The economic liberals have never forgiven the country for having been conceived in original sin. The national policy, whether for good or ill, rejected laissez-faire and pivoted on the tariff. The aim was to provide a material basis for Confederation by subordinating the economic to the political. There is nothing sacred about the mould in which we grew up and some of the tariff provisions are badly outdated. But neither are there magic formulas, especially those that run counter to the entire history and structure of the country. Professor Johnson knows this well enough:

Imitative magic describes the process of looking at other countries with currently more successful records than one's own, discerning some obvious institutional differences that seem to account for their freedom from the problems that plague oneself, and recommending the transplantation of the relevant institution to one's own country regardless of how it came to be established where it is or what makes it work.

A word on Professor Johnson's social philosophy as a whole. The reader should not get the impression that this is the old type of *sauve qui peut* economic liberalism. Professor Johnson subscribes to the thesis of the affluent society – to the point where he has 'rechristened' it the 'opulent society.' In the opulent society we can well afford abundant social welfare services as well as 'town planning, slum clearance and imaginative public works' – but not, apparently, independence. The fruits in the one case come from bolstering and manipulating the market – the sin in the second case is to interfere with it.

For economic liberals this book will have a superlative appeal, reminiscent of that bestseller *The Caine Mutiny*. On the face of it, Professor Johnson titillates the desire to be a nonconformist. With a bravado and a flourish he strikes out against the conventional economic wisdom in Canada, the many years of maladministration in this country, and even against Canadian capitalists ('the small, smug mind and large larcenous hands of Bay Street'). Yet just as in the novel, all this outspoken non-conformism is safe in the end. The economic liberal is deposited in the lap of an orthodoxy older even and more conventional than the national policy.

It is a radical position, implacably hewing to the free market regardless of the political consequences – but a radicalism that is neither the radical right nor the radical left. Thus, on Canadian economic policy, Professor Johnson stands for the radical centre.

DAVID BROMIGE
The Great Lover

The heroes of the old
west probably did step
that casual into
thin air

    to land in the saddle
feet slap on the stirrups
as the graceful creature
galloped past,
    into the leather
seems skin knitted to those muscles,
under groin & thigh

    The right moment, he thought,
        shifting
    feet on the firstfloor balcony, looking
    at their hooves, those hammers

    & went in & lay down to dream
    the compliant beasts came, their
        large soft
    eyes imploring, promising

Next morning, tho, they shook by
fierce as ever, the slim hipped heroes
whooping them on
to godknows what horizons

PADRAIG O BROIN
Railing at Byzantium

(on reading certain anthologized 'younger poets')

This is no country for old men. The young
in one another's sheets; strange birds
    in trees
— these dying generations — at their song
for which the presses gobble toppled trees;
the fishy flesh — or foul — all summer long
projecting verses loud as summer flies.
Caught in that sen-sen muzak none expect
monuments from too aged an intellect.

Quite right. An aged man a paltry thing,
a tattered poet upon a stick, unless
soul nod its solid head and loudly sing
every concept it can – or can't – express,
or study in a singing school to sing
cloacal monumental emptiness.
Therefore do I waive the seas; rehearse
a project: I project projective verse.

O images in TV's holy glare
gesticulant as shadows on a wall,
strut from the screen, twist pelvis in a gyre
and be the dancing masters of my sole
and heel. Cancel my heart. Sick of desire,
invalid in this dying metric style
yet knows what thing we are — but, swallow
    me
into your artifice of modernity.

So out of nature I shall no more take
poetic form from any natural thing,
but such a form as ayjayem-smiths make
of pummelled word and tired enamelling
hoping to get a Canada Council stake
and sit upon a pulpwood pile to sing
for edicrits and CBC, and crumbs:
'There is no past — in me the future comes.'

EDITORIAL
In the Bourassa Tradition

Out of the raucous babel of Quebec in search of its future in North America several voices of reason and realism have been gradually emerging over the past few months. The Committee formed around Pierre Trudeau has, as yet, had no measurable effect. Its impact can only be long run and come after careful detailed examination of Quebec's and Canada's current problems and proffered panaceas. The first step in this direction may be seen in Albert Breton's provocative analysis of 'The Economics of Nationalism' in the August number of the *Journal of Political Economy*. While the paper is too short to be a final statement on so large a subject, the general thesis is that such an action as the nationalization of hydro in Quebec has, in itself, done little more for the well-being of Quebeckers than to provide jobs for middle-class professional people. Indeed, in terms of increasing taxes, economic decisions taken for nationalist reasons seem detrimentally to affect the standard of life of the working classes. It is not surprising that Professor Breton's views have roused the ire of a certain Minister of Natural Resources! But the University of Montreal economist's thesis is all the more convincing in that it supports, through economic analysis, the concept of Quebec's essentially middle-class revolution as it is analyzed in sociological terms by Hubert Guindon in the summer issue of the *Queen's Quarterly*.

Perhaps more important in the present situation than the careful work of scholars and intellectuals is the attitude of people who contribute to the formation of public opinion through the mass media. For this reason it is all the more regrettable that Gérard Pelletier's sane and authoritative voice has been silenced for more than three months by an extremely complicated strike at *La Presse*. That strike has served to further increase the influence of that unique institution, *Le Devoir*.

It seemed for a time, a year or so ago, that *Le Devoir* was doomed to lose its influence in Quebec. Its director, Gérard Filion, left to take charge of the province's newly created General Investment Corporation. Then its editor, a man of enormous prestige in his province and the country at large, André Laurendeau, was enticed into Royal Commissioning. (He could hardly say no, since he had suggested the Commission in the first place.) The departure of these two strong personalities left *Le Devoir* not only weak, but suffering from a severe case of schizophrenia: one-half of which was the cold realism and slightly hesitant moderation of Claude Ryan, the other the flashy, emotional, and often elegantly written quasi-separatism of Jean-Marc Leger. Within the past few months that split has gradually been overcome, and one personality has emerged dominant. First, M. Ryan was appointed director of the paper over the protest of at least one important Quebec nationalist theoretician, the conservative F.A. Angers. Since the appointment of the new director, M. Leger's talents have been more and more directed to international, cultural, and other matters largely unrelated to the constitution. M. Ryan, ably assisted by the well-informed Paul Sauriol, has observed very well defined bounds in his discussion of the Canadian crisis. It was well summed up recently by M. Sauriol who wrote, almost as though he had his colleague Jean-Marc Leger in mind, 'Let's try co-operative federalism before we condemn it.'

In the current atmosphere in Quebec, an atmosphere so charged with emotion that words like 'colonialism,' 'centralization,' 'co-operative federalism' and Maurice Lamontagne set off one kind of unhealthy, hostile reaction, while 'an associate state,' 'a special status for Quebec,' 'autodetermination' and René Lévesque produce a more positive, but no less pavlovian, response, it takes a good deal of courage to swim against the mounting quasi-separatist tide. Claude Ryan made this point recently while taking part in the Tory 'Thinkers' Conference at Fredericton. The experience at Fredericton, and others recently, seem to have provoked M. Ryan into setting out explicitly the viewpoint which has guided his writing since he took over the direction of *Le Devoir*. In the first of three very important recent editorials he dared to express openly what few people on the reform side of Quebec politics, indeed few French Canadians, have found the courage to do: he severely criticized René Lévesque. This is the kind of anti-clericalism that is effective chiefly because it comes from within the community of true believers. This editorial was followed by two others delineating 'The Position of *Le Devoir* in the Present Canadian Crisis.'

Three moderate editorials do not, in themselves, build a bridge over the growing French-Canadian insistence on something near to separatism (but without its disadvantages) and English Canada's seeming satisfaction with the status quo. But the views expressed by M. Ryan, views which are firmly rooted in the tradition of *Le Devoir*'s founder, Henri Bourassa, represent an extremely important and timely expression of what an important but often quiet, or perhaps intimidated, group of French Canadians expect from the future. While to some English Canadians M. Ryan may seem to be asking for the moon, it would be well to remember that *Le Devoir*'s position is extremely moderate; in the present mood of Quebec, M. Ryan is asking for something very near to the absolute minimum. And that is what makes his statement both profoundly important and admirably courageous.

Only M. Ryan and other French Canadians can fight in Quebec the battle for sanity, realism and, to the liberally minded, the only sensible cure for the nationalist mania that afflicts the mid-twentieth century world. But there is little point in fighting that battle unless there is a willingness in English Canada to provide evidence that what M. Ryan calls 'the Canadian hypothesis' can be realized. M. Ryan's position is thus doubly dangerous for it depends not only on convincing French Canadians that the currently dominant tendency in their outlook is, in many respects, retrograde, but it also depends on the willingness of English Canadians to make the alternative workable. M. Ryan's courageous wager therefore deserves the most thoughtful attention throughout the country.

The Position of Le Devoir *in the Present Canadian Crisis (I)*
(Editorial in *Le Devoir,* September 18, 1964)

In the present Canadian crisis what is the basic position of *Le Devoir*?

This question has been asked by many readers in the course of the summer months. It became even more real following recent events to which few citizens remained indifferent: the *Pink* Conference, the Conservative meeting at Fredericton, the intervention of M. Lévesque, etc.

It is impossible to respond in a few lines, in a definitive manner, to a question so complex. The time has nevertheless come to proceed to certain clarifications.

There are for French Canadians two ways of approaching the Canadian problem.

One consists of identifying French Canada with Quebec and examining all our problems in relation to the interests of Quebec. At the heart of this hypothesis Quebec is first and foremost. It is necessary to pursue it and defend it, putting all other considerations in second place: that is the thesis of 'by itself and for itself' dear to M. Lévesque.

In this perspective the Canadian dimension appears a last resort. It is a rupture of the homogeneous order which would exist if Quebec was alone and completely master of its destiny; it is thus a weight from which it is necessary to strain in order to liberate oneself. Some are still prepared to accept the Canadian reality, provided that this reality does not hinder in any way the progress of Quebec, and that it serves Quebec's interests. Others have already concluded that the Canadian reality is injurious to Quebec, that it is necessary to put an end as soon as possible to an experiment which, in every way, has never been faithfully put to the test.

Between these two opinions there exists a difference of degree, not of nature. The two opinions accept, without discussion, the ideal of the primacy of Quebec. They separate at the chapter on means and strategy. In the long run the two opinions are destined to unite.

The second approach consists in envisaging the French-Canadian problem at the level of the whole country, that is to begin with the Canadian hypothesis.

At the heart of this hypothesis there is a place for a loyal admission of the difficulties that have sorely tried the French Canadians in Confederation. There is equally room for an explicit recognition of the special position that Quebec – as the principal political expression of the French fact in Canada – ought to occupy in the Canadian body politic.

But the perspective remains Canadian. Canada is accepted not as a last resort from which one would like to be liberated, but as a valuable political reality which one wants to improve. This viewpoint is not that of a supporter of a unitary system, but rather of a federalist. For him the federal regime is the one that best fits our geographic, historic, economic, and political conditions. Without wishing this regime to survive at any price, he rejects the global and defeatist interpretations that some propose about the history of the last century.

This viewpoint also takes account of the evolution which has taken place in English-Canadian opinion in the last quarter century. Those who adhere to this thesis believe that it is possible and desirable to reform our federation in a manner that will become effective and acceptable to Canadians of both languages. They see that this reform ought to be made up of conversations and faithful agreements between the two groups. They wish to obtain this objective by the road of dialogue rather than by the method of ultimatums. But they recognize at the outset that it is within the Canadian body politic that they look for a solution.

It is impossible, unless one wants to outsmart someone, to pretend to be inspired by both hypotheses. A newspaper should choose one of the two and defend it with courage and clarity. It should do this with the maximum loyalty and frankness. It should give all viewpoints a reasonable opportunity for expression in the news columns. But it would betray its mission if it avoided choice.

We will declare our choice tomorrow. We will indicate at the same time the range and the limits.

The Position of Le Devoir *in the Present Canadian Crisis (II)*
(Editorial in *Le Devoir*, September 19, 1964)

Between the two hypotheses which we traced yesterday, we choose the Canadian hypothesis. It remains for us to say why and to formulate certain nuances which mark our choice.

We choose the Canadian hypothesis for three principal reasons. The first reason relates to the very tradition of *Le Devoir*. The newspaper, under its first three directors, was a great Canadian newspaper. Henri Bourassa never wanted to limit his horizons to the province of Quebec. He considered that the whole of Canada was his country, that he ought to be at home everywhere in this country. Georges Pelletier also attached a great importance to Canadian realities. He liked to approach the most complex problems, for example those of transport, with an objectivity and a rigour that would have prevented him from closing them within a narrow compass. The third director, Gérard Filion, was of rural origin, but he had learned early at the school of the Catholic Union of Farmers the need for co-operation with the rest of the country. He was often severe toward Ottawa centralizers, but never negative or closed with regard to Canada itself.

The second reason lies in the economic order. It is sufficient to glance at a map of the country in order to establish that Quebec and Canada are tied together in many ways. Quebec's economy presents two important characteristics. It needs external markets for the dispersal of its products. It needs capital from outside for the development of its resources. Why should we say no to Canada today if that must only mean saying yes to others tomorrow? One does not deny his history for the simple pleasure of hypothetically changing partners.

Our most important motives lie in the political order. On the condition that Quebec enjoys all the autonomy which it needs to develop its own life and institutions, we believe that the preservation of the Canadian tie offers precious advantages. The first of these advantages is surely the possibility of maintaining and developing the French way of life in the rest of the country. *Le Devoir* has always maintained an attitude of solidarity with the French minorities in the other parts of the country. Whatever could have been said on this subject for some time, the present direction of *Le Devoir* holds that we must continue to support our compatriots in the other provinces. We refuse to join the prophets of doom who affirm, without ever having worked assiduously with these groups, that the French minorities of the other provinces are doomed to extinction.

The second advantage is less immediate, but no less obvious. Canada offers us the chance of constructing a new type of political society, that is a society whose political boundaries will be advantageous for the development of different cultures without being rigidly or exclusively conditioned by one culture alone. We are convinced that this type of society can be revealed as more advantageous to the cultivation of fundamental liberties, in the long run, than societies calculated too closely on the single reality of a particular culture. In affirming this conviction we are conscious of enunciating an ideal which is far from having been attained in the Canadian reality. But the difficulties and the checks of the past are not yet decisive enough to justify pure and simple abandonment of the ideal which presided at the birth of Confederation.

A durable political society is built neither on impulses nor on vague desires, but on rational ideas, on a certain conception of man and of life in society, on an objective assessment of reality. Nothing proves that men nourished in different cultures are incapable of co-operating on a certain conception of political life. The entente is surely more difficult when several cultures are called upon to cohabit, but it is not for all that purely and simply impossible.

That being said we insist on adding three qualifications.

We have said advisedly 'the Canadian hypothesis.' We have not spoken of dogma. It is possible that we are mistaken. If that is the case, the facts will indicate it to us in the proper time and place. Placed before the evidence we will not have the pretension of preventing history from fulfilling itself. But while waiting, the logic of events obliges us to fight firmly and frankly for the success of our hypothesis.

In choosing the Canadian hypothesis we are not opting for the status quo. If this hypothesis is to be realized, substantial modifications in the constitution of our country and in the functioning of our political institutions will have to be carried out. It will be necessary to rethink our federalism, to adjust it profoundly. It will be necessary to avoid the errors of the past, to correct the injustices of yesterday, to foresee new methods of work which will realize completely the equality of cultures.

Finally our choice will not prevent us in the least from approaching in Quebec the problems of Quebec. In the order of jurisdiction where it is and must remain (and even in certain areas become sovereign), Quebec has the right to our first allegiance. It will have it without restriction. In the discussion of the problems of education, social security, and the development of our resources and of our economy we will not act in the fashion of 'Canadians at large' who would like to solve our problems using norms borrowed from elsewhere rather than by the realistic examination of our situation and our resources. We will think and speak as Quebecois without misplaced pride, but without false humility.

These positions seem to us to conform best to the true reality of French Canada. We readily accept that they will be criticized and called in question. We will listen respectfully to the objections of our interlocutors.

But our position being clearly defined everyone will know what he can expect from *Le Devoir* and what he cannot demand from it.

A.W. PURDY

The Wine-Maker's Beat-étude

I am picking wild grapes last year
in a field
      dragging down great lianas of vine
tearing at 20 reluctant feet of heavy purple
having a veritable tug-o-war with Bacchus
who grins at me delightedly in the high
   branches
of one of those stepchild apple trees
unloved by anything but tent caterpillars
and ghosts of old settlers
become such strangers here —
I am thinking what the grapes are thinking
that is
    I am satisfied with the sun
and eventual fermenting bubble-talk together
then transformed and glinting with coloured
   lights in
    a GREAT JEROBOAM
that booms inside from the land beyond the
   world
in fact
I am satisfied with my own shortcomings
   letting
myself happen
        then I'm surrounded by COWS
black and white ones with tails –
At first I'm uncertain how to advise them
in mild protest or frank manly invective
then realize that the cows are right
it's ME that's the trespasser —
    Of course they are curious
perhaps wish to see me perform
   I moo off key
   I bark like a man
   laugh like a dog
   I talk like
   God — hoping
they'll go away so Bacchus and I can get on
   with it —
Then I get logical thinking if there was ever a
feminine principle cows are it and why not but
what would so many females want?
I address them like Brigham Young hastily
   'No, that's out! I won't do it!
   Absolutely not!'
Contentment steals back among all this
   femininity
thinking cows are together so much they must
   be nearly
all lesbians fondling each other's dugs by
   moonlight why
Sappho's own star-reaching soul shines inward
   and outward
from the soft Aegean islands in those eyes and
I am dissolved like a salt lick instantly oh
    Sodium chloride!
    Prophylactic acid!
    Gamma particles (in
      suspension)!
    After shave lotion!
    Rubbing alcohol!
        suddenly
I become the whole damn feminine principle
   so
happily noticing little tendrils of affection
steal out from each to each unshy honest
   encompassing
golden calves in Israel and slum babies in
   Canada and
a millionaire's brat left bawling on the toilet
   seat in
Rockefeller Center
    O my sisters
    I give purple milk!

LIONEL TIGER

Bennett and the Power and the Glory

If you do not believe that British Columbia's wildness and size and climate are for your benefit living here can intimidate you. This is why one of the crucial symbols of Premier Bennett's Government and a major recent reason for his success is his emphasis on hydro electric power. The turbines and high-tension cables suddenly and magically make of the rivers and mountains and rain a source of wealth and a reassurance of significance. Power is a link between man and environment and represents the extraction of a goodness from a complex, hostile terrain. In BC it is a potency on a grand scale which has been promoted and exploited so that now it possesses an almost mystic importance for many. In this domain of nature-lovers on the make it is an opportunity for a happy merger of pantheism and technology; it is both present reality and the foretaste of a future rich and sturdy.

Vancouver's most dramatic and contemporary building is the BC Hydro Building which rises crisply and confidently in a largely two-storey area of a largely two-storey town. The structure is brilliantly lit till midnight and dominates the city. The echoes of totem poles along its sides are appropriate because it is truly a place for a kind of god and nothing in the city can equal its symbolic force and arrogant millionaire's *panache*. When Bennett expropriated the BC Electric (and many of its plans he now claims as his own) he knew what he was doing. Jean Lesage's operation with Quebec's Hydro doesn't hold a candle to Mr Bennett's. Lesage is too interested in people; Bennett made a million selling hardware in the Interior and remains perhaps Canada's most successful hardware dealer. He specializes in electrical goods, and thinks big, and gives us all a charge.

Premier Bennett's 'policy' involves damming three rivers: the Peace, the Columbia, and (he has just announced) the Liard in the far north of the Province. The sums of money involved in these constructions and the amount of electricity which will result from them seem to assure a long-run economic boom in a province many of whose citizens see in this power and the wealth surrounding it a proof of their own promising affluence and of the correctness of their choice to live in BC and not 'back East' or in tempting California.

On the plane from Toronto to Montreal a BC booster urged a buddy to move to grand Vancouver and outlined all the virtues (no snow, free beaches, unbelievable gardens, everything always growing) and capped it finally with 'and then there's all that power.' Power is unbeatable, is lights today and brighter tomorrow, is industry and heat: power is POWER. Power provides us a year-round harvest festival. Go to bed and all night long the turbines pump money into provincial coffers; wake up and switch it on and there is power; even on Sunday in this grisly Presbyterian paradise the money pours in. We anticipate nothing less than 'the highest per capita energy development in the world.'

In fact, it's all a miracle. The Americans need power so they give us 274 million dollars to make jobs and roads with and dams, too, and then we give them the power for thirty years and don't have to do anything about it. Pearson and Johnson come to the Peace Arch to sign the treaties while Bennett huffs and puffs like a wind tunnel with a smile; live in a better province and the world will beat a path to your door; *being here* is all. And since even Bennett can't spend 174 million dollars in one time, simply lend 100 million to Quebec for a while – that'll show those Easterners.

The essential point is that like oil splashing out of the ground or the compound interest of a Rockefeller the money keeps coming in. It's good clean money because the product is hidden in wires and doesn't smell or make smoke; no one is exploited by the socially useful product which emerges from the spirited expenditure and vast machinery. It is all beautiful and it is not second-rate; Main Street power is as good as, better than, Bay Street power.

We're no socialists, of course, but all of this is ours. How can the NDP opposition, writhing with manifestos and growling dogmas, concerned with twenty cent raises for uninspiring workers, compete with this millionaire capitalist socialist who runs the 'world's biggest inland ferry system' (glistening white and on time), a massive power complex, a railway reaching to the north ('the brightest jewel in Mr Bennett's crown') and who is as likely as not to want to nationalize the high-profit BC Telephone Company (why send out of the province all those millions in Federal Taxes?). We're not socialists but we like the feel of ownership, particularly the ownership of the future; the future is ours and we'll supply the power.

Of course, there are a few minor inconveniences in the Dynamic Society which Bennett proclaimed when he announced a record 1965 Budget of $446 million. Though we're told the rates are low, somehow electricity still costs us quite a lot and it is with a touch of cynicism that we await the promised rate reductions which will come with Spring. The BC Hydro Authority runs the money-losing bus system in Vancouver and the fares have been put up; fewer people use buses and the service is even worse. But then, anyone worth anything has a car, and if Vancouver wants cheaper buses, it can vote Social Credit like other right-thinking people. Support for university education per student has been near the bottom of the Canadian list in this golden province and for a month the three Presidents of the universities ignominiously awaited news of the carve-up of a lump sum inadequate by national standards. Faculty Associations may vote resolutions but they can vote Social Credit, too; just because they're intellectuals doesn't mean they're smarter than us real folk. Anyway, H.R. MacMillan just gave UBC 8.2 million dollars and since that arose out of the favourable conditions the Government grants its friendly paper producers, doesn't it balance out? Does anyone really care that the Vancouver Prosecutor has been imprisoning Menaces to Society as Habitual Criminals despite the protests of criminal lawyers? Does it matter that the Head of the Narcotics Squad flatly contradicts all known information by asserting to UBCs pre-medical students that marijuana is addictive and that 'no male addict I have known has not been a criminal and no female not a prostitute'? Does it matter that his squad is engaged in a pointless rout of 'Intellectuals and Beatniks Found With Dope' as the clouded Vancouver *Sun* recently announced? If there's a bit of scandal with a mafia millionaire, the mountain peaks are still white, and so does it matter that drinking laws are abrasive and obscene while some 30 million dollars come in as taxes from something called 'Government enterprises?' Downhill, in mountainous country, a little hypocrisy goes a long way.

Bennett has been Premier longer than any BC leader to date and when that milestone was passed in February a tributary banquet was held for him in the Hotel Vancouver. A river of praise flowed and was carefully computed by one skilled in the hydraulics of power. Since then he has suddenly and capriciously issued several minor benefits from his seat in the Legislature and while one may be grateful for his quick largesse his methods of redistributing wealth are curious and few wait his whim with confidence. That it is the people's money he spends scarcely enters his head, so closely does he identify himself with Government in this bizarre polity. That anyone else will be Premier within quite a while enters some peoples' heads but few act upon it; when Don Smiley suggested the three opposition parties join to overthrow the government, the squeals from the local theologues of political dissent were round and final.

Bennett has been lucky and rides a boom time confidently and with a bright eye to the future. The composition of his Cabinet has been slowly changing; some professionally trained persons are creeping into a party that once greeted eggheads with bricks. Though he will never be a Medici, when enough voters want cheap higher education for their offspring, we can expect the Premier to flash the public bankroll he's appropriated and spend it on PhDs and labs. Meanwhile, Simon Fraser University flowers atop Burnaby Mountain, and UBC and Victoria sport new buildings all of which are far more visible and impressive than the demoralized staff and badly supported student bodies inhabiting them. Still, education expenditures have increased 749 per cent since Bennett took office. Vancouver has inadequate money for urban redevelopment which it painfully requires and unless fat grants are forthcoming its major development will continue to be private and there will still be nowhere lovely to walk in town. But what about Stanley Park and the beaches? The average income of West Vancouver is $10,000, of East Vancouver $3,000, and nothing Bennett does promises to reduce the gap significantly. But isn't the average *per capita* income higher than it ever was? And, each year, when the Premier mails his lavishly printed Budget Speech to thousands of not necessarily sympathetic 'influentials,' doesn't he clearly say how blessed are we who share in the benefits of his munificent expenditures of our money?

The Premier believes in bosses and is hostile to labour and yet suddenly, flashily invites a Chinese-Canadian shoeshiner from the bowels of the Hotel Vancouver to his testimonial banquet. He projects a pious domesticity while his development schemes are pagan and agnostically subvert the natural face of the earth. While his Budget Speech makes repeated reference to the need for creative Federal-Provincial relations, his is the glad Federalism of the rich scion who still lives at home and pays his rent but who feels affluence and integrity enough for a mansion of his own. While there is none of the silliness the Montreal *Star* expresses by its daily publication of the Buckingham Palace Court Circular, the profoundly provincial people of *British* Columbia talk familiarly about the 'old country' – even the children – and it is no wonder that Bennett had the new flag raised unceremoniously at about 6 o'clock in the morning when nobody was watching. To Victoria and Vancouver, London is more meaningful than Ottawa; and as for the 'Quebec Problem,' the UBC student newspaper dubbed the B and B report 'Frogwash.'

Bennett deals in paradox and this is both his appeal and the barrier to his deposition. Though the province is distant from everywhere he makes it appear the meaningful centre of the world to those many of his subjects who defensively rejoice in what they have. Underlying all this hard manipulation is his grandiose policy in hydro power. In the electronic age this is a real and symbolic accomplishment of perhaps decisive importance at least to his supporters, and also, I suspect, to many opponents, who see massive freedom in the dams and undefined gratuity in the slim wires. Which churl, which backward critic, will not plug into the grid of this Dynamic Society?

ABRAHAM ROTSTEIN & MELVILLE H. WATKINS

The Outer Man: Technology & Alienation

No civilization has been as rich as ours. Yet few have been as apprehensive.

Modern concern centres on our irreversible commitment to technology. Has a Faustian bargain been struck with the machine?

The most general theory of technology which we have is that of Marshall McLuhan. Technology is the extension of man. The wheel is an extension of the foot, the axe is an extension of the arm, print is an extension of the eye, radio an extension of the ear, and the computer is an extension of the nervous system.

Technology is regarded as an extension of the *individual* – his limbs, senses, and psyche. In McLuhan's world, man stands naked in the jungle of his technology. No institutions intercede to mediate or amplify the severity of the consequences. Social change is a stringent function of a changing technological environment. The progressive extension of man's being through his evolving technology rigidly sets the course he must travel.

Individualism, for example, is the product of a particular technology which generates a characteristic set of institutions. Print created literacy and increased specialization. This division of labour extended the process of exchange and the market system. Starting with the printed bible and the Protestant Reformation, there grew up the cult of achievement, accumulation and capitalism. With print, came the literate voter, the 'informed public' and liberal democracy. History is trapped in the ramifications of technology.

For Karl Marx, institutions intercede to mediate the effects of man's technology. Under the rubric of Marx's concept of externalization (*Entäusserung*) man projects his person naturally through his productive and creative activity; through his technology as well as through art, law and politics. But when a specific institutional framework, i.e., capitalism, despoils his human tie to these productive efforts through the impersonal and exploitative nature of his institutions, man becomes alienated. Alienation, or estrangement (*Entfremdung*) is not inherent in a given technology but only a consequence of the way that technology is instituted. 'The estrangement of man,' Marx states, is 'realised and expressed in the relationship in which a man stands to other men.' Thus, at least in the case of capitalism, institutions intrude between man and his technology so as to increase the social burden of his existence.

Marx is an optimist on the inherent consequences of technology itself. The fault under capitalism is purely institutional. He remains largely innocent in the area of technological constraints that transcend specific institutional forms whether capitalist or socialist.

A more general theory of technology and alienation proceeding beyond both Marx and McLuhan might begin by positing as the central proposition a mutual extension between man and his technology: while technology is an extension of man, man in turn may become an extension of his technology – the driver becomes an extension of the automobile, the factory worker an extension of the assembly line. The group of individuals linked to a given technology becomes a collectivity operating under the actual constraints and ties of that technology. In a technological society, institutions cease to be the voluntary contractual associations of individual atoms, but rather express in various ways the concrete concerns and constraints of persons tied by the hard realities of specific technologies.

The new technology erodes individualism and sets the central apprehension of the modern age – the loss of individuality. Symbol of the new technology is electricity operating as pure information in the form of the computer. It also creates the power grid on which the very sustenance of life depends. Food, heating, transport, light, and production rely on the grid. This overriding constraint of daily life effectively wires us all into the common circuit. Information moves with the speed of light and compresses time and space. Vital interdependence creates the collectivity as instant common fate.

Yet everywhere today we see not centralization and uniformity but protest – Quebec, Berkeley, Albania. The effective unit of action is the group, not the individual. The emerging pattern is the self-definition as well as the interdependence of collectivities. The result of the erosion of individualism is the creation of many tribes in the global village. Tribal involvements have become the prerequisite of personal identity.

All technology is man's externalization. To 'outer' oneself is to create new power and to risk losing control of it. Alienation is latent in the process of 'outering' but only comes to the fore with the machine. Karel Capek, in the play R.U.R., anticipated the final limits of 'outering' in the robot. The alienation of man from himself is complete. But it is the trauma of the individualist – the total externalization of the individual man.

Externalization today proceeds in the creation of the immensely complex and pervasive technologies and institutions of collective power. The robot, in fact, has a hundred thousand heads. With this insight Huxley and Orwell laid the basis for the modern vision of negative utopia. But the vision is necessarily a nightmare so long as one equates loss of individuality with totalitarianism and refuses to admit of meaningful collective existence.

Alienation is mass guilt. The technology that we have initiated, and assented to, may constrain not only ourselves but others. But we can neither relinquish it, nor contract out of our responsibility in an attempt to safeguard the sanctity of our individual consciences. The new institutions with their inherent potential for compulsion flow from the modern technology to which we have given our assent.

The moral issues of today are matters of the collective conscience; we are all involved in Hiroshima. The effective response to collective guilt is collective action.

The commitment to technology must be distinguished from the relinquishment of control over technology. It lies within our power to direct the process of invention and to mediate the social consequences of technological change. The absolute commitment to efficiency prevalent in North America amounts to saying 'let technology run free.' This is a cross that we need not bear.

With the new technology has come new philosophies. Existentialist philosophy focusses on the guilt and despair of the individual and misses the point. The philosophers of the absurd push our social diseases into high definition, thereby heightening social awareness and collective solutions. The philosophers of the new technology, notably McLuhan, make us aware of the environment, and thus increase our freedom to deal with it.

Technological determinism is fostered, albeit unintentionally, by those who merely cultivate apprehension in the name of the old moral absolutes of the individual conscience or who remain utopian with regard to the machine.

On one level, social reform focusses on existing patterns of income distribution, the paramountcy of property rights, and the premature lethargy of an affluent society. This affluence is itself the result of a more integrated and more interdependent industrial order, and thus provides a moral basis for institutional change. The new moral order bypasses the individualism of a competitive market society, but also challenges the individualism of our ethical commitments.

But the reform of the cash nexus can become a myopic endeavour if it ignores the hard and irrevocable reality of the machine nexus. On this level, the potential, if not the actual, endeavours toward reform of both capitalism and socialism draw more closely together. Neither can be utopian about the inherent consequences of the machine.

The human condition today is given by the certain commitment to technology and the uncertain limits of the loss of freedom. For those

March 1966

who are neither utopian nor in premature despair, these limits can only be known in the abiding commitment to social reform.

BP NICHOL

to islands rowboats stand on

(for mitzi)

```
                a
            rowboat
         an
       island
              o
         an
       island
              a
            rowboat
         row
              a
              boat
       to
         an
       island
            land
              is
       to
                       stand on
                    an
              island
       to
                   row
                     a
                     boat
                to
                and
                land
                              on
                        stand
                              on
                   islands
                   and

                     O
                         a
                     rowboat
                     row
                         a
                         boat
                to islands rowboats stand on
```

GEORGE BOWERING

The House On Tenth

I'm trying to tell the story of Ebbe Coutts, and I have to stop here and admit it's hard to tell a *story* about him. He comes to me in a strange mind picture, in which a background of scenes, apartments, parks, beaches, are moving back and forth in giant proportions, in and out among each other, like a deck of cards, fanned and interleaved, and in front of it all the figure of Ebbe Coutts, as I see him always, now hundreds of miles from him at least ... I see him angular, short and narrow-limbed, in skintight black pants and black turtleneck sweater, old soft leather shoes with pointed toes, but somehow heavy, blunt, suggestive of the heavy shoes of a grandfather who was once a strong labourer. The dark clothes gave his face a shadowed but small elegance. His hair was jet black, in long twists and waves. When he combed it with water in the morning it took on a sleek sheen, thick and wet around the ears and down the back of the neck. His face was too young for a beard, but a shadow clung to his angular jaw and below his sharply etched cat-like cheekbones. His eyes were black too, the eyebrows nearly meeting. Besides that there were his hands, thin and white, but too big. He could grasp a basketball and hold it with one hand on top of it, above the floor. His thumbs bent backward and bent in sharp degrees from their joints. When he moved his hands or his whole body, he did it with the spring and jounce you'd associate with a frog – suddenly gone, leaving an afterimage of bent limbs – back again, immediately icy still, face turned on an angle, comical glint in the eyes.

Or on his knees, crying tears down his soiled cheeks, hands out in front of him.

So I have to return to the night of that scene. Walking along Robson Street with Marce, I remembered it. That was a Christmas, too. There was the odd piece of tinsel flattened on a chair or crushed into the rug. It was at the big house the guys rented and destroyed on Tenth Avenue, in among the old stucco 1930 houses filled with retired peep from behind the curtains ladies tending the rhododendrons in the front lawn, this was the strangest house on the street, lived in by who knew how many people. It was a clearing house for students, ex-cons, weekend girls from the nurses quarters of distant crosstown hospitals, painters moving in and out, leaving garish canvasses when they left, but probably leaving with some books, one of the girls, or the telephone. No one actually knew how many people lived there – about five were paying the rent, but I had seldom been there of a night when there weren't at least twenty people showed up one after another all thru the night. This was one of the big 'parties' of gallon redwine jugs and clouds of pot smoke, upturned ashtrays on the wine-coloured rug, ashes squashed into the floor. Anything on the wall: paintings, chianti bottles hanging from spikes, a pair of mysterious black panties, blotch of red from glass of wine thrown at a face. In the kitchen there were many bags overflowing with garbage, lugubrious empty grapefruit skins plopped on top, people searching for wine glasses and settling for the sugarbowl, slurrp slurp slop – filled with red tokay and dribbling on the floor, later to be sticky black smear covered with grainy ashes and sand, while at the electric stove a scowling little guitar girl fries eggs, and in the kitchen alcove, bent heads together in conclave, marijuana joint passed around in a circle, finally too short, jammed in the end of a cigarette, a 'cocktail.'

At first Ebbe is seen once in a while thru the haze and darkness and moving across moviescene heads, dancing with bellies, people dancing with bellies and scissoring in and out knees, to the loud middle register of Miles Davis: 'Sooooo What?' Then I lose track of him, and I sit down on the ornamental stool – this is a toilet seat, that is, chair made out of whole toilet, plunked there, expressive of the house, like the row of cheerleader megaphones on the roof outside the top bedroom. I looked around. Charles is on the couch with Dorothy on one side and another guitar girl on the other. The guitar girl is smacking away on the strings and singing something that is smothered in the general noise, loud laughter, and the loud Miles Davis. Every once in a while a chair would tip over backward, or a bottle hit the floor, and the symphonic familiarity of the general noise would be punctuated with an unrealized thump.

My impression is that Ebbe is pretty happy. He is still in school and doing well, his poems showing up once every few months somewhere in a magazine, and Karen unabashedly loves him, a cool scene for him, walking into the party quietly with her by his side, expected there, smiling, learning the hipfringe jargon of pot, very much unlike Ebbe's former lost hopeless loves, like for instance once Dorothy, who wound up laughing at Ebbe and saying he couldn't manage a piece of ass, this right in front of his mother. Ebbe had responded by hitting her in the face and leaving the two women alone, impossibly together there, Ebbe loping down the street yelling inane gorilla noises.

That is, sitting there on the toilet in the livingroom I had seen Ebbe pass from the kitchen into one of the bedrooms, his hands up high so he could squeeze thru the crowd, a quarter-full bottle in one hand, pack of cigarettes in the other, making wide open surprised eyes and big grin which is a funny round hole in the middle of his slanty face.

I was all alone, as always about that time, having just finished a long stupid infatuation with opulence and free booze and long black hair. Enough. I'm talking about Ebbe Coutts, or, at least toward him, he is such a flitting night time figure.

Like Man Ray, Johnnie Ray, Aldo Ray, I was, you see, sitting there reading the paper now, opening at the classified ads where someone had fouled up the crossword puzzle, reading the In Memoriams, the true people's poetry of the day:

'This month comes with deep regret.
And brings a day we will never forget.
You fell asleep without good bye,
But memories will never die.'
– Lovingly remembered by the Frobush
family.

Aw, the Frobush family, family with unknown people's poet amidst, Wordsworth your ideal, you go remembered while Morris Frobush works unrecognized.

A lovely young late teenage girl I'd never seen before comes up to me somewhat drunk and asks where's Ebbe, so I told her, in the bedroom getting laid, and she turns around, drifting off toward the crush of bodies in the dining room, and before she got out of range in her aimless meander, I reached out with steady soft hand and placed its palm over the curve of her left buttock. She halted gently, hesitated, then proceeded on, propelling herself from the leverage of my tensile wrist.

'God knows how much we miss him.
Never shall his memory fade.
And loving thoughts will always wander
To the grave where he is laid.'

March 1966

*– Forever loved and remembered
by his Wife and Family.*

Touchingly mailed off to the paper with $1.75 once a year. God knows how much they miss him.

Even then, sitting on the white porcelain of the toilet seat and holding ragged newspaper in my hand, I wondered what it was I was looking for in Ebbe – he was five years younger than me, four years younger, four or five, and he came from Vancouver highschools of cool 1950s teenhood, long ducktail hair, glossy with Brilliantine, rat tail comb handle sticking from back pocket of denim pants properly faded, knowledgeable if not actually active, of hubcap sales to East End carparts dealers, and downtown rumbles in Chinatown of a Friday night. While me I came age seventeen down from the mountains and orchards to the big pigeon town, fog town silent smell of the early morning slap-wharf open town, city, big city for me, former town harmless rebel of a different clime...

*– In loving memory of Robert (Bob) who
departed this life February 27, 1960.
'There is a link death cannot sever,
Love and remembrance last forever.'
–Sadly missed by his wife Florence
and his daughter Eva.*

Death death death death death a newspaper item in the smallest possible print for your dollar seventy-five of a Tuesday morning. The party swirled more as people crushed in and Yehudi Bing the cool cool poet emerged from the drunk tank with disheveled and smiling nurse-girl and stood cool with crucifix hanging on naked chest, against a wall near the Miles Davis machine, looking to see who's here, George Delsing, nods to me, I nod back, looking askance at his girl. He wants me to know he has made his traditional strike in the drunk tank, the cold little room in the basement with moist mattress on the floor and pink thin wool blanket nailed over the door.

*'We miss you now, our hearts are sore.
As time goes by, We miss you more.
Your loving smile,
Your gentle face,
No one can fill your vacant place.'
Sadly missed by Otto, Marg and
grandchildren.*

Them cheap brothers and sisters, they leave everything up to Otto and Marg. Even when he was alive they wouldn't help take care of him. You'd think they could have offered to take him for a month so a person could have a decent holiday. The kids always talking about going to California because all the kids their age gets holidays in the summer, but oh no...

*'Your sweet face is still so clear,
It seems like yesterday,
When God needed another angel,
And called you home to stay.
We miss so much your ready smile,
The comfort of having you near,
We know you're with us every day,
And we miss you Mother dear.'
– Sadly missed by Christina, Peggy, Amie,
Lawrence, Terry, Jack and Peggy-Anne.*

Also:

RENT A TV
24-hour service
Rental Purchase Plan
Free Delivery
Reasonable Rates

Dear TV we miss you. Your ready smile, your gentle face.

I threw the newspaper into the general mess on the floor. Because there suddenly in the livingroom was one of the funniest things I'd seen for a long time. There was this big Juno girl, real name unknown, large blonde girl who said she was from southern Iowa and said they were all like her down there. She was six feet tall, with long hair coiled in a loose braid and dropped round her shoulder to the front down over a pair of enormous breasts, not enormous saggy, but sticking straight out under the thin wool of her sweater, great pointers ready to gun down the world. And in front of her little Billy Billy the English guy lately living in the house, as usual loudly drunk, standing in his bare feet, socks half off and dangling in loose emptyskeins in front of his toes, so everyone thought he would trip over them and fall on his pug nose. He was only about five foot two, but when he got drunk, which was almost every night, he got belligerent in the classic little guy way, and more ominous for us, he seemed to want to get someone mad at him, to desire a smash in the face or a noisy crashing of body among bottle-laden table. It was frightening, because he seemed to want it so much. There he was now, in front of Juno, drink in hand (secret personal scotch and soda!), eyes screwed up in the wild staring in two directions way the English drunk seems to have for himself, poking his forefinger out against the pointed breast tips of Juno, and each time he would teeter, as if he were indeed going to spring between her massive boobs, or backwards, on his ass. And as he poked, she waved and batted him away like a fly, swished him away with one long heavy sexy outstretched arm while she continued to listen to the conversation that buzzed among crowded heads in the middle of the livingroom floor. And Ebbe was there, past them, his grinning face with wide open eyes and black curly hair hanging over his forehead, his head bobbing up and down in the semi-shadow, his voice probably saying 'Yeah. Yeah. Hee he. Yeah.'

A kind of a skullface with black eyebrows. Smiling at the funny thing it is to be alive and little and pushing those most beautiful of all automation buttons. One time he had got me alone and started talking to me:

EBBE: About your poems, they stink.
GEORGE: Thanks a lot.
EBBE: No, be serious, I'm not jumping on you for god sake. But listen, listen.
GEORGE: Okay, so I listen.
EBBE: Goddam it, why don't you write more about fucking Gail or something, and be *serious* dammit, don't chicken out of your *feeling* until you really get into it, on your own terms.
GEORGE: That's what I'm trying to do ... there's other things...
EBBE: Your *own* terms. Not those you've madeup as yours: 'World-hugging ocean' is crap. Not your terms. I've never heard you talking like that. Expand your vision.
GEORGE: Maybe I'm working on another thing than you are.
EBBE: Moan Collins cuts the absolute shit out of you in that anthology, and he does it because he doesn't chicken out.
GEORGE: Moan Collins is different from me –
EBBE: Right. You're not doing it.
GEORGE: What?
EBBE: *Confess, confess, Confess.*
GEORGE: I don't write about sin, for christ sake. Sin has to do with death and fear of death. I want to write about something else. Like life.
EBBE: Your wit interferes with your feeling. That's the most obvious thing wrong. Poetry is not rhythmic reporting either. You can write about something you imagine as well as something you see. Don't give me your false and abstract sympathy in seeing the guy whose kid is going to die. Get into *him*, the dead kid – everything – Poems are made by leaving yourself vulnerable. Poems with you are too much of an objective diary, *the* thing you do rather than another aspect of your expressiveness.
GEORGE: Okay. I don't mind that. I don't mind being a poem writer, nothing else.
EBBE: That's where you're wrong. Because in California they got a machine can do that. George, you *risk* it with any of us, as you do with Gail maybe, as you have done with Maureen, as you did with Karen on the peyote. Get your *whole life* moving in the poem, not that isolated point to point reference of feeling that is prose, really.
GEORGE: Uh, uh, uh –
EBBE: When the *involvement* is real, the *sound* will be real, whether or not the concern is false: witness Pilgrim's Progress, John Donne, Keats versus Shelley.
GEORGE: Uh –
EBBE: I know you're going to argue. Don't be angry. Don't adopt the older and wiser attitude. Answer me, argue, but do it seriously. I don't want any more of these poems.

(And he handed me a handful of my poems, gave them to me angrily. I took them and folded them carefully and shoved them in my back pocket.)

EBBE: Give me the ones that were difficult, that hurt, that took something – I don't care what – work, blood, tears – that took something out of you other than words. I want poems that take something out of *me* – energy, love, tears. They should be a worthwhile *effort* to read.

We were by the beach at night, and I looked out at white moon slant. I felt the ocean in my eye. Inside I heard Ebbe's words whirling around in my hollowness, meeting other words there, agreeing.

'Aw, Ebbe, you're going to die,' I said.
I put my hand on his shoulder. Then I took it off.

What if the present were the world's last night?

I was still sitting on my toilet when the door opened and six or seven large bulky figures entered. The came into the crowded livingroom with a slow violence, and as they were noticed more and more there was a sequence of feelings that waved over the crowd: first uneasiness, the falling of quiet, then slight regrouping of figures in the dark, the guitar starting to sound again, Miles Davis again sinking into the larger middle register of the crowd, faces becoming the backs of heads. The guys said they heard Ebbe Coutts lived here, and it transpired that they had been school buddies of Ebbe, later jail buddies without him, out again now and looking for a good time, came at last to the house on Tenth. Formerly the House had seemed a wild after hours thing in the gloom night of college life. Now it was a genteel squire afraid of the hunch-shouldered violence of a beefy gangster man breaking his way into the family outing.

Ebbe tried to handle it as he handled everything – let it go, if you let it go and didn't hassle, things would work out fine. Like a huge horned bull. If you didn't get him riled he would get along with you fine. Live and let live. If you show welcome and humanness to the fierce killer he will soften to you. And everyone tried that. I walked out in the kitchen and saw their leader, drunk, wild prison lights in his eyes, asking Yehudi Bing for a glug from his bottle. Yehudi grinned and handed him the bottle. He walked away with it, and Yehudi grinned some more. His girl was watching him. He lit a cigarette and waited obviously. Maybe the guy would get a notion to give the bottle back.

I walked around the whole house, and they were all like that. They were wearing suits and ties, all of them except one, but the suits and ties that suggest the first kids to get out of school, quit, go to work, and dress up for the weekend dance in search of girls to screw or guys to beat up. They would never wear sweaters and suntans. Rather black pointed shoes, the kind you slip on, that looked like cowboy boots cut down for the city.

'God damn son of a bitch the whole fucking thing go to shit and blast I don't give a sweet goddam let it all fall down!'

'Shhh,' said Marce. The people on the bus were looking at us. I waited till they turned their heads back to the blank busrider stare in front of them.

'Marce, why are people here instead of not here? Why does human shit have to have a disagreeable smell?'

'Oh sure,' she said, 'that's the main problem.'

I finally got my wish then and asked Ebbe. 'Man, where did these zombies come from?' 'You just got to be careful,' said Ebbe.

'It's a wicked scene, Eb, I mean I don't *like* it. I want a peaceful time. I just want to sit and look and drink beer and smoke. There's going to be a hassle.'

'Or you could live with it, George.'

'Scared, Eb.'

'Well, I used to know them. They're a bad group. Maybe it'll be too dead for them. They want to see the beatnik scene. See if we're all fruits and commies.'

'What's bugging them?' I asked.

'Well, you know, man. Like they're the dark shadow of the Chamber of Commerce.'

Poor old Ebbe. I know how I would have felt. Like him. But he didn't know that.

Like a dog in the wind, dodging traffic on a busy intersection. Me, I'm sitting in a car, waiting for the green light.

I guess that was the way Ebbe felt about little Billy Billy the English guy, a hopeless deadbeat, trying to get people to include him in, all the time resentful of his own impulse, trying to keep them out. On me it worked: I didn't care too much about him at all. Ebbe stood and watched him, like when he was poking at Juno, and Billy Billy didn't even read poetry or pretend he did, it was okay, Ebbe saw something of himself there, I guess, maybe wanting to find out what it was about Billy Billy that held him. The way I had to find out about Ebbe.

So that was the way it was for Ebbe when the little guy took off after one of the guys that had crashed in, the one that wasn't wearing a suit. He had on a long soft doeskin jacket and a white turtleneck sweater underneath. There was something there that edged at my mind. The ugly cruelness and stupid malice on his face – the hint of sensitivity in the thin bony features and long eyelashes. This was the obvious leader of the group.

He killed a guy by accident, that's why he was in jail. He's bad when he drinks. This came through the air. I think Ebbe might have told someone, or one of the guy's friends. Everyone knew, except Billy Billy. Billy Billy was drunk, his eyes in strange miniature. Long John Silver ogle-stare.

'Hey, how about giving me a drink,' he was saying in his English accent, placing himself defiantly in front of the deerskin coat, waving slightly on his feet, his eyes in that cast.

'Sure,' said the guy, calmly, and handed Yehudi's half-gallon jug to the little guy. Everyone nearby was turning to look. There was a feeling went by me, reaching out to the fringes of hearing. Everyone knew it might get bad. Miles Davis was just blowing monotonous curses down deep in the horn, and the band, a pack of them in the smoky dank, beat out a Harlem jungle sound.

Billy Billy leaned back dangerously, glugging from the bottle. It swirled and went into his mouth, the red wine, looking like one of those old gasoline pumps with the gallons marked on the side of the glass. When he stopped and tried to lower the jug, the big guy reached out and gently held it up, forcing wine into Billy Billy's mouth and down the front of his throat and shirt. Billy Billy choked and pulled the jug away, teetering forward on his short legs.

Ebbe stepped forward and stood close to Billy Billy. 'Come on, I'm putting you to bed, Billy Billy,' he said.

'Man you better get him away right now,' said one of the guys in suits.

'Hey look, you guys, how about buggering off,' said Ebbe.

'*Forget* it. Just get the little fucker out of here.'

But Billy Billy moved then, stepped around Ebbe and flung the jug over three feet of air.

'Here, have a glug,' he said.

The guy in the deerskin coat caught the jug, but red wine slopped out onto the light tan coat. It looked like a deer, just been shot.

'Oh shit,' said a voice right behind me.

'Come on Frank,' said one of the guys in a suit, an unexpected voice of calm, or tense reason. I felt thankful there was that possibility.

Frank looked at Billy Billy, who was pushing against Ebbe's chest, trying to get by. Then he turned and went to the bathroom, to do something about the deerskin coat.

Ebbe was talking quietly to one of the guys in suits, trying to get him thinking along the lines that this was a drag and he should talk Frank into looking for action somewhere else, even, I think, suggesting a party he knew about on the North Shore, and I remember wondering at the time if he was lying – Ebbe? – asking anyway as a personal favour for something a long time ago, a link, that even now he couldn't break, not honourably. I understood that.

In the background, one of the guitar girls was sitting up straight on the couch, feet pulled under her wool skirt, eyes staring.

Billy Billy had filtered thru the crowd and was in the bathroom, yelling GOD DAMN SON OF A BITCH CAN'T PUSH ME AROUND COME ON NONE OF YOUR FRIENDS IN HERE WITH YOU, and there was a dull crash against the door, and then the door came open a bit and there was a long vertical flash of Billy Billy flying thru the air with a glass vase in his hand. Then a heel crashed against wood and the door slammed shut. There was a yell and a smash of glass. The door swung open again, closed, bounced open, settled back, closed. The lock shot – it was locked.

'He's smashing his head against the tub.'

'Frank! Frank!' Ebbe was shouting at the door.

The banging went on inside. There were no more shouts. Just the banging.

Ebbe faced the door, raised one foot and smashed it against the bottom panel. It cracked. He kicked and kicked, with the sole of his foot, the whole force of the leg, levered back and thrust, finally, thru the panel. The crazy Miles Davis horn blew then, loud, without the mute. Ebbe's foot kicked wildly, the door breaking in splinters. Finally, with a spring of his small body, he ducked his head and went into the bathroom, yelling in there, his voice unbelievably loud, a roar in there, it must have ached in his chest, echoed around and around in the tiled bathroom. Then his body came crashing out, miraculously through the jagged triangles of the broken door, sprawling on his knees outside the room. Ebbe kneeled there, his body splayed down, the feet spreading, knees together, arms hanging straight down beside him, fingers curled on the floor, face up, hair wild, tears splashing wet on the top curve of his cheekbones, under the sprinkled light of the party, crying, Miles Davis in his ears, sobbing.

In the bathroom the banging continued.

God Damn it!
I don't want to die!
When the phone rings
I ain't answering it
I've got forty years left
they'll think of something by then
But then it'll be too late
it'll only work on young men
What right have they got?
Just because they're younger
The hell with them!
Fuck them!
Kill them!
If I could live longer –
I'd kill them all!

The next morning I woke up and lifted the lid on the livingroom toilet seat. There was a thick turd in it.

RAMSAY COOK

'Un Québec fort dans une nouvelle Confédération'

'French and English-speaking Canadians have common ideals and share certain common values. They are not, however, identical and never will be. Quebec, as the centre of support for French Canada, asks today that this be recognized in fact and in law. In acting thus we will modify certainly an order of things which has already lasted one hundred years. It is this order of things that threatens us, not Canada itself. On the contrary, it is the latter which renders us the greatest assistance in attaining the dimensions of the ideal which presided at the birth of Confederation.'

Premier Jean Lesage,
Ste Foy, December 14, 1965

Premier Lesage, in announcing a Quebec election for June 5, claimed that his intention was to obtain a fresh mandate before entering negotiations with Ottawa and the other provinces on new fiscal agreements. Coming only three years after the famous hydro-nationalization election, the explanation, to some extent, lacks plausibility. That there will be new negotiations on fiscal arrangements is, of course, certain. Moreover, M. Lesage will doubtless be somewhat strengthened if he can point to a recent and resounding victory for his administration. But two other considerations doubtless weighed even more heavily in his decision. Like Mr Pearson last autumn, M. Lesage sees that magic date, 1967, looming ever nearer. He had no wish to hold an election during that *annus mirabilis* for a variety of obvious reasons.

To begin with, it appears that none of our politicians wants to clutter up John Fisher's scene with elections in 1967 when they can better spend their time attending festivites and dilating upon the capacity of the boys and girls of today to grow into the men and women of tomorrow. M. Lesage is no exception to the rule. But the Quebec premier has an even more important reason for viewing next year as an undesirable election year. In his province the Centennial will not, of course, be celebrated by everyone with total, ecstatic, enthusiasm. For separatists and others who believe they can make political yards out of *à bas*-ing Confederation, 1967 will be a potentially important year. M. Lesage quite naturally wants to be firmly settled in power, especially if he can first weaken further the Union Nationale and prove that the separatists are without significant electoral support, before the numerous nationalist societies begin their inevitable Centennial manifestations.

Over and above these speculations is the further fact that Jean Lesage, like democratic politicians everywhere, has chosen his election date with a sharp eye to the best chance of victory. Then, of course, there is the intriguing possibility that the Quebec premier is still dreaming dreams about a return to Ottawa after Mr Pearson's departure. Mr Pearson's other dauphins (apparently nearly every senior and some junior members of his cabinet), may be having some secret, ambiguous thoughts about Mr Daniel Johnson these days.

These political considerations aside, it is still true the Quebec election bears a heavy significance for the future of Canadian federalism. During the campaign itself, Quebec in particular and the country in general will certainly be treated to a number of declarations in favour of Quebec's autonomy, special status, 'associate' status, and independence, as well as the more usual remarks about motherhood and sin. (In selecting the date for his election, Mr Lesage has made it clear, on the other hand, that Quebec favours Sunday Sports.) English Canadians outside the province would be wise not to treat all of these declarations at face value. The real, as opposed to the rhetorical, problems will be debated and decided after the election. These issues will include division of spending and taxing responsibilities, provincial involvement in economic policies, manpower programmes, social welfare and perhaps even, again, external relations. It is therefore worthwhile to attempt some assessment of the present state of our famous constitutional debate as it effects parties, federal and provincial.

The first point which apparently still needs to be made, since some people still see the debate as one between Ottawa and Quebec alone, is that there is a widespread willingness in several provincial capitals to rethink federal relationships. Premier Robarts made this point plainly last October when he remarked that 'French-speaking Canadians are not alone in looking for changes in the basic structure of the Canadian nation.' Premier Roblin, speaking at

Three Rivers during the federal election campaign implied a similar view when he spoke of 'une nouvelle Confédération canadienne adaptée aux exigences d'un deuxième siècle de vie.' Premier Lesage, of course, takes a similar position. He has stated frankly and repeatedly that the time has not arrived for a thorough rewriting of the constitution. Instead, in the best tradition of Canadian politics, he has committed himself to an empirical approach to constitutional development. It is true that he has used that phrase 'status particulière,' especially in his important speech before the Ste Foy Chamber of Commerce last December. But even in that speech his emphasis appeared to be on the re-arrangement of administrative responsibilities rather than on fundamental structural changes or, even less, on a totally re-drafted constitution. In general these views appear to be shared by the Pearson administration.

What unites Messrs Pearson, Lesage, Robarts, and some other provincial premiers is, of course, power. It is noteworthy, for example, that during the federal election campaign when the Tories presented their new-found united front in Varsity Arena, Mr Robarts appeared to support the Diefenbaker call for a national constitutional convention. Since then, however, he has completely avoided, even rejected the suggestion. Constitutional revision always appears easy to those in opposition.

This rule applies to the parties at Ottawa. The Pearson government is committed to the existing constitution in a flexible and decentralized form, though the Prime Minister manifests a distressing incapacity or unwillingness to state his position in detail. Mr Robert Thompson's Socreds appear to share the government's view, though critical on some details. The Créditistes now support the 'Associate State' position in their provincial incarnation, at least. Mr Diefenbaker, on behalf of his party, recently repeated his proposal for a 'national constitutional Confederation conference.'

The Conservative leader's views are so vague and contradictory that the best one can say for his proposal is that it is a weak effort to provide his party with a policy different from that of his opponents. At worst, it is irresponsible, for surely not even Mr Diefenbaker believes that a constitution, an amending formula, national symbols, and the rest, can be instantly produced in a great national jamboree. The contradiction in his view is that while he condemns federal-provincial conferences as a method of settling matters between Ottawa and the provinces, he seems to believe that an enlarged Conference could redraft the entire constitution. One may be permitted to doubt that such a gathering could even produce a suitable constitution for the town of Prince Albert.

That Mr Diefenbaker's views are confused and contradictory is hardly novel. But to find the NDP open to the same charge is both surprising and distressing. Yet, if anything, Mr Douglas and his party appear to accept a position on constitutional revision that is so confused as to be little short of ludicrous. In a recent article in the Toronto *Globe & Mail* (April 13) Mr Douglas repeated the views on the constitutional question which his party first made public in a press release of February 11, 1965. He has added one touch, perhaps to go one better than Mr Diefenbaker: he wants to bring in 'the people' to a discussion held in a parliamentary committee.

The NDP insists that the country needs a new constitution because the existing one 'does not meet the needs of our modern technological society.' The particulars of this failing are not spelled out. The new constitution should include, according to the February 1965 statement, a federal government with power over matters of national concern including power to establish 'together with the provinces' full employment, medicare, overall social security, housing, manpower policy, and marketing boards for primary products. Moreover it must retain control over 'among other things' (a fine piece of constitutional precision) 'monetary and fiscal policy, banking, tariffs and transportation.' Ottawa must also have power to establish a Canadian Development Fund. A re-examination of taxing powers and financial resources is also necessary.

Two things are immediately striking about this proposal. First, that it sounds very much like the present distribution of powers in the BNA Act. That it is also very reminiscent of the legitimate, but traditional, CCF-NDP emphasis on centralization hardly needs to be underscored.

The catch is that the NDP also advocates a 'special status for Quebec.' And what does that mean? In Mr Douglas's words 'There must be a clear recognition of the special status of Quebec in respect of its language, culture and tradition.' (In his *Globe* article the NDP leader seemed to confuse completely the 'special status for Quebec' with equal status for French Canadians. On the latter point, forgetting the confusion, his views were wholly sensible, as were those expressed by Mr David Lewis in the recent debate on bilingualism in the federal civil service.) On the special status question Mr Douglas's proposal is that we should have a new constitution in which Quebec has a position like the one it has now – different from other provinces in language, culture, and tradition. Surely Mr Douglas and his advisers know that when Quebeckers these days speak of a 'special status,' they mean (the spectrum stretches from M. Lesage to Professor J.Y. Morin) increased Quebec control over economic policy, social welfare, manpower policy, social security, housing, and even external relations – all matters that the NDP statement places firmly in the hands of Ottawa.

The sin of the NDP is at least two-fold. It plays with words (special status) and panders to those who think constitutions can be changed as readily as dirty socks. (Mr Diefenbaker also plays with words. His counterpart of the NDP's 'special status' is 'ONE CANADA' (his capitals) which he uses to imply that his opponents believe in two or more Canadas. Not even separatists, of course, believe in two Canadas, though some good federalists believe in 'two nations,' and they are, frequently, playing dangerous word games, too. The CCF-NDP has a deserved reputation for clear, principled thinking. Its position on the constitution brings that reputation into question.

There are, in fact, only two seriously debatable positions in the present constitutional discussion (though there are several variations of each): the federalist position, and those who favour a 'special status' for Quebec. This point has been made obvious in several recent speeches by our most clear-minded constitutionalist: M. Pierre Elliott Trudeau. The federalist case is simple enough, though it involves a commitment to hard empirical thinking, and discussion. It means in essence an effort to work out institutions throughout Canada by which the equal status of French- and English-speaking Canadians can be ensured. It means further that constitutionally, though not necessarily administratively, all provinces will be treated as equals, with none more equal than others. It means that in a country like Canada with its strong regional, provincial and ethnic differences, consultation and co-operation among various levels of government is an inevitable, and not necessarily an unfortunate, fact of life.

The alternative, or 'special status' case, is one which looks towards the gradual emergence of two entities: English Canada, increasingly governed by Ottawa, and French Canada, increasingly identified with and governed by Quebec. M. Trudeau interprets the latter option, if adopted rigorously, as leading ineluctably towards the development of two political nations in Canada.

It is difficult to deny the view that these two positions represent, at least in theory, the only two realistic ones in the present situation. The federalist position requires a commitment to the existing, evolving constitution and rejects the idea of a constitutional convention either Diefenbaker or Douglas-style. The 'special status' view implies a radical revision of the constitution and the country. To the adventurous, or less kindly, the irresponsible, the Trudeau position, the federalist position, will appear prosaic and unadventurous. But constitutions are prosaic; it is only Declarations of Independence that are romantic and exciting. And even Trudeau's views require changes that may be too demanding for Canadians. As he told the Royal Society of Canada: 'la réforme que je propose paraîtra modeste par comparaison avec les chambardements énormes dont l'opinion québécoise est saisie depuis quelques années: c'est que je n'ai su parler que de l'essentiel. Ce modeste essentiel présuppose néanmoins une transformation gigantesque dans les mentalités, et de ce que j'ai appelé la règle du jeu social. Mais était-il atteint que le chauvinisme stérile disparaître des moeurs canadiennes, et les autres réformes constitutionnelles utiles suivraient sans trop de difficultés. Par contre, si cette essentiel n'est pas atteint, ce n'est vraiment pas la peine de parler du reste, car le Canada sera balayé périodiquement par le vent mauvais des querelles ethniques, et deviendra une terre stérile pour l'esprit, d'où toute paix et toute grandeur seront bannies.'

will be heard on the Quebec hustings in the next six weeks. But, then, electorates are not Royal Societies. It is, however, reassuring to know that those sentiments will be present when the next series of federal-provincial Conferences is called. They are, after all sentiments which Premier Lesage has never contradicted. It is for that reason that his almost certain re-election will be a victory for Confederation – for, as he has said, 'un Québec fort dans une nouvelle Confédération.'

DAVID W. SLATER

Gordon's New Book

Like many tracts for the times, Walter Gordon's *A Choice for Canada* is very biased and distorted. The central theme is of the extreme and immediate danger to the Canadian nation from United States economic imperialism, exercised through the increased American ownership and control of the Canadian economy that has developed during the last twenty years. According to Mr Gordon, this development overwhelms every other fact of change in Canada's political and economic independence in modern times. The 'Choice for Canada' is to adopt policies to induce many more 'Yankees to Stay Home' and to make those here now 'Be Good Yankees for Canada' – or to permit the disaster of Canada's disappearance as a nation.

The book can be attacked at an astonishingly large number of points of detail, about Canada's situation, about goals, and about specific policy recommendations. The book can also be readily attacked for its extremes of bias and distortion. But when one focuses on the central themes, when a reasonable discounting is made for the excesses permitted to a political advocate, what judgment does one come to? Is Mr Gordon's version of Canada's choices on ends and means essentially right? I think not. While the problems that he points to, of American ownership and controls over resources and activities in Canada, must be taken into account in our country's policy, I doubt that they deserve the weight he gives them. Other extremely important issues are neglected by Mr Gordon. And the means which he proposes for dealing with Canada's external economic requirements appear likely to do more harm than good.

Some personal, professional and 'good-citizen' matters should be disposed of at the outset. For a little time this writer saw Mr Gordon at close range. Very favourable impressions were formed of his intelligence, energy, courage, persistence, and long-standing devotion to Canadian affairs. There are many things to admire about his writing of the book. But some features are rather objectionable. In the book Mr Gordon, like some of his notoriously dirigiste friends in the journalistic community, denigrates the views of economists, political scientists, sociologists, etc., particularly those in universities. Up to a point this is good clean fun, but only up to a point. Canadian social scientists are well aware of their limitations and deficiencies. But their recent work displays attractive characteristics too: of intellectual honesty; of testing ideas by the available evidence; of painstaking effort to get the sums right within their respective disciplines. Admittedly these are modest and incomplete bases for understanding Canada's problems and contributing to development of policies. But they are not irrelevant. They are often preferable to habits of seeing only what one wants to see, and of hearing only what one wants to hear. One gets a little fed up too with being treated as, at best, a woolly unknowing fellow-traveller of the American imperialists (my words, not Mr Gordon's) whenever one challenges the pet ideas of those who see the shadows of American wolves around every corner.

The first half of Mr Gordon's book has been neglected by the press thus far. His discussion of 'Foreign Policy,' of 'Relations with French Canada,' of 'Social Security and Education,' of 'The Objectives of Economic Policy,' and the 'Supervision of Financial Institutions' have been submerged by the central themes of foreign investment, foreign control, and the balance of payments. As the Liberal Party found from neglecting to read *Troubled Canada* earlier, what Mr Gordon writes is ignored at one's peril. The chapter on foreign policy emphasizes Canada's interests: in support of the UN, particularly in its peace-keeping functions; in a continuous effort to help ease tensions in the world; and in maintaining contacts everywhere – without making deep commitments where we have little knowledge and little by way of vital interest. These views seem rather bland and reasonable. Mr Gordon offers a sympathetic, firm, optimistic, somewhat-fatherly view on 'Relations With French Canada.' He says that Canada is a bilingual country, but NOT a country of two nations. He hopes for much from the educational, social, technological, and industrial revolution in Quebec, and counsels patience from the rest of us. He is mindful of the interests of the non-English, non-French 'third' of the Canadian people (rounded to a third by lumping in the Scots, Irish, and Welsh), and of the needs for a strong national government. In the chapter on 'Social Security and Education' he is at his liberal best. Improvement in the structure of Canada's Unemployment Insurance system and increases in the scale of benefits are strongly recommended. He makes a strong case for the selective extension of old age assistance. He puts himself on the record favouring the war on poverty, public housing, improvements in hospitals, medicare and a very great improvement in Canada's educational system. The chapter on 'Objectives of Economic Policy' is principally a retelling of his 1965 budget story, which attributed much of Canada's improvement in employment and output since 1963 to Liberal government economic policies, in my view a fantastic exaggeration. Incidentally, in this chapter Mr Gordon takes a poke at the Economic Council of Canada for its efforts to counter some of the current panic about inflation; and at the bluntness of monetary policy (in this and many other respects the book reminds one of the speeches of the former Governor of the Bank of Canada).

In the chapter on 'Supervision of Financial Institutions' Mr Gordon argues against the Porter Commission's recommendations for integrating all Canada's banking-type institutions, no matter what government chartered them, into a national banking system, subject to federal government banking laws and regulations regarding their banking activity. His position is based on the contention that regulation of provincially-chartered institutions is beyond the constitutional jurisdiction of the Federal government. Reasonable arguments may be made for and against the Porter Commission's recommendations, but Mr Gordon's line is neither certain nor decisive and is seriously incomplete and unrealistic. When provincially-chartered institutions opt into activities which are federal government responsibilities, they must take the consequences. Provincially-chartered institutions have increasingly taken on, de facto, the status and functions of banks in Canada; they have taken on functions of creating money and near-substitutes for money and of participating in the payments mechanism. Judging by recent British judicial precedents, the legal dividing line between activities that are and are not banking is changing. In sharp contrast with the draft Bank Act which Mr Gordon introduced in 1965, prior to the troubles of Atlantic Acceptance and British Mortgage and Trust, he is now concerned with the safety of depositors in provincially-chartered loan and trust companies. He proposes the development of a federal deposit insurance system, with encouragement to provinces and to individual institutions to opt in. Deposit insurance has great attractions, but it does not rule out federal responsibility for deciding who is eligible and who not and on what terms; nor is it sufficient to provide an adequate system of protection against difficulties with domestic financial institutions, as United States experience has shown.

In chapters 6 to 8 the central themes are presented under the headings: 'Balance of Payments,' 'Foreign Investment' and 'What To Do About Foreign Investment and Balance of Payments.' About Mr Gordon's "Choice," one should probably state his own position a little before commenting on the book. I am prepared to concede that the present extent and form of foreign ownership and control is a limiting factor on the Canadian social and political choices. I believe that the net economic advantage of the size and form of Canada's net use of foreign capital in the postwar period has been, on balance, considerable. I am by no means convinced as yet that the degreee of change in the freedom of our social and political choices has been vitally altered by the increases in American ownership and control of resources and activities in Canada. I concede also that variability in capital flows into and out of Canada can sometimes cause problems for this country, and the instabilities in capital flows seem to have increased in recent years. Of course Canada encounters some vulnerability from these arrangements, in exactly the same sense as does a business firm within Canada when it borrows from a particular trust company or lends to some other business. But I reject categorically allegations of huge present balance-of-payments difficulties from this source.

Mr Gordon's chapters on 'Balance of Payments' and 'Foreign Investment' raise some of the most troublesome questions to a foreign-minded critic. What is fair game in an exercise of advocacy? Mr Gordon's book is seriously misleading, I believe, about the relationships between capital inflows and consumption in Canada, about the exchange crisis of 1962, about the returns to those who invest in equities as compared with fixed income securities, about the significance of bilateral Canada-US balance of payments relationships, about the mechanisms which relate Canada's current account and capital account transactions in balance of payments, about the relative burdens of 'servicing Canada's international indebtedness,' and many other factors. Is this fair game for somebody who is trying to stir up people about a problem that one considers serious? Is the 'May-Is game' fair within the rules? In discussing Foreign Investment, Mr Gordon introduces us to the myriad ways in which foreign-owned and controlled companies MAY limit Canadian exports, MAY be biased toward importing materials and capital goods from abroad, MAY be biased toward importing business services, MAY this, MAY that, MAY something else. In a cockeyed world, anything is possible; but what is the world really like? What are the fair rules of evidence in 'establishing the facts' in an exercise of advocacy? If you can find one or two examples to support your contention, can you reasonably argue that your case is proved?. Even if one concedes that it is bad analysis, is it acceptable by the rules of evidence in adversary proceedings? I don't know what the answers to these questions are. Most of us have been advocates, and we have shaped, selected, distorted, biased our arguments and evidence for the cause. Considerable latitude must be conceded to Mr Gordon in his advocacy. We should be skeptical of most things he says; but should we reply as in adversary proceedings? Sometimes yes.

Mr Gordon wants to reduce the size in relation to the Canadian economy of the net rate of capital inflow to Canada, and change its form too – so that more is borrowed under debt obligations and less carries ownership and control claims. The reduction in the size of the inflows would entail a reduction in the debit balance in Canada's current trade in goods and services. Mr Gordon's recommendations concentrate on decreasing Canada's imports and increasing Canada's exports of goods and services by a complicated, discriminatory set of policies. The most fundamental criticism of Mr Gordon's proposals is that they neglect the most important policies which would be required to achieve his objectives, namely a set of credit and tax policies to increase considerably private saving in Canada (especially by Canadian persons and companies), and a set of policies to raise government tax revenue relative to expenditure and carry out some form of 'forced public saving.' The other main criticism is of the rather extreme autarchical, complicated, discriminatory nature of Mr Gordon's recommendations. Maybe Canada should look at the way in which the Persians and the Mexicans and the Egyptians nationalized and repatriated foreign-owned and controlled ventures in their countries. Maybe Canada will want to do the same thing. Maybe we can be more ingenious than these other people were. But maybe what we should really learn from these other people is that the roads to economic development, and to such social and political independence and responsibility as we can have in the modern world do not really bear the signposts 'Yankee Go Home.' We ought to explore some of the other roads, and the considerable strengths of our vehicles.

DOROTHY LIVESAY

And Give Us Our Trespasses

1

Sometimes the room shakes
as the bed did shake
under love
sometimes
there's this
      earthquake.

2

As if at midnight
a socket
was plunged in the wall
and eyes sprang open.

3

Whenever I speak
    out of turn, is it?
you press your fingers
      against my mouth:
'Listen.'

I hear only your heartbeat.

4

My tongue
    is too long

my kiss
    too short
inadequate   I shrink
    from perfection.

5

Yet charged —
    your beauty charges me:

the receptor trembles

quivering water
    under the smite
        of sunlight.

6

The telephone
    hangs on the wall
always available
    for transmitting messages:

why is it
    to lift the receiver
is to push the weight
    of a mountain?

7

Between the impulse to speak
    and the speaking
storms crackle.

Forgive us our
        distances.

MELVILLE H. WATKINS
Is Gordon's Game Worth the Candle?

In last month's *Forum*, Professor David Slater commented on Mr Walter Gordon's views on foreign policy – as contained in the latter's new book, *A Choice for Canada* – that they were 'rather bland and reasonable.' That theme seems to me to be applicable to Mr Gordon's views as a whole. Since reason is a major virtue and blandness a minor vice, the book is praiseworthy. But too much of blandness engulfs like a fog and prevents one from seeing far enough. While Professor Slater wants us to explore other roads than Mr Gordon's, I would prefer that the fog lift the better to discover the real attractions that may lie ahead on Mr Gordon's route.

Much has been written already pro and con on the specifics of Mr Gordon's prescription for Canada – and more shall be added here. Little has been said of the premises from which Mr Gordon proceeds – yet they are easily discovered and the evidence that can be offered for the case of 'bland reason.' Witness the closing words of the preface:

... my premise is that Canadians wish their country to remain independent both economically and politically. Moreover, we want the benefits gained from developing our nation to be shared by Canadians - not handed over to enterprising people in other countries for a fraction of their potential value.

The assumptions are simple and straightforward: it is good to be a Canadian and to grow richer. The only thing wrong with such common sense is that it does not take us nearly far enough. One needs a grander *Weltanschauung* that at least tries to answer such questions as whether, on a shrinking globe, it is worthwhile being a Canadian – and not an American – and whether getting richer is really the overriding priority.

But let us retreat for a while to specifics. Everyone agrees that the most important issue for Mr Gordon is foreign ownership and control. Professor Slater reflects the majority view among Canadian economists in finding a predominance of unreason. Though an economist, I am inclined to disagree. The crux of the issue has to do with a distinction too infrequently made between the economic and political consequences of foreign ownership and control. The special competence of economists lies in discussing the former, and their findings – that foreign investment has been economically advantageous and probably substantially so – merit serious attention. It seems to me that on the whole Mr Gordon gives them that; if anything, he seems to be too unwilling, like most Canadian economists, to explore the alternative ways by which Canada could prosper with less foreign investment through increasing Canadian savings, through developing channels other than the parent-subsidiary relation for the inflow of technical progress, and through improving the home environment for scientific and technical research.

Mr Gordon's view that foreign control is disadvantageous and undesirable is based predominantly on political grounds – and here I think his case is more convincing than the economist's countercase, which rests on no special competence. His oft-quoted comment on American pressure, based as it is, on experience, is not easily disposed of:–

... I had not fully appreciated the depth and strength of these pressures until I became Minister of Finance in April of 1963. During the two-and-one-half years I held that office, the influence that financial and business interests in the United States had on Canadian policy and opinion was continually brought home to me ... American citizens and American corporations have enormous investments in Canada and ... they resent any measures that would interfere with or restrict the growth of such investments, or place obstacles in the way of making new ones.

A countercase must assume the burden of demonstrating that 'financial and business interests in the United States' are likely mostly to act in the Canadian interest. The easiest way to argue this is to insist that American corporations are innocent until proven guilty, but this has little to be said for it other than that it shifts the burden of proof away from the economist to the other side. American statesmen have provided ample evidence of late of their view that American corporations are the instruments of American foreign policy, not only in the narrow sense of defenders of the American balance-of-payments but also in the broad sense of propagators of American ideology. Nor will it do for the economist to fall back on the argument that Canada is politically sovereign, and that if foreign control were to create problems, then corrective action could be taken, for such an argument rests on the weak assumption that the capacity to take political action will survive the erosion caused by that unremitting pressure of which Mr Gordon writes.

Mr Gordon's other major preoccupation is the Canadian balance-of-payments. Professor Slater takes Mr Gordon severely to task for his muddled views on this matter and properly so. The adjustment-mechanism in the balance-of-payments is a highly technical matter and Mr Gordon should heed the experts when they doubt the existence of huge present difficulties simply because there is a large current account deficit. Mr Gordon's case against foreign investment is as seen above, a strong one based on political experience and premise, and deploring the current account deficit – which is mostly the consequence of the capital inflow, not the cause – only muddies the water.

It may be that Mr Gordon is mostly trying to get at the issue of Canadian-American trade and the consequences of its present extent, but if that is so, there are better ways to do it. Indeed, to do it Mr Gordon's way is to risk advocating exactly the wrong policy. The relevant example is the automobile industry agreement, which was justified as necessary to close the current account deficit, and in the process increased the extent of Canadian-American trade, and the integration of the Canadian and American economies which Mr Gordon is at such pains to deplore. While an increase in foreign control may be politically more costly than an increase in trade dependence, the latter does have political consequences, and Mr Gordon's case would be strengthened by consistently attacking both.

On the perennial issue of the tariff, Mr Gordon seems now to be somewhat more on the fence and less in the camp of the protectionists. One wishes he would pay even more attention to economists when they demonstrate the amount of inefficiency that thrives behind the tariff wall and the extent to which foreign control has been increased by the very existence of the tariff. Mr Gordon's case permits him to dispose of lowering tariffs bilaterally vis-a-vis the United States, but not of multilateral tariff reduction which may well offer the best possibility for decreased dependence on the United States.

Of the range of other specific topics on which Mr Gordon takes his stand, only one more will be considered here, and that is Canadian policy toward Asia. Here he is eminently reasonable; no military involvement in Asia, speak out against American policy in Vietnam, and recognize China. But the blandness creeps in, notably on China: recognize but now with the Americans escalating in Vietnam. This is only the most striking case where Mr Gordon seems to retreat from the strength of his own convictions. In the process one glimpses the manacle that restrains his hand – 'we do not wish to offend the United States unnecessarily' – and senses why Mr Gordon too often fails to live up to his promise.

Why the manacle? Mr Gordon, it seems to me, is a good and decent Canadian, who has no axe to grind except that the United States interferes with the quiet Canadian life. What seems to be missing is a sufficiently clear-eyed view of what this century is about.

Part of the problem is, not the fact that Mr Gordon often gets his economics wrong, but that he is too pre-occupied with economics. This is a Canadian disease, but one prefers political leaders who rise above the obsessions of the constituents. A strong case for taking action on foreign control would be based not on the prediction that it will make us better off – which could be true but only if a lot of other things were done at the same time – but that it might free us to pursue a foreign policy that differed substantially from the present disasterous American variety.

Another part of the difficulty is that, while Mr Gordon is a patriot, he is little more. In this age of nationalism, a vibrant Canadian variety – which is presumably what Mr Gordon wants – must come more to terms with the realities of the United States. On the one hand, there is, as just noted, the potential for deploring American foreign policy; Mr Gordon does – on Vietnam and China – but always cautiously and never fundamentally. On the other hand, there is the even more basic issue of how far to admire and emulate the American way of life. Here Mr Gordon – his critics notwithstanding – is very American. There is nothing in this book to upset American liberals, indeed, some of the latter have gone further in opposing the War in Vietnam, in pressing for the guaranteed annual income, and in raising troubling questions about the nature of America. With no desire to impugn Mr Gordon's motives, his nationalism reflects too much of the mentality of the petty bourgeoisie; he is suspicious of large corporations – they do not provide 'the best training for future heroes' – but he largely accepts the ideology of liberalism which permits them to thrive. His recommendations for reform run too heavily toward gimmickry – the usual failing of tax accountants – and not enough toward broad-gauged policies which are prepared to challenge the assumptions on which society – both American and Canadian – operates.

To question the influence of America today is instantly to conjure up General de Gaulle. Professor Stephen Clarkson – again in last month's *Forum* – posed the possibility of Gaullism as a prospect for Canada. With Mr Gordon today the leading advocate of Canadian independence, the question arises: is Mr Gordon a Canadian Gaullist? Professor Clarkson, it happens, has already given an answer: 'whereas our own Walter Gordon offers no choice for Canada in foreign policy, de Gaulle gives us a living case study of a middle power attempting to play a distinctive role in the age of atomic overkill.' But is it not possible that if Canadians would follow Mr Gordon on the issue of foreign investment, they – and Mr Gordon – might find a greater potential for autonomous action in foreign policy as well as in domestic affairs? Unless an independent foreign policy is made a primary and explicit objective for Canada, it is doubtful that Mr Gordon's game is worth the candle.

HELEN GOWANS

An Awfully Mature Person

Isobel brushed flour from her hands onto her apron and leaned across the kitchen table to look out the window for the postman. One of George's manuscripts was overdue. She watched the postman zig-zag back and forth up the block and thought that surely it would be faster if he just went straight up one side and down the other.

Now he was a block away, across the street at Lacey's. About five more houses to do – which gave her time to put the buns in before he arrived. She took rolls from the table, carried them to the stove and slid them into the oven. As she untied her apron she heard something crackle through the mail slot. She hurried to the hall and found on the floor an Eaton's flyer, three cake mix coupons, and a large manilla envelope. Seven years of marriage to an unsuccessful but sensitive writer had made her skilful at neatly opening and closing returned manuscripts so that George never knew she had previously opened them. Carefully she bent the pronged brass staple, unfastened the envelope flap and withdrew the thirteen pages of neatly typed, double-spaced, one-and-one-half inch margined manuscript that was 'The Loveseeker,' the short story George had submitted to the CBC.

Isobel took out a loose enclosure. A letter from Donald Grover this time, not a form rejection. That would give George a lift. She paused before reading, impressed by the CBC letterhead. Then she read:

Dear Mr Foster:

I was pleased to have an opportunity to read still another of your short stories, but while I found 'The Loveseeker' interesting, I am sorry to say that I have had to decide to return it to you. However, I must commend you for your perseverence, and encourage you to keep trying.

I hope you won't be offended if I begin by saying that the situation you are dealing with in 'The Loveseeker' isn't a very unusual one – that is, the infatuation of an imaginative adolescent girl with a sympathetic older man. I do think you show a good deal of insight. Somehow, however, it seemed to me that the general effect of the story was disappointing, and frankly I expected it to come to more than it does. I am not suggesting that you should have written a melodramatic ending, but the teacher's sudden decision to refer the girl to the guidance teacher – after he has begun to make love to her – strikes me as being anticlimactic. In its present form the story seems to fritter away, so that the overall effect is rather more one of embarrassment than poignancy.

I hope these comments will be of some help to you in your unrelenting efforts at writing, and that you will continue to send me your stories.

Meanwhile, will you give my best regards to your wife.

Yours sincerely,
Donald Grover,
Producer, 'Creative Canada.'

Well, Isobel thought, that was not too bad. He encouraged George to keep trying, and that was something. And it was friendly of him to remember her after all these years, lending a warm, personal touch to the rejection.

Donny had been a nice kid, even if he were too short and had worn those thick glasses. Isobel supposed he had never quite clicked with the kids because he had skipped grades and got socially unadjusted or something. But he was doing fine now – right in there with the CBC editing anthologies, and lecturing at Writers' Workshops. He was George's absolute oracle: 'I rank Grover as THE authority on the Canadian short story,' he always said.

She remembered how she had tried to shake Donny all through high school because of his height and those awful glasses. He had even written to her one whole summer when he was away at Banff summer school. She had laughed over one letter in particular that had begun, 'Dear Blossom Face.' Well, Donny Grover had sure shown her. Too bad a girl could not see how people would turn out before making up her mind.

Take George. Back at Varsity he had worn a beard, did not believe in marriage, and planned to 'hop a ship for Cuba to join Fidel in the mountains.' He never got that boat. Now here he was in Aurora, Ontario, teaching English to junior collegiate girls, sending stories to the CBC, and getting bronchitis every winter.

Poor George. He was going to feel just awful. 'The Loveseeker' had been out six weeks, and he was so sure it had been accepted that he was going to ask Grover not to let John Drainie read it, because he felt he could put it across better himself.

But she saw Grover's point about the anticlimax. When George came home one night and solemnly announced that he had something to disclose which he hoped she would forgive, she had waited with excited curiosity. Fumbling and painfully he told her about a sixteen-year old girl who had been writing him love letters. That afternoon, he said, she came into his office and behaved in such a way that he had, well, nearly forgotten himself.

'Just in time, Isobel, I took hold of the situation, made her button up her blouse and marched her right down to Miss Drysdale's office for counselling.'

Anguished, Isobel had moaned and blurted, 'Oh, no George! How cruel! You didn't! How could you!' And he had replied, 'Darling, I didn't ... but I'll be honest. I wanted to.'

She had raged at him. 'Not that, you idiot. I meant how could you send that poor lovesick girl to a guidance teacher! Oh George!'

He looked up, surprised and hurt, running long fingers through his crew cut as he explained. 'For God's sake, Isobel, I was thinking of you. And if you don't care about our marriage, consider the girl. It's probably one of those father image things, and the child needs help!'

Perhaps George had been right. At the school of social work she had attended the instructors claimed that Oedipal problems were dynamite. And even Miss Drysdale had felt the case was beyond her depth and was referring the girl to the new mental health clinic. But it all seemed so cruel and unpoetic.

The oventimer rang and Isobel returned letter and manuscript to the envelope, then left it on the bookcase where George picked up his mail. She hurried to the kitchen, turned off the oven and slipped on her oven mitts to bring out the tray of rolls. She brushed them with melted butter and lightly tipped them onto a fresh white tea towel to cool. Puffed high, and golden brown, they filled the kitchen with a tantalizing aroma. Isobel admired them with satisfaction. She would rather bake bread than do anything. Well nearly anything.

She smiled, recalling the adolescent crush she had had on Hans Goerts, the middle-aged German who had opened a bookstore back home in Nelson. He had not referred her to anyone. But gently led her by the hand into the back of the shop. Had anyone ever guessed? Like Grover – always barging in there after school to read Dostoevsky? He had been a pretty perceptive little guy. Was there a trace of amusement, even irony, in his letter to George? She chose a warm roll, broke it apart and buttered it, then eagerly took a bite. Oh well.

Nervously removing imaginary hang nails, George stood at the door of 312 waiting for the Grade 10 girls to file out. Clad in bright-coloured sweaters and the three patterns of skirts used in Sewing 10B, they sauntered past, poised purposefully for the sudden turn that made them brush pointed young breasts against his rough Harris jacket before they looked up, innocent-eyed and open-mouthed, to lilt at him, 'Oh excuse me, Mr Foster!' George stiffened himself against the wall, braced for repeated attacks on his self-control.

Hurry, hurry, hurry, you little bitches, I want to go home. Six weeks Grover had kept 'The Loveseeker.' He must have accepted it. Why not? It was a damn fine story, sensitively handled, and I know it. I don't need his opinion. He's keeping it. None of his patronizing little letters this time.

'Mr Foster, did you want us to memorize two stanzas or three of "The Skylark"? Mr. Foster?'

'What's that?' George looked down, way down, at Mavis Thompson, who peered up at him through harlequin glasses. Good old Mavis. Only twelve and in Grade 9 – straight As and no breasts yet.

'Oh, three verses, I think it was, Mavis.'

'Thanks,' she answered, then, man-to-man, asked, 'How do you think you're going to be this winter, Mr Foster? I hope you don't come down with pneumonia again. But then you are a bronchial type, so I guess you will.'

'Will what?'

'Be away again this winter. Well, take care of yourself.'

Et tu, Mavis. Christ. 'I feel fine, Mavis just fine,' he answered. He turned his back on her and walked to his desk to sit down.

He could hear MacGregor down the hall bellowing at the 9B boys. 'You lumberjacks stay in file, or I'll have the whole bunch of you in for detentions!' God, the way teachers forgot everything they ever learned at OCE! Temper, threats – what about motivation, self-discipline, logical consequences?

He fussed at his desk, tired, head-aching, trying to decide whether to dash to the staff room and leave early, but have to talk to people, or to wait until the rush was over and leave late but in peace. He chose the latter course, closed his door and sat down at his desk, eyes shut. God, what a headache! He opened the top drawer where he kept Kleenex, aspirins, antihistamine spray, and took out two 222's which he gulped down without water. There. That should help.

But the girls were pretty. He recalled how the coloured sweaters looked, milling about in the hall. 'Dizzy, his head aching, the girls in coloured sweaters spun before his eyes like dazzling shapes in a child's kaleidoscope!' Good. Get that down. He took a pen from his breast pocket and jotted the line in his notebook, then leaned on patched leather elbows and held his throbbing head between his hands.

I've got to stop kidding myself that I can write, he thought. I worked hard on 'The Loveseeker,' and I honestly think it's a pretty sensitive piece of writing – but if Grover rejects it, I quit. It's unrealistic to keep trying. Immature. I'll direct my energy to a more socially productive goal – newsletters for the Federation or something. They need me – and I think I've something to give.

He looked out the window at treetop branches against a pale, grey October sky. A pearly sky? No, better opal. Birthstone for October – nice touch. And the branches now. Filigree? 'Old gold filigree against an opal sky?' Absurd. Damn.

He looked at his watch. 4:20. He picked up his briefcase and started down the hall, body tense, anxious head thrust forward, his long light frame looking as though it threatened to zoom up and fly horizontally through the air like an arrow, were it not weighed down by his bulging briefcase. He felt awkward with his head, neck, shoulders, spine, arms, legs. He thrust up his head and was bothered by his Adam's apple, threw back his shoulders but felt them pulled by his heavy briefcase. Oh hell! On he soared into the staff room.

He felt more confident when he saw his new

brown Donegal coat on the rack. He set down his briefcase, removed the coat carefully from its hanger and put it on. Its newness and rightness comforted him, and its weight gave gravity something to work on, so that he lost the poised arrow look when he left the building and walked confidently to the parking lot where his little olive Volkswagen waited amongst the large cars. It pleased him to see it there – modest, functional, and unpretentious.

He unlocked the door and closed it after him as he jackknifed into the front seat, then inserted the key and started the motor.

Six weeks. Grover must have accepted 'The Loveseeker' for Creative Canada – perhaps also for *The Hemlock*, the little magazine he was editing. He would have to send some biographical information which it seemed presumptious to send with the manuscript. Should he mention Eric Desmond's creative writing course at Varsity? And his COTC experience?

Feeling brighter now, his headache gone, he signalled a turn onto Edward Avenue and spun along home.

Isobel lit a cigarette and looked out the picture window. Primrose Street. Why had the construction company called all the streets after wild flowers, when the only things that grew here were nursery shrubs and bulbs, and pavement? And why had they so inappropriately called the development 'Friendship Gardens,' when the houses were built so close together that the inhabitants just had to fight with each other all the time? She and George both hated it, but it was all they could afford. It was really hardest on George – he was a sensitive man and all those ridiculous repetitive three model houses must be awful for him, on top of teaching which he hated and did well, and writing which he hated and did badly – no wonder he was so tense all the time.

At least she could read when she felt like it, and bake when she felt like it, or just sit outside and breathe and not feel too badly about the world. But poor George. Tonight it was going to be simply terrible. She must help him feel better before she left for that damn Home and School meeting. It would be a complete bore but she had to show some positive interest in the school after the row George raised about the religious education Simone's kindergarten teacher was dishing out.

Wind swept up Primrose Street, seemed almost to blow the scurrying pre-schoolers into the houses. Isobel saw Simone with the Robertsons, scurrying into theirs. Razzle Park was on. 4:30. George would be along any minute.

Isobel returned to the kitchen and checked the barbecued spareribs and baking potatoes, set the table and hurried to the bathroom. She ran hot water and began to undress. As she stepped into the tub the Volkswagen crunched up the driveway. She lay in the hot water, aware of George's every move. Slam of car door, footsteps around to front, up the steps. Door open, door closed, coat onto hanger – oh hurry George and get it over with!

'Hi,' she called. 'I'm in the tub!'

'Hi, darling.' Footsteps over to bookcase, rattle of envelope. She splashed furiously, scrubbing soap over her body with the pink bath brush. She rinsed, sloshing water over the tub's edge, then began soaping all over again, listening. Slower steps to fridge, fridge door opening. Rattle. Glasses. Bottle opening.

'George?'

'Yes, Isobel?'

'Are you having beer? Will you bring me one? It's such fun drinking in the tub. Decadent.' Sound of footsteps to fridge, rattle, glasses, bottle opening. Footsteps down the hall. He was at the bathroom door.

She sat up, pink and tingling, and reached for the glass. 'Hello love. This is wonderful. Like that motel where we stayed in Minneapolis. Remember? With the square black tub? And I sat in it all day and drank American beer out of cans? Anything interesting mailwise? Was that your manuscript?'

'That bloody Grover. Just look.' He handed her the letter and sat down on the laundry hamper. She set her glass on the edge of the tub and took the letter.

'Gosh! A personal letter! He must have liked it.' She read the letter slowly, then thoughtfully handed it to George. 'Well, it's certainly encouraging. He went to all that trouble just to give you his opinion and everything.' She brushed wisps of bangs back from her forehead with a wet hand and said, 'I don't want to be critical of Grover or anything, George – I know what you think of him – but somehow I don't think he was quite fair, about your story. What he criticized was not the *story* – but the fact that nothing further happened between the man and the girl. Here these people are always telling you to write the truth about what you know, and when you do they don't like it because it's suburban Ontario truth – and that's what was so sad about the story, I thought. Nothing could happen ...'

'Isobel, that's just it. I didn't know what was wrong with Grover's letter – but you've got it.' Isobel relaxed in the tub. 'If he had criticized my technique, or style, or something – but he criticized content. That's pretty naive of Grover, and frankly, I'm disappointed in him.'

'Well to be perfectly honest, George, I never did get all this Grover worship of yours. It's just because he edits all those anthologies and because he's a name to you. If you knew him like I know him ... '

'"AS I know him."'

'All right. AS I know him.' She looked up at George and smiled. Everything was going according to plan, so far.

George tilted his head back and drained the last of his beer, then poured the rest of the bottle into his empty glass. Isobel was no intellectual, he thought, but she was amazingly perceptive about some things. Put my feelings about Grover's letter into words in a flash – before I had intellectualized them myself. God, beer was good – relaxing. His headache was completely gone. He looked down at Isobel as she splashed water over her stomach. 'My, you look charming in that outfit,' he said.

She laughed. 'Why, this old outfit? I've had it for years! You really like it?' She felt George's hand caressing her wet shoulder. 'George? Simone is watching TV with the Robertsons. So we'll eat late. Why don't you lie down and have a rest, I'll be out of here in a minute.'

He bent down and kissed her on the mouth. 'Good idea,' he murmured, then walked to the bedroom, smiling.

At least he had a realistic evaluation of Grover now, he thought, as he began to undress. He got under the covers, and with happy anticipation heard the water draining from the tub. That crazy Isobel. A minute later she was crawling in beside him, warm and round and soap-smelling.

Afterwards she snuggled close and kissed his shoulders, and knew she would not feel so mean, leaving him for the Home and School. He bent his head down and rubbed his face in her tousled hair and murmured, 'You know, Isobel, you're an awfully positive and mature person.'

ALDEN NOWLAN
Rivalry

The nurse, who is neither young nor
　　pretty,
warms the cold lotion with the friction of
　　her palms,
massages my flesh as though coaxing a
　　tired lover,
leans so close I can tell her belly is
　　without fat,

her breasts firm and, perhaps, beautiful

and smiles mysteriously across my naked
　　body
at my wife, who holds my hand in both
　　of hers,
her own smile becoming tighter and
　　tighter.

MICHAEL ONDAATJE
Peter

I

That spring Peter was discovered, freezing
the maze of bones from a dead cow,
skull and hooves glazed
with a skin of ice.
The warmth in his hands
carved hollows of muscle,
his fingers threading veins on its flank.

In the attempt to capture him
he bit, to defend himself,
three throats and a wrist;
that night villagers found the cow
frozen in red, and Peter
eating a meal beside it.

II

They snared him in evening light,
his body a pendulum
between the walls of the yard,
rearing from shrinking flashes of steel
until they, with a new scince,
stretched his heels and limbs,
scarred through the back of his knees
leaving his veins unpinned,
and him singing in the evening air.

Till he fainted, and a brown bitch
nosed his pain, stared in interest,

and he froze into consciousness
to drag his feet to the fountain,
to numb wounds.

III

In the first months of his capture
words were growls, meaningless;
disgust in his tone burned everyone.
At meals, in bed, you heard Peter's howl
in the depths of the castle like a bell.
After the first year they cut out his tongue;

difficult
to unpin a fish's mouth
without the eventual jerk
to empty throat of pin and matter.

There followed months of silence,
then the eventual grunting;
he began to speak with the air of his body,
torturing breath into tones; it was despicable,
they had made a dead animal of his throat.

He was little more than a marred stone,
a baited gargoyle, escaped
from the fountain in the courtyard:
his throat swollen like an arm muscle,
his walk stuttered with limp, his knees straight,
his feet arcing like a compass.

IV

They made a hive for him in the court,
Jason throwing him bones from the table,
the daughter Tara tousling in detail
the hair that collapsed like a nest
over his weaving eyes.
She, with bored innocence,
would pet him like a flower,
place vast kisses on his wrists,
thrilled at scowls and obscenities,
delighted at sudden grins
that opened his face like a dawn.

He ate, bouldered at their feet,
vast hands shaping rice,
and he walked with them on grit drives –
his legs dragged like a suitcase behind him.

V

All this while Peter formed violent beauty.
He carved death on chalices,
made spoons of yawning golden fishes;
forks stemmed from the tongues of reptiles,
candle holders bent like the ribs of men.

He made fragments of people: breasts
in the midst of a girl's stride,
a head burrowed in love,
an arm swimming – fingers heaved
to nose barricades of water.

His squat form, the rippled arms
of seaweeded hair,
the fingers black, bent from moulding silver,
poured all his strength
into the bare reflection of eyes.

VI

Then Tara grew.

When he first saw her, tall,
ungainly as trees,
her fat knees dangled his shoulders
as her hips rode him,
the court monster, she
swaying from side to side, held
only by the grip of her thighs
on his obtuse neck –
she bending over him,
muttering giggles at his eyes,
covering his creased face with her hair.

And he made golden spiders for her
and silver frogs, with opal glares.

And as she grew, her body
burned its awkwardness,
The full bones roamed
set in autumn – the brown, the warm air.
The ridge in her back broadened,
her dress hid seas of thighs,
arms trailed to adjust hair that paused
like a long bird at her shoulder;
and vast brown breasts
restless at each gesture
clung to her body like new sea beasts.

And she smiled cool at Peter now,
a quiet hand received gifts from him,
and her fingers, poised,
touched
to generate expressions.

VII

An arm held her, splayed
its fingers like a cross at her neck

March 1967

till he could feel fear thrashing at her throat,
while his bent hands tore the sheet of skirt,
lifted her, buttock and neck to the table.
Then laying arm above her breasts
he shaped her body like a mould,
his tongue sharp as a cat, cold,
dry as a cat, rasping neck and breasts

till he poured loathing of fifteen years on her,
a vat of lush oil, staining,
the large soft body like a whale.

Then he lay there breathing at her neck
his face wet from her tears
that glued him to her pain.

RAYMOND SOUSTER

Rags-and-Bones Man

Maybe if I get it down right this time, O rags-
    and-bones man,
maybe, just maybe, once and for all you'll cease
    to be my all too-recurrent nightmare ....

London, wartime, the Tube, close to midnight,
    somewhere Waterloo to Shepherd's Bush,
faces blurred or clear always moving, signs
    beckoning, lights flasing, doors sliding,
the train gathering speed, coaches rocking,
    wheels screeching high on the turns, again
    hell of faces ghostly-lit between light and
    dark,
with me, strap-hanging airman, beautiful in
    beer fog –

And suddenly at coach end, you, man or part
    of a man, caricature of something of a
    human –
wild hair, eyes glazed or not seeing at all, sickly
    drunken smile over pasty face, cheekbones
    cutting through like knives,
skeleton of shoulders holding up a coat or rags
    of a coat, pockets bulging, rags of trousers
    on spindly legs, toes showing out of shoes
    or shreds of sole and leather:

the whole thing doing a dance, a neck-shaking
    round, a ghostly shuffle, three steps up,
    three steps back, the whole thing shaking
    to music leaking out of a long-lost brain,
grinning faces of the passengers grotesque
    with the ghost-light on them, pale, over-
    rouged, but no face anywhere matching
    his own with its mask of pure raptured
    madness,
and all the time the train is roaring on
    through the earth, speeding through its
    burrow under rivers, sewers, rot of cities,
    knifing the mole-dark of tunnel, shaking
    deepest rat holes of hell,
but always that shuffle at the coach-end, that
    mad, crazy dance going on and on, three
    steps up, three steps back, dance of death
performed with all the lighthearted
    brightness of life, dance without reason,
    without end ....
Maybe if I get it right this time, O my rags-and-
    bones man,
maybe if I say it true enough your dreams will
    fade tonight and forever, I'll sleep with no
    sweat to soak through my bed, no crazy fear
    left there in the past,
maybe you'll visit me no more, your one and
    only too-patient victim,

O let it be so, rags-and-bones man!

EUGENE McNAMARA

To Burn

That day had been overcast, warm, muggy, when the weather wraps people in damp and they feel that all the air has been pumped out of the sky and they breathe water. Dave had been sent out from the hiring hall as a helper on a construction truck; all that day his senses were strung tight, over-aware, preternatural, abnormal. Because of the weather. As he got off the bus down on the South Side and looked across the vacant lots towards the loading yard he caught his first sight of the fire. It was a pile of debris from wrecked houses; smashed lath, old doors, beams, boards, all piled up and burning, sending a slow, oily cylinder of smoke into the grey sky. His eyes stinging in the muzzy haze, he made a wide curve around the pile and walked through the gate.

'You the man from the hall?' It was an older man in a corduroy shirt and a hard hat. He had *boss* written all over him, from his yellow-laced roofer's shoes up.

'Yes.' Dave handed over the card with his name, book number, and the union seal on it. Magic horses. The boss jabbed it under the spring on his clipboard without looking at it, then pointed his pencil out the gate. 'OK. Now you and Big Bill will burn wood today. You got gloves?'

'No.' Burn wood? What the hell –

'No gloves?'

'Don't need no gloves on the trucks.'

'Well you sure need em burnin wood fella. You better get some tonight.' The boss turned towards the office shack. 'Bill! Here's your helper!' A large blue-black Negro came out of the shack. He held a paper cup of coffee in one hand.

'This here is Big Bill. You'll be helpin him.'

Resentment. Not because the guy was black. But because *he* wasn't a wood-burning janitor but a truck helper and had been sent out from the hall to work on a truck, not to burn crap in a vacant lot. But he wasn't sure that the union would back him up if he balked. The ways of the union were strange and dark. They might pull a strike and pull every driver out of this lot. But they just as easily might screw him up, take his book away, blackball him. Hell, only for a day. He shrugged.

'Bill you got an extra pair of hand shoes for this man?'

'I got none for myself Eddie.'

'No gloves?' It was the same shocked tone, as if he expected every man in the world to be born wearing them, or had them presented at manhood, guaranteed to last to the grave, or even beyond, buried with you, to help you dig into the next world.

'We'll manage,' drawled Bill, with a slow wink aside at Dave. 'Les get at it son.'

They moved to the pile of rubble and bent to a cracked eight by eight.

'Watch them splinters.'

They humped it to their mid-thighs, half-turned and walked it towards the fire. The heat got more intense as they got nearer, nearer, and he squinted his eyes. 'Close enough,' called Bill, '*Now*.' And they heaved in unison. Back to the pile. Broken chairs. Warped boards. A darkwood varnished mantel from a house that must have been a hundred years old. After it landed, bounced, slid, settled, he watched for a moment as the layers of varnish bubbled, shrank, and boiled away. The fire licked around the wood, hugging it in a curled grip. Back again. Each trip back to the pile of junk seemed to take longer and longer. Then back with another piece of stuff, parts of walls even with the plaster hanging off, brown-stained wallpaper flapping. All morning back and forth, mechanically, not talking much, saving breath, moving slower and slower.

Noon whistles shrilled all over the South Side, and suddenly as if by signal a wind sprang up from the west. Overhead the curtain of clouds began to stir, rolling back as if thrust by a giant hand. A patch of blue appeared, growing larger, broader. The wind kept blowing and the fire leaped higher, the smoke mixed with sparks and crackling shards of paper, flakes of flame. Now all the clouds had been shoved to the horizon and the sky, hard-blue and bright opened to the smoke from their fire. They looked at each other, chests heaving, sweat running through the soot that covered them and laughed. All of a sudden it was much better. They sat down on a door to eat lunch.

'Son of a bitch,' Bill said and chuckled. Then Dave laughed too. He didn't know why, but he felt very happy. Even when the whistles blew again and he got up, his legs almost buckling, weak, he felt good. His knees trembled, locked stiff, as they bent to the door they had been sitting on, half-walked, half-dragged it to the fire. Back again. The wind still blew from the west, so they walked in from the east. After the door, another eight by eight, then some boards, the stiffness worked out and it was easier again. He wondered, looking up into the sky, if from up there, a watcher peering down at the bent black figures would think they were savages in some dim ritual, placating a stern god, burning a sacrifice. They kept burning. The wind was steady and strong from the west. The fire leaped higher. When the four o'clock whistles blew, he had almost stopped feeling or thinking. They were half in the act of lifting a broken segment of wall when the whistles blew and they halted in the midst of their motion, eyes locked. Simultaneously, laughing, they let go and danced back as it fell on the pile. 'E-*nough*,' said Bill. 'Time to *re*-tire.' And together they walked towards the office. Bill kept on walking past the office between two trucks, calling back, 'See you tomorrow man.'

'Oh. Yeah. Sure.' But he knew he wouldn't.

After he got paid off, back down to the hall for him.

And that's what he did. The next morning, sore as all hell, even sunburned through all that soot, splinters in his palms, even a bruised thigh, he went back down to the hall. This time he was sent out on a truck. And finally in a week or so he landed a steady job on a pop truck. A few years and he'd get a route of his own.

It was about a year later, while he and the driver were having coffee about half-way through the route as he read a paper that his day of burning wood came back.

'Hey, I think I know this guy,' he pointed to a picture of a crowd in the Detroit riot. '*This one.*' he prodded a picture of a man struggling between two policemen. Two angry-eyed women stood behind the contorted group; a fire hose snaked in front of the whole scene. A burning building lit it all up. DETROIT POLICE SUBDUE RIOTER. 'I think I worked with him a while ago.' The driver frowned at the picture, face a grimace of concentration. 'That's a bad picture. How can you tell?'

'I don't know. I *think* it's him.'

'They all look alike anyway,' the driver dismissed the whole thing and finished his coffee, a subtle signal to finish his, which he did, and they went back on the route. Maybe it wasn't Bill. What the hell would Big Bill be doing in Detroit anyway? He almost forgot it during the press of work, as he hauled empty cases out of tavern cellars and the back store rooms of groceries, as he wheeled in the full cases, and redistributed the load on the truck. And, by the time they were back at the warehouse, unloading at the dock, it had slipped his mind.

But then that night he dreamed that he and Big Bill were back in the vacant lot burning the wood again. Together they lifted the boards, the cracked beams, the splintered doors, heaved in unison. The fire grew larger and more intense. The pile was very high now and they had to sling the stuff harder to make sure it would hit the top. But strangely, the more fierce the fire became, the darker all around it seemed to grow. By now he could no longer see what it was they were throwing into the fire. Nor could he see Bill at the other end of a board or door. They moved more slowly, each gesture of bending, hauling, heaving, mired down in fatigue, made mechanical and stiff in the gathering darkness. It seemed to him that they were throwing larger and more cumbersome objects into the fire. But the only way he could tell was by the increasing intensity of the heat and the deepening gloom. Perhaps they were shoving the houses and stores of Detroit into the fire. Maybe construction trucks, pop cases, movie screens, furniture. Burn it all. New energy seemed to course through whatever it was they were holding, running like a humming current into his hands, down his arms, nerves, brain, a silent *yes* from Bill sent back *yes*.

And now they were pulling at the very earth itself, wrestling it into position. Bill hunched at one end, and he knew that this was so he could get purchase on the other. Now they had it firmly in hand, and squeezing it between them, half-dragging, half-rolling it, they shoved it into the sun.

ALDEN NOWLAN

The Unnatural Son

Occupational therapy, it's called. There are about a dozen of us who trundle carts similar to those you've seen on railway station platforms from the great, underground kitchen with its huge, steaming pots, mounds of peeled vegetables, and hairy-chested cooks in open shirts and tall, white hats, down a long, white, crypt-like tunnel to the dumbwaiters that carry baskets of boiled eggs, vats of Irish stew and, on Sundays, hot roast beef wrapped in tinfoil up to the wards. Twice a week, on Mondays and Wednesdays, we go from ward to ward, supervised by an attendant with a jangling key-ring, each team of two men carrying a hamper, made from canvas sewn on a square steel frame, into which are stuffed bundles of filthy clothing and bedding, tied up in sheets, which we carry back downstairs to the laundry.

We leave our own wards at eight o'clock in the morning and go back to them at five in the afternoon. Since we don't work more than three or four hours a day, we spend more than half of the time sitting around in the tunnel or, rather, in one of the many storerooms, most of them empty, joining it. We're all of us on ground parole, which means we can come and go much as we like so long as we don't leave the grounds, so the attendants don't watch us as they do the inmates from the back wards who sandpaper furniture and rake leaves off the superintendent's lawn.

The storeroom where we usually spend much of the day is situated far down the tunnel and contains several hundred bedsprings in stacks five or six feet high, with spaces like passageways, about four feet wide on all four sides of each stack.

We play cards – poker in all its forms from five-card stud to hooks, crooks, one-eyed-jacks, mustached kings, and a pair of natural sevens takes all; cribbage, casino, blackjack, Russian bank, rummy, bridge and, even, euchre. We analyze the previous night's game between the Boston Bruins and the Montreal Canadiens. We debate whether or not Joe Louis, in his prime, could have beaten Cassius Clay. We discuss women or, more accurately, Woman. Czerny tells us how he once spent a weekend in Havana in bed with a jug of sherry and two beautiful nymphomaniacal Spanish sisters. Fullerton disgusts Dominic, who, as always, sits very close to Jimmy, whom he has re-christened Giacomo, by saying that his own tastes are so catholic that the inaccessibility of women does not disturb him. 'I don't think we should talk about that kind of stuff in front of the kid,' Dominic says. Jimmy-Giacomo blushes as prettily as a pageboy in a novel by Baron Corvo, and Fullerton laughs.

And we have Belafonte, the West Indian, who is called Belafonte because sometimes he claims to be Belafonte, and sometimes he says that he is Belafonte's son or younger brother, and sometimes he says simply that Belafonte is the greatest singer in the world. Belafonte – our Belafonte – sings calypso songs and folksongs, accompanying himself on the guitar. His favourite is 'Island in the Sun.'

When we're wanted, Mickey Levesque, the attendant in charge of our detail, goes into the furnace room near the mouth of the tunnel and blows three times on a steam whistle. 'Boots and saddles,' Fullerton calls it. Usually, we hasten to respond, for Mickey, retired foreman of a railway section gang, has no patience with loafers and while he can't fire us he can put us on report, and a man who is put on report almost invariably is confined to his ward.

The only part of the job I heartily dislike is collecting dirty laundry in the female wards. The back wards in the male section are horrible, too, full of creatures that look, act, and smell like Swift's Yahoos. But they don't disturb me as much as even the best of the female wards.

When I was on Ward 63, the insulin ward, the women undergoing insulin shock were in a ward adjoining ours and there was glass in the door between us. The door was near the chief attendant's office and so we could go near it only when the attendants changed shifts and, for a few minutes, left the office empty. Then some of the men would talk to the women through the glass. It was adolescent teasing, mostly, which was natural enough because none of us on Ward 63 was much older than twenty. But the women – girls, really – frightened me. I knew they had equal right to be afraid of me. I was an inmate just as they were. But their hysterical eyes and moist lips terrified me in almost the same way that the novels of Bram Stoker and H.P. Lovecraft had terrified me when I was younger. Looking through the glass at them I could believe in hags and vampires, and if that sounds ridiculous, well, as Czerny says: 'What's the use of being crazy if you can't act like it?'

At times I suspect that every system of sexual morality since the beginning of civilization has been an outgrowth of man's secret fear of woman.

But let me tell you about a strange incident that occurred recently. One morning about a month ago we were gathering up dirty laundry as usual when a woman on one of the back wards came rushing up to me, shouting: 'Nicky! It's you! Nicky, I knew you'd come. Oh, Nicky, Nicky, Nicky!' And before I realized what it was she was up to she had thrown her arms around me and kissed me on the cheek. Of course, the female nurses dragged her away, and there was a good deal of laughter at my expense. 'She thinks you're her son,' one of the other women explained, grinning scornfully. 'Every once in a while she sees somebody she thinks is her Nicky. The last time it was an interne.' The rest of the day, Czerny and Fullerton called me 'Nicky.'

I thought that would be the end of it, but the next time we went through her ward, the woman spoke to me again.

This time, she sidled up to me and addressed me in a whisper: 'Nicky Darling, I knew you'd come back. I knew you'd never forget me. You're all I have now that your father's gone. This is a terrible place, Nicky. You'll get me out of here, won't you? Won't you, Nick?'

April 1968

April 1968

She had been beautiful once and would have been handsome even now if it hadn't been for the wildness of her hair and eyes and clothing. As it was, she looked like a great city tormented by riots. Anarchy had broken out in her mind and spread throughout her body. 'Don't leave me here, Nicky,' she pleaded as I stood staring at her, hoping guiltily that the nurses would overhear and again take her away.

'I'm not your son,' I told her.

'Don't say things like that, Nicky. Please don't talk to your mother that way.'

'Listen, I'm not who you think I am. You don't know me. I'm a patient here the same as you are.'

'Oh, Nicky, do you think the time will ever come when I can't recognize my own son? Why are you pretending you don't know me, Nicky? Tell me why.'

By now we were ready to leave. I pulled away from her and picked up one end of a hamper, while Fullerton lifted the other.

'Don't leave me, Nicky! Please don't leave me!'

I had to calm her. I was afraid that she would grab me again.

'It's all right; I'll be back,' I said. 'Don't worry.'

'Say you love me Nicky! Say you love me!'

'Yes, yes, I love you,' I said, as we followed the attendant out the door. And didn't Fullerton laugh at that one! But what else could I do?

After that, there was no escaping her, and I found myself fostering the delusion; at first simply to calm her, and then, I suppose, from pity. I never actually told her that I was her son, but I no longer denied it. I'm ashamed of that now. Perhaps, unconsciously, I encouraged her not because I pitied her but because it amused Fullerton and Czerny, and caused Dominic to tell me repeatedly that I was a most compassionate young man. What schizophrenic could resist starring in a drama in which he played both Lucifer and Christ?

It was all very silly. It embarrasses me a little to talk about it.

She was always near the door, waiting for me. Her appearance began to improve. She combed her hair, put on a little make-up, and wore a clean and rather attractive housecoat. Lindsay, the nurses called her – so I must be Nicholas Lindsay. Well, I hadn't been very successful playing the part of Kevin O'Brien: as Nicholas Lindsay, I was unlikely to do worse.

'Good morning, Nicky Darling,' she would say.

'Good morning. You're looking very well this morning.'

'I feel much better, Nicky. The doctors tell me there's been a big improvement. But I don't need them to tell me that. I can feel it.'

'Well, take care of yourself ... That's the important thing.'

'Nicky?'

'Yes?'

'When are you going to take me home? I try not to be impatient, but I'd like to know.'

'The doctors ... they'll have to decide that. But you're looking better every day. You really are.'

'Don't let them keep me here a day longer than they have to, Nicky. Please.'

'It's up to the doctors ...'

'Please, Nicky.'

'I'll do my best.'

Occasionally, the women from one of the churches in the city send us boxes, and the contents are often incredible: a jar of peanut butter, a package of pipe cleaners, a rosary, a pair of mittens, a package of chewing gum, and a tin of anchovies may be found in one box, while another contains a copy of *The Imitation of Christ*, a wedge of cheddar cheese, a jar of cold cream, a penlight, a bottle of Pepsi Cola, and a Red Sox baseball cap. The last time these boxes were distributed, about two weeks ago, I actually found a rose in mine – a single, long-stemmed red rose – which I could not resist giving to Nick Lindsay's mother.

I had become quite fond of her, you see. I suppose it flattered me to see how her face lit up when I entered the ward. It was like giving a coin to a beggar and buying a moment of sainthood for a quarter. Although that is not the way I thought of it at the time. I was giving her happiness and if it was based on a delusion, what the hell, wasn't all human happiness based on delusions of one kind or another. Wasn't sanity, ultimately, the perpetration of delusions, as opposed to the suffering of them?

In a little while I might have started calling her 'Mother.' It's even possible, God knows, that I might have entered into her dream and come to believe that I was her son: here, we're constantly becoming participants in one another's illusions and hallucinations. You may find it difficult to believe this, but I have often seen doctors, nurses, and attendants gradually assume, in reality, the role that some schizophrenic inmate, or group of inmates, had created for them. I am quite sure that if I believed, fervently believed, that Dr Stoddard, superintendent of this institution was Napoleon, or Hitler or, even God, the time would come when he began to believe it, too.

Last Wednesday, we collected the laundry as usual, and, as usual, the woman was waiting when we entered her ward. That morning, however, she had not combed her hair, and her eyes were bright and weird as they were the first time I saw her.

'Good morning,' I said.

'Good morning, Nicky.' She stared at me contemptuously. 'That is your name, isn't it?'

'My name...?' I edged farther away from her. What was she up to now?

'You bastard,' she said. 'You dirty little bastard!' Her voice rose and an old woman walking by with a towel and a bar of soap in her hands, stopped, looked at me with red hateful eyes and laughed loudly.

'Don't get upset,' I pleaded. Fullerton was observing everything with a smile of pure delight. Czerny and the others were already in the bathroom, filling their hampers.

'Don't get upset, he says! The nerve of the son of a bitch. He lies to me, tries to convince me he's my son, and then he says "don't get upset." What kind of a fool does he take me for, the miserable little jerk!' She raved on and on, berating me. A crowd of women gathered around us, some of them simply watching and listening, others urging her on and cursing me for a fraud and a liar.

'Look,' I said, helplessly, 'Listen...'

While four of the nurses subdued her and took her away she kept shouting 'You bastard! You lying bastard!' over and over. I could hear the other women screaming it even after we went outside and the attendant locked two heavy doors behind us.

PAUL FOX

The Liberals choose Trudeau - pragmatism at work

True to its nature as part of an intrinsically pragmatic society, the Canadian political system has just passed through one of its periodic mutations in which the system is renewed, recharged, and reformed from the inside out, rather than from the outside in – by a process of ingestion and auto-genesis rather than by the operation of any external dialectic.

To those who view dialectical materialism as a universal first principle and to ideologues who have been urging the regeneration of Canadian politics by a simple polarization into left and right, the choice by the Liberal Convention on April 6 of Pierre Elliott Trudeau as their new leader and prime minister will be dismaying for it belies the dialectic and forestalls the process of simple division. Once again our political system has refreshed itself at the highest level of leadership without a sudden dramatic shift from one extreme to the other in the party in power but rather by the system opening up and elevating a relatively non-partisan outsider who seemed best suited to new conditions.

The absence of ideological concern amongst those who made the choice illustrates once more the fact that every society is *sui generis* and that Hegel and Marx cannot be transposed to North America with any more universality than the pragmatism of North America might be transferred to Mao's China.

With that strange, half-conscious, half-accidental groping that is so characteristic of Canadian politics, the country's interest came to focus on Trudeau as the man who should be chosen to fulfil the aspirations of a burgeoning generation. To the ideologues it was a peculiar choice. Three years ago Trudeau was not even a member of the party he was destined to lead. A labour union lawyer and economist, he campaigned for the CCF-NDP. A staunch defender of provincial rights in the fifties, he entered national politics in the sixties to strengthen waning federal power. A French Canadian who urges the extension of French linguistic rights throughout the country, he opposes special status for Quebec. Touted as an individualistic 'swinger' in style and dress and thought, he turns out to be a sober man with very orthodox views on many issues – on the extension of universal social welfare benefits, on the sale of Canadian war material to the United States, on American investment in Canada, on votes for 18-year olds, and on the abolition of the monarchy.

An intellectual of genuine distinction – political theorist, professor of constitutional law, and writer-editor of the praiseworthy progressive journal *Cité libre* – he has a gift for communicating with very ordinary people. Middle-aged, of medium stature, and no matinee idol, he lights up dark rooms when he enters, sends the teen-age mouse pack that pursues him everywhere into squeals of frenzy, and draws older women palpitating in his wake. A man of reason who appeals only to logic in politics, he arouses more emotion than all of the rest of the candidates put together. A cool man, he has plugged a generation of Canadians into politics for the first time. A John Stuart Millite liberal in his intellectual persuasion, he is, by his own admission, a pragmatist of the Benthamite sort when it comes to political action.

A man full of contradictions. It is his 'sign,' he says. Yet, as it turns out, he is the consensual man, because there is something in him for everybody. The winner embodies a mixture of contradictory truths, like the Canadian political system and reality itself. There is the key. Trudeau is not a comfortable middle-of-the-roader. He is not a bland average which is an artificial concoction with highs and lows eliminated. He is an aggregate of conflicting interests, which is very different.

Whether or not Trudeau reflects in this respect his party as well as his country is open to greater and more partisan consideration. After observing both the Liberal and Conservative parties at work – and play – in their most recent conventions, I am inclined to conclude that the Liberals are the most broadly-based political party in Canada. They have their stereotyped members – determined Toronto business men, earnest young lawyers, French-speaking Canadians, Jews, prosperous wheat farmers, professors, and beautiful (and no doubt brainy) young women in dark glasses – some of whom are also to be found amidst the Conservatives, but somehow among the Liberals the types are more varied and more numerous and the ethnic and class differences are more obvious. The Liberal delegates ranged from aged senators who had attended the 1919 Convention to a bunny girl from an Ottawa night club. The Tories were more decorous, more orderly, more proper. It is not true to say, as it might have been once, that the difference between the two parties' conventions was something like the difference between an Anglican cathedral and a revival meeting, but it is remarkably similar to the difference between the Republican and Democratic parties in the United States.

Trudeau may have appealed to this broader spectrum in the Liberal party. It is certainly hard to conceive of his being elected leader of the Conservative party, or even becoming a candidate for its leadership. But whatever the breadth of his consensual appeal, it was clear from the moment he appeared in company with the other candidates that he stood head and shoulders above them. He was distinguished by a capacity and excellence in mind, in speech, and in deportment that his rivals either did not possess or could not manifest. While the others (with the rare exception of Joe Greene) hacked their way tediously through dense verbal jungles of their own making, Trudeau blazed a trail with an economy of words laced with a wryness of humour that never broke the mould he had cast for himself as a rational man discussing the serious business of politics with an intelligent audience.

There was a great irony and even greater satisfaction in the fact that not all the tens of thousands of dollars spent by candidates on bands and booze, placards, pretty girls, demonstrations, organization, hoopla, and Mother Bell's best in telecommunications could overcome the countervailing attraction of sheer ability. It is still not possible to buy political power in this country with money alone, though Trudeau's forces undoubtedly spent as much as many of his competitors.

Finally, Trudeau's victory can be attributed to the stark confrontation at the end between him and Robert Winters. When after three ballots, the 2,378 delegates were faced with a clear choice between backing Trudeau, who, however inexperienced he was, appeared at least to be on the wavelength of tomorrow, or supporting Winters who was riding the eddy of a Liberal tide of a decade ago, the delegates decided in favour of progress. To many present it was inconceivable that a political party that called itself Liberal could even contemplate reestablishing an Establishment Man from a disestablished age, who still believed in balancing budgets and selling Air Canada and the CBC to private enterprise, but 27 votes cast the other way would have forced a fifth ballot, although it seems likely in the final crunch most of Turner's votes would have gone to Trudeau.

Yet the fourth ballot victory for Trudeau was close enough that it showed how slim the consensus for change was. The process of autogenesis that alters the Canadian political system does not seem to work by large numbers. When, in somewhat similar circumstances, the Liberal party changed leaders in 1919 and opted for a new phase in Canadian politics by selecting Mackenzie King and his program of social welfare, the 44-year old King, who had also begun as a dark horse, triumphed over his older rival Fielding only after three ballots and by a margin of 38 votes.

Like King and all new leaders under such circumstances, Trudeau now faces very difficult problems. He not only has to fulfil the expectations of the rising generation that has plumped for him but he must heal the rifts in his own party. The divisions are real and deep. The most serious of them arise from the contrasting cultural and social elements that make up the Liberal party. An elderly Cape Breton delegate who was all for Winters bemoaned the choice of Trudeau. 'Ah,' he said to me in his heavily accented, Gaelic sorrow, 'my old woman won't let me in when I go home. This man will never win an election in Nova Scotia. We've just delivered the province to Bob Stanfield.'

Undoubtedly many of the prairie delegates felt the same way. The choice of Trudeau does not by any means solve for the Liberals the dilemma that has faced every party in the last ten years, the difficulty of overcoming differences in regional outlooks, which are largely cultural, and building a viable national party.

In his favour, however, Trudeau possesses a remarkable combination of talents that are reminiscent of the best of both Laurier and King: Laurier's charm and intellect and King's reserve and astuteness. One of his greatest problems will be to prevent his own assets – his pragmatism, his wit, his intellect, and his grace – from being turned into liabilities by his opponents and his critics, particularly by the media, which having adopted him early on as their favourite son will now pick holes in him like a reproving parent.

How fast the symbols of victory can be converted into the stigma of defeat was demonstrated by the young man at the Liberal Convention who, every time Stanfield's name was mentioned, raised derisively a placard which proclaimed 'Yes, we have no bananas.'

Pragmatic politics in Canada can raise a man almost overnight to the heights but they provide no protective cloak of ideology when he is assailed from all sides. The test of pragmatism is success not logic, and success is harder to come by.

GAD HOROWITZ

Trudeau vs Trudeauism

The author of *Federalism and the French Canadians* has been elevated, with a little help from his friends (including some readers of *The Canadian Forum*) to the highest political office in Canada. The Canadian intelligentsia must now turn its energies to the study and exegesis of the Thought of Prime Minister Trudeau.

The two basic principles of Trudeauism are:
1 'Political freedom finds its essential strength in a sense of balance and proportion. As soon as any one tendency becomes too strong, it constitutes a menace. ...' We must 'create counterweights.'
2 'The first law of politics is to start from given facts. The second is to take stock of the real relationship between forces.' We must forget 'historical might-have-beens,' reject 'impossible dreams,' and accentuate the feasible.

It should be obvious that the application of these principles to a specific problem is no simple matter. Rational, unemotional, pragmatic liberal minds can easily differ in their assessments of the relative strength of 'tendencies' and the relative given-ness of 'facts.' Trudeau himself believes that Trudeauism leads inexorably to the condemnation of state sovereignty in the world arena and to the sanctification of something like the present division of powers in Canadian federalism. But it may be that Trudeau misinterprets Trudeauism. Let the Prime Minister consider carefully the true implications of his own Thought!

It is Trudeau's contention that the peace of the world is threatened primarily by nationalism. The idea of state sovereignty leads to bloody irrational conflict among nations. The idea of national self-determination leads to the disruption of existing states and prevents the emergence of functional governmental structures. The necessary 'counterweights' are internationalism and polyethnic federalism. The implications for Canada are first, that we must not allow the defence of Canadian sovereignty against continentalism to become an important issue and second, that we must resist the transformation of the French Canadian sociological nation into the political nation of Quebec. Special status for Quebec would be, in Trudeau's opinion, nothing but an essential phase of this transformation.

Trudeau's interpretation of Trudeauism is incorrect because it ignores or underestimates the weight of a number of hard facts:

1 It is the chauvinism of the superpowers which is the *primary* threat to the world. The sovereignty of smaller states is an essential counterweight to American, Russian, and Chinese imperialism.

Trudeau looks forward, with most liberals and social democrats, to the establishment of the federal republic of mankind. He does not understand, however, that Canadian Liberal 'internationalism' has always been, in the main, a rhetoric rationalizing our subservience to nationalist Empires. He does not understand that a strong Canadian nationalism capable of reversing the absorption of this country into the United States, is an essential first step towards the emergence of the kind of Canada that could possibly make some small contribution to the realization of the anti-nationalist ideal. Canadian sovereignty is not being eroded by the republic of mankind; it is being eroded by the American Empire. A Canadian elite which permits increasing integration of this country with the United States, whether or not it does so under the cover of well meaning cosmopolitan slogans, will be serving not the interests of humanity, but those of the most powerful and possibly the most dangerous nationalism in the world. The point of Canadian nationalism is not to preserve a sovereign Canadian nation state forever and ever no matter what, but to preserve it so long as the only unit capable of absorbing it is a larger and more terrible nationalism. Trudeau has not taken stock of the real relationship between forces.

2 Trudeau applied all the powers of his considerable intellect and wit to the demolition of the separatist principle of national self-determination. Almost every state in the world would be reduced to chaos by the rigorous application of this principle. If any geographical area could secede from any state for ethnic-cultural reasons, 'what a lovely lot of separations there would be.' 'Why Norway and not Brittany, Ireland and not Scotland, Nicaragua and not Quebec?' The principle of national self-determination, if it means that every state *ought* to be based on a single homogeneous ethnic or cultural entity, must obviously lead to ruin. Reason points to federalism as the inescapable compromise between the understandable desire of every sociological nation to have a state of its own and the practical necessity or desirability of sharing a state with other sociological nations. If the French- and English-speaking peoples of Canada cannot share one political nationality in a federal state what hope is there for the world?

Trudeau recognizes that the people of Quebec *may* choose to become independent, that they have the power and therefore the 'right' to do so. The state is based not on any principle, but on 'consensus' – on the *will* of groups of people occupying a given geographical area to form a state. When consensus has been achieved, 'no group ... feels that its vital interests and particular characteristics could be better preserved by withdrawing from the nation than by remaining within it. A state ... must continually persuade ... the people that it is in their best interest to continue as a state.' The separation of Quebec would mean that the Canadian consensus has finally been disrupted. But Trudeau refuses, correctly in my opinion, to see this disruption as either desirable or inevitable. Most Canadians, French- and English-speaking would consider the logic of his position to be irrefutable: An independent Quebec, although it is a legitimate option in principle, is fraught with countless dangers. The path of reason is that which seeks to preserve a Canadian federal compromise, a single state which can equally serve our two sociological nations.

From this point onward Trudeau errs. For he absolutely identifies the notion of 'federal compromise' with the division of powers of 1867. He absolutely refuses to grant to any other kind of federalism the status of rational compromise. He absolutely refuses to entertain the possibility that some units of a federal state might have a significantly greater degree of power than others. These refusals do not flow with inexorable logic from his basic principles, but from his failure to give sufficient weight to the *established, given* tendency of French Canadians in Quebec to expect more from their provincial government than is expected from any other provincial government.

The Quebecois may be prepared to waive their right to *independence*, but they do not appear to be prepared to give up their ambition to be, in some sense, a political nationality. This is as clear and as hard a fact as any. There is a great deal of evidence for the argument that the only 'consensus' upon which a viable Canadian federal compromise can be built is a consensus that permits the provincial state of Quebec to serve, for some but not all important purposes, as the national state of the French Canadians. Therefore, unless *every* province of Canada is to be permitted to be a sort of quasi-nation state, the rational solution is a special status for Quebec within Canadian federalism. Trudeau's gallic rationality is offended by the notion of a French Canadian quasi-national state within the Canadian federal state, but this only indicates that his rationality may be greater than his realism. The ideal of Canada in which French Canadians will 'scrap the very idea of the nation state once and for all,' which is what Trudeau says they must do, is in all likelihood a wish dream, a historical might-have-been.

3 Trudeau recognizes that the terms of the Canadian federal compromise must permit *both* sociological nations 'to develop the body of laws and institutions essential to the fullest expression and development of their national characteristics ... to protect and realize their own special ... qualities.' But his case for the preservation of the compromise of 1867 as interpreted by the Judicial Committee of the Privy Council rests almost entirely on its usefulness to the French Canadians of Quebec.

The constitution of 1867, Trudeau argues, is an ideal one because by its terms 'French Canadians have all the powers they need to make Quebec a political society affording due respect for nationalist aspirations.' The constitution of 1867 creates a situation in which 'an enormous amount of power is being transferred to provincial governments by the natural operation of demographic, social, and economic forces, without the necessity of amending a single comma of the constitution.' Trudeau points out that of sixteen items of economic reform proposed for an independent Quebec by separatist Marcel Chaput, all but one (the abolition of federal taxes) 'could be undertaken under the present constitution.'

So far so good. The federal compromise is shown to permit the fullest expression and development of French Canada's national characteristics primarily in that it gives tremendous power to a single province in which they are the majority. But there is nothing in Trudeau's writings about the requirements of the other party to the compromise. It is simply *assumed* that an extremely decentralized federalism, which fragments the English Canadian sociological nation into nine provinces, each having as much power as Quebec, is the ideal vehicle for the expression and development of the special qualities of the English Canadians. English Canadians are not likely to allow this assumption to go unchallenged in any renegotiation of the federal compromise, which is precisely why Trudeau advises the French Canadians to avoid renegotiation: 'Natural forces are presently favouring provincial autonomy. It is the centralizers who should be pressing for constitutional changes.'

Perhaps it is time for English Canadians to ask what centralized state machine *they* – having given up their unfair domination of Ottawa – are to use to 'protect and realize their own special ... qualities.' Again, the rational solution would appear to be a special status for Quebec, which would permit the English speaking provinces to avoid the degree of decentralization which is required by Quebec alone. But Trudeau opposes this solution precisely because it would 'break the opposition of the provinces as a whole to centralization.' The present constitution is good *because* it 'creates a country in which Quebec may call upon the support of nine allies to protect provincial autonomy.' Moreover, 'those who encourage other provinces to establish interprovincial or federal-provincial relationships that differ from those used for Quebec, thereby fostering the isolation of this province,' are accused of doing 'a very great disservice to the country they claim to serve.'

Evidently the sole criterion which English Canadians may legitimately employ in assessing the usefulness of the present constitution is its usefulness in assisting Quebecers, for particularly French-Canadian reasons, to preserve 'provincial autonomy.' Evidently there is no need to assure English Canadians that '*their* vital interests and particular characteristics' can be better preserved by the present compromise than by any other. Any English Canadian who proposes a different federal compromise – such as special status for Quebec, which would allow the other provinces to centralize a bit, in line with *their* particular *characteristics* – is doing a 'very great disservice' to his country.

This is not the spirit of rational compromise. Neither does it take into account a certain 'given' which is as unlikely to disappear as the 'given' of provincialism in Quebec – the desire of English Canadians to develop national policies on matters of national importance (matters which are now formally under provincial jurisdiction), not in nine bits and pieces, but through one federal government.

Whether Trudeau likes it or not, the princi-

December 1968 ples of Trudeauism, applied to the 'given facts' and 'real relationships' of the Canadian situation, point to a special status for Quebec within a radically restructured Canadian federalism.

HANS WERNER
Sonnet for Monika

One more cigarette. A glass
Of wine at Leydickes where you
Brush laughter with friends.
I feel the glass and test
The strength of my hand against it. It
Does not break.

Bus number 62 comes in seven minutes,
Cold March whistle from Bahnhof Zoo.
   I
Hold you close into my coat to
Feel your thighs warm a last
Attempt to reach you
A quick kiss that was not meant, and
   you

Fold back behind the pneumatic hiss
Of doors.

JOYCE WIELAND
Cover illustration June 1968

DALTON C. CAMP

Canadian-American Interdependence: How Much?

How much interdependence is possible between Canada and the United States? I have concluded that the United States can be as interdependent as it likes, and Canada also can be as interdependent as the United States would like.

I have long ago resigned myself to the view that the better way to approach the matter of relationships with the United States is to accept the posture of a client state. All the covert, secret aspects of our relationship have been laid bare – there is nothing left to hide. If we have not learned the facts of life from President Kennedy, it is easily demonstrable on notice, and the question for our lifetime is not whether we live in cultural interlock and increasing economic sync with the United States. The perpetual question is how; how to endure, how to survive, how to maintain some kind of purchase against the sheer face of gravity, upon the glacial surface of American power, presence, and pervasiveness. As Canadians, representing a subcontinental mass of as yet unrevealed historic experience, we do not suffer the master-slave relationship, with the suggestive presumption of brutality, but we are more the mistress of dominant power – available, timid, sensitive to indifference, and demanding.

Indeed, our only power, the single influence we have, is to withhold approval, to deny the permissiveness of tacit consent. But we are periodically taught the limitations of our influence and the inner realism of the relationship – we can have our way about the Mercantile Bank, but not about Bomarcs. But yet we have a hold upon the dominance of America – not for our present, but for our potential, even though there is, in the existing relationship, a useful subsidiary role, and, don't forget, whatever else we are, we are not ugly.

Nor is America. After all, we do protest too much. We are, as Frank Underhill has said, the first anti-Americans, the primeval anti-Americans, the anti-Americans with the longest experience – indeed, the archetypal anti-American, the ideal anti-American in the mind of God. There are those who believe this is the first article of our citizenship: to be distinguished as Canadians for the reason of our stubborn resolve not to be Americans. Professor William Kilbourn suggests we may make our mark in the world as the authentic critics of America. In the age of Joe McCarthy this might have been a credible destiny, but not in the age of Eugene McCarthy. America is producing its own best critics and, as is its custom, producing them in abundance. It is that economic principle of the largest market and the longest runs.

No, with respect to Professor Kilbourn, we need not be second best in criticism too. It is presumptuous to assume the role of McCarthy, Cleaver, Murray Kempton, Norman Mailer – a short list for you to expand upon. Instead, I have in mind a more cunning strategy. It is in two parts.

The first part is exhortation, and it embraces all matters substantive and political. Idealism is the luxury of the weak, for those who dream of perfection in themselves but demand it in others. Idealism without realism is sentimentality, and nothing has been better for Canadians than their present disillusionment and concern with America which is the consequence of an idealistic expectation flawed by sentiment.

The patriotic fervour has been fanned by the thousands of tongues of American politicians; their words borne on the prevailing winds of their righteous oratory have taken flight and, like the neighbour's dandelions gone to seed, have settled next-door on Canadian soil, and taken root. Take your average Canadian, as the saying goes, and beneath that light crust of bravado, defiance, and incipient envy there is conviction – about America, her strength, power, potency, versatility, and eternal potential. The Canadian has not only swallowed the received opinion of the *New York Times*, but he believes all the historians, from Parson Weems to Arthur Schlesinger, Jr. In short, there has been hardly a Canadian who has ever given a thought to the prospect of America being anything else but the best in everything and a lifetime friend in the bargain.

But the word is leaking out. The birds come back from the south in springtime; the jets swoop in to Dorval and Malton and disgorge cargoes of observers of the foreign scene; the electronic mailbag brings a thousand messages from strangers in alien ports – and the message is simple, from those who knew of Napoleon and the age of Victoria, and now of Russia and America: a super power is a super power. Not just a neighbour, friend, ally, or pal, but a super power. And when the sea is rough, and you are in her company, swing out the lifeboats on their davits and be prepared.

And so I say to my student friends and my political peers – do not expect so much from America as you would from yourself, for there is now a fundamental, functional difference. By an accident of history, America has become a super power – a trite, vague generality to encompass a dark range of formidable possibilities. The world knows this has special, present poignance for Canada, as well as future terrors. (I am not sure we are as envied as we like to think we are.)

Be realistic about America. Be realistic about Canada; we are a minority share-holder and we have the inevitable options of the minority share-holder – the limited powers of persuasion and the unfathomable powers of prayer. (Indeed all our domestic talent, when it achieves the status of stardom, becomes American – the best of all worlds – a Canadian childhood and an American audience.) Suffice it to say, we live at a time when the United States of America will never, never, never hazard its security, restrain its response to crisis, or menace the prospects of its success because of Canadian sensitivity, anxiety, or sovereign pride.

It is easily possible to be sentimental about American-Canadian relations. Presumably, it is as easy to be despairingly resigned and concede, *a posteriori* to George Ball. It is better to be realistic, and be neither.

So the second part of my advice is taken from the inspiration of Harold Macmillan. I recall him commenting on the lessons of history and the flux of national destiny. There was the Egypt of the Pharaohs, Caesar's Rome, Napoleon's France, Elizabeth's England – and other empires and epochs less salutary and more short-lived – but there are lessons in history, and surely one must be that predominant power is predominantly transient.

Whether you say it with furtive satisfaction or nervous regret, the omnipotent America of Harry Truman – of all people – and the America of Richard Nixon is not the same, and while the shrinkage in her power is relative, it is inexorable. And history, a century from now, will measure it more precisely and wonder how little the world took note of it.

So I say to my student friends and political peers, do not exhaust yourself in this ritualistic habit of your fathers, exorcising the ghost of anti-Americanism. Instead, take profit from the knowledge of her experience, explore the outer limits of your own freedom, and patiently await the day when Canada will no longer be the natural accessory after the American fact, the assumed acolyte in her procession, but rather the full-blooded, rising, muscular equal in a partnership of immeasurable and unimagined enterprise and endeavour. Then we can really talk on interdependence – and 'how much.'

To the warrior, to the politician, to the nationalist – and are we not all something of each? – survival is the sweetest triumph; to outlive the present danger, to quit the battle only to resume the course. You may say or think to yourselves, such a day is a long way off. Yet, how many days has it been, in history, between Harry S. Truman's America and Richard Nixon's?

In Canada, we are busy reappraising our role in the world. What we are doing, I hope, is what I have been shouting from the rooftops we must do: examine our options. Dispel the public illusions as to their variety and number. Inform the public as to our central realities, as to the consequences of our actions within the narrow range of our options. Then we shall have the beginning of understanding, understanding of ourselves and of those essential relationships with America, which are, in the immediate circumstances, all that is truly vital to us. Then, let us carefully begin to cast ourselves in the image of what we want to become – without all this baggage of our mythology, and these layers of pretence, prejudice, and pretention.

I saw in the Kingston *Whig Standard* recently a headline which read: 'Canada, NATO Allies Warn Soviet Union.' Imagine – and we do imagine – Canada warning the Soviet Union, presumably rattling America's nuclear sabre. I hear our Canadian politicians cheerfully committing the next Canadian generation to some unspecified act of belligerency with fearsome rhetorical courage.

Why doesn't someone talk sense? We have a truncated brigade in West Germany, where the action isn't, and is unlikely to be, serving as part of a truncated British division which, in the event of Russian aggression, would serve as butter for the knife. And I am not detracting from the courage or efficiency of Canadian men-in-arms. Canada has no reserve, or back-up because the 're-inforcements' back home are being equipped for a different role – which has been our furtive way of opting out. We have a shrinking air division with a nuclear strike role sufficient, on a clear day and allowing for minimal resistance, to desolate any city in central Europe, a contingency for which no sane person has yet been able to write a scenario. We have an anti-submarine role in the Atlantic, for which we are painfully short of men and ships, and we have a pending order for four more destroyers, estimated cost $200 million, but the decision awaits, apparently, the flipping of a coin in the office of Treasury Board – heads they win, tails we lose.

The day will come, I hope and expect, when even our American friends will take note of our present posture, suspended as we are on the hook of obsolescence and unable to find our footing in the rapidly shifting ground of technology. And my hope then is that they, the Americans, will also come to their senses and say to us, quite candidly, honestly and mercifully: 'Look, there must be something better you can do.' That will be the beginning of wisdom.

The most alarming aspect of present American policy, to me, is the reduction of its foreign aid expenditures and operations. Let me add at once that I understand the brutal reality of American life – the need to re-equip, modernize, and make more efficient its military apparatus. After all, if they are going to end the draft, as Mr Nixon has pledged, the difference must be made up in hardware, if that is not too crude a way of putting it.

But I should think, since we have been priced out of the market for some years, in the military sense, that America would become more interested in seeing us assume some greater responsibilities in aid and assistance, which we could do, if I may say so, with greater efficiency and with fewer complications than can the United States in some areas of the world. Nothing would be so salutary to Canadian-American relations – to say nothing of the business of interdependence – than that the United States send a few spies into Canada, to join the Soviet, French, and Gabonese ones apparently already here, and undertake a genuine appraisal of our potential military capacity in today's terms, for service in Western Europe, or elsewhere. And, after that, assuming a sensible conclusion, encourage Canada to do something substantive in the world which will be of greater value to each and all of us.

To summarize my view: we are, for all significant purposes, in matters of security, dependent upon the United States, as we will be for some time. The responsibility is, therefore, not especially or uniquely Canada's, regardless of the bravura of our politicians to determine our role in the world. We have in the past needed help – such as the generous provision of free Bomarcs, and other hardware, at reasonable cost. But the help we most need is a genuine understanding by America – understanding of the sort that a great power can afford – of the enormous potential Canada has for bringing stability and re-inforcing freedom in the world, short of doing so with armed forces. At present, we are a misallocated resource and our efforts are in danger of being, insofar as our mutual relations are concerned, counter-productive. Thinking Canadians – including some enlightened ones in our government – would like another role. This seems to me, at any rate, so natural as to be inevitable.

I simply wish it would come sooner, and not later.

PAUL BIDWELL

God Bless Americaw

Look. There on the fence.
More of those damn feathers.
And there, above that maple,
   ragged shifting shadows
     darken roofs and supermarket
       parkinglots.
Aquila, reconnoitring the shops.
Never satisfied.

He's got some odd habits.
Lives south of here (that land is full of
   birds),
But migrates everywhere in trading
   season.
Old Baldy doesn't live alone. Oh no.
Bring me, he cries, your hawks, your
   doves,
your broken wings and claws,
but keep your dead phoenixes.

The whole country's starting to
   resemble one stinking aviary.
Lucybirds and Lindabirds nest in
   current issues

of third-rate magazines, and moulting
    in suburbia
is a relentless process.
Why must birds of a feather squawk
    together?

And overseas. Squadrons of eagles
drop napalmic eggs gathered hardboiled
from dupont henhouses.
And the Pope unwittingly prays for
    more birds.

'Aves,' 'Aves.'

I understand that we've been lucky.
Managed to lure an expert
Ornithologist from Yale.
Even got a yankee birdseed plant.
But all these damn feathers!
It's getting hard to breathe.

GLEN SIEBRASSE

La Plaza de Toros, Madrid

The bull had done with the picadores
and banderillas sucked
on the pelt of blood
coursing over its flank;
it turned to face the crowd.
Together they were man, woman;
heat and the still laying of spent muscle
or anything, opposite, that joined we
    despise.
    Bull drummed at the cape.
In the stands men sold rolls of chocolate
    drops;
grey beards lapped at the scent of
    younger backs;
a whittle of blood coloured my mouth.

The torero passed and
rising hard as any cock

slipped the sword under the pillows
of muscle bridging the heart.
Legs snapped, head nuzzled between
    the knees;
a midwife from Chicago (seven
    children lost)
left with her young lover.
The bull staggered, fell again
and we set to it with picks and jibes
until the legs rose slowly from the sand;
a patch of tongue crept between the
    white teeth.

When the mules hitched the thing away,
its hooves, biting into the court,
trailed a faint scar on the loose sand
    dumb
    pools of water in our mouths.

ABRAHAM ROTSTEIN

Running from paradise

Upon the rivers of Babylon,
there we sat and wept:
when we remembered Zion...
How shall we sing the song of the Lord
in a strange land?

                        PSALM 136

The year 2000 these days glows brightly in the distance. Its sanguine supporters remain undeterred by current upheaval or prospective revolution. Technology is the balm to make the wounded whole.

But there are dissonant voices outside this world of positive thinking. George Grant's new book (*Technology and Empire:* House of Anansi; pp. 143; $5.50) is not about the external revolution — the third world, imperialism, poverty, or participatory politics. It is about an internal revolution and one that we have lost — the destruction of man's inner life in a technological society. The outer man has won spectacular victories over nature; the inner man, while hardly being aware of his loss, has suffered something ultimate and irremediable.

Grant is not a revolutionary, he is a Prophet and he calls us to account for what we have done to the world, in the biblical terms of good and evil. He is no naive fundamentalist for he knows our century and its origins in that incisive and sweeping way which is given to very few. This is no milk-and-water sermon about morality lagging behind technology; no insipid call from the research establishment for more 'research' in the social sciences. It is a universal cry in a technological jungle which is already triumphant and irreversible. For Grant, our century is a paradigm of ultimate deprival; we cherish the idols of efficiency and liberalism, the pragmatism of our political and economic order, and all of it is empty of significance.

Grant's is a moving plea, evocative, passionate, and deeply human. It sounds those hidden chords in all of us that could turn atheists religious and socialists conservative, and have them discover that against the common condition, their own divisions are insignificant.

The theme is not new. A powerful literary tradition has sounded this note many times: something central and precious in the life of man has eroded and we are helpless before an autonomous and runaway technology. Huxley, Orwell, Karel Capek, Kafka, Beckett, Dudintsev, Sartre – the list is long and eminent, each with his own form of allusion and indirection, but all pointing to a negative utopia. But we have a segregated compartment in our mind where we can isolate and contain the early warning signals from literary quarters. Are they merely products of the imagination? Literary license?

Grant sounds the same message in a different key, but this shift from art to life has yet to find an adequate vocabulary. It is a shift from allusion to present condition and from warning to lament. It is a lament not for nation, but for mankind; a Pilgrim's Progress in reverse. It is not a nostalgic reverie for a medievalism that never was, nor for a world of taboo, magic, and superstition, of class cruelty and master-slave exploitation. It is not about the evils or benefits of capitalism. It transcends all of these but we barely have the vocabulary to stand outside and view our deepest selves. Gropingly, we search for metaphors such as 'deprival'; we formulate disturbing questions: What, if anything, is there to seek beyond the liberal virtues of freedom and equality? Was there ever something else?

Technology and Empire is a collection of five essays and an epilogue, four of which have been published previously. The most notable essay, 'In Defence of North America' is new and is first in the volume. It is a masterful apologia and a powerful indictment both, and no Canadian has written with such sweeping insight on this subject before. Grant moves beyond the perspectives of both Louis Hartz and Jacques Ellul to trace the origins of the American destiny in the interweaving of history, ideology and technology. He writes as a Canadian closely identified with the North American experience:

We are still enfolded with the Americans in the deep sharing of having crossed the ocean and conquered the new land ... the majestic continent which could not be ours in the way that the old had been ... because the very intractability, immensity and extremes of the new land required that its meeting with mastering Europeans be a battle of subjugation. And after that battle we had no long history of living with the land before the arrival of the new forms of conquest which came with industrialism ... There can be nothing immemorial for us except the environment as object.

While for Hartz America is frozen as a Lockean 'fragment,' for Grant it is shaped by a Calvinist Protestantism of the seventeenth century. Grant has in mind not only the connection between Calvinism and capitalism which Max Weber expounded, but the 'deeper level of the matter which is the connection between Protestant theology and the new sciences.' The connection is complex but its essence – following Troeltsch – was:

the emphasizing of the individual and empirical, the renunciation of the concepts of absolute causality and unity, the practically free and utilitarian individual judgement of all things. The influence of this spirit is quite unmistakably the most important cause of the empirical and positivist tendencies of the Anglo-Saxon spirit...

Benjamin Franklin provides a perfect illustration with his public virtues drawn directly from the Protestant ethos and his scientific drive a prime example of Troeltsch's analysis.

The moral and historical climate of America was highly favourable to the development and diffusion of technique. This diffusion was required in the subjugation of the environment and came to be regarded as an exercise of freedom. The drive of technology was so powerful because its purveyors could identify their activities with a beneficent progress and with the liberation of mankind. A sense of 'unappeaseable responsibility' became the secular version of Calvinist predestination.

The end result is a spiritual wasteland:

... an immense majority who think they are free in pluralism, but in fact live in a monistic vulgarity in which nobility and wisdom have been exchanged for a pale belief in progress, alternating with boredom and weariness of spirit; when the disciplined among us drive to an unlimited technological future, in which technical reason has become so universal that it has closed down an openness and awe, questioning and listening; when Protestant subjectivity remains authentic only where it is least appropriate, in the moodiness of our art and sexuality, and where public religion has become an unimportant litany of objectified self-righteousness necessary for the more anal of outer managers...

America is a closeup of our global destiny as the technological society spreads. There is no 'saving remnant' in Grant's vision and no way out:

The drive for radical change in this society tends only to harden the very directions the society is already taking ... the source of revolutionary fervour [arises] finally from a further extension of the very modernity which has brought us where we are...

Radicals are caught in an insoluble contradiction:

They want both high standards of spontaneous democracy and the egalitarian benefits accruing from technique. But have not the very forms of the bureaucratic institutions been developed as necessary for producing those benefits? Can such institutions exist as participatory democracies?

Little can be expected from social scientists either. They are deluded by their claims to 'objectivity,' specialized to the point of myopia by their vested interests, and act as dilettantes picking 'values' in a fabian garden. Grant's essay on the university reads like an Epistle to the Philistines. Research factories are the order of the day:

If one has steady nerve, it is useful to contemplate how much is written about Beowulf in one year in North America. One can look at the Shakespeare industry with perhaps less sense of absurdity; but when it comes to figures such as Horace Walpole having their own factory, one must beware vertigo.

The essay 'Religion and the State' shows up the kind of Christianity which is taught in the schools as a 'facade of tradition' which 'serves the passing interest of the state without really serving the interests of the churches.' 'Tyranny and Wisdom' is a commentary on the debate between Leo Strauss and Alexandre Kojève about the universal and homogeneous state. The debate and commentary about this ideal of the liberal internationalists centers around the question of whether such a world implies nothing less than an appalling world tyranny. The debate is highly technical and Grant's commentary is inconclusive on the main issue, while touching only incidentally the major theme of the rest of this book.

On the question of the future of Canada, Grant is less passionate than he was in his *Lament for a Nation,* but no less resigned to the end of an independent Canada. She has no alternative vision to sustain her and is bound to be swept into the American vortex:

To most Canadians, as public beings, the central cause of motion in their souls is the belief in progress through technique, and that faith is identified with the power of leadership of the English-speaking empire of the world. ... The very substance of our lives is bound up with the western empire and its destiny, just at a time when that empire uses increasingly ferocious means to maintain its hegemony.

But prophecy is one thing and policy another; they can in fact point in opposite directions:

Nothing here written implies that the increasingly difficult job of preserving what is left of Canadian sovereignty is not worth the efforts of practical men.

It is a dim candle to light the way.

We were seduced by Liberal ideology and now we suffocate in the grip of the cast-iron maiden of technique. Grant offers little to qualify his message of total despair. Is he the ultimate realist among us?

In the century and a half since the onset of the first industrial revolution, we have been given reasons to doubt the double-barrelled determinism of ideology and technique. Some lessons of that experience may be revealing. The official credo, derived from English political philosophy, pictured a society of atomistic individuals seeking their just reward on the market, with laws of property and contract guaranteed by the state. The feeding of the new machines with raw materials and labour required at the time, that both man and his habitat be governed by self-regulating labour and land markets respectively. Their disposition was to be solely the verdict of the mindless new order known as the market economy. Left to its own devices, the supply-demand mechanism for the 'factors of production,' produced the disastrous dislocations of the early industrial revolution. Had matters rested there, ideology and technology would have produced a negative utopia matching any of Grant's deepest apprehensions.

But this was only the beginning of the first round, and the 'fictitious commodities' labour and land were still to be heard from in their own right. The countervailing and spontaneous reactions of a society arising to protect itself, created the human and social history of that century. The extension of the market in regard to genuine commodities was accompanied by its restriction in regard to 'fictitious' ones and created a 'double movement.' Trade unions, child labour laws, factory legislation, and later, minimum wage laws, zoning regulations, and housing standards intervened as an institutional buffer in this unprecedented attempt to cast society into a mold suitable to the needs of the machine.

There seems little room in Grant's view of the world for the role of institutions mediating between ideology and technique and being acted on in turn by both. Before this first century of 'modernization' was over, even more substantial institutional and moral forces were released. It became the age of universal suffrage, the beginnings of mass literacy and mass education, and flowering of civil liberties and the freedom of the press. Some of the developments are to be ascribed to the reigning liberal ideology, others to the reaction against it with roots in a Western moral heritage that was older. Certainly it was the century of the birth of socialism.

Who could have predicted this outcome? The assumptions of liberal ideology were only a tissue of shallow fictions on the nature of man and society, but because they offered permissive ground for the spread of the machine, they were, in a sense, wrong for the right reasons. But neither the moral nor institutional history of that first round of industrialization were contained within the bounds of the liberal premises. We can hardly expect these premises to last a second round which is now under way.

The new wave of globe-girdling computer and communications networks and the octopi of multi-national corporations are phenomena far more implacable seemingly, than the institutional enormity of the market economy. Countervailing institutions and the indigenous traditions of nation-states are not so clearly suited to become the protective barriers in the second round. The requirements of control, co-ordination, and expansion of the system create a proliferating bureaucracy which operates as an anonymous tyranny for which no one can answer.

But the reaction nevertheless escalates in proportion to the spread of the technological society. There is a global explosion of moral passions in which we seem to have discovered, virtually for the first time, social wounds that are as old as mankind itself: poverty, racism, inequality, national oppression and exploitation and our intolerance of them is fierce and unbounded. The phenomenon is universal. Our universities and churches will never be the same, and we may witness, for the first time, the resignation of a Pope. In the early throes, these movements are often blind or groping. But can we rule out a creative institutional and moral transformation out of the anguish and upheaval? Will total despair turn out to be as myopic a verdict in 1969 as it was in 1820?

It is precisely the fact that we cannot answer this question either way that produces the basic tension of the technological society. No one knows the limits to which it can be reformed nor indeed, how. For some, this provides a precarious but sufficient basis for hope without illusion and for action.

But I doubt that all this goes to the heart of George Grant's complaint, the sense of ultimate deprival. The term is a metaphor, but a metaphor for what? Grant is barely articulate on this question and the reader can only attempt with some hesitation, to reconstruct his meaning.

When Grant writes that 'technique is ourselves' and that it 'comes forth from and is sustained in our vision of ourselves as creative freedom,' he goes to the heart of the question of technology. But he has eminent predecessors. For McLuhan, technology is the extension of man in a literal but far-reaching sense. For Marx, the concept of externalization (*entausserung*) refers to the projection of man through his technology but also through his laws, his art and his institutions. A theory of technology as the projection of man, helps to explain the irreversible impetus which the technological thrust has acquired.

Marx follows up the moral implications of his theory in the specific critique of capitalist alienation (*entfremdung*). Grant fails to do likewise, but one can imagine that his sense of deprival must be linked in some way with his view of technology. To recognize on the moral plane that 'technology is ourselves' is to stagger under the burden of an immense responsibility. We can no longer dissociate ourselves from, or contract out of the vast network of compulsion and anonymous tyranny that the technological society creates. We ourselves are its source when we opt for the reign of the machine. We cannot escape through non-recognition, the burden of what we do to others. We are helpless in the defence of that citadel of conscience which is the core of inner life and the foundation of religious existence as we have known it.

Grant's inarticulate anguish and despair may be foreshadowed in the single sentence:

I could not face the fact that we were living at the end of Western Christianity.

DAVID MCFADDEN

Get Your Feet Off the Coffee Table

Room temperature is about 16 degrees
lower than body,
and today in late September
the leaves turn brown
as if being digested
by the bright cool fall air
which is about 16 degrees
lower than room temperature

and I walk along Garside Avenue
in my maroon jacket, proud
and swinging an empty milk jug.

I have to get baby food, eggs,
cigarettes and milk and the poor widow
who runs the tiny corner store
is directly delighted
with such a big order,

she nods at me with friendly
openness and says her eggs
are a loss leader, she loses
three cents a dozen, so I
only get six.

As usual
she doesn't have my preferred brand
of cigarettes, and says look!
here's the Palmolive soap you wanted
– big pile of wrapped soap bars.
No no, I say, not Palmolive soap,
it was Pall Mall smokes I wanted
and still do.

I better write that down
she says, how do you spell it?
P, A, L (thinking deeply, double L?), L,
M, A, L, L, and she writes it down,
puts the scrap of paper in a little box
of little scraps of paper.

He'd only died about an hour before
and she probably hadn't heard, so I said
instead of commenting on the weather
Did you hear the bad news from
    Quebec?
No, what's that?
        Premier Johnson
had another heart attack and this time
    died
I said, weakly.
        O that's too bad, said she,
but that's life, it has to end some time.

Walking home with my bag it hit me
she probably never heard of Daniel
    Johnson
and sort of envied her, wished I'd never,

and thought how great it would be
if I could get a small guitar
for each of my two small daughters

and they could learn to sing me songs
like Judy Collins and make money
so I could retire and change seasons,
just turn brown like the leaves.

ABRAHAM ROTSTEIN

The Search for Independence

Canada has become the land of the *cri de coeur*. Across the political spectrum and on the most varied occasions the listener will pick up the cries of the heart, now as a manifesto, now as a personal credo, occasionally as an editorial outburst. The cries are worth listening to and pondering, for the barely ruffled political waters conceal some deeper currents running beneath the surface.

The most important *cri de coeur* last month was 'For an Independent Socialist Canada' (The Watkins Manifesto). The title was the message: Canadian independence from the American empire could only be achieved by socialism. The Manifesto was a measure of the growing impatience of a segment of the left in the NDP including Melville Watkins, Laurier Lapierre, Charles Taylor, and Cy Gonick; time was running out as the American economic takeover moved ahead, and no effective action was to be seen on the horizons.

The document was addressed to members of the NDP with the aim of creating a 'left grouping' within the party. We will know more about the fate of the Manifesto and its adherents at the end of this month when the NDP's national convention takes place. Our concern for the moment is with the national significance of the document rather than the party verdict of the NDP.

A surprisingly large number of subjects are touched upon in the Manifesto apart from the issue of independence: the extension of workers' control in industry, regional disparities, Quebec ('two nations, one struggle'), the extension of public services, and the erosion of the Canadian business class. The hysterical tirade of the daily press from coast to coast against the Manifesto, failed either to take note of some of the genuine merits of the document or to argue the issues as presented. (George Bain's column in *The Globe and Mail*, Sept. 6, and Dalton Camp in *The Telegram*, Sept. 8, are the two exceptions.)

I write as a critic of the document and as one who is unable to endorse its major formulations however urgent and well-intentioned the cry for Canadian independence. My reservations centre first on the kind of socialism which is proposed namely, full-scale nationalization:

Capitalism must be replaced by socialism, by national planning of investment and by public ownership of the means of production in the interests of the Canadian people as a whole.

This has a ring about it that is more fundamentalist than radical. We are back to the socialism of the Regina Manifesto but attempting to apply it to a different problem than was originally intended. The early thirties witnessed the collapse of Canadian capitalism with massive unemployment and hunger as the main issues. In the days preceding Keynes and prior to the economic stimulus of military spending, the nationalization of industry appeared to be the only solution to the creation of jobs and the restoration of production. Economic independence was not an issue at the time and there is not a word in the Regina Manifesto about foreign control of the economy.

Admittedly, there are additional problems that are inherent in a capitalist economy. The distortion of priorities (as between the public and private sectors) is a problem common to 'corporate capitalism' regardless of its nationality, as the authors of the Manifesto indicate. It is not clear, however, why this distortion requires the same solution as was advocated for depression of the thirties. Some discrimination in technique is required related to the problem at hand. This applies as well to the problem of economic independence.

Toward the end of the Manifesto the authors do qualify their position:

... extensive public control over investment and nationalization of the commanding heights of the economy, such as key resource industries, finance and credit, and industries strategic to planning our economy.

It seems to me that all of this requires rethinking. There is the question of financing the massive nationalization which the authors contemplate; the cost of buying out the Americans as a start, boggles the mind. How to retain access to the stream of new technology generated by the multi-national corporation is a second question. It is odd moreover, that the authors of the Manifesto hardly take note of the trends in socialist thinking in the West in the last two decades that provide for alternatives to nationalization. One broad stream of socialist thought distinguishes between *titles* to property and property *rights* or *functions* that attach to the titles. In the industrial sphere for example, titles to property include the right to set wages and working hours, to allocate capital, to establish new investment, to set prices on the product, to distribute dividends, to invest abroad, etc. Individually and together these powers can be modified, controlled, or subsumed altogether by legislation and regulation. It is not necessary for the government to acquire the *titles* to property in order to exercise these functions on behalf of the public interest. They are powers equally available for the control of foreign and domestic corporations. Such an approach requires that objectives be spelled out in specific terms, and appropriate regulatory functions selected to meet these objectives. Different controls for example, may be needed for 'distortion' than are needed for 'independence.' Future takeovers that are not in the national interest may be blocked by such devices as the proposed monopolies commission recently suggested by the Economic Council (although needless to say, this was hardly the Council's intention). The expansion of the public sector and the establishment of development corporations offer a further range of possibilities.

The fact that the present Liberal Government shows not the least inclination to exercise these prerogatives is no reason to dust off the battering ram of wholesale nationalization. But I doubt that any of this is new to the authors of the Manifesto. Why then take the road back to nationalization? Is there a hidden political rationale which governs this unexpected economic logic?

My second reservation about the Manifesto is its reaction to the United States which is placed at the forefront of the argument. When the Manifesto characterizes America as 'militarism abroad and racism at home,' it utters an obvious truth but neither a comprehensive nor necessarily an enduring one. The phrase comes out of the handbooks of the American left, and the present reality is obvious for the world to see. But we should remember the implicit message of the American left: 'there is another America out of which we have sprung and to which we shall return.' With apologies to H. Rap Brown, both violence *and* Staughton Lynd are as American as cherry pie. Is the raison d'être of Canadian independence to be based on the permanent victory of violence and the permanent failure of the American left? If by chance America were to change course and become a social democracy, would the authors of the Manifesto logically be required to go continentalist? A Manifesto which pivots on a reaction to America at a low point in its history is, in my view, not an enduring basis on which to construct the edifice of Canadian independence.

The political significance of the Manifesto, however, does not lie entirely in the strength or weakness of its substantive formulations. Its stated objective is to create a new and coherent political grouping on the Canadian left, more radically committed to the issue of Canadian independence. But how is such a group to be crystallized out of the scatter of diverse elements in the NDP and out of a party platform that has 'everything'? The political genesis of such a group can only be accomplished by a signalling process based on symbols that would render an unambiguous message to the sympathetic listener. It is in the end, a sign of the weakness of the Canadian left, that the only two such unambiguous signals are on the one hand, classical and outdated – the Regina Manifesto – and on the other, external and derivative – America as 'militarism abroad and racism at home.' The authors of the Manifesto gave prior importance to the clarity of the signal over the substance of the text. From a purely political standpoint, they may have been correct, for the crystallization of this political grouping has now begun to move swiftly. (I do not mean to imply incidentally, that the centre and the right in Canada could be rallied by symbols that are less cliché-ridden. The opposite is probably true.)

The national importance of such a new grouping goes beyond the number of adherents it will manage to secure. It is a fringe development, but a movement on the fringe is itself of substantial significance. It may be the clearest indicator of what is happening in the less articulate median, a bellwether of the silent centre. We should read it as an early warning.

It is no coincidence that the Manifesto comes at a time when the Prime Minister has abnegated any direct action on the issues surrounding Canadian independence. The limits of the Government's aspirations are defined by the Prime Minister's declaration of the 10 to 15 per cent by which Canada can be independent. The Watkins Manifesto is now the major reaction to this position. A brief review of the Canadian political scene reveals the backdrop against which the movement for left-wing solutions to independence is evolving.

When John Porter published *The Vertical Mosaic* in 1965, it was already to be read as history. The Upper Canada College-Rosedale-Bay Street axis had passed its apogee and we were living amidst the decline of this country's political and economic elite. The great takeover by American business was both a symptom of this decline and hastened the process further. It was a rare event in the global annals of capitalism for the top business echelon of a country to preside gracefully over its own liquidation, but that is precisely what happened. Apart from the industrial performance of the elite, which was second rate when judged by American standards, its will to survive had eroded.

No obvious class or grouping was available to replace it and only a nascent populism, sporadically erupting on the provincial fringes could fill the gap. First Diefenbaker and later Trudeau found the key to tap this pent-up populist undercurrent. The Diefenbaker fiasco need not be recapitulated here. The important question today is the shape which Trudeau will give to the populist upsurge which brought him to power. Populism is in its essence a vaguely defined political movement, deriving in this country from a mixture of agrarian and urban grass roots elements, united in their resentment against a declining establishment. Such a movement coheres well with Trudeau's slogan of 'participatory democracy,' but is remarkably open-ended on specific commitments and policies.

The only determination of concrete policy in the situation is the cast of mind that the Prime Minister brings to bear, his own vision of the rightness of things and the tasks to be accomplished. The Prime Minister's anti-nationalism is well known, but not so apparent is the classical liberalism out of which this derives and how that shapes his basic outlook. A man of many sides claiming a pragmatic approach to politics, he is the most deeply ideological of Canadian prime ministers. This surfaces rarely, but when it does in an unguarded moment of candour, the statement may be a revelation (even after the PR types have rushed in to set the statement 'in context.') The most famous of his personal *cris de coeur* is the query to Western farmers, 'Why should I sell your wheat?'. It is the perfect embodiment of the ethos of the market economy – it expresses the PM's personal sense of the rightness of things economic. It is worth reflecting on how deep-seated a commitment it would require to wash out even momentarily, seventy-five years of history of the Canadian West – the wheat pools, the battle around the Winnipeg grain exchange and finally the Canadian Wheat Board itself!

The new policy toward Canadian Indians provides a second case. The attempt to have Canadian Indians 'sink or swim' in five years, is reminiscent only of the Poor Law Reform Act of 1834– the pivotal legislation for the creation of a free labour market in England's emergent laissez-faire economy. To be told further, as we have been, that one section of Canadian society cannot form treaties with another section, is to wash out in an instant another two hundred years of Canadian history. The valuable civil rights legislation of the last session of Parliament, in itself a great achievement, rounds out the picture. The cast of mind is unmistakeably that of classical liberalism. Despite the PM's personal motto – *la raison avant la passion* – he himself expresses the triumph of ideological passion, not only over reason but over history as well. This stance is his personal privilege, but in the circumstances it is also the country's burden. No ideological determinism need be invoked to appreciate that his anti-nationalist obsession is part of a coherent and unshakeable philsophy of atomistic individualism and that little support can be expected from the present Government in the battle for Canadian independence. In spite of all this, can the PM maintain the support of a populist electorate without taking a stand on the issues of independence? I doubt it. New issues and new incidents crop up continuously. Trade with China is on the immediate horizon and some brisk winds have been blowing from the north.

As our final example we turn to the *cris de coeur* of Canadian newspapers that accompanied the voyage of the United States tanker *Manhattan* through our Arctic waters. It was a remarkable spectacle. The Toronto *Telegram* demanded hysterically that the Manhattan fly the Canadian flag. *The Globe and Mail* proclaimed that she 'ploughs through Arctic ice to what might well be history – and a nasty precedent.' The message was echoed from coast to coast, some newspapers printing two or three editorials on the subject in the same issue. The peculiar shape of the concern for Canadian independence was suddenly revealed –a classic territorialism. The newspapers, it seemed, rose to the defence of every ice pack, inlet, and practically every ocean wave that touched our shores. The very newspapers who offered only a blithe unconcern or hesitant commentary on the loss of control over our economy and technology became militant to the point of hysteria when the fate of the polar region was at stake. It was incredible to see into what peculiar channels the independence issue had been shunted and where it had burst forth. Seemingly, only territoriality and extra-territoriality have become the active issues in the minds of the Canadian public.

How much of this sentiment grows out of the unease and confusion that has let the major issues thus far go by default? For the issues that matter in the twentieth century are the control of technology, communications, and decision-making power, and these centre on economic life.

The Prime Minister tried to calm down the popular eruption by invoking (not unexpectedly) the dangers of 'ultranationalism,' and promising a statement at the opening of Parliament. To the layman it appeared that the legal position of our Arctic claims was not at all assured. A variety of international precedents and criteria might be invoked. If the issue then shifted from the legal sphere to the diplomatic, to negotiations with the United States, that was hardly the area of Canada's greatest strength. This country seemed to be on the high road once more to its traditional solution of 'quiet diplomacy,' and that was hardly reassuring to public opinion.

Mr Sharp attempted to deal with the public outcry by a statement on Sept. 18 that moved in two directions at once. On the international plane he welcomed 'vessels of all flags' to use the Arctic route, glossing over the substantive issues such as whether the limits of Canadian sovereignty were to be defined by the three-mile limit around the Arctic islands or not, as the Americans had contended last June. For purely domestic consumption he injected the military factor into the situation, referring to the Prime Minister's statement on defence policy last April 3rd which promised 'an effective multipurpose maritime coastal shield.' When the Minister of Defence announced the following day that our aircraft carrier, the Bonaventure, was to be taken out of service, leaving us with 30 aging Argus aircraft for the task and little more planned, one defence analyst commented: 'given that Canada has 7,000 miles of coastline to protect, the (original) objective is in any case unattainable.' The addition of Arctic surveillance to an already 'unattainable' task, turns Mr Sharp's statement into a purely symbolic gesture.

It is the nature of the symbol, however, which is of interest for the moment – territory and coastline. No doubt it was reassuring, even though we were without the adequate means in the twentieth century to achieve the objective. This statement had simply followed the note which the PM had struck last April when justifying our partial withdrawal from NATO. One might have expected at that time some reference to the international political situation, the changed climate of the cold war, how circumstances had altered the reasoning behind Canada's initial sponsorship of NATO, or possibly what a 'middle power' might achieve by loosening its ties with military alliances. None of these were deemed appropriate for public consumption. Vestigial symbols alone were offered. The PM's statement referred simply to 'the surveillance of our own territory and coast lines in the interest of our own sovereignty.'

It was an act of homage to the national icon but little else. The gap between the symbolic and the substantive issue was at least half a century greater than the one on the Canadian left to which we referred earlier.

Thus we have the *cris de coeur* in Canada of the politics of independence, – a debate that is incoherent, outbursts that are sporadic, issues that are out of focus, and an inadequate political vocabulary in which all this is expressed. Politics outside of the electoral system has become highly volatile, and even the Prime Minister may be unable to defuse the situation. If he persists in his non-recognition of the issue of independence, he can only succeed in the long run in making his Government irrelevant, however successful his short term tactics. The political tides will turn elsewhere. That is the real significance of the Manifesto. For however incoherent in its expression, this country has a rage to live.

COLLEEN THIBAUDEAU
February 20th

The day before yesterday
my daughter and a friend
decided to put a curse on the neighbour boy,

they made a mudball with extra gravel
from the cemetery, welded in burdock,
blackberry thorn and the wing
of a moulty bird,

   they threw
it into a willow tangle on the creekbank.

Yesterday the neighbour boy
limped going to school as if he
had fallen off his bike or got
checked too hard at hockey;

this morning he came the two miles home
from school at 11 a.m.
kicking a stone and expecting a licking.

They got their sweaters full of sticktights
and their hair full of burrs
and their faces full of scratches
finding that mudball,

which dissolved in the creek and the feather
bubbled off to the sewer, and like tears
over a body cold creek waters
kept laving the mudball.

KENNETH McNAUGHT

The Permanent Colony

We have not yet, mercifully, achieved a consensus view of Canadian history. For a while in the forties and fifties a number of anglophone historians thought they were moulding such an interpretation based upon the idea of a long, almost excessively patient and nearly inevitable progress from colony to nation. But the sixties revealed much that was both inadequate and misleading about such a view – just as that decade challenged even more violently the consensus view within American historiography.

In Canada, Quebec's increasingly unquiet revolution has demonstrated that the liberal-conservative anglophone story of steady growth to political independence, economic competence and national unity was a kind of non-self-fulfilling prophecy rather than penetrating historical analysis. It was a version of our history which could be sustained only by assuming that the angular historical manifestations of racial friction, colonial-mindedness and economic dependency had all more or less passed away with the ultimate defeat of the integrated Empire-Commonwealth, the successful weathering of the second conscription crisis and our emergence as a 'leading industrial state.' Without recognizing the dangerous extent to which our 'maturity' and 'unity' were based upon the twin bases of anglo-saxon superiority and unlimited American investment, we religously celebrated our new and influential independence. We had shared in the secret development of atomic energy, we were equal partners in NATO and in NORAD, we were righteous leaders in a multi-national Commonwealth of Nations and in international peace-keeping and we had produced another francophone prime minister who had threatened to build the St Lawrence Seaway entirely in Canadian waters – thus forcing the mightiest nation in the world to co-operate with us and proving our talents in the field of racial conciliation. We had entered a new and glittering Laurier era.

Well, it is now clear that the bases of an anglophone consensus history were being disastrously undermined at the very time that we were celebrating unity and the final success of the good old east-west economy. Instead of listening to the heart-warming assurances of Uncle Louis and Lester B. we should have been reading *Cité Libre* and Frank Underhill. Especially Professor Underhill who told us clearly enough that 'in 1940 we passed from the British century of our history to the American century. We became dependent upon the United States for our security. We have, therefore, no choice but to follow American leadership.' Of course this did not bother Mr Underhill, although he did warn that our American century would be a tough one. It didn't bother him – or his new and somewhat surprised friends in Canadian Liberalism – because they all believed that fighting against the inevitable is futile. They believed, too, that the best way we could use our independence was in close, voluntary co-operation with the United States. Only thus could we derive the full economic benefits of superior American technology and investment. And, in any event, we should act upon our recognition that the best in American culture was the best in the West – was, in fact, the complement of an essential American military defence against an illiberal and brutalizing communism.

It was this kind of reasoning that led most anglophone Canadians (save for a nervous twitching of their political subconscious in the Diefenbaker elections) to accept a new colonialism. Like the colonialism of our British era, our relationship to the American empire is based upon a perception of personal interest by the Canadian anglophone economic elite. And as in our previous colonialism the life-styles and social values of the imperial power tend to become the success criteria of the colonial elite. But it is now evident, also, that the comparison of our British and American colonial periods does not end with the facts of economic-military integration and of social emulation.

In both colonial periods resistance to 'foreign domination' is to be found spearheaded by French Canadians, more-or-less vigorously supported by the political Left in English-speaking Canada, and occasionally endorsed by establishment politicians who sense the cyclical mood of their constituents and do not wish to be too obviously at variance with it. The most essential point about recurring Canadian resistance to domination from abroad is that it is based firstly upon a cumulative desire for the survival of basic identities – regional, cultural, provincial, and even, on occasion, national. The second most important characteristic of such resistance is that it holds suspect the nature and purposes of the dominating imperial power. This was true of the attitude to imperial Britain expressed by French Canadians, the Progressives, and the CCF. It is equally true of their successors who now look with dismay at the new imperial power – an empire even more violently discordant in its own homeland and at least as ruthless in exercising its power abroad as was Britain in South Africa or India.

But here a comparison between our British and American colonial relationships leads to a fundamental and ominous point of difference. We released ourselves from the British relationship with comparative ease, despite a lot of political clamour which was useful principally to Mackenzie King. This was possible largely because Britain was losing her power much more rapidly than most Canadians at the time realized and because we were able to tie ourselves economically and militarily to the 'countervailing power' of the United States. Any attempt to shake free of the American empire will be almost infinitely more hazardous for more reasons than appear at first glance.

Not only is the United States at the peak of its power (one may hopefully assume) but also the nature of its domination of Canada is both more subtle and more complete than was Britain's at any time in the twentieth century. In the case of our British colonial relationship, political, military, and economic dominance were present from the beginning. Political dominance slipped away almost automatically with the erosion of Britain's economic and military power. This can scarcely be the case with our American colonial relationship. In the American case political domination has followed economic and military dominance. And it has followed in a way that is normally so subtle that it is frequently indiscernible. Only occasionally is it felt necessary that a general or a State Department spokesman should openly point out the error of our ways.

Like American reformers in the Progressive era, most Liberal and Conservative Canadians feel that they still have the political power to impose mastery over drift – to legislate regulation of business while leaving business to create ever larger corporate structures whose control of public appointments and public policy became virtually complete. Like the American reformers, however, many Canadians are now awakening to the fact that if you permit great 'private' corporations to own your economy you also grant to them the control of public policy. You grant to them the right to use your resources to protect the 'right' of multinational corporations to operate and regulate their own world-wide market system. You grant to them the right to impose upon the areas within their writ their own technological values and their own definitions of liberalism and freedom. American reformers discovered too late that they had been hoodwinked by regulatory reforms which were merely provisions by which a corporate elite could use the power of the state to rationalize its market operations. As they take to the streets, or flee to Canada, in opposition to the corporate-military values of their kept government, they almost scream their warning to those who inhabit the provinces of the informal American empire.

And we live in the most important of those provinces. Just as we were the 'senior Dominion' of the Empire-Commonwealth, so now we are the most reliable of the American provinces. As a Dominion we gratified ourselves by saying 'no' to proposals for formal integration, and finally we broke the relationship altogether – but only when our economic elite no longer needed money from British investment houses. Now we find ourselves within an even more powerful empire and the recipient of four times as much investment from our metropolitan centre as is bestowed upon any other country. Occasionally we say 'no' to requests for *formal* commitments, as in Vietnam. But we are clearly nowhere near breaking the colonial relationship. Because our economic elite (including a number of trade union leaders) find it to their advantage to co-operate with multinational corporations, the most strenuous opposition to serious countervailing measures comes from inside the colony itself. As it did also in the days of Sir John A.

As in our former colonial experience, it is the French Canadian and the anglophone Left that perceive what is necessary if their various versions of survival and the good society are to retain meaning. Each recognizes that it is not enough to say that American corporations in Canada act like good citizens – for this merely means that they convey to us whatever modicum of their technological expertise they find convenient, while excercising a vast, if indirect political influence, the precise nature of which remains to be documented. Each recognizes, too, that however beneficial the technological fall-out it more often than not inhibits the central purpose of a liberal society which is self-fulfillment – in both the individual and collective sense. Self-fulfillment (let alone the good society), as the humane sector of American society has discovered, is not possible within even the metropolitan country as long as it is dominated by politically irresponsible corporations. Much less are the essential liberal goals attainable in a wholly dependent colony.

It is because of these obvious considerations that the Left in Canada (both English- and French-speaking) has given a nationalist and a *nationaliste* tone to its demands for public ownership of those debatable 'key' sectors of the economy and for stringent regulation of foreign investment. And it is the Left's growing awareness of the nature of the multinational corporate agents of the American empire that leads to doubts about the absolute need of the Canadian economy for unlimited foreign investment when already the dividends flowing south are greater than the annual rate of foreign investment.

In the circumstances it is scarcely surprising that the tentative anglophone consensus history of Canada failed to survive the fifties. It now appears that a consensus version of our history would have to be built upon the assumption that Canadians have always really wanted to be colonials – whereas, in fact, it is only our elites that have enjoyed the colonial condition. That kind of consensus history would do as much, or greater violence to the facts than does American consensus history.

WITHDRAWN BY
WHITMAN COLLEGE LIBRARY